Third Edition

MASS COMMUNICATION
An Introduction

JOHN R. BITTNER

The University of North Carolina
at Chapel Hill

Prentice-Hall Inc., Englewood Cliffs, N.J. 07632

Library of Congress Cataloging in Publication Data

BITTNER, JOHN R.
   Mass communication, an introduction.

   Bibliography.
   Includes index.
   1. Mass media.   I. Title.
P90.B515–1983   302.2′34   82-13146
ISBN   0-13-559286-0

Editorial/production supervision
   and interior design by Joyce Turner
Cover design by Jeannette Jacobs
Cover photos by Royal Ontario Museum, Library of Congress, A.T.&T.,
   Office of Information of the University of Houston, Dow Jones,
   Independent Broadcasting Authority, Mergenthaler Linotype
   Company.
Manufacturing buyer: Ron Chapman
Page makeup by Rita Schwartz

Printed in the United States of America

10   9   8   7   6   5   4   3   2   1

ISBN 0-13-559286-0

Prentice-Hall International, Inc., *London*
Prentice-Hall of Australia Pty. Limited, *Sydney*
Editora Prentice-Hall do Brasil, Ltda. , *Rio de Janeiro*
Prentice-Hall Canada Inc., *Toronto*
Prentice-Hall of India Private Limited, *New Delhi*
Prentice-Hall of Japan, Inc., *Tokyo*
Prentice-Hall of Southeast Asia Pte. Ltd., *Singapore*
Whitehall Books Limited, *Wellington, New Zealand*

for
Denise, John, Donald, and Stormy

Other books by John R. Bittner

Each Other: An Introduction to Interpersonal Communication, Prentice-Hall, Inc.

Broadcast Law and Regulation, Prentice-Hall, Inc.

Professional Broadcasting: A Brief Introduction, Prentice-Hall, Inc.

Broadcasting: An Introduction, Prentice-Hall, Inc.

Radio Journalism (with Denise A. Bittner), Prentice-Hall, Inc.

CONTENTS

16 LEGAL ISSUES AND THE WORKING PRESS 406

17 AUDIENCE AND EFFECTS OF MASS COMMUNICATION 433

PREFACE

Strengths from the second edition of the text have been retained in this new edition. At the same time, important changes have been made and new material has been added.

The text remains written for readers who aspire to be responsible consumers or practicing professionals of mass media in society. Like the earlier editions, it is designed for introductory courses studying mass communication and courses studying mass media in society.

Among new features are:

* A comprehensive chapter on mass communication and new technologies, including teletext, videotex, the impact of home computers, and electronic publishing.
* A separate chapter devoted to public relations with an inside look at a public relations campaign.
* A restructured chapter on ethics and social issues.
* Material on radio and television syndication.
* A "preview" page of learning objectives preceding each chapter.
* An expanded bibliography, "Opportunities for Further Learning," concluding each chapter.
* Improved graphic and photo layout design for easy reading and comprehension.
* A complete updating of all areas important to the study of mass communication.

The text continues to examine the many different mass media, including newspapers, magazines, radio, television, motion pictures, book publishing, and the recording industry.

It also examines such areas as advertising, photography and photo-journalism, mass media news, networks, syndicates, cable, satellites, legal issues and the working press, regulatory control of mass media, the audience and effects of mass communication, and a glossary of media terms.

A comprehensive instructor's manual accompanies the text.

ACKNOWLEDGMENTS

Over the three editions and seven years this book has been accepted, I continue to accumulate a list of people to thank which far exceeds the space available. Faced with the risk of missing someone, I instead choose to generalize with a blanket thank you, appreciation, and deep indebtedness to my colleagues who have spent long hours reading drafts of manuscripts, checking facts, making recommendations, and providing feedback on every aspect of the book. Your time, commitment, and dedication to what has now become a collective, continuing project is one of the most precious gifts and rich rewards this author enjoys. Not the least of this is the warm, unselfish friendships that accompany that commitment.

For the many people, including both instructors and students, who have written and called with compliments, criticism, and questions, I also offer a heartfelt thank you. Somehow, there is nothing quite so refreshing as personal calls or letters from students or teachers thousands of miles away who are faced with completing an assignment or preparing a lecture. You never impose. You always enrich.

The domestic and international acceptance of the text continues to exceed the author's and publisher's highest expectations. For this, I must credit the professional staff of Prentice-Hall, Inc. Few authors enjoy the support and friendship of an organization of this high caliber. John Davis and Robert Haltiwanger deserve special mention.

Commitment and consistency belong to Bobbie Christenberry, Joyce Turner, Barbara Kelly Kittle, Colette Conboy, and Gert Glassen.

Ed Stanford, Stan Wakefield, and Steve Dalphin continue to find new frontiers.

Lisa Femmel's contagious enthusiasm and ability are crucial.

Bryce and Pam Dodson deserve their own special thank you.

At the heartbeat of this edition and earlier ones are special friends and supporters. Jim Parker, Charles Briqueleur, Jim Panther, Jack McGarrie, Bill Firth, Ben Nowell, and others are extremely important. John Paul Jones, Willis Bliderback, Tom Kubiak, Richard Crean, Bill Wicker, Dave Morris, Tim Moore, Bob Thorensen, Paul Rosengard, Bill Kestle, Christine Beranek, Martin Tenney, Cindy Jennings Meuer, Joellen Sesker, Judy Mortell, Michael Sutton, Walter Welch, Jon Nissenblatt, Candy Cotton, Cindy Marione, Dianne Werder, Lyle Clark, and Gordon and Jerri Johnson deserve special mention. Also important are Greg Michael, Dale Brown, Terry Brennan, Rita Vale, John Davis, Jr., Bob Molitar, and John Allison.

In addition, many others have devoted energies on the book's behalf, and your work and efforts do not go unnoticed.

Lucy Weeks is thanked for being there when needed.

Tommi Jones and others of the Jefferson-Pilot organization contributed more than they know.

Randi helped Tommi.

A special acknowledgment is made to Robert Allen, whose expertise and keen pen made important contributions to the chapter on motion pictures.

At a time when inspiration was needed, Doris Betts and John Jakes came through with flying colors.

This edition of the text started on Ocracoke Island and ended with *E.T.* Both are magical.

No one deserves more credit than Denise.

J.R.B.
Chapel Hill

CHAPTER

WHAT
IS
MASS COMMUNICATION?

PREVIEW

After completing this chapter, we should be able to:

Trace the development of communication from the beginnings of language to today's new technologies.
Define intrapersonal communication.
Define interpersonal communication.
Define mass communication.
Distinguish among intrapersonal, interpersonal, and mass communication.
Explain the gatekeeper concept.
Understand semantic noise and physical noise.
Explain delayed feedback.
Discuss the social forces that affect mass communication.
Be aware of the new technologies that are redefining "mass communication."
Understand the concept of specialized media in postindustrial society.

WHAT IS *Mass Communication?* It is the deadline of the investigative journalist, the creative artistry of documentaries, the bustle of a network newsroom, the silence of a computer, the hit record capturing the imagination of millions, the radio disc jockey setting the pace of a morning show, and the advertising executive planning a campaign. It is radio, research, recordings, resonators, and ratings. It is television, teletext, talent, telephones, and tabloids. It is satellites, storyboards, systems, and segues. It is all these things and many more. It *is* dynamic and exciting, but it is *not* new. Let us go back for a moment to the dawn of civilization— more than two and a half million years ago.

THE EVOLUTION OF MASS COMMUNICATION

If you will, try to imagine our prehistoric ancestors emerging from their caves and reacting to their environment. Archeologists, who refer to this era as the Ramapithecus age, tell us that cave people possessed the basic senses of sight, hearing, touch, smell, and taste. Different from creatures of the twentieth century, their brains and central nervous systems began slowly to evolve, and later generations gradually acquired the basic tools for communication (Figure 1–1). They began to distinguish between pleasurable and unpleasurable experiences. More refined perception and a more sophisticated brain and central nervous system developed simultaneously and aided in satisfying basic needs—light to see, air to breathe, food to eat, water to drink, sleep to strengthen, and shelter to protect them from the environment. By about 300,000 B.C., their nervous systems and brain, as well as their genetic features began to resemble those of present humans.

Figure 1-1 Stone tablets from the Middle East are believed to contain the first elements of written language. Those studying such tablets, as seen in this illustration, suggest they were primarily used to record units of land and agricultural products, such as grain. Additional importance is attributed to the belief that such tablets represent the last stages of simple counting that mathematicians conjecture preceded the use of abstract numbers. (Courtesy of the Royal Ontario Museum, Toronto, Canada)

Two hundred thousand years later an embryonic language began to develop, replacing a communication based mainly on touch. Regardless of whether this language developed through learning or instinct, genetic evolution had now been joined by language evolution. By about 7000 B.C., homo sapiens had evolved genetically to their present form, and the ability to communicate had gained another medium, *pictographics*. These wall etchings inside caves and temples remain vivid picture messages that depict the life and religious beliefs of these first humans. In the period from 3000 to 2000 B.C., these etchings became highly stylized, and the first symbols came into existence. Primitive alphabets, sometimes consisting of more than 600 characters, marked the beginning of recorded history (Figure 1–2).

Humans were now able to record sociocultural events, attitudes, values, and habits and to trace the development of moral codes. Many of these techniques continued into modern cultures, such as those of the North American Indians who recorded famous battles, songs, and the lives of chiefs for posterity. Cultures learned about and studied other cultures. Historical perspectives developed so that, when plotting our futures, we could examine our past.

Figure 1-2 Drawings on the inside of caves, such as these from Lascaux, France, depict lifestyles, people, animals, and in some parts of the world, religious beliefs. Some were elaborate scenes illustrating motion. (Peter Buckley)

Functional
Requirements
of Society

Society's survival and growth depended on a number of things, among them a *system of communication* through which people could exchange symbols and thus propagate learning at a much accelerated rate; a *system of production* to create goods and services both for their needs and for barter and exchange; *systems of defense* to protect their domain against intruders; a method of *member replacement* sufficient to counteract disease and other elements of member destruction; and a method of *social control* to maintain order in the society. In the following centuries each of these functional requirements was, and is still, fulfilled by ever more sophisticated and efficient systems, especially in communication.

Figure 1-3 A paper mill showing the paper-making process—from dipping the screen into a vat of paper pulp, to new sheets being stacked and readied for pressing. (From DIDEROT and courtesy: *The Printer in 18th-Century Williamsburg*. Williamsburg, Va: Colonial Williamsburg, 1955)

Figure 1-4 Major advancements in printing were made when paper was applied to printing presses. Cylinder-fed paper rolls and type cylinders continued to advance printing technology.

As civilization continued to expand, interpersonal communication was used cross-culturally. Relay runners would carry messages to distant places and different people. Learning about people living in different ways was still very slow, however, mostly determined by how fast a messenger could run or ride. In some cases the messages took months and even years to reach their destination.

Print Technology

In the fifteenth century human ingenuity created a major breakthrough in technology—the invention of movable type—and introduced it to the European continent. People could now produce and send messages much faster. From this point on, breakthroughs in communication technology mushroomed because accelerating the recording of knowledge made possible a much more rapid exchange of information.

Two important developments followed the invention of movable type. First, the use of a *paper-making machine* (Figure 1–3) in the eighteenth century made it possible to mass produce and cut paper in specific sizes, reducing the cost of production. Second, the application of steam power to the printing press, an alternative to human labor, made possible true mass production of printed material. Sources of power, improved printing presses and improved paper manufacturing processes developed continuously during the nineteenth century. Such devices as cylinder-fed paper rolls and type cylinders continued the advancement of printing (Figure 1–4). Mechanical typesetting machines also became part of the printing process. With the aid of larger and faster presses, newspapers could print editions with as many as a dozen pages.

New Distribution Systems

Three other nineteenth century inventions further aided the ability to communicate. First, the development of *major transportation systems* permitted large quantities of newspapers to be carried to people residing outside the major cities. Railroads, aided by the ever-present delivery entrepreneur (Figure 1–5), became the key to this network and distribution system. Second, just as railroads began to prosper, the *telegraph* arrived. In widespread use (Figure 1–6) by the late 1800s, it permitted people to communicate over long distances with considerable speed. By means of the mechanical transmission of short and long sounds—dots and dashes—representing the letters of the alphabet, a skillful telegraph operator could easily send or receive twenty words per minute, although only those centers equipped with telegraph lines could receive messages. Newspapers used the telegraph to communicate bulletins, and when the Atlantic Cable was completed, news of commercial and political events could be exchanged between the United States and England via Newfoundland. By the late nineteenth century a network of telegraph lines had developed over the United States.

The third major development of this century, the device that enabled people to send voices over the wires, soon supplanted the telegraph signal because of its immediacy of communication. Although Alexander Graham Bell's *telephone* (Figure 1–7) helped people to communicate vocally with each other over long distances, its impact was minor compared to that of the next technological revolution that loomed on the horizon.

Figure 1-5 While printing technology and transportation aided the development of the newspaper, few contributed as much as the fledgling entrepreneur who delivered the newspapers. This photo, taken about 1900, remains a symbol of the many people who have been part of newspaper distribution. While technology has made giant strides in the way news is reported and printed, the newspaper delivery process has remained essentially the same. (Library of Congress)

Figure 1-6 Samuel F. B. Morse's first telegraph. The needle protruding from the horizontal bar caused a perforation in a paper tape, permitting a "coded" record of the message. (Smithsonian Institution)

Figure 1-7 Alexander Graham Bell's liquid-electrical telephone of 1876. "Mr. Watson, come here, I want you!" These words were spoken by Bell when he spilled sulfuric acid on himself and called to his assistant in another room. Watson heard the words through the crudely tuned reed in the receiving device. (Courtesy, A. T. & T.)

Electronic Communication

Just as the twentieth century dawned, a system was perfected by which electromagnetic impulses could be sent through the air without wires, carrying voice transmission over long distances (Figure 1–8). This new invention was to become known as *radio*. Low-cost receivers were developed which could be purchased by almost everyone for a few dollars, enabling them to listen to mass-produced messages from thousands of transmitters located all over the world. Societies and cultures were within an instant of communicating with each other; a news event on one side of the world could be transmitted almost simultaneously to any other point in the world. For the first time in civilization, people had a medium of *mass communication* that just a century before had belonged to the world of science fiction.

In the same century the ability to capture moving visual images with the camera was perfected. People also discovered ways of capturing movement as well as sound on film (Figure 1–9) to produce the motion picture and the electronic system called *videotape*. Scientists, in deciding how these motion pictures could be transmitted over wires and subsequently without wires, created a new medium called *television*. In much the

Figure 1-8 Men of the British Post Office examining the apparatus used by Guglielmo Marconi for his experiments in wireless across the Bristol Channel, the first time wireless successfully worked across water. (The Marconi Company Limited, Marconi House, Chelmsford, Essex)

Figure 1-9 Lee De Forest with a sound motion picture camera. De Forest's three-element audion tube contributed to advancements in both broadcasting and the motion picture industry. (Courtesy, A.T.&T.)

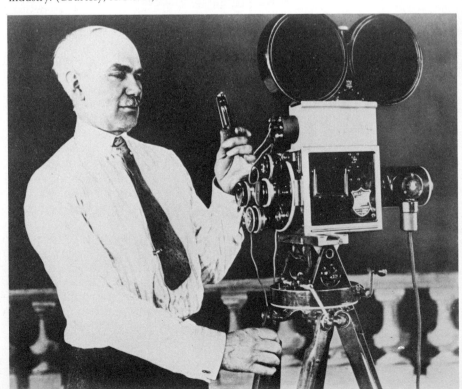

Figure 1-10 Since the early unmanned voyages around the moon, to moon landings, and later space probes, television has explored the outer reaches of the solar system. New advancements in television technology now make scenes from space common, yet no less spectacular. Space shuttles, shown in this illustration, promise to offer still new opportunities to witness our exploration and application of science in space. (Courtesy, NASA)

same way that steam aided the printing presses, rocket propulsion (Figure 1–10) took television to the galaxies and beyond. Using computers in mass communication has aided in the transmission, monitoring, and logical development of information (Figure 1–11).

But let us stop for a moment. Have we answered our question of what mass communication is? We have, partially.

We have learned it includes such entities as newspapers, radio, and television, what we call the *mass media*. But we still need to distinguish it from two other types of communication—*intra*personal and *inter*personal communication.

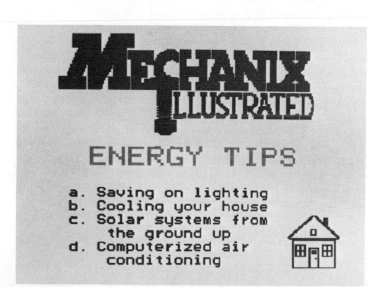

Figure 1-11 New information technologies provide textual and graphic materials via combinations of television, computers, and telephones. The texts of newspapers, magazines, and other "print" material are stored in computers, then accessed through home video display terminals. (Courtesy, CBS)

DISTINGUISHING AMONG TYPES
OF COMMUNICATION

One of the best ways to distinguish among different types of communication is to use a *communication model*. This *pictorial representation of the communication process* contains the basic components of communication. Figure 1–12 shows the relationship among the parts of the model: sender, medium, message, receiver, feedback, and noise. With this model in mind, let's begin by discussing *intra*personal communication.

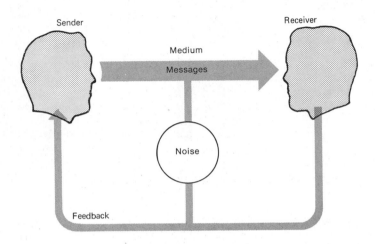

Figure 1-12 Basic Model of Communication. The process of communication is a dynamic process of sharing information between individuals.

Intra-personal Communication

We can assume that, even before history recorded such things, early humans used their senses to help them understand their world and thus to perceive, to judge, and to act accordingly. They learned that on a hot, rainy day, they should go outside the cave to cool off. When it was cold, they should build a fire. The process of sunlight entering the eye and communicating brightness to the central nervous system, the tactile sense organs communicating the feeling of cold air, the thought processes of deciding whether to brave the cold or build a fire, stay inside or walk in the rain—all were the result of communication taking place *within* the individual. This is the electrochemical action of the body taking part in the process of *intrapersonal communication—communication within ourselves.*

Intrapersonal communication is the basis of all other forms of human communication. Without an effective system of intrapersonal communication, an organism is unable to function in its environment—that is, to be open to external forms of communication. Ideally this communication system allows one to make decisions based on information received through the senses. For instance, when you watch television, your eyes and ears receive information and communicate it to your brain. If what you see and hear is pleasurable or interesting, your intrapersonal communication system indicates that, and you attend to it. If you do not like it, your brain sends a message to your muscles which results in a decision to change stations or to push the "off" button.

Just as the electronic components in your television set prohibit more than one station from being received at a time, your central nervous system also sorts out the different stimuli so that you can concentrate on one immediate thought—which station to watch. Perhaps the telephone rings just as you begin to think about changing stations. Instead of answering the phone, your central nervous system may give priority to the television message, and you may continue to pay attention to that. However, if you had been anxiously awaiting a call from a close friend, then your central nervous system will probably give the telephone message priority, and you will answer its ring. The entire process requires intrapersonal communication. Now imagine the phone rings, and just as you get up to answer it, the doorbell rings. You stop. You cannot decide whether to answer the door or the telephone. You just stand there. The doorbell has interfered with your intrapersonal communication processes. Or perhaps just as you get up to answer the phone, you drop back in your chair with a splitting headache. Again you cannot concentrate. The headache has also interfered with your process of intrapersonal communication.

Applying our example of watching television to the components of our basic model of communication (Figure 1–12), we can see that your eyes and ears become the *senders* or transmitters of electrochemical impulses (*messages*) through a *medium* of communication, which in this case was your central nervous system. Your brain becomes the *receiver* of these impulses which transmits additional electrochemical impulses in the form of *feedback* to muscles, producing such physical activity as changing stations or answering the telephone. We also saw interference to successful intrapersonal communication. The doorbell produced external *noise* which interfered with this process. You also experienced internal noise in the form of a headache. The headache and doorbell interrupted the normal flow of electrochemical impulses, thus adding new factors to your decision-making task and temporarily distorting the process of intrapersonal communication.

Interpersonal Communication

With the crude beginnings of language, the process of *interpersonal communication*—communication in a face-to-face situation—bridged the gap from the concrete to the abstract. It became possible to communicate about persons or things not directly in view. If we apply our basic model to interpersonal communication, a typical situation might be as follows: You (sender) may speak (medium) words (message) to a friend (receiver) across the room, and the friend replies with an approval (feedback). While you are speaking and while your friend is reacting, intrapersonal communication is also taking place. When the two of you are talking, if a baseball (noise) comes flying through the window, it will disrupt both the process of intrapersonal communication and that of interpersonal communication. Perhaps one of you uses a cliché or a phrase which the other person does not understand; then, *semantic noise* interferes with the communication process. The possibility of semantic noise is one reason why a basic rule of journalism is to avoid using clichés.

For example, put yourself in the position of the television reporter from Idaho who visited New York to be interviewed for a job with a major television network. During the interview the reporter commented how after a hard day on the job, he would literally "come apart at the seams" before sitting down for dinner. The network executive conducting the interview jotted down in her notes that the reporter "can't withstand pressure, becomes mentally deranged, and goes berserk before dinner!" To the Idaho reporter, "coming apart at the seams" simply meant totally relaxing before eating dinner. Obviously the reporter did not get the job. Semantic noise obstructed the process of interpersonal communication and consequently the job interview.

Important to understanding interpersonal communication is to recognize that each of us possesses what communication researcher, Wilbur Schramm, calls a *field of experience* (Figure 1–13). Our background, knowledge, beliefs, and virtually anything about us make up our field of experience. When we communicate interpersonally, our fields of experience begin to overlap. A reporter who does not share common knowledge about political issues with a politician cannot ask intelligent questions, and thus the politician and the reporter cannot carry on an intelligent dialogue. The further a relationship between two people advances, the more fields of experience will overlap. This overlapping of fields of experience is called *homophily*. The greater homophily that is present, the more chance for effective meaningful interpersonal communication.

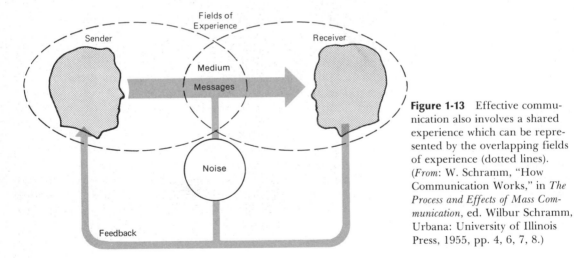

Figure 1-13 Effective communication also involves a shared experience which can be represented by the overlapping fields of experience (dotted lines). (*From*: W. Schramm, "How Communication Works," in *The Process and Effects of Mass Communication*, ed. Wilbur Schramm, Urbana: University of Illinois Press, 1955, pp. 4, 6, 7, 8.)

Every day we use interpersonal communication. However, the number of people we can reach with our ideas is limited if this is the only means of communication available to us. To understand the full potential of our communication processes, we need to look beyond interpersonal communication to the process of mass communication.

Mass Communi- cation

To understand mass communication as a process distinct from interpersonal and intrapersonal communication, imagine that you are attending a party where a politician is mingling and conversing with guests. About an hour later the party ends, and you join a few thousand people in an auditorium to hear the politician deliver a major address. Stop and ask yourself whether mass communication was taking place either at the party or in the auditorium where a large number of persons was present. The answer is *no*. For mass communication to exist, we need an intermediate transmitter of information, a *mass medium* such as newspapers, magazines, film, radio, television, books, or combinations of these. The politician who delivered a major address without the aid of the mass media would be forfeiting his chance to reach thousands, even millions of persons not physically present. Essentially, then, *mass communication is messages communicated through a mass medium to a large number of people.* For further clarification we shall use the word *mass* to refer to a large body of persons. Although by definition we have answered our question of what mass communication is, we need to examine more closely the specific characteristics of the process.

CHARACTERISTICS OF MASS COMMUNICATION

A number of characteristics distinguish mass communication from other types of communication.

*Mass
Medium*

We have already distinguished one characteristic of mass communication— the presence of a mass medium. A mass medium makes it possible for the message to reach far beyond the immediate proximity of the sender. A few hundred feet may be all the distance the human voice can project to a crowd without the aid of public address system. A mass medium can take that same message around the world.

*Limited
Sensory
Channels*

The presence of a mass medium also limits the number of sensory channels upon which we can draw. When we sat in the auditorium and listened to the politician, all of our senses could take part in the communication process. For example, after the speech we might have shaken hands (touch) with the politician. With mass communication we might only be able to hear and see the politician. Even then, we may be at the mercy of a producer's or director's decision of whether to take a close-up or distant shot, whether to concentrate on the crowd or the speaker.

*Impersonal
vs. Personal
Communi-
cation*

Still another characteristic of mass communication is that it is largely impersonal. To understand this concept, compare messages exchanged through interpersonal communication. Although first meetings between strangers are relatively impersonal, as the relationship continues, the communication becomes more and more personal. With mass communication, since participants in communication are usually unknown to each other, messages are more impersonal.

*The
Gatekeeper
Concept*

The process of mass communication requires additional persons, most often complex societal organizations and institutions, to carry messages from the speaker to the audience. Returning to our simplified examples, sitting next to you in the auditorium is a reporter who hears the politician's speech, writes a story about it, and delivers it to the local newspaper that publishes it the next morning. In this example, relay people aid in carrying the speaker's remarks beyond the auditorium to the reading public. The reporter who wrote the speech, the newspaper editor who edited the reporter's remarks, the typesetter, and the printer all helped relay this information through a medium of mass communication. Both the individuals (termed *relay people*) and the organizations are called *gatekeepers*. The term *gatekeeper* was first employed by the Austrian psychologist Kurt Lewin to refer to individuals or groups of persons who govern "the travels of news items in the communication channel." We will expand Lewin's definition and define gatekeeper as *any person or formally organized group directly involved in relaying or transferring information from one individual to another through a mass medium.* A gatekeeper can be a film producer who cuts a scene from the original script, a network censor who deletes a scene from a prime-time show because it is perceived as being too sexually explicit, a director who determines what segment of film to use in a documentary, a newspaper executive who determines the topic for an editorial, or any other individual in the processing or control of messages disseminated through mass media to the public.

We can readily see that such an individual has the ability to *limit* information we receive from the mass media. A reporter may edit a story about the work of a congressional committee or a meeting of Parliament by deleting parts of the story he or she feels may be irrelevant. On the other hand, a gatekeeper can also *expand* information to the public by supplying facts, attitudes, or viewpoints his or her audience would not usually receive. The reporter who covers the congressional hearing or reports on Parliament's deliberations increases the total amount of information we receive—in this case, in absentia—from our environment. The reporter may also *reorganize or reinterpret* the information we receive. Facts may be rearranged or a new slant may be given to the story of the politician's speech. This is not always the case, but it can happen.

It is important to remember that there are three functions of the gatekeeper: (1) to *limit* the information we receive by editing this information before it is disseminated to us; (2) to *expand* the amount of information we receive by giving us additional facts or views and (3) to *reorganize* or *reinterpret* the information.

Delayed Feedback

Returning to our example of the politician, perhaps the next day after reading about the speech in the local newspaper, an angry constituent writes a letter to the editor of the newspaper criticizing the politician's stand on an issue. Another constituent, somewhat more upset, decides to write directly to the politician. A lobbyist who heard the speech on radio may personally approach the politician and express approval of the speech. Each example is a form of *delayed feedback,* which differs from the immediate feedback the politician received from the members of the live audience. In the auditorium, for example, reporters could ask questions about certain ideas they did not understand. The politician could, in turn, clear up any misunderstandings or project new messages for further thought. The difference between the reporters' responses and those of the constituents and the lobbyist may be accounted for by the time delay.

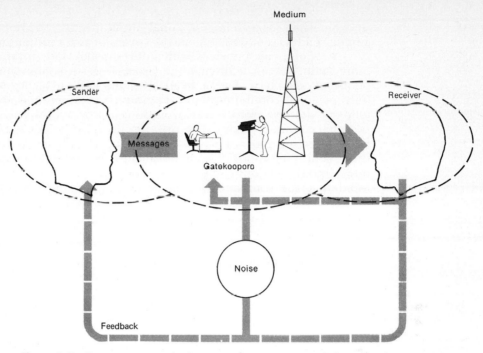

Figure 1-14 In mass communication, a gatekeeper processes information between sender and receiver. Feedback is thus delayed; whereas in interpersonal communication, feedback is instantaneous.

Delayed feedback is not unique to the mass communication situation. It can occur on an intrapersonal level, as when one is temporarily baffled by an optical illusion. It also occurs often on the interpersonal level when one person temporarily refrains from commenting about another's remark or suggestion. However, since delayed feedback will in many cases result from the mass communication situation, we shall use it as one of our distinguishing characteristics. Adding the concepts of the gatekeeper and delayed feedback to our basic model of communication gives us the model of mass communication illustrated in Figure 1–14.

Figure 1-15 Components of the process of communication.

	Intrapersonal	Interpersonal	Mass
Sender	Sense Organs	Politician	Politician
Receiver	Brain	Reporter	Public
Messages	Electro-Chemical Impulses	Language	Language
Medium	Central Nervous System	Voice	Newspaper
Feedback	Electro-Chemical Impulses	Questions	Letters
Noise	Headache	Breaking Glass	Blurred Printing

Similarly, as with interpersonal communication, homophily can exist among senders, gatekeepers, and receivers of mass communication.

As noise can interfere with interpersonal and intrapersonal communication, so can it disrupt the process of mass communication. The politician may have had a headache and had difficulty concentrating (intrapersonal communication). The air conditioner may have been too loud for the reporter to hear everything the politician was saying (interpersonal communication). The printing press as the newspaper may have failed, creating blurred pages and making it difficult to read the story (mass communication). Figure 1–15 shows the politician's speech broken down into the various components of our communication model. Keep in mind that the components present in intrapersonal and interpersonal communication are also part of mass communication. Note, for instance, that in the case of the receiver, for there to be a "public" to receive mass communication, there also has to be a "reporter" to receive interpersonal communication and a "brain" to receive intrapersonal communication. All three components are part of the process of human communication.

THE SOCIAL CONTEXT OF MASS COMMUNICATION

Up to this point, our model of mass communication has been primarily concerned with how we send and receive messages. But forces also affect the messages themselves, in addition to how consumers react to these messages. Specifically these forces consist of society's social groups and systems.

Mass communication does not operate in a social vacuum as a machine does. When a computer receives a message, for instance, it will provide an answer based on that original message. If the computer is functioning properly, the same answer will appear every time we send it the identical message. Now contrast this process with what occurs in mass communication. Imagine that you, a consumer of mass media, read the newspaper story about the politician's speech. After you talked with your family, friends, and co-workers about it, you decided to write a letter to the politician. It is thus possible that three social groups—your family, friends, and co-workers—affected your reaction to the speech.

Now imagine that you are the newspaper reporter responsible for writing about the speech. Social groups will affect your reporting of the story to the public. Perhaps you are a member of a union that goes on strike just as you return to your office to write the story. Perhaps you belong to a journalism association with a code of reporting ethics to which you personally adhere. The code states that you cannot accept gifts as part of your job as a reporter. Your morning mail brings an invitation from a major oil company to be their guest on a flight to Kuwait for an on-the-spot story about oil exploration. You are faced with accepting the free trip and doing the story or rejecting the free trip and permitting other media in your city to obtain the story. You obviously are faced with a dilemma attributable at least in part to the influence various social groups have on you.

CHANGING DEFINITIONS: SPECIALIZED AUDIENCES

Because mass media are such an important part of our lives, we tend to think of media audiences as being total populations or mass national audiences. Although to some degree this is correct, we should also understand that today the *mass audience* is becoming a *specialized audience*. Similarly many *mass media* are also very *specialized media*.

Although some magazine publishers may want to reach as many readers as possible, others may want to reach only specific readers. For example, if you published *Dallas* (Figure 1–16) magazine, you would want to concentrate your efforts on reaching people who lived in Dallas, or if you published *Ohio*, your primary audience would be residents of Ohio. Moreover, your advertisers would not be interested in paying high rates to reach an audience that had no interest in buying their products, and you would not want to spend the additional money to print the magazine for these disinterested readers.

Radio represents another example of specialized media. When radio's golden age began in the 1930s, it was truly a mass medium. By the 1950s it began to develop different programming formats. Drama programs

Figure 1-16 Magazines directed at specific audiences offer advertisers the opportunity to direct their messages to "specialized" as opposed to "mass" audiences. (© 1980 DALLAS Magazine. Reprinted by permission of the Dallas Chamber of Commerce and *Ohio* Magazine)

aimed at the mass audience, which once predominated, have been replaced by rock and roll, top-forty, and other musical trends meant to reach a specialized younger audience. Phrases such as the "18–24-year-old" and *"target audiences"* are commonly applied to radio. Network programming primarily directed at mass audiences has become local programming directed at specialized audiences. Radio network programming has diversified. Larger networks have broken up into smaller demographic networks. State radio networks directed at audiences in specific geographical regions have also developed.

Television also appeals to diversified audiences. Cable television, for instance, can provide a multitude of channels with different types of programming for different viewers. Besides the major network programs, special broadcasts can be produced by local colleges and universities, corporate programs can be used to train employees, and still other presentations can include citizen discussion groups talking about community issues. No longer does television simply aim at the "masses."

Consider newspapers. Although the large metropolitan dailies still mainly serve mass audiences, new computer technology permits many to reach specific audiences with area edition inserts and refined distribution systems. Smaller suburban and foreign language (Figure 1–17) newspapers, edited for communities adjacent to the metropolis, attribute their success to news of interest to their own particular community.

Figure 1-17 Foreign-language newspapers reach specialized audiences and are many times the preferred advertising media, because they can identify with the culture of a foreign-speaking population.

Wire services have also changed. At the turn of the century the United States was served primarily by two wire services—Associated Press (AP) and United Press International (UPI). In a sense they were directed at the mass national audience through their subscribing newspapers. Today, however, although the two major wire services still function, numerous specialized wire services have come into existence. Some deal exclusively with weather information and news of prime importance to agricultural regions. Others, directed at the business audience, deal with stocks and commodities. Grain farmers, chicken farmers, and people in the lumber business have specialized wire services. Even AP and UPI have become specialized. Both print and broadcast wires for subscribers are offered, in addition to audio services and special services to cable television operators.

Look at the recording industry. Back when the early television program *The Hit Parade* was popular, the ten songs performed each week were accorded a "mass" national audience. Today a similar program would have a hard time finding an audience large enough to justify its staying on the air. For there now are top-forty charts, top country and western charts, top classical charts, top easy listening charts, and even videodisc and videotape charts.

NEW TECHNOLOGIES
AND PERSONALIZED MEDIA

Videodisc and videotape are only some of the new technologies which may revolutionize our use of media and further alter the definition of mass communication. Direct broadcast satellites, for example, make it possible for us to purchase a small dish antenna and receive hundreds of television channels (Figure 1–18). The choices on what and when to watch become much wider than those listed in the evening newspaper. We can go to a local electronic store and purchase a home computer (Figure 1–19) which uses a television set or video display terminal (*VDT*) to display a host of functions, from plotting complex business statistics to playing electronic games.

By purchasing a *modem,* a device that connects your telephone receiver to a computer, we can hook up to such other services as stock market reports, gardening information, or the latest news headlines. Using telephone interconnects, we can interact with other users of the system and exchange information. The decision on how to use these new interactive technologies are much more complex than simply deciding on whether to operate the on-off button on our television set. We are making highly individual *personalized* choices. We become not only the receivers of communication but also the senders and the gatekeepers. As these new technologies make an increasing impact on our lives, we will not only want to keep alert to how "mass" media change but also to how we use these "new" media.

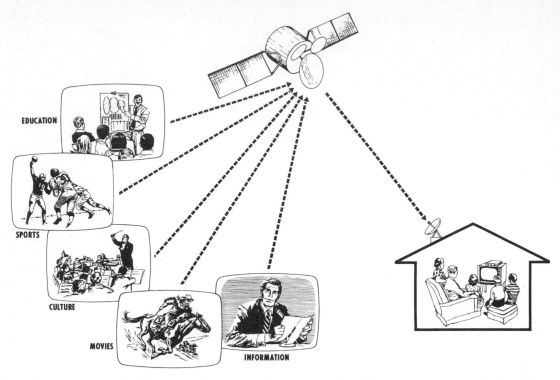

Figure 1-18 Direct broadcast satellites can send television signals directly to home antennas. Increased clarity through large-screen, high-definition transmitting and receiving systems, increased channel capacity, and the ability to reach rural areas more efficiently than cable television are just some of the advantages which may evolve with this new technology. (Courtesy, COMSAT)

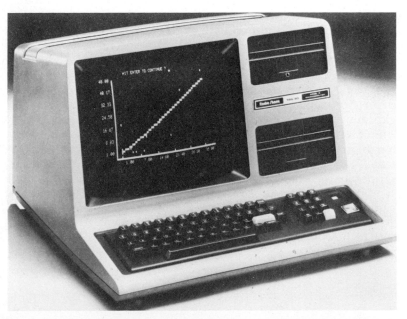

Figure 1-19 Home computers are among the changing uses for the home television screen and also part of the two-way interactive home information systems which could become the "media" of the future. (TRS-80* Microcomputer. Used with permission of Radio Shack and Tandy Corporation. *TRS-80 is a trademark of Tandy Corporation.)

Theorists have predicted this trend toward specialized and personalized media. For example, Richard Maisel has theorized that industrial society eventually necessitates the creation of specialized media. He contends that our present "postindustrial" society results in the growth of service industries, which are "great consumers of specialized media." He states, "The needs and tastes of specialized groups can only be satisfied by a form of specialized communication designed for a homogeneous audience."[1]

Although Maisel may seem to be referring to the industrial consumption of media, his concept applies just as well to many facets of nonindustrial consumption of media—for example, the entertainment function of media. Even the radio commercials that inform us of vital "services" in our postindustrial society are directed to local audiences.

Although it may at first seem that the growth of specialized media conflicts with the truly mass media, this is not necessarily the case. We now have the *choice* of attending to the older, more generalized mass appeal media or to the newer specialized media. The future of mass communication in the very broad sense is still open to speculation. Our society is centuries old; yet with the exception of books and newspapers, we are mere infants in our experience with mass media. What effect the growth of specialized media will have on society is open to further study.

SUMMARY

Mass communication evolved from the fundamental process of human communication—people exchanging messages through verbal and written symbols. Technology increased the efficiency of mass communication so that today the process can send messages around the world and into space.

We defined mass communication as messages communicated through a mass medium to a large number of people. We also learned how to distinguish mass communication from other types of communication by examining the components of human communication as represented in a communication model. These components include senders, receivers, messages, and medium of communication. Two additional components are feedback, which occurs when a receiver reacts to a message, and noise, which is anything that interferes with the communication process.

Mass communication is one of three basic types of human communication, the other two being intrapersonal and interpersonal communication. Intrapersonal communication is communication within ourselves, electrochemical impulses sent from the sense organs of sight, sound, touch, smell, and taste through the central nervous system to the brain. The brain, in turn, generates electrochemical impulses that activate the muscular system. Interpersonal communication is communication in a face-to-face situation. It contains the same basic components of the communication model as does intrapersonal communication.

Mass communication differs from both intrapersonal and interpersonal communication in that it requires a mass medium, such as television or newspapers. It also necessitates the presence of gatekeeper(s), people, and/or systems that control and process the information before it is disseminated to the public. In addition, mass communication almost always has delayed feedback rather than the immediate feedback present on the other two levels of communication. We learned that media messages are more impersonal than the interpersonal messages of face-to-face communication.

Mass communication also operates within a complex social context. Messages are affected by the attitudes of the various gatekeepers, and audience response in turn is affected by social context. How we react to mass media is partially self-determined, however. To some extent we choose to associate with specific social groups, friends, neighbors, co-workers, and members of professional, religious, and political organizations. The people and groups we associate with influence how we respond to messages received through the mass media.

Mass communication increasingly is becoming a process designed to reach specialized audiences through specialized media. Virtually every medium is in some way directed toward specialized audiences. Researcher Richard Maisel views this changing definition of mass as a natural function of our postindustrial society.

OPPORTUNITIES FOR FURTHER LEARNING

Austin-Lett, G., and J. Srague, *Talk to Yourself: Experiencing Intrapersonal Communication.* New York: Houghton Mifflin Company, 1976.

Bormann, E. G., *Communication Theory.* New York: Holt, Rinehart & Winston, 1980.

Bittner, J. R., *Each Other: An Introduction to Interpersonal Communication.* Englewood Cliffs, N.J.: Prentice-Hall, 1983.

De Lozier, W. M., *The Marketing Communications Process.* New York: McGraw-Hill, 1976.

Del Polito, C. M., *Intrapersonal Communication.* Menlo Park, Calif.; Cummings Publishing Company, 1977.

Dervin, B., and M. J. Voigt, eds., *Progress in Communication Sciences*, Vol. II. Norwood, N.J.: Ablex, 1980.

Gumpert, G., and R. Cathcart, *Inter/Media: Interpersonal Communication in a Media World.* New York: Oxford University Press, 1979.

Hanneman, G. J., and W. J. McEwen, *Communication and Behavior.* Reading, Mass.: Addison-Wesley, 1975.

Harper, N., *Human Communication Theory: History of a Paradigm.* Rochelle Park, N.J.: Hayden Book Co., 1979.

Laswell, H. D., D. Lerner, and H. Speier, eds., *Propaganda and Communication in World History, Vol. 1: The Symbolic Instrument in Early Times.* Honolulu: University of Hawaii Press, 1979.

Lesly, P., *How We Discommunicate.* New York: American Management Associations, 1979.

McCombs, M. E., and L. B. Becker, *Using Mass Communication Theory.* Englewood Cliffs, N.J.: Prentice-Hall, 1979.

MITCHELL, W. J. T., *The Language of Images*. Chicago: University of Chicago Press, 1980.

MORTENSEN, C. D., ed., *Basic Readings in Communication Theory*. New York: Harper & Row, 1978.

Planning Methods, Models, and Organization: A Review Study for Communication Policy Making and Planning. Honolulu: East-West Center, East-West Communication Institute, 1978.

POOL, I. D. S., *Handbook of Communication*. Skokie, Ill.: Rand McNally, 1973.

SCHRAMM, W., AND D. LERNER, eds., *Communication and Change: The Last Ten Years— and the Next*. Honolulu: East-West Center, University Press of Hawaii, 1976.

SCHROEDER, F. E. H., ed., *5000 Years of Popular Culture: Popular Culture before Printing*. Bowling Green, Ohio: Bowling Green University Popular Press, 1980.

SEVERIN, W. J., AND J. W. Tankard, Jr., *Communication Theories: Origins, Methods, Uses*. New York: Hastings House, 1980.

STEVENS, J. D., AND H. D. GARCIA, *Communication History*. Beverly Hills, Calif.: Sage Publications, Inc., 1980.

CHAPTER

NEWSPAPERS

PREVIEW

After completing this chapter, we should be able to:

List Otto Groth's criteria for determining a true newspaper.

Be aware of the Roman and Chinese contributions to the newspaper.

Trace the European and English foundations of the modern press.

Describe and identify the early colonial newspapers and their publishers.

Discuss the significance of the John Peter Zenger case.

Explain the advantages that both the telegraph and the Atlantic Cable provided for the newspaper industry.

Understand the contributions of the penny press to modern newspapers.

Understand the beginnings of the black press, American Indian press, and the role of women in journalism.

Explain how the War Between the States, Reconstruction, and westward expansion affected American newspapers.

Discuss yellow journalism.

Realize the significance of professional associations to newspapers.

Trace the early development of United Press.

Determine how economic indicators, newsprint, labor, computer and satellite technology, and advertising affect the newspaper industry.

Know about suburban, foreign, and international newspaper editions.

Discuss the concept of newspaper sectionals.

Realize the advantages to newspapers of adopting standard advertising units

Explain newspapers' expansion into corporate conglomerates

Describe the electronic newspaper.

Newspapers are an economic and social phenomenon of our society. They are a major force in forming public opinion the world over and thus mightily affect national and international efforts toward economic progress and global understanding. Specialty newspapers exist for elementary school students, major financial dailies appeal to the commerce tycoons of the world, tabloids dress the newsstands of city transportation hubs, and popular underground publications appear or disappear at the change of a trend or movement. Newspaper stories have turned ordinary men and women into heroes and have removed world leaders from power. Huge presses spew out hundreds of pages in a single edition, and modern transportation and communication systems can put that same edition on a breakfast table 3000 miles away. Today the newspaper industry has become one of the largest in the world. It employs hundreds of thousands of people, from managing editors, to investigative reporters, to carriers. It has survived wars, economic collapse, and social destruction, yet remains essentially the same type of medium that it was centuries ago—pages of print communicating information to readers.

Before beginning our discussion of early newspapers, we should first define what a true newspaper is.

CHARACTERISTICS OF A NEWSPAPER

In 1928 a German scholar, Otto Groth, developed a set of five standards which modern scholars generally hold as acceptable criteria for determining a true newspaper.[1] Groth's first standard was that a newspaper must be *published periodically* at intervals not less than once a week. Second, *mechanical reproduction* must be employed. Early Roman and Chinese publications would not qualify here. Third, anyone who can pay the price of admission must have *access to the publication*. In other words, it must be available to everyone, not just a chosen few. No organization can have an exclusive right to read or obtain the publication. Fourth, it must *vary in content* and include everything of public interest to everyone, not merely to small, select groups. Finally, publication must be *timely* with some *continuity of organization*.

Keep Groth's definitions in mind as we read about early newspapers, since the true beginnings of the press are found in many publications that may not meet Groth's standards. Yet his standards remain important to our study as a point of reference that historians use to refer to the newspapers' true impact on our society.

Scholars have never quite agreed on what could be considered the first true newspaper, partly because they could not reach a consensus on how to define the beginnings of the press.

The Posted Bulletins

In Italy messengers disseminated mass news as early as 59 B.C. with the publication of daily events bulletins called *Acta Diurna*. They were posted in a public place for all to read and were kept on file as an official record of historical events (Figure 2–1). There are indications that the bulletin may have been copied and reproduced by hand for distribution to other countries by messenger and ship. Obviously the ability of the publication to transmit messages to a mass audience was minimal based on today's standards. The number of "subscribers" were the number of persons who happened to read the poster. Almost 1800 years later, posted bulletins were a source of news during the American Revolution (Figure 2–2).

The Romans also developed a system of news dissemination in which a "reader" would announce the day's news events at a given time and place, and those wishing to hear it would be charged admission. You would have paid one Italian *gazetta* to hear the news. Such contemporary newspapers as the *Sydney Gazette* of Australia and our own *Georgia Gazette* and *Colorado Springs Gazette* trace their name to this ancient custom. No one country can claim the foundation of the modern press. The earliest *forerunner* of the modern newspaper can, however, be credited to the Chinese. A publication resembling a court journal appeared about 500 A.D., entitled *Tsing Pao*. The publication began in Peking and remained in publication into the twentieth century.

European Foundations of the Modern Press

As the technological advances of printing made their way across Europe, newspapers cropped up frequently in almost all areas. Certain political atmospheres helped and in some cases hindered the development of the press, but for the most part it flourished. The seventeenth century was deluged with this medium. During this period the press flourished in England, the Scandinavian countries, France, Germany, and the United States. The turmoil of the Thirty Years' War during the first half of the seventeenth century contributed to the development of journalism in Europe mostly by providing a background against which many different issues could be aired. In general, the war did more to liberate journalism than to hinder it.

The first newspaper published in Germany was founded in 1609 by Egenolph Emmel, a bookseller, who started a weekly in Frankfurt in 1615. A competing Frankfurt newspaper published in 1617 by Johann von den Birghden led to the first legislation over a newspaper monopoly. In a lawsuit brought by Emmel, von den Birghden asserted that, as postmaster he had an exclusive right to publish a newspaper. Similar controversies did not in any way discourage entrepreneurs from entering the business, however, as is indicated by the fact that in 1633 there were no fewer than 16 newspapers in Germany.

Figure 2-1 Early distribution of news occurred with the posting of "bulletins" on the sides of buildings in public places. There, passers-by could read about the events of the day. (John W. Houck, *Outdoor Advertising: History and Regulation.* Notre Dame, Ind: University of Notre Dame Press, 1969)

Figure 2-2 Posted bulletins remained a source of news, including this poster engraved, printed, and sold by Paul Revere and distributed during the American Revolution. (Institute of Outdoor Advertising)

In England the press developed under the authoritarian atmosphere of the early seventeenth century. A product of the Tudor system designed to "license" official government printers, a free press was virtually nonexistent. In fact, some whose fever for free expression became too much to hold back found themselves at the end of a hangman's noose. William Caxton had established the first English printing press in 1476, but not until 1621 did "sheets" of news begin to appear sporadically across the English countryside. Called *corantos*, they still were not true newspapers by today's criteria. They usually skirted the restrictions against a free press by publishing news from outside the country.

The Thirty Years' War is credited for the flourishing of the early English press. During that period, from 1618 until 1648, news of the war became both popular and profitable.

The voices calling for a free press were growing more strident. Most noted among these was the poet John Milton. Milton had been educated at Cambridge and had traveled widely in Europe, meeting many of the noted politicians, artists, and church leaders of his time. He had become disenchanted with the church's ritualism, and this had germinated similar feelings against government's control over its people. In his famous *Areopagitica*, Milton stated, "And though all the winds of doctrine were to let loose to play upon the earth, so Truth be in the field, we do injuriously by licensing and prohibiting to misdoubt her strength. Let her and Falsehood grapple: who ever knew Truth put to worse, in a free and open encounter?"

The licensing to which Milton was referring was an order issued one year earlier, in 1643, making the government-approved stationers' company responsible for putting its official stamp on anything printed in England. The company also had the right to search and seize publications which did not have its approval. Milton's argument for a free press became the foundation for arguments used by Thomas Jefferson in colonial times and even for contemporary lawyers championing the rights of the First Amendment.

In 1694 the licensing of the press finally ended in England. The powers of Parliament were beginning to conflict with those of the Crown and with rivaling factions competing for the same constituency, and none wanted its views muzzled. This freedom of expression increased the thirst for news, and eight years later, in 1702, the *Daily Courant* became the first, although not continuous, newspaper published in the English language. But between the edicts of the 1640s and the end of licensing, those most affected by both church and state had already ventured to a new world called America.

NEWSPAPERING IN EARLY AMERICA

If you had been among the first colonists in America, publishing a newspaper would not have been one of your priorities. There are a number of obvious reasons why not, even though skilled printers were among the first people to arrive from England. Basic needs of survival had to be met first: forests had to be cleared, fields plowed, houses built, and crops harvested. Second, news of international events arrived regularly via ships from London. In addition, you would have had little need for news about your own government, because that scarcely existed. Fourth, the closely knit geographical location of the New England communities facilitated news dissemination through interpersonal communication. Town meetings thus became the colonists' primary means of communication. Based on today's standards, early America was a closed society.

Early Colonial Newspapers

The first attempt at a newspaper in the colonies was one started by the English printer Benjamin Harris. Harris had been banished from England for operating the modern equivalent of an underground newspaper. Coming to Boston, he published in 1690 an edition of a newsletter entitled *Publick Occurrences, Both Forreign and Domestick* (Figure 2–3). In the publication he made the mistake of taking a stance not favorable to the Indians in the area. The government of Massachusetts, one of whose primary aims was to win the favor of the Indians, did not appreciate Harris' ill-timed and undiplomatic remarks. As a result Harris' publication was promptly confiscated, but the government gave him a subsidy to continue printing.

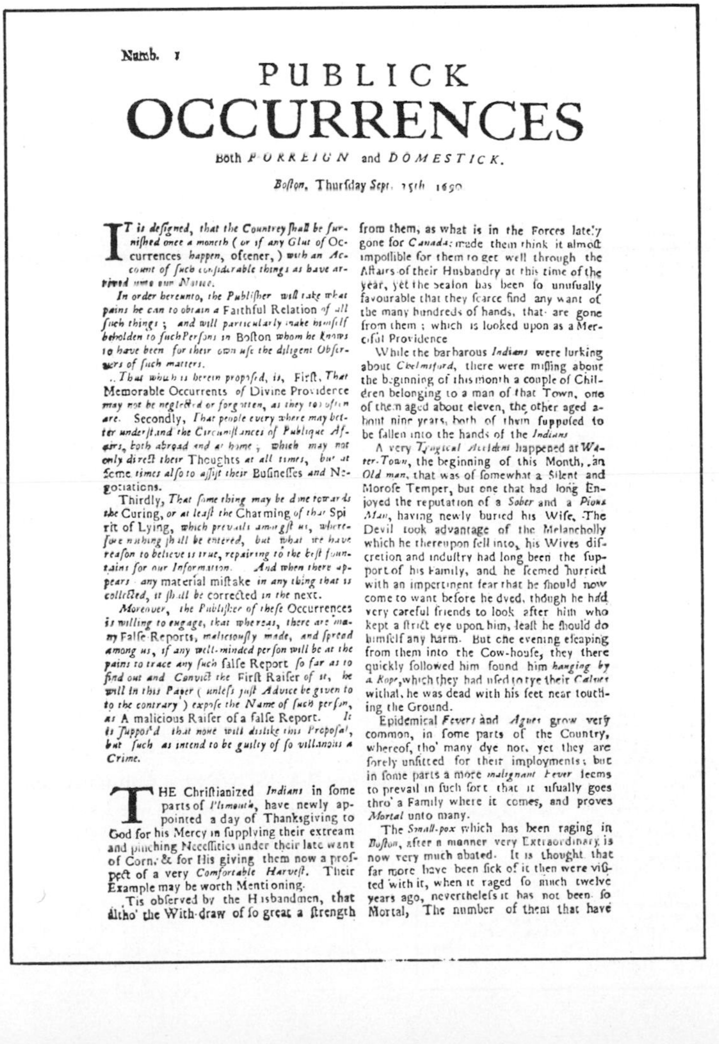
Numb. 1

PUBLICK OCCURRENCES

Both FORREIGN and DOMESTICK.

Boston, Thursday *Sept.* 25th 1690.

It is designed, that the Countrey shall be furnished once a month (or if any Glut of Occurrences happen, oftener,) with an Account of such considerable things as have arrived unto our Notice.

In order hereunto, the Publisher will take what pains he can to obtain a Faithful Relation *of all such things; and will particularly make himself beholden to such Persons in* Boston *whom he knows to have been for their own use the diligent Observers of such matters.*

That which is herein proposed, is, First, *That* Memorable Occurrents *of* Divine Providence *may not be neglected or forgotten, as they too often are.* Secondly, *That people every where may better understand the Circumstances of Publique Affairs, both abroad and at home; which may not only direct their* Thoughts *at all times, but at some times also to assist their* Businesses *and* Negotiations.

Thirdly, *That some thing may be done towards the* Curing, *or at least the* Charming *of that* Spirit of Lying, *which prevails amongst us, wherefore nothing shall be entered, but what we have reason to believe is true, repairing to the best fountains for our Information. And when there appears any* material mistake *in any thing that is collected, it shall be* corrected *in the* next.

Moreover, the Publisher of these Occurrences *is willing to engage, that whereas, there are many* False Reports, *maliciously made, and spread among us, if any well-minded person will be at the pains to trace any such* false Report *so far as to find out and Convict the* First Raiser *of it, he will in this Paper (unless just Advice be given to the contrary) expose the Name of such person, as* A malicious Raiser of a false Report. *It is suppos'd that none will dislike this Proposal, but such as intend to be guilty of so villanous a Crime.*

THE Christianized *Indians* in some parts of *Plimouth*, have newly appointed a day of Thanksgiving to God for his Mercy in supplying their extream and pinching Necessities under their late want of Corn, & for His giving them now a prospect of a very *Comfortable Harvest*. Their Example may be worth Mentioning.

'Tis observed by the Husbandmen, that altho' the With-draw of so great a strength from them, as what is in the Forces lately gone for *Canada*; made them think it almost impossible for them to get well through the Affairs of their Husbandry at this time of the year, yet the season has been so unusually favourable that they scarce find any want of the many hundreds of hands, that are gone from them; which is looked upon as a Merciful Providence

While the barbarous *Indians* were lurking about *Chelmsford*, there were missing about the beginning of this month a couple of Children belonging to a man of that Town, one of them aged about eleven, the other aged about nine years, both of them supposed to be fallen into the hands of the *Indians*

A very *Tragical Accident* happened at *Water-Town*, the beginning of this Month, an *Old man*, that was of somewhat a Silent and Morose Temper, but one that had long Enjoyed the reputation of a *Sober* and a *Pious Man*, having newly buried his Wife, The Devil took advantage of the Melancholly which he thereupon fell into, his Wives discretion and industry had long been the support of his Family, and he seemed hurried with an impertinent fear that he should now come to want before he dyed, though he had very careful friends to look after him who kept a strict eye upon him, least he should do himself any harm. But one evening escaping from them into the Cow-house, they there quickly followed him found him *hanging by a Rope*, which they had used to tye their *Calves* withal, he was dead with his feet near touching the Ground.

Epidemical *Fevers* and *Agues* grow very common, in some parts of the Country, whereof, tho' many dye not, yet they are sorely unfitted for their imployments; but in some parts a more *malignant Fever* seems to prevail in such sort that it usually goes thro' a Family where it comes, and proves *Mortal* unto many.

The *Small-pox* which has been raging in *Boston*, after a manner very Extraordinary is now very much abated. It is thought that far more have been sick of it then were visited with it, when it raged so much twelve years ago, nevertheless it has not been so Mortal, The number of them that have

Figure 2-3 Some consider it the first American newspaper. *Public Occurrences Both Forreign and Domestick* appeared on September 25, 1690 from the print shop of R. Pierce and under the editorship of Benjamin Harris. The publication, printed on three sides, was 6″ × 10¼″ and had the fourth page blank so the reader could add more information before passing it along to another person. However, it was banned after the first issue. (Source: E. Emery and M. Emery, *The Press in America.* Englewood Cliffs, N.J.: Prentice-Hall, Inc., 1978)

He accepted. This may seem a rather cowardly act by today's journalistic standards, but the seriousness of Harris' financial position dictated a practical response. According to Groth's standards, Harris' publication would not have been considered a true newspaper since it appeared only once before its publisher returned to England. The first publication to meet all of the standards of a true newspaper made its appearance 14 years later.

In 1704 postmaster John Campbell joined with printer Bartholomew Green to publish a newspaper called the *Boston News-Letter*. Campbell had several advantages, including a postmaster's free use of the mails. He also had been appointed by the Crown and reported directly to the governor of Massachusetts, and when he ran into financial trouble, a government subsidy was waiting. The *News-Letter* received competition from the *New England Courant* published by James Franklin, the older brother of Benjamin Franklin. The *Courant* distinguished itself as being independent from the publishing enterprises approved by the Crown's governors and carried forth numerous editorial crusades against both church and state.

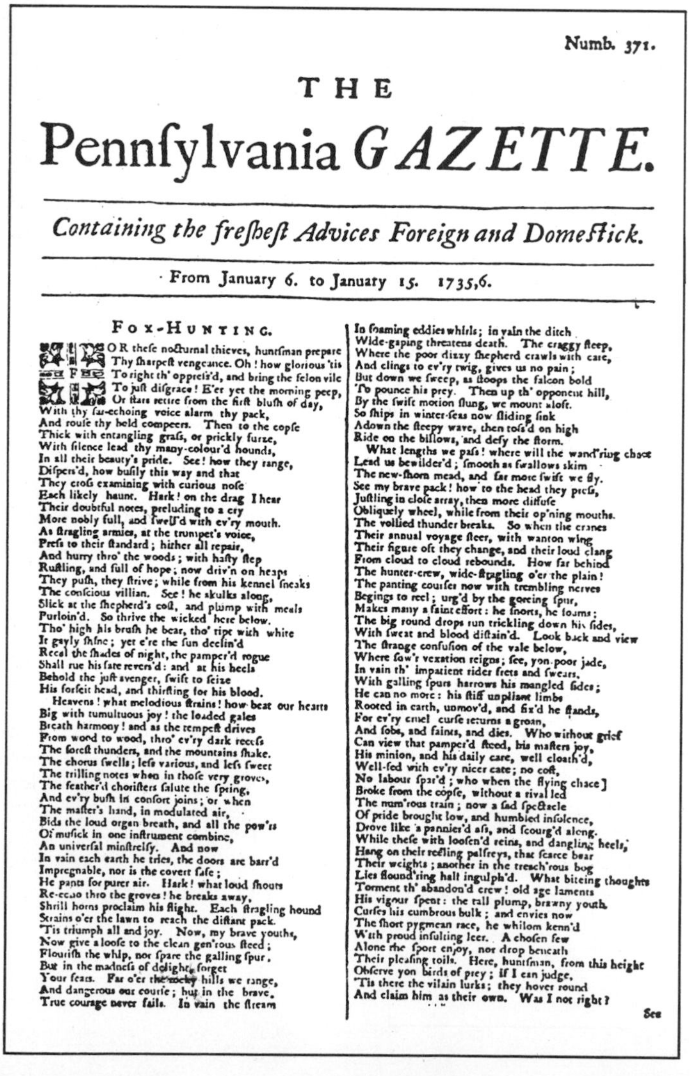

Numb. 371.

THE

Pennſylvania *GAZETTE*.

Containing the freſheſt Advices Foreign and Domeſtick.

From January 6. to January 15. 1735,6.

FOX-HUNTING.

FOR theſe nocturnal thieves, huntſman prepare
Thy ſharpeſt vengeance. Oh! how glorious 'tis
To right th' oppreſs'd, and bring the felon vile
To juſt diſgrace! E'er yet the morning peep,
Or ſtars retire from the firſt bluſh of day,
With thy far-echoing voice alarm thy pack,
And rouſe thy bold compeers. Then to the copſe
Thick with entangling graſs, or prickly furze,
With ſilence lead thy many-colour'd hounds,
In all their beauty's pride. See! how they range,
Diſpers'd, how buſily this way and that
They croſs examining with curious noſe
Each likely haunt. Hark! on the drag I hear
Their doubtful notes, preluding to a cry
More nobly full, and ſwell'd with ev'ry mouth.
As ſtragling armies, at the trumpet's voice,
Preſs to their ſtandard; hither all repair,
And hurry thro' the woods; with haſty ſtep
Ruſtling, and full of hope; now driv'n on heaps
They puſh, they ſtrive; while from his kennel ſneaks
The conſcious villian. See! he skulks along,
Slick at the ſhepherd's coſt, and plump with meals
Purloin'd. So thrive the wicked here below.
Tho' high his bruſh he bear, tho' tipt with white
It gayly ſhine; yet e're the ſun declin'd
Recal the ſhades of night, the pamper'd rogue
Shall rue his fate revers'd: and at his heels
Behold the juſt avenger, ſwift to ſeize
His forfeit head, and thirſting for his blood.
Heavens! what melodious ſtrains! how beat our hearts
Big with tumultuous joy! the loaded gales
Breath harmony! and as the tempeſt drives
From wood to wood, thro' ev'ry dark receſs
The foreſt thunders, and the mountains ſhake.
The chorus ſwells; leſs various, and leſs ſweet
The trilling notes when in thoſe very groves,
The feather'd choriſters ſalute the ſpring,
And ev'ry buſh in conſort joins; or when
The maſter's hand, in modulated air,
Bids the loud organ breath, and all the pow'rs
Of muſick in one inſtrument combine,
An univerſal minſtrelſy. And now
In vain each earth he tries, the doors are barr'd
Impregnable, nor is the covert ſafe;
He pants for purer air. Hark! what loud ſhouts
Re-echo thro the groves! he breaks away,
Shrill horns proclaim his flight. Each ſtragling hound
Strains o'er the lawn to reach the diſtant pack.
'Tis triumph all and joy. Now, my brave youths,
Now give a looſe to the clean gen'rous ſteed;
Flouriſh the whip, nor ſpare the galling ſpur,
But in the madneſs of delight, forget
Your fears. Far o'er the rocky hills we range,
And dangerous our courſe; but in the brave,
True courage never fails. In vain the ſtream
In foaming eddies whirls; in vain the ditch
Wide-gaping threatens death. The craggy ſteep,
Where the poor dizzy ſhepherd crawls with care,
And clings to ev'ry twig, gives us no pain;
But down we ſweep, as ſtoops the falcon bold
To pounce his prey. Then up th' opponent hill,
By the ſwift motion flung, we mount aloft.
So ſhips in winter-ſeas now ſliding ſink
Adown the ſteepy wave, then toſs'd on high
Ride on the billows, and defy the ſtorm.
What lengths we paſs! where will the wand'ring chace
Lead us bewilder'd; ſmooth as ſwallows skim
The new-ſhorn mead, and far more ſwift we fly.
See my brave pack! how to the head they preſs,
Juſtling in cloſe array, then more diffuſe
Obliquely wheel, while from their op'ning mouths
The vollied thunder breaks. So when the cranes
Their annual voyage ſteer, with wanton wing
Their figure oft they change, and their loud clang
From cloud to cloud rebounds. How far behind
The hunter-crew, wide-ſtragling o'er the plain!
The panting courſer now with trembling nerves
Begings to reel; urg'd by the goreing ſpur,
Makes many a faint effort: he ſnorts, he foams:
The big round drops run trickling down his ſides,
With ſweat and blood diſtain'd. Look back and view
The ſtrange confuſion of the vale below,
Where ſow'r vexation reigns; ſee, yon poor jade,
In vain th' impatient rider frets and ſwears,
With galling ſpurs harrows his mangled ſides;
He can no more: his ſtiff unpliant limbs
Rooted in earth, unmov'd, and fix'd he ſtands,
For ev'ry cruel curſe returns a groan,
And ſobs, and faints, and dies. Who without grief
Can view that pamper'd ſteed, his maſters joy,
His minion, and his daily care, well cloath'd,
Well-fed with ev'ry nicer cate; no coſt,
No labour ſpar'd; who when the flying chace]
Broke from the copſe, without a rival led
The num'rous train; now a ſad ſpectacle
Of pride brought low, and humbled inſolence,
Drove like a pannier'd aſs, and ſcourg'd along.
While theſe with looſen'd reins, and dangling heels,
Hang on their reeling palfreys, that ſcarce bear
Their weights; another in the treach'rous bog
Lies flound'ring half ingulph'd. What biteing thoughts
Torment th' abandon'd crew! old age laments
His vigour ſpent: the tall plump, brawny youth
Curſes his cumbrous bulk; and envies now
The ſhort pygmean race, he whilom kenn'd
With proud inſulting leer. A choſen few
Alone the ſport enjoy, nor drop beneath
Their pleaſing toils. Here, huntſman, from this height
Obſerve yon birds of prey; if I can judge,
'Tis there the vilain lurks; they hover round
And claim him as their own. Was I not right?

See

Figure 2-4 Started by Samuel Keimer, the *Pennsylvania Gazette* was later acquired and managed by Benjamin Franklin.

Samuel Keimer started the *Pennsylvania Gazette* (Figure 2–4) which was later managed by Benjamin Franklin. William Parks founded both the *Maryland Gazette* and the *Virginia Gazette*. The latter proved especially important because of Virginia's influence on American independence and because the paper was published in Williamsburg, the capital of the Virginia colony.

The John Peter Zenger Case

In 1733 there was a landmark case concerning freedom of the press. It involved John Peter Zenger, an immigrant from Germany who had been a colleague of William Bradford, a printer in the New York colony. Bradford's newspaper, the *New York Gazette*, mostly expressed the government line. A group of business and political leaders wanted another voice in the affairs of state and convinced Zenger to start an opposition paper to Bradford's. Zenger's paper, the *New York Weekly Journal*, became critical of the colonial government. Specifically, the December 3, 1733 issue got him into trouble and almost a year later he was arrested. In 1735 he was brought to trial for *seditious libel*, publishing false and defamatory statements against the government. The famous Philadelphia lawyer Andrew Hamilton defended him in one of the classic cases of American journalism. Hamilton argued that the jury had the right to determine (1) whether Zenger printed the paper, and (2) whether the material was in fact libelous. Hamilton fully admitted that Zenger had published the paper and the criticism of the governor. However, he also argued that the material was true and therefore could not be libelous. As the jury had the right to determine whether the material was true, it therefore had the right to determine whether Zenger had committed libel. The prosecutor in the case took the position that, although the jury could determine whether Zenger had in fact published the paper, it remained the judge's prerogative to determine whether the material was indeed libelous. When Hamilton argued that the jury had the right to *both* decisions, he won its favor; a not guilty verdict established, at least in principle, the freedom to criticize public officials.

Surviving the Revolution

With the American Revolution the press became noticeably more political. Strife between the colonies and the Crown was bound to be aired in a press that reflected the colonists' deep mistrust of the political control they had fled. The Crown's attempt to place controls on the press was also a natural reaction. Newspapers, the stalwart of information during the Revolution, quenched the people's thirst for information during a time of crisis. Thus despite all the economic tribulations of war, 75 percent of the newspapers that commenced production during the Revolution were still in existence at its conclusion. Those that survived were healthier for the experience because the war had made them more aware of their responsibility in a free society and their content had become much more than just a regurgitation of commerce and government news. The press was on its way to becoming a true political force. Although not the most objective press by modern standards, these newspapers were nevertheless the training ground for several notable persons who raised the prestige of the early colonial printer to that of publisher and editor.

Figure 2-5 The telegraph and news of war were powerful ingredients to interest readers in the newspaper. In many communities, the arrival of the newspaper was a major event. A painting by Richard Canton Woodville graphically captured the excitement and showed the reading of news about the Mexican War (1846–1848).

The Telegraph and Instant News

During the nineteenth century technology significantly aided the newspaper industry. In 1844 Samuel Morse invented the telegraph, and news could now be transmitted rapidly over long distances to major cities, rural communities, and the Western frontier. No longer did important information have to wait for ship, pony express, or stagecoach that sometimes took weeks and months to reach its destination. The era of the "bulletin" meant that news could be reported on the same day (Figure 2–5) that it occurred. Consider your reaction if you had been used to receiving news from distant places weeks and months after it happened, when suddenly you could be in touch with events the day they occurred. Certainly your awareness and desire for information would increase. The desire for "instant" news often resulted in the common practice of newspapers' preceding their headlines by the word *Telegraphic*.

The Atlantic Cable: A Link With Europe

Along with an improved domestic relay system, another development, the Atlantic Cable, provided the international link for news coverage. Completed in 1866, the Atlantic Cable prompted predictions that the European mails would become little more than waste paper. "The profound discussions of the old world press will pass un-read," stated the *New York Times*. Although plagued with periodic breakdowns, the cable provided the first direct link between the United States and Europe and helped disseminate news of international events both in the United States and abroad. The American student of economics and politics could open the *New York Times* and read news of British commerce and the activities of Parliament. The student in England could check the latest edition of the *Times of London* to learn the actions of Congress and the going price of cotton. Clearly the newspaper had become an international organ.

The Penny Press

Although the press was becoming well accepted, its appeal still was limited to society's elite. Written in dense prose and dealing with what often were complex political issues, the average American found little interest in these "statesmen" newspapers. All this began to change in the 1830s with the introduction of a new style of journalism and a new style of newspaper. Small newspapers with a lighter style, stressing not political issues but the crime, sex, and gossip of the day, sold for one cent. The new publications ushered in the era of the *penny press* which, although the price has increased, still sees its brand of journalism alive in certain contemporary tabloids.

The earliest penny press, the *New York Sun*, began in 1833 out of the desperation of an all but bankrupt printer named Benjamin H. Day. Day quickly left the impoverished ranks and, with news of immediate interest, achieved almost overnight success. The *Sun* was quickly copied by similar ventures, including one in 1835 by another hard-pressed editor named James Gordon Bennett. Bennett founded the *New York Morning Herald* which became eminently successful, even though it experienced a 100 percent price increase. Philadelphia with its *Public Ledger* and Baltimore with its *Sun* also joined the ranks of successful penny newspapers.

What the penny press managed to do was increase newspaper circulation to all-time highs, which meant that advertisers started paying attention to these penny newspapers, even if the social elite found them abhorrent. The penny press was distributed on sidewalks, not through subscriptions. Bought wholesale by vendors, they were peddled on the streets by hucksters. Along with the cry of the newspaper vendor came bigger headlines, all designed to attract the attention of the readers.

The penny press, in content, did not vanish from the scene. It convinced many nineteenth-century publishers that the penny press' style of reporting, and its content based more on features and a variety of news rather than merely on political and business news, could be a powerful and profitable voice.

THE MINORITY PRESS

The history of American newspapers is dotted with publications directed to specialized audiences, specifically racial minorities. Today we can find newspapers published in many different languages appealing to the various ethnic populations of the United States and Canada. Two early newspapers that stand out in history belonged to the black and the American Indian populations.

The Black Press

The first black newspaper, dated March 16, 1827, was *Freedom's Journal* (Figure 2–6) and was edited by the Reverend Samuel Cornish and John Russwurm. The newspaper began publication in the politically restrictive atmosphere of New York City in the late 1820s. Slavery had been partially abolished by a new law that was to take effect on July 4, 1827, but it applied only to those over forty. White slave owners were prohibited from transporting slaves outside New York State, but that had not stopped the practice. The right to vote, which had belonged to free blacks in both the North and the South, was beginning to be withdrawn by new state laws, and there were no newspapers to plead the cause of the black people. In fact, some of the newspapers were even making vile attacks on blacks. The time was ripe for a newspaper directed to and published by blacks.

The first issue had a four-page, four-column format. The headlines, small and brief, read "To Our Patrons," "Common Schools in New York," and "The Effects of Slavery," among others. The newspaper told its readers: "We wish to plead our own cause. Too long have others spoken for us. Too long has the publick been deceived by misrepresentations, in things which concern us dearly, though in the estimation of some mere trifles." Carrying news of foreign countries of special interest to blacks, the first issue had news of Haiti and Sierra Leone as well as the "Memoirs of Captain Paul Cuffee," who led a trading ship staffed by free blacks. *Freedom's Journal* went on to clash openly with other newspapers of the day. Russwurm remained with the paper for only about a year. When he left, Cornish continued the publication under another name, *Rights for All.*

Figure 2-6 *Freedom's Journal* appeared on March 16, 1927, edited by Samuel Cornish and John Russwurm. Right to vote laws for free people were beginning to be retracted by some states, and New York was politically charged with issues of slavery and voting. The time was right for a newspaper representing the cause of blacks to succeed.

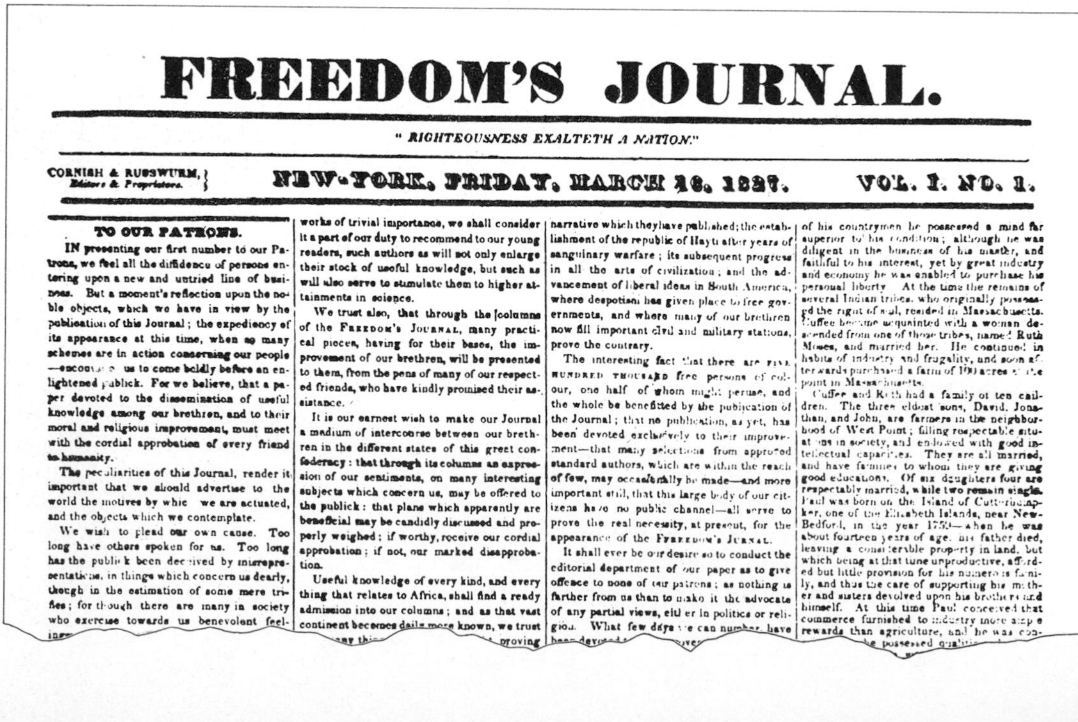

FREEDOM'S JOURNAL.

" RIGHTEOUSNESS EXALTETH A NATION."

CORNISH & RUSSWURM, Editors & Proprietors. NEW-YORK, FRIDAY, MARCH 16, 1827. VOL. I. NO. 1.

TO OUR PATRONS.

IN presenting our first number to our Patrons, we feel all the diffidence of persons entering upon a new and untried line of business. But a moment's reflection upon the noble objects, which we have in view by the publication of this Journal; the expediency of its appearance at this time, when so many schemes are in action concerning our people—encourage us to come boldly before an enlightened publick. For we believe, that a paper devoted to the dissemination of useful knowledge among our brethren, and to their moral and religious improvement, must meet with the cordial approbation of every friend to humanity.

The peculiarities of this Journal, render it important that we should advertise to the world the motives by which we are actuated, and the objects which we contemplate.

We wish to plead our own cause. Too long have others spoken for us. Too long has the publick been deceived by misrepresentations, in things which concern us dearly, though in the estimation of some mere trifles; for though there are many in society who exercise towards us benevolent feelings ...

... works of trivial importance, we shall consider it a part of our duty to recommend to our young readers, such authors as will not only enlarge their stock of useful knowledge, but such as will also serve to stimulate them to higher attainments in science.

We trust also, that through the columns of the FREEDOM'S JOURNAL, many practical pieces, having for their bases, the improvement of our brethren, will be presented to them, from the pens of many of our respected friends, who have kindly promised their assistance.

It is our earnest wish to make our Journal a medium of intercourse between our brethren in the different states of this great confederacy: that through its columns an expression of our sentiments, on many interesting subjects which concern us, may be offered to the publick: that plans which apparently are beneficial may be candidly discussed and properly weighed; if worthy, receive our cordial approbation; if not, our marked disapprobation.

Useful knowledge of every kind, and every thing that relates to Africa, shall find a ready admission into our columns; and as that vast continent becomes daily more known, we trust ... proving

narrative which they have published; the establishment of the republic of Hayti after years of sanguinary warfare; its subsequent progress in all the arts of civilization; and the advancement of liberal ideas in South America, where despotism has given place to free governments, and where many of our brethren now fill important civil and military stations, prove the contrary.

The interesting fact that there are FIVE HUNDRED THOUSAND free persons of colour, one half of whom might peruse, and the whole be benefitted by the publication of the Journal; that no publication, as yet, has been devoted exclusively to their improvement—that many selections from approved standard authors, which are within the reach of few, may occasionally be made—and more important still, that this large body of our citizens have no public channel—all serve to prove the real necessity, at present, for the appearance of the FREEDOM'S JOURNAL.

It shall ever be our desire so to conduct the editorial department of our paper as to give offence to none of our patrons; as nothing is farther from us than to make it the advocate of any partial views, either in politics or religion. What few days we can number, have been devoted ...

of his countrymen he possessed a mind far superior to his condition; although he was diligent in the business of his master, and faithful to his interest, yet by great industry and economy he was enabled to purchase his personal liberty. At the time the remains of several Indian tribes, who originally possessed the right of soil, resided in Massachusetts. Cuffee became acquainted with a woman descended from one of those tribes, named Ruth Moses, and married her. He continued in habits of industry and frugality, and soon afterwards purchased a farm of 100 acres ... point in Massachusetts.

Cuffee and Ruth had a family of ten children. The three eldest sons, David, Jonathan, and John, are farmers in the neighborhood of West Point; filling respectable situations in society, and endowed with good intellectual capacities. They are all married, and have families to whom they are giving good educations. Of six daughters four are respectably married, while two remain single.

Paul was born on the Island of Cutterhunker, one of the Elizabeth Islands, near New-Bedford, in the year 1759—when he was about fourteen years of age, his father died, leaving a considerable property in land, but which being at that time unproductive, afforded but little provision for his numerous family, and thus the care of supporting his mother and sisters devolved upon his brothers and himself. At this time Paul conceived that commerce furnished to industry more ample rewards than agriculture, and he was con... he possessed qualities ...

Figure 2-7 More than any-one in the Indian nation, "Se-Quo-Yah" was responsible for developing the alphabet for the Cherokee Tribe and thus helped to make possible the first Indian newspaper, the *Cherokee Phoenix*. The newspaper was first published on February 21, 1828 by a mixed-blood tribe member named Elias Boudinott. (Library of Congress)

The American Indian Press

At about the same time *Freedom's Journal* was championing its cause, another minority, the American Indians, was the object of similar oppression. In Georgia the government was trying to move the Cherokees out of the South and into the Midwest to free southern lands for farming. An Indian named Sequoyah (Figure 2–7), a Cherokee, was laboring amid skepticism from the tribe to try to develop a code of symbols that would permit the Indians to communicate as the white people did, in written prose. He worked on this for almost 12 years. Finally, in a special demonstration for the tribal elders, Sequoyah watched as his sons demonstrated the new Cherokee alphabet of 86 symbols. Immediately the rather speedy transition to literacy began to take place, and special arrangements were made to obtain a printing press capable of printing the new alphabet. The first Indian newspaper, the *Cherokee Phoenix* (Figure 2–8), was published on February 21, 1828, by a mixed-blood tribe member named Elias Boudinott. White printers friendly to the Indian cause were hired to print the newspaper. Written in both Cherokee and English, the first issue of the newspaper had four pages.

Figure 2-8 The *Cherokee Phoenix*, Indian Newspaper of the Cherokee Tribe.

Although the crusade to force the Indians from their land continued, the militia moved in approximately ten years later and drove the Cherokees westward. In what became known as the Trail of Tears, the Indians gradually settled in Oklahoma territory. Accounts of what happened to both Sequoyah and Boudinot are conflicting. Sequoyah fell out of favor with the tribe over his views on the western emigration. History records that he either crossed the border into Mexico or was labeled a traitor by the tribe and had his ears cropped and his forehead branded. Boudinot, whose favor with the tribe was equally perilous after the move west, is reported to have suffered a brutal death at the hands of his political tribal opponents.

WOMEN IN JOURNALISM

While the black and the Indian press were playing important journalistic roles during the early nineteenth century, women were also beginning to enter the profession and make their mark. Both as reporters and publishers, women carried not only the issues of the country but also those of their own cause to the readers. In 1831 Anne Royall, at age 61, founded a publication entitled *Paul Pry*. Another newspaper under Royall, called *The Huntress*, followed this example and bannered the cause of equal rights for Indians and immigrants. By 1850 the Washington press corps was beginning to accept women in its ranks. Jane Grey Swisshelm paved the way by entering the Senate press gallery on April 17, 1850.

At about this time Ida Minerva Tarbell (Figure 2-9) was born in Erie County, Pennsylvania. Educated at Allegheny College in Pennsylvania, she came from one of the old American oil families who made their fortunes from the Pennsylvania oil fields. By the turn of the century Tarbell was writing for such major magazines as *McClure's*, and she was turning the oil industry's heads, and much of the journalism profession's as well, with her investigative reporting and her stories about big business.

Figure 2-9 Ida Tarbell, early journalist and author who wrote about the industrial life of Western Pennsylvania. (Allegheny College Archives)

Another famous woman reporter of the late nineteenth century was Elizabeth Cochrane Seaman. Under the pen name Nellie Bly (Figure 2–10), she became famous for her escapades in the interest of her employer, *The New York World*. Some of these escapades included being admitted to a New York insane asylum so that readers could have a firsthand report of the care of the mentally ill and being arrested so that she could report how police treated women prisoners. But the feat which gave Bly her greatest reputation was her around-the-world trip that beat the time described in Jules Verne's famous novel, *Around the World in Eighty Days*. By every conceivable means of transportation, including ships and handcarts, she made the trip in just over 72 days. Her career started at the age of 18 with the *Pittsburgh Dispatch*, and she died in 1922.

Figure 2-10 World traveler and journalist, Nellie Bly achieved fame for, among other things, her around-the-world reporting assignment for *The New York World.*

Figure 2-11 Eliza Jane Nicholson came from Mississippi and a family steeped in tradition. She became head of the *New Orleans Picayune* in 1876 and continued to run the paper until her death in 1896. (Courtesy, *New Orleans Picayune*)

Eliza Jane Nicholson (Figure 2–11) became the head of her husband's *New Orleans Picayune* after he died in 1876 and continued to run it until her death in 1896. The job was not an easy one. New Orleans in the late 1800s was famous for being a rough town, and she accepted the job in opposition to the advice of friends who suggested newspaper publishing was no place for a woman. Despite debts, libel charges from a rival paper's editor, and suits challenging her ownership, the editor and her newspaper survived.

Ida Tarbell, Nellie Bly, Jane Grey Swisshelm, Anne Royall, and Eliza Jane Nicholson are just a few of the many women who contributed to journalism. From colonial printers to today's newspaper executives in charge of some of the largest and most influential papers in the world, women have been and continue to be tremendously important to the newspaper industry

THE WAR BETWEEN THE STATES

The mood of the country was much different during the War Between the States than it was during the Revolution. The country was fractured in the middle, not unified from the center. The war was a trying time for editors and readers alike. The entire philosophy upon which the war was fought gave editors a variety of choices. The foremost one was choosing between two presidents—Abraham Lincoln and Jefferson Davis. In addition, within almost any readership could be found opponents to any war effort, significant in number and vocal in presence, Or, as in the border states, sympathy toward both sides could be equally strong. Thus while their newspapers carried local news of this local war being fought by local troops, editors could choose among supporting two different armies, two different presidents, and three different causes—the North, the South, and the Union.

Many newspapers distinguished themselves for their war coverage. As wars had in the past, the war created an almost insatiable thirst for news. Newspapers such as the *Cincinnati Gazette*, the Richmond Enquirer, the *New York Herald*, and *New Orleans Picayune*, the *Memphis Appeal*, the *Savannah Republican*, and the *Charleston Courier* were lifelines of information to troops in the field, families, and businesspeople. Papers such as Horace Greeley's *Tribune* carried persuasive editorials. Names of correspondents such as Peter W. Alexander at Gettysburg and Antietam, B. S. Osbon at Fort Sumter, Whitelaw Reid at Shiloh, and Lawrence A. Gobright at Lincoln's death became historical bylines. Newspapers were also sources of information for the enemy, and a war correspondent's publicity of impending military campaigns tipped off more than one officer. The result was government censorship of the press during wartime. Unfortunately the ability of the telegraph to speed news thousands of miles in a day suddenly became a liability for the press. With generals putting pressure on the government, some newspapers were temporarily suspended. Although war news continued to flow, the prepublicity of military maneuvers came to a halt.

The war also changed the style of American journalism. The demands of battlefield dispatches and the unreliable transmission systems that could be cut off at any moment created a new breed of writer. Concise leads and headline formats became standard, and that style continues today in both print and broadcast news.

RECONSTRUCTION AND WESTWARD EXPANSION

With the War Between the States behind it, the United States moved toward a new union, western expansion, and the industrial revolution. With all three traveled the newspapers.

The West also spawned its share of great journalists and editorial writers. Harvey W. Scott (Figure 2–12) of the Portland *Oregonian* was such an editorialist. The *Oregonian* had been founded in 1850, but it was not until the full effect of the western movement was felt that Scott's editorials began to be taken seriously east of the Mississippi River. He saw the industrial revolution from a viewpoint both touched by eastern technology yet tempered by the great expanses of the Northwest and its close proximity to the lumber industry. Perhaps through Scott's eyes, unfilled with the crowded populations of the East and the factories of New England, came some of the most intelligent writing of the day. Other early newspapers famous in the West included the *Sacramento Union* started in 1851, Salt Lake City's *Deseret News* in 1850, and *Dallas News* in 1885.

Figure 2-12 Harvey W. Scott of the Portland *Oregonian*. Scott first edited the newspaper and then joined with Henry L. Pittock to become a joint owner. (Courtesy, The *Oregonian-Oregon Journal*)

Figure 2-13 William Allen White stands as one of the pioneer editors of the "Western frontier." From the town of Emporia, Kansas, he became a national legend. At age 24, he was an editorial writer in Kansas City. When he was 27, he had managed to get enough money together to buy the *Emporia Gazette*. He became a leading spokesperson of Republican politics, and his editorials were reprinted throughout the United States in newspapers and magazines. His friends included Presidents of the United States, and he became especially close to the family of Theodore Roosevelt. (Courtesy, *The Emporia Gazette*)

In the Midwest and South, newspapers made the transition from the Civil War to an industrial economy. Many began their publishing ventures in the fresh atmosphere of economic recovery. In Milwaukee the *Journal* was founded in 1882 with its famous publisher, Lucius W. Nieman. Under Nieman's guidance, the newspaper became a respected voice, both nationally and internationally. Nieman later helped advance journalism education by establishing the Nieman Fellowships at Harvard University.

The Midwest also boasted such names as William Allen White and Joseph Medill. Medill's association as editor with the *Chicago Tribune* brought a conservative stance to the city. Another conservative stance, one which reached a national readership but started in the small town of Emporia, Kansas, belonged to William Allen White (Figure 2–13). White bought the *Emporia Gazette* for $3,000 in 1895. After his editorials were reprinted in a number of leading newspapers, he and his newspaper achieved national prominence. He became a friend to leading journalists and political families, including the Theodore Roosevelts.

In St. Louis another publisher was making his mark, Joseph Pulitzer (Figure 2–14), for whom the Pulitzer Prizes in journalism were named. Born in Hungary in 1847, Pulitzer came to America and worked on some German-language newspapers. After serving a term as a state officer in Missouri, he managed to buy the *St. Louis Dispatch* at a bankruptcy auction. It became the *Post-Dispatch* and, although filled with its share of sensationalized reporting in its infancy, matured into a respected daily. Pulitzer broadened his journalism base in 1883 by buying the *New York World*.

Figure 2-14 Born in Hungary, Joseph Pulitzer built a publishing career which, at one time or another, included such newspapers as the St. Louis *Post-Dispatch* and the New York *World*. He is also remembered for the heated competition which developed between him and his competitors in the era of "Yellow Journalism." (From a portrait by John Singer Sargent. Photo by D. Bulick)

Figure 2-15 Henry W. Grady assumed the editorship of the *Atlanta Constitution* in 1880. (Courtesy, *The Atlanta Journal-The Atlanta Constitution*)

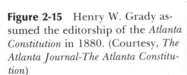

In Kentucky Henry Watterson of the *Louisville Journal-Courier* exerted a major influence on reconstruction. A border state, Kentucky felt the pressures of both the North and the South. Watterson, who became editor of the *Journal Courier* in 1868, called for a united nation and garnered respect from both sides. Farther south, Henry W. Grady (Figure 2–15) in 1880 assumed the managing editor's position of the *Atlanta Constitution*. He increased the staff of the newspaper and strengthened the editorial page, bringing it up to a par with the *Louisville Journal-Courier*.

YELLOW JOURNALISM

The penny press not only proved that "light" news sold at an inexpensive price could be highly successful, but it also laid the groundwork for an era of journalism that was to arise some forty years later. The star participants were Joseph Pulitzer, who published the *New York World*, and William Randolph Hearst (Figure 2–16), who in 1887 became the editor of the *San Francisco Examiner*. Hearst's association with the newspaper business came from his father, who was more an aspiring politician than a journalist and had originally acquired the *Examiner* for political purposes. William Randolph Hearst ventured east to Harvard where he gained fame more for his pranks than for his studies and was eventually expelled. He did manage to acquire newspaper experience on Pulitzer's *World* and, on his return to San Francisco, took the lessons of sensationalism from the penny press and applied them to big-city journalism. With bold, eye-gripping headlines and various escapades to generate or report the news, Hearst's *Examiner* began to climb in circulation. The result? It doubled—then tripled—both circulation and profits.

Figure 2-16 Few people have left more of a legacy in newspaper publishing than William Randolph Hearst. At one time an employee of Pulitzer, Hearst managed to extend his newspaper investments from the *San Franciso Examiner* to buy the *New York Morning Journal*. He later battled with Pulitzer in a war of sensational journalism that firmly placed Hearst's identity with the era of "Yellow Journalism."

But San Francisco was not the only place Hearst set out to tame. He had studied the ways of his old boss Pulitzer and had watched the new technology and somewhat sensational journalism already practiced by the Boston newspapers. His lessons, already learned and proved workable in San Francisco, were brought to New York to do battle with Pulitzer. Hearst used *Examiner* money to buy the faltering *New York Morning Journal* and most of the good newspaper talent in New York City. The result was a steady climb in the *Morning Journal's* circulation as Hearst splashed more and more sensational headlines. Pulitzer himself could not even match the brazen Hearst.

When Hearst hired away one of Pulitzer's top illustrators, Richard F. Outcault, it was the beginning of a battle that left an imprint on journalism that remains today. Outcault had drawn a cartoon about life in New York's crowded tenements that featured a child cartoon character. The extremely popular "kid" appeared in a yellow dress and became known as "the Yellow Kid." When Outcault came to the *Morning Journal*, the kid came too, almost. She also stayed behind to be drawn by George B. Luks of Pulitzer's newspaper. Appearing in the promotional literature of both newspapers, the "circulation war" was in full force, and a new title had been given to this era of sensational, competitive, and in many ways irresponsible journalism—*yellow journalism.*

It remained as a way of selling newspapers well into the 1900s and can still be seen today. National scandal sheets use the technique as common practice. Characterized by large headlines and sensational reporting, yellow journalism is credited by some with starting the Spanish-American War when it sensationalized the sinking of the warship *Maine* in 1898. Hearst and his empire became the subject of a famous movie, *Citizen Kane,* and most responsible journalists would rather the era of yellow journalism were banished to the archives.

A PROFESSIONAL IDENTITY

Despite the era of yellow journalism, newspapers have become a viable economic force and began to develop a professional identity among its practitioners.

American Newspaper Publishers Association

In 1887, the American Newspaper Publishers Association (*ANPA*) was organized as a trade association of dailies. Its presidents were seasoned veterans in newspaper publishing. Men like Don C. Seitz of the *New York World* and John Norris of the *New York Times* were typical of the leaders who made the ANPA a viable organization. Today the ANPA offers members a number of services including weekly bulletins on management, circulation, law, and advertising. Organized efforts in research through the ANPA Research Institute and in public information through the Newspaper Information Service have continued to serve members, education, and the profession.

The Society of Professional Journalists, Sigma Delta Chi

The impact of new printing technology, the increase in the number of newspapers, and the jump in readership also spawned a new emphasis on the "profession" of journalism. In 1909 Sigma Delta Chi was formed, later to have its name changed to the Society of Professional Journalists, Sigma Delta Chi. Originally begun as a secret fraternity, it grew in numbers and opened campus and professional chapters. It publishes *The Quill* and lobbies for First Amendment issues in legislatures and the legal arenas.

The American Society of Newspaper Editors

The American Society of Newspaper Editors, under the leadership of Casper S. Yost (Figure 2–17) of the *St. Louis Globe-Democrat,* was organized in 1922. Operating primarily as an organization of editors, it passed its own code called the "Canons of Journalism" in 1923. The Canons also contain a First Amendment ring with the statement, "Freedom of the press is to be guarded as a vital right of mankind. It is the unquestionable right to discuss whatever is not explicitly forbidden by law, including the wisdom of any restrictive statue."

Figure 2-17 Casper S. Yost of the *St. Louis Globe Democrat* led the formation of the American Society of Newspaper Editors in 1922.

The presence of professional organizations and the subsequent criticism of the press that began to appear in other media, namely magazines, began to temper the sensational "yellow" reporting. World War I arrived, and there was enough action to report without emphasizing the crime-sex-sin syndrome that splashed earlier front pages. World War I also prompted, as wars always do, a new public desire for news, and newspapers began to rely heavily on syndicated news services. Today such services as United Press International, Associated Press, and Reuters are right hands to newspapers, which rely on them not only for national and international news but also for high-speed data networks and photographs.

E. W. Scripps   Roy Howard

Figure 2-18 The *Cincinnati Post* and the *Cleveland Press* numbered among E. W. Scripp's chain of newspapers. After an outstanding career with UPI, the *St. Louis Post-Dispatch,* and the E. W. Scripps newspapers in Indianapolis and Cincinnati, Roy Howard became the partner in the Scripps-Howard newspaper empire. (Courtesy, Scripps-Howard and Jack Shannon)

Typical of the wire services that have evolved through the twentieth century is United Press International. UPI was born as the brainchild of an aggressive newspaper executive named John Vandercook of the E. W. Scripps (Figure 2–18) newspapers. Scripps had been operating news services for his own newspapers when Vandercook convinced him of the wisdom of merging his news services with the Publishers Press Association to form the United Press Associations. Vandercook died a year later, and the United Press operations came under the directorship of Roy W. Howard (Figure 2–18). World War I brought the United Press into its own with the establishment of foreign bureaus serving both American and foreign newspapers. Roy Howard left United Press in 1920 and became an executive in the Scripps newspapers. United Press continued its expansion and pioneered such services as a broadcast news wire and the United Press Audio Service in 1956. In 1958 the service merged with the International News Service to become United Press International. It currently provides news pictures, a television news service, a cable television news service, and is pioneering efforts in high-speed news transmission.

Roy Howard, meanwhile, continued to move up the ranks of the Scripps newspapers—newspapers that were in many ways indicative of the style of journalism that evolved from the industrial revolution. A large class of factory workers had emerged from this revolution as a powerful but disorganized political force in America. E. W. Scripps, like many other publishers of his time, exercised a strong *personal* editorial influence on the American labor movement and called for the organization of the working class. Scripps took newspapers, some of them the outgrowth of the penny press, and began to direct their content to the less-educated working class. He personally and directly influenced editorials and viewed the newspapers as the true means of communication about the political system. Scripp's son, Robert Paine Scripps, continued the newspaper legacy when his father died. When Robert died in 1938, one of the three key people to take over the newspapers was Roy Howard. Howard remained influential in what became the Scripps-Howard Newspapers, owned by the parent E. W. Scripps Company.

The E. W. Scripps Company, like many other major publishing enterprises, has now diversified into additional communications media, including broadcasting. But the personal style of journalism, evident when entrepreneurs such as E. W. Scripps were in *direct* control of their newspapers, has been replaced by corporate mergers and public ownership in which parent companies may look more closely at profits than at editorial lines. Surviving as a remnant of that past are some small-town dailies, which in certain parts of the country still exercise that personal style of journalism so popular with big dailies of the past.

THE CHANGING INDUSTRY

As we look at the growth trends of the newspaper over the past 25 years, we notice that circulation rose very slowly (Figure 2–19). The increase in circulation between 1946 and 1980 did not keep up with the general population growth. This did not, however, spell financial gloom, quite the contrary. Income of most newspapers, through both advertising and sales, increased steadily. Newspapers still claim the major share of the advertising dollar. Economic data show that the growth of the newspaper industry has generally equaled and in several ways exceeded the growth of the economy (Figure 2–20). Expenditures for advertising, for instance, have more than kept pace with the gross national product, and employment in the industry has expanded at a more rapid rate than have composite United States employment indicators. The success of the industry is due in large part to its adaptability to the new technology developed over the last fifty years.

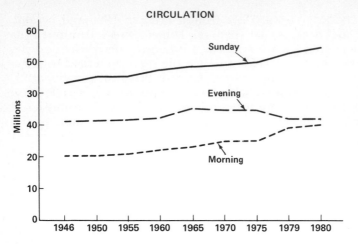

CIRCULATION

Figure 2-19 Circulation growth of Sunday, evening, and morning newspapers between 1946 and 1980. (Courtesy, ANPA)

Figure 2-20 Newspaper advertising volume compared to the Gross National Product (GNP) between 1946 and 1980. (Courtesy, ANPA)

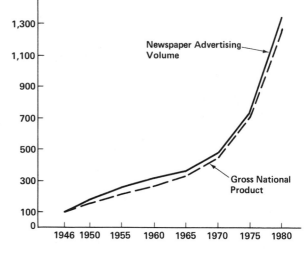

INDEX OF GROWTH (1946 BASE)

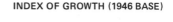

Economic Indicators Along with the positive indicators have come signs of caution for newspaper publishers. A research study by the Bureau of Business Research and Service at the University of Wisconsin highlighted these concerns.[2] *First,* as consumers we are finding it increasingly difficult to read more than one newspaper per day. We are even finding it difficult to read one newspaper per day. Newspapers are becoming larger; a major city edition may include sixty pages instead of the ten or twenty that comprised the major city editions at the turn of the century. *Second,* other media vie for our attention. We have at our disposal a wealth of magazines; we listen to the radio; we watch television; we receive direct-mail literature; and we go to the movies. *Third,* the shorter workweek of many businesses and the new technology gives us more free time, longer vacations, and higher income to spend on recreational activities. Again these activities take away

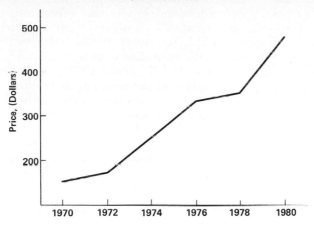

(Per Metric Ton)

Figure 2-21 Price per metric ton of paper. (Courtesy, ANPA)

from time spent reading. *Fourth,* deterioration of the central city means that we are not as apt to go downtown after dark and purchase an evening edition from the corner newsstand. The convenience of listening to the radio on the drive to work is another factor to be considered. *Fifth,* wire services carrying news and information from around the world are available at moderate fees to even the smallest newspapers, and these papers are taking advantage of this. Thus their ability to carry national and international news cuts into the circulation of the major metropolitan dailies. *Sixth,* paper costs (Figure 2–21) and labor costs are steadily increasing. Let's examine paper costs in more detail.

Newsprint: Cost and Supply

Newsprint, the paper upon which newspapers are printed, has reached record consumption (Figure 2–22). But increase is only part of the story—cost of newsprint has also jumped because supply has not kept up with demand. There are many reasons for this economic disparity. One is the profit margins of paper manufacturers and suppliers. In the past these

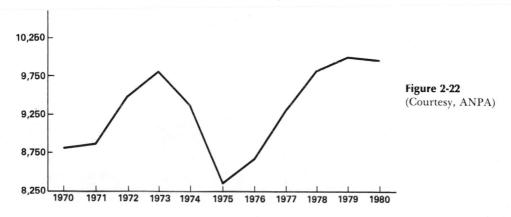

NEWSPRINT CONSUMPTION AS REPORTED (thousands of metric tons)

Figure 2-22
(Courtesy, ANPA)

merchants have proposed various cost-per-ton price increases. The news-paper industry justifiably complained loudly and effectively postponed rate increases for some time. Gradually, however, economic factors in the paper manufacturing and supply segments of the industry became de-pressed. With reduced profits the manufacturers and suppliers could not expand and increase production. Finally, about 1971, everything came to a head. The gap between supply and demand began to close. Manufac-turers and suppliers increased prices. The energy crisis arrived, and labor disputes developed which affected everyone from lumberjacks to shippers. Supplies dwindled. Costs soared.

As Canadian supplies began to dwindle, the United States' suppliers had to make up the difference.[3] The north central states, with newsprint production up 1151 percent, carried most of the burden. To cut shipping weight and to make the same tonnage produce more paper, the industry is experimenting with new ways to retain paper strength while making it lighter. Breakage, however, is a big problem. The lighter stock cannot withstand the stress of high-speed presses. Moreover, very thin newsprint causes a "see-through" effect which makes the finished newspaper difficult to read.

Labor and New Technology

New techniques in printing mean new equipment, new expenses, and new personnel to learn the trade. If labor unions are affected, technology can be forced to creep at a snail's pace when the unions try to protect jobs. The threat of strikes is common when skilled workers are fired because technology has made their jobs obsolete. When such strikes do occur, the result has been serious damage to the newspaper. Strikers have been accused of smashing presses to stop a newspaper from being printed by scab (nonunion) employees. This action may have several consequences: the newspaper may either shut down, print the editions elsewhere, bow to union demands, or a combination of all three. Personnel costs for the average newspaper now run between 50 and 60 percent of the total operating expenses. The largest share (48 percent) of the newspaper workforce belongs to production and maintenance (Figure 2–23). When profit margins shrink, the expense of new technology can become prohib-itive.

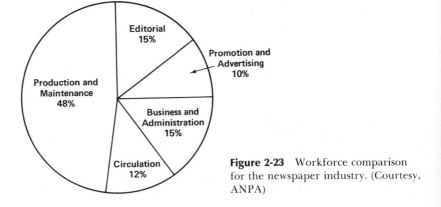

Figure 2-23 Workforce comparison for the newspaper industry. (Courtesy, ANPA)

Computers and Satellites   Computer technology has become a part of many phases of newspaper publishing, such as advertising and distribution. If you are a business executive and want to place an advertisement in the evening edition of your local paper but want to reach only one part of the city, a computer-based distribution system will put your ad in newspapers going exclusively to that section of the city, and you will be charged for the appropriate circulation. Even satellites and microwave transmission systems are part of the production of large newspapers. A facsimile of a major metropolitan daily can be sent via satellite to another country and be incorporated into one of its newspapers. It is now possible for newspapers with regional editions, such as the *Wall Street Journal,* to use computers and satellite technology to transmit entire pages from one city to another, electronically, in a matter of minutes (Figure 2–24).

Figure 2-24 Newspapers such as the *Wall Street Journal* can be sent via facsimile transmission over satellite communication systems and printed almost simultaneously in different parts of the world. (Courtesy, Western Union)

Electronic distribution systems give newspapers a flexibility never before possible. Little more than a century after a crude method of dots and dashes was utilized to send individual letters across a telegraph wire, satellites now link news bureaus all over the nation and can almost instantaneously transmit news stories to any of these bureaus. Computers can automatically set the stories into type and start the presses rolling.

Figure 2-25 The *Suburban Trib*, a regional newspaper distributed as an insert in the *Chicago Tribune*. Different tabloid-sized newspapers are prepared for different suburban areas surrounding Chicago. The process is one way for major metropolitan dailies to compete for audiences and advertising dollars in the suburbs. Suburban businesses or businesses wanting to reach a specific suburban audience can advertise in the *Suburban Trib* and reach that specialized audience for less money than it would cost to run ads in the metropolitan edition. Although the metropolitan edition would reach a larger audience, many of those people may be too far away to patronize the suburban business. (Copyrighted, *Chicago Tribune*. Used with permission.)

Figure 2-26 Foreign-language newspapers with specialized features reach specialized audiences. The cartoon pictured in this illustration appears regularly in *El Miami Herald*, a Spanish-language newspaper serving southern Florida. (Courtesy, the Miami Herald Publishing Company)

Suburban, Foreign, and International Newspapers

Some suburban newspapers are distributed as part of larger metro editions. For example, the *Suburban Trib* (Figure 2–25), which is part of the *Chicago Tribune,* is printed in different editions to reach different suburbs around Chicago. For smaller businesses, suburban newspapers are a localized advertising vehicle, allowing them to reach local audiences at a reduced cost, a favorable alternative to paying for expensive ads in larger papers which reach customers who are too far away geographically to patronize a local business.

Spanish-language newspapers are being published in many parts of the United States where large Spanish-speaking populations are located. One example is the *Miami Herald's* Spanish edition *El Herald,* complete with editorial cartoons (Figure 2–26) and features seen in its English-language edition. Other Spanish-language newspapers are found in major cities and the areas of the Southwest. International editions also reach specialized audiences. For example, the *Wall Street Journal* publishes an Asian daily and weekly edition specializing in the economic news of Asia (Figure 2–27).

Figure 2-27 The *Asian Wall Street Journal* serves Asia with international economic news and news of particular interest to Asians. (Courtesy, Dow Jones)

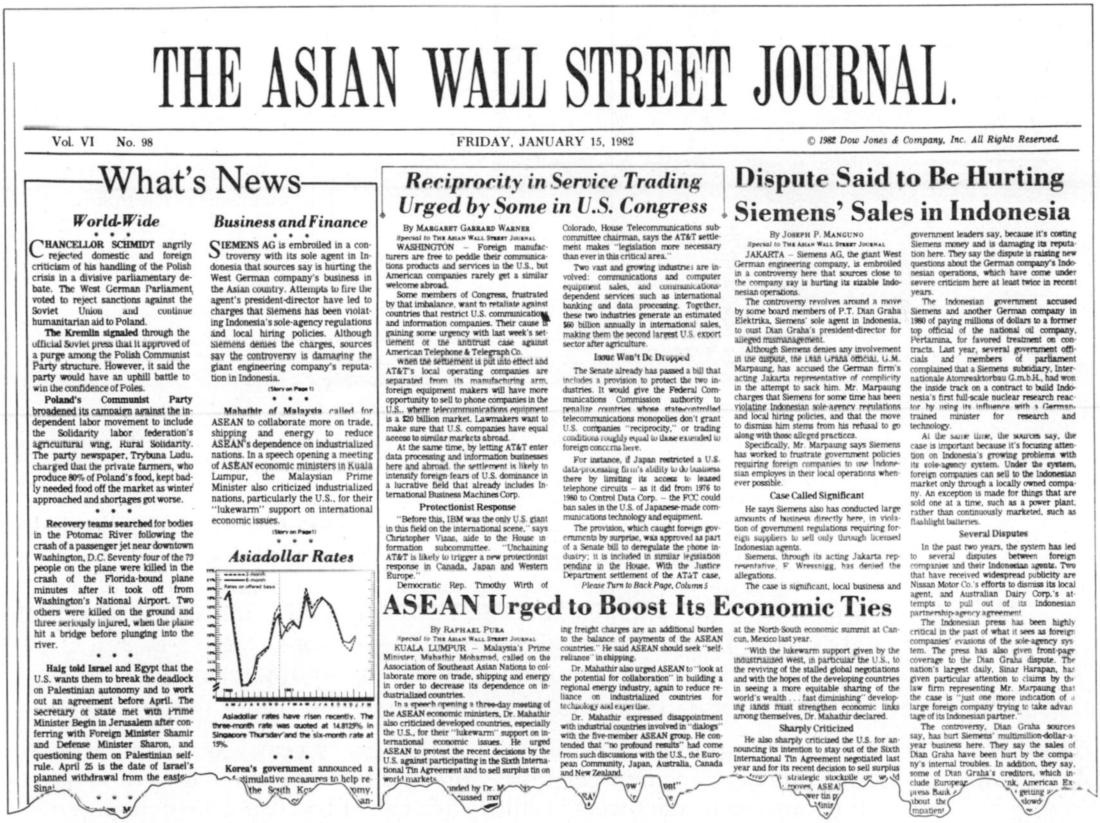

THE ASIAN WALL STREET JOURNAL.

Vol. VI No. 98 FRIDAY, JANUARY 15, 1982 © 1982 Dow Jones & Company, Inc. All Rights Reserved.

What's News

World-Wide

CHANCELLOR SCHMIDT angrily rejected domestic and foreign criticism of his handling of the Polish crisis in a divisive parliamentary debate. The West German Parliament voted to reject sanctions against the Soviet Union and continue humanitarian aid to Poland.

The Kremlin signaled through the official Soviet press that it approved of a purge among the Polish Communist Party structure. However, it said the party would have an uphill battle to win the confidence of Poles.

Poland's Communist Party broadened its campaign against the independent labor movement to include the Solidarity labor federation's agricultural wing, Rural Solidarity. The party newspaper, Trybuna Ludu, charged that the private farmers, who produce 80% of Poland's food, kept badly needed food off the market as winter approached and shortages got worse.

Recovery teams searched for bodies in the Potomac River following the crash of a passenger jet near downtown Washington, D.C. Seventy four of the 79 people on the plane were killed in the crash of the Florida-bound plane minutes after it took off from Washington's National Airport. Two others were killed on the ground and three seriously injured, when the plane hit a bridge before plunging into the river.

Haig told Israel and Egypt that the U.S. wants them to break the deadlock on Palestinian autonomy and to work out an agreement before April. The Secretary of State met with Prime Minister Begin in Jerusalem after conferring with Foreign Minister Shamir and Defense Minister Sharon, and questioning them on Palestinian self-rule. April 25 is the date of Israel's planned withdrawal from the easte[rn] Sina[i].

Business and Finance

SIEMENS AG is embroiled in a controversy with its sole agent in Indonesia that sources say is hurting the West German company's business in the Asian country. Attempts to fire the agent's president-director have led to charges that Siemens has been violating Indonesia's sole-agency regulations and local hiring policies. Although Siemens denies the charges, sources say the controversy is damaging the giant engineering company's reputation in Indonesia.

(Story on Page 1)

Mahathir of Malaysia called for ASEAN to collaborate more on trade, shipping and energy to reduce ASEAN's dependence on industrialized nations. In a speech opening a meeting of ASEAN economic ministers in Kuala Lumpur, the Malaysian Prime Minister also criticized industrialized nations, particularly the U.S., for their "lukewarm" support on international economic issues.

(Story on Page 1)

Asiadollar Rates

Asiadollar rates have risen recently. The three-month rate was quoted at 14.8125% in Singapore Thursday and the six-month rate at 15%.

Korea's government announced a [...] stimulative measures to help re[...] the South Ko[...]

Reciprocity in Service Trading Urged by Some in U.S. Congress

By MARGARET GARRARD WARNER
Special to THE ASIAN WALL STREET JOURNAL

WASHINGTON – Foreign manufacturers are free to peddle their communications products and services in the U.S., but American companies rarely get a similar welcome abroad.

Some members of Congress, frustrated by that imbalance, want to retaliate against countries that restrict U.S. communications and information companies. Their cause is gaining some urgency with last week's settlement of the antitrust case against American Telephone & Telegraph Co.

When the settlement is put into effect and AT&T's local operating companies are separated from its manufacturing arm, foreign equipment makers will have more opportunity to sell to phone companies in the U.S., where telecommunications equipment is a $20 billion market. Lawmakers want to make sure that U.S. companies have equal access to similar markets abroad.

At the same time, by letting AT&T enter data processing and information businesses here and abroad, the settlement is likely to intensify foreign fears of U.S. dominance in a lucrative field that already includes International Business Machines Corp.

Protectionist Response

"Before this, IBM was the only U.S. giant in this field on the international scene," says Christopher Vizas, aide to the House information subcommittee. "Unchaining AT&T is likely to trigger a new protectionist response in Canada, Japan and Western Europe."

Democratic Rep. Timothy Wirth of Colorado, House Telecommunications subcommittee chairman, says the AT&T settlement makes "legislation more necessary than ever in this critical area."

Two vast and growing industries are involved: communications and computer equipment sales, and communications-dependent services such as international banking and data processing. Together, these two industries generate an estimated $60 billion annually in international sales, making them the second largest U.S. export sector after agriculture.

Issue Won't Be Dropped

The Senate already has passed a bill that includes a provision to protect the two industries. It would give the Federal Communications Commission authority to penalize countries whose state-controlled telecommunications monopolies don't grant U.S. companies "reciprocity," or trading conditions roughly equal to those extended to foreign concerns here.

For instance, if Japan restricted a U.S. data-processing firm's ability to do business there by limiting its access to leased telephone circuits – as it did from 1976 to 1980 to Control Data Corp. – the FCC could ban sales in the U.S. of Japanese-made communications technology and equipment.

The provision, which caught foreign governments by surprise, was approved as part of a Senate bill to deregulate the phone industry; it is included in similar legislation pending in the House. With the Justice Department settlement of the AT&T case,

Please Turn to Back Page, Column 5

Dispute Said to Be Hurting Siemens' Sales in Indonesia

By JOSEPH P. MANGUNO
Special to THE ASIAN WALL STREET JOURNAL

JAKARTA – Siemens AG, the giant West German engineering company, is embroiled in a controversy here that sources close to the company say is hurting its sizable Indonesian operations.

The controversy revolves around a move by some board members of P.T. Dian Graha Elektrika, Siemens' sole agent in Indonesia, to oust Dian Graha's president-director for alleged mismanagement.

Although Siemens denies any involvement in the dispute, the Dian Graha official, G.M. Marpaung, has accused the German firm's acting Jakarta representative of complicity in the attempt to sack him. Mr. Marpaung charges that Siemens for some time has been violating Indonesian sole-agency regulations and local hiring policies, and that the move to dismiss him stems from his refusal to go along with those alleged practices.

Specifically, Mr. Marpaung says Siemens has worked to frustrate government policies requiring foreign companies to use Indonesian employes in their local operations whenever possible.

Case Called Significant

He says Siemens also has conducted large amounts of business directly here, in violation of government regulations requiring foreign suppliers to sell only through licensed Indonesian agents.

Siemens, through its acting Jakarta representative, F. Wressnigg, has denied the allegations.

The case is significant, local business and government leaders say, because it's costing Siemens money and is damaging its reputation here. They say the dispute is raising new questions about the German company's Indonesian operations, which have come under severe criticism here at least twice in recent years.

The Indonesian government accused Siemens and another German company in 1980 of paying millions of dollars to a former top official of the national oil company, Pertamina, for favored treatment on contracts. Last year, several government officials and members of parliament complained that a Siemens subsidiary, Internationale Atomreaktorbau G.m.b.H., had won the inside track on a contract to build Indonesia's first full-scale nuclear research reactor by using its influence with a German-trained minister for research and technology.

At the same time, the sources say, the case is important because it's focusing attention on Indonesia's growing problems with its sole-agency system. Under the system, foreign companies can sell to the Indonesian market only through a locally owned company. An exception is made for things that are sold one at a time, such as a power plant, rather than continuously marketed, such as flashlight batteries.

Several Disputes

In the past two years, the system has led to several disputes between foreign companies and their Indonesian agents. Two that have received widespread publicity are Nissan Motor Co.'s efforts to dismiss its local agent, and Australian Dairy Corp.'s attempts to pull out of its Indonesian partnership-agency agreement.

The Indonesian press has been highly critical in the past of what it sees as foreign companies' evasions of the sole-agency system. The press has also given front-page coverage to the Dian Graha dispute. The nation's largest daily, Sinar Harapan, has given particular attention to claims by the law firm representing Mr. Marpaung that the case is "just one more indication of a large foreign company trying to take advantage of its Indonesian partner."

The controversy, Dian Graha sources say, has hurt Siemens' multimillion-dollar-a-year business here. They say the sales of Dian Graha have been hurt by the company's internal troubles. In addition, they say, some of Dian Graha's creditors, which include Europea[n] [...]nk, American Express Bank [...]

ASEAN Urged to Boost Its Economic Ties

By RAPHAEL PURA
Special to THE ASIAN WALL STREET JOURNAL

KUALA LUMPUR – Malaysia's Prime Minister, Mahathir Mohamad, called on the Association of Southeast Asian Nations to collaborate more on trade, shipping and energy in order to decrease its dependence on industrialized countries.

In a speech opening a three-day meeting of the ASEAN economic ministers, Dr. Mahathir also criticized developed countries, especially the U.S., for their "lukewarm" support on international economic issues. He urged ASEAN to protest the recent decisions by the U.S. against participating in the Sixth International Tin Agreement and to sell surplus tin on world markets.

[...]ing freight charges are an additional burden to the balance of payments of the ASEAN countries." He said ASEAN should seek "self-reliance" in shipping.

Dr. Mahathir also urged ASEAN to "look at the potential for collaboration" in building a regional energy industry, again to reduce reliance on industrialized countries for technology and expertise.

Dr. Mahathir expressed disappointment with industrial countries involved in "dialogs" with the five-member ASEAN group. He contended that "no profound results" had come from such discussions with the U.S., the European Community, Japan, Australia, Canada and New Zealand.

[...] at the North-South economic summit at Cancun, Mexico last year.

"With the lukewarm support given by the industrialized West, in particular the U.S., to the reviving of the stalled global negotiations and with the hopes of the developing countries in seeing a more equitable sharing of the world's wealth . . . fast diminishing" developing lands must strengthen economic links among themselves, Dr. Mahathir declared.

Sharply Criticized

He also sharply criticized the U.S. for announcing its intention to stay out of the Sixth International Tin Agreement negotiated last year and for its recent decision to sell surplus [...] strategic stockpile o[n] w[orld] [...]

Sectionals   Newspapers have found the use of *sectionals* a way to attract both specialized audiences and the advertisers who want to reach them. Some of the more popular sectional inserts include those on sports, entertainment, food (Figure 2–28), business, and recreation.

Readership surveys allow the newspaper to match those readers with an advertiser's *target audience.* In this way the newspaper can recommend the most efficient and effective media buy for the advertiser.

Figure 2-28   Special sectional inserts, such as *Taste* in the *Chicago Tribune,* serve audiences with special features on foods and dining out. Advertisers, such as restaurants, find these inserts an effective and cost-effective means to reach their audiences. (Copyrighted, *Chicago Tribune.* Used with permission.)

MARKETING/PROMOTION

Increased competition from other media, battles over circulation, and increased costs have been a big concern of publishers; many have not hesitated to move aggressively toward advertising and promotion campaigns. Reaching potential advertisers with effective messages, sometimes unabashedly frank with headline-grabbing slogans (Figure 2–29), is part of the way newspapers are using modern marketing techniques.

Newspaper Advertising   Before the impact of television, the fall of every year was a boom time for newspapers. It was new car time, and to announce their new models, the major auto manufacturers would purchase advertising in newspapers of every size. For the smaller newspaper, it was big and important money. Yet in the last ten years the small newspapers have seen the auto makers' money vanish. Most national advertisers have changed their media buying habits. They have concentrated their purchases on the larger metropolitan dailies and television, while withdrawing their national advertising from smaller newspapers. Newspaper advertising in general, however, is increasing, and newspapers still outdistance radio and television in their share of the advertising dollar (Figure 2–30).

Figure 2-29 Major advertising and sophisticated marketing campaigns are becoming an essential part of modern newspaper promotion efforts. (Courtesy, *Chicago Sun-Times*)

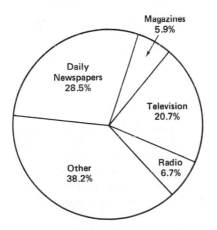

Figure 2-30 Newspaper share of advertising. (Courtesy, ANPA)

Standard Advertising Unit	Width	Depth	Standard Advertising Unit	Width	Depth
1	13" (Full)	21" (Full)	17	4-1/4"	10-7/16"*
2	13" (Full)	18"	18	4-1/4"	6-15/16"*
3	13" (Full)	10-7/16"	19	4-1/4"	5-3/16"*
4	10-5/8"	21" (Full)	20	4-1/4"	3-7/16"*
5	10-5/8"	18"	21	1-3/8"	6-15/16"*
6	10-5/8"	15-5/8"	22	1-3/8"	5-3/16"*
7	9-5/8" (Tab Full)	13-15/16"* (Tab Full)	23	1-3/8"	3-7/16"*
8	9-5/8" (Tab Full)	6-15/16"*	24	1-3/8"	2"*
9	8-1/16"	21" (Full)	25	1-3/8"	1"*
10	8-1/16"	10-7/16"*			
11	6-5/16"	21" (Full)			
12	6-5/16"	13-15/16"* (Tab Full)			

In addition to the above 25, 6-col. newspapers offer the following alternate sizes:

Standard Advertising Unit	Width	Depth
13	6-5/16"	10-7/16"*
14	6-5/16"	5-3/16"*
15	4-1/4"	21" (Full)
16	4-1/4"	13-15/16"* (Tab Full)
21A	2-1/16"	6-15/16"
22A	2-1/16"	5-3/16"
23A	2-1/16"	3-7/16"
24A	2-1/16"	2"
25A	2-1/16"	1"

* Fits tab

Figure 2-31 Standard Advertising Units have permitted standardization of ad dimensions for newspapers and opened the way for more efficient use of facsimile transmission of ads via satellite.

Despite the increase in advertising expenditures, some forecasters offer only cautious optimism about the future of the newspaper industry.[4] Not that an immediate danger of depression looms, but the industry must realize that it is living in an era of rapidly changing social and economic conditions. In Chapter 1 we studied the theoretical development posited by Maisel that would link our existence in a postindustrial society with an increase in specialized media. With the advent of new technology and changing life styles, will we change the way we "consume" today's typical newspaper? Will our life style changes also evolve more rapidly than the newspaper industry can compensate for them? The ability of a newspaper to survive thus will depend on facing the reality of competing media and understanding the changes that may have to be made. An indication that this sensitivity exists came with the cooperative efforts of different newspaper organizations in developing Standard Advertising Units (Figure 2–31).

Standard Advertising Units

In the design of newspapers, few changes have been more important than the adoption of Standard Ad Units. Placing advertising in more than one newspaper or trying to design an ad which would run in more than one newspaper was in the past difficult because newspapers use different size pages and columns. Enlarging or reducing an ad to fit a particular newspaper also involved a corresponding change in rate.

Gradually the industry began to standardize the dimensions used in the layout and design of advertising, and many newspapers have adopted Standard Advertising Units. This change means that while a rate may differ, an advertiser can buy a given size ad in many different newspapers which use the Standard Advertiser Unit system and know the ordered size will appear. This also means that, besides saving advertisers time and money used in preparing different sizes of ads, newspapers can now compete more effectively for advertising dollars with other media, such as radio and television. These media had long ago adopted standardized advertising in the form of 10, 30, and 60-second commercials.

The new system will also aid in the satellite transmission of newspaper pages permitting an ad to be composed and then transmitted via satellite to newspapers anywhere in the world.

EXPANDING ENTERPRISES

Independent newspapers are finding themselves the target of acquisitions by large newspaper corporations who are expanding their influence and ownership.

Newspaper Chains

Major companies such as the New York Times Company, the Times Mirror Company, Scripps-Howard, and Gannett are just some of the companies who own much more than either a single newspaper or, indeed, just newspapers. In fact, 60 percent of the daily newspapers in the United States are owned by newspaper chains. Chains have proliferated because of the need to invest operating profits from existing papers which may average as high as 25 percent to 30 percent. One of the more publicized acquisitions was when Australian businessman Rupert Murdock took over a myriad of New York publishing interests, including the *Village Voice*. Murdock's previous publishing record of borderline sensationalism worried some American journalists that too many media and their accompanying influence were in his hands.

Diversified Holdings

Many modern newspapers, much like other corporate conglomerates, have diversified into areas surprisingly different from publication of the local edition. Dow Jones and Company gives the reading public the *Wall Street Journal* and *Barron's National Business Financial Weekly*. In addition to publishing, its specialized services include the Dow Jones News Retrieval Service, a jointly operated computerized news retrieval service available to stock brokerage firms, banks, and other businesses. The AP-Dow Jones Economic Report in conjunction with the Associated Press operates an international wire service. Operating 24 hours a day, six days a week, news is gathered by AP and Dow Jones and sent out around the world through AP facilities. Also part of the Dow Jones enterprises are the Ottaway Newspapers, a wholly owned subsidiary, Dow Jones Books, Dow Jones Information Service, and Dow Jones Cable.

Pros and Cons of the Media Conglomerate

There are arguments both for and against the wisdom of such major holdings under one roof. Some argue that this arrangement seriously hampers the public's *ability to gain access* to the media. This is especially true when the media holdings are in the same community. Concerned over this issue, the FCC has moved in to break up combinations of newspapers, television, and radio outlets when all are owned by the same party and serve the same people.

What the increase in newspaper chain acquisitions means to the public is still open to question. Certainly serious dangers can result. The tip-off comes when the ownership of the chain decides to use the newspapers as a unified editorial voice. A head office directing all newspapers in the chain to carry a certain editorial or to take a specific editorial line is all that is necessary to put the Justice Department on the alert for antitrust violations, to say nothing of the serious implications of monopolistic control of information.

Despite these drawbacks of monopolistic ownership, other examples reveal that rival media under the same owner can be as fiercely competitive as two football teams. When the same boss oversees both and can readily make a comparison, the incentive for excellence can far outweigh any concern over the identity of the owner.

The newspaper industry has remained prosperous, in some instances because of these diversified investments. Moreover, there is no indication that the public's desire for news is waning. For as both government and international politics become more complex and as new communication technology puts each individual in touch with people all around the world, newspapers and their allied services will continue to be a vital and prosperous part of the world economy.

THE ELECTRONIC NEWSPAPER

While few are predicting that the newspaper as we know it will vanish, new technology is creating the potential for expanded distribution of newspapers. Publishers are watching closely the developments in new technology such as cable origination programming, discussed in more detail in Chapter 13.

Two experimental distribution systems are *teletext* and *videotex*. The teletext system sends "electronic pages" over frequencies used for television signals. These pages can be selected to appear on a home television set with a special decoder. Whereas teletext systems are one-way systems, videotex systems are two-way "wired" systems so that a home television set or video display terminal (*VDT*) can be connected to a central computer via cable or telephone lines. The consumer can call up pages of text and can conduct business through the system, such as shopping or banking.

SUMMARY

Newspapers are an important social and economic force in society. An outgrowth of the "posted bulletins" of early Italy, newspapers evolved from single sheets of paper locally distributed to multipage products with international distribution. In Germany the first newspapers appeared in the early seventeenth century; in England the single-sheet corantos were being published by 1621. These were among the first newspapers to fit Otto Groth's standards for a true newspaper, which included being published periodically, mechanically reproduced, accessible, timely, and having varied content with continuity of organization.

American colonial newspapers contained mostly commercial news and were published by licensed printers who received government subsidies. Yet that content was changing. John Peter Zenger was tried for seditious libel after criticizing the governor's stand toward the Indians. Found not guilty, the Zenger case was indicative of the changing face of journalism which eventually culminated in a free press.

The minority press in America developed in the nineteenth century with such newspapers as *Freedom's Journal* published by blacks and the *Cherokee Phoenix* published by American Indians. Women journalists also made their mark on early newspapers, with such names as Nellie Bly and Ida Tarbell becoming legends in their own right. It was also the era of the "penny press," inexpensive newspapers with sensational news stories. Big-city dailies that adopted the style of the penny press introduced "yellow journalism."

By the twentieth century, newspapering was gaining credibility with the founding of professional associations. The first half of the twentieth century also saw a decline in the individual influence of the early publishing entrepreneurs, a gradual change to newspapers owned by large corporations with public stockholders, and newspapers as expanding enterprises. Newsgathering also changed with the growth of press associations.

Current economic indicators have seen a continuation of newspaper profits but only a gradual climb in circulation. To help the latter, newspapers are attempting to reach specialized audiences with suburban editions and increased use of sectionals.

As an industry, newspapers are changing. Newsprint costs are rising, other media compete for our attention, and labor and technology clash over innovations. To emphasize the positive, newspapers have adopted Standard Advertising Units, making it easier for advertisers to place one ad in several newspapers.

Electronic newspapers are also springing up in many parts of the country. Major newspapers have joined forces with the computer to offer electronic pages of text.

OPPORTUNITIES FOR FURTHER LEARNING

BAILYN, B., AND J. B. HENCH, *The Press and the American Revolution*. Worcester: American Antiquarian Society, 1980.

BLASSINGAME, J. W., AND M. G. HENDERSON (eds.), *Antislavery Newspapers and Periodicals*. Boston: G. K. Hall, 1980.

BOLLIER, D., *How to Appraise and Improve Your Daily Newspaper: A Manual for Readers*. Washington, D.C.: Disability Rights Center, 1978.

BOND, D. H., AND W. R. MCLEOD, *Newsletters to Newspapers: Eighteenth Century Journalism*. Morgantown: West Virginia University School of Journalism, 1977.

CHANEY, L., AND M. CIEPLY, *The Hearsts: Family and Empire—The Later Years.* New York: Simon & Schuster, 1981.

CURL, D. W., *Murat Halstead and the Cincinnati Commercial.* Gainesville: University Presses of Florida, 1980.

DOWNIE, L., *The New Muckrakers.* New York: Mentor Books, 1978.

EMERY, E., AND M. EMERY, *The Press and America.* Englewood Cliffs, N.J.: Prentice-Hall, 1978.

FILLER, L., *The Muckrakers.* University Park: Pennsylvania State University Press, 1976.

FOX, W., *Writing the News: Print Journalism in the Electronic Age.* New York: Hastings House, 1977.

GIES, J., *The Colonel of Chicago.* New York: Dutton, 1979.

GOTTLIEB, R., AND J. WOLT, *Thinking Big: The Story of the Los Angeles Times, Its Publishers and Their Influence on Southern California.* New York: Putnam's, 1977.

HOHENBERG, J., *The Professional Journalist.* New York: Holt, Rinehart & Winston, 1978.

KERBY, W. F., *A Proud Profession: Memoirs of a Wall Street Journal Reporter, Editor, and Publisher.* Homewood, Ill.: Dow Jones–Irwin, 1981.

LEWIS, A. A., *Man of the World: Herbert Bayard Swope: A Charmed Life of Pulitzer Prizes, Poker and Politics.* Indianapolis: Bobbs-Merrill, 1978.

LOVELL, R. P., *The Newspaper: An Introduction to Newswriting and Reporting.* Belmont, Calif.: Wadsworth, 1980.

MARSCHALL, R., ed., *The Sunday Funnies, 1896–1950.* New York: Chelsea House, 1978.

MARZOLF, M., *Up from the Footnote: A History of Women Journalists.* New York: Hastings House, 1977.

PICKETT, C., *Voices of the Past: Key Documents in the History of American Journalism.* Columbus, Ohio: Grid, Inc., 1977.

RIVERS, W. L., AND S. SMOLKIN, *Free-Lancer and Staff Writer: Newspaper Features and Magazine Articles,* 3rd ed., Belmont, Calif.: Wadsworth, 1980.

ROBERTS, C., *The Washington Post: The First Hundred Years.* Boston: Houghton Mifflin Company, 1977.

SALISBURY, H. E., *Without Fear or Favor: An Uncompromising Look at The New York Times.* New York: Times Books, 1980.

SHAW, D., *Journalism Today: A Changing Press for a Changing America.* New York: Harper & Row, Pub., 1977.

SMITH, A., *The Newspaper: An International History.* London: Thames and Hudson, 1979.

WENDT, L., *Chicago Tribune: The Rise of a Great American Newspaper.* Skokie, Ill.: Rand McNally, 1979.

WILLIAMS, H. L., *Newspaper Organization and Management.* Ames: Iowa State University Press, 1978.

CHAPTER

MAGAZINES

PREVIEW

After completing this chapter, we should be able to:

Trace magazines' basic beginnings from their English heritage to early American publications.

Describe the reasons for the mass circulation magazines' prosperity and their subsequent decline.

Discuss the reintroduction of magazines.

Be familiar with special editions, regional editions, and international editions.

Identify the four major types of magazines and their corresponding subcategories.

Understand the differences between vertical and horizontal business publications.

Explain the marketing dilemmas faced by magazines and some of the solutions to these dilemmas.

Appreciate the concept of magazine readership loyalty.

Describe the economic considerations of a magazine and their future implications.

Talk about the characteristics of the magazine audience.

Know how an advertiser monitors magazine circulation.

Outline the concept behind a magazine network.

Be aware of magazines' satellite era.

Historians date the origins of magazines back to the 1600s and the emergence of catalogues of books for sale and pamphlets, mostly designed as literary publications. Then it was difficult to distinguish magazine publishing from what we consider newspaper publishing.

BASIC BEGINNINGS

Many consider the first magazine to be Daniel Defoe's *Review*. Defoe had been jailed for his opinions against the Church of England, and either from prison or immediately after his release in 1704, he began issuing the weekly periodical. What seemed to distinguish Defoe's *Review* from the newspapers of the era was the fact that not only did he publish considerable news, but his publication also contained feature material. Increasing its frequency to three issues a week, the *Review* was published for nine years. Defoe remained its only editor and contributor.

English Heritage

Out of the journalistic style of Defoe came two other publications, the *Tatler* and the *Spectator*. Richard Steele began publishing the *Tatler* in 1709 with a broader editorial scope than had been characteristic of the *Review*. Moral issues ranging from gambling to dueling were the target of the *Tatler*'s biting prose, although foreign news, theater reviews, and even humor were also included.

A partner of Steele, Joseph Addison joined him to publish the first edition of the *Spectator* in March, 1711. The content consisted of humorous coffeehouse sketches and short advertisements. Yet the *Spectator* produced two magazine "firsts." With the informal essay, the *Spectator* became the first magazine to make a contribution to literature. The polite English upper class was entertained with *Spectator* essays on vanity, affection, discourse, and behavior. With its London circulation reaching 3000, the *Spectator* published the first magazine fiction which was a tale of a whimsical knight named Sir Roger.

Soon imitators of both publications emerged, such as the *Guardian*, the *Englishman, Town Talk, Tea Table, Chit Chat*, the *Plebeian*, and *Grub Street Journal*.

Early American Magazines

In the United States, while he was still publishing the *Pennsylvania Gazette*, Benjamin Franklin began publication of the *General Magazine*. Designed as a collection of articles from books, pamphlets, and newspapers, the publication reached residents of the American Colonies as early as 1741. Political documents and news of Parliament's actions which affected the Colonies were among its content, making it one of the first magazines to truly attempt an editorial content for the mass audience.

Even though its publication life was brief, Thomas Paine's *Common Sense* was the document which polarized the opinion of the Colonists to separate from England. As much a pamphlet as it was a magazine, the publication appeared between January, 1775, and July, 1776.

In 1830 Louis Godey founded *Godey's Lady's Book* (Figure 3–1), an American magazine for women, which some consider as truly ushering in the era of the magazine in America. *Godey's Lady's Book* was edited by Mrs.

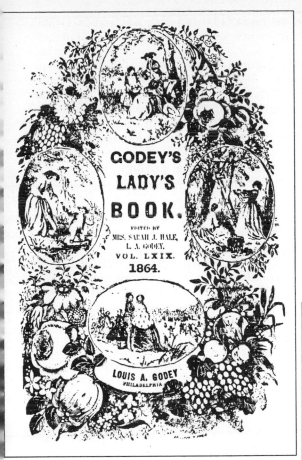

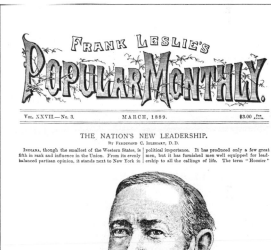

Figure 3-1 Louis Godey's *Godey's Lady's Book* is considered by some as the publication that ushered in the era of the American magazine. (Courtesy of *Matrix* and Women In Communications, Inc. Source: K. Endres, "Women's Press During the Civil War," *Matrix* (Winter 1981), p. 24)

Figure 3-2 *Frank Leslie's Popular Monthly* represented an illustrated magazine of the later 1880s.

Sarah Josepha Hale, a Boston feminist. The popular publication, which dealt with women's fashions, manners, and home matters, became an institution during the 1800s.

With the development of photography, illustrations became as important as the content of magazines. Both Frank Leslie's *Leslie's Weekly* and *Harper's Weekly* served to pictorially and historically record the late 1800s. Frank Leslie's *Popular Monthly* (Figure 3–2) was also available.

In this 1800s atmosphere of economic and geographical expansion, magazines prospered, and their content expanded. From *The Dial* to *Everybody's Magazine* to *McClure's Magazine,* a reader could find articles on New England intellectualism, hazardous industrial working conditions, or life in the West.

FINDING AN AUDIENCE

As the nation prospered, a growing audience began to yearn for entertainment, entertainment that took the form of magazines. Entrepreneurs immediately realized that if they could provide light, diversionary reading at nominal prices, they could capture this mass audience. And they did. The magazine publishing boom began. Between 1865 and 1885 the number of periodicals jumped from 700 to 3300.[1]

As competition developed, so did trends in pricing and content. The name of the game was circulation. Circulation lured advertisers who could pay to reach a mass audience. The price was high enough to allow a decrease in subscription prices, making magazines still more attractive to the public. Distribution also became more efficient, as the rails spread their network into hitherto inaccessible rural areas. Many magazines specifically sought a mass audience, just the opposite of what happened fifty years later.

PROSPERITY AND TRANSITION

America's phenomenal industrial growth during the early twentieth century also helped spur the magazine publishing industry. The era saw major strides in corporate expansion and the ability to produce mass goods for the consumer. With that ability came the need to make the consumer aware of these goods and of the various brand names of the products on grocery shelves, in new car showrooms, on clothes racks, and in furniture stores. Magazines filled the bill, and advertisements filled magazines. Although there were ups and downs, many of the publications achieved wide national acclaim. Among them were *Life, Look,* and *The Saturday Evening Post* (Figure 3–3). The classic issue of prosperity was the *Saturday Evening Post* of December 7, 1929. "Weighing nearly two pounds, the 272-page magazine kept the average reader occupied for twenty hours and twenty minutes. From the 214 national advertisers appearing in it, the Curtis Publishing Company took in revenues estimated at $1,512,000."[2]

For the mass circulation magazine, the glory of that era did not survive. Television already loomed on the horizon. It signaled the growth of specialized magazines and the decline of mass circulation publications.

Figure 3-3 Representative issues of the *Saturday Evening Post* that have appeared since 1900. The magazine was once a publication directed to a mass audience. It folded and was reintroduced and directed to a more specialized audience, yet it retained the high quality illustrations and many of the feature stories that had originally made it famous. See also Figure 3-6. (Reprinted from the *Saturday Evening Post*. © 1900 & 1954, The Curtis Publishing Company)

The exact time of this turning point is debatable. The mass national magazines survived the golden era of radio and at first seemed to hold their own with television. Advertising revenues for *Life* increased in the early 1960s. "A single issue of *Life* in October, 1960 carried $5,000,000 worth; another in November, 1961 had revenues of $5,202,000.[3] But the figures were deceiving. A period followed in which many industry spokespersons argued that television was making gains on the magazine publishers; magazine publishers countered that more than ever was being spent on advertising—magazines were not only holding their own, but gaining. To some extent, both arguments were correct. Magazines in general were still experiencing a period of growth, but television and skyrocketing postal rates finally dealt a fatal blow to the mass circulation magazines.

Inability to direct themselves to a specialized audience was another reason for the demise of such well-known magazines as *Look* (Figure 3–4) and *Life*. These were magazines in the true sense of the word *mass,* having something within their pages that was of interest to everyone. With the advent of television, however, advertisers could reach the same mass audience as *Look* and *Life* (Figure 3–5) did, but more cheaply and more efficiently. In addition, television offered visual messages on a mass scale with both motion and sound accompaniment. With increased operating costs, mass circulation magazines folded. The *Saturday Evening Post* shared the fate of the other mass circulation magazines.

Figure 3-4 *Look* was another mass-circulation magazine which eventually folded due to such factors as high postage rates and television's competition for the advertising dollar.

Figure 3-5 Introduced in 1936, *Life* magazine was well-known as a showcase for photojournalism. (Margaret Bourke White, LIFE Magazine © 1936, Time, Inc.)

REINTRODUCING FAMILIAR PUBLICATIONS

After reading the last paragraph, you may stop and say, "Wait a minute. I just saw *The Saturday Evening Post* on the newsstand." You are right. In the past few years you probably have spotted some of these magazines, such as *Life* and *Country Gentleman*. Each represents an unusual trend in publishing that applies to a select few of some of the biggest titles to grace magazine history. But do not be deceived into thinking those editions are reaching the same mass audience they did thirty years ago. They are not. What publishers have done is to purchase the names of the major publications and then reintroduce them into the marketplace, but to a much more specialized audience. What has been created instead are specialty magazines with familiar titles.

For example, after *The Saturday Evening Post* folded, it was purchased by the Ser Vaas family of Indianapolis. The new Curtis Publishing Company, operating out of a different city and with a different staff, introduced a new edition of *The Saturday Evening Post,* (Figure 3–6) with quality articles and top illustrators (Figure 3–7). Instead of trying to reach the mass audience of the former publication, the new *Post* is directed at a more conservative element of American life and contains many of the same sort of illustrations that its predecessor had. Its secret is that it has been able to control its circulation and distribution systems. Had the old *Post* been able to accomplish this same feat early enough, it might never have disappeared from the scene. But most of the circulation magazines persisted too long in trying to reach a mass audience so that they were unable to make the drastic shift to a specialized audience in time to avoid insolvency.

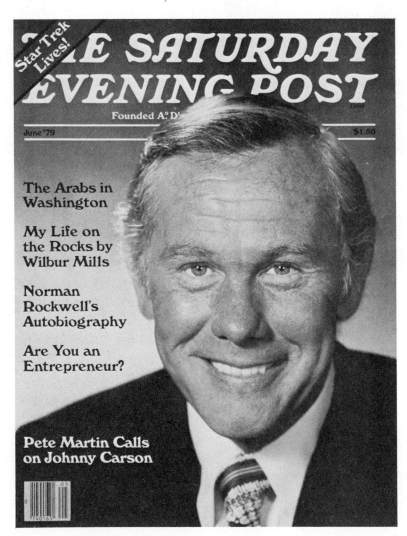

Figure 3-6 The "reintroduced" *Saturday Evening Post,* which targets to a more specialized audience than its predecessor. (Reprinted with permission from the Saturday Evening Post Company, © 1979)

Figure 3-7 Talented artists, such as Lucian Lupinski, artist in residence at the *Saturday Evning Post,* have made magazines an attractive and popular medium. Lupinski has become recognized for illustrations gracing the inside pages of the *Saturday Evening Post* as well as cover portraits of famous religious and political figures.

The *Saturday Evening Post* was not the only magazine revived by the Curtis Publishing Company. A very shrewd gamble paid off when the company reintroduced *Country Gentleman* magazine (Figure 3–8). Initial circulation had reached more than 100,000 before the new magazine ever left the printer. That continued to swell to more than 300,000 as *Country Gentleman* effectively reached the "gentleman farmer" of the 1970s and 1980s. Advertisers of such products as building supplies for home repair and remodeling, lawn seed, and other suburban homeowner products found the *Country Gentleman* the ideal medium to reach this specialized audience.

In 1978 Time-Life brought back *Life* magazine. Based on the experience of other popular publications such as *People,* the new *Life* was designed for the more contemporary life style and the affluent reader than its mass circulation predecessor was. Advancements in printing and photojournalism permitted the new *Life* to be even more "picture-oriented" than the old *Life* was.

Still famous magazine titles like *Collier's* remain to be reintroduced. But the potential is there, so do not be surprised if you happen to spot them at the newsstand someday.

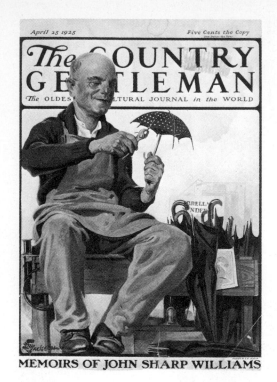
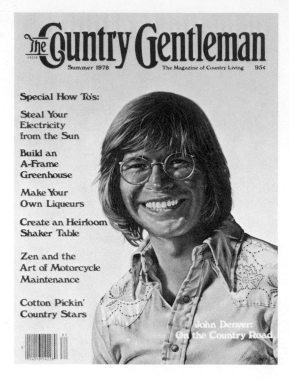

Figure 3-8 Reintroduced as a publication for the suburban reader, *Country Gentlemen* retained the recognition of a famous-name publication but with altered content. (Reprinted from *Country Gentleman.* © 1925 The Curtis Publishing Company. Reprinted with permission from The Country Gentleman Company, © 1978)

MODERN MAGAZINE PUBLISHING:
THE SPECIALIZED AUDIENCE

Not all publications were destined for the fate of the old mass circulation periodicals. Many made the necessary changes to reach the highly specialized audiences that modern magazine publishing demands. For example, *Business Week* offers advertisers a select group of management-level readers by regularly refusing to take subscriptions from nonmanagement-level readers. Even living in a certain section of the country may determine if you qualify for a specialized magazine subscription. *Sunset* magazine (Figure 3–9), called "the magazine of Western living," is directed to readers in the Pacific coast states and Nevada, Arizona, Idaho, and Utah. If you want to subscribe to the publication but do not live in the West, you have to pay more. As a result, advertisers know that by purchasing an ad in *Sunset,* they can concentrate on this western audience and will not be paying for circulation to other parts of the country that might not be as interested in their advertising. The same is true for *Southern Living* magazine (Figure 3–10) for the southern audience.

Figure 3-9 *Sunset* and *Southern Living* (seen in Figure 3-10) are examples of regional magazines. (Used with permission, Lane Publishing Co.)

Figure 3-10 *Southern Living* carries features on a variety of subjects of interest to readers living in the South. (Copyrighted by Southern Living, Inc., Nov. 1981)

Special Editions

Many magazines publish numerous special editions to reach those specialized audiences. What may appear to be one nationally distributed magazine is actually several specialized publications under the same cover. For example, *Time* magazine publishes both demographic and regional editions. An advertiser wanting to reach college students can advertise in the *Time* which is distributed primarily to college students, or *Time* offers its *Time Z* and *Time A+* editions. *Time Z* stands for "zip codes." Time Z is directed to subscribers in 1414 of the United States's most affluent zip code areas within metropolitan markets. Thus if you were an advertiser with a product appealing to high-income buyers, the *Time Z* edition might be a good place to put your advertisement. An even more elite audience can be reached through the *Time A+* edition. The A+ edition is directed at business and professional people, 600,000 of them.

Another example of specialized editions is *Sports Illustrated*. Not only does the magazine publish four regional editions—East, West, South, and Midwest—but it also publishes a "homeowners edition," limited to 640,000 subscribers in zip code areas that show the highest concentration of homeowners. In addition, it offers special "insert editions" to advertisers, with such special insert features as the U.S. Tennis Open and the Grand Slam of Golf. A manufacturer of tennis rackets, for instance, might find the U.S. Tennis Open insert edition an excellent place to advertise.

Regional Editions

We mentioned the regional editions of *Sports Illustrated*. Other publications are realizing the advertising appeal of regional editions. *Playboy* has eastern, central, western, southeastern, southwestern, New York metropolitan, Chicago metropolitan, Los Angeles metropolitan, San Francisco metropolitan, and urban market editions. The centerfold is the same in the New York metropolitan edition as in the Los Angeles metropolitan edition, but an advertiser wanting to reach only the New York audience can do so by buying advertising space in just the New York metropolitan edition.

International Editions

Playboy, along with its regional editions in the United States is also among those magazines that publish international editions. Along with its overseas military edition, *Playboy* publishes foreign editions for France, Italy, Germany, Japan, Mexico, and Brazil, but this time different centerfolds do appear in certain foreign editions because some countries prohibit the bold displays used in the United States. The magazine also has different titles, being called *Caballero* in Mexico and *Homen* in Brazil.

Two other familiar publications with international editions are *Cosmopolitan* and *Good Housekeeping*. Both have Spanish-language editions which Spanish and American advertisers find ideal for reaching Spanish-speaking audiences both inside and outside the United States. *Cosmopolitan's* Spanish edition looks much like the English-language edition. The front cover is identical, but a closer look reveals the Spanish-language subtitles (Figure 3–11). The *Good Housekeeping* version is titled *Buenhogar* (Figure 3–12), and is independently edited. It stresses family life, children, and self-improvement and is sold in 22 countries.

Figure 3-11 *Cosmopolitan's* Spanish-language edition. (Courtesy, Editorial America, S.A.)

Figure 3-12 *Buenhogar,* the Spanish-language edition of *Good Housekeeping.*

New Target
Audiences:
New
Publications

The magazine industry is much more than a series of specialized editions. New publications are cropping up which are devoted entirely to very select audiences.

Perhaps nowhere is this trend more evident than in magazines directed toward today's changing woman, following her every mood from sports to professions. One of the first of these publications was *Ms* magazine, followed by *City Woman* (Figure 3–13) published for professional women living and working in the city, *Professional Women,* and *Woman. Essence* appeals to an even more select audience—black professional women.

Business executives have always been a prime *target audience* for magazines. These individuals usually make major buying decisions and have higher than average incomes. Reaching this audience is the first aim of another specialized magazine. *Chicago Business.* Published by Crain Communications, *Chicago Business* is an example of a magazine appealing not only to the specialized audience of business people but also refining that even further to reach business people in Chicago. Geared to more general audiences are the many city magazines that have appeared in recent years (Figure 3–14).

Magazines devoted to audiences in a particular state are becoming prevalent (Figure 3–15). Features on tourist attractions, politics, and business and industry are commonly found in these publications which may be published by private enterprise or by agency of the state government. While the state magazine itself reaches a specialized audience, other publications reach specialized audiences within the state. One example in the state category is *Texas Sports* (Figure 3–16).

Figure 3-13 Reflecting the degree to which magazines target their editorial content to specialized audiences is *City Woman,* which actually targets to three levels of specialization: women, professional women, and professional women living and working in the city. (COMAC COMMUNICATIONS, LIMITED)

Figure 3-14 City magazines have enjoyed healthy growth and acceptance. Some are published by private firms, while others are produced by the municipalities themselves, many under the editorship of a local Chamber of Commerce.

Figure 3-15 *Tar Heel* is representative of a state magazine that has now been combined with *Sandlapper* into a new publication titled, *Carolina Lifestyle*.

Figure 3-16 This advertising represents a specialized state magazine, which not only directs its contents to residents of a single state, but further specializes in the sports of that state.

How can you sell 4000 hockey pucks ...in El Paso?

Or how about your "ancient" collection of baseball cards. Or maybe those five six-week-old Labrador pups that are eating you out of house and home.

If you've got something to sell, and you want to do it fast, you need the **TEXAS ★ SPORTS Classifieds.**

That's right. **TEXAS ★ SPORTS Classifieds** are designed to reach the Texas sports fan with information on products and services ranging from fishing to football. Vacation or travel opportunities, hunting leases, sports tickets, sports films, club memberships and many more are to be found in this unique section for our unique reader.

TEXAS ★ SPORTS Classifieds are a monthly feature beginning in May. Classified advertisements are accepted subject to the publisher's approval. Rates are $1.50 per word with a 15 word minimum. Abbreviations and zip codes count as one word; post office boxes and telephone numbers as two words. There is a 10% discount for three time insertions.

Checks or money orders must accompany all copy and orders, and must be received on or before, the twentieth, two months preceding issue date (April 20 for June issue).

Classified display advertising with special logo, art, etc., must be ordered by the inch and is available at $75 per inch, one inch minimum. Please send camera-ready copy with payment.

So if you've got something to sell, from hockey pucks to hungry pups, put the **TEXAS ★ SPORTS Classifieds** to work for you. Call or write our Classified Manager, Windsor Communications, P.O. Box 402086, Dallas, Texas 75240; (214) 385-8040.

TEXAS ★ SPORTS
The Sports Magazine of the Lone Star State

The College Market: It's Big Business. Today!

Today, more than ever, college students have the inclination and the dollars to build markets: they travel by plane, own cameras and stereo components, drive cars *at almost twice the rate of* non-college youth.

It's BIG Business Tomorrow, Too.
When you sell college students today, you sell them for tomorrow. Brand loyalties are just forming. So what they learn about you today will affect you tomorrow. When they'll be even bigger customers than they are now.

Time Is Precious for this Elusive Audience.
With classes, papers and extracurricular interests, a myriad of

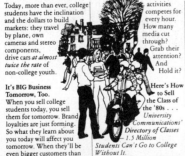

activities competes for every hour. How many media cut through? Grab their attention? And Hold it?

Here's How to Sell the Class of the '80s . . . *University Communications' Directory of Classes* — 1.5 Million *Students Can't Go to College Without It.*

Here's a truly unique publication. *The Directory of Classes* is the one – the only – source for course listings and summations for over 1.5 million students at over 70 major colleges and universities. And each school guarantees full distribution to their entire enrollment.

Since the *Directory of Classes* is so vital to these students they not only read it, they devour it — an average of 13 times per

issue, every issue — Fall, Winter and Spring.

Reach Them, Teach Them, and Sell Them In The Directory of Classes.
Published 3 times a year: must reading for over 1.5 million students; 100% guaranteed circulation; an official university publication — the *Directory of Classes* is the one publication they must read. The Classes of the '80s are The *Class of the '80s.* Reach them, teach them, and sell them — in University Communications' *Directory of Classes.* It's your Phi Beta Kappa key to sales.

UNIVERSITY COMMUNICATIONS' DIRECTORY OF CLASSES
For information, call
NEW YORK
Jerry Koffler (212) 725-8706
CHICAGO
Richard Spengler (312) 346-2600
DETROIT
Marty Toohey (313) 649-1950
LOS ANGELES
Lowell Fox (213) 990-2950

Ziff-Davis Publishing Company. One Park Avenue, New York, N.Y. 10016

Figure 3-17 Reaching the college student audience, whose media habits usually change when attending college, is particularly difficult. Through the *Directory of Classes*, advertisers are assured of a certain level of college student readership and attention.

We discussed *Time's* ability to reach college students through a specialized edition, but one of the more novel examples of reaching college students is the *Directory of Classes* (Figure 3–17) for selected colleges published by University Communications. The college supplies the company with its class schedule, and the company, in turn, sells advertising in the *Directory*. Reaching the college student is a difficult media problem since media attention habits change at that time. The hometown newspaper may no longer be available, the hometown radio station may not be within range, and loyalty to other media may vary since class schedules and different living conditions can intervene.

CHARACTERISTICS AND TYPES OF MAGAZINES

Magazines are of four principal types—*farm, business, consumer,* and *religious*. Each has subcategories. For example, farm publications consist mainly of *state* and *vocational* publications. State publications are directed toward a particular geographic area, such as the *Montana Farmer-Stockman* and *The Pennsylvania Farmer*. Vocational farm publications, on the other hand, are directed toward a particular type of farmer and include such magazines as the *Citrus and Vegetable Magazine* and *Dairy Herd Management* or *Beef*.

Figure 3-18 Some regional publications, such as the *New England Journal of Medicine*, have acquired a national readership and respect. This publication is also representative of a "professional" magazine.

Business publications include *professional magazines* such as those pertaining to law, medicine (Figure 3–18), or education. Here the publisher may be a professional organization such as the American Dental Association. *The Quill,* official publication of the Society of Professional Journalists—Sigma Delta Chi, is an example of a professional magazine. Another subcategory of business publications includes *trade magazines* for specific businesses, such as the *Hardware Retailer* and *Today's Office* (Figure 3–19).

A third subcategory consists of *industrial publications.* Edited for specific industries, they can include magazines directed to specific processes, for example, manufacturing or communication. Two examples of industrial publications of the printing and broadcasting industries, respectively, are the *Printing News* and *Broadcast Management and Engineering. Institutional business magazines* also abound, such as *Hotel-Motel News.* Publications that are sent to a group of people belonging to an organization are usually termed *house organs.* Copies of house organs may be sent to the news media for public relations purposes. The content of the house organ is usually information of special interest to its select readers.

In addition to these major categories of business publications, you should understand the difference between *vertical* and *horizontal publications.* Vertical publications reach people of a given profession at different levels in that profession. For instance, a major vertical publication of the radio and television industry is *Broadcasting.* Its content is geared to every person working or interested in the broadcasting industry, whether it be

Figure 3-19 "Trade" magazines, such as *Today's Office,* are "business" publications directed toward a specific segment of a business or industry. (Steve Sint Photo)

the television camera operator, the radio station manager, or even the advertising executive who needs to know about new FCC regulations affecting broadcast commercials. Horizontal magazines, on the other hand, are aimed at a certain managerial level but cut across several different industries. *Business Week,* for example, is directed at management-level personnel in many different facets of the business world. Two other examples of magazines directed at management include *Forbes* and *Fortune.*

Consumer magazines are usually of two types: specialized and general. Magazines directed at audiences with an interest in a special area, such as *Sailing* or the *Model Railroader,* are *specialized* magazines. *General* magazines are directed to people with more varied interests.

Religious publications also have various subdivisions, usually based on specific religious denominations. Typical religious publications include *The Catholic Voice, The Jewish News, The Episcopalian, The Lutheran,* and many more regional publications that deal with specific denominations within a city.

MARKETING MAGAZINES

Magazine publishing overall has enjoyed a steady growth both in number of publications and in circulation. Considering the increasingly competitive state of mass media, the growth is commendable, and many factors have contributed to this growth. In marketing a magazine to its intended audience, many marketing considerations must be kept in mind, such as reader loyalty, the audience, the advertiser, and economic considerations.

The Audience and the Advertiser

Tough problems and decisions await the publishers of magazines. For instance, when a market analysis reveals that an audience profile is changing, both publisher and advertisers may need to take immediate action, most of it based on hypothetical projections. Advertisers who buy space in the hope of reaching a specific audience as verified by market data must now decide whether to switch media.

Put yourself in the position of an advertising manager, say, of your school magazine. According to market data, the audience you are reaching is the school audience. Suddenly your audience begins to shift. Your magazine's circulation remains the same, but student interest now begins to ebb while subscriptions among the housewives living near campus increase. Your first reaction may be, "So what?" Your advertisers simply do not want to reach housewives, that's what. They want to reach the students. What do you do? Do you change the editorial or news content of the magazine to reflect the needs of the student audience? That might work, but what if the trend is already too deeply rooted? By changing the content you would not regain the students, but you would lose the housewives in the process. By now your circulation has dwindled and advertising rates must be cut, but in order to stay in business and to meet expenses you must keep the same advertising rate. Tough decisions? Absolutely. Now imagine how hard it is for magazine publishers dealing with millions of dollars in revenue and millions of readers.

A major reason for the overall steady growth of magazines has been their ability to adapt with remarkable efficiency to the changing media habits of readers and to the unpredictable changes in the economy. Magazines have also fared well because of their ability to reach specialized audiences, audiences whose *loyalty* is considered fairly steadfast. Stop and consider your own media experiences. Naturally you watch television, if not as much when in school, then certainly when you are at home in the evening, on weekends, during the summer, or on vacation. But do you have a loyalty to one channel? Probably not. You switch freely from channel to channel. However, if you have a keen interest in a hobby, you may very well have a strong loyalty to a magazine devoted to your hobby. For example, if you enjoy skiing, you might regularly read *Ski;* if you are a gun enthusiast, you might regularly read *Shooting Times;* a horse enthusiast might subscribe to *Western Horseman* or the *Chronicle of the Horse.* You may even be so involved in your hobby that you avidly read the editorial content of the magazine, such as editorials championing financial support for the United States Olympic team, gun control, or new interstate commerce regulations for transporting horses over state lines.

How strong is your loyalty to a magazine? Would you sacrifice reading one issue of the newspaper each week to continue the opportunity to read your favorite magazine? Would you give up the chance to watch a TV channel one or two nights a week so that you could continue to receive your favorite magazine? Regardless of your own answers, keep in mind that millions of people would react with a definite "yes" to these questions. A business executive, for example, might need an industry publication to understand business trends and to ensure his or her continued livelihood.

Additional evidence of the important relationship between a magazine and its reader is seen in a research study by Opinion Research Corporation, released through the Magazine Publishers Association. It indicates that over a six-month period 72 percent of the male readers and 79 percent of the female readers kept an issue of a magazine for future reference, 79 percent of the men and 78 percent of the women discussed an article or feature with another person, and 51 percent of the men and 68 percent of the women tried an idea suggested in an article.

ECONOMIC CONSIDERATIONS

In today's world of rapidly increasing costs for labor and paper, an acute awareness of the expenses of magazine production is also important.

Postage

Postage costs are continuing to spiral upward. As they do, money must be subtracted from other areas of production. Postage rates are forcing publishers to look for ways to cut the costs of distribution through such means as newsstand sales. *People* magazine, for example, is sold principally through newsstands. Yet for other magazines, their limited appeal prohibits this means of distribution. The average newsstand would sell so few issues of the publication that the use of shelf space to display it would be unjustified.

Paper Costs   Paper costs also continue to eat away at the production dollar. Many magazines are reducing their actual dimensions in an effort to save paper costs and to prevent their magazines from being listed as "outsized" by the Post Office. In fact, many publications on today's newsstands are at least one-third smaller in width and length than they were ten years ago.

Cost Sharing   Costs have prompted some magazine publishers to join together to help each maintain a strong position in the market and cut costs. The Society of National Association Publications (*SNAP*) is one vehicle that helps publishers cut costs, in this case by sharing cover designs. The magazine *Hardware Retailing* published an issue featuring a cover design of Uncle Sam eyeing a consumer. The title of the special issue was "Consumer Protection . . . How Far Is Too Far." This cover was subsequently made available to any other member of SNAP who wanted to copy it. The other publishers needed only to substitute the title of their own magazine. Four others did, including *Mutual Review*, whose issue was entitled "A Look at Government-Industry Cooperation."

Cost Per Thousand (CPM)   Despite these higher costs, magazines are predicted to fare better than both newspapers and network prime-time television in offering advertisers a lower cost per thousand in the coming years. Cost per thousand (CPM) is the cost of reaching one thousand people with one advertisement.

This does not necessarily mean that if you were to go out and purchase a commercial on television or an advertisement in the newspaper that it would necessarily cost more than a magazine advertisement. We are talking about projected increases in CPM, not necessarily in the cost of advertising. But in an era of increased advertising costs, the cost of magazine advertising is not expected to increase at the rate that other media will. One major reason is the availability of magazines and the increasing number of magazines creating a good competitive climate. In many large markets you have only one choice in purchasing newspaper advertising. Moreover, until we have many more commercial television networks, there is no indication that the cost of prime-time television is going to level off significantly.

THE AUDIENCE

The magazine audience is comprised, overall, of affluent, well-educated readers—readers that advertisers pay premium dollars to reach. Although more expensive on a cost-per-thousand basis, advertising in specific small circulation magazines that reach a specific target audience which has the interest and the money to spend on a particular product or service usually gets results. A drug manufacturer trying to sell its products to doctors would find advertising on network television which is viewed by many who have no interest in the products to be much less cost efficient than advertising in a medical journal which aims its editorial content right at the drug manufacturer's target audience.

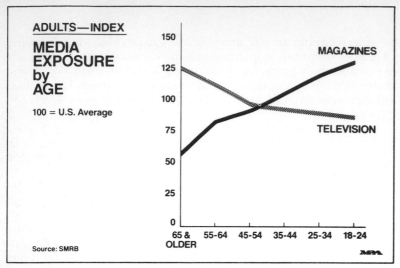

Figure 3-20 (Magazine Publishers Association)

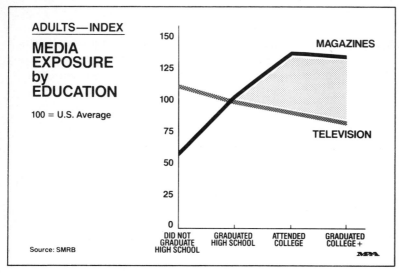

Figure 3-21 (Magazine Publishers Association)

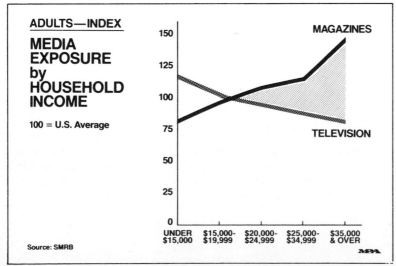

Figure 3-22 (Magazine Publishers Association)

In the important advertising *demographics* of age, income, education, and occupation, magazines compete well with television, particularly for the younger audience (Figure 3–20) whose buying habits are not firmly set and who are thus important prospects for advertisers. Magazines remain dominant for those aged 18 to about 50, at which point television gradually takes over.

Better-educated readers also favor magazines over television (Figure 3–21). For goods or services which require more detailed explanations or which appeal to the more educated, magazines offer a medium to present that detail and an audience that can understand it.

Another category important to advertisers is high-income households. Here, again, magazines fare well (Figure 3–22). Looking at our graph, we find that at a family income of about $17,000, the consumption of magazines overtakes that of television. This is followed by a sharp increase in magazine consumption at about the $28,000 income level. At this level a family's income is high enough to allow it to purchase various magazines, and such people often seek information found in professional magazines associated with their job or profession. This association with magazines and the higher-income professional is also seen in Figure 3–23, which explains the magazine industry's dominance over television among people in professional or managerial occupations.

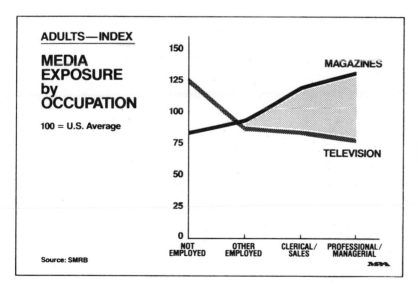

Figure 3-23 (Magazine Publishers Association)

MONITORING CIRCULATION

An advertising executive wanting to place an ad for a product might consider any number of media. With radio and television, for example, the executive could consult ratings services, such as Nielsen or Arbitron, to determine the estimated number of listeners or viewers.

To find the circulation of a magazine, or how many copies are sold and read, the executive could consult the Audit Bureau of Circulation (A.B.C.) which handles only publications which have 70 percent or higher paid circulation. The executive could also consult the *Business Publications Audit of Circulations* for controlled-circulation magazines, those which distribute their copies to selected groups of people who may or may not pay for the publication, or the *Verified Audit Circulation* which bases its data on *random samples* of subscribers and mailing lists, the demographic characteristics of the recipients, and whether they actually receive the publication.

Most people buying space in a magazine refer to the *Standard Rate and Data Service* (SRDS) which publishes descriptions of magazines, among other media, listing their circulation, intended audiences, key personnel, latest rates, mechanical specifications, and other pertinent information for advertisers.

MAGAZINE NETWORKS

While we tend to associate networks with radio or television, they also thrive in the magazine field. The term *network* in magazine publishing refers primarily to a group of magazines owned by the same company or represented by the same agency or buyer. For example, if you were a manufacturer of sporting goods, you might advertise in a series of magazines reaching sports enthusiasts. The Times Mirror Magazine Network, publishers of *Outdoor Life, The Sporting News, Golf,* and *Ski,* may be under your consideration in this instance. To help your decision making, Times Mirror, as do most other magazine networks, offers advertising discounts for ads placed in two or more of its magazines. Perhaps you were interested in reaching people with certain demographic characteristics, such as high-income business executives. Knowing that such executives fly a great deal of their jobs, you might advertise in a series of in-flight airline magazines, many of which are published by the same company.

Even cruise ships have magazine networks (Figure 3–24). If you were to take a Princess Cruise, you would find the magazine *Embark* waiting in your room. The company which publishes *Embark* also publishes *Azure Seas* and *Emerald Seas* for passengers of Eastern Steamship Lines, *Sunway* for passengers of Home Lines, and *Odyssey* for passengers of Royal Cruise Lines. The individual editorial content of the magazines includes information about ports of call and on-board activities.

THE SATELLITE ERA

Just as newspapers have commissioned satellites to transmit pages to different editions, so have magazines turned to this new technology. For example, the western and midwestern editions of *Time, People,* and *Sports Illustrated* are distributed via Western Union's Westar satellite. Time's earth stations in Chicago and Los Angeles receive the respective facsimile pages, including four-color illustrations, which are then converted from data to hard copy for press runs. The color pictures are sent via a high-speed digital format with a capacity of 112,000 bits of information per second. The ability to print late-breaking information, the speed of transmission, and cost effectiveness are just some of the reasons satellite transmission is making an impact on magazine publishing.

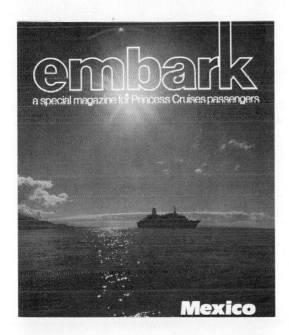

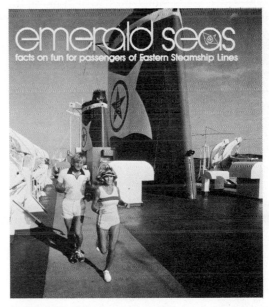

Figure 3-24 Magazine networks can consist of different magazines with similar content reaching readers with similar but specialized interests. These cruise ship magazines contain much of the same information and advertisements, but each is directed at the passengers on a particular cruise ship or ships cruising a particular region. (Courtesy, In-Cruise Network)

Whether magazines can retain their competitive edge over television is uncertain. While magazines have traditionally sought to reach a highly specialized audience, television is also evolving into a highly specialized medium, seeking magazines' audiences. More channels of communication created through cable and home information systems will also offer advertisers alternative specialized audiences. To combat this new technology, some magazines, such as *Better Homes and Gardens,* are entering the field of electronic publishing by offering information through home information systems.

The entire magazine field with its specialized audience characteristics will bear watching in the electronic publishing future. Will those "tele-magazines" which make the new technology jump prosper? If a publication does not make the jump, will it survive?

SUMMARY

Modern magazines trace their roots to the latter part of the nineteenth century when they became the first true entertainment medium, for at that time no radio or television signals crowded the air waves, and not every community was blessed with a movie theater. Magazines began to fill the void and gradually attracted advertising. As they grew in size and popularity, their success was closely tied to circulation. The more issues the magazines sold, the more advertisers they could attract and the more they could charge for advertising. But by the 1950s television had acquired a sure foothold as the new "mass" medium, and it was not long before advertisers who wanted to reach a mass audience could do it more cheaply on television than in magazines. As a result some of the true mass circulation magazines, such as *Life, Look,* and *The Saturday Evening Post,* were forced out of business. Even though some of these were later revived, they were completely new magazines, for television had ushered in the era of specialized publications.

Today magazines have at their disposal a variety of methods to reach specialized audiences. *Time,* for example, publishes special editions to reach the college student and the business person, among others. *Sports Illustrated* publishes special insert editions containing special information on the U.S. Open Tennis Championships or the Indianapolis 500. Regional editions permit advertisers to reach readers in certain select regions of the country. *Playboy* and *Reader's Digest* are two magazines that utilize the international edition option. Reaching special target audiences is still another way that specialized magazines flourish. For example, *City Woman* and *Woman* are published for the working woman.

Tough decisions await publishers of specialty magazines. Reader loyalty, competition, and economics are just some of these considerations. On the other hand, magazines have a projected lower growth in CPM than television or newspapers, and magazines reach an audience with higher education and income than television does.

Magazine circulation is monitored through the Audit Bureau of Circulation. Other services such as the Standard Rate and Data Service (SRDS) are also available. Magazines are also organized into networks which are groups of magazines owned by the same company or represented by the same agency or buyer.

Satellite transmission has aided magazines in publishing regional editions and therefore reaching more specialized audiences and loyal readers.

OPPORTUNITIES FOR FURTHER LEARNING

HAMBLIN, D. J., *That Was the Life*. New York: W. W. Norton & Co., Inc., 1977.

Handbook of Magazine Publishing. New Canaan, Conn.: Folio Magazine Publishing Corp., 1978.

How and Why People Buy Magazines: A National Study of the Consumer Market for Magazines. Port Washington, N.Y.: Publisher's Clearinghouse, 1977.

KELLEY, J. E., *Magazine Writing Today*. Cincinnati: Writers Digest, 1978.

KIMBROUGH, M., *Black Magazines: An Exploratory Study*. Austin: Center for Communication Research, University of Texas, 1973.

Lieberman Research, Inc., *How and Why People Buy Magazines: A National Study of the Consumer Market for Magazines*. Port Washington, N.Y.: Publisher's Clearinghouse, 1977.

MAYES, H. R., *The Magazine Maze*. Garden City, N.Y.: Doubleday, 1980.

MEYER, S. E., *America's Great Illustrators*. New York: Harry Abrams, 1978.

MOGEL, L., *The Magazine: Everything You Need to Know to Make It in the Magazine Business*. Englewood Cliffs, N.J.: Prentice-Hall, 1979.

MYERSON, J., *The New England Transcendentalists and the Dial: A History of the Magazine and Its Contributors*. Rutherford, N.J.: Fairleigh Dickinson University Press, 1980.

NELSON, R. P., *Articles and Features*. New York: Houghton Mifflin Company, 1978.

RANKIN, W. P., *Business Management of General Consumer Magazines*. New York: Praeger, 1980.

RIVERS, W. L., *Free-Lancer and Staff Writer: Newspaper Features and Magazine Articles*. Belmont, Calif.: Wadsworth, 1976.

SCHACHT, J. H., *A Bibliography for the Study of Magazines*, 4th ed. Urbana, Ill.: College of Communications, 1979.

SCHREINER, S. A., *The Condensed World of the Reader's Digest*. Briarcliff Manor, N.Y.: Stein & Day, 1977.

STEINBERG, S. H., *Reformer in the Marketplace: Edward W. Bok and the Ladies' Home Journal*. Baton Rouge: Louisiana State University Press, 1979.

WOLSELEY, R. E., *Understanding Magazines*, 2nd ed. Ames: Iowa State University Press, 1969.

WOLSELEY, R. E., *The Changing Magazine: Trends in Readership and Management*. New York: Hastings House, 1973.

CHAPTER

BOOK PUBLISHING

PREVIEW

After completing this chapter, we should be able to:

Trace the development of book publishing.

Describe publishing and bookbinding in colonial America.

Know that William Holmes McGuffey was responsible for early American textbooks.

Connect the name of E. F. Beadle with the introduction of the dime novel.

Discuss the distribution system for paperback books.

Identify methods used to promote books.

Distinguish between the media event and the media marketing in the process of book marketing.

Explain the concepts of the personalized book and the fotonovel.

Discuss the current issues facing the book publishing industry.

Describe regional publishing.

When radio and then television became mass media, pessimists made dire predictions about the future of books, similar to the prognosis they had made for the mails upon completion of the Atlantic Cable. They suggested that we would become a visual society attuned to the giant screen instead of to the printed page. The satirical movie *Fahrenheit 451* portrayed a future in which television would be the giant controlling medium and in which it would be illegal to possess books.

Although such a state is not beyond the realm of possibility in anything less than a free society, books have stood the test of time. They have survived and carry with them an important part of society's development. From Chaucer's *Canterbury Tales* to the latest best seller, books have remained an important part of our lives. We learn from them, we are entertained by them, and we possess them. They have survived major reforms among people and nations. Books have been the object of political suppression and the stimulus for champions of liberation. They have been among the cherished possessions of kings and have helped lay the foundations of republican government. Radio and television programs come and go; at best we may remember a catchy word or phrase, or a fleeting image may haunt our memory. A book, however, like a good friend, can be looked up again and again without tiring of its acquaintance.

BEGINNINGS OF BOOK PUBLISHING

The first books were actually large rolls of paper attached to two rods that permitted the book to be held and rolled from either end. Each manuscript contained a tag which served as a label for the book. Although lengths of a manuscript varied as they do today, sometimes entire books were contained on a single roll. In Rome around the time of Christ, history records a brisk book-selling business; some households were recorded as having libraries containing thousands of volumes. Caesar commanded the founding of public libraries, some of which were estimated to contain hundreds of thousands of volumes. In the cloisters and abbeys of medieval Europe, monks laboriously copied the Scriptures, embellishing them with crude hand-engraved illustrations. These early scrolls contained script sometimes extending their entire length, much of which was arranged in columns. These rolled scrolls were gradually replaced by manuscripts folded in accordionlike stacks, with wooden boards attached to the first and last pages. Then came the idea to punch holes into and stitch one side of the folds. From this process came the practice of "binding" individual sheets of paper between covers. Early binding actually consisted of flexible hinges to which the pages were attached with linen threads. When leather became the chief material used for book covers, bookbinders began bordering these covers with their trademarks of patterns rolled on with small wheellike tools called *rolls*. These rolls were similar to those used by today's leathercraft workers to engrave belts, wallets, and other products. Needless to say, with so few books available and with considerable time and effort expended in their production, they were very valuable.

With increased use of the printing press during the sixteenth century, composition changed drastically. Engraved wooden blocks became printing plates to produce illustrations. Books could now be mass produced—of course on a scale we would consider moderate indeed. These early books were mostly hardback volumes, with content concentrating on religion,

Figure 4-1 This early bookbinding shop shows the workers (left to right) beating the folded sections of the book, stitching the book, trimming the edges on a ploughing press, and pressing the edges on a standing press. (From DIDEROT and courtesy of *The Printer in 18th Century Williamsburg*. Williamsburg, Va.: Colonial Williamsburg, 1955)

Figure 4-2 Notice in this illustration of a colonial bookbindery, the hand tools on the back walls. The tools are used to "engrave" the ornate borders on leather-bound books. The standing press is at the left, and immediately behind it are shelves with sheets of uncut leather. (Courtesy, Colonial Williamsburg)

the writings of the ancient Greeks, and the trades. The audience for the early hard-bound volumes again was not the mass audience. It consisted mostly of students who would borrow the books and pass them on from one class to another, the religious orders of the day, or the elite and wealthy who could afford the luxury of buying books.

The book publishing industry was centered on the local bookbinder's shop. Figures 4–1 and 4–2 show two views of an early bookbinder's shop. In Figure 4–1 the man on the left is heating the folded sections of a book so that they will lie flat. He is using a wooden hammer and large wooden block in much the same way a blacksmith uses a hammer and anvil to shape metal. The folded sections of the book are then stitched on a crude stitching frame, operated by the woman on the right.

The two people at the right of Figure 4–1 are using a ploughing press (also seen in Figure 4–3) and a standing press (also seen in Figure 4–4). The ploughing press sat on a rectangular frame and was used to trim the edges of a newly sewn book. The worker on the far right is using the standing press to press a stack of bound and trimmed books. The standing press used a large corkscrew to press a plate against the stack of books.

Figure 4–2 shows a typical Colonial bookbinder at work. Here you can see a closer view of the standing press with its large wooden corkscrew. Notice that on the table there is a much smaller press used to hold a single book. On the shelves by the window are uncut sheets of leather used for book covers, and on the wall behind the bookbinder are the rolls used to imprint borders and designs on the covers. The bookbinder usually was in the village printing shop which, naturally, also sold books.

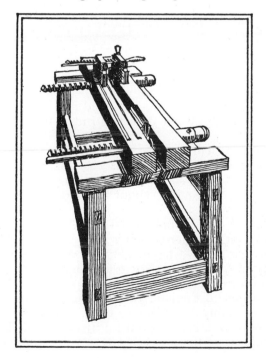

Figure 4-3 A closer view of the ploughing press which "trims" the book. The pages are clamped firmly between the two top horizontal beams, then the knife secured in the "plough" cuts the rough, uneven pages, leaving the edges of the pages even and smooth. (*The Bookbinder in 18th-Century Williamsburg.* Williamsburg, Va: Colonial Williamsburg, 1959)

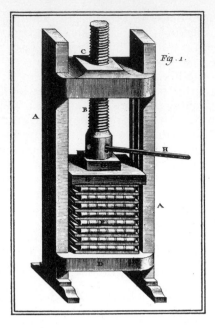

Figure 4-4 A closer view of the standing press shows the books stacked with "press boards" between each book and the large handturned wood screw applying pressure to the wood block on top of the stack. (*The Bookbinder in 18th-Century Williamsburg*. Williamsburg, Va: Colonial Williamsburg, 1959)

PUBLISHING IN COLONIAL AMERICA

The roots of book publishing in America can be traced back to the early English expeditions of the mid to late 1500s.

Writing about the New World

Although not published in America, one of the first books about early settlements on the North American continent was Thomas Harriot's *Brief and True Report of the New Found Land of Virginia* (Figure 4–5). First published in 1588, an illustrated edition appeared two years later containing 28 engravings by artist John White depicting Indian life styles and customs as well as maps of the new land.

The book was primarily a public relations piece to encourage people to settle the American continent. After unsuccessful and tragic expeditions during the era of Sir Walter Raleigh, its publication was a gallant attempt to lessen the fears of the English about the promises of the American continent.

Sir Walter Raleigh had commissioned John White to head a company and locate a settlement in America. White's fleet went to sea in April of 1587, headed for what is now Chesapeake Bay. Mutiny forced him to the Island of Roanoke in what is now North Carolina. There he deposited a group of people which included his daughter, her husband, and their daughter. He returned to England for supplies, but upon returning to America, found the colony deserted. No trace of the settlement has ever been found. This news and the news of the difficulties of earlier expeditions dampened the enthusiasm that Harriot's book was supposed to generate.

Colonial Bookbinders

The beginnings of the book publishing industry in America can be traced as far back as the seventeenth century, when the developing Colonies needed to distribute laws, propositions before government, and other official documents approved by the Crown.[1] Often these "booklets" were published by officially approved printers in whose shops the bookbinders also worked. In fact, government printing and publishing contracts constituted the major trade of Colonial printers. Additional income was obtained by printing religious publications, such as psalm books or collections of sermons. Often these "published" books were single copies, nothing resembling mass distribution.

Figure 4-5 *A briefe and true report of the new found land of Virginia* represents one of the first books ever to be published about the "New World." First published in 1588, an illustrated edition with sketches by artist John White appeared two years later in 1590. (From the Dover edition, the Rosenwald Collection Reprint Series)

Bookbinders in Colonial America spent much of their time binding publications for private citizens who retained the only copy of the work. Some jobs were binding books written by the customer ordering the binding. Other books were Bibles, which often were rebound and passed on from generation to generation. If we had walked into the bookbinding shop of Joseph Royle in Williamsburg, Virginia, in the summer of 1765, we could have visited with a customer wanting a song book bound, another wanting a prayer book bound, or even Thomas Jefferson might have stopped by to request that a history of Virginia be bound.

In addition to customer-ordered books, a lucrative side of the business was the publication of blank ledgers and account books. These, along with stationery items, kept the Colonial bookbinder in business. If we had read the *Virginia Gazette* on August 19, 1780, for example, we would have seen an advertisement placed by Thomas Brend offering to sell spelling books, psalm books, pocket books, blank books, and account books (Figure 4–6).

The changes in early colonial bookbinding followed those of early colonial newspapers. After independence was declared, both increased the diversity of their content and their distribution.

THOMAS BREND,
BOOKBINDER AND STATIONER,
HAS for SALE, at his shop at the corner of Dr. Carter's large brick house, Testaments Spelling Books, Primers, Ruddiman's Rudiments of the Latin Tongue, Watts's Psalms, Blank Books, Quills Sealing-Wax, Pocket-Books, and many other articles in the Stationery way. Old books rebound; and any Gentlemen who have paper by them and want it made into Account Books, may have it done on the shortest notice.

Figure 4-6 (Courtesy, Colonial Williamsburg)

MASS TEXTBOOK PUBLISHING

A quarter-century after American independence, William Holmes McGuffey was born in Claysville, Pennsylvania. He later became known as one of the great educators of the time and advanced through various positions including public school teacher and professor of languages and then served as president of Cincinnati College and later Ohio University. But what McGuffey was best known for was his creation of elementary school textbooks known as the McGuffey Eclectic Readers (Figure 4–7), readers designed to teach good pronunciation and reading ability. McGuffey readers were an institution, not only in education but in book publishing as well. In all, between 1836 and 1857, McGuffey wrote six readers designed for different levels of achievement. Based on gradual learning and always carrying a moral message, they were designed so that

LESSON XXXIII.

pu̱ll   càrt   gōats   Bĕss

ŭp   rīde   hĭll

u̱

Figure 4-7 A page from the *McGuffy Reader.* The *Reader* became one of the most widely read and universally adopted early elementary textbooks.

Bess has a cart and two goats.
She likes to ride in her cart.
See how the goats pull!
Bess is so big, I think she should walk up the hill.
The goats love Bess, for she feeds them, and is kind to them.

the student could graduate to the next level of reader after completing the preceding one. As they became increasingly popular, new editions were published and survived well into the first decade of the twentieth century.

Considering the times, the approximate circulation of 122 million copies of McGuffey's readers is phenomenal. Today the original readers are collectors' items and are on the shelves of antique shops. In their time they set the stage for a new era of book publishing that went beyond the classroom to the general public.

THE DIME NOVELS

The impetus for publishing on a mass scale occurred shortly after 1850 when there were both the means and the desire to produce books that would become the foundation for much of the current publishing industry. At that time a New York publisher named E. F. Beadle decided that he could sell books if they were cheap enough and if they satisfied the public's desire for entertainment and good literary prose. He started with the publication of a ten-cent paperback song book. Shortly thereafter he ventured into other paperback "dime novels" (Figure 4–8), which became best sellers even by the modest standards of the late 1800s. Beadle's novels were not long—only about 75 pages—and most of them were about the American pioneer.

Figure 4-8 Beadle's "dime novels" were the forerunner of the modern paperback books. Their content ranged from Western tales of adventure beyond the Allegheny Mountains to "Dialogues" which could be adapted for amateur theatrical productions.

A search for an escape into fantasy was what made dime novels into best sellers. They contained little truth but continued to prosper even into the Civil War when troops found the books good company on long hikes. Many other companies also ventured into dime-novel publishing, and although the thrill of the original dime novel diminished, it left a sizable impression on the history of book publishing. To it we owe the modern concept of the book as a medium of mass communication.

In a suburb of Dayton, Ohio, a former advertising executive sat down at his typewriter in the mid-1970s and began writing a series of paperback books. Under contract to his publisher and stringent deadlines, author John Jakes (Figure 4–9) typed the first pages of the American Bicentennial Series. The series would shake the roots of the book publishing industry.

The American Bicentennial Series was released first in paperback. That in itself was a first in American book publishing, since the common practice for major best sellers was to release them originally in hardback and later in paperback. But then no one knew Jakes's novels would be best sellers.

Finally, the first of the series rolled off the presses. Titled *The Bastard*, it traced the beginnings of the fictitious Kent family from their roots in France and England and then to America. It also triggered a chain of events that set records in American book publishing. *The Bastard* (Figure 4–10) was followed by other titles—*The Rebels, The Seekers, The Furies, The Titans, The Warriors, The Lawless,* and *The Americans.* The series became so popular that Jakes became the first author to have three books on the *New York Times* best seller list within one year. It was not long before the series had sold more than 30 million copies, and the publishing industry was taking another look at paperback book publishing. Some of Jakes's novels were later combined and released in hardback, and syndicated television features beginning with *The Bastard* were released to independent television

Figure 4-9 The paperback books by John Jakes which traced the lives of the fictitious Kent family set paperback-book publishing records. This series, which became known as the "Bicentennial Series" and also "The Kent Family Chronicles," made publishers realize that major novels could succeed when first published in a paperback edition. The standard practice had been for a major novel to first be published in hardback, then reintroduced in paperback. (Provided through the courtesy of JOVE Publications, Inc.)

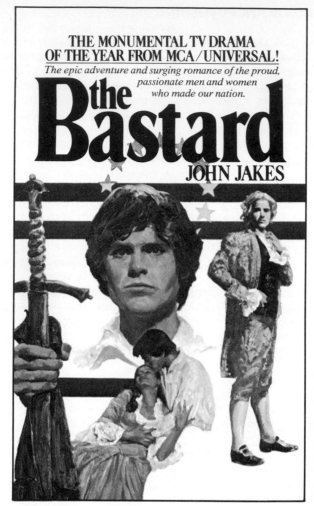

Figure 4-10 *The Bastard* was the first book of the "Bicentennial Series" written by John Jakes. When the television miniseries for *The Bastard* was aired, the book cover was adapted to reflect the characters in the television production. (JOVE Publications, Inc.)

stations, achieving a ratings success. Jakes later began work on a trilogy, the first of which was released in hardback in 1982 and titled *North and South*. The whetted appetite of the readers for his paperbacks gobbled up the first of the trilogy and sent it immediately to the top of the *New York Times* best seller list.

The success of John Jakes and his Bicentennial Series was indicative of both the potential and the present appeal of paperback book publishing. Today it is a major part of the book publishing industry and is receiving increased distribution, production, and promotional support.

Distributing Paperbacks

One reason for the success of today's paperback book industry is its distribution system. If you can distribute easily and inexpensively information that the public wants, you have a chance for success. The first chapters of the paperback book success story are easy transportation and wide availability. The distribution system, although not as efficient perhaps as that of radio or television, is still not cumbersome by any means.

Because of this ease of distribution, paperback books have also become an instrument of persuasion and, in some cases, propaganda. For example, politicians running for office may find that they can add to their prestige by writing a book that details their career in office. The book can be assembled into approximately one hundred pages and distributed on a mass scale to as many potential voters as funds permit. The cost of producing the book is minimal, and distribution can be through political workers carrying an armload door to door.

Portability is part of the reason you, as a consumer, chose a paperback book to accompany you on your last trip. It was light, and you could carry it for a long time even though you were walking through bus stations or airport corridors. You also could hold it easily or set it on the edge of your seat.

Paperback books can also be bought at places other than bookstores. Sir Allen Lane, publisher of the famous Penguin books, during a visit to America in the early 1930s, surmised that if he could make buying books as easy as buying any other novelty, he could reach a substantial, untapped market of readers. Sir Allen managed to negotiate a contract with the Woolworth stores to distribute his Penguin books.[2] The venture proved successful, and the new distribution system clinched the success of his enterprise. Today you can find paperback books in virtually every type of retail establishment imaginable, from gas stations to grocery stores.

*Promoting
Paperbacks*

Along with distribution advantages, mass market paperbacks now emphasize promotion that rivals the best of Madison Avenue's marketing schemes. Today a paperback book reaches the marketplace with a coordinated effort including everyone from the bookstore to the consumer (Figure 4–11). For example, the best seller *Coma*, a medical thriller, was released to bookstores with a whole array of promotional aids. *"Tie-ins"* included an attractive floor display for bookstores to increase reader interest at the place of purchase. A special marketing booklet with scenes from the film was included. That in itself was a new phenomenon in book publishing— having book and film (sometimes even television) rights and production schedules all completed before the book was released. *Coma* T-shirts were part of the campaign, and posters showing movie scenes were available for bookstores, as were shopping bags with *Coma* printed on them and a special gimmick, *Coma* surgical masks. For the bookstore with the best display came a prize from the publisher.

Other promotional tie-ins also contribute to a book's success, whether paperback or hardback. The appearance of authors on television talk shows can definitely boost sales. Promotional agents work hard to get the authors on programs that can promote the books at both local and national levels. Advance copies of the book are distributed to reviewers, bookstore clerks, and other people who can promote the book. Radio, television, and *billboard* advertising can also be part of the marketing campaign. All combine to make contemporary book publishing a radically different business from what it was twenty years ago. Literary agents auction off top

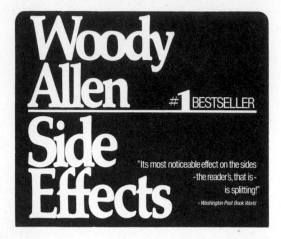

Figure 4-11 Successful book sales require major advertising and promotion efforts inside the bookstores at the point-of-purchase.

manuscripts in the millions of dollars, television rights can bring even more money, and movies add still more to an industry that certainly has adapted well to the competition of new media in the marketplace.

BOOK MARKETING AND THE MASS MEDIA

Few forces have affected book publishing more than its mass media competitors. With marketing strategies hinging on millions of dollars, no publisher or marketing executive can afford to overlook the staggering ability of newspapers, radio, television, and other mass media to publicize and transmit information. Book publishers are teaming up with television and motion picture producers to coordinate the release of a book with the release of the corresponding motion picture or television series. Each complements the publicity of the other so both can gain more of the reading and viewing public. We can view this media phenomena through two ways: (1) the media event and (2) media marketing.

The Media Event	Modern technology has made it possible for a book to be published at a speed unheard of a few years ago. With the ability to ship paperbacks by air and the readily available data to make intelligent marketing decisions, a book publisher can turn a major news event into a publishing bonanza almost overnight. In some cases, especially when tragedy is involved, it may seem like crass commercialization, but the procedure will continue as long as it is profitable.

An example of how quickly and efficiently news events can turn book publishers into profit hunters occurred with the shooting death of former Beatle star John Lennon. Many publishers immediately checked with bookstores to see if Lennon's death meant an upsurge of public interest in books about the Beatles subsequently sent shipments to stores within one week after Lennon's death. Reissued existing paperbacks made up part of the lot, but new books were also published.

These "instant books," so called because they are rushed to publication in the instant an event occurs, included *Strawberry Fields Forever* (Bantam) with an initial press run of 350,000.

Media Marketing Even though a book can be promoted with television commercials, talk show appearances, and shows with book tie-ins, the publisher only benefits if the book is available for purchase in the bookstores when the public is ready to buy it. Book publishing has two distinct customers: the reading public and the bookstore owners. Thus book merchandisers and distributors make special efforts to attract both the public's and the bookstore owner's attention, often by using the mass media approach.

An example of this sensitivity to media is seen in Waldenbooks' media table campaign in which the "media-hot" books are grouped together at a special table with labels such as "As seen on *Today*" or "Now a Movie" decorating the tables and books to alert potential customers. A *Media Merchandising Manual* is even available to help bookstore owners and managers recognize which books are truly media-hot and how best to make them attractive on store counters.

NEW FORMATS

In addition to paperbacks, publishers have started experimenting with new formats in book publishing. Two of these are personalized books and "fotonovels."

Personalized Books *Personalized books* are composed and printed entirely by computer. The computer stores a complete text of the book but with programming arranged so that specific names and places can be inserted into the text. Suppose a parent wants to order a book for a child. Let us assume that the child has a family pet, a brother, and a sister and lives in a small community. We shall call her Nancy Smith, the dog will be named Laddie, and the family will live on Peach Street. When Nancy's parent orders the book, all of this information is given to the publisher, who in turn

Figure 4-12 Promotional tie-ins for fotonovels often include the practice of releasing the book at the same time the motion picture or television program airs. In-store marketing displays have been effective for some titles and are part of the point-of purchase advertising and marketing strategies. (Courtesy, Bantam Books)

programs the computer to personalize the book for Nancy. When Nancy opens the book, it reads: "This morning, Nancy and her dog Laddie were walking home on Peach Street when Laddie began barking loudly." The story then continues with the names of the characters the same as those of Nancy's actual brothers, sisters, and relatives. There is more to this concept than novelty, however. What has given them significant educational value and use as learning tools are the interest and motivation that children acquire when they see their names in print.

Fotonovels
The fotonovel is part printed text, part picture book, and part comic book. It developed as a spin-off to television and movies and includes still pictures from the movies or programs, accompanied by short lines of text or dialogue. *Star Trek* recently provided some of the most popular material for fotonovels. Acclaimed for years in Europe, fotonovels are relatively new to North America. But with the increased use of television, they are a natural commercial complement to entertainment programming. Promotional tie-ins often include releasing both the fotonovel and the television series at the same time and coordinating bookstore and retail outlet advertising (Figure 4–12) with television promotional efforts.

ISSUES IN THE BOOK PUBLISHING INDUSTRY

In the rapidly changing world of corporate decisions, the future of the book publishing industry hinges on many important issues.

Distribution, Printing, Paper

The energy crisis has taken its toll in book publishing expenditures as it has on the costs of operating other print media. Unlike radio and television, however, which can broadcast their messages over the airwaves, the book publishing industry must transport its messages by truck, ship, train, and plane. These sources of transportation will naturally continue to increase their rates as the cost of fuel continues to rise. When a book leaves the warehouse, many people handle it, and many vehicles transport it. The labor costs of loading books onto trucks, the cost of purchasing the trucks to haul them, the cost of gasoline to run the trucks, the salaries paid to drivers, the cost of labor to unload the books, and the increased rental costs to display them in a bookstore or wherever else they are sold have all burgeoned. This has triggered everything from bankruptcy to consolidation.

More and more printers are realizing the value of their skills and the importance of good printing to the overall production of a book. Labor unions are negotiating contracts that add higher salaries and new fringe benefits.

As other print media do, book publishers also face soaring paper costs. The chief villain is the inflated cost of energy and natural resources necessary to manufacture paper. Added to this are higher labor costs. In many cases the market for books simply will not bear the essential price hikes to offset completely these paper costs. As a result the difference has appeared in shrinking profit columns. This does not mean that book publishing is about to vanish from the American scene. It can, however, translate into lean years for stockholders until prices level off, for paper can represent as much as one-half the expense of publishing a book.

New Ventures: New Income

We already have seen how the paperback book industry is booming because of major promotional efforts. In addition, the industry is branching out into new, profitable areas. For instance, Bantam Books has developed a new gift-books division. In a major commitment to this type of publication, Bantam hired Ian Ballantine, the founder of Ballantine Books, out of retirement to head the new division, called Peacock Press. The Peacock Press publishes gift books with excellent reproductions of quality art prints.

Retailing for a fraction of the cost of competing publications, these specialty items have literally stolen the market. Paperback originals by established authors are also increasing the potential of this upcoming offshoot of the industry.

Even unusual undertakings can become profitable with imagination, research, and a little luck. Ballantine Books, for example, published a packet of blueprints for the starship *Enterprise* from the popular *Star Trek* television series. More than a half-million packets were sold. Publishing sets of books or reissuing books in gift covers has also proved successful. A popular book may beget sequels, and after five or so have been published, a gift-box arrangement of an entire set can lure new readers and new buyers to bookstore shelves. Even the illustrations can turn into popular collection pieces. Norman Rockwell's paintings, which for many years decked the covers of the *Saturday Evening Post*, have been published and republished in collectors' editions. Special collections of circus stories, Christmas stories, Easter stories, recipes, and numerous other items have proved interesting reading and profitable book publishing ventures.

REGIONAL PUBLISHING

Some publishers predict that future economic constraints on distribution will generate growth in regional publishing—books appealing to a particular region (Figure 4–13). As a regional book publisher, you would not seek out manuscripts that appeal to a national readership but, rather, to a specific regional market. For example, instead of publishing a book about farming, you might publish one about farming in New England or in the Midwest. Although the market for regional books is more limited, sales density can be higher because of generally greater interest. Most important, distribution costs drop as the publisher concentrates on a specific region, say the East Coast. Many major publishing companies have already developed regional distribution systems, and some smaller companies are exclusively regional. One of the more successful regional presses is the Caxton Press of Caldwell, Idaho. Its primary distribution area, the Northwest, is also the focal point of its readership. Caxton has made recent inroads into *coffee table books*—handsomely designed, oversized volumes with color pictures—selling for as much as fifty dollars or more. Other

Figure 4-13 Some publishing efforts base their success upon high interest by readers in a specific geographic region. One example is this publication by Lee Enterprises, Incorporated, which details the devastating eruption of Mt. St. Helens in the state of Washington. (Courtesy, Lee Enterprises, Incorporated)

publishers focus on material about a specific area. The University of Tennessee Press, for instance, concentrates on books on the heritage and people of that region. Its list of titles also includes books on the War Between the States.

FUTURE MANAGEMENT DECISIONS

The future manager of any publishing enterprise will need to monitor constantly the industry's cost factors. Besides production and distribution costs, the industry has fundamental cost factors such as sales and advertising. Here the key is to attract and to keep enthusiastic and dedicated people who have the discipline to work well without much supervision and who enjoy working on a commission basis. These people keep a firm in business. But as with every other cost, the expenses incurred by a sales staff are increasing. In any publishing venture, there are only so many excess dollars to go around after basic publishing expenditures. Thus at some point management must decide if it can raise the commission paid to the sales staff without raising the price of the book.

Other management decisions also will affect profit. Knowing a book's market is crucial because the larger the number of volumes that are printed, the smaller the cost per copy. However, it costs just as much to print books that do not sell. One key to success in a new venture is not to overrun the initial printing—that is, to avoid unsold books being returned from bookstores. Management also faces unexpected costs that might develop before the book reaches the bookstores, such as a truckers' strike that would necessitate shipping some books by air freight. All of those factors can dramatically change the economic picture of any publishing venture.

SUMMARY

The roots of book publishing can be traced to the Saxons in the fifth century. Making accordionlike folds and binding the edges, the book concept gradually evolved because of the advantages of stitching the loose pages together. From the limited distribution of hand-copied manuscripts of the monks, the printing press and movable type began to transform book publishing into a mass medium.

Book publishing's Colonial American roots were closely tied to the printing industry. Colonial bookbinders using such equipment as ploughing and standing presses bound books on special order for individuals and the government. Mass production books as we know them today could be bought only in England.

The first real impact on mass publishing came with the work of E. F. Beadle, who pioneered the famous "dime novels" which became popular in the late nineteenth century. Beadle's novels were short, sold for a dime, and contained plays or tales of the West. Lane discovered the secret of modern paperback book publishing—that inexpensive works available in many different retail establishments could be a profitable publishing venture.

Author John Jakes is responsible for introducing a new era in contemporary paperback publishing with his American Bicentennial Series. It proved that a major novel could be successfully released in paperback without first appearing in hardback. Jakes's Bicentennial novels, the first of which was titled *The Bastard*, not only sold in the millions of copies but also had some of the largest first printings in book publishing history.

Paperbacks have succeeded because of their inexpensive price, inexpensive distribution costs, and multiple places of sale, such as drugstores and grocery stores. Major promotional efforts are also closely tied to a book's success and can include everything from T-shirts to television commercials.

Other media are part of the book publishing industry's efforts to promote and sell books. Creating tie-ins to major television programs and motion pictures, publishing books which dovetail with major media events, and helping bookstore managers to be responsive to customer demands for "media-hot" books are all part of the media marketing strategies.

New book formats, such as personalized books and fotonovels, are also appearing on bookseller's shelves. With high risks and increased costs, future managers in book publishing are going to be making tough decisions which may make it difficult for books with marginal sales potential or by untried authors, to find a publisher.

OPPORTUNITIES FOR FURTHER LEARNING

ALTBACH, P. G., AND E. M. RATHGEBER, *Publishing in the Third World: Trend Report and Bibliography*. New York: Praeger, 1980.

ANDERSON, C. B., ed., *Bookselling in America and the World: Some Observations and Recollections*. New York: Quadrangle/The New York Times Book Co., Inc. 1975.

ARMOUR, R., *The Happy Bookers*. New York: McGraw-Hill, 1976.

ARNDT, K. J. R., AND M. E. OLSON, *The German Language Press of the Americas, Volume I: History and Bibliography. 1732–1968, United States of America*. New York: Unipub, 1976.

BARKER, N., *The Oxford University Press and the Spread of Learning: An Illustrated History*. New York: Oxford University Press, 1978.

BENJAMIN, C. G., *A Candid Critique of Book Publishing*. New York: R. R. Bowker, 1977.

BRUCCOLI, M., AND E. E. F. CLARK, JR., *Pages: The World of Books, Writers, and Writing*. Detroit: Gale Research Co., 1977.

COCHRAN, W., *Into Print: A Practical Guide to Writing, Illustrating, and Publishing*. Los Altos, Calif.: William Kaufmann, Inc., 1977.

CRUTCHLEY, B., *To Be a Printer*. London: Bodley Head, 1980.

DESSAUER, J. P., *Book Publishing: What It Is, What It Does*. New York: R. R. Bowker, 1974.

DUKE, J. S., *Children's Books and Magazines: A Market Study*. White Plains, N.Y.: Knowledge Industry Publications, 1979.

EISENSTEIN, E. L., *The Printing Press as an Agent of Change*. New York: Cambridge University Press, 1980.

FEBVRE, L., AND H.-J. MARTIN, *The Coming of the Book: The Impact of Printing 1450–1800*. Atlantic Highlands, N.J.: Humanities Press, 1977.

FITZGERALD, F., *America Revised. History Schoolbooks in the Twentieth Century*. Boston: Little, Brown, 1979.

HACKETT, A. P., AND J. H. BURKE, *80 Years of Best Sellers: 1895–1975*. New York: R. R. Bowker, 1977.

JONES, H. H., *Butterworths: History of a Publishing House*. London and Boston: Butterworths, 1980.

LANE, M., AND J. BOOTH, *Books and Publishers: Commerce Against Culture on Postwar Britain*. Lexington, Mass.: Lexington Books (Heath), 1980.

PETERS, J., *Book Collecting: A Modern Guide*. New York: R. R. Bowker, 1977.

RICE, S., *Book Design: Systematic Aspects*. New York: R. R. Bowker, 1978.

RICE, S., *Book Design: Text Format Models*. New York: R. R. Bowker, 1978.

STEINBERG, S. H., *Five Hundred Years of Printing*. Baltimore: Penguin, 1974.

TEBBEL, J., *A History of Book Publishing in the United States, Volume I: The Creation of an Industry, 1630–1865*. New York: R. R. Bowker, 1972.

TEBBEL, J., *A History of Book Publishing in the United States, Volume II: The Expansion of an Industry, 1865–1919*. New York: R. R. Bowker, 1977.

TUROW, J., *Getting Books to Children: An Exploration of Publisher-Market Relations*. Chicago: American Library Association, 1979.

WINSBURY, R., *The Electronic Bookstall: Push Button Publishing on Videotex*. London: International Institute on Communications, 1979.

CHAPTER

RADIO

PREVIEW

After completing this chapter, we should be able to:

Connect the name of Guglielmo Marconi with the birth of wireless.

Identify the contributions of J. Ambrose Fleming, Lee De Forest, Nathan B. Stubblefield, Reginald A. Fessenden, and Ernst Alexanderson to the development of radio.

Name four pioneer radio stations in the United States.

Discuss the cooperation and competition between RCA, GE, A.T.&T, and Westinghouse for dominance of the early radio industry.

Trace the history of NBC, ABC, CBS, MBS, and NPR.

Explain the concept and history of FM.

Identify the inventor of FM radio as Edwin Armstrong.

Discuss the development of radio as both an entertainment and a news medium.

Explain radio syndication.

Speculate on the future of radio.

While the print media continued to influence world opinion, reaching millions of people with information and entertainment, the twentieth century signaled the era of electronic communication. The habits of media consumers changed as people began to spend more time with a new novelty called *radio*. Although they temporarily left it for the phenomenon of television, they returned, and radio once again prospered. Today over 9000 radio stations operate in the United States alone. Radio reaches every corner of the globe, bringing the latest pop music to a large metropolis or information about fertilizer to a remote tribal village. Radio is unique in its portability as well as its ability to reach us while we do different things or even while consuming other media. The soothing background music of a classical FM station adds to the atmosphere of a library reading room. The latest rock music bounces from the speaker of a nearby transistor while a teenager leafs through a favorite magazine at the beach. And a car would practically be naked without its radio.

Much different from the tubes and wires that held together the early stations of the 1920s, today's radio station is a complicated combination of electronic sophistication and creative mastery. Radio commands more than just the attention of the audience; it also commands the imagination. But radio's ability to conjure up creative imagery also has disadvantages. Images triggered by auditory stimuli, perhaps more than visual cues, depend heavily on the listener's own experience. For the child in the ghetto, for example, the sound of a crackling fire might create a vision of a burning tenement house. For a child from a well-to-do family, it might recall an open fireplace in a living room or the crackling logs of a campfire. Radio's coverage of civil unrest has suffered from the same drawback, resulting in the criticism that it is not objective and accurate. A news report about a shouting demonstrator and a milling crowd could easily give the impression of a mob out of control to many listeners.

With all of this criticism, though, radio has the ability to communicate messages with special qualities. Intangible products, for instance, can sell well on radio, making the added "visual costs" of television unnecessary. Radio journalism is also experiencing considerable new growth and recognition. When did this medium of radio begin? We shall begin our discussion in the late nineteenth century.

THE BIRTH OF WIRELESS: MARCONI

By the standards of the late nineteenth century, Guglielmo Marconi was born of wealthy parents. On their estate in Italy, he experimented with the theories of Heinrich *Hertz* Figure 5–1 until his father's patience grew thin with the boy's constant dinner conversations of wireless telegraph possibilities. Finally, hoping to either encourage him or to apply the experiments to some constructive conclusion, Guglielmo's father loaned him the money to buy equipment necessary to outfit an attic laboratory. Equipped with the basics (Figure 5–2), Marconi successfully proved Hertz's theory of *electromagnetic waves* by making a compass needle turn at the same time a spark jumped between two wires on the other side of the room. Constructing a more elaborate transmitter, Marconi successfully sent signals across the hillside outside the family home near Bologna. With his mother he then traveled to England and successfully demonstrated the

Figure 5-1 Heinrich Hertz, discoverer of electromagnetic waves, which were used as a basis for Marconi's early wireless experiments and are the basis of much of today's communication systems. Hertz's early experiments began in his home laboratory. After he died in 1894, some scientists picked up on the theoretical foundation of his work while others, such as Marconi, made practical applications of Hertz's findings. (der Universität Karlsruhe)

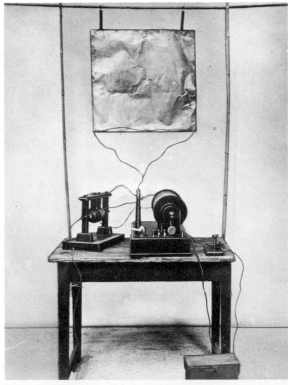

Figure 5-2 Marconi's first transmitter used in his early experiments in 1895. The large piece of tin suspended above the table served as the antenna. (The Marconi Company Limited, Marconi House, Chelmsford, Essex)

device to and received support from the British Post Office Department. He patented the new "wireless telegraph" on June 2, 1896.

At age 23, Guglielmo Marconi was fast gaining world recognition for his experiments that linked islands off the British Isles to communication with ships at sea. Familiar with the work of Samuel F. B. Morse in America, Marconi realized the full potential of his invention would occur only with a transatlantic wireless link. After an unsuccessful attempt at a broadcast between England and the New England coast, he later tried again from Signal Hill, Newfoundland (Figure 5-3). There on December 12, 1901, using a kite antenna and crude spark-gap receiving unit, he heard transmitted from across the Atlantic the letter S. Newspapers and magazines throughout the world heralded the historic event. With this success Marconi developed a series of companies which dominated the wireless market. In fact, he was accused of monopolistic tendencies because of his refusal to permit ships with other companies' equipment to communicate with shore stations and other ships equipped with his wireless equipment. But despite criticism, his work brought wireless far beyond the realm of experimentation.

Figure 5-3 Guglielmo Marconi. As much a business executive as an inventor, Marconi created a worldwide wireless empire with companies in England, the United States, Canada, and other countries. (Courtesy, RCA)

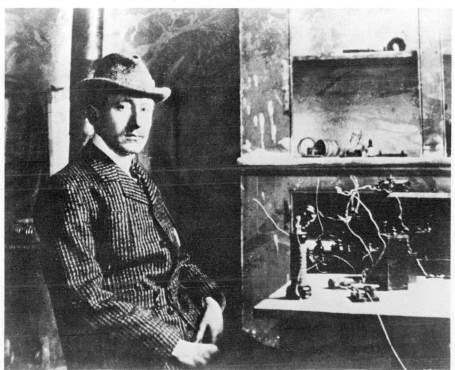

Marconi's invention was the application of a basic principle, sending electromagnetic Morse code. But Marconi was only the first in the long line of contributors to the invention of radio.

Fleming and De Forest

One of the biggest hurdles to be conquered was the receiving apparatus. It was bulky with an enormous antenna necessary to receive the minute electrical impulses. One of the early breakthroughs in this area is credited to J. Ambrose Fleming, who in 1904 patented a special, two-element receiving tube called the Fleming Valve. The device controlled the "flow" of electricity much like a valve controls the flow of water, greatly amplifying the incoming radio signals. It was improved upon by another inventor, Lee de Forest (Figure 5–4), who added a third element. His tube, the *audion*, in principle is still in use today and was the main component of radio before the invention of the transistor. Although both De Forest and Fleming ended their careers still feuding with each other over the patent rights to the vacuum tube design, the work of both men was critical to radio's development.

Figure 5-4 Lee de Forest invented the "audion," a three-element vacuum tube. He based his work on the foundation laid by Hertz, titling the Ph.D. dissertation he produced for Yale University in 1899, "Reflection of Hertzian Wave from the Ends of Parallel Wires." Much of his career was marked by legal feuds with J. Ambrose Fleming. De Forest is seen here at the 1939 World's Fair with a display tracing the evolution of the vacuum tube. (Courtesy, A.T.&T.)

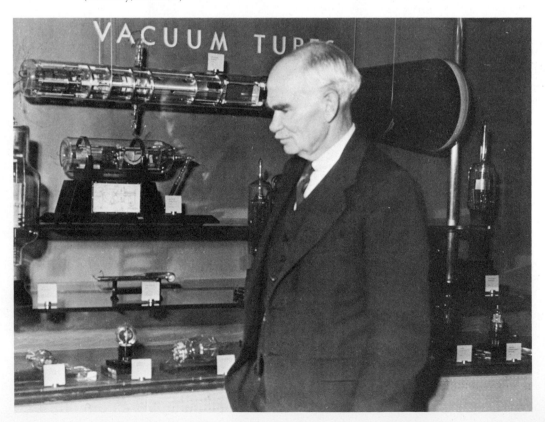

Figure 5-5 Nathan B. Subblefield (left) with his wireless telephone. As early as 1892, Stubblefield is reported to have sent voice by wireless over a short distance at his farm in Murray, Kentucky. His son, Bernard (right), later became an employee of Westinghouse. (Courtesy, Murray, Kentucky Chamber of Commerce)

Voice Broadcasting

While Fleming, de Forest, and even Marconi were conducting their historic experiments, a Kentucky farmer named Nathan B. Stubblefield (Figure 5–5) also made history by transmitting the first voice via wireless using a method called *induction*. It had little promise because it worked well only over short distances. Stubblefield's first demonstrations took place in 1892, but his work never had any significant application. He was still experimenting with his little publicized device when a professor at the University of Pittsburgh named Reginald A. Fessenden joined with some local entrepreneurs and successfully broadcast music to ships at sea on the night of Christmas Eve, 1906. With the help of a General Electric engineer named Ernst Alexanderson, a large alternator (Figure 5–6) was used successfully to transmit the sounds of "O, Holy Night" between the coast of Massachusetts and the West Indies. In 1908 De Forest also conducted experiments in voice broadcasting with successful demonstrations from Europe.

Figure 5-6 Dr. Ernst Alexanderson, a General Electric engineer who developed the high-frequency alternator that gave America a substantial edge in early long-distance voice broadcasting. The alternator shown here, one of several developed by Alexanderson between 1905 and 1920, was used to send transatlantic broadcasts from the RCA station at Rocky Point, Long Island. (Courtesy, General Electric Research and Development)

RADIO COMES OF AGE

With the advent of voice broadcasting, radio matured quickly. The takeover of the industry by the federal government during World War I actually gave broadcasting an additional boost. Although the efforts were directed to war defense communication, the takeover forced all companies that were once competing with each other to share their knowledge. Everyone was thus immune from patent infringement suits, and thousands of amateur radio operators and war-trained telegraph operators swelled the ranks of early radio experimenters.

The Early Stations

It was not long before people began to envision radio as much more than just ship-to-shore communication, and experimenters began to apply radio as a medium for the masses. Generally recognized as the first commercial station to sign on the air was an experimental venture in 1909 built by Dr. Charles David Herrold, which later evolved into KCBS. With studios in San Jose, California, the station broadcast mostly advertisements of Dr. Herrold's School of Radio.

Another pioneer station signed on as WHA at the University of Wisconsin at Madison, becoming the first major noncommercial broadcasting station. Its regularly scheduled programming dates back to 1919, the same year RCA was formed. Today WHA continues as one of the leading public broadcasting stations in the United States. Under its experimental call letters 9XM, early listeners heard such programs as extension college courses, the University of Wisconsin Glee Club, farm news, and even courses on how to build your own radio receiver. It eventually was joined by WHA-TV.

Two other stations are included in what historians consider the foundation of radio in America. On August 20, 1920 at 8:15 P.M., two records were played on an Edison phonograph with the speaker horn directed into a microphone connected to a De Forest transmitter. This experimental broadcast of WWJ, the *Detroit News* station, worked so well that it was followed the next day by a broadcast of the Michigan election returns. The station captured attention with its newspaper-radio mobile unit (Figure 5–7).

Figure 5-7 The "mobile news" truck of the *Detroit News* and WWJ. (Courtesy, the *Detroit News* and WWJ)

In November the same year, station KDKA in East Pittsburgh, Pennsylvania, signed on with the election returns of the Harding-Cox race. The flagship station of what was to become known as the Westinghouse Broadcasting stations, or "Group W," KDKA (Figure 5–8) has frequently been dubbed the first radio station in the United States. Actually it was the first station with regularly scheduled continuous programming, but the publicity surrounding its inaugural broadcast that November night began its claim to fame. However, if you were to travel to either San Jose, Madison, Detroit, or Pittsburgh, you would find commemorative plaques claiming *first* broadcasting honors for each of these pioneer stations.

Figure 5-8 Harold W. Arlin became KDKA's first full-time announcer. In addition to introducing many well-known personalities to KDKA listeners, he is also credited with broadcasting the station's first play-by-play football game. (Courtesy, KDKA)

Competition and Cross-Licensing

In 1916 a former employee of the American Marconi Company, David Sarnoff (Figure 5–9), wrote his new boss at RCA (Radio Corporation of America) a memo:

> I have in mind a plan of development which would make radio a "household utility" in the same sense as the piano or phonograph. The idea is to bring music into the house by wireless. . . . The receiver can be designed in the form of a simple "Radio Music Box"; . . . supplied with amplifying tubes and a loud speaking telephone, all of which can be neatly mounted in one box. . . .
>
> Aside from the profit derived from this proposition, the possibilities for advertising for the company are tremendous for its name would ultimately be brought into the household, and wireless would receive national and universal attention.

Like many memos, this one went largely unheeded. But KDKA's broadcast quickly changed all of that. Even GE (General Electric), RCA, and A.T.&T. (American Telephone and Telegraph), which had envisioned themselves the triumvirate of radio as a form of marine communication, what these companies thought the future of the medium would be, stopped short. Westinghouse had something here, something profitable.

The four companies soon secured agreements to share patents, manufacturing, and distribution. But the honeymoon ended when GE, RCA, and A.T.&T. also decided to sign on the air with their own stations. Westinghouse increased its broadcasting chain by adding such stations as WBZ, then in Springfield, Massachusetts, and now in Boston; WJZ in Newark, New Jersey; and KYW in Chicago, later assigned to Philadelphia. RCA started WDY in New York, and GE went on the air with WGY in Schenectady, New York.

The big headline of early radio, however, belonged to A.T.&T. It signed station WEAF on the air in 1922 with the idea of toll broadcasting, meaning that anyone wanting to use the station's airwaves could do so by paying a toll. Queensboro Corporations, a local real estate company, was the first to try out the idea. It was not long before the print media began to criticize the practice, realizing the dangers of radio competition. The printing trade journal, *Printer's Ink*, said that advertising on radio would be offensive. WEAF disagreed. It secured a more favorable, less crowded frequency, and the advertising continued to roll in. It was evident A.T.&T. had discovered what David Sarnoff had predicted, commercial broadcasting was where the action was. Not satisfied with just WEAF, A.T.&T. began to license other stations, charging them a fee before permitting them to hook up to its long distance lines. It then organized groups of stations to give advertisers a discount on advertising, creating the first true broadcasting network, called "chain" broadcasting.

Finally, the agreements among the four companies began to erode as each started to pave its own way into the future of commercial broadcasting. The end result was the involvement of the Justice Department, charges of antitrust by the Federal Trade Commission (FTC), and A.T.&T.'s decision that the negative public opinion and expensive legal battles were not worth the trouble. The telephone company bailed out of the broadcasting business in 1926 and sold WEAF to RCA's separate subsidiary company, the National Broadcasting Company (NBC).

Figure 5-9 Young David Sarnoff taught himself Morse Code and landed a job with the American Marconi Company as a wireless operator for the station on Nantucket Island. (Courtesy, RCA)

The start of NBC began a new era in broadcasting—the networks.

NBC

Two networks operated as part of the NBC system: the Red and the Blue. The Blue Network served stations on an exclusive basis as did the Red, but some stations negotiated contracts permitting them to draw programming from both. Both operated until the Federal Communications Commission (FCC) became involved in 1941. In a special report titled the *FCC Report on Chain Broadcasting*, NBC was criticized for its financial holdings in a talent company that steered the best stars over to NBC. Finally, the breakup of the Red and Blue Networks was inevitable, and NBC reorganized the Blue Network into a separate corporation in order for it to be sold.

ABC

He made his money in Lifesavers candy, but when Edward J. Noble bought NBC Blue in 1943, he turned much of Lifesavers' assets toward broadcasting. It was a sizable challenge for the times. World War II was raging, and the country was in a state of economic uncertainty. But Noble pulled together his own management team, and on June 15, 1945, *affiliates* heard the network announcer open with, "This is the American Broadcasting Company."

In what turned out to be one of the most novel decisions ever to affect radio network programming, on January 1, 1968, ABC split its operation into four different networks. These were the American Contemporary Radio Network, the American FM Radio Network, the American Entertainment Radio Network, and the American Information Radio Network. The idea was to develop new programming to meet the needs of different types of radio formats. For example, the American Contemporary Network was designed to match the programming of contemporary-sounding stations. Sharp, quick tones preceded and concluded the newscast; stories were shorter and more direct; and the entire newscast was shortened to fit into the quick changes in sound and the fast transition that occurs on the contemporary station. The four-network concept proved to be extremely successful and additional specialized networks were added later.

CBS

CBS has its roots in a cigar company with an advertising manager named William S. Paley (Figure 5–10). Paley's cigar company had experimented with sponsoring a program on the UIB/Columbia radio network in 1927 and saw its business more than double. Paley, a year later at the age of 27, arrived in New York and bought the network that later became CBS.

Like the other networks, besides its regular entertainment and news programming, CBS experimented with broadcasts from trains, balconies, and underwater bathyspheres. There were some unexpected outcomes. A 1930 broadcast featuring George Bernard Shaw aired the playwright's comments without approving them beforehand. CBS officials gasped as Shaw began with, "Hello America! Hello, all my friends in America! How are you dear old boobs . . ." and ended up by praising Russia. When the

Figure 5-10 William S. Paley guided the corporate development of CBS after his father's cigar company purchased the floundering network in 1928. (Courtesy, CBS, Inc.)

broadcast was over, CBS decided it was in everyone's best interest to provide equal time for an opposing opinion.[1]

In 1930 Paul Kesten joined CBS as promotion manager and immediately began to whittle away at powerful NBC. First came a survey on radio listenership that refuted NBC's claim to be the "most-listened-to" network. Next came an era highlighted by a policy of attracting big-name radio personalities to CBS. This concept of using major entertainment to build up the business saw such stars as Bing Crosby and Kate Smith join CBS.

In 1935 a 27-year-old instructor from Ohio State University received a telegram from CBS. It read, "I don't know of any other organization where your background and experience would count so heavily in your favor or where your talents would find so enthusiastic a reception."[2] The instructor's name was Dr. Frank Stanton. He accepted CBS's invitation and began to work for $55 a week doing audience measurements and research. Later he too climbed CBS' success ladder to become one of the leading spokesmen for the broadcasting industry.

When World War II broke out, many CBS employees began to make names for themselves in broadcast journalism. Correspondents Eric Sevareid, Richard C. Hottelet, H. V. Kaltenborn, and many others reported from the front lines—a first in providing up-to-date wartime news coverage.

Figure 5-11 Jack Benny is representative of the early stars of radio who also made the transition to television.

When the war ended, there again was a movement to develop competitive programming, and CBS spared little in competing head-on with NBC. In what became known as the great "talent raids," CBS literally bought such NBC talent as Red Skelton and Jack Benny (Figure 5–11). CBS also developed a sizable chain of its own radio and television stations serving major markets. The combination of CBS' own stations, its network affiliates, and creative programming placed the network at the top in national popularity.

Mutual

The Mutual Broadcasting System (MBS) started in 1934 as a cooperative arrangement among four stations: WOR in Newark, WXYZ in Detroit, WGN in Chicago, and WLW in Cincinnati. Mutual was the *time-broker* for all four stations. Advertisers buying commercial time on all four stations would pay the regular advertising rate, and Mutual would take 5 percent to handle the cost of promoting the network, line charges for network programs, and other expenses.

In 1936 Mutual added 13 stations in California and 10 in New England. Two years later it assimilated a *regional network* in Texas, adding 23 more stations to the chain. By 1940 Mutual had grown to 160 outlets.

Remaining an exclusively radio network, Mutual is owned by the Amway Corporation, known for direct sales of home cleaning supplies. Its programming includes such names as newscaster Fulton Lewis III, son of the famed Fulton Lewis, Jr., who for years was a major attraction of

Mutual. Also included in the Mutual programming schedule are such major sports events as Notre Dame football, championship boxing, NFL football, PGA golf, and the Sugar Bowl.

National Public Radio

The roots of public radio go back to WHA at the University of Wisconsin, which signed on the air as the first noncommercial station. Noncommercial radio was soon trying its microphones on college and university campuses all across the country. Then in 1965 the Carnegie Commission for Educational Television conducted a major study of noncommercial broadcasting in the United States and recommended providing financial support for a national system of *public broadcasting* stations. The Public Broadcasting Act of 1967 appropriated $38 million for improving existing noncommercial stations and building new ones. Also formed was the Corporation for Public Broadcasting (*CPB*), a quasi-government agency selected to administer funds to public broadcasting stations.

The 1967 legislation made possible a special category of stations, called CPB-qualified stations, which met certain operating criteria, such as specified hours of operation and transmitter power. Although not all noncommercial stations are CPB-qualified, the 1967 act made all noncommercial stations "public" stations, in that they can secure grants from individuals and corporations to provide operating expenses. National Public Radio (NPR) is the organization linking together all CPB-qualified stations by direct lines and satellite connections permitting network programming to reach all of those stations simultaneously.

The Role of Radio Networks

The role of radio networks in broadcasting is similar to that of television networks, except that the individual station is not as dependent on the network for programming. Radio has become a very specialized medium with considerable local programming directed to specialized and local audiences, and it is much less expensive to program local radio than to program local television. The recording industry provides countless hours of inexpensive recorded music which can fill local programming schedules. In addition, a single disc jockey can operate virtually all the controls in a radio station, including the transmitter, and originate local programming as well, all at the same time. Larger stations naturally require a larger number of personnel, but the operation of a radio station is much less complicated and less expensive than that of a television station, overall.

Radio affiliates are sometimes reimbursed for airing network commercials, although the contractual agreements with stations vary greatly. In many cases the station may not realize a profit from affiliating with a network, but it feels that the network programming adds to the overall image of the station.

Despite their supplementary role, radio networks have thrived, even though many radio stations have no network affiliation. If the future of radio networks can be predicted from their ability to specialize, plus the burgeoning number of FM stations, all indications are that they will prosper. Also we must keep in mind that the cost per thousand persons reached by radio advertising is low and that advertisers can aim at specific markets.

FM RADIO

Frequency modulated, or *FM*, radio operates at a higher *frequency* than *AM*, or amplitude modulated, radio does. The higher frequency permits the signals to travel in a straight line, rather than bouncing them off the atmosphere in a zigzag pattern. As a result and because of the type of modulation employed, FM signals are less susceptible to atmospheric distortion than AM signals are. That, plus other advantages, has made FM radio a growing, popular medium.

FM was invented by Edwin Armstrong while he was working at Columbia University in 1933. Its early application met with little enthusiasm because of the developing war and the radio industry's preoccupation with the threat of television. But after World War II ended, both the FCC and the industry began to take another look at FM. That second look became even more appealing in the 1970s, because the FCC had already allocated most of the available AM frequencies during the previous decade. FM still had a wide range of frequencies open for expansion.

The development of FM stereo also gave FM stations the ability to broadcast music of a quality and distinction previously limited to the stereo record player. FM stereo broadcasts the two tracks of a stereo record on two separate FM frequencies. A special FM stereo receiver picks up these signals. Even stereo news is coming into its own. With stereo speakers, a morning news interview with a local politician assumes immediacy as the interviewer's voice emanates from one speaker and the politician's from the other.

Many industry professionals expect the real growth of radio audiences to be in FM. Today it is not unusual for FM broadcasting stations to sell for millions of dollars, a price inconceivable in the 1960s.

PROGRAMMING

In 1923 Robert McCormick, editor and publisher of the *Chicago Tribune*, wrote his mother saying, "I have written to arrange to have an operator come to your room with a radio set and give you an exhibition. I don't think you will want to keep one, but you cannot help being thrilled at the little box that picks sounds from the air. . . ."[3] McCormick's *Chicago Tribune* had its own station, WDAP, which later became WGN, a major station in American broadcasting. The ambitious and creative people at WGN helped bring radio into its own. A warm May afternoon brought the microphone of WGN's A. W. "Sen" Kaney to the famed Indianapolis 500 auto race for seven hours of live sports broadcasting, the first time the Indy 500 had ever been heard on radio. In October of 1924 a crack of the bat kept listeners glued to their radios as sounds of Chicago Cubs and Chicago White Sox baseball came over WGN's airwaves. That same month the University of Illinois and the University of Michigan met for a football clash, again broadcast by WGN. The famed Scopes trial of 1925 heard WGN broadcast the voices of Clarence Darrow and William Jennings Bryan as they argued the case of the Tennessee school teacher, John Thomas Scopes, accused of teaching the theory of evolution.

*Becoming a
Mass
Medium*

The next decades saw radio blossom into mass popularity. Variety shows, dramatic productions, and comedy series elevated such radio personalities as Jack Benny and George Burns to national stars. Radio heroes dominated the medium. "The Lone Ranger," "The Shadow" and many more kept listeners spellbound. Radio also developed as a news medium. A study by educator Wilbur Schramm in 1945 asked college students what medium they would most likely believe in the face of conflicting news reports. Radio led by far.[4] Broadcasts of events as they happened—the actual "sounds" of the news—made radio one of the most credible news sources. The radio schedule of the evening newspaper became important and popular reading for everyone, especially the radio critics' columns. When WSB in Atlanta pioneered the airways, the *Atlanta Journal* noted in wordy prose:

> As may be instantly surmised by a casual glance at telegraphic tributes printed elsewhere on this page today, Sig Newman, astonishing virtuoso of the saxophone, and his orchestra of New York, entrancingly aided by the vocal brilliance of Mrs. Susan Reese Kennedy, Atlanta soprano, not only took Atlanta but half of the United States by storm at WSB's 10:45 concert Monday night, following proportionate glittering success at the 7:00 radio debut of the *Journal's* radio telephone station.[5]

For the time being, the thrill and novelty of radio were conveyed to the public by a press only too eager to cover every new programming and technical development of the new medium.

*The Medium
Becomes
Specialized*

This massive audience appeal began to waver, however, when television made its appearance. Forced into new formats, radio began a period of transition. It found its niche as a "specialized" medium (Figure 5–12). Major radio networks that once carried entertainment programming began to specialize in news. Each station began to forge its own individual identity. An examination of radio stations in any major metropolitan area illustrates the extent to which this specialization has been accomplished.

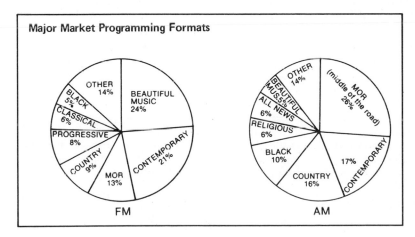

Major Market Programming Formats

FM

AM

Figure 5-12 (Courtesy, Cox Broadcasting Corporation)

Figure 5-13 Larry Lujack, nationally famous disc jockey long affiliated with the Chicago area. (Courtesy, Larry Lujack)

One station may specialize in top forty or rock music with top disc jockeys (Figure 5–13) while another may devote itself exclusively to foreign broadcasts. Still others may concentrate on educational programs or all-news formats. Starting at one end of the AM spectrum, your first encounter might be a "personality" station. By the time you had turned the dial to the other end of the spectrum, you would probably have heard a country-western station, a station that plays only hit records from the past, an automated station, a foreign-language station, a top-forty station, and more than a dozen others. If you were to turn to the FM dial, you would hear an equally large selection among almost three dozen stations, each with its own identity.

Educational Radio

In many countries where television systems are not well developed, radio remains the dominant medium. Consequently it has become a major teaching medium for people in these underdeveloped nations. Researchers at the Institute for Communication Research at Stanford University have compared the effectiveness of instructional media in various international locations. The institute has tested both instructional radio and instructional television. In a summary report, researchers concluded:

> There is nothing in the research to cast doubt on the proposition that a motivated student can learn from any medium. One of the most surprising results to researchers was the absence of any clear and consistent evidence of difference between the efficiency of learning from the complex and costly media like television and the less costly ones like radio.[6]

Installation of relatively inexpensive transmitters in local areas enables radio to disseminate information in the local language and to reflect local cultures. This is especially important in areas in which social and cultural identities are threatened. In the United States many colleges and universities offer special courses by radio. The University of Wisconsin School of the Air pioneered in this area, and other schools that followed, such as Purdue University's WBAA, offer credit by examination for radio courses. Public schools also have found radio an inexpensive alternative to television. The South Carolina Educational Radio Network serves public schools in South Carolina. Special multiple-earphone listening systems (Figure 5–14) permit teachers to use radio as a supplement to classroom activities and learning experiences.

Figure 5-14 While educational television has received considerable attention, educational radio has also contributed its share of instructional programming. (South Carolina Educational Television and Radio Network and the South Carolina State Department of Education)

RADIO SYNDICATION

With thousands of radio stations operating in the United States and Canada, competition becomes very real; a few *rating* points can mean the difference between profit and loss. To successfully compete, many stations are turning to *syndicated programming*. Produced by professionals who have large musical libraries, the syndicated programming is prerecorded on high quality equipment and then sent, usually on large reel tapes, to stations for airing.

Scope of Radio Syndication

A wide variety of formats exists from which the local radio programmer can choose. In consultation with the syndication company consultant, the local station program director can choose from progressive rock, easy listening, middle of the road, country rock, and soft rock formats, for instance. Or, wanting something specialized, the program director can even specify such formats as middle-of-the-road string orchestras or upbeat string orchestras.

Syndicated talk-radio formats usually originate from and are recorded in a large market where a popular talk-radio personality's program is aired, then edited, and made available for syndication. In the editing process any material directly relating to the city where the show originates is eliminated. For example, if one of the show's call-in listeners discuss a local landmark, the reference to the landmark must be deleted before the show is syndicated. To make as much of the original program available for syndication as possible, the host will try and keep the topics general, such as talking about the economy or national politics, something to which any listener in any locale can relate.

The Consultant-Syndicator Relationship

In addition to helping program directors choose what type of syndicated programming would compete best in the station's local market, the syndication company consultant will also assist the local station in producing commercials which fit the sound (Figure 5–15) of the syndicated program-

Figure 5-15 A typical hour of one company's syndicated musical format shows the different time segments allocated to music and local commercials. Most syndication companies can tailor exact "sound" hours to the individual needs of a particular station and market. (Courtesy, Century 21 Productions & Programming, Inc.)

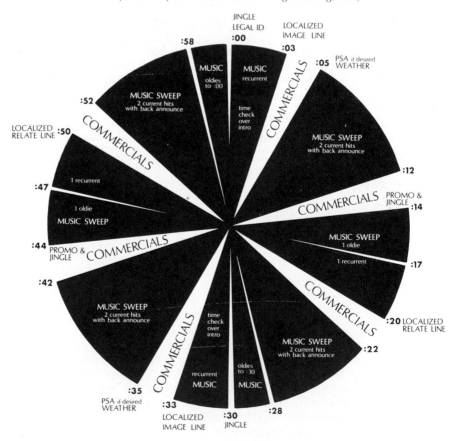

ming. In this way both the musical and commercial programming blend, which is appealing and effective in holding an audience. If the syndication company can help a station attract and hold an audience, it will be more likely to have its contract renewed. The syndication company, in turn, can use such a success in one market to boost its publicity and to attract stations in other markets.

IMPACT OF RADIO

The medium that was once merely a theoretical vision of the late nineteenth century has now achieved a major impact throughout the world.

Radio's Acceptance and Potential

Despite the enormous impact of television in the 1950s, radio has continued to grow and prosper. Since its early development in 1920, it has achieved and maintained growth rivaling that of all other media in the history of mass communication. Estimated percentages through the 1980s see growth up over 225 percent from that of the early 1950s. Despite a penetration of more than one radio for every person, radio set sales continue to climb. Almost 95 percent of all automobiles have radios, up from 55 percent in 1952.

We might well ask, with virtually every household equipped with more than one radio, why people continue to buy radios. One reason is that a transistor radio has become a widely accepted gift, coming in all shapes and sizes from complex shortwave sets, to combinations of radios and other gadgetry such as cigarette lighters, liquor decanters, and pencil sets. Miniaturization of parts has made it possible to place a radio in all kinds of imaginable items in the home, from intercoms to popular home entertainment combinations of television, AM/FM radio, and stereo record players. Moreover, increased use of FM bands has sparked still more sales.

Radio is an especially strong medium among both the general population and specialized audiences. For example, the overall radio listening audience is larger than the television audience for a sizable

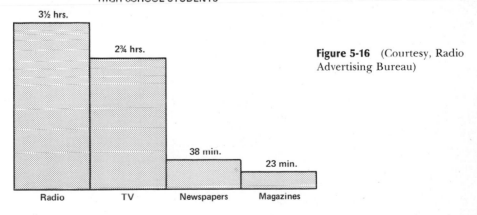

AVERAGE DAILY TIME SPENT WITH MEDIA:
HIGH SCHOOL STUDENTS

3½ hrs.

2¾ hrs.

38 min.

23 min.

Radio   TV   Newspapers   Magazines

Figure 5-16 (Courtesy, Radio Advertising Bureau)

portion of the day. The highest audience measurement comes at approximately 8:00 to 9:00 A.M., then it tapers off, climbing back up to a plateau between 3:00 to 7:00 P.M. These "highs" are commonly called *drive-time*, when many people listen to radio while commuting to and from work. Television begins to take over the audience after 8:00 P.M. But among both high school and college students, radio is the primary mass medium. High school students spend an average of three and one-half hours per day with radio compared to two and three-quarters hours for television, 38 minutes with newspapers, and 23 minutes with magazines (Figure 5–16). College students spend an average of two and three-quarters hours per day with radio compared to two hours with television, 31 minutes with newspapers, and 21 minutes with magazines (Figure 5–17).

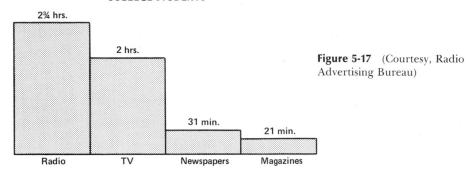

AVERAGE DAILY TIME SPENT WITH MEDIA:
COLLEGE STUDENTS

2¾ hrs.

2 hrs.

31 min.

21 min.

Radio   TV   Newspapers   Magazines

Figure 5-17   (Courtesy, Radio Advertising Bureau)

Radio's Future Perspective

The future of radio is bright both in terms of technological developments and the all-important economic considerations that face any mass medium. The ability of radio, for example, to reach a great number of people at a comparatively small cost has a distinct advantage over television. For companies with small to moderate advertising budgets, radio affords the opportunity to reach their public. Many radio news departments operate with a small number of personnel, a few inexpensive cassette tape recorders, and an automobile equipped with a two-way radio. For television news to function, it takes thousands of dollars worth of equipment, trained personnel for operating the equipment, and a costly television transmitter and studio equipment to edit, compose, and send the program to the viewers.

Stereo FM will continue to develop. The full potential of stereo news has yet to be tapped. It will permit radio to develop and stretch the audio picture of an event beyond what television can do as a single video dimension. The medium has come a long way since Marconi first lifted his kite antenna above Newfoundland and received signals across the Atlantic. Throughout the world, radio serves the masses with entertainment, news, and instructional programming. It survived television and gained its own identity as a medium with distinct advantages and the ability to reach specialized audiences in our society.

SUMMARY

With over 9000 stations operating in the United States alone, radio penetrates the lives of virtually the entire world population. The development of the medium is credited to a number of countries. In Italy Guglielmo Marconi experimented with a crude spark-gap transmitter and sent signals over the hillside near his home. He later captured world attention by sending and receiving wireless signals across the Atlantic. In America Fleming gave radio his two-element valve, and De Forest contributed his three-element audion. Voice broadcasting began as early as 1892 using a process called induction, but the primitive process had little promise. Practical voice application of the methods employed by Marconi were made by Reginald Fessenden in 1906.

As radio moved out of the experimental era, early radio stations began to apply the technology by bringing music and news to large numbers of people. In 1909 Charles David Herrold's station signed on the air in San Jose, and in 1919 WHA at the University of Wisconsin became the nation's first recognized noncommercial station. A year later both WWJ in Detroit and KDKA in Pittsburgh crackled onto the airwaves. The KDKA venture signaled a new entertainment and commercial application for radio, and it was quickly followed by other stations. A.T.&T. signed WEAF on the air but sold it to RCA in 1926. Out of that sale came NBC. NBC operated two networks until 1943 when it was forced to sell one of them, which became ABC. Two others, CBS and Mutual, also were part of the development of early commercial radio. For noncommercial stations, the National Public Radio began regular programming in 1971.

FM radio, once shelved by the industry in favor of the development of television, has overtaken AM radio in listener popularity. Both AM and FM have prospered because of radio's ability to adapt its programming to both the competition and the audience. Programming drama in the 1920s, 1930s, and 1940s, radio began to direct its programming to a specialized audience in the 1950s.

Syndication is becoming an important part of radio programming. Syndication companies offer prerecorded programming which can be interspersed with local programming. Syndication company consultants work closely with local stations to properly blend local production with syndicated production.

Today the medium has reached nearly 100 percent saturation in the United States and is found in 95 percent of the country's automobiles. It commands our attention for the majority of the daytime hours and is the most-listened-to medium among high school and college students.

OPPORTUNITIES FOR FURTHER LEARNING

AITKEN, H. G. J., *Syntony and Spark—The Origins of Radio. New York*: John Wiley, 1976.

BAKER, J. C., *Farm Broadcasting: The First Sixty Years*. Ames: Iowa State University Press, 1981.

BARNOUW, E., *A Tower in Babel*. New York: Oxford University Press, 1966.

BARNOUW, E., *The Golden Web*. New York: Oxford University Press, 1968.

BARNOUW, E., *The Image Empire*. New York: Oxford University Press, 1970.

BITTNER, J. R., *Professional Broadcasting: A Brief Introduction*. Englewood Cliffs, N.J.: Prentice-Hall, 1981.

BITTNER, J. R., AND D. A. BITTNER, *Radio Journalism*. Englewood Cliffs, N.J.: Prentice-Hall, 1977.

CLAUDE, B. H., *The Business of Radio Programming*. New York: Billboard Publications, 1977.

DELONG, T. A., *The Mighty Music Box: The Golden Age of Musical Radio*. Los Angeles: Amber Crest Books, 1980.

DREHER, C., *Sarnoff: An American Success*. New York: Quadrangle/The New York Times Book Co., Inc., 1977.

DUNLAP, O. E., *Marconi: The Man and His Wireless*. New York: Arno Press, 1971.

FANG, I. E., *Those Radio Commentators!* Ames: Iowa State University Press, 1977.

FORNATALE, P., AND J. E. MILES, *Radio in the Television Age*. Woodstock, N.Y.: Overlook Press, 1980.

HOOD, S., *The Professions: Radio and Television*. North Pomfret, Vt.: David and Charles, 1975.

JULIAN, J., *This Was Radio: A Personal Memoir*. New York: Viking, 1975.

KLEINFIELD, S., *The Biggest Company on Earth: A Profile of AT&T*. New York: Holt, Rinehart & Winston, 1981.

LEINWOLL, S., *From Spark to Satellite: A History of Radio Communication*. New York: Scribner's, 1979.

LICHTY, L. W., AND M. C. TOPPING, eds., *American Broadcasting: Book on the History of Radio and Television*. New York: Hastings House, 1975.

MACFARLAND, D. T., *The Development of the Top 40 Radio Format*. New York: Arno Press, 1979.

ROBINSON, S., *Radio Advertising: How to Sell It and Write It*. Blue Ridge Summit, Pa.: TAB Books, 1974.

ROSEN, P. T., *The Modern Stentors: Radio Broadcasters and the Federal Government, 1920–1934* (Contributions to Economics and Economic History, No. 31). Westport, Conn.: Greenwood Press, 1980.

SMITH, V. J., *Programming for Radio and Television*. Washington, D.C.: University Press of America, 1980.

STERLING, C. H., AND J. M. KITTROSS, *Stay Tuned: A Concise History of American Broadcasting*. Belmont, Calif.: Wadsworth, 1978.

TAYLOR, G., *Before Television: The Radio Years*. Cranbury, N.J.: A. S. Barnes, 1979.

ULLYETT, K., *Ham Radio: A Practical Guide and Handbook*. North Pomfret, Vt.: David and Charles, 1977.

VYVYAN, R. N., *Marconi and Wireless*. Yorkshire, England: E. P. Publishing Limited, 1974.

WATSON, K., A. SUNTER, AND F. ERMUTH, *A Financial Analysis of the Private Radio Broadcasting Sector in Canada and the United States*. Ottawa: ABT Associates Research of Canada, for the Department of Communication, Social Policy and Programs Branch, 1978.

CHAPTER

6

TELEVISION

PREVIEW

After completing this chapter, we should be able to:

Discuss the contributions of Paul G. Nipkow, Vladimir K. Zworykin, and Philo Farnsworth to the development of television.

Explain the effects of the FCC's decision on a compatible color transmission and receiving system, its freeze on licenses, and its support of UHF.

Describe television's golden era and the "Red scare" of the 1950s.

Discuss the transition television underwent in the 1960s.

Reflect upon television of the 1970s and 1980s.

Define public broadcasting.

Describe early noncommercial television and how it was influenced by the recommendations of the Carnegie Commission.

Be aware of the Corporation for Public Broadcasting, the Public Broadcasting Act of 1967, the Public Broadcasting Service, and the Carnegie Commission II.

Explain television syndication.

Speculate on television's impact and future.

Television has been called everything from an educational panacea to a "boob tube" projecting images of a vast wasteland. People have labeled it biased, accurate, liberal, conservative, and have accused it of everything from wrecking the family structure to robbing us of our individuality. Somewhere in between all this lies the truth. One thing is certain. The medium has become one of the most powerful communicative forces in the history of civilization.

EARLY DEVELOPMENT

To appreciate the great technological strides television has made in the past decades, we need to examine the history of the medium. The concept of television can be traced back to 1839. In that year French physicist Alexandre Edmond Becquerel observed the electrochemical effects of light.

Nipkow's Scanning Disc

In 1884 German scientist Paul G. Nipkow devised a method by which a spiraling disc would pass over a picture and create a scanning effect. Nipkow punched holes in his disc to create the pattern of a spiral, beginning at the outer edge and circling toward the center of the disc. When the disc revolved, the holes would pass over the picture, and in one complete revolution of the disc, the total picture would be scanned. Nipkow transferred the light passing through each hole into electrical energy and transmitted this electrical energy through wires to a receiver that also had a synchronized disc connected to a transmitter. When the transmitter changed pictures at rapid intervals, a very crude picture with a semblance of motion could be achieved. Nipkow's device represented a mechanical adaptation of the principle used in the old penny arcade in which a series of cards would turn down, each with a slightly different picture than the one before it, thus creating the illusion of movement.

Mechanical television and the scanning disc processes continued to improve. Television entered into new experimental eras with greater picture clarity. By the 1920s, although very crude, pictures could be reproduced with high intensity lighting. Felix the Cat was the first star of the system which made Felix look more like a venetian blind than a cat, and the sixty-line (Figure 6–1) system was a long way from the picture clarity that would follow with major developments in electronic television.

Zworykin and Farnsworth

It was not long before the television experimenters realized that the future of the industry could not be tied to the mechanical reproduction of visual images. The breakthrough into electronic television came in the 1920s and is credited to two men, a Russian immigrant, Vladimir K. Zworykin (Figure 6–2), and an American, Philo Farnsworth. Zworykin was an employee of Westinghouse in Wilkensburg, Pennsylvania, in 1919. It was there that the company gave him permission to work on a new device which used electrons to detect and transmit pictures instantly. The device was patented in 1923 and named the iconoscope television pickup tube. It signaled the end of television's mechanical era.

Improving the system was left to a schoolboy from Rigby, Idaho, who at age 15 drew a blackboard sketch of a high-resolution scanning system. The boy was Philo Farnsworth, and he later shared the credit with

Figure 6-1 The year was 1928, and television was in its experimental stages. A 60-line black and white picture was successfully obtained by turning Felix the Cat on a mechanical turntable in front of four, high-intensity spotlights. (Courtesy, RCA)

Figure 6-2 Vladimir K. Zworykin is credited with inventing the "iconoscope," an all-electronic television pickup tube. (Courtesy, RCA)

Zworykin for fathering modern television. Farnsworth formed the Crocker Laboratories in San Francisco, later the Capehart-Farnsworth Corporation. Farnsworth eventually held more than 150 patents related to television, some common to all television receivers.

RCA, meanwhile, continued its own television experiments, which included opening an experimental television station, W2XBS, in New York on July 30, 1930. In 1931 the company placed an experimental transmitting tower on top of the Empire State Building. These experimental transmissions permitted the development of a system producing a clearer picture than had been possible previously. Continuing its television experiments, RCA announced in 1935 that it would spend one million dollars for television field testing. It was a sizable business venture at a time when there were few viewers and much progress still to be made before the system could approach significant home use.

Experimental Programming Succeeds

In 1936 television receivers were able to pick up signals from a distance of one mile. In 1937 the antenna atop the Empire State Building went into "public" use, and NBC and RCA took television to the people. In an arrangement set up on the streets of New York, passersby could stop and see the operation of the new invention. A Broadway play, *Susan and God*, was televised from the NBC studios on June 7, 1938. It was also the year David Sarnoff, president of RCA, announced to a meeting of the Radio Manufacturers Association that television sets would go on sale to the public when the World's Fair opened in 1939 (Figure 6–3). During that year television signals were transmitted a distance of 130 miles from New York City to Schenectady, New York. A year later on February 1, 1940,

Figure 6-3 One of television's first public appearances was at the 1939 World's Fair. The set on display had an 8″ × 10″ screen reflected on a mirrored cabinet top. (Courtesy, RCA)

Figure 6-4 RCA's first color television receiving sets are seen coming off the assembly line in Bloomington, Indiana. (Courtesy, RCA)

as members of the FCC watched, television pictures were sent from New York to Schenectady and then *rebroadcast* to other points in upstate New York. Although on a small and experimental basis, the first television network was born.

Color, the Freeze, and UHF

Three FCC decisions greatly influenced television's growth from the early 1940s through the early 1950s. They included the decision on a compatible color transmission and receiving system, the freeze on licenses and the resultant allocation of *frequencies*, and the support of UHF television stations.

Two broadcasting giants, CBS and RCA, battled for supremacy in color transmissions. Both had systems that produced color programming with acceptable results. CBS got the FCC's first go-ahead with a noncompatible system, one which permitted color pictures to be received on special sets that could not receive the same pictures in black and white. Meanwhile RCA was developing a compatible system which permitted color programs to be transmitted so that they could be received in black and white on sets already in use. RCA sued CBS, and the appeals went to the Supreme Court where CBS's noncompatible system received its blessing. But CBS's jubilation was short-lived. The FCC, realizing the advantages of RCA's system and wishing to avoid a disruption of the industry's manufacturing efforts, reversed itself. Thus RCA's system became the standard color system of modern television (Figure 6–4).

As the color debates were brewing, the FCC meanwhile had frozen all new television licenses in 1948 until it had time to study a plan for television's orderly development. It lifted the freeze in 1952. The results were that 12 channels were assigned to the very high frequency (VHF) band (channels 2 through 13), and 70 channels (14 through 83) were assigned to the ultrahigh frequency (UHF) band.

Although the freeze cleared the way for the development of both VHF and UHF television, UHF stations operated at a disadvantage. Few sets had channel selectors beyond channel 13. Thus, although in theory the FCC hoped that television set manufacturers would keep up with the demand for UHF, the demand could not materialize because UHF stations could not stay on the air for financial reasons. It was a vicious circle. As a result, everything stood still until 1964 when the FCC required set manufacturers to install both UHF and VHF tuners on all sets. Although UHF stations still do not have as many viewers as VHF can muster, many are gaining in the marketplace as viable competitors. Many UHF stations are independent and, as independent stations, obtain quality programming through syndication.

Recording the Television Picture

Early attempts to record the television picture used film. The first successful demonstration was in 1950 using Kodak film, a Navy camera, and a CBS receiver. *Videotape* recording was demonstrated by RCA in 1953, but it was Ampex Corporation's demonstration in 1956 at a NAB meeting that received the publicity. From that point on, videotaped recording continued to be improved through systems which now include cassette recorders and videodiscs.

TRENDS IN TELEVISION PROGRAMMING

Television networks were essential to early programming. NBC, with the backing of RCA's financial support and technology, was one of the top competitors. CBS, with William Paley's administrative abilities, had by the 1950s become a powerful force in the industry. ABC, although an infant, kept pace with innovative programming, especially with sports programming in the 1960s and 1970s.

The Golden Era

The 1950s are generally considered television's golden era. It was a time of continual experiments, and the experiments were live. Television was innovative because almost everything was a "first." One of the pioneer stars was Milton Berle with his "Texaco Star Theater." The show was so popular that on Tuesday nights, restaurant owners without a television set could expect vacant tables. Comedy was also king with programs like "I Love Lucy," built around a zany redhead and her band leader husband. William Bendix starred in "The Life of Riley," one of the first shows to bring blue-collar comedy to television.

Children had the puppet show of "Kukla, Fran, and Ollie." For the slightly more serious child there was Jack Barry's "Juvenile Jury," and for

Figure 6-5 (Left) A number of live children's programs were included in the early television fare, and among them was the popular "Howdy Doody Show." With such characters as Buffalo Bob and Howdy (both shown), the show featured a "peanut gallery" of children who witnessed the comical suspense antics of puppets, clowns, and Indians. (Photo courtesy of Jack Drury Associates)

Figure 6-6 (Below) The original "Mickey Mouse Club," produced by Walt Disney Productions, included such regulars as Jimmie Dodd and Roy Williams. The television program created cross-publicity for many of Disney's other projects, including films and amusement parks. (© Walt Disney Productions)

the budding scientist there was "Mr. Wizard." Perhaps the most famous early children's program was "Howdy Doody" (Figure 6–5), featuring a puppet with a sidekick named Buffalo Bob and a group of kids in the studio audience called the "peanut gallery." The "Wonderful World of Disney" and the "Mickey Mouse Club" (Figure 6–6) were two other famous shows; the Disney show still remains popular. Even the original "Mickey Mouse Club" and "Howdy Doody" returned to modern television through syndication.

The "Red Scare"

As a social force, television news received attention and respectability in the 1950s. It was an era beset with irrational, patriotic fever, worried that the Communist movement had infiltrated into every segment of American society, including the entertainment industry. Senator Joseph McCarthy used the "Red scare" as a platform for political expediency, and his rhetoric persuaded both the government and a number of private businesses to fire certain employees. The entertainment industry was hard hit by the impact of his purge when a right-wing publication, entitled *Red Channels*, published in June, 1950, the names of 151 people associated with the Communist movement who were also in the radio and television industry. Many entertainers found themselves suddenly without work and with their professional careers ruined.

It was television journalism that finally brought these abuses of civil liberties to the attention of the public and signaled the beginning of the

Figure 6-7 Edward R. Murrow set many of the standards for early television journalism. (Courtesy, WNET and CBS)

end for McCarthy. Career journalist Edward R. Murrow (Figure 6–7) hosted the television news show "See It Now." After an Air Force officer was asked to resign because of his relative's questionable Communist activities, Murrow went on national television presenting the case that the officer had been the victim of innuendo. Another show covered the case of nuclear physicist J. Robert Oppenheimer, who lost his security clearance because of a political stand on nuclear energy. The *See It Now* program cast the first shadows of doubt about the McCarthy purge. When the senator took on the United States Army in congressional hearings, television was there, and the public, already skeptical of McCarthy, watched his radical accusations. When it was over, McCarthy had been reduced to humiliation, and television journalism had gained a new legitimacy.

Politics and Space

If television were said to have been "in training" in the 1950s, it went to war in the 1960s. Few could have predicted the turmoil that television would capture in the 1960s. For the first time in history, it brought the trauma of political assassination to the world with the coverage of the assassination of President John F. Kennedy. It repeated the horror as it covered the assassination of civil rights leader Martin Luther King, Jr. And then Senator Robert Kennedy met death by an assassin's bullet while he campaigned in California for his own presidential bid. By this time television was beginning to be blamed for the outbursts of violence that began rocking the country. As the decade drew to a close, that violence had spilled onto the streets and into living rooms as television covered the civil rights riots in the Watts section of Los Angeles and the student protests at the 1968 Democratic National Convention in Chicago. But most of all, it covered the bloody agony of American servicemen fighting an impossible, unpopular war in the jungles of Vietnam. Yet, although most of the decade it had been covering conflict, television ended the period with a triumph—live coverage of the first man on the moon.

Situation Comedy and Concerns for Quality

The trends of the 1960s, both in national events and television's coverage of them, continued into the 1970s. The winding down of the Vietnam War and the pullout of American forces, the last remnants of campus protests, and the continuing saga of space travel all were a part of 1970s television. But that decade had its own version of conflict—that of a nation testing the very roots of its foundation through the impeachment hearings of a president. Television was there, giving us continuity through Richard Nixon's resignation, Gerald Ford's succession, and Jimmy Carter's election to the White House.

Major new efforts in programming developed as the situation comedy, so popular in the 1950s, found its way back to television. Perhaps the leader in this trend was "The Mary Tyler Moore Show" (Figure 6–8). The program made a successful run on CBS as the fictitious crew of a TV news department brought laughs and some serious issues to television. Audiences watched Mary Richards, played by Mary Tyler Moore, grow from a trauma-ridden single girl to a mature professional woman. The program became as popular in syndication as it was in its network run. Mini series, such as "Roots," also drew large audiences (Figure 6–9).

Figure 6-8 Situation-comedy reigned supreme during the 1970s and continues to keep a hold on television programming. Among the most successful programs, and one of many which have reached syndication, was M-T-M's "The Mary Tyler Moore Show." The show was set inside the newsroom of a fictitious Minneapolis television station. This scene features a guest appearance by long-time CBS news commentator, Walter Cronkite (second from left). Many of the original cast went on to star in their own television series. (Courtesy, M-T-M Productions)

Figure 6-9 Of television's miniseries, few have achieved the success of "Roots." Based on Alex Haley's novel of the same name, the program traced the heritage of a family from Africa to colonial America and through the War Between the States years to the present. (Courtesy, ABC; Wolper Productions, Inc; Warner Bros.)

The 1970s also heard continuing criticism of television programming and saw a growing consumer movement. A critical and also popular view of television was offered by Canadian philosopher Marshall McLuhan, who said that the media was massaging us into a rear-view way of thinking. More direct criticism of television began to develop as groups, such as Action for Children's Television, began to examine what was being shown to children and what could be done about it. Direct communication with and lobbying efforts at both the FCC and the networks made the organization and the consumer movement in general a visible force in the television industry. Some of the public's reaction to violence on television resulted in some major corporations issuing public statements that they would not sponsor violent programming.

In the 1980s there is some indication that serious attention can possibly be paid to higher quality programming. ABC rose to the top of the ratings under the direction of programming executive Fred Silverman. When NBC lured Silverman away, Silverman suggested that in contrast to the action-filled (some called it "sex and guts") programs that put ABC on top, NBC would reach the top slot through a new wave of quality programming that Silverman predicted would materialize in the 1980s.

Before NBC had achieved the goal of being the top-rated network, Silverman left the network. Grant Tinker, who had achieved the respect of the television industry as head of Mary Tyler Moore Productions (M-T-M), took over and engineered the network's first critically acclaimed success with "Hill Street Blues." After capturing the attention of the public through its many awards, "Hill Street Blues" did manage to survive its first major season.

Magazine programs such as "60 Minutes" and some experiments in live studio drama were also showing promise. But the appeal of prime-time "soap opera" programs such as "Dallas" indicated that viewers still wanted television to provide escape as well as information.

PUBLIC BROADCASTING

Along with the commercial networks, public broadcasting systems also are an essential part of the overall structure of broadcasting. Public broadcasting as defined here means *the operation of the various noncommercial radio and television stations in the United States*. The depth to which the public participates in these broadcasting complexes varies considerably, but the underlying purpose of these stations is to serve the public—not to operate at a profit. This does not mean that commercial radio and television stations do not serve the public; it means simply that staying in business—that is, making a profit—must be their primary concern. In many cases commercial stations may be owned by a parent corporation that views them first as profit-making instruments. If they are not, then there is a good chance that they will be sold for more profitable ones. Since public radio stations are not under the same financial pressure as their commercial counterparts are, they can program to more select audiences without as much concern over losing a mass audience or winning a spot in audience ratings. Public broadcasting stations usually operate with a sizable portion of their budget coming from listener contributions, direct appropriations, and grants from foundations and corporations.

Early Stations and NET

Although public broadcasting has attracted serious attention only in recent years, as we learned earlier, the roots of the system began back in 1919 at the University of Wisconsin in Madison when the experimental radio station 9XM went on the air. In 1952 the FCC allocated exclusive channels for noncommercial television. Of these, 80 were located in the VHF range and 162 at the UHF end of the spectrum. This was just the help that noncommercial television needed to develop along with radio. Also in 1952 noncommercial broadcasting received a major financial boost when the Ford Foundation created the Educational Television and Radio Center. This later became the National Educational Television (NET), involved in producing educational programs for public television stations. In 1953 station KUHT (Figure 6–10) at the University of Houston was the first noncommercial, educationally licensed television station to sign on the air. WQED-TV in Pittsburgh became the first community-owned, noncom-

Figure 6-10   The first educational television station in the United States, KUHT-TV, signed on the air at the University of Houston. (Office of Information, University of Houston)

Figure 6-11 Fred Rogers, star of "Mr. Rogers' Neighborhood," is one of the pioneers of public broadcasting. (Copyright, Family Communications, Inc.)

mercial television station to sign on the air. WQED-TV is also credited with supporting one of the earliest quality children's television programs on a noncommercial television station. One of the station's employees was Fred Rogers who took part in the creation of a show called "Children's Corner." The program first appeared in 1954, but it sparked a much more lasting and creative effort that materialized into a program called "Mister Rogers" on the Canadian Broadcasting Corporation and eventually "Mister Rogers' Neighborhood" (Figure 6–11) in 1965 on WQED-TV. Fred Rogers was directly responsible for all of the programs and has continued to star in "Mister Rogers' Neighborhood" while working closely with child psychologists in developing the popular program on public broadcasting. His programming inventiveness led the way in showing noncommercial television what the medium could accomplish.

The Carnegie Commission and CPB   The next nine years saw noncommercial broadcasting develop rapidly. In 1962 Congress passed the Educational TV Facilities Act which provided $32 million over a five-year period to develop state systems of educational broadcasting.

In 1965 planning began for what was to become a major policy document affecting the development of public broadcasting in America.

A major industry-wide study of public television was undertaken by the Carnegie Commission for Educational Television. The Commission was "asked to 'conduct a broadly conceived study of noncommercial television' and to 'focus its attention principally, although not exclusively, on community-owned channels and their services to the general public.'. . . The Commission will recommend lines along which noncommercial television stations might most usefully develop during the years ahead." The Commission, whose report was published in 1967, was made up of a broad spectrum of industry leaders. It reached the conclusion that a "well-financed, well-directed educational television system, substantially larger and far more persuasive and effective than that which now exists in the United States, must be brought into being if the full needs of the American public are to be served."[1]

The Public Broadcasting Act and CPB

Acting on that recommendation, Congress passed the Public Broadcasting Act of 1967. Among other things, the act allocated an appropriation of $38 million for the construction of facilities and the formation of a nonprofit corporation called the Corporation for Public Broadcasting (CPB). Specifically CPB was charged with authorization to:

> Facilitate the full development of educational broadcasting in which programs of high quality, obtained from diverse sources, will be made available to noncommercial radio or television broadcast stations, with strict adherence to objectivity and balance in all programs or series of programs of a controversial nature;
>
> Assist in the establishment and development of one or more systems of interconnection to be used for the distribution of educational television or radio programs so that all noncommercial educational television or radio broadcast stations that wish to may broadcast the programs at times chosen by the stations;
>
> Assist in the establishment and development of one or more systems of noncommercial educational television or radio broadcast stations throughout the United States;
>
> Carry out its purposes and functions and engage in its activities in ways that will most effectively assure the maximum freedom of the noncommercial educational television or radio broadcast systems and local stations from interference with or control of program content or other activities.[2]

The concept of public broadcasting had received the beginnings of a financial base. Now it could prosper and expand.

The Public Broadcasting Service

To help meet these goals, the CPB joined in cooperation with many of the licensees of noncommercial television stations in the United States in 1970 and formed the Public Broadcasting Service (PBS), which became the primary distribution system for programs serving public broadcasting stations. PBS is responsible for obtaining programs for national distribution from its member stations (Figure 6–12) as well as from independent suppliers. PBS has been responsible for a number of award-winning special programs as well as regular series, the most famous of which is "Sesame Street" (Figure 6–13).

Figure 6-12 (Above) Considered the first series on educational television, Julia Child's "The French Chef" began at WGBH-TV in Boston. (Courtesy, WGBH Educational Foundation)

Figure 6-13 (Left) "Sesame Street" combined popularity, creativity, and instructional effectiveness to become a major programming force in noncommercial children's television. (Courtesy, Children's Television Workshop)

In 1979 the PBS membership of *affiliate* stations voted the recommendation to split PBS into three primary services with different programming and distribution responsibilities. A national or primary service is designed for prime-time entertainment and cultural programming; a regional and special-interest service is designed to feature the works of independent producers; and an informational and instructional programming service is designed to provide both in-school and home-study offerings.

Affiliates, Organizations, and Licensees

In addition to NPR, PBS, and CPB, other key components of public broadcasting include affiliated stations, state systems of educational radio and television, program libraries, and producers. Noncommercial radio and television stations are of four basic types: those licensed to state authorities or commissions; community stations licensed to nonprofit community corporations; school stations licensed to school corporations; and university stations, usually licensed to the boards of trustees of both public and private colleges and universities.

Carnegie Commission II

A second study of public broadcasting was made in 1978 and was released in 1979. Officially titled "The Carnegie Commission on the Future of Public Broadcasting," it criticized the system now in operation and suggested numerous changes. Among these was eliminating the Corporation for Public Broadcasting and replacing it with a Public Telecommunications Trust, with a Program Services Endowment as a subsidiary of the trust. The trust would be a nonprofit, private, nongovernmental corporation, and the endowment would be dedicated to underwriting and developing qualtiy programming for public radio and television.

Funding for public broadcasting would come partly from licensee or "spectrum" fees paid by commercial broadcasters. At the same time the Carnegie II report took some potshots at commercial broadcasters for not providing quality programming. Comments such as "the growing degradation of America's commercial communications media" and other phrases did not sit well with commercial broadcasters. At the very least they showed little political expediency since Congress will make the final changes in the system and since commercial broadcasters through the NAB can be a powerful lobby on Capitol Hill.

The Funding Crunch

While money to support public broadcasting has always been a problem, the tough economic times of the 1980s have sent especially strong caution signals to public broadcasting stations. The Economic Recovery Act of President Ronald Reagan's administration changed the tax status for charitable contributions, making such contributions less attractive for taxpayers. It also slashed funds for the Corporation for Public Broadcasting, the avenue through which public radio and television stations received most of their federal subsidies. Seeing the economic handwriting on the wall, public broadcasting began to experiment with something it had vigorously condemned in its more affluent days—advertising. But even though it faces stiff competition from commercial broadcasting for these advertising dollars, public broadcasting's financial future may be much different than it is today. The nagging question is, what will the quest for advertising dollars do to the programming content? Will public broadcasting succumb to the Nielsen ratings?

TELEVISION SYNDICATION

While much of television programming comes either from the networks or is produced locally, a rapidly growing number of programs are reaching us via the syndication route (Figure 6–14). Syndication refers to a program distribution system whereby prerecorded programs are sent directly to stations, bypassing the networks. Many programs which air successfully on networks are later sold into syndication. Others go directly into syndication.

Figure 6-14 Syndicated programs, such as "Hee Haw," fill local stations' time slots with programming alternatives to network shows. (Courtesy, Junior Samples)

Direct Syndication

Until the 1970s direct syndication was extremely rare, operating primarily on a limited distribution schedule of independent stations which had no network affiliate. The program "Mary Hartman, Mary Hartman" (Figure 6–15) changed all that. Producer Norman Lear had enough faith in the program even after the networks rejected it to make the show available to stations via syndication. Although the show's popularity diminished after its first year, Lear's initial success alerted producers to the vulnerability of the networks' dominance over program distribution. *Production companies* began to see the economic advantages of producing shows for this distribution system.

Figure 6-15 Direct syndication made its mark when the program "Mary Hartman, Mary Hartman" debuted. (Courtesy, T.A.T. Communications Company)

The Network Route

While some production companies have been successful in putting their programs into direct syndication, many find success by syndicating programs which first appear on networks. Network distribution offers many advantages, not the least of which is the network's ability to build an audience for a program, which then finds a waiting audience after it leaves the network. Some programs have made as much, or more money for the production company in syndication than they did through network release. Some have also had exceptional staying power. The cartoon program "The Flintstones" aired on the network almost 25 years ago, and since that time has earned more than $30 million in syndication.

Regional Audience Appeal

One advantage of syndication is that programs do not need national exposure to be successful. With syndication, programs can reach regional audiences. If we were to offer a program on salmon fishing to stations in New England, in areas surrounding Lake Michigan, and on the Pacific Coast, all areas where salmon fishing exists, we might find enough stations buying the program to make it a profitable production venture.

Syndication permits many stations not only to specialize geographically but also to specialize demographically. Perhaps a program appeals to families, and a station knows of a sponsor who likes to buy advertising on family-oriented programs. The station first approaches the sponsor to gain a commitment to buy advertising on the show, then it contracts with the syndicator to buy programming. The end result is a satisfied sponsor, who can reach a specialized audience, and a satisfied station, which is able to provide the sponsor with programming the network might not have provided.

The
Economics of
Syndication

Syndication production companies realize that hard economic decisions must precede success. First, they know that stations, often competing with other stations that may be airing network or already proven syndicated programming, will not risk buying an unseen, untried product. Therefore syndicators must produce a sample or *pilot* program, even though it is expensive.

Second, syndicated programming must develop its audience through promotion and advertising in local markets, but sometimes the promotion costs, when added to the purchase price of the series, makes the project less attractive for a station. Selling the series in certain major markets is important because they have the most viewers and because stations in smaller markets are sometimes influenced by the decisions of broadcasters in larger markets.

Syndication
and New
Distribution
Systems

Syndication can be described as a television distribution system in transition. The new channels opened up by cable television currently offer production companies new outlets for programming, but with satellite technology, a producer of the future will be able to send programs to stations via a leased satellite circuit, instead of "packaging" them on prerecorded tapes and mailing or shipping them to stations. When direct-to-home satellite broadcasting becomes operative, the same production company will in effect have its own satellite television station beaming straight to the home consumer, thus offering a host of new channels to the television viewer.

TELEVISION'S IMPACT AND FUTURE

The public has widely accepted the medium ever since its first year of significant operation in 1948. Television's Bureau of Advertising estimates that television commands 48 percent of our time as opposed to 32 percent for radio, 13 percent for newspapers, and 7 percent for magazines. Television set ownership increased dramatically after World War II. Networks began to develop major distribution systems at that time to reach affiliate stations in most areas of the United States and in many foreign countries. A. C. Nielsen estimates that over 43 million households had televisions in 1950. Today that figure has increased to approximately 70 million. In the United States we averaged more than five hours of television consumption per day, per household, in 1963, and today this has increased to over six hours. This translates into actual years spent in front of television by the time we reach adulthood.

Educational television (*ETV*) and instructional television (*ITV*) have been designed specifically to capitalize on the teaching-learning process in both education and industry. ETV refers to *any noncommercial television program*, whether or not the program is used for direct classroom instruction. ITV refers to *programming especially tailored for use in the classroom or in direct teaching*. Industries have also incorporated ITV into many areas of training. The ability to transmit ITV programs directly into the home makes it possible for many corporations to conduct home training programs. Similar programs have been developed through colleges and universities.

Much of the medium's impact cannot be measured in statistics. The changes in our life styles since the advent of television are too numerous and in some cases too subtle to measure fully. An international television spectacular from one country can set a new trend in another country's clothing styles. A breakfast cereal commercial may show someone participating in the sport of hang-gliding. The sale of the breakfast cereal soars, and so does the sale of hang-gliders. A student sits in the classroom and has little desire to learn from lectures. The teacher introduces a televised segment into the lesson, and the student's interest and attention span increase. Researchers in a university prepare a comedy series to teach reading to underprivileged children. When their examples seem unreal to the children's preconceptions of television, the series fails miserably. All of these examples show that at present we are still unaware of the total impact of the medium. It has only been during the last decade that college students have become the first total-television generation, living with the medium from birth. What will occur when you become the first television-parent generation, and your children will be part of a family in which every member has been affected by television since birth? It is easy to see why it is so important to realize the impact of the medium now and to become responsible consumers and molders of its future.

What television holds for society as it approaches the end of the twentieth century is open to considerable speculation. Already we can sit in front of "big screen" television, which can cover an entire wall. A special television receiver collects the signal and then projects it onto a wall like a slide projector. Research has also developed slim-screen television to replace the cumbersome models of the past that had television tubes as large as two feet thick. The new picture tubes are not much thicker than a picture frame and can be hung on the wall in much the same manner. Portable "mini-cams" and "microcams" (Figure 6–16) give television reporters the flexibility of the radio journalist, although they still are not at the reduced cost that radio enjoys. Although we may not see the wholesale marketing of Dick Tracy-type wrist televisions in our lifetime, the miniaturization of electronic components will increase the portability of television.

Television programming also will change. As cable television grows, more channels will be available than are possible with direct, over-the-airways reception. Local access to cable television will increase, and community groups will be responsible for this programming. Public television supported through public contributions and government subsidies from the Corporation for Public Broadcasting will be providing more alternatives to the mass appeal programs seen on commercial network television. Pay television may be in the future; limited experiments have proved successful in a number of communities.

New technologies will also affect our viewing habits. A national system of low-power television (LPTV) stations may enable smaller communities to have locally owned and operated stations. The use of the television screen for video games and as a visual display terminal for a home computer will mean even more time spent watching television. Such new transmission systems as direct broadcast satellites (DBS) and multipoint distribution services (MDS) will offer even more ways to reach an audience.

Figure 6-16 Smaller circuit and component design and its related equipment allow television journalism to be a flexible, portable force. With satellites, live news reports can originate almost anywhere in the world where reporters and equipment can be transported. (Courtesy, Thomson-CSF Laboratories, Inc.)

Over-the-air *teletext* and the wired *videotex* distribution of textual material will also stimulate new programming formats.

All these possibilities add up to more selective viewing which, along with technological improvements, will be important to television's development as a medium of the future.

SUMMARY

Television's debut can be traced back to the work of Alexander Edmund Becquerel and the electrochemical effects of light. Practical application of principles transmitting visual information took place in 1884 with Paul Nipkow's scanning-disc transmitter and receiver. Vladimir Zworykin with his iconoscope tube and Philo Farnsworth with his improved, high-resolution scanning system made the transition to electronic television.

Television was introduced to the public at the 1939 World's Fair. Surviving the FCC's decision on an industry-wide color system, a freeze on licenses, and rules improving the development potential of UHF, the medium enjoyed its golden age in the 1950s. Programming ranged from the variety shows and comedies of the fifties, to the political turmoil of the sixties, and to the consumer movement of the seventies. Television journalism gained respect in the 1950s with such programs as "See It Now" and explored new horizons in the 1970s with electronic newsgathering. Television's impact on our lives has been substantial, with steadily increasing amounts of time being spent with the medium.

Syndication enables stations to have a wide selection of programs, some of which are available via direct syndication and still others which are available after their successful network airings. The economics of syndication demand production companies invest money in pilot programs. Both production companies and local stations must consider the costs of promoting and selling the programs. For the production company, selling the program means finding enough stations willing to buy the program to make it a viable production venture. For the local station, selling the program means finding enough sponsors who want to buy commercials on the program.

Changes in television, in programming as well as in new technologies, will offer new ways for us to use television in the future.

OPPORTUNITIES FOR FURTHER LEARNING

A Public Trust: The Report of the Carnegie Commission on the Future of Public Broadcasting. New York: Bantam, 1979.

ADLER, R. P., ed., *"All in the Family," A Critical Appraisal.* New York: Holt, Rinehart & Winston, 1979.

AVERY, R. K., AND R. M. PEPPER, *The Politics of Interconnection: A History of Public Television at the National Level.* Washington, D.C.: National Association of Educational Broadcasters, 1979.

BARCUS, F. E., AND R. WOLKIN, *Children's Television: An Analysis of Programming and Advertising.* New York: Holt, Rinehart & Winston, 1977.

BARNOUW, E., *Tube of Plenty.* New York: Oxford University Press, 1975.

BITTNER, J. R., *Broadcasting: An Introduction.* Englewood Cliffs, N.J.: Prentice-Hall, 1980.

BOTEIN, M., AND D. RICE, *Network Television and the Public Interest: A Preliminary Inquiry.* Lexington, Mass.: Lexington Books, 1980.

BOWLES, J. A., *A Thousand Sundays: The Story of the Ed Sullivan Show.* New York: Putnam's, 1980.

BRADY, B., *The Keys to Writing for Television and Film*, 3rd ed. Dubuque, Iowa: Kendall/Hunt, 1978.

BROWN, L., *Keeping Your Eye on Television.* New York: Pilgrim Press, 1979.

CANTOR, M. G., *Prime-time Television: Content and Control.* Beverly Hills, Calif.: Sage Publications, Inc. 1980.

CATER, D., AND R. ADLER, EDS., *Television as a Social Force: New Approaches to TV Criticism.* New York: Holt, Rinehart & Winston, 1975.

COLE, B., *Television Today: A Close-Up View.* New York: Oxford University Press, 1981.

COMSTOCK, G. A., *Television in America.* Beverly Hills, Calif.: Sage Publications, Inc., 1980.

COMSTOCK, G., S. CHAFFEE, N. KATZMANN, M. McCOMBS, AND D. ROBERTS, *Television and Human Behavior.* New York: Columbia University Press, 1979.

EASTMAN, S. T., S. W. HEAD, AND L. KLEIN, *Broadcast Programming: Strategies for Winning Television and Radio Audiences.* Belmont, Calif.: Wadsworth, 1981.

ETTEMA, J. S., *Working Together: A Study of Cooperation among Producers, Educators, and Researchers to Create Educational Television*. Ann Arbor: Center for Research on Utilization of Scientific Knowledge, Institute for Social Research, University of Michigan, 1980.

FIREMAN, J., *TV Book: The Ultimate Television Book*. New York: Workman Publishing Co., 1977.

GEOTHALS, G. T., *The TV Ritual: Worship at the Video Alter*. Boston: Beacon Press, 1981.

GERLACH, V., AND D. P. ELY, *Teaching and Media: Systematic Approach*, 2nd ed. Englewood Cliffs, N.J.: Prentice-Hall, 1980.

GREENBERG, B. S., *Life on Television: Content Analysis of U.S. TV Drama*. Norwood, N.J.: Ablex, 1980.

HINDMAN, J., L. KIRKMAN, AND E. MONK, *TV Acting: A Manual for Camera Performance*. New York: Hastings House, 1979.

HOWARD, H. H., *Multiple Ownership in Television Broadcasting: Historical Development and Selected Case Studies*. New York: Arno, 1979.

HYDE, S. W., *Television and Radio Announcing*, 3rd ed. Boston: Houghton Mifflin, 1979.

KAPLAN, D., *Video in the Classroom: A Guide to Creative Television*. White Plains, N.Y.: Knowledge Industry Publications, 1980.

KEIRSTEAD, P., *Modern Public Affairs Programming*. Blue Ridge Summit, Pa.: Tab Books, 1979.

KELLY, K., *My Prime Time: Confessions of a TV Watcher*. New York: Seaview Books, 1980.

KRAUS, S., ed., *The Great Debates: Carter vs. Ford, 1976*. Bloomington: Indiana University Press, 1979.

MAHONEY, S., N. DEMARTINO, AND R. STENGEL, *Keeping PACE with the New Television: Public Television and Changing Technology*. New York: Carnegie Corporation of New York, VNU Books Int'l, 1980.

MASTERMAN, L. *Teaching about Television*. London: Macmillan, 1980.

METZ, R., *The Tonight Show*. New York: Playboy Press, 1980.

MORGENSTERN, S., ed. *Inside the TV Business*. New York: Sterling Pub. Co., 1979.

NEWCOMB, H., ed., *Television: The Critical View*. New York: Oxford University Press, 1979.

OWEN, B. M., *Structural Approaches to the Problem of TV Network Economic Dominance*. Durham, N.C.: Center for the Study of Business Regulation, Graduate School of Business Administration, Duke University, 1978.

PEPPER, R. M., *The Formation of the Public Broadcasting Service*. New York: Arno, 1979.

PRIMEAU, R., *The Rhetoric of Television*. New York: Longman, 1979.

QUINLAN, S., *Inside ABC: American Broadcasting Company's Rise to Power*. New York: Hastings House, 1979.

REISS, D. S., *M*A*S*H: The Exclusive, Inside Story of T.V.'s Most Popular Show*. Indianapolis: Bobbs-Merrill, 1980.

SINGER, D. G., J. SINGER, AND D. M. ZUCKERMAN, *Teaching Television: How to Use TV to Your Child's Advantage*. New York: Dial Press, 1981.

SKLAR, R., *Prime-Time America: Life on and behind the Television Screen*. New York: Oxford University Press, 1980.

SMITH, R. R., *Beyond the Wasteland: The Criticism of Broadcasting*. Falls Church, Va.: Speech Communication Association, 1976.

STEDMAN, R. W., *The Serials: Suspense and Drama by Installment.* Norman: University of Oklahoma Press, 1977.

STEIN, A. H., AND L. K. FREIDRICK, *Impact of Television on Children and Youth.* Chicago: University of Chicago Press, 1975.

WILLIS, E. E., AND C. D'ARIENZO, *Writing Scripts for Television, Radio, and Film.* New York: Holt, Rinehart & Winston, 1981.

WURTZEL, A., *Television Production.* New York: McGraw-Hill, 1979.

CHAPTER

PHOTOGRAPHY AND PHOTOJOURNALISM

PREVIEW

After completing this chapter, we should be able to:

Identify the contributions to photography made by Johann H. Schulze, Karl W. Scheele, Joseph N. Niepce, and others.

Connect the process of daguerrotype with Louis Daguerre.

Describe tintypes and the dry-plate process.

Discuss the contributions of George Eastman to the photography industry.

Explain the role of book artists, sketch artists, and early photojournalists.

Understand the historical impact of the landscape photographer, Plains Indian photographer, and railroad photographer.

Link the name of Mathew Brady to photography of the late 1800s.

Identify the first halftone picture.

Realize the contributions of tabloids to photojournalism.

Discuss the use of photographs in *Newsweek, Life,* and *Look* as well as their use in documentary photography.

List some of photojournalism's "great" pictures.

Discuss contemporary photography.

Describe electronic camera systems.

Figure 7-1 Camera obscura, a box-like room, was used to project images on the inside walls of the room. Artists used it as a guide for paintings and sketches. (International Museum of Photography at the George Eastman House)

We may not always think of photography as being a mass medium. After all, our snapshots of the last campus holiday or a family picnic may be seen by only a few close friends. But when we consider that a news photo may travel around the world on a *picture wire* and appear in hundreds of newspapers which are read by millions of people, we can see that photographs and the work of the photojournalist quickly become mass communication.

CAMERA OBSCURA

History's first record of images being reproduced with light dates back to the ancient Greeks. Aristotle described light waves and how they behaved when projected through a small opening called an *aperture*. Later applications of Aristotle's principles were recorded in the Middle Ages when Francis Bacon used a dark room with a tiny opening in one wall to permit light to enter from the outside and to project an image on the opposite wall. The device used for these experiments became known as the *camera obscura*, which in Latin means "darkened chamber." Artists, including Leonardo da Vinci, are reported to have used the camera obscura to project images (Figure 7–1) into the darkened chamber where the artist would trace the image.

Gradually the camera obscura began to be improved and reduced in size. What started out as a room became a large box. Then a piece of glass was added to the aperture, and a mirror was placed inside the box. The mirror reflected the image to the top of the box where another lens permitted it to escape and to be projected onto a wall. By looking directly into the lens on top of the box, the image could be viewed from outside the camera obscura. This latter principle is the same used in early cameras held at chest level while the photographer looked down into the viewfinder.

A PERMANENT IMAGE

Although the camera obscura had considerable use for the artist, it was not a camera capable of capturing permanent images. That did not occur until 1727 when German scientist Johann H. Schulze discovered that silver salts were sensitive to light. The process Schultze used, however, was not stable, and although a crude image could be captured, it could not be preserved. Closer scrutiny of the process resulted in Karl W. Scheele's 1777 discovery that the image captured on silver salts could be preserved longer with ammonia.

Niepce and Daguerre

Progress was slow until 1826 when, after a series of experiments, Frenchman Joseph N. Niepce succeeded in producing a permanent photograph (Figure 7–2), but the exposure time ran as much as eight hours.

Figure 7-2 The first photograph, "Image from Nature," produced by Niepce in 1826 was called a heliograph. The gray area of the sky is actually the impurities of the metal. In the original, the sky appeared white, and the dark shadows revealed more contrast. (Gernsheim Collection, Humanities Research Center, The University of Texas at Austin)

Three years later Niepce joined in partnership with another French-man, Louis Daguerre. Daguerre, like Niepce, was also attempting to create permanent photographs. Using copper coated with silver and exposed to iodine vapors, a photosensitive plate was produced. When exposed to light through a camera obscura and then brought into contact with mercury vapors, the plate produced the image seen by the camera obscura. The process was both quicker and of better quality than the process originally used by Niepce. Called *daguerrotype* (Figure 7–3), the process became popular in Europe and America and was even used for portrait photography. It was not long before explorers' expeditions were carrying daguerrotype cameras to capture the landscape of unexplored territory.

Figure 7-3 The Daguerreo-type camera contributed significantly to photography's ability to record history in everything from portraits to landscapes. (International Museum of Photography at the George Eastman House)

The only disadvantage of the daguerrotype was that only one daguerrotype could be made at a time. There was no process for reproducing more than one image, such as multiple positive prints from a single negative. That hurdle was overcome by British scientist William H. F. Talbot, who invented a light-sensitive paper, coated with salt and silver nitrate. From a single negative, multiple positive prints could be made. Talbot's process was christened *photography*. By 1841 Talbot had received a patent on an improved version of his paper film, calling the improved process *calotype*, and by 1844 Talbot's photographs had appeared in *The Pencil of Nature,* the first major book containing photographs. For the early world of photography, however, Talbot's ability to make multiple copies from a single negative of marginal quality did not appeal as much as Daguerre's single prints of almost perfect quality.

*Improving
the
Photosensi-
tive
Plate*

The next two developments in photography were in the substance of the photographic plate. Frederick Scott Archer took glass and coated it with a wet substance called *collodion*. The *wet-plate* process was later applied to metal by an American, Hamilton Smith, who called them *tintypes*. There were further improvements in photography in 1871 when Richard L.

Maddox invented a *dry-plate* process which meant less cumbersome developing equipment which in the past resulted in a wagonload of chemicals and apparatus when the photographer ventured into the field.

Improved camera design followed the developments in photographic plates, and although it took George Eastman to make photography popular for the masses, the late 1800s still saw many affluent subjects posing for portraits.

GEORGE EASTMAN AND KODAK

Although history records Hannibal Goodwin as the inventor of celluloid film, George Eastman (Figure 7–4), founder of the Eastman Kodak Company, will always stand out as having the greatest impact on photography and motion pictures. The year was 1877 when Eastman took an amateur interest in photography and discovered the craft entailed being part chemist, part artist, and part mechanic. Producing pictures required much equipment and luck. Eastman, who at the time was working as a bank clerk in Rochester, New York, began experimenting with manufacturing "dry plates." Eastman invented a machine to manufacture the dry plates and with a partner, H. A. Strong, opened a business in a third-floor loft in Rochester to begin manufacturing the plates on a mass scale. The Eastman Dry Plate Company opened for business on January 1, 1881.

Figure 7-4 George Eastman, founder of the Eastman Kodak Company, made photography a medium available to the masses. From inexpensive box cameras to modern instant cameras, Eastman left an important imprint on the field, both as a hobby and as a commercial enterprise. (Courtesy, Eastman Kodak Company)

Roll Film   Three years later Eastman jolted the photographic industry with his announcement that he had invented film rolls and a roll adapter which fit virtually every dry-plate camera. Not having to change plates after every picture was a significant improvement but not as monumental as what happened in 1888. It was in that year that Eastman introduced a light, portable camera priced at $25 and capable of holding film for 100 exposures. When the exposures were taken, the customer sent the entire camera back to the company where the film was extracted, developed, and the camera with new film was returned to the sender. The cost for replacing and developing the film was $10. A year later Eastman introduced the first commercial roll of film on transparent nitrocellulose backing.

        The impact of his organization's inventive and marketing skills became apparent in 1895 with the introduction of the Pocket Kodak which sold as fast as they could be manufactured.

The Brownie   Not satisifed with manufacturing a camera that contained film for 100 exposures, Eastman set out to make photography a truly "mass medium" (Figure 7–5). What was needed was a camera that anyone could afford

The . . Pocket Kodak

1896.

Was the Photographic Success of 1895.

In the hands of the absolute novice it produced a larger percentage of perfect pictures than any camera, big or little, had ever produced before. The "cartridge system," did away with the necessity of a dark room, and made photography simple and easy, with a Pocket Kodak.

THE 1896 MODEL

Retains the simplicity and daylight loading features of the original, and combines with them an

IMPROVED ROTARY SHUTTER,
SET OF THREE STOPS FOR LENS,
RECTANGULAR FINDER, . . .
IMPROVED RATCHET. . . . .

1896.

The new shutter is always set—push the lever—that makes the exposure. The set of stops adds greatly to the capabilities of the camera, especially for interiors and snap shots on the water. (No other manufacturers fit stops to cameras listing at less than $12.00 to $15.00). The rectangular finder gives a more exact scope of view than a round finder. Exquisite finish—Dainty yet strong.

Price, loaded with film for 12 exposures, - - $5.00.

EASTMAN KODAK CO.

Free Booklet.   Rochester, N. Y.

Figure 7-5 The pocket Kodak, "the photographic success" of 1895, continued for years to bring a succession of models to the amateur photographer. The 1896 model claimed an "improved rotary shutter." (Eastman Kodak Company)

Figure 7-6 Not all of Kodak's success was attributed to its products. Effective marketing and advertising programs contributed to public acceptance of the cameras. (Courtesy, Eastman Kodak Company)

and simple enough for anyone to use. The price of his early camera, $25, was inexpensive compared to previous studio models but still out of reach of the average person. For the most part the only people really engaged in photography were studio photograhers and people who could afford the high-priced camera with roll film. Finally after much product research and testing, in February, 1900, Eastman introduced the Brownie camera, a simple box camera with a price tag of only one dollar. Now photography was available to almost everyone, and the company that had started as a manufacturer of dry plates was into worldwide distribution and improved products.

Advertising and Slogans   Major advertising efforts helped the company succeed. In 1889 Eastman placed the slogan "You Press the Button, We Do the Rest" (Figure 7–6) into distribution. By 1897 a huge sign with the word "Kodak" appeared in lights over Trafalgar Square in London. The company later published numerous trade publications and consumer materials and, with the help of ad agencies, became a giant in photography.

Despite the changes in the development of still photography in the 1800s, photographs were not used in the daily production of the newspaper until later. The roots of photojournalism grew from the work of artists, not photographers. Although the War Between the States spotlighted sketch artists' contributions to mass communication, especially because of the widespread use of their work in newspapers, this era was by no means the first to bring the artists to the attention of the readers.

Book Artists

Book publishing had previously used the sketch artist to illustrate current events. For example, the book mentioned earlier titled *Briefe and True Report of the New Found Land of Virginia,* published in 1590, contained illustrations (Figure 7–7) sketched by John White. White is hailed today as one of the early artists to record life on the new continent.

About 300 years later when photographs did come into widespread use in newspapers and other publications, they were used as guides for engravers to make woodcuts, which in turn, were printing plates. A debate ensued between photographers and printers alike on which method, the sketch artist or photographer, would become the mainstay of the illustrated press.

Figure 7-7 Early "photojournalism" was not the work of photographers but rather of sketch artists. A book titled *Briefe and true report of the new found land of Virginia* was illustrated by John White and depicted scenes found when an early expedition under the direction of Sir Walter Raleigh landed on the coast of what is now North Carolina. (Courtesy of the Rosenwald Collection Reprint Series and Dover Publications, Inc.)

Newspaper Illustrators

But while the debate continued, events meant that illustrated newspapers and their artists would flourish. Often criticized for glorifying battle and portraying an unrealistic picture of events, the sketch artists still found a waiting public. Illustrated newspapers, started in the 1850s, flourished with the war. Most prominent were titles such as *The Southern Illustrated News*, *Harper's Weekly*, and *Frank Leslie's Illustrated News* (Figure 7–8).

Figure 7-8 The illustrated newspaper did much to make pictures an important part of journalism and paved the way for acceptance of photographs as illustrations. (Courtesy, Leanin' Tree Publishing Co.)

Even papers not accustomed to using pictures became conditioned to new layout styles. For these papers, the maps of the War Between the States battles and troop movements demanded composition different from the thin columns commonly used for type. Gradually two and three columns were used to display maps large enough to identify roads, paths, and tiny, unknown hamlets made famous by the war.

Capturing scenes from the era between the late 1850s and the early 1900s, including the War Between the States, was Winslow Homer. His engravings are somewhat overshadowed by his paintings of ships and seacoasts of the East and New England, but they still stand as some of the best records of social (Figure 7–9), economic, and military history. Many of his drawings were featured in *Appeltons' Journal of Literature, Science and Art*.

Figure 7-9 Winslow Homer's engraving of "The Boston Common" which appeared in *Harper's Weekly*, May 22, 1858. (Source: P. C. Beam, *Winslow Homer's Magazine Engravings.* New York: Harper and Row, 1979)

Illustrators of the West

The movement to the western frontier created another appetite for illustrations. Again the sketch artist prevailed. Names such as Charles Graham and Allen C. Redwood embellished weeklies with drawings of outlaws, cowboys, and the western experience. Graham, who was one of the best-known national news artists of the late 1800s, traveled throughout Montana and Idaho sketching Indians. Redwood, who fought with the Confederates, traveled and sketched Idaho and Washington after the war.

Although better known for his famous paintings than his work as a sketch artist for newspapers, Frederic Remington helped bring scenes of the West (Figure 7–10) to eastern newspapers and magazines. One of the most responsible artists of his day, his scenes were not the glorified exaggerations produced by some of his peers. Illustrations by Remington appeared in such publications as *Century Magazine* and *Collier's Weekly*. When the Spanish-American War broke out, he was sent to Cuba as a war correspondent by the Hearst papers.

Another product of the West was artist Charlie Russell. Like Remington, he is more famous for his paintings than his illustrations, although Russell's pictures did appear in publications. Longing to be a cowboy, Russell left home in St. Louis for the West and remained to live among the cowhands of Montana and the Indians of Canada. For capturing the life style of both groups, few equaled Russell's talent for depicting the hard, calloused, but sometimes fun-loving life of the open range. While writers created glamour and intrigue of the West, Russell, Remington, and others made a realistic appraisal of a land that many easterns say only in pictures.

Much of the credit for photographing the westward expansion belongs to the United States government. Supported by sponsored geological surveys, such photographers as Timothy O'Sullivan, A. J. Russell, William Henry Jackson, Carleton E. Watkins, and Eadweard J. Muybridge captured images of the western landscape. Being hundreds of miles away from the nearest outpost or town, these pioneer photographers had to use improvised darkrooms, usually a tent or wagon equipped with bottles and chemicals for processing the plates, often as big as 20×40 inches.

Congress used Jackson's 1870 photographs of the Wyoming and Montana wilderness to proclaim Yellowstone a National Park in 1872. Jackson became so synonymous with that pristine area that an area and later the town of Jackson Hole bore his name. The work of these photographers opened up a new era of wilderness photography for others, such as Ansel Adams, who would later make western landscapes their subject.

Figure 7-10 Frederic Remington illustrated a number of scenes from the American West, but it was Charles M. Russell, who actually lived as a cowboy and with the Indians, who is responsible for the most complete eyewitness drawings of the American frontier.

Photographers of Plains Indians

Stretching west of the Mississippi River into the Dakotas, the Wyoming Territory, and what were later the western states, exploration parties, settlers, and railroad personnel found themselves dealing with the West's original occupants—native Indians. Early photographers gave us an anthropological view of these residents of the Great Plains, their life styles, and some distinguished portraits of their leaders.

Some of the earliest Indian photographs came from the work of Albert Bierstadt. He ventured into this virgin territory in 1859 when Fort Laramie in Wyoming Territory was considered the "capital" of the West. Bierstadt was an artist by trade and used stereographic techniques, photographing dual images with a special camera, to make photographs which he later used as references for his paintings. One of his first pictures was of a Sioux village outside of Fort Laramie.

Alexander Gardner, who had become well known for his photographs of the War Between the States, was present with his camera in 1868 when the Indian Peace Treaty Council was held at Fort Laramie. He focused upon intimate views of the Indian life style—the interior of an Indian teepee council chamber, Indian women packing hides, and an Indian burial tree.

Other photographers captured the images of the great Indian chiefs, often in that sometimes stilted, studio tradition. Perhaps the most famous chief, Sitting Bull (Figure 7–11), sat before photograher D. F. Barry's camera in 1885, slightly less than a decade after Sitting Bull's visions of a great victory over the white man united the tribes at Little Big Horn and ended General George Custer's career. Another Hunkpapa Sioux Chief, Rain-In-The-Face, was photographed in a portrait by L. A. Huffman, the post photographer at Ft. Keogh, Montana Territory in 1880. Red-Armed panther, also known as "Red Sleeve," sat for a portrait photograph made by Huffman at Fort Keogh in 1879.

The peaceful portrait photographs of the Indians in the late 1800s were a strange contrast to the legends and reality of the war paint and the bloodshed which had been both suffered and inflicted during the beginnings of the westward expansion.

The Railroad Photographers

In addition to the United States government, the Union Pacific Railroad also fostered the medium of photography. By 1868 when Wyoming was becoming a territory, the Union Pacific was stretching westward to meet the Pacific Railroad in Utah. An experienced photographer from the War Between the States, A. J. Russell, was hired by the Union Pacific to make a still documentary (Figure 7–12) of the railroad's construction progress. Other photographers, such as John Carbutt and Arundel C. Hull, rode with the trains and captured much of the human effort that accompanied railroad construction. Among Hull's prominent photographs were the Union Pacific's first engine, the first engine crossing, and the trestle of Dale Creek Bridge, Wyoming. Scenes photographed by Russell included a railroad-owned windmill and water tank outside Laramie, Wyoming; railroad workers camped on top of boxcars; and stone masons constructing a permanent stone railroad bridge at Green River, Wyoming.

Figure 7-11 Sitting Bull of the Hunkpapa Sioux was photographed by D. F. Barry in 1885. (Courtesy, The Smithsonian Institution)

Figure 7-12 Railroad photographers were an important part of the early photographic history of the West. (Used with permission of the Union Pacific Railroad Museum Collection)

Figure 7-13 "Bridge Wreck," one of over 5,000 photographs which were the work of pioneer photographers T. N. Bernard and Nellie Jane Stockbridge. (Courtesy, Bernard-Stockbridge Photographic Collection of the University of Idaho Foundation, Inc.)

However, not all of the photographs from the western collections of Hull and Russell were of the railroad. Outlaw "Big Steve" Young was captured and hanged from a telephone pole outside a Laramie train station in 1868, and Hull recorded his corpse and some distant onlookers. Freund's Gun Store, famous for supplying "guns and ammunition to vigilantes and outlaws impartially," was also seen through the lens of Hull's camera.

Portraits and Places

One of the most complete chronicles of western life in the late 1800s and 1900s occurred, not on the pages of newspapers, but in a tiny photographic studio located in Wallace, Idaho. There, T. N. Bernard photographed not only commissioned portraits of the people of the rich silver-lead mining region, but also the town, its surrounding area, the mines, and anything else that made a good subject. When his business of the 1890s grew too busy to manage, he telegraphed his photographer sister-in-law in Chicago and asked her to join him. She did, and Nellie Jane Stockbridge continued to photograph the people of northern Idaho well into the 1960s (Figure 7–13). But it wasn't until her death in 1965 that her work gained recognition on a wide scale. At that time the University of Idaho became the beneficiary of over 200,000 negatives from the Bernard-Stockbridge photography business, and through the efforts of the University of Idaho Foundation, cataloguing and copying of the negatives began in earnest. The result is a rich depository of material for scholars of both early photography and the history of the Pacific Northwest.

PHOTOGRAPHY MAKES AN IMPACT

By the late 1800s the photographer had managed to become part of the reporting process, albeit not in newspapers. Government collections, books, and private exhibits were the showcase of the photographer-reporters. What the photograph could do for reporting, however, was shown by a massive photo project headed by Mathew Brady.

Mathew Brady

Many illustrators captured the Civil War, but Mathew Brady and his staff did it on a grand scale. Brady's interest in photography grew from a boyhood fascination that matured through associations with Samuel Morse, who, along with inventing the telegraph, had an interest in optics. Morse introduced Brady to Daguerre in Europe, and in 1844 Brady came back to New York and opened his own photography studio using daguerrotype. By 1860 he had met and photographed Abraham Lincoln. When the Civil War broke out, Brady received presidential approval to photograph it.

Figure 7-14 Two of Mathew Brady's famous photographs are these of Abraham Lincoln (left) and Jefferson Davis (right). (Courtesy, International Museum of Photography at the George Eastman House)

With Secret Service protection and now using the improved wet-plate process, he and his assistants traveled from battlefield to battlefield bringing reality to a war which the sketch artist often misrepresented. Although the newspapers did not benefit from his photographs, since there was no rapid photoengraving process, his work remains one of the important beginnings of photojournalism.

Brady also left his mark on photography and photojournalism by giving us some of the best photographs of prominent figures (Figures 7–14). Along with Lincoln, he also photographed Jefferson Davis, John Tyler, John Quincy Adams, James Polk, and Franklin Pierce. Brady, or his assistants, are also credited with photographs of such noted people as Mary Lincoln, wife of the President, and Susan B. Anthony, women's suffrage leader.

Mathew Brady brought photography out of its experimental stages into its place as a recorder of history, but the invention that brought photographs to mass communication was the *halftone*.

The Invention of the Halftone

For the newspaper publisher of the 1870s, photographs were nice, but there was no fast and practical way to put them in print. Even when used as tracings for engravers, the cutting and edging of a good engraving took time—too much time for the demands of instant news the telegraph brought to newspapers. But all that began to change in March, 1880, when the *New York Daily Graphic* published its first line halftone picture showing a scene in Shantytown, New York (Figure 7–15). The halftone process permitted the printer to capture the full tonal range of a photograph, something not possible before. An improved halftone process used two

Figure 7-15   A halftone engraving of a photograph titled "Scene in Shantytown" appeared in the *New York Daily Graphic* on March 4, 1880. It sparked a new era in newspaper illustrations. (Courtesy, Newspaper Collection, The New York Public Library, Astor, Lenox, and Tilden Foundations)

pieces of acid-coated glass with tiny parallel lines cut on the glass. When the two pieces of glass were placed so the lines were perpendicular to each other, it formed a "screen" effect that in turn was used to impose the tonal variations of a photographic negative onto a printing plate.

There is a debate over who contributed the most to developing the halftone. Two people stand out as particularly important. One is Frederic E. Ives who worked at Cornell University and is credited with making the first halftone reproduction in 1878. He continued to improve the process, while simultaneously a photographer named Stephen H. Horgan worked on a way to use the halftone process in newspaper publishing, specifically for his employer, the *York Daily Graphic*. It was Horgan who prepared and published the Shantytown picture and made the use of halftone practical on the rotary press.

With the ability to publish quality photographs with speed, the importance of the photographer to journalism increased dramatically.

THE TABLOIDS

As photography began to improve, more and more people became aware of the capabilities of the medium, and organized professionals banded together to promote their craft. Early efforts by Alfred Stieglitz resulted in the formation of Photo-Session, a cooperative group of photographers who, through 1917, published and displayed a wide variety of photographs.

After World War I, newspaper publishers took time to view the growth of the illustrated tabloid newspapers of England and realized that a handsome profit awaited the publisher who could combine good photography with reporting. Unfortunately it was not journalism's finest hour. With strong competition among tabloids, sensationalism became the norm. Motion pictures were just coming into their own, and the life of the celebrity filled gossip pages. Using a new, smaller, 35mm camera from Germany, called the Leica, photographers took candid shots of politicians, movie stars, and everyone else who could be caught in an embarrassing position.

Edwin and Michael Emery in their book *The Press in America* succinctly describe the era:

> The national experiment called Prohibition brought rumrunners, speakeasy operators, and gangsters into the spotlight, and they were interesting people. Al Capone, Dutch Schultz, Waxey Gordon, Legs Diamond, and their rivals were sensational copy. Socialites caught in a speakeasy raid made good picture subjects.
>
> Tabloid editors feasted, too, on stories about glamorous and sexy Hollywood and its stars—Rudolph Valentino, Fatty Arbuckle, Clara Bow. They glorified in the love affairs of the great and not-so-great—Daddy Browning and his Peaches, Kip Rhinelander, the Prince of Wales. They built sordid murder cases into national sensations—Hall-Mills, Ruth Snyder. They glorified celebrities—Charles A. Lindbergh, Queen Marie of Rumania, Channel swimmer Gertrude Ederle. They promoted the country's sports stars— prizefighter Jack Dempsey, golfer Bobby Jones, tennis champion Bill Tilden, football coach Knute Rockne, and home run hitter Babe Ruth.[1]

Figure 7-16 Few scenes from photojournalism in the 1920s were as sensational as the photograph of the electrocution of Ruth Snyder. (Copyright 1928 by Pacific and Atlantic Photos)

Figure 7-17 Gracing everything from barbershop walls to hotel and store windows, the news poster became a popular attraction of early photojournalism.

With Joseph Medill Patterson at the helm, the *Illustrated Daily News* became one of the first New York tabloids, with its inaugural issue on June 28, 1919. Hearst launched another tabloid, the *Daily Mirror*, in 1924. Magazine publisher Bernarr McFadden bought the *Daily Graphic* and turned it into a tabloid. But the pinnacle of the photo-oriented tabloids came on January 14, 1928, when a full-page picture of convicted murderer Ruth Snyder (Figure 7–16) being electrocuted at Sing Sing appeared with a caption reading "exclusive closeup of Ruth Snyder in death chair at Sing Sing as lethal current surged through her body."

Photojournalism had gained such popularity by the late 1920s that some publishers had syndicated photographs of major news events (Figure 7–17) and would send them to subscribers for posting in such places as hotel lobbies, restaurants, and barber shops. These "instant news" one-page sheets lasted until radio news began to take over as the new instant medium.

MAGAZINES AND DOCUMENTARY PHOTOGRAPHY

Other tabloids in other cities prospered, but many eventually went out of business, including New York's *Mirror* and *Graphic*. But photography and photojournalism were growing, and it was the magazines that brought the camera to new heights in mass communication.

Newsweek

On February 17, 1933, a new magazine rolled off the presses. Its name was *Newsweek*, and it brought to magazines the benefit of the photojournalist's sharp eye. Its front cover displayed photos of the week in review, two additional photopages were inside the cover, and candid shots of the week's newsmakers were sprinkled throughout the magazine's pages. Three years later, *Newsweek* was faced with competition from another magazine specializing in photojournalism.

Life and Look

When Henry R. Luce launched *Life* magazine in 1936, it quickly became the standard of photojournalism. Although showing its own brand of sensationalism by printing such things as sequence pictures of the top of a man's skull being removed for a brain operation, it prospered with the expert photographic talents of such well-known names as Margaret Bourke-White and Alfred Eisenstaedt. Eisenstaedt has one of the longest associations with the magazine, over thirty-six years. He is credited with over 1700 stories and 90 covers for *Life*. He joined *Life* eight months before its first issue and rejoined them at the age of eighty when *Life* was reintroduced. As we learned earlier, the original *Life* fell victim to the mass appeal and lower cost-per-thousand of television. *Look*, first appearing in 1937, copied *Life's* picture style. It also succumbed to television but appeared again in 1979 with different covers for different regions of the country. Both magazines are considered standards in photojournalism.

Figure 7-18 Dorothea Lang's photograph from the Farm Security Administration's Program is perhaps one of the most famous representations of the Great Depression. Titled "In This Proud Land," the photo was of a migrant woman and her children. (Library of Congress)

Still Photography as Documentary

While *Life* and *Look* radiated the importance and acceptance of photography magazines, a man named Roy Emerson Stryker made history in the photographic division of the Farmers Home Administration. Founded in 1935, it showed what could be done with documentary photography, the graphic recording of events, conditions of society (Figure 7–18), and its people. Documentary photography is a statement, an impact, a commentary, yet an accurate portrayal. And for documentary photography, few eras could equal the Great Depression of the 1930s. Roy Stryker made a permanent history of these tragic times of poverty and gave documentary photography a permanent place in modern photojournalism.

More recently Documerica, a project of the 1970s, brought photographers together to record the ecological condition of the country. Stryker in the 1930s and Documerica added still more to the importance of photography and photojournalism.

LANDMARKS IN PHOTOJOURNALISM

Within any profession there are always the "classics," the best examples of a trade and its most memorable moments.[2] The work of the pioneer photographers like Mathew Brady are, of course, among these, but others through the years have also left indelible impressions, often of major news event.

One such event was the San Francisco earthquake on April 18, 1906. The earthquake and resulting Great Fire left 452 people dead and burned through 28,000 buildings. Edward Rogers of the *San Francisco Morning Call* photographed the destruction but when he returned to his office, it also was in flames. He managed to get across San Francisco Bay to Oakland to have the photos developed in time to be included in a special newspaper edition called the *Call-Chronicle-Examiner* which eight enterprising newspapermen from the three papers managed to print.

Assassinations have left their mark on photojournalism as well as on history. William Warnecke of the *Evening World* had been assigned to cover the departure on vacation of New York Mayor William J. Gaynor on August 9, 1910. Arriving late for the assignment, he found the other photographers had already left. Just then a man appeared with a pistol and shot the mayor twice. As the mayor staggered, Warnecke took the photograph which later appeared on page one of the paper.

President John F. Kennedy was assassinated on November 22, 1963, in Dallas, Texas, but the photograph which made history came later as the accused assassin, Lee Harvey Oswald, was himself shot to death. Robert Jackson, a photographer for the *Dallas Times-Herald*, had been assigned to cover Oswald's transfer from the County Jail to the City Jail. As the transfer began, Jackson heard someone yell and by instinct snapped the shutter, just as a heavyset man emerged from the crowd and shot Oswald. The photograph of the shooting won Robert Jackson the Pulitzer Prize.

War, along with death and mangled bodies, has also provided some of photojournalism's most memorable photographs. Possibly the most well known belongs to Joe Rosenthal of the Associated Press. Taken in 1945, the photo depicts the United States Marines raising the flag at Iwo Jima (Figure 7–19).

Figure 7-19 The "Flag Raising at Iwo Jima" by Joe Rosenthal of the Associated Press is one of the memorable and frequently reproduced photos of World War II. (Courtesy, Naval Photographic Center, Official Navy Photograph)

Sports photograhs have also made photojournalism history. Perhaps the most famous was made of baseball star Babe Ruth. After 15 years of playing baseball for the New York Yankees, the "Babe" retired on June 13, 1945. Nat Fein, a photographer for the *New York Herald Tribune*, instead of taking a head-on shot of the Babe and using a flashbulb to compensate for the gloomy day as the other photographers did, moved to the back of Babe Ruth. There he captured the moment of emotion as Babe Ruth leaned on his bat with his right hand, shoulders stooped, the retired number "3" showing prominently on his jersey. The photograph (Figure 7–20) is displayed next to Babe Ruth's uniform at the Baseball Hall of Fame in Cooperstown, New York. For Nat Fein, the sports photograph meant the Pulitzer Prize.

Photojournalism is filled with hundreds of other landmarks. Los Angeles *Examiner* photographer Sam Sansone's picture of California center Roy Riegels wrong-way run in the 1929 Rose Bowl game against Georgia Tech and J. Parke Randall's photograph of a scaffolding collapse at the Indianapolis Motor Speedway in 1960 are two more examples from sports. Remember, the examples here are only an attempt to show how the photojournalist's craft, combined with talent and perhaps good timing can bring readers the visual highlights of the news.

Figure 7-20   In sports photojournalism, they remember "The Babe." Nat Fein of the *New York World-Telegram* had moved away from the other photographers at Yankee Stadium that day in 1948. Shooting behind, not in front of Babe Ruth, he snapped this scene the day Babe Ruth retired. (Used with permission of the Baseball Hall of Fame and Museum, Inc.)

Figure 7-21 Modern industrial photography provides career opportunities for skilled photographers. This scene is of the Getty-operated production platform in the Gulf of Mexico. (Courtesy, Getty Oil Company; Lon Harding, photographer)

CONTEMPORARY PHOTOGRAPHY

Today a skilled photographer practices his or her craft in a wide variety of settings. New printing processes have made it easier and less expensive to print pictures so that photography is more widely used. Some of the most talented photographers either work for or freelance for major corporations. Industrial photography captures everything from seascapes (Figure 7–21) to magnifications of computer chips. Major magazines offer photographers opportunities from snapping fashion to freezers.

Richard Avedon's photograph (Figure 7–22) of actress Nastassja Kinski attracted much attention when it first appeared in *Vogue* and was

Figure 7-22 Richard Avedon's photograph of actress Nastassja Kinski first appeared in *Vogue*. Later highlighted in such publications as *Newsweek*, the response to the photograph titled "Natassja Kinski and The Serpent" prompted Avedon to issue a large color poster of the photograph which was distributed through art and poster galleries in signed and unsigned editions. (Used with permission of Richard Avedon)

later highlighted in such publications as *Newsweek*. The response to the photograph titled "Nastassja Kinski And The Serpent," was so great that Avedon issued a large color poster of the photograph which was distributed through art and poster galleries in both signed and unsigned editions.

For the average consumer, recent popularity and pricing of the 35 mm camera has called new attention to amateur photography. The major mass marketing strategy of the Canon AE-1 camera set the stage for other manufacturers to follow.

THE FUTURE

With newspapers becoming involved in cable television and satellite distribution and programming, print and electronic journalism may begin to complement each other in the future. Evidence of the way technology may contribute is seen in the electronic camera systems which have been produced by RCA and Sony.

Electronic Camera Systems

The merging of still camera photography with electronic journalism has been attempted successfully by more than one company. Both RCA and Sony (Figure 7–23) have systems which use the hardware and size of a 35mm camera but the "recording" system of videotape. Sony's Mavica system combines the portability of the 35mm camera with the ability to produce instant "electronic" pictures on a video screen. The Mavica system employs a single lens reflex camera and records the image on a small, spinning magnetic disc. The disc is then transferred to a special player which reproduces the picture on a screen.

Since the clarity of the Mavica's still photographs is approaching print photojournalism standards, inherent advantages exist for the photojournalist. For example, photographs could be developed immediately and sent over telephone lines to a waiting newsroom, where the image

Figure 7-23 Sony Corporation's electronic "MAVICA" camera. (Photo used courtesy of Sony Corporation of America)

could be reproduced on a printing plate and be on the press within 15 minutes after it was shot. With such systems it is becoming increasingly difficult to distinguish between print and electronic photojournalism.

Kodak's Disc Camera

Keeping competitive in the age of rapid change, Kodak has introduced a disc film and accompanying camera which could, if successful, eliminate the roll film traditionally used in many cameras. Instant automatic focusing, a perpetually charged flash that never needs to be turned on, automatic winder, an optical finder defining picture area, are just some of the features touted by Kodak.

Color and Specialized Publications

Color photography is a vital, if not major, force in photojournalism. Such scientific breakthroughs as Polaroid's instant developing and the printing industry's color offset presses promise to bring more and more color photography to a variety of publications.

Today, just as media are becoming more specialized, so is the work of the photograher. Depending on the publication or the company, a photographer can specialize in specific types of photography such as food, fashion, or farming.

What about the future? Will new media delivery systems mean new demands and markets for the photographer? What will the new technological advances in photography mean? Alfred Eisenstaedt was asked that question and replied, "You can buy the most modern equipment, lenses, cameras, etc., but you still need the eye and the brain behind the camera. It's not the camera that takes the picture, it's the person with the brain and the eye."[3]

SUMMARY

Photography had its beginnings with the camera obscura—a crude, boxlike device used to project inverted images. A lens was added to the camera obscura, and photosensitive plates were invented to capture the image permanently. The first permanent photograph is credited to Joseph Niepce who later, with his partner Louis Daguerre, perfected the photosensitive plate and shortened the exposure time necessary to take pictures. The photosensitive plate was improved still further by such people as Frederick Scott Archer, Hamilton Smith, and Richard Maddox. George Eastman produced an inexpensive camera and roll film, bringing photography in reach of the average citizen.

The roots of photojournalism go back to the early illustrators who drew pictures to highlight books and newspapers. During the War Between the States, photographer Mathew Brady made realistic pictures of battle scenes, tempering the exaggerated and glorified examples drawn by some sketch artists of the period. After halftone printing processes made rapid and accurate reproduction of the photograph possible in newspapers and other publications, photography became much more a medium of mass communication. Although it suffered from the sensational reporting techniques of the early tabloids, photojournalism matured and was represented with distinction in such publications as *Life* and *Look* and in the documentary photography of Stryker in the Great Depression and the

1970s Documerica Project for ecology. Today new technology in camera, lens, and film have aided the photographer. As other forms of mass communication have become more specialized, so has the work of the modern photographer.

OPPORTUNITIES FOR FURTHER LEARNING

The Best of Photojournalism, 5: People, Places, and Events of 1979. Columbia: University of Missouri Press, 1980.

BLODGETT, R., *Photographs: A Collector's Guide.* New York: Ballantine, 1979.

CAVALLO, R. M., AND S. KAHAN, *Photography: What's the Law.* New York: Crown Publishers, Inc., 1976.

COE, B., *Cameras From Daguerreotypes to Instant Pictures.* New York: Crown Publishers, Inc. 1978.

COLEMAN, A. D., *Light Readings: A Photography Critic's Writings, 1968–1978.* New York: Oxford University Press, 1979.

CRAVEN, G. M., *Object and Image: An Introduction to Photography.* Englewood Cliffs, N.J.: Prentice-Hall, 1975.

CURL, D. H., *Photocommunication: A Guide to Creative Photography.* New York: Macmillan, 1979.

CURRENT, K., *Photography and the Old West.* New York: Harry N. Abrams, 1979.

DAVIS, P., *Photography.* Dubuque, Iowa: Wm. C. Brown, 1975.

EDEY, M., AND C. SULLIVAN, eds., *Great Photographic Essays from Life.* Boston: New York Graphic Society, 1978.

EDON, C. C., *Photojournalism.* Dubuque, Iowa: Wm. C. Brown, 1976.

EISENSTAEDT, A., *Witness to Our Times,* rev. ed. New York: Viking, 1980.

FREUND, G., *Photography and Society.* Boston: David R. Godine, 1980.

GOULD, L. L., AND R. GREFFE, *Photojournalism: The Career of Jimmy Hare.* Austin: University of Texas Press, 1977.

KERNS, R. L., *Photojournalism: Photography with a Purpose.* Englewood Cliffs, N.J.: Prentice-Hall, 1980.

KOZLOFF, M., *Photography & Fascination.* Danbury, N.H.: Addison House, 1979.

LANGFORD, M., *The Step-by-Step Guide to Photography.* New York: Knopf, 1978.

MALCOLM, J., *Diana & Nikon: Essays on the Aesthetic of Photography.* Boston: David R. Godine, 1980.

POLLACK, P., *The Picture History of Photography: From the Earliest Beginnings to the Present Day.* New York: Harry N. Abrams, Inc., 1977.

ROTHSTEIN, A., *Photojournalism,* 4th ed. Garden City, N.Y.: Amphoto, 1979.

SCHWARZ, T., *How to be a Freelance Photographer.* Chicago: Contemporary Books, 1980.

STARK, R., AND L. DANCE, *Nebraska Photographic Documentary Project.* Lincoln: University of Nebraska Press, 1977.

STOCKWELL, J., AND B. HOLTJE, eds., *The Photographer's Business Handbook: How to Start, Finance, and Manage a Profitable Photography Business.* New York: McGraw-Hill, 1980.

THOMAS, A., *Time in a Frame: Photography and the Nineteenth-Century Mind.* New York: Schocken Books, Inc., 1977.

WELLING, W., *Photography in America: The Formative Years, 1839–1900.* New York: Harper & Row, Pub., 1978.

CHAPTER

MOTION PICTURES

PREVIEW

After completing this chapter, we should be able to:

Describe the contributions of William Dickson and Thomas Edison to motion pictures.

Cite the contributions of the Lumière brothers, George Méliès, and Edwin S. Porter to early motion pictures.

Distinguish between the vitascope, nickelodeon, kinetograph, and kinetoscope.

Explain the contributions of D. W. Griffith to the silent era of film.

Acknowledge the importance of such films as *The Birth of a Nation* and *Intolerance*.

Name four silent comedy film stars.

Talk about the influence of stars, producers, and directors on the fledgling motion picture industry.

Describe the mood, sets, and scenery of the early film studios.

Discuss the international development of film.

Explain the transition film had to undergo to survive the arrival of sound.

List some of Walt Disney's early animated films.

Name some famous film stars of the 1930s.

Discuss the impact of such films as *Gone with the Wind* and *Citizen Kane*.

Describe how the film industry dealt with the arrival of television.

Talk about the bank financing and the film industry.

Trace trends in film through the 1960s, 1970s, and into the 1980s.

Contrast film with video.

If we walk back to the nineteenth century, we will not see shopping centers with movie theaters tucked away between department store entrances and ice cream shops. We will not see neon signs flickering names like Roxy or Rivoli between rows of flashing lights. We will not see marquees listing the choices at Cinema I, Cinema II, Cinema III, and Cinema IV. Neither will we find plush cushioned seats, wide screens, or sound-encased theaters. What we will see are movie parlors and curious theaterlike establishments called *nickelodeons* and storefront theaters. We will encounter people like Thomas Edison. And as we begin our walk toward today, we will meet other familiar people like Lee de Forest and George Eastman.

TOWARD REPRODUCING MOTION

Film really began in the minds of people who came long before the film pioneers. The attempt to capture and recreate motion can be traced to the beginnings of civilization when cave drawings depicted a horse with eight legs, the fleeting arrow from a hunter's bow, or carefully detailed drawings of kings with one foot outstretched to suggest a walking motion.

Images and Sequence

Early attempts at photographing and reproducing motion were crude. Eadweard Muybridge came close when he photographed a running horse (Figure 8–1) with a series of cameras. Connected to each camera along a track was a trip cord, and when the horse ran by, it tripped the cords and the cameras, giving Muybridge a series of photographs of the horse in various stages of running. The French next developed a single camera that could take 12 pictures in a second. What was still lacking, however, was a film and a camera capable of taking rapid pictures of moving objects, pictures that when developed could be "played back" for an illusion of motion.

Figure 8-1 Some of the first attempts at photographing motion occurred when Eadward Muybridge used a series of cameras and a trip cord to capture the movement of a horse.

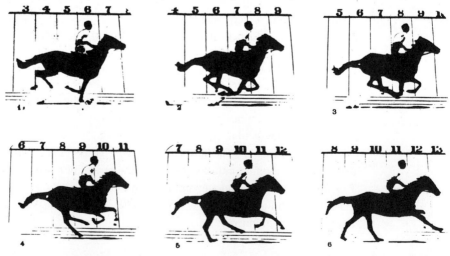

Camera and Viewing Mechanisms

History is somewhat unclear about exactly who deserves credit, but two people, William Dickson and Thomas Edison, both of Edison's laboratory, we know are associated with efforts to move George Eastman's contributions in photography beyond the world of the still camera. From the Edison labs came a workable motion picture camera, the *kinetograph* in 1889.

Figure 8-2 "Black Maria," the kinetographic theatre at Edison's laboratory. (Courtesy, Edison National Historic Site)

A year later the two men were successfully taking motion pictures. By 1891 Edison had constructed a crude motion picture studio at his workshop and headquarters in West Orange, New Jersey. The studio was a tarpaper shack dubbed "Black Maria" (Figure 8–2), but it was the beginning of the commercial motion picture industry in America. From Black Maria came a series of very short films on such subjects as Buffalo Bill, a strong man, a dancer, and a Chinese laundry. The films were shown on a large contraption called a *kinetoscope* (Figure 8–3), which had a peephole to look into and view the moving images. Kinetoscope parlors were popular viewing areas housed in everything from buildings to storefronts which were converted into rooms where dozens of the machines were lined up for paying patrons.

Thomas Edison, the inventor, was interested in making improvements on his devices and moving any product from the shelf to the marketplace. He introduced a new projector, the Projecting Kinetoscope, in 1897 and took out patents on the kinetograph and the projector. He did not secure international patents on the camera, however, and that oversight allowed two brothers from France to develop their own system.

Figure 8-3 Edison's peep-hole kinetoscope. (Edison National Historic Site)

Projection:
The Lumière
Brothers

Auguste and Louis Lumière were brothers who worked with their father's business manufacturing photographic plates and film. Using the technology they learned from Edison's work, they set out to improve both the kinetoscope and kinetograph. They succeeded in developing a camera much more portable and less cumbersome than Edison's, one that could print and project pictures with a crude yet intermittent motion. The invention was named the *cinematographe*.

In 1895 the Lumière brothers produced their first film, titled *Leaving the Lumière Factory*, the content of which was what the title implied. On December 28, 1895, they began showing films in the basement of a Paris cafe, and the motion picture industry began. The impact of the new medium, even with its shaky photography, caused quite a stir. One of the Lumières' most famous films, *The Arrival of a Train*, made theatergoers cringe in their seats as they watched the huge steam locomotive approach on the screen. Other famous *Lumière* films included *Feeding Baby* and the more humorous *L'Arroseur arrosé*. The latter showed a gardener with a water hose and a boy coming behind the gardener and stepping on the hose. When the water stops, the gardener looks down the nozzle of the hose at the moment the boy steps off the hose. The gardener gets wet. The audience laughs. As you can probably detect, even simple humor was amusing since the mere presence of motion before the eyes of the audience created a heightened emotion capable of being triggered by the slightest response.

For the Lumière brothers, the potential of the new invention was never fully realized. They were far more impressed with the mechanical workings of their "scientific" discovery than they were with its ability to make money. They produced films that used the reality of the outdoors and the real lives of people. Most were between thirty and sixty seconds long and sufficient to entertain early film enthusiasts. Critics view the films of the Lumières as being much more creative than those of Edison who used more stilted presentations suitable to the confines of his early makeshift studio.

The Vitascope

Back in the United States, the kinetoscope was running into trouble. The novelty of the machines wore off, and by 1895 their popularity had reached a plateau. The licensing agents for the kinetoscope, Norman Raff and Frank Gammon, saw the advantage of screen projection over the peephole viewing of the kinetoscope. In December, 1895, they began negotiations with Thomas Armat and Francis Jenkins who had invented their own projection system. Realizing Edison's value to the marketing of the system, Raff and Gammon convinced him to take over manufacturing the machine and to lend his name to the product. The *vitascope*, as the device was called, was introduced as part of a vaudeville program on April 23, 1896, at Koster and Bial's Music Hall in New York.

Nickelodeons

The vaudeville theaters and locations used by itinerant show people were the showplaces of motion pictures until about 1905 when the nickelodeon era arrived. These projection parlors where a nickel was the price of admission spurred new efforts in motion picture production to satisfy the increasing demand for films. By 1905 the average length of a motion picture was 1000 feet on a single reel with a running time of about 12½ minutes. Most nickelodeons had showings of 30 minutes or longer.

Edison's Patent Suits

Edison aggressively tried to gain a stronghold on the industry and in 1897 began filing patent suits. He claimed a patent on film stock and cameras that used intermittent motion. One mechanism, among others, of which Edison claimed ownership was the Latham loop, a small loop used on the projector to permit a flexible tension of the film as it passed in front of the lens. The loop is still used today, and although a rather simple principle, it was the cause of countless legal battles. Armat later fell out with Edison and sued him over ownership of the vitascope. But whatever the outcome of these power plays, the motion picture business was now an established entity.

Expanding The Story Line: Méliès and Porter

Among many, two other people left their imprint on early motion pictures. One was a Frenchman named Georges Méliès who added the dimension of special effects to film. A magician by trade, Méliès secured a camera and projection device, began producing films about 1897, and soon became an international distributor.

Méliès's most famous film, *A Trip to the Moon*, showed a group of scientists and chorus girls launching a rocket to the moon. The rocket is seen hitting the "eye" of the man in the moon, and the space people encounter moon people. Some of the special effects Méliès incorporated in the film include the earth rising on the horizon and a trick photography scene of moon people disappearing in smoke. Méliès went on to produce numerous fanciful pictures showing his talent for special scenery, if not the most imaginative use of the camera.

Another landmark film was the product of one of Edison's employees, Edwin S. Porter. Porter produced *The Great Train Robbery* (Figure 8–4) and numerous other films that were a direct product of Méliès's influence on world cinema. *The Great Train Robbery* is famous for its introduction of narrative to early films. It told a story and inaugurated the technique of *cross-cutting*, piecing together different scenes in a composite story line, to a 14-scene film which lasted just short of 12 minutes. An earlier Porter film, *The Life of an American Fireman*, used similar editing techniques, but not knowing exactly how the last scene was edited caused *The Great Train Robbery* to emerge instead as the singular example of the narrative style. A sequence of scenes was not new to film. That had appeared before in Méliès's films, but in Méliès's films, especially *A Trip to the Moon*, the action progressed from one scene to another—from constructing and launching the rocket on earth to its landing on the moon. In *The Great Train Robbery*, viewers visit the telegraph office not once but twice at different times in the film, first for the outlaw to tie up the operator and later for the operator to be discovered. For the nickelodeon audience, this scene was a marvel, and people could not get enough. Thus began an industrial revolution in the production, distribution, and showing of motion pictures. Silent films had arrived.

Figure 8-4 Scene from "The Great Train Robbery," produced by Edison employee Edwin S. Porter. (U.S. Department of the Interior, National Park Service, Edison National Historic Site)

D. W. GRIFFITH AND THE SILENT ERA

By the turn of the century, the technology and creativity of motion pictures were beginning to mesh. Longer narratives and sophisticated techniques became the norm. But for the industry, this meant stiff competition, so stiff that nine companies, including Edison's, joined together in 1908 to form the Motion Picture Patents Company to oversee all aspects of the motion picture industry. At this time also the talents of motion picture producers and directors were given their just recognition. Perhaps none was more highly regarded than David Wark Griffith.

The Technique

Intending to be a serious stage actor and playwright, D. W. Griffith found his aspirations and the demand for his work somewhat at odds. After he unsuccessfully tried to sell some of his material to the Edison studio, Edwin S. Porter convinced him to try his hand at film acting. He did and played the lead role in the film *Rescued from an Eagle's Nest*. But more importantly, Griffith landed a job as assistant to a director when a shortage of help and a demand for films gave many studio employees a jack-of-all-trades experience. Griffith was no average assistant, however. He had an energy and a will to learn that gave him a reputation among studio people that he could be counted on and that he would put in the hours to get the job done. It paid off.

He was given a chance to direct, and his attention to dramatic flow impressed even the studio heads. With more and more films under his belt, Griffith was slowly beginning to change the way motion pictures were made. He scheduled rehearsals before final shootings and concentrated on producing scenes that carefully followed the progress of the film. His first film, *The Adventures of Dollie*, utilized a high-angle shot that gave the film a new dimension. But this was only a hint of the man's talents.

Gradually Griffith graduated from single-reel films to the longer versions that gave him more latitude for experimentation. By 1914 he was firmly entrenched as a brilliant director, respected by the motion picture industry around the world. He had realized not only the tremendous potential of the camera to capture the intense emotions of the actors but also the flexibility of different camera angles and shots to communicate these emotions to the audience. Until Griffith's time, the camera had been primarily a silent witness to theaterlike productions. It was not any longer. Griffith carried three important elements to their full potential: (1) the use of the camera, (2) scene and costume design, and (3) editing. In using the camera, he effectively employed the close-up, medium, and long shot to give the audience many different perspectives on a scene. Such shots were designed to add to the story line as well as to the feeling of the picture. A battle scene shot from a distance, for example, could show the size of the armies and the terrain on which they fought. A medium shot could show the fierce fighting in the trenches, and a close-up could show the emotion on a soldier's face as he met the enemy and death.

Similar mastery was displayed in his editing techniques, Louis D. Giannetti, in his book *Understanding Movies*, classifies Griffith's editing techniques as *cutting to continuity*, *classical cutting*, and *thematic montage*.

Cutting to continuity is editing the action so as to preserve its flow without showing all of the action. In its very simplest form, a modern example would show someone boarding an airplane, the airplane taking off, a shot of the person in his or her seat, the plane landing, and the person walking out of the airport. Griffith brought to the screen a smoother yet more dramatic continuity than had been seen previously. The "dramatic" aspects of his films were highlighted further by his classical cutting. Some of Griffith's most famous scenes were chases or rescues that he carefully edited to control both time and space to prolong the climactic moment of suspense. Or, using the thematic montage technique, Griffith would unify a central theme of his film, regardless of the different scenes or camera shots. For example, different periods in time can be edited together to capture a central theme. Actors in a live scene while the camera flashes back to one actor's memory of previous romantic encounters is an example of thematic editing.

The Birth of a Nation and Intolerance

Of all the films produced by Griffith, he displayed the greatest talent in *The Birth of a Nation* and in *Intolerance* (Figure 8–5). They remain today the most discussed and studied of Griffith's works. *The Birth of a Nation* traced in dramatic terms the history of the United States through the Civil War and Reconstruction. That in itself was a first, because history had previously been limited to books. Although critics deplore the blatantly racist theme of the picture, which centered on the Ku Klux Klan and postwar racial strife, it is still considered a brilliant cinematic work. Costing $125,000 and requiring 15 weeks to shoot, it opened in Los Angeles in 1915.

In comparison, Griffith's film *Intolerance* presents some of the best cinematic examples of thematic montage. *Intolerance* was an extravaganza even by today's lavish standards. Originally begun as a film titled *The Mother and the Law* that dealt with life's injustices, the piece was expanded into four scenarios in different time periods which were edited together in an attempt to show the existence of injustice over time. The four scenarios consisted of the city of Babylon constructed with lavish sets and hundreds of extras, the age of Christ and the conspirators against him, Protestant-Catholic strife in Renaissance France, and murder and child stealing in modern America. In typical Griffith fashion, the four parts of the film that kept the audience jumping between each period all were brought together by editing a "unified" conclusion.

For all of its acclaim over the years, however, *Intolerance* had its pitfalls. *The Birth of a Nation* had brought Griffith considerable criticism because of its social implications; *Intolerance* was an attempt to show that social strife had been with us through the ages. Unfortunately it did not refute the criticism of *The Birth of a Nation*. In addition, it proved to be too complex for its audience. Griffith had attempted to carry even further his skills in camera technique, editing, and lavishly detailed sets. But in doing so, he went beyond the ability of his audience to understand the film. In other words, it flopped. Because it was so lavish, Griffith had to put his profits from *The Birth of a Nation* into *Intolerance*, which spelled financial trouble. No longer a financially independent producer, Griffith was forced to seek outside financing for future films.

Figure 8-5 Although the audience found it difficult to comprehend, "Intolerance" was a classic example of an early film spectacular. (National Film Information Service, Academy of Motion Picture Arts and Sciences)

Ironically the motion picture industry went through a similar experience in the late 1960s when *The Sound of Music* was produced with a budget in the range of $20 million. It was highly successful. Believing that the key to big audiences and big profits was similar spectaculars, the industry spent huge sums on films that, like *Intolerance*, flopped and placed some of the biggest motion picture companies on shaky financial ground.

The *Birth of a Nation* and *Intolerance* were the pinnacle of D. W. Griffith's career as a director. By having to secure outside financing, he lost some of the independence of producing what he wanted, how he wanted, and with the production schedules he wanted. But besides this, times were changing. The Roaring Twenties were not noted for their love of Victorian theatrical epics of the kind that Griffith produced. Two of his films that were popular just as the twenties arrived were *Broken Blossoms* and *Way down East*. The former showed rare compassion and gentleness somewhat unusual for Griffith's tradition of social upheaval. *Way down East* presented one of the most popular rescue scenes complete with a damsel in distress heading over a giant waterfall.

The arrival of sound in motion pictures signaled the beginning of the end for Griffith, for it was a technology that he did not master as he had the camera lens. The powers in the movie industry also felt that Griffith had failed to sense the changing tactics of the movie audience. Nevertheless, the man had a profound effect on the entire concept of film and still does.

SILENT COMEDY: SENNETT AND CHAPLIN

It was one of D. W. Griffith's understudies who began a silent-era tradition of bringing comedy to the silver screen. Mack Sennett was much like Griffith in the paths their cameras took and what led them to fame as directors and producers. With a background in acting and little success in vaudeville, Sennett ended up at Biograph working under Griffith as an actor. It was with the Keystone Film Company that Sennett was able to begin producing his first love—silent comedy.

Sennett paid little attention to the narrative storytelling and continuity for which Griffith was noted. Rather, he had one objective—to produce comedy through purely physical action. It was not important if the scenes fit together in any real sense of forward motion, nor critical that a social message be presented. Sennett cared only that actors and objects be combined in a way that gave the audience as many chuckles as possible in as little time as possible. The famous Keystone cops became one of his trademarks, the focus of his directing style being on three primary

Figure 8-6 Beginning his career with Keystone at a salary of $150 a week, Charlie Chaplin rose to become a star of silent films. His image has remained imbedded in the character he portrayed first in Essanay's production of "The Tramp."

methods. One method was to take a melodramatic plot and insert strategically placed gags in it. Another was to take a particular location and stage all the gags there. For example, a single room might contain a slippery banana peel, a board ready to knock someone on the head, a bucket placed where someone will step in it, and glue all over the floor. Another approach was to fit individual gags into the theme of the picture, such as a movie director trying to instruct a half-witted actor.

Two other Sennett trademarks were his use of fast-motion film and characters whose fast-paced antics tickle the funny bone. The secret was to direct an actor to act out gags in a mechanical fashion, record the action at one speed, and project it at a faster speed, thus achieving the robotlike comic effect. Machines were also important to a Sennett comedy. An automobile crashing into and knocking over everything in its path was even more outrageous with an illusion of a fast speed of eighty miles per hour.

Of all who worked with Sennett, none captured the hearts and box office popularity of American more than Charlie Chaplin did (Figure 8–6). It was 1913 when Chaplin went to work for Keystone at a salary of $150 per week and a year's guaranteed salary. His small, thin frame was perfect for the mechanical tin-soldier look Sennett wanted, and the director used Chaplin effectively in a number of comedies. While with Keystone, Chaplin began to develop a character called the "tramp" that would make him a star. As the little man with a cane, moustache, derby, and baggy pants, Charlie Chaplin shared with audiences the disappointments, frustrations, and constant confrontations with the obstacles of life. But it was after leaving Keystone that he was able to realize his potential.

In 1915 he was offered and accepted a salary of $1,250 per week to act, direct, and produce for the Essanay company. In Essanay's *The Tramp*, Chaplin comes to the rescue of a beautiful woman, played by Edna Purviance, only to lose her love to her handsome boyfriend. Yet unlike the Sennett style that progressed rapidly from gag to gag, Chaplin moved with more deliberation, milking a scene for all the humor it could offer before going on to the next one. His films also contain more continuity and composition than Sennett's do. For instance, in *The Tramp*, Chaplin acted through four complete scenarios protecting the girl from other tramps, working for the girl's father on their farm, stopping a robbery of the farm, and losing the girl.

The pretty girl and the downtrodden tramp became the theme of many Chaplin pictures. Chaplin himself came from a life of poverty and had a keen awareness of social injustices. This added quality, well portrayed in his pictures, made him a popular favorite. Today his films are still studied and enjoyed in theaters, and on college campuses.

LAUREL AND HARDY, KEATON, AND LLOYD

The popularity that Sennett and Chaplin brought to comedy was echoed by other stars of the silent era. Among comedian teams, two men named Stan Laurel and Oliver Hardy were among the best (Figure 8–7). Laurel and Hardy's comic style was in the tradition of Sennett and Chaplin.

Figure 8-7 Laurel and Hardy were two of many comedians of early motion pictures. Others who contributed to the development of the comedic acting style included Buster Keaton and Harold Lloyd. (© Freelance, Lansdale, PA)

Downtrodden and against the world, they managed to tackle it head-on. Although starting out in pictures separately, they worked well with each other. Critics did not regard them as having the depth of style of Chaplin, but their "team" approach nevertheless kept audiences entertained well into the sound era.

Called the "Great Stone Face," Buster Keaton began in pictures in 1917 and became a master at portraying an individual able to succeed through ingenuity. Many times confronted with mechanical obstacles, from trains to boats, he would use them to get an upper hand. His appeal was his straight-faced reaction to unsurmountable circumstances while keeping audiences on the edge of their seats with his hair-raising stunts. In *Sherlock Jr.*, we see a movie projectionist fall asleep, dreaming that he is playing the hero in a series of daredevil stunts. Critics consider Keaton's best film to be *The Navigator*. Here he ends up as a dumbfounded millionaire adrift on an ocean liner with one other passenger, played by Kathryn McGuire. Before the picture ends, they end up in the water after being attacked by cannibals. Unfortunately the one hurdle Keaton could not conquer was sound. When talkies arrived, he moved behind the camera and worked as a script doctor, never to have his talents extended beyond a few short appearances as an extra.

A third well-known comedian of the silent era was Harold Lloyd, who combined some of Chaplin and Keaton in a straight-man image. For Lloyd, the character was Lonesome Luke, also the title of many single-reel films produced between 1915 and 1917. Movie scenes carried Lloyd, however, more than Lloyd carried the scenes. In *The Freshman*, a tiny thread on his tuxedo begins to unravel and carries the action through a hilarious romp in which the tuxedo falls apart. With the public taste whetted by Chaplin and Keaton, Lloyd had no trouble finding an audience for his antics.

OTHER STARS, PRODUCERS, DIRECTORS

This also was the era of giant epics, lavish sets, and big money, especially with the monumental *Ben Hur*. Begun in Italy, it was finished in California where M-G-M's home office could keep an eye on expenditures. The total cost of a staggering $6 million was not entirely recovered from box office receipts.

Horror films had their day with Lon Chaney starring in such pictures as *The Monster*, a story about a mad doctor who captures motorists for experiments in bringing back the dead. Other Chaney hits included his 1923 *The Hunchback of Notre Dame* and his 1925 *The Phantom of the Opera*.

Sex made its appearance in a number of early films. *Sinners in Silk* in 1924 had Hedda Hopper's drinks spiked so that the villian could take her home for the evening. In those days wild intentions were mostly thwarted, however. Greta Garbo excited early audiences in such films as *The Temptress*, in which she played a loose woman who drove men to murder. In *Flesh and the Devil* Garbo teamed up with John Gilbert for some of the hottest love scenes of the era.

Pickford and Fairbanks

The "sweetheart" of early films was Mary Pickford. Labeled "the first movie star" and "America's Sweetheart," her Hollywood ventures included marriage to Douglas Fairbanks and life on their estate named Pickfair. Born in Canada, she started her career acting with stock companies before she joined D. W. Griffith. She later became one of the partners with Griffith in founding United Artists. Her "sweetheart" role was nurtured by such films as *Tess of the Storm Country*, *Rebecca of Sunnybrook Farm*, *Poor Little Rich Girl*, and *Little Lord Fauntleroy*. In 1929 her performance in *Coquette* won her an Academy Award.

Douglas Fairbanks was a hero with so much energy that Griffith's directing seemed to confine rather than to display his talents. With physical attractiveness and roles that made him the chief romper through pirate ships and Sherwood Forest, Fairbanks was a movieland star of the first order. He was at his best when he was physically involved in the scene, whether it was crashing through windows or swinging from ceilings. He was John Wayne, Tarzan, and a Latin lover all rolled into one. *Robin Hood*, *The Three Musketeers*, and *The Mark of Zorro* all made Fairbanks a famous male symbol of the 1920s.

The king of the silent Western thrillers was Thomas Ince. Known more as a producer than as a director, he realized early the power of the great outdoors, especially the West. With stagecoaches, posses, Indians, and blazing but mute gun battles, he brought the Western hero to the silent era. Ince is respected for his ability to combine shoot'-em-up action with a tight story line that did not get lost in the shuffle. Careful editing to preserve that story line also became his trademark, instead of editing for emotional highlights as Griffith and Sennett did. Representative of his major Westerns are *War on the Plains, Custer's Last Fight*, and *Hell's Hinges*, all produced between 1912 and 1916. So intent on producing films set in lavish landscapes, he arranged for 18,000 acres of land on the Pacific to be leased for *War on the Plains*. The tract was christened Inceville.

Also realizing the lavish possibilities of the West was Cecil B. De Mille. De Mille became famous for his spectaculars, such as *The Ten Commandments*, and his films that catered to liberal morals as in *Why Change Your Wife?* Although his films received high praise when they were released, he slipped out of grace among contemporary critics for his appeal to the masses and his preoccupation with studio profits. Nevertheless, just his longevity as a director has made him an indelible part of film history.

Somewhat in contrast to De Mille was Eric von Stroheim. Von Stroheim, a popular actor and later director, brought some very long, yet quality films to the early screen. *Foolish Wives* and *Greed* were two of his longest films, running seven and nine hours, respectively. He also brought *uncompromising detail* to films and would sacrifice nothing to create the tiniest display of realism. Although his films have not played to nearly as many audiences as De Mille's have over time, the critics have been kinder to von Stroheim because of his devotion to this detail while remaining at odds with studio accountants over costs and shooting times.

The public's hunger for movies, the overnight profits, and the bullish attitude toward the future of films are readily seen in some of the lavish expenditures and sets that the major studios constructed. For example, Universal Studios kept a complete zoo, drawing on everything from elephants to pets. At one time it housed thirty lions, ten leopards, a sizable share of elephants, numerous monkeys, horses by the hundreds, and an array of dogs and cats.

Fox Films, which became Twentieth-Century Fox in the 1930s, had entire streets and villages constructed for its productions. It started in 1925 when William Fox purchased a ranch for cowboy star Tom Mix. A western street became part of the Mix set and was shortly joined by a European city for *Sunrise*, a French village and battleground for *What Price Glory?*, and a Parisian set for *Seventh Heaven*, all on the back lot. A scale model of an ocean liner seen from blocks away was constructed for *Metropolitan*. Surviving for thirty years because of its flexibility was the famous New England street with its stone church, courthouse, and gabled houses. The Erie Canal set was constructed for Henry Fonda's *The Farmer Takes a Wife* and a Honolulu set was constructed for Warner Oland's *Charlie Chan* series.

THE INTERNATIONAL INFLUENCE

Although our discussion of motion pictures to this point has centered on American actors and directors, we need to mention the impact that motion pictures made in other parts of the world. Two countries stand out for their cinematic contributions—Germany and the Soviet Union.

Germany and The Cabinet of Dr. Caligari

Shortly before the end of World War I, Germany began to bring its film industry under partial government control. After the war it was under complete control of the state and organized around the Universum Film, A.G. (UFA). With massive studios at Neubabelberg near Berlin, UFA's goal to join the power of film to domestic "uplifting" and international influence. Although originally more a war policy than a creative one, the latter eventually materialized as German directors captured the desolate state of the German people following the European conflict. The emotional impact they made stirred sensations in international film circles, beginning with *The Cabinet of Dr. Caligari* in 1920. Dr. Caligari, played by Werner Krauss, is a demented physician with mental powers over his patients, powers that can hypnotize them into performing lunatic acts in the most grotesque fashion. This was a horror film like nothing the American directors had dared to make. For the unsophisticated viewer, the film is an escape into fantasy. For the critic in search of symbolism, the film unearths a wealth of comparison to political suppression and tyranny.

If *Caligari* jolted the senses, other German films went on to show a mastery of technology that the Americans found tough to match. Cameras were used in every conceivable way to illustrate emotion. Strapped to an actor's chest, placed on camera dollies to follow the action, and hung from a trapeze, they went everywhere a viewer or a viewer's eyes could go.

Dominating German films was the theme of a depressed people caught in hopeless straits against both the real and surreal. Fritz Lang's *Destiny* with souls going through a stone wall surrounding a cemetery, Paul Leni's *Waxworks*, and F. W. Murnau's *Nosferatu* on the Dracula theme are all representative of the oppressed horrific themes. Even the future world of Lang's *Metropolis* reflects a city with human catacombs beneath the street.

As German films began to play in America, they not only became popular but also spurred American directors to become more creative and bold in their own endeavors. For Germany, however, the creative era was short-lived and is considered to have ended when Hitler took power in the 1930s.

Russia and Potemkin

Like Germany, the Soviet Union developed a sizable state-controlled film industry after the Russian Revolution. By 1917 film was an instrument of propaganda but one that still nurtured creative talents. International acclaim was achieved through the successful use of the thematic montage, refined and perfected from the foundation laid by Griffith. Carefully editing for sequence and emotion, the Soviets used the broad expanse of natural scenery with the thematic montage to capture a new realism in film. It was perhaps best displayed in Sergei Eisenstein's *Battleship Potemkin* (Figure 8–8). This story of revolt and revolution depicts an event from the Russo-Japanese War, the mutiny of the crew of the battleship *Potemkin* in Odessa harbor. In the film the mutiny symbolizes revolution against oppression, a fitting theme for the postrevolutionary Russia of 1925. Five parts of the film are skillfully edited through thematic montage into a theme of *unity* against political dictatorship. The film is further heightened by classical cutting techniques. In a scene from the first part of the film, a sailor eating infested meat sees the words "Give us this day our daily bread" inscribed on a plate and smashes the plate in frustration as the action is highlighted by ten different camera shots.

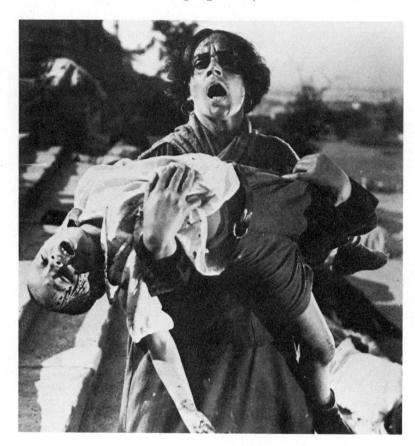

Figure 8-8 The Mother and child from "Potemkin." (National Film Information Service, Academy of Motion Picture Arts and Sciences)

Other Soviet films and personalities displayed similar creativity. Vsevlod I. Pudovkin brought a more relaxed approach to film with attention to the individual. Comedy in *Chess Fever* and empathy in *Mother* were part of his repertoire. Although clinging to the revolutionary themes of Eisenstein and Pudovkin, Alexander Dovzhenko chose surrealism in which people and objects are distorted from reality. In his *Arsenal*, bullets from a firing squad have no effect on a prisoner, symbolizing the ability of the spirit to withstand the oppressor.

France and Un Chien Andalou

In France, surrealism reached its height with the work of artist Salvador Dali and director Luis Buñuel. Their film, *Un Chien Andalou*, carries the shocking and absurd to new peaks with objects out of place and the camera deliberately focused on special effects to jolt the audience. A dead donkey on a piano is one example, but tame compared to a portrayal of a straight razor slicing across a woman's eyeball.

French surrealism treated life as an irrational dream with its directors making no apologies for their film's content or even trying to justify any symbolism. The shocking scenes of *Un Chien Andalou* have somewhat masked the displays of other French films.

The Passion of Joan of Arc

Climaxing the silent era was a French film of international proportions. *The Passion of Joan of Arc* was produced by Carl Dreyer whose association with the UFA brought his talents to France where he was joined by German craftsman and designer Hermann Warm and Polish photographer Rudolph Mate. Starring as Joan was the Italian actress Falconetti. The key to *Joan's* success, even in the beginning days of sound, was the use of the camera to catch facial expressions. For instance, the close-up shot masterfully captures every turn of her eye, every tear, and every agony. The special effects of Joan burning at the stake, not so much gruesome as they were expressionist and packed with intense empathy, brought audiences the world over to appreciate what the camera could do. Audiences would need to remember that versatility, because with the arrival of sound would come a degree of restraint on directors and producers that had been present only at the very beginnings of film.

THE ARRIVAL OF SOUND

Sound joined film as early as 1889 when William Dickson introduced sound on a disc system to Thomas Edison, but not until the end of World War I was there any significant development.

Technology

Two different systems premiered in early sound pictures. The famous "audion" tube that Lee de Forest invented to amplify the incoming *electromagnetic waves* of a radio receiving set appeared again in the 1920s as an amplification system for sound motion pictures. De Forest also invented a method through which sound could be recorded directly on the film in perfect synchronization with the picture. This system, introduced in 1922, was called *phonofilm* and was similar to a German process called the *tri-ergon process*. The other system was developed by Western Electric and used a disc recording in synchronization with the picture. Called *vitaphone*, it would not become the standard of the industry, but it would drastically change it.

Vitaphone, after being offered to numerous studios, was finally purchased by Warner Bros. Warner started out by producing a series of sound short subjects, or "shorts," with vitaphone, using a few talking dignitaries of the film industry and some musical scores. The first feature-length film with the system was *Don Juan* in 1926. Warner's almost instant success came on the night of October 6, 1927, when the film *The Jazz Singer* starring Al Jolson opened in New York (Figure 8–9). Although not the first sound film, it did use synchronized sound to tell a story. Audiences loved it.

Meanwhile, Fox started producing sound films with a system closely resembling Lee De Forest's. Called Fox Movietone News, the early "journalism" shorts were gradually replaced by feature films produced in Fox's Movietone City, a studio complex built for sound in 1928. By 1930 movie theaters around the country had converted to sound. While technically it moved motion pictures far into the future, artistically it left them behind.

Figure 8-9   Al Jolson starred in "The Jazz Singer," which was the first feature-length film to use the Vitaphone sound system. The "talkies" had arrived. (Warner Communications, Inc.)

Cameras that had once roamed sets and had gone along with riding posses now were frozen in cement. They had a new device to contend with—a microphone. The camera could not rove because the microphone could not rove with it. In addition, the director's habit of shouting directions now had to be muzzled. But they adapted. The camera became encased in a special soundproof box, and the director learned to use everything from signs to sign language to communicate with the actors. And the studio audience, which once had filled the balconies of the silent movie studios, was kept out entirely. The most abused character in all of this was the cameraperson who had to be locked up inside the soundproof cage with the camera.

Unfortunately movie audiences did not give the studios much incentive to adapt to sound creatively. Early sound films with their stilted camera shots and lack of action were a novelty, just as film itself had been in the days of the Black Maria. People came to hear actors talk and guns shoot. Never mind that actors huddled together straining their voices toward a concealed microphone; never mind the crackling quality of voices picked up and reproduced on primitive equipment; never mind the return of the theater sets. Stars and directors of the silent era cringed at what was happening to the medium. There was no place for the trifles of Chaplin's tramp nor the stunts of Buster Keaton.

For actors, sound became a frightening experience of mammoth proportions. Stars of the silent era dropped like flies, victims of the new technology. When a hero of action sounded like a whimpering coward, his career could end with a ten-minute audition. When a romantic actress talked with sloppy English and battered accent, beauty could not salvage a crumpled career.

Reliance on theater for scripts, however, also brought new stars with the voices to make the transition. One of vitaphone's finds was Lionel Barrymore. For Barrymore, the microphone was a friend. It captured his resonance and gave the audience just what it wanted. Dolores Costello starred with Conrad Nagel in *Glorious Betsy* and brought a contrast of the male and female voices to the screen. In *The Lights of New York* in 1928, Helene Costello and Cullen Landis sat "very close" so the single microphone could pick up their dialogue, even though the picture consisted of little more than the camera shots of the pre-Griffith era.

Fortunately the creative void did not last too long. Soundproof cages were replaced by more manageable soundproof camera covers. Two directors unshackled the industry with their creative and technical breakthroughs. Rouben Mamoulian accomplished with *Applause* in 1929 a feat that sounds simple by today's standards. First, he separated sound from picture in the original filming. Using a camera crane for aerial shots of New York's Penn Station, he added the sound later. Second, Mamoulian used two microphones instead of one. Using a sound mixer, dual microphones permitted new latitudes in positioning actors as well as scenery.

The second director to break the sound barrier was King Vidor. With his production of *Hallelujah!* Vidor put the camera into a chase through a swamp, then later added the sound of squishing mud and animals.

Distant shots of blacks in the fields of the South were accompanied by the singing of spirituals, which made it seem as though microphones were in the cotton bushes.

At last the motion picture industry was managing to wed sound to film, even though the products were a bit like a newborn fawn, beautiful to look at but awkward.

HOLLYWOOD: THE 1930s TO WORLD WAR II

With the creativity of sound released from its cages and an audience again becoming sophisticated, film moved into its second generation. Some critics feel that film grew faster in these years than it ever would again. As a new medium experimenting with itself, virtually all of the shots used in today's pictures and many of the sound techniques came from this time. By the 1930s the town called Hollywood was a lavish dreamland where millions were made and stars were born. To examine this era, let's look at some of the producers, the films, and the stars that were part of it. Keep in mind that it was a time when the big Hollywood studios like M-G-M, Warner Bros., Columbia, and Twentieth-Century Fox were big, big business. Movies were mass produced, and their audiences clamored to the theaters. Remember also that television was not around to keep audiences at home. That came later and drastically altered the motion picture industry.

Film in the 1930s had reached a Waterloo with sex and violence, just as television today is feeling the pangs of citizen group pressure. After the risqué 1920s, civic and religious leaders began blaming the movies for society's ills. In 1934 a Catholic lay leader, Joseph Breen, was added to the board of the Motion Picture Producers and Distributors Association, which had been founded as a self-regulatory commission in 1922, headed by President Harding's postmaster general, Will Hays. Although there was still plenty of action, it was Breen's responsibility to determine what society should see and what it should not. Fortunately for Breen and the industry, the lack of competition from television, the novelty of sound, and the new achievements in color photography kept people interested in the movies.

Animation: The Work of Walt Disney

Walter Elias Disney (Figure 8–10) entered Hollywood not as an actor or director like so many before him, but as an artist. A cartoonist from Kansas City, Disney started producing short, animated cartoons called Laugh-O-Grams. Then with animal characters, he set out to produce cartoons which mimicked the real world. By the time his career had matured, Disney had collected a record number of Academy Awards and had moved beyond cartoons to feature films known for their family entertainment value. The profits his company amassed stand today in such monuments as Disneyland in California and Walt Disney World in Florida.

What brought Walt Disney's productions to the national public's eye was his 1928 cartoon, *Steamboat Willie*. It introduced a character eventually named Mickey Mouse (Figure 8–11) who went on to become one of the biggest stars in motion picture history. In *Steamboat Willie*, Disney put

Figure 8-10 Walt Disney. The studios Walt Disney built produced feature films which established animation as both a contemporary art form and an important part of the motion picture industry.

Figure 8-11 MICKEY THROUGH THE YEARS: (top left) His screen debut in "Steamboat Willie," 1928; (top right) As a policeman in "The Dognapper," 1934; (bottom left) As "The Sorcerer's Apprentice" in "Fantasia," 1940; (bottom right) With Minnie Mouse in "Mickey's Birthday Party," 1942. (© Walt Disney Productions)

Figure 8-12 Walt Disney's "Fantasia" combined the work of the artist and the musician in what some consider to be the Disney Studio's best example of animation. (© Walt Disney Productions)

Mickey on a steamboat, bringing music out of everything from cow's teeth played like a xylophone to the drumming sounds of garbage cans. The picture was a success because cartoon characters did not need the peculiar microphone arrangements of real characters; sound could complement, not constrain. Following the success of *Steamboat Willie*, Disney's *Silly Symphonies* series combined music with animated dance and preliminary attempts at color. Then after three years of work on the project, Disney captured the hearts of the world as he set to animation *Snow White and the Seven Dwarfs*. Here the screen could capture much of the great techniques of directors and actors alike. With the use of animated close-ups, the audience was able to see the flawless beauty of Snow White and the varied expressions of the Seven Dwarfs. After all, how could any real-life film character compete with Sleepy, Dopey, or Grumpy? Disney was showing Hollywood and the world what he could do, and there was no one who could match him.

Many critics feel that his most creative efforts were unleashed in his 1940 production of *Fantasia* (Figure 8–12). Here Disney set his cartoon characters loose to dance and to act out the themes of great works of classical music. For example, Hyacinth Hippo dances with Ben Ali Gator to Ponchielli's "Dance of the Hours." Then Mickey Mouse, as Dukas' "Sorcerer's Apprentice," bewitches brooms to do water-carrying chores. Filmed in Technicolor, which now was able to bring the complete spectrum of color to the screen, *Fantasia* still stands as a classic example of the unique ability of animation to mix sound, sight, and color.

Disney continued to produce cartoon features. The little fawn *Bambi* both enchanted and scared the daylights out of young audiences in 1942.

Pinocchio made any child think twice about telling a lie, and *Dumbo* became a symbol of hope for children who doubted their importance. After World War II, Disney began adding real people to his cartoons. In *Song of the South*, animated birds and animals flirted with real people. By the 1950s Disney was working on Disneyland, and his films had expanded to include family features and nature documentaries.

The Stars

The 1930s also proved that the silent films did not have a corner on the comedy market. Comedy was alive and well, even among the female stars like Mae West. Her original roles displayed her buxom appearance and unrestrained sex appeal, but restrictions from the Hays office and Breen kept her reined in through much of her career. One of her best appearances was in *My Little Chickadee* (Figure 8–13) with comedian W. C. Fields. Fields was to sound what Chaplin had been to silents. He possessed both the voice and the physique to garner a laugh. He became known for his highly articulated speech and natural deviousness in cosmic portrayals. Along with *My Little Chickadee*, some of his most famous films include *The Bank Dick* and *Tillie and Gus*. Matching Fields in comic routines were the Marx brothers. Groucho, Harpo, and Chico had the irreverence of Fields, the style of Chaplin, and the ability to play one against the other in such films as *A Night at the Opera* and *Duck Soup*.

Figure 8-13   Mae West and W. C. Fields teamed up in "My Little Chickadee." Fields was to sound what Chaplin had been to silent films; the combination of his voice and physique added up to comedy. (© Freelance, Lansdale, PA)

Romance and intrigue arrived when Paramount Studios director Josef von Sternberg found Marlene Dietrich. The match worked financial wonders for Paramount. Dietrich became the star of shadows and mystery, lover and loved. Among others she played in *The Blue Angel*, *Blonde Venus*, and *The Devil Is a Woman*. Born in Berlin, Dietrich became an American citizen in 1937 and was honored during World War II for her overseas entertainment efforts.

Gary Cooper and Clark Gable also entered films in the thirties. Cooper, playing in famous roles opposite Dietrich, and Gable, who won an Academy Award in 1934 for *It Happened One Night*, were symbols of the macho male.

Other stars making their presence felt in the thirties and early forties included Jimmy Stewart, Jean Harlow, Spencer Tracy, Jackie Cooper, John Wayne, James Cagney, Humphrey Bogart, and Rita Hayworth. Joan Crawford starred in *No More Ladies*, while Robert Young of modern television fame and Betty Furness of consumer fame starred together in the 1936 M-G-M production of *Three Wise Guys*. Johnny Weissmuller, meanwhile, romped through the jungle in the *Tarzan* movies. Then Myrna Loy starred in *The Barbarian* which included a racy, nude bathtub scene. Fred Astaire and Ginger Rogers entertained audiences whenever they danced together, and Edward G. Robinson entertained them by being the original tough guy. Names such as William Powell in *The Thin Man*, Peter Lorre in *Mad Love*, Judy Garland in *Broadway Melody 1938*, and Greta Garbo in *Ninotchka* and *Camille*, all kept movie audiences flocking to the theaters. Even with the Great Depression of the early thirties, when attendance took a massive but temporary dip, the movies survived.

But the stars were only one of the attractions. It was the directors who made the industry and, consequently, stardom possible.

The Directors

In addition to being known for consistently casting Marlene Dietrich in his films, Josef von Sternberg was most at home with intrigue set in seamy places. From the foreign legion to the back street nightclub, von Sternberg loved focusing his shadows and dull lights on shady characters and bewitching women.

Breaking out of the studio into the freedom of the open spaces, John Ford used people and scenery in contrast with each other. In films like his most notable *Informer*, Ford used the camera to emphasize the facial expressions of the middle class in their life of survival and fight against the idle rich or political injustice.

Carrying contrast to the inner self, Howard Hawks (Figure 8–14) was most comfortable with actors of the Douglas Fairbanks era. Hawks went beyond action to the psychological, however, and contrasted courage and cowardice.

The year 1939 saw the arrival in the United States of Alfred Hitchcock.

The master of such later shockers as *The Birds* and *Psycho*, Hitchcock (Figure 8–15) brought these audiences such thrillers as *The Man Who Knew Too Much* and *The Thirty-Nine Steps*.

Figure 8-14 Director Howard Hawks was comfortable with the swashbuckling actors of the Douglas Fairbanks era.

Figure 8-15 Alfred Hitchcock became one of the great directors of movie intrigue. Some of his more familiar films include "Psycho," "The Birds," and "Frenzy."

Figure 8-16 "Gone With the Wind" was an epic production of the late 1930s, famous for numerous cinematic accomplishments. Well publicized was this embrace between Rhett Butler (Clark Gable) and Scarlett O'Hara (Vivien Leigh). (From the MGM release GONE WITH THE WIND © 1939, Selznick International Pictures, Inc. Copyright renewed 1967 by Metro-Goldwyn-Mayer, Inc.)

Figure 8-17 Orson Welles in "Citizen Kane." (National Film Information Service, Academy of Motion Picture Arts and Sciences)

Two films that stand out as "the" movies of the early sound era, however, are *Gone with the Wind* (Figure 8–16) and *Citizen Kane* (Figure 8–17). The former is considered so because of its lasting appeal to the masses, the latter because of its lasting appeal to critics and students of film.

Based on Margaret Mitchell's book of the same title, *Gone with the Wind* was the dream child of producer and studio head David O. Selznick. As soon as Mitchell's book became a best seller, Selznick bought the screen rights for $50,000, intending the movie to be his company's masterpiece. Later he voluntarily doubled the amount after profits on the film soared. Soon, however, the Selznick organization needed both financial and artistic help. The public wanted Clark Gable for the leading role, but Gable had a contract with M-G-M. Undeterred, Selznick convinced M-G-M to place $1 million into the picture and release Gable to star in it, giving the film company the distribution rights and half the profits in return. Even the *New York Times* became interested in the picture, lamenting in an editorial that the first actress chosen to play opposite Gable, Norma Shearer, declined the role. Vivian Leigh became the beguiling Scarlett O'Hara instead.

Throughout its production the American press constantly ran stories about the upcoming event, generating enough anticipation that regardless of what the final product was, America was ready to see the movie. Sidney Howard was hired to do the screen play but died before the picture was finished. Such well-known writers as Ben Hecht and F. Scott Fitzgerald were called in to finish the script. When the picture was officially released in 1939, it immediately filled theaters both in America and abroad. During World War II there were lines at box offices in England even during the raids. Among the records set by the film were its running time of 2 hours and 42 minutes and its collection of ten Academy Awards. Since its release, it has also chalked up the distinction of being one of television's biggest film spectaculars and has earned M-G-M close to $200 million.

If *Gone With the Wind* stands as the picture of this era with the most mass appeal, *Citizen Kane* stands as the film most heralded for its accomplishments in cinema. The director, who also saw to it that he starred in it and had a direct hand in virtually every phase of the production, was young Orson Welles. Welles had become famous through theater and his 1938 *War of the Worlds* radio broadcast. *Citizen Kane* was his first, his best, and practically his last fling at pictures.

Opening with shots of Charles Foster Kane near death, recalling his life, it moves to a shot of a small sled bearing the name of "Rosebud." Rosebud becomes a symbol of the film, contrasting the love and play of Kane's childhood to his adult life in pursuit of material things. Kane becomes a powerful and ruthless newspaper executive who will do anything to create a story, increase circulation, and boost profits. He tries to buy everything, including love, and spends much of his life in a California castle filled with museum artifacts, the symbols of his materialist life. Faintly resembling the life of William Randolph Hearst, Sr., the picture uses lighting and angle shots to the limit to accentuate the ferocious temperament of Kane and the massive walls of his castle. The film, despite its dismal box office showing, is still a popular favorite of film studies programs.

FILM THROUGH THE FIFTIES: CHANGES
AND TRENDS

World War II had an unusual effect on the movies. Directors produced government films, people escaped the realities of war by attending those pictures that Hollywood did turn out, and it postponed the inevitable breakup of the theater chains and distribution systems that the antitrust forces soon dissolved. It also took the industry's mind off a new invention that RCA's David Sarnoff had introduced at the 1939 World's Fair. That invention arrived in the fifties and with it, dramatic changes for motion pictures.

Transition to
Television

A business faced with monumental and almost overnight competition will do some unusual and hasty things to survive. Some work; some do not. Film was no exception. What could the industry do to counteract a movie screen that had been reduced to 21 inches and placed in the living room? How could motion pictures compete with "I Love Lucy" and the "Texaco Star Theatre," with Ed Sullivan and Milton Berle? It tried novelty, novelty in the form of *cinerama*.

Cinerama was more a process than a picture. Using multiple cameras and projectors, the audience was offered a visual spectacular with a huge screen expanded to ten times its usual size and "wrapped around" the audience. Peripheral vision made it all seem incredibly real. The first cinerama captured the visual feeling of clutching in the front seat of a roller coaster as it thundered up and down and around the curves, all in living color. Cinerama worked, but on a limited scale because only a select group of theaters were big enough or went to the trouble of buying equipment for it.

The next novelty was three-dimensional pictures, or *3-D*. Using separated images on the screen and bringing them together with the muted hues of a pair of special 3-D glasses, the audience looked more like a group of Martians with space goggles than like theater patrons. The idea did not work well because the movies that used the process were as bad as the glasses. Some of the most famous 3-D films were *It Came from Outer Space, Bwana Devil, House of Wax*, and *Creature from the Black Lagoon*.

Creature from the Black Lagoon, however, managed to take its place among some of the better science fiction features of the 1950s. John Baxter writing in *Science Fiction in the Cinema* called it "brilliant underwater photography." Even the relationship between the creature, Gill-Man, and the woman he desires managed to elicit positive reactions from critics. The film is still a popular feature of science fiction festivals and is distributed in its original 3-D version.

With the expense of cinerama and its limited distribution possibilities, and the short-lived novelty of 3-D, the industry next tried *cinemascope*. First introduced by Twentieth-Century Fox in the biblical story *The Robe*, cinemascope expanded the width of the screen to a two to five ratio but did not wrap it around the audience as cinerama did.

Along with cinemascope came new sound systems with names such as Warnerphonic and Kinevox Stereo. Other marketing labels attached to sound-visual sensations included Visterama, Vista Vision, Vectograph, and Vitascope. But through all the gimmicks and all the novelties, it became clear that if audiences were going to keep coming back, the industry needed more than wide screens, glasses, and fancy names. It needed big pictures.

Spectaculars

One solution was to produce epic pictures of proportions too big to be ignored by the public and the press. One of the first of the fifties was *Quo Vadis*. At a cost of $7 million, it was filmed in Rome where a cast of 5500 extras took part in a march to Nero's palace. Director Mervyn LeRoy guided Robert Taylor, Deborah Kerr, Peter Ustinov, and Leo Genn through scenes that saw them costarring with no less than twenty lions and two cheetahs. The success of *Quo Vadis*, which earned for M-G-M the most money it had seen since *Gone with the Wind*, made it clear that spectaculars had promise.

Another profitable spectacular was a remake of *Ben Hur*. This time M-G-M sunk $15 million into it as Charlton Heston raced chariots, again on location in Rome. Back home the movie won 12 Academy Awards.

The lure of the spectacular created a different kind of reaction at Twentieth-Century Fox. There *Cleopatra* went into production on the basis that a big event picture could not go wrong. It did. *Cleopatra*, starring Elizabeth Taylor, Richard Burton, and Rex Harrison, came out as the first and most lavish spectacular of the 1960s, but it flopped and cost the studio millions.

Other Solutions

Another solution to television, and something the movies did rather well, was social commentary. *Blackboard Jungle* brought to the screen the theme of juvenile delinquency with switch-blades and confrontations in schools. Then an unknown actor from a small town in Indiana came to the screen in *Rebel without a Cause*. James Dean (Figure 8–18) became the symbol of the teenager searching for identity, adventure, love, and life. After Dean was killed in an automobile crash, he became almost a spiritual guru of the teenage scene, and movie magazines played up his image for years.

Because television was faced with even more content restrictions than the motion picture industry was, movies sought to exercise what freedom of expression they did have to the limit. Elizabeth Taylor and Paul Newman starred in Tennessee William's play *Cat on a Hot Tin Roof*. From the plantation country of the deep South, a story of romance and tension unfolds as Paul Newman, the husband, refuses to make love to his wife, played by Elizabeth Taylor. Implied homosexuality is the result with outstanding performances by both stars. Taylor had also teamed up with Rock Hudson and James Dean for a temptuous love affair in the movie *Giant*. Sex symbol Mamie Van Doren also kept the theaters steaming with *The Beat Generation*, *Girls Town*, and *Born Reckless*.

The ever popular Westerns padded the box offices, especially when cast with major stars with John Wayne. Jimmy Stewart ended up in the Alaska gold fields in *The Far Country* and on the railroad in *Night Passage*. Western hero Audie Murphy starred in such films as *The Duel at Silver*

Figure 8-18 Natalie Wood starred with James Dean in "Rebel without a Cause."
(© Warner Bros.)

Creek and *Destry*. Victor Mature rode along in *Chief Crazy Horse*, Rock Hudson trailblazed in *Seminole*, and Jeff Chandler shot it out in *Pillars of the Sky*. By the time the 1960s rolled around, motion pictures had adapted to television so well that they were beginning to permit the medium to buy selected films for broadcast use and even attempted to produce some television movies themselves.

THE MODERN ERA: FINANCIAL TRANSITION

Financially the movie industry also began to change after the 1950s. In a nutshell, box office flops and big expenditures spelled financing.

Big Bank Financing

Sharp financial business managers have not always sat behind the desks of the motion picture corporations. Before television, creative geniuses, or "movie barons" as they were known, ruled the movie kingdom, and there was nothing that could not be sacrificed for the sake of creativity. If a picture went over its budget in adding the necessary glamour to suit the director's whim, over it went. The difference between then and now was that money seemed to stretch farther in those days.

Competition from television, however, required new management and new thinking within the industry. It thus entered a transitional period that brought management keen financial minds, people who could talk the language of accountants and bankers. Although creative talent was and continues to be the backbone of the industry, "dollars and cents" people began to make the final decisions.

The industry had changed in other ways as well. Because of required divestitures resulting from the 1948 decision of *U.S.* v. *Paramount et al.*, the motion picture companies were no longer in control of their own chains of theaters. No longer was a film assured a booking and an audience. The studies had been divorced from their distribution system, and a new element of risk was now involved.

At the same time, money became scarce, and financial risks became much greater. And remember, the industry was entering the era of the spectacular. The *Sound of Music* (Figure 8-19) was a typical example of a picture that went all out with script, stars, and financial backing in the $20 million range. Fortunately it was extremely successful at the box office. As we have seen, such movies created the theory that big scripts, big stars, and big money automatically meant big box office receipts.

Figure 8-19 Julie Andrews starred in "The Sound of Music," one of many big-budget, bank-financed movie spectaculars. (SOUND OF MUSIC, Copyright © 1965 Twentieth Century-Fox Film Corporation)

To obtain big money, the industry approached leading financial institutions to secure loans, but banks were not used to lending money under the risks common to the motion picture industry. So the industry had to prove that responsible management and financial safeguards were inherent in any given film enterprise. One of the banks' greater concerns was budget overruns. To counter this, film companies had to show that even though a director or producer might have a tremendous desire to shoot a special scene for a special effect, he or she would not jeopardize the budget. After all, the financial luxury of waiting thirty days for the weather to clear to achieve the proper lighting and scenery was not something upon which banks looked favorably. In order to further appease the banks, the industry also rearranged its contractual agreements with actors and actresses. The rule had been to guarantee a star a certain amount of money before the picture ever went into production, regardless of how well the movie did at the box office, but now film companies began to offer the stars a percentage of the box office receipts.

Some banks did give credit to come of the larger film makers on the basis of past film successes. For instance, a typical film company may produce 25 films in a year, five of which may prove quite successful, another five may be financial disasters, and the rest may come somewhere near the break-even point. On balance, then, the company's profit record seems a reasonable credit risk.

Film companies could also offer the banks collateral in the form of *in-the-can films*—movies which already had been run in movie theaters but whose income was still assured from re-releases and release to television. This was the type of collateral that appealed to banks. The fallacy, however, was in the formula. Big money did not necessarily mean big profits. Three New York banks found that out after they arranged a credit line of over $70 million to one major company for four movies, only one of which was profitable. In fact, some of the most popular bank-financed titles, such as *Hello Dolly*, did not live up to their financial expectations. As a result, some banks backed out of the movie financing business.

Low Budgets and Big Profits

A happy ending was in sight, however. Although some of the big-budget movies were bombing at the box office, some low-budget pictures were on the upswing. Turning the heads of the industry was *Easy Rider* which came in at a cost of about $500,000 and made about $20 million. Two others in the $3 million to $5 million range were *M*A*S*H* and *Butch Cassidy and the Sundance Kid*. Paul Newman and Robert Redford helped the latter considerably. It meant a new formula was possible, one with only one of the formerly essential ingredients—big stars.

Today movies in the $7 million range are permitting many producers and directors to experiment with their creative talents without endangering the financial structure of a movie company. This development has also allowed individual investors to get back into the movie financing business. People and organizations with a few million dollars to lend can reap tremendous profits if the movie is a success, yet they need not place their own corporate structure on the line in case of failure. This attitude has also given rise to more creative production flexibility, for if too tight a financial rein is placed on a production, creativity can suffer as well as quality. Today's producers have found that they can produce pictures of exceptional quality on reduced budgets, and the public is willing to accept them, sometimes even more eagerly than the spectaculars.

ACCENT ON YOUTH

The 1960s brought turmoil to America with the unpopular Vietnam War, the civil rights movement, the drug scene, and campus protests. Perhaps at no other time in recent history was a generation of young adults in such a quandary. The movies, which had been trying to find a theme and an audience to match it, stumbled onto this young adult audience.

First came the beach movies of the early 1960s with themes of California and sun. Teenagers were dancing, loving, swimming, and playing volleyball by the ocean, while bikinis were featured in such films as *Beach Party*, *Beach Blanket Bingo*, and *How to Stuff a Wild Bikini*. Elvis Presley took up the role in *Spinout* playing a singer and race driver.

Then as the decade progressed, an unknown star named Dustin Hoffman teamed up with Anne Bancroft and Katherine Ross, another unknown, in the picture *The Graduate* (Figure 8–20). Hoffman, who was an instant hit, portrayed a young college graduate who finishes his senior year without a job and little more going for him than his parents' rich friends, all giving him advice. His problems are compounded as he falls emotionally for Mrs. Robinson's daughter, played by Katherine Ross, and

Figure 8-20 Dustin Hoffman and Katherine Ross in "The Graduate." (Avco Embassy Pictures Corporation)

sexually for Mrs. Robinson, played by Anne Bancroft. Hoffman followed *The Graduate* with a starring role in *Midnight Cowboy*, a story about a male derelict and his friend, played by Jon Voight.

Even though low budget, the epitome of pictures of the sixties generation was *Easy Rider*. It brought to the screen the contrast between the establishment and the nonconformists, between clean living and drugs, all wrapped in the theme of directionless youth.

Thomas Laughlin continued the nonconformist theme in his portrayal of *Billy Jack*, a nonviolent hero who, when pushed far enough, could still stand up and fight. The story of an Indian war veteran on a reservation, *Billy Jack* became a cult movie by the 1970s, spawning two sequels, *The Trial of Billy Jack* and *Billy Jack Goes to Washington*. Word-of-mouth promotion campaigns and surprisingly low production costs made these films a huge success.

DIRECTORS LEAVE THEIR MARK

While movies were catering to their young adult audience with nonconformist themes and low budgets, still other films reassured the critics that creative directors had not all gone to the beach. The genius of Stanley Kubrick had emerged as early as 1962 in the movie *Lolita*. He enhanced that recognition, although not necessarily for a better picture, in *Dr. Strangelove, or How I Learned to Stop Worrying and Love the Bomb*. In *Dr. Strangelove*, country-western star Slim Pickens portrays a crew member on an Air Force bomber that mistakenly heads to Russia to drop its load. But the movie that propelled Kubrick into world fame was his 1968 production of *2001: A Space Odyssey* (Figure 8-21). Stars did not make the picture; Kubrick's creation of future interplanetary civilizations did, and without gimmicks. Kubrick carried his wild illusions further in *A Clockwork Orange*, a film about a futuristic society with sexual mannikins and violent perversions.

Figure 8-21 Stanley Kubrick's "2001: A Space Odyssey." (From the MGM release 2001: A SPACE ODYSSEY, © 1968 by Metro-Goldwin-Mayer, Inc.)

Figure 8-22 George C. Scott in "Patton." Expert use of camera technique placed Scott in the role of a larger-than-life leader who simultaneously displayed a love of war and a contempt for the bureaucracy which creates it. (PATTON, Copyright © 1969 Twentieth Century-Fox Film Corporation. All rights reserved.)

Examining the inner self and the search for reality, Italian director Michelangelo Antonioni brought to the screen such well-known pictures as his 1966 *Blow Up*. Two sex scenes in the movie caused such a stir that in South Dakota, a local Baptist minister demanded the film be banned from the city theater. A much deeper meaning than the sex, however, is the search by a photographer to find meaning in his life. That meaning had been treated earlier in Antonioni's *Red Desert*, in which a woman examines her life in relation to the people and things surrounding her.

Director Federico Fellini's films brought an explicit visual realism to the screen, achieving a height of emotional vigor difficult to match. The human condition reflected in both individuals and society in his films was presented in sometimes shocking form. Fellini explored the mind in his 1963 production of *8½*, dwelt on fanciful illusions in *La Dolce Vita*, and expanded this in *Juliet of the Spirits*. On location in Rome, Fellini shot *Fellini Satyricon* and *Roma*, which display the cynicism and grotesqueness for which he is noted.

Other directors of the 1960s and 1970s who stand out for their individual achievements include Franklin Schaffner, who directed George C. Scott in *Patton*, one of his most powerful roles (Figure 8-22). The expert use of camera techniques created a larger-than-life leader of men who displayed both a fanatical love of war and an equal contempt for the bureaucracy that created it. Interestingly enough, it managed to appeal to both the hawks and doves of the Vietnam War era. Roman Polanski received rave reviews directing Mia Farrow in *Rosemary's Baby* and brought the underworld of the 1930s to life in *Chinatown*. William Friedkin directed *The French Connection*, a powerful film about an international drug ring, and the *Exorcist*, an equally powerful movie about mental powers. Francis Ford Coppola brought us *The Godfather*, while Alfred Hitchcock directed Tony Perkins and Janet Leigh in *Psycho*. Peter Bogdanovich's *The Last Picture Show* was another favorite of the film set. And David Lean, who had been well accepted as a director in the 1940s and 1950s, directed the beautiful 1965 production of *Dr. Zhivago* as well as the 1970 production of *Ryan's Daughter*.

DRAWING CARDS: VIOLENCE AND SEX

While the peace movement was flourishing, the motion picture industry was swelling with violence. In the bullet category, *Bonnie and Clyde* took top honors. Directed by Arthur Penn and starring Faye Dunaway and Warren Beatty, the gangster movie climaxed with machine guns riddling the two stars. More vintage firearms were used in director Sam Peckinpah's *The Wild Bunch*. Raw guts and guns came to the screen as a new star named Clint Eastwood spent time looking down both ends of a gun barrel in such pictures as *Hang 'Em High* and *Dirty Harry*. Steve McQueen starred as a police officer in *Bullet*, noted for its famous chase scenes.

The audiences that violence could not lure to the box office, sex did. *Midnight Cowboy* had an X rating. Jane Fonda lay nude inside a science fiction love-making tube in *Barbarella*, and *A Clockwork Orange* detailed future sex. Swapping sex was the theme of *Bob and Carol and Ted and Alice*. Prostitution appeared in such films as *Irma La Douce*, starring Jack Lemmon, and sexual fantasy was the theme of *Belle de Jour*. Two films, *I Am Curious Yellow* and *Carnal Knowledge*, contained such explicit scenes that they provoked court cases testing the power of censorship. Yet even harder-core sex appeared in the 1973 production of *Last Tango in Paris* starring Marlon Brando. Receiving attention as more serious X-rated films of the era were *Deep Throat* and *The Devil in Miss Jones*.

EMERGING BLACK FILMS AND BLACK STARS

By the 1960s and 1970s race relations were being treated with some degree of reality. Stars such as James Earl Jones, Lola Falana, Roscoe Lee Browne, and James Brown helped to focus this reality.

Of all the black stars, however, Sidney Poitier probably did more to call attention to the black actor as a serious star with major audience appeal. Poitier was a hit in Ralph Nelson's production of *Lilies of the Field*. He then played a powerful role in *In the Heat of the Night* as a black New York police detective who is stranded in a small southern community. While he is there, the detective finds himself working on a murder case with the town's bigoted white police chief, played by Rod Steiger. The film brings realistic racial tension to the screen but concludes with a lesson in racial harmony. Still another Poitier film was *To Sir with Love*, in which he played a schoolteacher who wins the respect of white students in trouble. In *Guess Who's Coming to Dinner* he portrayed a doctor marrying into an aristocratic, white family.

Other black stars followed Poitier's lead. Singer Diana Ross starred as Billie Holiday in the well-received *Lady Sings the Blues*, and Pamela Grier played in *Coffy, Foxy Brown,* and *Sheba Baby.* From television to recordings, Richard Roundtree's role in M-G-M's *Shaft* had audiences intrigued with a new "hip" private eye. The actor even starred in two spin-off sequels: *Shaft's Big Score* and *Shaft Goes to Africa.* Diahann Carroll and James Brown appeared in *The Split.* The screen had come a long way from the racist 1915 production of *The Birth of a Nation.*

RECENT EPICS

If three types of films could best represent the 1970s, they would be disaster films, shark films, and science fiction. The former found their way onto the screen with *The Poseidon Adventure*, which showed an ocean liner sinking with most of its passengers trapped inside. This ocean adventure was followed by fire in *The Towering Inferno* and by crumbling buildings in *Earthquake.* Airplanes and dirigibles also became part of the act. Fear at 30,000 feet was so successful for the movie *Airport*, starring Dean Martin and George Kennedy, that it begot *Airport 1975, Airport 1977,* and yet another, *Airport '79,* which featured the fast-flying Concorde jet.

A movie realistic approach to big-action suspense was played by George C. Scott in his role of a German colonel assigned to travel with the dirigible *Hindenburg* to try to prevent sabotage. Using original footage from the actual Hindenburg crash, the picture was one of the better disaster epics, winning an Academy Award for special effects.

Although they produced their own low-budget copies, *Jaws* and *Jaws II* kept many theaters in the black during the seventies. *Jaws* was the brainchild of author Peter Benchley who wrote the book and publicized it in serial form in a leading magazine. Released at the beginning of the summer of 1975, it was not long before the "Jaws" fad took the country by storm. The film was successful enough to give Universal City Studios a 25 percent share of the United States and Canadian film market for 1975 and to become the all-time box office record breaker. For producers Richard Zanuck and David Brown and director Steven Spielberg, it meant millions in personal income.

Science Fiction and Special Effects

As for science fiction, few films could equal the dazzling display of special effects in *Star Wars*. With a likable pair of robots, *Star Wars* (Figure 8–23) was the sleeper film that broke all-time box office records. It was pure fantasy, but it brought forth a new wave of interest in science fiction and a definite wave of profits. Followed by the more realistic but equally majestic *Close Encounters of the Third Kind*, creatures from outer space were becoming bigger stars than earthlings.

Similar science fiction fare arrived with *Meteor, The Humanoid,* in which a world of tomorrow is menaced by a super human force. The tale

Figure 8-23 (Left) Science fiction and special effects combined to offer a dazzling display of cinema in "Star Wars." The movie led a string of science-fiction features, which included sequels as well as other themes, including "Close Encounters of a Third Kind."

Figure 8-24 (Below) Using a collection of some of motion picture history's classic suspense techniques and special effects, "Raiders of the Lost Ark" succeeded at both the box office and in the critics' columns.

of a professor looking for ultimate truths in drugs and isolation tanks appeared in *Altered States*, Sean Connery came back from space in *Outland*. The success of *Star Wars* was followed by sequels, including *The Empire Strikes Back* and *The Revenge of the Jedi. Star Trek, The Motion Picture* beamed upon the screen and was followed by *Star Trek II, The Wrath of Khan*. Steven Speilberg followed *Jaws* with the successful *Close Encounters of the Third Kind* and *Poltergeist*, a science fiction-horror combination. But the movie which encompassed the magic of Disney-like fantasy and employed the gamut of human emotions as well as special effects was Speilberg's *E.T.* A lovable creature from outer space is stranded in a California suburb. Befriended by a neighborhood child and his friends, *E.T.* is protected from harm until a space ship returns and rescues the lost alien. In *E.T.*, Speilberg proved he was equally capable of capturing hearts as he was of controlling his medium.

SUSPENSE TO SENTIMENTALITY

From the archives of what made the movie thrillers of the past, the spectacular *Raiders of the Lost Ark* (Figure 8-24) emerged, starring Harrison Ford with the team of George Lucas of *Star Wars* fame and directed by Steven Spielberg of *Jaws* fame. Also released were such spine-tingling horror films as Brian DePalma's *Dressed to Kill* and Stanley Kubrick's *The Shining*. The former played on suspense and quick action, the latter on the naturalistic portrayal of a berserk middle-age male. On the lighter side, the award-winning Broadway play *Annie* was adapted to the screen by Columbia Pictures.

FILM AND VIDEO

The motion picture industry has experienced a number of technological changes during its brief history. Some have spurred the industry forward, as sound did, moving the industry out of silence and into the "talkies," and color, which was shown in all its early majesty in *Fantasia* and *Gone with the Wind*. Other technology, such as television, added a new way to distribute programs but also competed for theater's audiences.

The Technology

The "video revolution" has resulted in new ways to distribute visual art forms such much different from the 35mm film used to show the latest features in a shopping center movie house. The consumer is increasingly tempted by other viewing experiences. By purchasing a home videotape recorder, people can rent or purchase feature-length films (Figure 8-25) and watch them at home as often as they like. Even videotape rental costs are competitive with movie theater admission tickets.

Videodisc, a platter about the size of a phonograph record, permits still another means of distribution. By using light through different optical reproduction systems, damage to the disc, such as scratches, do not affect the quality of the reproduction. Both videotapes and discs provide a secure means of storing color images which can fade when stored on film.

Billboard R — Survey For Week Ending 12/19/81

Videocassette Top 40 ™

These are best selling videocassettes compiled from retail sales, including releases in both Beta & VHS formats.

This Week	Last Position	Weeks on Chart	TITLE Copyright Owner, Distributor, Catalog Number
1	1	5	KRAMER VS. KRAMER Columbia Pictures 10355
2	4	9	STIR CRAZY Columbia Pictures 10248E
3	2	9	THE BLUE LAGOON Columbia Pictures 10025E
4	3	7	FRIDAY THE 13TH II Paramount Pictures, Paramount Home Video 1457
5	5	9	ENDLESS LOVE MCA 77001
6	7	5	THE THIEF Magnetic Video 4550
7	6	12	THE JAZZ SINGER Paramount Pictures, Paramount Home Video 2305
8	10	17	RAGING BULL United Artists, Magnetic Video 4523
9	13	5	THE POSTMAN ALWAYS RINGS TWICE CBS 700077
10	8	12	BUSTIN' LOOSE Universal City Studios, MCA Dist. Corp. 77002
11	18	6	MEATBALLS Paramount Pictures, Paramount Home Video 1324
12	19	17	NIGHTHAWKS Universal City Studios Inc., MCA Dist. Corp. 71000
13	14	19	CASABLANCA United Artists, Magnetic Video 4514
14	11	6	ATLANTIC CITY Paramount Pictures, Paramount Home Video 1460
15	16	17	TESS Columbia Pictures 10543
16	12	13	DRESSED TO KILL Warner Bros. Inc./Warner Home Video 26006
17	17	8	THE COMPETITION Columbia Pictures 10124E
18	9	5	THE GOODBYE GIRL CBS 700069
19	15	28	ORDINARY PEOPLE (ITA) Paramount Pictures, Paramount Home Video 8964
20	24	4	BACK ROADS CBS 70071
21	23	7	SEEMS LIKE OLD TIMES Columbia Pictures 10475E
22	27	5	USED CARS Columbia Pictures 10557
23	28	45	AIRPLANE (ITA) Paramount Pictures, Paramount Home Video 1305
24	NEW ENTRY		AN AMERICAN WEREWOLF IN LONDON MCA 77004
25	32	4	CHITTY CHITTY BANG BANG Magnetic Video 4557
26	NEW ENTRY		BREAKER MORANT Columbia Pictures 8300
27	26	5	THE MALTESE FALCON Magnetic Video 4530
28	33	3	DOGS OF WAR Magnetic Video 4569
29	38	3	THE GOOD, THE BAD & THE UGLY Magnetic Video 4545
30	34	8	HAPPY BIRTHDAY TO ME Columbia Pictures 10595
31	NEW ENTRY		FOUR SEASONS MCA 77003
32	22	6	THE FAN Paramount Pictures, Paramount Home Video 1469
33	20	5	BANANAS Magnetic Video 4555
34	30	23	BLACK STALLION (ITA) United Artists, Magnetic Video 4503
35	21	7	HALLOWEEN Media Home Entertainment M131
36	29	22	AND JUSTICE FOR ALL Columbia Pictures 10015
37	31	42	FAME (ITA) MGM/CBS Home Video M70027
38	37	2	GOING APE Paramount Pictures, Paramount Home Video 1398
39	25	28	ELEPHANT MAN (ITA) Paramount Pictures, Paramount Home Video 1347
40	39	2	ORCA: THE KILLER WHALE Paramount Pictures, Paramount Home Video 8935

Figure 8-25 With new technologies opening up new opportunities for viewing, the marketing and popularity of feature-length films through video-cassette and other media offer new outlets for producers and the motion picture industry. Although the traditional movie theatre will be competing for the box-office dollars, the opportunity for income from other "video" outlets shows promise. (© Billboard publications)

Although some people believe video has advantages over film, others strongly disagree. Some artists who work with film and have learned to appreciate its unique qualities as an art form resist using video such as tape or discs. Others have bridged the gap and have combined both video and film, especially for special effects work. At the heart of the medium, however, is the projection system and the viewing experience.

Projection Systems

While video has provided alternatives to film as a means of capturing visual images, projections systems have also changed. Large-screen television projections are becoming more commonplace, if not in the average home, at least in restaurants and in the media rooms of some more affluent video consumers. Large-screen, high-definition television permits video viewing to approach the size qualities of the movie theatre. Cable television, the plush lounge seats of a living room or den, and a large-screen television with a videotape recorder or videodisc can be a tempting alternative to getting in the car, driving to a movie theater, and paying admission prices for a one-time viewing. High-definition television will soon give large-screen television much greater clarity than current large-screen images, thus erasing some of the competitive edge of 35mm film.

The Viewing Experience

How is the motion picture industry adjusting to these changes in recording and distribution? Some theaters are making major investments in redesigning theaters and the technology they house, such as larger viewing screens, improved sound systems, and even three-dimensional viewing without glasses. Still other alternates will be to switch to the high-resolution television projection systems. Instead of shuffling first-release films between theaters, these $1000-plus prints may be replaced by satellite-fed systems or video recordings which would be less costly but would retain picture quality.

Also needed are sophisticated studies using the latest techniques of behavioral science research to determine exactly what an individual experiences when he or she sits in a darkened theater and watches a motion picture. What psychological factors operate to make the experience more satisfying than sitting at home watching the same program? When these questions can be answered, the studios may be on their way to understanding and capitalizing on the future, whatever that means in terms of technology and viewing experiences.

SUMMARY

In theory, we can trace motion pictures back to the era of pictographics when cave paintings attempted to express the illusion of motion. By the 1800s motion pictures became a reality as Thomas Edison invented the motion picture camera in America, and the Lumière brothers in France invented a projection device. Early films were short and easily satisfied their patrons. Gradually, as directors like D. W. Griffith and Mack Sennett offered more creative camera techniques and story lines, the public thirst for films grew, and makeshift studios were built to accommodate production of these new films. People especially developed an interest in movie stars. Charlie Chaplin, Buster Keaton, Laurel and Hardy, Mary Pickford, and Douglas Fairbanks were among the early idols.

In 1927 sound was introduced to motion pictures, and they became a novelty all over again. Creativity stood still as sound moved forward, but finally, Mamoulian placed two microphones at different locations, thus unleashing the constaints that had plagued directors and actors.

Even through the depression of the 1930s, the movies flourished. Studio profits were plowed back into bigger productions and lavish sound stages. World War II promoted the boom. Then in the 1950s, film met a new competitor—television. Panic attempts to lure audiences back to the movies came up with such novelty technology as 3-D, cinerama, and cinemascope. Movies also adapted with a series of low-budget films, a few spectaculars, and themes of juvenile delinquency.

The 1960s and 1970s witnessed changes in the financial structure of movies as studios were purchased by corporate conglomerates more concerned about profits than about creativity. Bank financing also became common, although some box office failures were too much for conservative financiers. The movies themselves began to search for an audience and found it in young adults. Pictures about the "now" generation thus became the vogue, followed by sexual liberation and violence. Disaster epics, shark films, and science fiction seemed to characterize the 1970s, and prospects for the early 1980s see a new trend in full-length feature cartoons.

Video may play a significant role in the future of motion pictures. The technology of videotape, video discs, and high-resolution and big-screen television—all available to consumers for home use—will compete with the motion picture theater. Changes in theater design, projection systems, and the merger of film and videotape in studio production may make motion picture distribution and viewing a different experience in the future.

OPPORTUNITIES FOR FURTHER LEARNING

ALLEN, R. C., and D. GOMERY, *Film History: Theory and Practice.* Reading, Mass.: Addison Wesley, 1983.

BOHN, T. W., AND R. L. STROMGREN, *Light and Shadows,* 2nd ed. Sherman Oaks, Calif.: Alfred Publishing Co., Inc., 1978.

BONDANELLA, P., ed., *Federico Fellini: Essays in Criticism.* New York: Oxford University Press, 1978.

DICKSTEIN, M., ed., *Great Film Directors: A Critical Anthology.* New York: Oxford University Press, 1978.

EIDSVIK, C., *Cineliteracy: Film among the Arts.* New York: Random House, 1978.

FIELD, S., *Screenplay: the Foundations of Screenwriting—A Step-by-Step Guide from Concept to Finished Script.* New York: Delta, 1979.

GIANNETTI, L. D., *Understanding Movies,* 2nd ed. Englewood Cliffs, N.J.: Prentice-Hall, 1976.

GIUSTINI, R., *The Filmscript: A Guide for Writers.* Englewood Cliffs, N.J.: Prentice-Hall, 1980.

GOLDBERG, R., *Performance: Live Art 1909 to the Present*. New York: Abrams, 1979.

GRANT, B. K., ed., *Film Genre: Theory and Criticism*. Metuchen, N.J.: Scarecrow, 1977.

GUNTER, J., *Super 8: The Modest Medium*. Paris: UNESCO, 1977.

JOWETT, G., and J. M. Linton, *Movies as Mass Communication*. Beverly Hills, Calif.: Sage Publications, Inc., 1980.

KINDEM, G. A., ed., *The American Movie Industry: The Business of Motion Pictures*. Carbondale, Ill.: Southern Illinois University Press, 1982.

LEESE, E., *Costume Design in the Movies*. New York: Ungar, 1977.

LONDON, M., *Getting into Film*. New York: Ballantine, 1977.

MARILL, A. H., *Movies Made for Television: The Telefeature and the Mini-Series, 1964–1979*. Westport, Conn.: Arlington House, 1980.

MAST, G., *A Short History of the Movies*, 3rd ed. Chicago: University of Chicago Press, 1981.

MAST, G., AND M. COHEN, eds., *Film Theory and Criticism*. New York: Oxford University Press, 1979.

MAY, M., *Screening out the Past: The Birth of Mass Culture and the Motion Picture Industry*. New York: Oxford University Press, 1980.

McCABE, J., *Charlie Chaplin*. New York: Doubleday, 1978.

MERCER, J., *Glossary of Film Terms*. Philadelphia: Department of Radio-TV-Film, Temple University, 1978.

MONACO, J., *American Film Now: The People, The Power, The Money, The Movies*. New York: Oxford University Press, 1979.

MUYBRIDGE, E., *Muybridge's Complete Human and Animal Locomotion: All 781 Plates from the 1887 Animal Locomotion*. New York: Dover, 1979.

RYAN, R. T., *A History of Motion Picture Color Technology*. New York/London: Focal Press, 1978.

SAMPSON, H. T., *Blacks in Black and White: A Source Book on Black Films*. Metuchen, N.J.: Scarecrow, 1977.

SITNEY, P. A., *Visionary Film: The American Avant-Garde, 1943–1978*. New York: Oxford University Press, 1979.

TYNAN, K., *Show People: Profiles in Entertainment*. London: Weidenfeld and Nicholson, 1979.

WILLIAMS, C. T., *The Dream beside Me: The Movies and the Children of the Forties*. Rutherford, N.J.: Fairleigh Dickinson University Press, 1980.

CHAPTER

THE RECORDING INDUSTRY

PREVIEW

After completing this chapter, we should be able to:

Understand the scope of the recording industry.

Trace the history of the recording industry back to broadsides and sheet music.

Discuss Thomas Edison's contribution to the recording industry.

Distinguish between the graphophone and gramophone.

Identify the role Joseph P. Maxfield played in perfecting electrical recording.

Describe the "battle of the speeds."

Discuss the impact that tape, television, and stereo had upon the recording industry.

Talk about the development of rock and roll, disco, and country music formats.

Explain the process of making a hit record.

Understand charts and playlists.

Be aware of the economic issues facing the recording industry.

What images come to mind when we think of the recording industry? The support for virtually every type of electronic mass communication, the industry is synonymous with multimillion-dollar studios, rock bands, promoters, albums, concerts, stars, excitement—and perhaps heartbreak.

To the musicians it means Nashville, London, Chicago, New York, Paris, and Los Angeles. To the electronic engineer it is echo chambers, reverbs, microphones, and synthesizers.

SCOPE OF THE RECORDING INDUSTRY

The recording industry today is an international, billion-dollar enterprise. In the United States alone, more than 1200 companies are producing and releasing records and tapes; approximately 2600 different record and tape labels are sold; 60,000 stores sell records and tapes; approximately 73 million phonographs are in use; and in any one year, as many as 2600 albums and 6200 singles will be released. Retail sales of records in the United States are in excess of $2 billion annually. In fact, the United States is the largest consumer of recorded music with approximately 36 percent of the world market. What types of music are the most popular? Contemporary music by far, accounting for over 61.4 percent of sales. Country music follows with 11.7 percent. Figure 9–1 examines other musical types, showing that middle-of-the-road music accounts for 11.1 percent, classical for 5.4 percent, jazz with 4.6 percent, children's music at 2.3 percent, and comedy with 1.6 percent.

To understand how the recording industry achieved such success, we need to go back before radio, before disc jockeys, even before the phonograph.

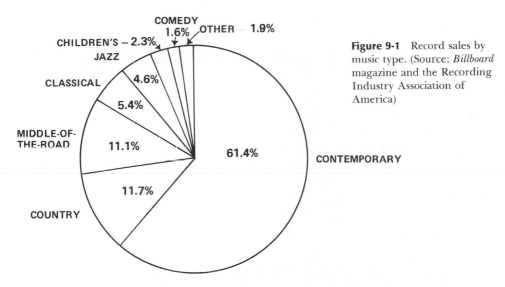

Figure 9-1 Record sales by music type. (Source: *Billboard* magazine and the Recording Industry Association of America)

PRERECORDING ERA: BROADSIDES AND SHEET MUSIC

The first use of music as a means of mass communication is credited to the print medium. Long before the concept of electronics, a new song was published on paper and inserted inside a decorated cover to be played on the piano or other appropriate musical instrument of the time. *Published* meant just that, produced by a printing press and distributed the same way a book was. Music publishing in the eighteenth century took the form of *broadsides*, which were musical editorials on some important political event of the day and were printed on a rather large sheet of primarily rag content paper, hence its name.[1] The broadside's purpose was not actually to publish music but rather to act like a newspaper "extra." Inside would be news of the day and the accompanying comical verse set to a familiar tune satirizing some newsworthy event.

Sheet music, those separate publications devoted entirely to musical selections, arrived later as the American Revolution whetted appetites for patriotic songs. *The Yankee Man of War*, in honor of the deeds of the famous Captain John Paul Jones, and *The Liberty Song* were typical of songs in the late eighteenth century. Some of the songs first appeared in newspapers; then if their popularity warranted it, they received separate publication status as sheet music. Typical of these was the song *Independence*, first published in the *Freeman's Journal*, a full month before the signing of the Declaration of Independence in 1776. Another popular tune of the era was the famous *Yankee Doodle*. Actually this song was in existence before the American Revolution, having been part of a larger selection published as part of a comic opera in 1767. It evolved as a separate song about 1780, published in London under the title *Yankee Doodle or (as Now Christened by the Saints of New England) The Lexington March* (Figure 9–2). Instructions were given to the effect that "the Words to be sung thro' the Nose, & in the West Country drawl and dialect."

Figure 9-2 The first separate version of "Yankee Doodle" published as sheet music in London about 1780. Numerous variations of the verse were published in later years in Boston, New York, and Philadelphia. (Source: Harry Dicter and Elliott Shapiro, *Handbook of Early American Sheet Music 1768–1889*. New York: Dover Publications, Inc. 1977)

Figure 9-3 The phase "music publishing," which today involves records, originated from the publication of songs as sheet music. To entice people to purchase sheet music many published selections were decorated with photographs and ornate borders. (Source: R. A. Fremont, ed., *Favorite Songs of the Nineties.* New York: Dover Publications, Inc., 1973)

The War of 1812 also produced its share of sheet music favorites. The most famous American tune is credited to author Francis Scott Key, who wrote what became our national anthem during the defense of Fort McHenry near Baltimore. Although the verse is credited to Key, the tune itself had appeared in many versions prior to 1814. Titled *Anacreon in Heaven*, the tune was composed by the Englishman John Stafford Smith and appeared as early as 1798.

Sheet music (Figure 9–3) remained the usual method of music distribution in the nineteenth century, and the politics of the times produced a wide selection of popular songs. Presidential campaigns were naturals for sheet music publishers. The most popular selections were marches such as *President John Quincy Adam's Grand March*, published by G. E. Blake of Philadelphia about 1825, and then there was the *Fillmore Quick Step*, published by Miller & Beacham of Baltimore in 1856, and the *Lincoln Quick Step*, published by Lee and Walker of Philadelphia in 1860.

Even tobacco provided themes for such sheet music as *The Light Cigar* and *Think and Smoke Tobacco*.

The War Between the States continued the sheet music craze, and both the war and the celebration of its conclusion packed music sellers' shelves. One of the most enduring songs appearing in sheet music between 1860 and 1869 was *Dixie* by Dan Emmett, appearing under the original title of *I Wish I Was in Dixie's Land* by Firth, Pond & Co. of New York and later reproduced, some say *pirated*, by P. P. Werlein of New Orleans. Werlein changed some of the lyrics, as typified by this first line of the Firth edition, "I wish I was in de land ob cotton," which the Werlein edition changed to, "I wish I was in the land of cotton." Another popular favorite was *The Little Brown Jug*, published by J. E. Winner of Philadelphia.

Sheet music continues to be sold by most major retail stores, and the recording industry is still plagued by people pirating songs and selling them through infringing on their copyright. But the widespread practice of pirating began to diminish when the international copyright agreements were reached in 1891 and President Benjamin Harrison issued the U.S. International Copyright Proclamation on July 1 of that year. By then the era of sheet music was beginning to feel the effects of competition from an odd-looking machine called the *phonograph*.

BEGINNINGS OF ACOUSTICAL RECORDING

The story of the phonograph began in Thomas Edison's small laboratory in West Orange, New Jersey (Figure 9–4) where he worked on a device to improve the telegraph.

The Phonograph: Edison and Cros

The problem was to devise a way in which the dots and dashes of the Morse telegraph could be captured on a paper that later could be played back. Edison was fascinated by communication. The Western Union Telegraph Company was using his improved carbon transmitter in competition with Bell and had developed a system in which four telegraph signals could be sent over the same wire. As Edison played the "paper tape" back to hear the Morse code, the increased speed sounded much like rhythmic tones of the voice. An idea developed. Why not record the human voice in the same way that the Morse code had been recorded? In 1877, although the exact date is somewhat obscured by history, Edison sketched a crude drawing and had his assistant manufacture the machine that Edison envisioned would "talk back" to its speaker. The device consisted of a metal cylinder around which Edison wrapped a form of tin foil. Connected to a diaphragm was a needle which touched the tin foil. A second diaphragm and needle was used for playback. As the cylinder turned, the needle would vibrate on the tin foil, making an indentation. This indentation would then reproduce the sound after the needle was returned to its starting position, then played back over the cylinder. The question was, would it work? With exacting care, Edison placed the needle in position, and as he hand-cranked the cylinder, recited the poem, "Mary Had a Little Lamb" into the diaphragm. The playback stylus was placed in position, and as Edison turned the crank, he was "taken aback" by the

Figure 9-4 Thomas Edison in his lab in West Orange, New Jersey. On the table is an improved version of the cylinder phonograph he invented in 1877. (U.S. Department of the Interior, National Park Service, Edison National Historic Site)

Figure 9-5 Edison's original phonograph, patented in 1877, consisted of a piece of foil wrapped around a rotating cylinder. The sound waves of his voice, as Edison spoke into a recording horn (not shown), caused a vibration, which in turn caused the stylus to cut grooves into the tin foil. The first sound recording was Edison reciting the poem, "Mary Had a Little Lamb." (U.S. Department of the Interior, National Park Service, Edison National Historic Site and the Recording Industry Association of American)

little machine saying, "Mary Had a Little Lamb." Using the Greek words for "sound writer" the new invention was christened the *phonograph* (Figure 9–5).

History has confirmed that Edison later took the machine to the editorial offices of *Scientific American*. There under the witness of eager reporters, he demonstrated the phonograph. One eyewitness said, "The machine inquired as to our health, asked us how we liked the phonograph, informed us that *it* was very well, and bid us a cordial good night. These remarks were not only perfectly audible to ourselves, but to a dozen or more persons gathered around." On Christmas Eve, 1877, Thomas A. Edison filed for a patent on the phonograph. Sound recording was born.

It is interesting to note that while Edison was busy inventing the phonograph, a Frenchman had already conceived the idea, although he had never managed to apply it practically. Charles Cros, a poet and tinkerer, wrote a paper in which he envisioned a "phonograph" that would record speech and play it back for the listener. Cros' idea was quite similar to Edison's and used a stylus to imprint a groove in a disc. Edison's machine used a cylinder. Cros never built the device that he imagined but did file a sealed paper describing it with the Academie des Sciences. He later requested the paper be read, presumably on hearing the news of Edison's machine in the United States. Although both men had the same idea and both used the term *phonograph*, Edison remains the recognized inventor of sound recording with the cylinder machine that cited, "Mary Had a Little Lamb."

Despite its accomplishments, the phonograph was far from becoming the medium of home entertainment that it is today. The little tin foil cylinder wore out after a few plays, and it only took a couple of minutes for the stylus to travel the length of the cylinder. Still, it looked profitable, and Edison formed the Edison Speaking Phonograph Company in 1878. One of his backers was none other than Gardner Hubbard, Alexander Graham Bell's father-in-law. The phonograph became the hit of the vaudeville circuit as entertainers demonstrated it to audiences willing to pay for the privilege of hearing a few words of prose or a few measures of song. The entire venture lasted less than a year, and although it was profitable while the novelty lasted, Edison's commitment to the electric light, plus a lack of time and resources, sent the whole idea into early retirement, at least temporarily.

The Graphophone: Bell and Tainter

It is understandable that with Alexander Graham Bell's father-in-law backing Edison's venture, Bell would keep an eye on the phonograph's development. After winning the $10,000 Volta Prize from the French government for the invention of the telephone, Bell founded the Volta Laboratories in Washington, D.C., in 1880. There he hired an English relative, Chichester Bell (Figure 9–6) and an American technician named Charles Tainter to begin work improving the Edison machine. They developed an improved version of the phonograph and called it the *graphophone*. The graphophone differed from the phonograph in two important ways: (1) the cylinder used a wax coating instead of tin foil, which permitted a clearer sound though one not as loud as the phonograph,

Figure 9-6 Chichester A. Bell, cousin of Alexander Graham Bell, who worked on sound recording in the Volta Laboratories. He teamed up with Charles Tainter to improve on the Edison machine by developing the graphophone. (Courtesy, A.T.&T.)

and (2) the stylus or needle encasement floated on the wax cylinder. Bell and Tainter were not interested in stealing Edison's idea, but Edison apparently did not think so. When Bell and Tainter visited him with their new invention, he decided that the two men had invaded sacred territory.

Bell and Tainter wanted Edison to help them perfect, market, and manufacture their graphophone. But Edison, suddenly faced with competition, developed a new interest in the phonograph. Meanwhile Bell and Tainter gained financial support from a group of Washington, D.C. business executives and formed the American Graphophone Corporation in 1877. Acquiring a treadle to replace the hand crank, the new graphophone hit the market as a definite step above the phonograph. Edison counterattacked by adding an electric motor to his phonograph and incorporating solid wax cylinders that could be shaved and reused. Subsequent refinements resulted in a machine with multiple earphones which permitted upwards of ten people to listen at the same time (Figure 9-7).

Before the corporate war heated up, a Philadelphia businessman decided to enter the sound recording business and gained control of the distribution rights for both the phonograph and the graphophone. Jesse Lippincott had the right idea, but he went about it the wrong way. Taking his cue from the telephone company, he decided the best way to make money was to lease the machines instead of letting people buy them. Lippincott divided the country into territories, but it was not long before the whole venture began to collapse. The only territory making any money was that assigned to the Columbia Phonograph Company, which had secured the distribution franchise for Washington, D.C., and could service the government offices with dictating machines.

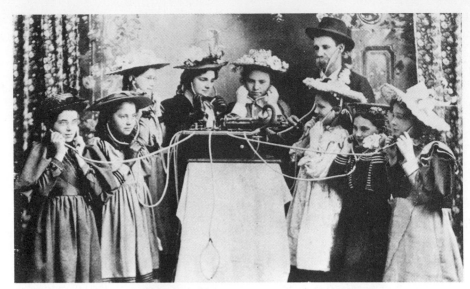

Figure 9-7 An improved version of the cylinder phonograph with multiple earphones, permitting up to ten people to listern at the same time. (Recording Industry Association of America)

Figure 9-8 A view of one of the phonograph parlors which helped to popularize recordings during the 1890s. These machines were the forerunners of the home phonograph and the jukebox. (Library of Congress and the Recording Industry Association of America)

Soon some poor, rebellious salespersons on the West Coast threw corporate image to the wind and started leasing the machines to a San Francisco saloon. There, patrons began to stand in line to plug a nickel into the machines and be "talked to" by the phonograph (Figure 9–8). What was supposed to be the distinguished mechanical contribution to the offices of the country became the bawdy boon to the saloon business. Yet, despite their interest in the amusing apparatus, saloons did not rescue the American Graphophone Company. It went the way of the tin foil phonograph. The lone survivor was the Columbia group which kept its fiscal head above water and gained control of the Bell-Tainter patents. The new venture became known as Columbia-Graphophone.

The Gramophone: Berliner and Johnson

While the graphophone and phonograph were confronting each other, a German immigrant and a machine shop operator were preparing to steal the show with the third addition to the sound recording family, the *gramophone*. Emile Berliner (Figure 9–9) landed in America as a penniless immigrant from Germany and was self-educated in the science of physics. He first invented an improved telephone transmitter, which was the forerunner of the modern microphone. Bell Telephone paid him for the patent and put him to work. Almost ten years later he took a leave of absence from Bell and went to work improving the phonograph. The most dramatic improvement came in changing the way that the stylus recorded sound. The second change was to use a disc instead of a cylinder.

Figure 9-9   Emile Berliner, who arrived a penniless immigrant from Germany, educated himself in physics. He invented an improved microphone for the telephone. But his most famous work was the invention of the disc recording device called the gramophone. (RCA)

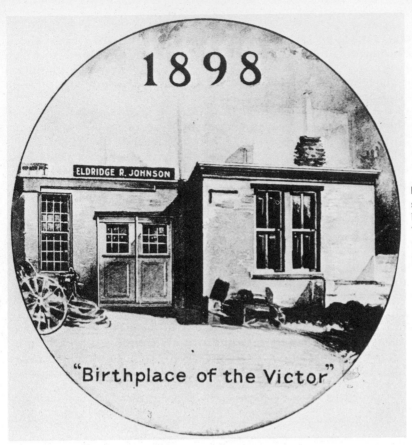

Figure 9-10 Eldridge Johnson's machine shop, the birthplace of the Victor Talking Machine Company, which eventually became RCA Victor. (RCA)

It was now time to begin marketing and selling the new device. For that, a Camden, New Jersey machinist named Eldridge Johnson joined Berliner, and the two formed the Victor Talking Machine Company (Figure 9–10). Berliner received 40 percent and Johnson 60 percent of the stock. Not only did the gramophone (Figure 9–11) ornament poeple's living rooms, but Johnson also began importing the famous European Red Seal records of famous opera stars. They were expensive, about $5. Enrico Caruso was one of the first to record, and the event in 1902 gave a new legitimacy to sound recording. Other opera stars were quick to follow. Now the public could obtain quality recordings and purchase reasonably priced machines with which to listen to them. Along with good music, Victor also obtained a world famous trademark, "His Master's Voice," the picture of a terrier named Nipper listening to a gramophone. The trademark (Figure 9–12) was originally painted by Francis Barraud and sold to the European affiliate of Victor. Johnson realized the appeal of the art, secured an American copyright for the logo, and used it on Victor records.

The final breakthrough in early acoustical recording came in 1905 when Columbia introduced disc records with songs on both sides. The dual-sided records originally sold for 65¢ and could be played on any disc machine. Columbia promoted the dual-sided recordings in ads which read,

Figure 9-11 The gramophone, first exhibited in 1888. Later models were manufactured by the U.S. Gramophone Company of Washington, D.C. and were some of the earliest disc phonographs on the market. Hand powered, it required the operator to crank the handle up to a speed of about 70 revolutions-per-minute in order to produce a satisfactory playback. (Smithsonian Institution and the Recording Industry Association of America)

Figure 9-12 Original painting of "His Master's Voice," which later became the trademark of the Victor Talking Machine Company and later, RCA Victor. (RCA)

"Columbia *Double*-disc Records! Double discs, double quality, double value, double wear, double everything except price! Don't put your record money into any other!"

THE ELECTRICAL ERA

Although the popularity of acoustical recording spread widely, it was seriously limited in its reproduction of quality sound. Because the sound was imprinted on the record through the impact of sound waves on the recording stylus, performers literally had to shout into the microphone.

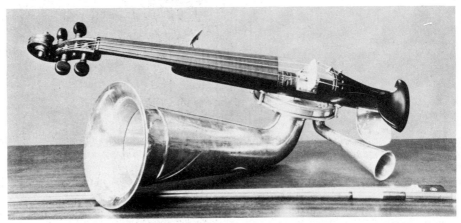

Figue 9-13 Because cylinder records could not capture string sounds faithfully brass and woodwinds were frequently substituted for strings at recording sessions. The Stroh-violin, an acoustically amplified instrument, was designed especially for cylinder recordings. (Smithsonian Institution and the Recording Industry Association of America)

Heavily draped and highly confined recording studios were employed, and, in some cases, even the musical instruments were altered so that a satisfactory recording could be made. Sounds from string instruments could not be reproduced clearly; thus many orchestras would substitute brass and woodwind instruments for better sound reproduction. One altered instrument was the Stroh-violin (Figure 9–13), which employed a special acoustical horn permitting directed amplification of the sound and greatly aiding the recording process. Because of all the makeshift apparatus, though, inventors realized that the future of recorded sound was in finding a way to record and amplify sound through an electrical, not an acoustical process. The breakthrough came just as radio was becoming a home medium.

Joseph P. Maxfield and Electrical Recording

Joseph P. Maxfield and other members of the Bell Laboratories began experimenting with electrical recording processes in 1919. Other companies were also working on this, including the English Columbia and His Master's Voice, formerly the Gramophone Company, Limited. Their main goal was to find a means of electrically amplifying sound. Three things were needed to accomplish the task: (1) a condenser microphone that would provide greater clarity than the horn did and would reduce the loss of volume and quality of sound as it passed to a (2) vacuum tube amplifier that would amplify the sound and transmit it to (3) an electromagnetically powered cutting stylus. If perfected, listeners could hear everything from the most subtle sounds of a symphony orchestra to the true undistorted sounds of a marching band.

By 1924, Maxfield had perfected the process, and recording companies quickly jumped in line for licenses permitting them to develop commerically the new process for the home consumer. The first company to reach the home playback market was Brunswick with its Panatrope machine in 1926. Soon such names as Electrola and Radiolas began to crop up in advertisements as companies such as Victor marketed the home playback devices. Prospects looked promising enough for RCA to purchase a major portion of Victor in 1929 and to move for a formal merger in 1930. Although the long-term benefits were substantial, the short-term were disastrous.

Rise and Fall of Depression Profits

Neither radio nor the recording industry foresaw the economic consequences of the 1929 stock market crash. For the recording industry, it was a catastrophe, primarily caused by radio, which was free to the listener. The medium that was to be the "advertiser" for the recording companies' products appeared at first to be its demise. Movies did not help either. Escaping the realities of famine and unemployment, crowds flocked into theaters to watch the silver screen. Based on figures of the Recording Industry Association of America (RIAA), recording industry retail sales, which had reached $75 million in 1929, had plummeted to $5.5 million by 1933.

In the same year, however, the industry started to regroup. With the repeal of Prohibition in 1933, the nightclubs, the bars, and the cocktail lounges once again returned to the neon facade of the business district. With them came juke boxes. First manufactured in 1927 by Automatic Music of Grand Rapids, Michigan the names on the flashing, push-button record players were such industry standards as Capehart, Seeburg, and Wurlitzer. Through juke box (Figure 9–14) exposure, record sales began to climb back to respectability, reaching $26 million in 1938. Radio networks, meanwhile, were beginning to see future tie-ins with the broadcasting industry. CBS purchased the Columbia Phonograph Company. Recordings by major stars made famous by radio were snatched up quickly in the record stores, and familiar corporate names, such as RCA Victor, Columbia, and Decca, began to appear on recording labels.

Battle of the Speeds

Also brewing at this time was the "battle of the speeds." RCA in 1931 had unsuccessfully launched a long-playing 33 1/3 rpm (revolutions per minute) record, substantially improving the ability to record such major productions as musicals and symphonies. The trouble was that the records wore out after a few plays. Some 33 1/3 recordings were used in World War II to send radio programs overseas, but for the most part, the long-playing record was of little value to either the recording industry or the broadcasters. Then in 1948 Peter C. Goldmark (Figure 9–15) of CBS invented a long-playing, long-lasting 33 1/3 rpm record. Accompanied by lightweight tone arms and special microgroove cutting techniques, the new records began to catch on. Success did not come overnight, however, because arch rival RCA created chaos one year later by introducing the 45 rpm disc. With three speeds to choose from—78, 33 1/3, and 45—the public reacted by not buying much of anything. Finally Columbia released its famous 33 1/3 recording of *South Pacific*, and the public demand for the disc sent the era of 78 rpm into the past. RCA was not licked, however. Juke box operators found the durable, lightweight 45s with the big holes just right for the coin-operated machines. To be safe, radio stations bought equipment with all three speeds. Finally 45s found a home in single hit records, and 33 1/3 records were ideal for musicals, symphonies, and operas.

Figure 9-14 With the repeal of prohibition, night clubs and other establishments flourished. With them came the juke boxes. As much care went into the visual design of the machines as in their components. "The Bubbler" had a built-in bubble effect which sent multi-colored liquid rising from both sides. Models of the 1940s included such features as florescent tube lights and a larger window "bomber nose" which evolved from the design of the World War II warplanes. (Source: *JUKEBOX: The Golden Age.* Published by Lancaster-Miller Publishers, Berkeley, CA 94705. Photographs by Kaz Tsuruta)

Figure 9-15 Dr. Peter C. Goldmark dramatizes the increased capacity of the long-playing 33⅓ r.p.m. record, which he helped to develop. The music contained in the stack of 78 r.p.m. records on the left, can be recorded on the long-playing albums Dr. Goldmark is holding. (Columbia Records)

TAPE, TELEVISION, AND STEREO

The recording and broadcasting industries became involved with much more than just discs. The Allied forces during World War II discovered that the Germans had made great strides in recording on magnetic tape, and the technology was brought to America. For broadcasting, even the 33 1/3 rpms were running second to what the capabilities of tape could offer. Tape gave even the smallest radio stations the ability to record, playback, erase, and rerecord everything from local newsmakers to studio trios. Editing was also possible, down to a note or syllable. Radio newscasts began to use the actual sound of the news, edited into short *audio* "*actualities*" which fit easily into the shorter time slots evolved during radio's competition with television. Today the cartridge tape plays inside the radio studio, the home, the car, and the boat. Radio broadcasting and sound recording have achieved not just a relationship, but a marriage.

What about television? It sent radio into a tailspin, and the recording industry did not have much comfort either. There were dire predictions once again for both industries. RIAA figures show that record sales, which had hit $224 million in 1947, plunged to $173 million in 1949; they did

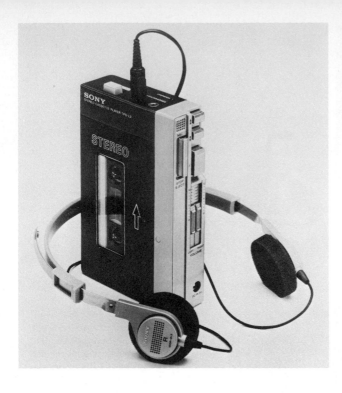

Figure 9-16 Miniaturization of electronic components has made portable cassette tapes popular. (SONY Corporation of America)

not return to 1947 levels until 1955. Radio advertising fell, and the radio networks consequently could not afford live talent. What they desperately needed was a cheap supply of quality radio programming. Coming to the rescue was the 45 and the 33 1/3 which had made significant inroads into the home market. The two industries started to revive.

Moreover, television did not have stereophonic sound, which had been successfully developed in 1931 by Englishman A. D. Blumlein. Stereo records made their debut in 1958, led by Audio Fidelity, a small recording company. As people began to understand the possibilities of sound separation, the demand for stereo records increased. FM stereo received the FCC's approval in 1961, opening up more new stereo avenues.

More recently, consumers have added the small, easily portable cassette player (Figure 9–16) to their "must have" list of popular electronic playback devices. The player with accompanying earphones can go along on a bike ride, a ski run down the mountain, or a morning jog.

With the increase in home video devices, video rock is becoming more accessible. Sophisticated sound systems can be complemented by big-screen video, by which the consumer can watch as well as listen to favorite stars.

THE RECORDING ARTIST: A RISING IDENTITY

Although the changing technology of the recording industry was an important part of the history of recorded music, the transition between songs and performers was equally important. At the turn of the century when the novelty of the phonograph was in full bloom, people were not as interested in performers as they were in specific songs. Today a recording artist is what the public wants; the songs follow. People pay as much as $25 to attend a rock concert, not because they want to hear a given song but because they want to hear and see the star. The same holds true when someone enters a retail establishment and buys an album; it is the artist who counts.

Back in the 1880s, however, records did not even carry the name of the artist. George W. Johnson, a popular black performer, George Schweinfest, a piccolo soloist, and George J. Gaskin, an Irish tenor, were distined to obscurity although their recordings were hits at the turn of the century. Then there was Russell Hunting who recorded Irish dialect stories and received fame in recording industry management circles but never as a recording star. It took opera favorites like Enrico Caruso to change the industry, to see the name of the recording artist appear on the record label, and to see performers paid royalties instead of a fee for each recording session.

Entrepreneurs also capitalized on the industry's growth. An enterprising Englishman named Louis Sterling became rich by recording musical shows and selling the recordings to lonely soldiers in World War I. These were the first of the "original cast album shows," which included such favorite tunes as Irving Berlin's *Watch Your Step*. World War I also saw the introduction of jazz recordings, with the public snapping up those by jazz artists King Oliver, Kid Ory, and later Louis Armstrong (Figure 9–17).

Figure 9-17 Recording artists, such as Louis Armstrong, have left as much of an impact on music as music has on the public. His popularity as a jazz musician places him among the greats of the music industry.

Changes in technology, specifically electrical recording, brought a new wave of artists called *crooners*. Crooners were performers who sang in soft romantic tones, something that was impossible with acoustical recordings. Among the early favorites were Rudy Vallee, Bing Crosby, and Frank Sinatra. When film began to incorporate sound, recorded music again received attention as musical scores from motion pictures came into vogue. When Al Jolson appeared in the movie *The Jazz Singer* in 1928, every song in the film became an instant hit.

By the 1930s the big bands were in full swing—Benny Goodman, Jimmy and Tommy Dorsey, Harry James, Glen Miller, Artie Shaw, and Woody Herman. Their popularity continued through the 1940s, receiving a big boost from radio which, ironically, also signaled their demise by ushering in the next big era, the age of rock and roll.

DEVELOPING FORMATS: SUCCESSES AND FAILURES

When radio was forced by the advent of television to specialize its programming formats, it had the good fortune to be helped by the burgeoning popularity of rock and roll. After a few years rock and roll itself diversified into soft rock, hard rock, acid rock, punk rock, and various combinations of these. Disco was born, and some say it subsequently died; country music experienced a new emergence and importance.

Rock and Roll

The 1950s brought forth a revolutionary new musical concept—"rock and roll." It changed the music industry, it helped change radio, and it provided some of the largest profits that the entertainment world had ever seen. Its beginning is credited to a combination of fast-paced country-and-western music combined with rhythm and blues. Its first international hit belonged to Bill Haley and the Comets and their song "Rock around the Clock." Rock and roll also belonged to such names as Chuck Berry, Little Richard, Fats Domino, Chubby Checker, Bo Diddley, The Shirelles, The Coasters, Jan and Dean, Buddy Holly, and Danny and the Juniors. Rock and roll also began to narrow its appeal to teens and young adults. Middle-aged people were attracted to the novelty by Elvis Presley's (Figure 9–18) first appearance on national television, but it was the younger audience that became devoted fans of rock music and performers. By the time the Beatles (Figure 9–19) arrived in the 1960s, these young fans were complete rock converts. Meanwhile, the middle-aged recording fan had become a voice almost too small to be heard in the consumer market.

Disciples of the new music made up the larger portion of the population who tuned in rock radio stations to hear the "Top 100," the "Top 40," the "pick hit of the week," the "number one song" in the area, and the occasional "oldies but goodies" which were never too old to be out of the real era of rock music. The music industry's new commodity commanded a loyalty and a following that sent thousands to concerts from Woodstock to the Thames. Because of radio's adaptability, it drew the same overwhelming loyalty, and disc jockeys became popular stars in their

Figure 9-18 Popular stars such as Elvis Presley brought rock-and-roll to new heights of international popularity.

Figure 9-19 British rock followed on the heels of the rock-and-roll popularity in the United States. With their son, "I Want to Hold Your Hand," and television news coverage of their appearances in the pubs of Liverpool, the appetite for the British rock group, The Beatles, skyrocketed. Their first American tour in the early 1960s set the stage for many British rock groups to follow, among them, The Rolling Stones.

own right. Transistors even made it possible to take rock music and a favorite radio station almost anywhere.

But rock music did more than acquire its devotees—it also changed our culture. With the Beatles came long hair and then still longer hair with the countless rock groups that followed. People began to realize that rock and roll was a true cultural expression and not a passing fad.

From its beginnings with Bill Haley and the Comets through Elvis Presley, rock and roll itself began to specialize. Today there are different rock forms from middle-of-the-road rock, which has a beat not unlike that of the original rock, to hard rock, and the even harder acid and progressive rock. Groups such as Kiss brought a new dimension to rock with wild costumes, popular music, and broad appeal to a contemporary audience. Punk rock emerged in the late 1970s, featuring performers clad in outfits of leather jackets, boots, mini skirts, and sporting Mohawk haircuts.

Disco

While rock and roll played to the beat of the young audience of the fifties and sixties, the late seventies spawned a new generation of music lovers. They listened, danced, bought records, and danced some more to disco. Disco music had its roots, much like rock and roll, in the beat of rhythm and blues, the repeated tempo, and the sounds of drums and brass fermented by synthesizers.

New stars emerged as charter members of the disco era. Expressing the animal beat of a bump-and-pump rhythm, Donna Summer began to capture the sensuous side of the disco beat with her recording "Love to Love You Baby" released in 1975. Donna Summer was as hot on stage as on an album. Tour and television appearances soon added to her mass appeal. Even in small-time nightclubs, amateur talent tried to woo audiences by imitating Summer and her sound.

From the solo performances of Donna Summer followed The Village People—six men whose on-stage costumes produced a cowboy, construction worker, Indian, policeman, motorcycle jockey, and soldier. Their 1978 songs "Y.M.C.A." and "Macho Man" became instant hits.

As the 1980s arrived, disco's popularity faded. People still wanted to dance, but the songs became more mellow, and the influence of country music became more distinct. For radio stations and nightclubs that had thrown heart, soul, and money into a quick conversion to disco, the waning popularity spelled financial trouble. Seeing the "handwriting on the wall," disco's giant billboards, neon lights, record albums, and stars began to adapt to new musical tastes. Those who didn't adapt were left behind to salvage what they could.

Country Music

What has heritage, fans, its own city, and means big business to the recording industry? Country music is the answer, which today sports the greatest musical popularity next to rock and roll. Country music is in an era of new maturity, having grown from the guitar-pickin' hill country of Appalachia to emerge on the Grand Ole Opry stage of Nashville. The singing cowboys like Gene Autry and the countless bands that played the less glamorous nightclubs all produced extremely loyal fans, laying a strong foundation which many predict will enjoy lasting success.

Figure 9-20 Kenny Rogers is an example of the modern country-western artist with the versatility to reach many different audiences and achieve mass popularity. He started working small fairs and stayed with the music business through rough times. Gradually, his talent and loyal following could not be overlooked. The result was international stardom. (Courtesy, Kragen and Company)

Artists who grew out of the country tradition, like Dolly Parton and Kenny Rogers (Figure 9–20), have expanded their music and their popularity to cut across musical formats once reserved for pop artists. Radio stations, capturing the versatility of these artists, play more of their songs, which in turn contribute to the artists' success. Industry reports from the Country Music Association place the growth in country music radio stations from about 700 in 1973 to almost 1600 by the early 1980s.

Motion pictures, just as they publicized rock and roll in the 1950s and 1960s, have supported the country music image even more. *The Electric Horseman, Coal Miner's Daughter, Urban Cowboy,* and others have helped portray country music as more than a backwoods phenomena. Riding the mechanical bull at Gilley's Club in Texas became much more than just a backdrop for *Urban Cowboy.* Gilley's-styled clubs sprang up all over the country so hard core country fans and inquisitive onlookers could gather for a taste of this important musical genre.

Television stars have given the music further luster. Barbara Mandrell's (Figure 9–21) network program with her sisters' managed to keep the "family roots" tradition alive and appealing to a mass audience.

For the recording industry as a whole, country music became a financial base for new profits at the turn of the decade. The industry suffered a drop-off in 1979 from the high-growth cycle that began in the 1950s, and the lavish demands of stars could no longer be met by open

Figure 9-21 Like Kenny Rogers, Barbara Mandrell has achieved fame beyond the circles of country music fans. Versatility, talent, television exposure, and persistence have brought her rewards. (Courtesy, Mandrell Management)

checkbooks. As a whole, country stars have not required the huge technological support of rock groups, which require massive sound stages and expert editing and dubbing to get a song ready for release. The simplicity of production plus country's popularity simply translated into more profit.

MAKING A HIT RECORD

How does an idea become a hit record? It starts at one of the *performance rights societies*, such as Broadcast Music, Inc. (*BMI*) or the American Society of Composers, Authors, and Publishers (*ASCAP*). Association with these organizations is important because they become responsible for collecting royalties. They collect licensing fees from broadcast stations, airlines, or rock groups that perform songs.

Demo and Master Recording Sessions

After the performing rights societies comes the *publishing company*. The publishing company arranges for a *demo session* and provides the basic accompaniment to put a song on tape. After the manager and some of the staff of the publishing company listen to the tape, they decide whether or not to arrange for a *master session*. This session is immensely important. To achieve authentic reproduction of every sound, the recording is done on a *master control console* having as many as thirty or more channels with a trained recording engineer and full orchestral accompaniment (Figure 9–22). The master session requires an investment by the publishing company of many thousands of dollars. After the master session, the tape is sent to be made into a *master record*, usually a 45 rpm, and from this, thousands of records are pressed and readied for distribution. Modern production methods also employ a process called *direct-to-disc* that eliminates the tape-to-disc transfer.

Computers have also entered the very foundation of the recording process with *digital recording* becoming the wave of the future. With digital, the range and clarity of reproduction is greatly enhanced. High and low notes are virtually distortion free, a feat with which other methods cannot compete. With digital, the distortion occurring from standard recording onto magnetic tape—mixing sounds in the studio, transferring the tape to a master disc, using the master disc to press other records—is eliminated. As the sound is originally produced by, say, an orchestra, the computer can sample the sound waves picked up by the microphone as many times as 50,000 times in one second. Each *sampling* is assigned a numerical value and, along with other "samplings," produces a numerical model of the sound. The numerical values comprising the model can be stored in the computer and called back when the recording is made. Sounds can still be mixed, just as they can with magnetic tape, but distortion—creating characteristics of magnetic tape such as flutter and varying tape speed— is eliminated. Although direct-to-disc methods also eliminate many of the problems encountered with tape, the need still arises for the artist to perform perfectly, since postperformance correction cannot be made on the disc.

Figure 9-22 Recording studio control console. (Photo: Yael Brandeis, Courtesy, Le Studio)

Promotion is the next step. So far, there is no one interested in buying the record. The publishing company plans to change that and sends complimentary copies of the record to radio stations all over the country, hoping the disc jockeys will listen to it, like it, and begin to play it. This process is not as easy as it sounds. At an average radio station, the record will be in competition with more than 200 other records each week. At many stations, unless the artist is known, the record will not even be taken out of its cover. If someone does decide to play the record, and if it begins to generate requests for air play, the next step is watching for it to appear on the *charts* of the industry's trade magazines.

Survey For Week Ending 12/19/81

Billboard® Best Selling Jazz LPs™

This Week	Last Week	Weeks on Chart	TITLE Artist, Label & Number (Dist. Label)
1	1	17	BREAKIN' AWAY ● Al Jarreau, Warner Bros. BSK 3576
☆	3	7	CRAZY FOR YOU Earl Klugh, Liberty LT 51113
☆	5	4	THE GEROGE BENSON COLLECTION George Benson, Warner Bros. 2HW 3577
4	4	16	FREE TIME Spyro Gyra, MCA MCA 5238
5	2	11	SOLID GROUND Ronnie Laws, Liberty LO 51087
6	6	10	STANDING TALL ● Crusaders, MCA MCA-5245
☆	25	2	COME MORNING Grover Washington Jr., Elektra 5E-562
☆	10	4	SOMETHING ABOUT YOU Angela Bofill, Arista AL 9576
9	9	32	THE DUDE ● Quincy Jones, A&M SP-3721
10	7	15	SIGN OF THE TIMES ● Bob James, Columbia FC 37495
★	12	5	EVERY HOME SHOULD HAVE ONE Patti Austin, QWest QWS 3591 (Warner Bros.)
12	13	13	REFLECTIONS Gil Scott-Heron, Arista AL 9566
13	8	22	THE MAN WITH THE HORN Miles Davis, Columbia FC 36790
14	11	8	LOVE BYRD Donald Byrd, Elektra 5E-531
★15	17	6	PIECES OF A DREAM Pieces Of A Dream, Elektra 6E-350
16	14	11	TENDER TOGETHERNESS Stanley Turrentine, Elektra 5-E535
★17	20	5	FREE LANCING James Blood Ulmer, ARC/Columbia 37493
18	18	6	MONDO MANDO David Grisman, Warner Bros. BSK 3618
19	19	57	WINELIGHT ▲ Grover Washington Jr., Elektra 6E-305
20	15	9	ANTHOLOGY Grover Washington Jr., Motown M9-961A2
21	21	27	AS FALLS WICHITA SO FALLS WICHITA FALLS Pat Metheny & Lyle Mays, ECM 1-1190 (Warner Bros.)
22	16	8	ENDLESS FLIGHT Rodney Franklin, Columbia FC 37154
23	23	5	A LADY AND HER MUSIC Lena Horne, QWest 2QW 3597 (Warner Bros.)
24	24	11	MAGIC WINDOWS Herbie Hancock, Columbia FC 37387
☆	35	2	SHE SHOT ME DOWN Frank Sinatra, Reprise FS 2305 (Warner Bros.)
26	26	19	FUSE ONE Fuse One, CTI CTI 9003
☆	40	2	BELO HORIZONTE John McLaughlin, Warner Bros. BSK 3619
28	28	5	SPLASH Freddie Hubbard, Fantasy F-9610
29	22	36	VOYEUR David Sanborn, Warner Bros. BSK 3546
☆	NEW ENTRY		SOLO SAXOPHONE II-LIFE John Klemmer, Elektra 5E-566
31	29	15	MISTRAL Freddie Hubbard, Liberty LT 1110
32	32	4	WANDERLUST Mike Manieri, Warner Bros. BSK 3586
33	36	13	ORANGE EXPRESS Sadao Watanabe, Columbia FC 37433
34	31	33	RIT Lee Ritenour, Elektra 6E-331
35	27	24	APPLE JUICE Tom Scott, Columbia FC 37419
36	34	11	THE LEGEND OF THE HOUR McCoy Tyner, Columbia FC 37375
37	37	9	MORNING SUN Alphonse Mouzon, Pausa 7107
38	33	7	TRAVELIN LIGHT Tim Weisberg, MCA MCA-5245
39	38	22	MECCA FOR MODERNS Manhattan Transfer, Atlantic SD 16036
40	30	6	UNTOLD PASSION Neal Schon And Jan Hammer, Columbia FC37600
41	41	15	BLYTHE SPIRIT Arthur Blythe, Columbia FC 37427
42	39	20	YELLOW JACKETS Yellow Jackets, Warner Bros. BSK 3573
43	42	20	THIS TIME Al Jarreau, Warner Bros. BSK 3434
44	43	18	BLUE TATTOO Passport, Atlantic SD 19304
45	NEW ENTRY		I REMEMBER DJANGO Stephane Grappelli/Barney Kessel With The New Hot Club Quartet, Jazzman JAZ 5008
46	45	32	THE CLARKE/DUKE PROJECT Stanley Clarke/George Duke, Epic FE 36918
47	46	3	PASSAGE William Ackerman, Windlam Hill WHSO-C-1014
48	47	29	HUSH John Klemmer, Elektra 5E-527
49	48	19	INVOCATIONS THE MOTH AND THE FLAME Keith Jarrett, ECM-D-1201 (Warner Bros.)
50	50	30	LIVE Stephanie Grapelli/David Grisman, Warner Bros. BSK 3550

Figure 9-23 One of the weekly *Billboard* charts indicating a song's popularity. Appearing on the charts and rising into the top slots can translate into big money for the people involved in producing the record. Fees charged for concert appearances, frequency of a song's airplay, and record sales all can be influenced by a song's position on the *Billboard* charts. (© Billboard Publications)

The Charts   The *Billboard* charts are a detailed summary of a recording's popularity. Let's assume that it does appear on one of *Billboard* magazine's hit charts (Figure 9–23). Now the chances for success, although not guaranteed, suddenly become a thousand times greater. Once a song appears on the chart, it has a much better chance of receiving air play on radio stations, of being recognized by program directors and disc jockeys, and finally of being purchased by the public.

However, before you run out to buy a guitar and head for Nashville, remember two things: those who do make it to stardom are few and far between, and the time that transpires between the first signing with the publishing company and reaching stardom may be decades. Although glamorous and profitable, the recording industry has many risks.

UNDERSTANDING CHARTS AND PLAYLISTS

It is Monday morning, and every disc jockey, radio program director, recording company executive, artist, composer, and everyone who has anything to do with the music industry is literally consuming every word of the *Billboard* chart published in *Billboard* magazine.

Billboard   The typical *Billboard* chart lists ten important pieces of information which, when surveyed over time, can indicate how well a particular performer or group is doing, how well a particular recording company is faring, and the prospects for a record becoming a hit. For instance, assume the hit song you are following is "Sunset," recorded by Mary Doe. It might appear on the chart as follows:

675 SUNSET
Mary Doe, Apple 1201 (Capitol) (Tre-Hollis, BMI)

The first two numbers on the chart indicate the record's standing for the current and the previous week, respectively. In our example, "Sunset" has moved up from seventh place to sixth place. This information immediately tells you that the recording is becoming more popular or is "climbing the charts." As program director at a radio station that is airing "Sunset," you might, on the basis of this listing, increase the frequency of air play of the song, for example, from one to two air plays every hour. You might also give it some additional buildup, such as your own station's "pick hit of the week." All of these decisions, which may seem little more than radio "jargon," are daily judgments that can actually be reflected in profits or losses of hundreds of thousands of dollars, for the slightest change in a radio station's programming can prompt the listener to switch stations or to change listening patterns entirely. When this decision is translated into ratings which then affect advertising dollars, you can see how this "jargon" becomes very expensive.

The third important number on our listing represents the number of weeks the song has been on the charts, in our example, five weeks. This information indicates how fast the song climbed to its present position. The remainder of the information tells the name of the song; the label and order number, which in our example is Apple 1201; the distributor's label, which in our example is Capitol; the publisher of the song, which for "Sunset" is a company called Tre-Hollis; and the licensee, which is BMI.

Playlists

Playlists are similar to the *Billboard* charts except that they are published by individual radio stations and reflect the popularity of songs in that station's immediate listening area. They are usually found in most record stores posted in a conspicuous place next to the record display racks. Many times they contain supplementary information, such as the latest "gossip" on station air personalities. They are distributed by direct mail and are important promotional literature for many radio stations. Playlists are also an excellent way for stations to assure themselves of obtaining free records for air play. In fact, when the energy crisis created a shortage of the petroleum products used to make records, some recording companies informed campus radio stations that they could not afford to send them any more free promotional records unless they received playlists in return.

Along with retail record outlets in any market, station playlists are usually mailed to major recording companies, record distribution companies, certain artists and performers, and other radio stations. Just as the recording industry scans the *Billboard* charts, it also reviews playlists, especially those of the major radio stations. In essence, being first on the playlist of some of the larger radio stations in the United States is equal in importance to being first on the *Billboard* charts.

Syndicated Charts and Playlists

In addition to station playlists and the *Billboard* charts, other charts and services are used by the industry to gauge the success of its products. Some private individuals, mainly authoritative and knowledgeable program directors or disc jockeys, make up their own syndicated record charts and playlists. Such charts and playlists are detailed and can reflect the rise of an obscure recording in a small market, thus indicating how it might do nationally.

ECONOMIC ISSUES

The road to a hit record is becoming more expensive, affected by everything from price wars among record distributors to shortages of vinyl, the material used to manufacture records. In between is the consumer, whose fickle buying habits send many a recording artist into unemployment and promoters back to the drawing board. To the average consumer, records are a luxury, and the industry tends to sway with the economy. When the economy is up, record sales are up; when the economy is down, then record sales either drop or consumers change their buying habits. For instance, singles may outsell albums simply because they are cheaper, and people wanting a certain hit may not want to spend the extra money for other songs. The segments of the industry are interrelated. Artists, through their contracts with recording companies, are not as flexible in the marketplace as artists in some other media are. Whereas an author may easily go to different publishing companies, a recording artist is usually signed to one company and remains there until his or her contract runs out or is bought out by another company. The companies themselves are also involved in related areas of the industry, such as distribution, retail sales, and promotion. As a result, the entire industry is affected by its component parts, many of which may be controlled by a single corporation. Expenses are mostly in two areas—promotion and distribution.

Promotion Costs

Only on rare occasions does a record make it big on its own without the recording company launching a major promotional campaign. The cost of these promotional campaigns and all of their various aspects can be in the millions of dollars. For example, recording companies purchase a substantial number of commercials to introduce new artists. They also pay fees for performers to appear on prime-time television programs. They purchase blocks of tickets at rock concerts to give away to fans and purchase outdoor advertising (Figure 9–24). Large record companies will join with promoters to stage concerts and dance fests featuring major rock stars. All of these promotional efforts have a single goal: to give the artists ample exposure and thus attract attention to their recordings.

Figure 9-24 Generating sales of a major recording requires a well-coordinated advertising campaign. Here, a billboard advertisement is used to promote the rock group, CHICAGO. The billboard has a gold background with red lettering showing a mock bar of chocolate candy being unwrapped. (Institute of Outdoor Advertising)

Another heavy expense is keeping an artist or rock group soluble until they have a major hit record and can pay their own expenses. The recording industry is much like a crowded airport with planes flying in a holding pattern. With only so much room for planes to land at any one time, the rest stay airborne until they have the opportunity to land. Similarly many recording artists are kept in business until there is an opportunity for them to penetrate the market; public demand dictates that only so many of them can be popular at any one time. All recording companies make major investments in talent, some of which never pay off.

The distribution system for records is quite similar to that for books and has many of the same costs. Transportation is one. Shipping of recording discs and cassettes is done by truck, and increased fuel prices affect the distributors' and eventually the consumers' costs. The distributor must also estimate the demand for the recording to avoid the costly process of returning unsold recordings. On top of this, price wars have complicated the distributors' woes. Record retail outlets are very much like gas stations. They buy from wholesalers but can also discount their merchandise. A market that has price and time limitations placed on it can suffer considerable loss from such tactics. A popular recording artist, for example, will have a hit on the charts for a limited time only, during which the public will purchase his or her record. Stores displaying the signs "big tape discounts" and "cut-rate prices" abound, and consumers invariably find that shopping around does pay. Although the record companies have been accused of cooperating in this, the FCC has been strongly against interfering, stating that recording companies must compete in a free market.

Overall the recording industry has shown the ability to weather most of the economic storms it has faced—partly because it also has a system of royalty agreements suited to different outlets such as bands, juke boxes, radio stations, and airline music systems, to name a few.

Pirating

In addition to price wars, the recording industry also must contend with *pirated records and tapes*—illegally recorded music sold in violation of copyright agreements and contractual agreements with artists. Pirate companies have been the target of both the industry and the Justice Department. Although there have been some major crackdowns, the practice continues. Pirate operations (Figure 9–25) will record songs of

Armed guards protect latest Elvis record

INDIANAPOLIS (AP) — Elvis Presley fans can rest assured that the latest of The King's posthumously released records will get the ultimate in security treatment.

Officials at RCA Records say the production of 250,000 numbered copies of "Elvis Aron Presley" at the company's Indianapolis plant will be attended by armed guards and armored trucks to prevent theft or counterfeiting of the limited edition 25th anniversary Presley album.

"We don't want any advance copies to fall into the hands of counterfeiters," said RCA vice president of manufacturing Joe McHugh, who has charge of the added security measures. "Nor do we want thieves sneaking in and making off with copies. Our security is further intended to guard against any possible hijacking of the vans between our factory and our warehouse."

As soon as it is packaged, the album is transferred in specially sealed Brinks security vans to the warehouse for national distribution.

Figure 9-25 Theft and piracy are continuous threats to record manufacturers. As this story explains, extra measures are often taken to secure that a record shipment reaches its destination. Such stories, well-placed in the media, can also add up to a promotional boost for the record's popularity and sales.

popular artists directly from a broadcast or from other recordings and then sell the tapes at a big discount. Profits are considerable, since pirate companies pay neither royalty fees nor the cost of distribution. Most are operated on a regional or even local basis with few outlets, thus eliminating most wholesaler fees. All that is needed is duplicating equipment and a retail outlet to sell the mechandise. After that, it is mostly profit. Offenders, can get stiff fines, however, and sometimes a jail sentence.

SUMMARY

Chapter 9 examined the billion-dollar recording industry, starting with its roots in the seventeenth century when musical selections first appeared in broadsides and as published sheet music. Thomas Edison is credited with inventing the first workable phonograph in 1877, which used a tin foil cylinder upon which indentations were made from a stylus connected to a large recording horn. Chichester Bell and Charles Tainter made substantial improvements on the machine and named their improved recording device the *graphophone*. It also used a cylinder, but one made of wax.

A German immigrant named Emile Berliner teamed up with craftsman Eldridge Johnson and invented the first workable disc recorder, called the *gramophone*. Commerical development of acoustical recording devices continued through the early twentieth century while the machines tried to find a profitable market, appearing as everything from dictating machines to fads of saloons and phonograph parlors.

By 1924 radio had become a home medium, and Joseph P. Maxfield introduced the first electrical recorder. Now sounds could be amplified much more than was possible with acoustical methods, and the result was a tonal clarity never before achieved. The improvements made the phonograph the newest home entertainment medium. Although the Depression slowed the growth of the industry, it bounced back and remains an important part of both home entertainment and broadcasting.

Along with the technology came the identity of recording stars. Early opera favorites such as Enrico Caruso were to be followed by such greats as Al Jolson, the big-band sounds, the jazz favorites, and crooners. By the 1950s rock and roll arrived.

The making of a hit record is part of a step-by-step process that has many more failures than successes and is tied to the economic issues facing the recording industry. The concept of a hit record starts at the performance rights society and goes from there to the publishing company, where recording sessions are followed by major promotional efforts, possibly leading to retail sales.

OPPORTUNITIES FOR FURTHER LEARNING

CARR, P., ed., *The Illustrated History of Country Music by the Editors of Country Music Magazine*. Garden City, N.Y.: Doubleday, 1979.

CHAPPLE, S., AND R. GAROFALO, *Rock 'n' Roll is Here to Pay*. Chicago: Nelson-Hall Publishers, 1977.

CLARK, D., AND R. ROBINSON, *Rock, Roll & Remember*. New York: Harper & Row, Pub., 1976.

CLARKE, G. E., *Essays on American Music*. Westport, Conn.: Greenwood Press, 1977.

CSIDA, J., *The Music/Record Career Handbook*. New York: Billboard Publications, Inc., 1975.

DAVIS, C., WITH J. WILLWERTH, *Clive: Inside the Record Business*. New York: Billboard Publications, Inc., 1975.

DENISOFF, R. S., AND R. A. PETERSON, eds., *Change*. Skokie, Ill.: McNally, 1972.

DICHTER, H., AND E. SHAPIRO, *Handbook of Early American Sheet Music 1768–1889*. New York: Dover, 1977.

DUNN, L., *On the Flip Side*. New York: Billboard Publications, Inc., 1975.

GELATT, R., *The Fabulous Phonograph: 1877–1977*. New York: Macmillan, 1977.

HENDERSON, W. *How to Run Your Own Rock and Roll Band*. New York: Popular Library, 1977.

MCCUE, G., ed., *Music in American Society, 1776–1976: From Puritan Hymn to Synthesizer*. New Brunswick, N.J.: Transaction, Inc., 1977.

PALMER, T., *All You Need Is Love: The Story of Popular Music*. New York: Viking, 1976.

RUST, B., *The American Record Label Book*. New Rochelle, N.Y.: Arlington House, 1978.

SHEMEL, S., AND M. W. KRASILOVSKY, *This Music Business*. New York: Billboard Publications, Inc., 1977.

SMITH, B., *The Vaudevillians*. New York: Billboard Publications, Inc., 1976.

STAMBLER, I., *Encyclopedia of Pop, Rock and Soul*. New York: St. Martin's Press, 1976.

TITON, J. T., *Early Downhome Blues: A Musical and Cultural Analysis*. Urbana: University of Illinois Press, 1977.

WEISSMAN, D., *The Music Business: Career Opportunities and Self-Defense*. New York: Crown Publishers, Inc., 1979.

WHITCOMB, I, *After the Ball: Pop Music from Rag to Rock*. Baltimore: Penguin, 1974.

CHAPTER

ADVERTISING

PREVIEW

After completing this chapter, we should be able to:

Name and discuss the four functions of ad agencies.
Know the difference between market research and product research.
State the sources of advertising agency income.
Discuss the future costs of making advertising impressions.
Describe and give an example of each of the different types of advertising.
Explain the different advertising appeals.
Be aware of our perceptions of advertising.

As either industry professionals or future consumers of mass communication, we should be aware that there are many people responsible for the messages disseminated by mass communication. There are people and organizations whose primary responsibility is to produce and prepare messages, especially commercial messages. Advertising agencies are one of the most important and active organizations that influence every facet of mass media.

FUNCTIONS OF AD AGENCIES

Ad agencies first appeared in the late nineteenth century when newspapers began to rely less on government subsidies and more on commercial advertising to survive. The improved distribution systems of railroads and highways made newspaper advertising an attractive means of reaching a large number of people. Yet agencies still met resistance, not from consumers but from merchants who felt it was unorthodox to market their products in any way other than in a storefront display or a simple paragraph in the paper. The creative ads in the pages of today's newspapers and magazines were mostly absent in the eighteenth and nineteenth centuries, mainly because the foundation for such an inventive service had yet to be laid. The newspaper publisher's chief concern was with publishing, as the merchant's was with running a business. Many manufacturers worked cooperatively with retailers to aid the acceptance of new products and companies themselves retained talented copywriters who produced some of the more memorable slogans (Figure 10–1) gracing ads in the early 1900s. With the growth of magazines and new opportunities for design and layout (Figure 10–2), it became clear that talent and creativity were not only at a premium but also necessary to compete in the marketplace.

Basically there was a need for someone in the middle, someone who could work between the media and the manufacturer or retailer and develop the creative messages necessary to bring the product to the reader's attention. Some early efforts at advertising came from copywriters at local papers. Some of them realized the importance of advertising, and became independent agents, specialists whose talents were in great demand.

This modest beginning was the foundation of modern advertising as a business and a profession. Today advertising agencies are found in virtually every major city in the world, and their role in stimulating economic growth is solidly established. To understand advertising, we need to examine the four functions an agency performs.

Figure 10-1 Many companies retained talented copywriters who produced some of advertising's most memorable slogans. (Courtesy, Campbell Soups and the Allegheny College Alumni Magazine)

YOUNG folks with their fresh, unspoiled palates are the real judges of *flavor*. They enjoy the crispness, the wonderful good taste of Kellogg's Toasted Corn Flakes—and they are the ones who keep the imitations away from the table. The crispness and flavor of Kellogg's are *there*—five million breakfasts a morning—and no telling how many times between meals.

It is a remarkable fact that there is no storage space at Kellogg's. Each day's production is shipped crisp from the ovens in the Kellogg *WAX-TITE* package — that keeps the fresh, good flavor in and all other flavors out.

W.K.Kellogg

Kellogg's
TOASTED
CORN
FLAKES

W.K.Kellogg

KELLOGG TOASTED CORN FLAKE CO.
BATTLE CREEK, MICH.

Figure 10-2 The growth of magazines provided new opportunities for layout and design of advertising.

Talent   The basic function of an ad agency is providing *talent*. The creative efforts of the art director, the marketing savvy of the media buyer, the detailed analysis of the research director, and the political understanding of the campaign director are just a few examples of the many abilities ad agency personnel have to offer. A business, organization, or person will contract the services of an ad agency to help market a product. The product may be soap, the corporate image of a multimillion-dollar company, a political figure, or a nonprofit organization.

Research   The second function is *research*. In order to distribute the message to the public successfully, the agency must first know all that it can about the product. Imagine you are responsible for handling the advertising for a major lumber company. The company wants to develop an advertising campaign for a new byproduct it has developed. This byproduct is small chips of bark which previously have been burned as a waste. It is your job to plan the advertising campaign.

One of your first jobs is to research the product and the company. You must learn everything you possibly can about both. Your research must even take you close to the heart of the firm's inner operations. In order for you to make effective advertising judgments that may involve thousands of dollars, you must know how that firm works. Occasionally research may reveal certain questionable business operations, dealings that may force your agency to withdraw from handling the campaign. Handling a disreputable firm's advertising may leave your agency with the problem of collecting money for your services, to say nothing of a lawsuit for fraudulent advertising and possible tangles with the Federal Trade Commission. This research into the company and its product is called *product research*.

Market research, the second type of research, aims at finding the potential market for the new product. You will need to know if there are other products on the market that can successfully compete with your client's product. You will want to know where the customers for the product can be found. You will want to know the characteristics of your potential customers. Are they home owners? Are they apt to do their own gardening and yard work, or do they hire professional gardeners to do these tasks? Answers to these questions are part of market research.

Distribution   The third important function is *distribution*. Here you will decide what type of *message* you are going to create for the company and what *media* (Figure 10–3) will be most helpful in sending this message to the public.

Figure 10-3   Creative outdoor ads embellished with special materials provide eye-catching advertisements. (Robert Keith & Co.)

Let's assume that your research into the company's background gives it a clean bill of health and that you decide to continue with the account. You have learned that the bark chips make a good bedding to place around shrubbery. Next, you conduct further research into a possible name for the bark chips. Your research strikes a positive note on the name "Barko!" The name is catchy, is easily remembered, and carries the substance of the product into the name.

Now comes the decision on how to tell the "Barko!" story to the public. It is time to call a meeting of the agency's department heads.

Account Executive: The lumber company has decided to market the small wood chips that are waste material when bark is ground off the logs. The chips are a few inches long and come in all shapes. They'll bag them in fifty pound sacks, and we're calling it "Barko!"

Research Director: We've investigated the product and the market as thoroughly as possible. The bark chips are great for placing around shrubbery. We see the market as basically home owners who do their own gardening and yard work.

General Manager: It's a good account all around. The lumber company has been in business for fifty years, and they have an excellent credit rating. Any ideas on how to tell the story?

Art Director: I think some pictures toned with soft brown shades will tell the story best.

Production Director: OK, but don't go too far; color television has more potential than brown. Let's consider using some bright yellows, oranges, and greens.

Art Director: Since this stuff comes in all shapes and sizes, perhaps we could arrange a cartoon character around it.

General Manager: That's cutting our budget close. Cartoon production is too expensive with this account.

Photographer: We could shoot some sharp photography of sunlit patios with "Barko!" around the shrubbery.

Copywriter: That might work well. We could develop a series of commericals to stress seasonal outdoor decorating.

Media Buyer: I envision running some ads in the syndicated section on gardening in the Sunday paper and tying in the theme to evening television and radio. Perhaps some *billboards* would also be helpful. In addition, I feel a brochure sent to all the gardening outlets in the state would be an excellent sales piece.

This conversation illustrates some of the numerous considerations in planning an advertising campaign. Notice how the development of the commercial message encompasses the creative talents of many people. Precisely because it would be too time consuming and costly to develop this expertise within the lumber company, its management hired the ad agency. Moreover, the people at the ad agency can look at the company's product objectively. They are not as closely associated with the product or the company so they can point out possible positive and negative aspects of the product that should be considered.

Figure 10-4 Mail Pouch Tobacco signs painted on the sides of barns became a form of logo in themselves. (General Cigar & Tobacco Co.)

Figure 10-5 Spanish language advertising retains a cultural identity while reaching a specific audience. (OMAR)

Monitoring	The fourth function of an advertising agency is *monitoring feedback*. Al-
Feedback	though this may be accomplished in various ways and is not always

Monitoring Feedback   The fourth function of an advertising agency is *monitoring feedback*. Although this may be accomplished in various ways and is not always included in the ad agency's contract, it can be an important part of the business-media relationship. Perhaps retailers receive complaints about "Barkos!" Perhaps there is a rival product, and the public is confusing your product with its competition. By monitoring consumer *feedback*, a decision on whether to revise the message, the medium, the target audience or all of them can be made.

The preceding paragraphs have given us a brief look at the operation of an ad agency. As the business of reaching the public with information about new products becomes increasingly complex, the work of ad agencies becomes more and more important. No longer can a firm make a decision merely to advertise in a storefront window or in the local newspaper. Complex multimedia buying decisions, the psychology of attitudes toward styles and color combinations, and the ability to coordinate advertising messages across many different media all demand talent—talent based on the ad agency's years of expertise.

Many large, diversified corporations supplying national and international markets are developing their own ad agencies right within the company. These *in-house* agencies serve much the same function as an independent ad agency except that they deal exclusively with that company's products. Although there is some danger in being "too close" to the company and its line to treat them objectively, such dangers have not deterred the growth of in-house agencies.

If an advertising campaign has the backing of effective talent, research, distribution, and feedback, it has the best chance of succeeding. Today more and more specialized advertising is developing, demanding new creativity by advertising personnel. Although some of the simplest campaigns have, over the years, been tremendously effective—campaigns like Mail Pouch Tobacco (Figure 10–4) and its painted barns—new campaigns demand specialized talent. For example, in many areas attorneys are advertising for the first time, and special consulting and advertising firms are devoting their talents to the law profession. Celebrities are increasingly being used in ads, and not only the creative talents of an ad agency but legal talents are required to understand the regulations of complex contracts between stars and the products and agencies with which they are associated.

Ad agencies are developing to reach ethnic audiences and some of the most effective advertising includes ads written in the native language of the target audience (Figure 10–5). All of these specialized campaigns are creating new demands on agencies and are requiring new talents for people who work in advertising.

ECONOMICS OF AD AGENCIES

Two arguments can be heard by agency personnel whenever they gather. One executive will claim his or her agency is doing well because the economy is doing well. Another will claim that because the economy is in bad shape, businesses are advertising more, and thus the agency is doing well. Both arguments are valid and reflect some of the concerns of being in a business that is "in the middle."

Much of the income of an agency comes from the discounts it receives from media. Most discounts, which are in effect agency commissions, are approximately 15 percent. With the exception of newspapers, which generally still refrain from giving agency discounts, this percentage is fairly standard in all media. By the way of illustration, assume that you are advertising "Barkos!" and that your ad agency is going to spend $10,000 advertising "Barkos!" in a gardening magazine. You contact the gardening magazine and purchase a $10,000 full-color insert. After the ad runs, the gardening magazine bills your ad agency for $8,500 ($10,000 minus 15 percent). Your ad agency pays that bill and then bills the company that manufactures "Barkos!" for $10,000. When the manufacturer pays its account, your agency has received $1,500 income in the transaction. Of course, the agency's costs must come out of the $1,500, so that this is by no means clear profit. The American Association of Advertising Agencies estimates that in a typical large agency, media commissions represent about 75 percent of the agency's income. In smaller agencies the percentage drops to as low as 55 percent. The reason for this difference is that large agencies usually cater to large markets where a thirty-second radio commercial may cost $250. Fifteen percent of $250 makes a nice commission. But smaller agencies in markets where $10 buys a thirty-second spot simply cannot exist on the commission alone. They must have other income.

Other income can be realized through an agency's own percentage charges. For instance, an agency may have a printing job to complete for a client. The printer allows the agency a 20 percent discount on the job to attract and keep the agency's business. We shall assume the nondiscount rate for the printing job is $500. With the 20 percent discount, the agency is billed only $400 ($500 minus 20 percent). The agency then bills the client for $475, keeping $75 as a commission. Although the client still pays a fee over and above what the agency is charged, the client is still receiving the service at less cost ($25 less) than if he or she had placed the printing order directly with the printing company.

Some ad agencies have even entered into special arrangements with manufacturers in which they not only handle a company's advertising but also process orders for goods and services provided or sold by that company. For instance, an ad agency might handle the advertising for a new cooking utensil. In the media campaign, the agency purchases ads in leading homemaker magazines and issues press releases to media outlets that might give the new product free publicity. The agency then processes the orders for the new product and takes a commission on the gross sales, such as $5 on each utensil sold. These arrangements are not a general practice with all ad agencies, but they have proved successful for smaller agencies that have a limited market in which to secure accounts. Other income has been realized by agencies conducting executive workshops, sales training seminars, and other activities.

Within the agencies, there are many different arrangements for commissions and income. Any agency-client relationship, of course, rests on an agreement that is mutually satisfactory. Some agencies, for instance, provide different classes of service in accordance with clients, needs, wishes, and, most importantly, budgets. More experienced personnel and those with proven creative abilities may be enlisted to serve clients wanting the best service possible. Newer personnel may be engaged for lower quality, less expensive projects. Some large accounts from which the agency receives a major share of its income will receive top-of-the-line service simply because of the importance of retaining such a lucrative account. Different services within the agency can also affect the final cost to the client. For example, additional use of the secretarial force does not raise the cost of the total package anywhere near as much as extra hours of an art director's talent.

Public Relations

Agencies with extensive public relations work will command a larger proportion of their client's dollars than agencies concerned mostly with placing media buys. Public relations services for a client include such things as meeting with media representatives on behalf of the client, sending press releases to media, visiting trade fairs, organizing promotional luncheons, and so on. Whenever such activities are involved, there is less outflow of cash for media buys and more retained within the agency. The actual amount of these "services" can account for as much as 50 percent of an agency's income. We'll learn more about public relations in Chapter 11.

Future Costs of Making Impressions

One factor that will largely determine this income of ad agencies in the future is the actual cost of advertising—placing a message with a particular medium to reach a *target audience*. Let's examine how one medium, television, will require more of the ad dollar to reach a target audience, women, between now and 1985. This future perspective was offered at a meeting of the Association of National Advertisers by Andrew Kershaw.[1] It illustrates how the cost of reaching women is increasing, but that the *impressions*—the number of times a person is reached by an ad—are decreasing. Figure 10–6 shows that in 1965, a $5 million ad budget spent

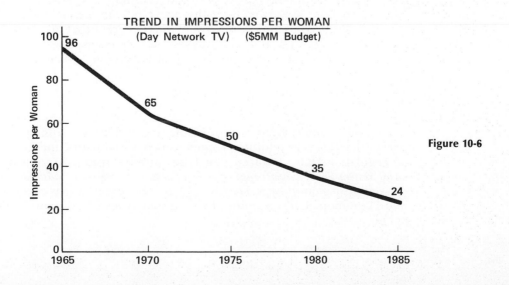

TREND IN IMPRESSIONS PER WOMAN
(Day Network TV)   ($5MM Budget)

Figure 10-6

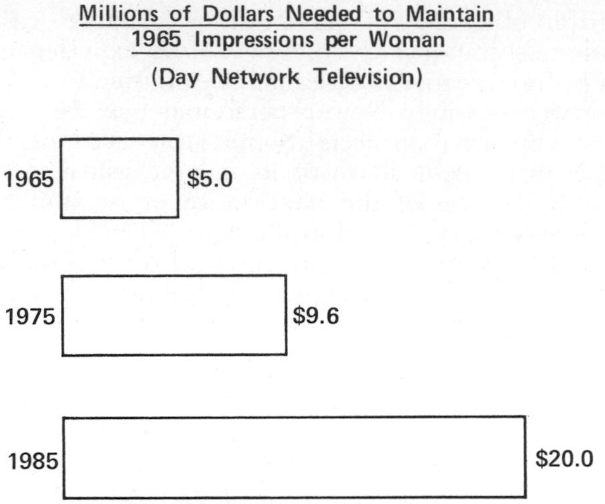

1965	$5.0

Figure 10-7

1975	$9.6

1985	$20.0

on daytime network television would have reached all women, 18 years old and over, 96 times that year. However, that same ad budget in 1985 will reach that same audience only 24 times. The cost of keeping up with the 1965 impressions also becomes substantial. Figure 10–7 illustrates how the increase will be almost 300 percent for daytime network television. In other words, in 1985 it will be necessary to spend $20 million in daytime network television to make the same 96 impressions per woman that $5 million bought in 1965. A similar problem exists in nighttime network television. Kershaw's prediction for the future?—a necessity for more effective advertising and, in the case of television, shorter commericals. The talents of the ad agency seem to be assured of an even more receptive market.

The Agency's Position   The agencies themselves, however, are in the unique position of remaining flexible and of still making money despite increasing costs. There are two important reasons for this. One is that the ad agency takes its commission from the overall purchase price of the advertising. If the cost of purchasing advertising time increases, then the agency's commission increases proportionately. Second, in a highly competitive market that takes advertising glamour for granted, most businesses find themselves willing to spend gigantic sums to obtain the most for their advertising dollars.

TYPES OF ADVERTISING

The most common types of advertising are *standard advertising* and *public service advertising*. In addition, contemporary social issues and governmental regulations have induced new types of advertising. Among these are *social responsibility advertising, counter-advertising, corrective advertising, advocacy advertising,* and *image advertising. Municipal advertising* is also becoming more common. Let's examine the different types of advertising in more detail.

Standard Advertising

Standard ads (Figure 10–8) appear in all media and are financed by the company or organization that has products to sell or services to render. The motive is to sell and to create in the consumer a feeling of need and desire for a product or service. Decisions as to the type of message the ads will use, in what media they will be placed, and how often they will appear in the media are usually made by the manufacturer or distributor, sometimes in conjunction with an ad agency. Once these decisions are made, time or space is purchased, and a contract is signed specifying such things as the number of times the ad will appear, when it will appear, in the case of billboards, at what location. There is usually some type of tangible market feedback to judge the ads' effectiveness, such as the number of sales resulting directly from the ad. Standard advertising is the financial lifeblood of commerical mass media.

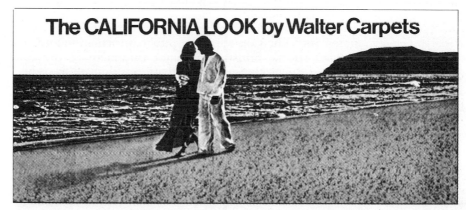

Figure 10-8 Standard advertsing appears in all media and is financed by the company or organization with products to sell or services to render.

Public Service Advertising

Public service advertising supports nonprofit causes and organizations. Time or space for this type of advertising is provided free as a service to the public by the print or broadcast media. Most public service advertising is to solicit contributions of either time or money for the nonprofit enterprise. Contributions to organizations such as the Red Cross are received almost exclusively through public service advertising.

Most broadcasting stations provide a certain amount of broadcast media time for public service programming. Public service announcements (PSAs) run a regular schedule with the commercials. They usually last anywhere from a few seconds to five minutes, the most common lengths being thirty or sixty seconds.

Prime time on broadcasting networks devoted to PSAs is a valuable commodity worth many thousands of dollars. As a result, there is considerable competition among nonprofit organizations to obtain exposure for public service advertising.

Public service advertising in the print media is concentrated mainly in those magazines that devote free space to nonprofit organizations. Although there is no legal requirement for the print media to do so, most magazines cooperate with the Advertising Council and contribute advertising space. Major outdoor companies also cooperate with nonprofit organizations and provide public service space. Outdoor companies, however, expend considerable effort in designing and pasting up the bulletin. Moreover, they must usually foot the rental for the property on which the bulletin is displayed.

Social Responsibility Advertising

A screech of tires, the sound of smashing glass, twisting metal, and the plea to "drive safely." This message is the subject of radio and television messages which are especially plentiful during holiday seasons. The safe driving ads and others which admonish us to act responsibly belong to social responsibility advertising. These ads are usually sponsored by either a nonprofit organization such as the National Safety Council, not linked to any one industry, or special public relations organizations representing a particular industry.

An example of the latter is the Distilled Spirits Council of the United States, Inc. The Council is the public information and research arm of the distilled spirits industry. A major campaign of the Council through its Licensed Beverage Industries division is to instill responsibility in drinking (Figure 10–9). Its advertisements have a dual purpose: raising the public's consciousness about drinking, and informing the media that the industry

Wet your whistle but don't drown it.

Don't drink too much of a good thing.
The Distilled Spirits Council of the United States.
1300 Pennsylvania Building, Washington, D.C. 20004

Figure 10-9 Responsible alcohol consumption and safe driving are examples of social responsibility advertising.

is taking an active role in promoting a responsible attitude toward alcohol consumption. The major thrust of this campaign came just after cigarette commercials were banned on television. Although, because of the NAB Codes, advertisements for hard liquor seldom appear in broadcasting, there is nothing to prevent a major antidrinking campaign from developing in a fashion similar to the antismoking campaign. Perhaps if the cigarette industry had provided a "responsibility in smoking" advertising campaign, cigarette ads would still be running on radio and television. The distilled spirits industry is thus applying the extremely effective public relations technique of combating poor publicity before a significant image problem can arise.

There are many other types of social responsibility advertising besides the two we have already mentioned. Significant campaigns to use natural resources responsibly have become common, and land use planning, fire prevention, and wildlife management are just three examples. Energy conservation has also received wide exposure in ads sponsored by nonprofit industries and in some cases the energy companies themselves.

Counter-Advertising

One of the most controversial types of advertising is counter-advertising, advertising directed *against* a product or service. Counter-ads directed against *specific* products are rarely seen on a national scale. Nevertheless, industry and public concern over such ads has become significant. Advocates of counter-advertising claim that standard advertising does not sufficiently inform the public to enable consumers to make intelligent buying decisions; counter-ads are therefore necessary to counteract some of the allegedly unwarranted claims found in standard advertising. Some familiar counter-ads are those which warn against abusive collection practices by credit agencies, the dangers of air and water pollution and cigarette smoking.

Broadcasters have put up considerable resistance to counter-advertising. The National Association of Broadcasters as well as the Television Information Office, both professional groups representing the broadcasting industry, have opposed widespread requirements for stations to run counter-ads.

The effectiveness of counter-advertising is still moot despite recent research efforts. Bayer aspirin counter-ads apparently made Bayer users adopt a more cautious attitude toward the product, but the statistical figures were not significant.[2] There was no indication that in real-life situations attitudes would have changed significantly, that peer group decisions about the product might have contradicted the effectiveness of the ads, or that the decrease in favorable attitudes would have remained over time.

Counter-advertising remains a concern for advertisers. The interpretation of the Fairness Doctrine in broadcasting, the possibility of lawsuits against other media, and the liability for broadcasting and printing unfounded claims in product advertisements certainly are not taken lightly by media executives. At the very least, the issue of counter-advertising has made media management stop, consider, and scrutinize the content of advertising.

Corrective Advertising

"Super bloopers make your feet run faster." "This vitamin cures all ills." "Thirst-quench has better nutrients than any other drink." Exaggerated claims such as these are prime targets for corrective advertising, which are attempts, usually instigated by regulatory orders, to correct false or misleading advertising.

Many government agencies participate in policy advertising claims, including the FCC, FTC, and the Food and Drug Administration, but the agency responsible for ordering corrective advertising is the FTC. The others assume more of a preventive role. The Food and Drug Administration, for instance, has established strict rules for ingredient disclosure, thus guarding against deceptive food and drug labeling. Similarly the FCC strongly encourages radio and televison station management to reject advertising that may be deceptive.

The classic case of corrective advertising occurred in 1971 when the FTC reached an agreement with the ITT Continental Baking Company to correct advertising that implied that eating the company's Profile Bread would result in weight loss. According to the FTC, Profile Bread was no different from other breads except that the slices were thinner. The baking company was ordered to stop using weight loss as a pitch and to spend part of its advertising budget over a one-year period to tell the public that its bread was not an effective weight reducer. The result was a television commercial with the script:

> I'd like to clear up any misunderstandings you may have about Profile Bread from its advertising or even its name. Does Profile have fewer calories than other breads? No, Profile has about the same per ounce as other breads. To be exact, Profile has 7 fewer calories per slice. That's because it is sliced thinner. But eating Profile will not cause you to lose weight. . . .

The FTC also ordered the maker of Listerine mouthwash to start including in its advertising a statement to read, "Contrary to prior advertising, Listerine will not prevent colds or sore throats or lessen their severity." The company denied that it had claimed the mouthwash was a cold cure and readied an appeal.

Obviously there are arguments for and against corrective advertising. Supporting arguments claim that the ads are necessary to put the "bite" on companies that readily defy regulatory measures. In addition, they are necessary to inform the public that misleading claims do appear and that therefore the consumer should be more critical of advertising. Negative arguments say that years will have passed by the time the wheels of the enforcement process begin to turn and a misleading advertiser has been made to retract claims it has made for its product. Others claim that people are attracted by the novelty of the corrective ads, which call their attention to the product rather than to the corrective message and that the regulatory purpose of the ad is therefore defeated.

Advocacy Advertising

Closely related to counter-advertising is advocacy advertising. Whereas counter-advertising is normally directed at a particular objectionable product, a company producing such a product, or an industry responsible for creating a societal ill, advocacy advertising champions preventive action against conditions affecting the public welfare. Ads raising our awareness of heroin addiction, the rising crime rate, and impoverished conditions in the ghetto are all examples of advocacy advertising. In most cases advocacy advertising is sponsored and paid for by an organization which wants to be associated with community involvement. The ads may or may not be directed toward the sponsor's own business interest. The Distilled Spirits Council, which we learned has sponsored the responsibility in drinking ads, has also warned against the ills of moonshine liquor. Moonshine is illegal but can also cut into the profits of licensed distillers.

Advocacy advertising is finding more and more sponsors as companies and organizations want to gain the added benefit of directing a message against a common fault of society while at the same time keeping their name visible to the public.

Image Advertising

For many corporations image advertising (Figure 10–10) has become very important and is part of their natural public relations function. For example, oil companies may go to great lengths to show how they are working to protect or reclaim the environment during drilling and exploration. Such scenes as waterfowl flying in front of an oil rig or the rays of a setting sun across reclaimed grassland are designed to create a favorable corporate image. Other image advertising is more direct and deals head-on with issues confronting a particular company or industry. Mobil Oil has taken a particularly strong stand in its ads, frequently clashing with the mass media, television networks being one example (Figure 10–11).

Figure 10-10 Image advertising is an important part of corporate marketing and advertising campaigns. Acceptance of corporate products, employee morale, and prestige are some of the reasons why this particular advertising is undertaken.

TOWARD RIGHT CONCLUSIONS

"...right conclusions are more likely to be gathered out of a multitude of tongues, than any kind of authoritative selection."

– Judge Learned Hand

As an oil company, we've felt obliged to speak out on energy and economic issues that affect our business. Very often, our contribution to the "multitude of tongues" takes the form of advocacy advertising.

But the TV networks refuse to accept advocacy commercials. Isn't that dismissal precisely the kind of authoritative selection that Learned Hand was warning against?

The best contribution any business can make to the public discourse is to say what it truly thinks about public policies and decisions. The position that Mobil or some other business takes may sound controversial or even outrageous to the press; indeed, sometimes our position has outraged members in our own industry. But shouldn't a responsible press, electronic as well as print, foster the dialogue of many voices that helps the people and their leaders advance toward right conclusions?

We believe the press should encourage a multitude of tongues, and never act as an instrument of silence.

Mobil

© 1981 Mobil Corporation

Figure 10-11 Mobil has taken particularly strong stands in some of its advertising. In this ad, Mobil criticizes television networks for their refusal to accept advocacy advertising. (© 1981 Mobil Corporation)

Figure 10-12 Municipal advertising is important for attracting everything from tourists to new businesses. This ad appeared in a publication for convention planners. (Courtesy of the Greater Cincinnati Convention & Visitors Bureau)

Cincinnati.
A city you can afford to enjoy.

Big league sports... Award-winning restaurants
Museums... World-renowned symphony
Convention Center... Skywalks

Greater
Cincinnati
Convention and
Visitors Bureau

Write or call and we'll send you our Facility Guide.
200 W. Fifth St., Cincinnati, Ohio 45202 (513) 621-2142

Dynamic Pittsburgh

With 28 colleges, four universities and renowned programs in robotics, medicine, science and engineering. It's a very bright place to live and work.

Clustered in the city's Oakland section are Carnegie-Mellon University, Carlow College, and the University of Pittsburgh. More than 26,000 students attend Pitt's 16 schools in law, engineering, international affairs, medicine, dentistry, public health and more. And its business school offers graduate programs designed for executives.

Carnegie-Mellon University, in collaboration with Westinghouse, leads the nation in robotics research. CMU offered the country's first degrees in music and drama; its MSIA, chemical, electrical and metallurgical engineering and computer science programs are among the country's top five.

Seventy area vocational schools offer state-of-the-art training in industrial skills. The State Employment Service works with business and industry to develop new programs that meet specific employer needs.

This dinosaur collection (funded by Andrew Carnegie) is one of the most complete in the world. The Museum of Natural History of Carnegie Institute is part of a network of libraries and galleries that enrich secondary education.

Duquesne University supplies more MBAs to the Big 8 accounting firms than any other graduate business school. A leading Catholic university, Duquesne is also known for programs in music, pharmacology, philosophy and law.

Indiana University, women's colleges Chatham and Carlow, Robert Morris, Point Park, Slippery Rock, Allegheny Community College and four Penn State branches offer higher education throughout the nine-county region.

Education: it's the second strength of a region whose first strength is business. Here you'll find economics Nobel laureate Herb Simon. A public school system whose team teaching and Head Start programs are among the country's first. And a trained work force that beats the national average in percentage of high school and graduate degrees.

They're the people who staff 70 American multinationals headquartered here and 150 foreign-owned firms operating here. Living in a nine-county region that offers a below-average cost of living. Top recreation and outstanding programs in the arts.

Innovative. Educated. Dynamic. Pittsburgh. To find out more about locating your company here, write on company letterhead to: Jay D. Aldridge, Executive Director, Penn's Southwest, One Oliver Plaza, Pittsburgh, Pennsylvania 15222 USA. Or call at (412) 281-4741, Telex 86-6149.

This ad, fifth in a series, is sponsored by National Steel, one of the major corporations proud to call Pittsburgh its headquarters city.

Figure 10-13 An ad for Pittsburgh, Pennsylvania. Ask yourself if you hold a stereotype image of this "steel city" and if the content of this ad presents a different image.

Municipal
Advertising

Municipal advertising (Figure 10–12) refers to the promotion of municipalities as attractive places to live and work. Municipal advertising has become important because locations of manufacturing plants, executive offices, and distribution centers can be as crucial to a company's success as the quality of its products. Sometimes the ads will tout the affordability of living in a particular city; in others, the educational (Figure 10–13) and cultural opportunities; in still others, recreational opportunities. Although the ads are generally directed at the people who will actually choose the location for a plant or office, the ads also serve to "prime" the public opinion of workers who may be transferred to the new locations.

ADVERTISING APPEALS

As consumers of mass communication, understanding advertising is also understanding the different appeals used in advertising messages. Two of the most common appeal to an individual's values and basic needs.

Vail.
A mountain, a village,

a world of warmth.

The mountain is big . . . a playful medley of silky smooth forest trails and challenging powder bowls.
The village is enchanting . . . cozy lodges, intriguing boutiques, mouth-watering restaurants, all in abundance and mingled with laughter-filled nights.
And the warmth is so special that it seems to reach out and touch you. Come ski with us. Feel the warmth of a Vail winter.

Please send me a Vail Vacation Planning Kit describing the best times to ski from November to April.

Name
Address
City   State   Zip
Vail Resort Association, Box CO5S,
Vail, Colorado 81657 (303) 476-5677

Figure 10-14 Aesthetic appeals stress beauty and are frequently employed in ads which publicize the attractiveness of an area. Examine the ad for Cincinnati in Figure 10-12 and notice the aesthetic qualities of the ad. Similarly, notice how "a world of warmth" in the Vail ad also appeals to humanitarian values and sex appeal. (Produced for Vail Associates, Inc. by Advantage Vail. Photo by Peter Runyan)

"We're 2,000 miles apart now, but still just as close."

Before I could tell time, I knew when my dad would be home from work. I'd be waiting at the window, watching for him to turn the corner.

When I was old enough, I'd run to the bus stop to wait for him. And we'd race each other to the porch, then sit on the steps and talk about everything from football to cowboys.

That part of the day was ours. Now, we're 2,000 miles apart, but I still get a kick out of sharing my day with him.

Long Distance is the next best thing to being there.

🔔 Bell System

Figure 10-15 This ad for the Bell System shows strong humanitarian value appeal. (American Telephone and Telegraph Company, Long Lines Department)

Value Appeals

Values are broad-based characteristics of a population defined as *standards that influence individuals to choose between alternative behaviors*. Values are a product of our early childhood development and hence are not easily changed. Since they form the basis for many of our decisions, appeals to our *value structures* are very common in mass communication.

Most researchers have defined the range of values into six broad categories: *aesthetic, humanitarian, intellectual, materialistic, prestigious*, and *religious*.[3] Looking at each of these values separately, we can recognize the value-oriented appeals found in advertising. For example, aesthetic appeals attempt to evoke a sense of beauty and grace in our environment (Figure 10–14). Humanitarian value appeals are some of the most widely used in advertising and can reach across cultural boundaries. Love and respect of people are the basis of humanitarian appeals (Figure 10–15). Intellectual appeals, on the other hand, are based on an individual's love and respect for knowledge.

Some of the most dominant and most frequent value appeals found in advertising are those directed to materialistic and prestige values. We are an acquiring people who enjoy having possessions and the money to purchase them. Our orientation into materialism begins when we acquire our first toys and continues from there. Regardless of whether materialistic values are dominant, people usually make decisions based on their "money's worth." Similarly prestige values are closely matched to our desire to obtain some form of power and position among our peers. When an advertising campaign equates wearing a certain suit with leadership, it is appealing to our desire for prestige.

Appeals to religious values are not used as frequently in advertising as other value appeals are. It is difficult to relate consumer product demand to the worship of a supernatural being. Religious appeals are used principally to persuade people to attend church or to make religion more relevant to their daily lives.

Appeals to Basic Needs

Everyone shares certain biological and psychological needs. The three basic ones are *food*, *shelter*, and *sex*. We need food to live, we need protection from the elements to survive, and we have a biological sex drive to enable the species to survive. Much of the content of advertising is designed to appeal to these needs. Food products, for instance, consume a sizable portion of most media advertising income. It is no accident that among children, Ronald McDonald is the most recognizable character next to Santa Claus. Breakfast cereals predominate on Saturday morning television, and savory sauces precede, permeate, and parcel the evening news. Exhausted athletes quenching their thirst with fruit drink and families barbecuing steaks in the back yard are all part of food product advertising.

Another common appeal, and sometimes a controversial one, is sex appeal in advertising (Figure 10–16). It can be subtle, as in a commercial for eye glasses, or more direct, as in some advertisements in leading men's and women's magazines. All are based on the fact that people are sexually attracted to each other. Multimillion-dollar industries have developed around cosmetics, hair coloring, after shave lotions, padded bras, toothpaste, bikinis, toupées, perfume, and hard liquor, to name a few. Some of the most successful sex appeal themes have been used to market health foods and diet drinks.

The women's rights movement has had some strong criticism for sex appeal advertising. In one state protests arose over the use of a billboard advertisement in which a woman dressed in black velvet was used to sell hard liquor, likening its taste to the soft touch of velvet. In another case when singing star Susan Anton showed up in a men's locker room selling Muriel cigars, one television network even refused to air the commercial (Figure 10–17).

When actress Brooke Shields appeared in ads for Calvin Klein jeans, a network and two New York television stations rejected the ad because they thought it was too suggestive and "feminist." Another New York television station restricted the ads to run only between 7:00 A.M. and 9:00 A.M. and after 9:00 P.M.

**Give him a Christian Dior shirt and tie for Christmas.
And stay home New Year's Eve.**

*Think of the most elegant name in fashion.
Think of the man in your life. Wouldn't they look great together?
Christian Dior for this Christmas, this New Year's Eve,
and all year long. At fine stores everywhere.*

Figure 10-16 Sex appeal in advertising. (C. F. Hathaway Company)

Shelter, like food, is somewhat limited and is usually directly related to building products or similar items. Often combined with materialistic values, such shelter-oriented ads as good investments in a home, long-lasting weather siding, leakproof shingles for the roof, or dual-pane insulated windows are common. Occasionally motels and hotels have also used the shelter appeal on a theme of "coming in out of the storm."

Again it is important to remember that seldom are any of the appeals we have discussed used exclusively. For instance, as you sit in front of your television set or read the evening newspaper, the message that states that the new car is priced $500 cheaper also says it will add prestige to your life, will probably enhance your sex appeal, and has beauty equivalent to a fine artistic masterpiece. Likewise, the appeal for your vote on the city bond issue will more than likely stress that your children's health and education are at stake and that you will save gasoline by not having to take

Figure 10-17 Criticism of sex appeal advertising caused one television network to refuse to air this ad for Muriel cigars, featuring Susan Anton. (DKG Advertising, Inc. and Consolidated Cigar Corporation)

your garbage to the city dump. As consumers of mass communication, you should become familiar with these various appeals and learn to identify them. With this knowledge you will be able to make more intelligent and critical judgments of the issues and products the appeals are designed to support.

OUR PERCEPTIONS OF ADVERTISING

How do we feel about advertising? The answer to that may depend on how we have been taught to react to advertising and to the quality of advertising in the area in which we reside. The American Association of Advertising Agencies (*AAAA*) has studied the issue and found that our opinions of advertising are principally influenced by the advertising we see on television. Naturally, newspaper, radio, and magazine advertisements also have their effect. Direct mail and billboards contribute the least to our opinions of advertising. The AAAA study also showed that the issues about which we are most concerned are advertising's credibility, entertainment value, advertising as a social force, and consumer benefits (Figure 10–18). We are concerned about how advertising manipulates and motivates us, its clutter and intrusiveness, its content, and media support of advertising as an institution. Of these, our negative opinions center on its credibility, content, intrusiveness, and its ability to manipulate and motivate us.

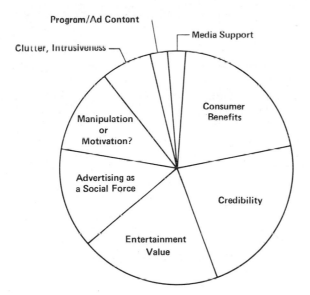

Figure 10-18 The extent to which opinion about each issue contributed to overall attitudes about advertising.

Advertising has been criticized by some for turning us into a materialistic society, isolating the poor who cannot afford the majority of products splashed across billboards, the television screen, and countless other media. Advertising has also been held responsible for creating an artificial demand for products that we do not need and in some cases are actually harmful to us. Counter-advertising, corrective advertising, and social responsibility advertising have emerged from this concern to change the tide of mass persuasion more toward the public's welfare and away from commercial exploitation. Ad executives speaking on college campuses are fielding questions about why the agencies are continually producing ads that show women in their traditional roles as housewives and childbearers, thus supporting the status quo and perpetuating traditional role models for young children. These and many other considerations will remain important concerns. One thing is certain—advertising is a major force in our society. It is an important part of media content and has perhaps a greater effect on our lives than any other type of media message. For this reason, it is important to know as much as possible about all types of advertising messages.

SUMMARY

Advertising agencies are responsible for many of the commercial messages in the mass media. The main asset of the advertising agency is talent. The creative talents of such people as the production director, research director, general manager, photographer, copywriter, media buyer, and account executive are all combined. This "team" of creative people works to call the attention of the public to a product or service. Along with talent, the ad agency uses research, distribution, and monitoring feedback to create its services.

There are also many different types of advertising. Standard advertising attempts to persuade us to purchase certain products and services. Public service ads are those devised by nonprofit organizations to answer a public need. Social responsibility ads seek to warn us against the dangers inherent in the excessive use of some product or service. Counter-advertising concentrates on warning consumers about alleged fraud or misrepresentation in advertising. Corrective advertising is employed when an enforcement agency has determined that a previous ad has misrepresented a product or service. Image advertising is a term primarily applied to messages sponsored by corporations to improve their corporate images. Municipal advertising is becoming more frequent as cities turn to modern marketing techniques to publicize their favorable business climates and opportunities for life style, both of which help to attract new industry to municipalities.

Overall, advertising is accepted as an important part of any economic system, and a large majority of the population feels that it creates better products and services for society. Advertising messages continually surround us. Our value structures, attitudes, and basic needs affect how we perceive these messages.

OPPORTUNITIES FOR FURTHER LEARNING

AAKER, D. A., AND J. G. MYERS, *Advertising Management*. Englewood Cliffs, N.J.: Prentice-Hall, 1975.

ALBION, M. S., AND P. W. FARRIS, *The Advertising Controversy: Evidence on the Economic Effects of Advertising*. Boston: Auburn House, 1981.

ARLEN, M. J., *Thirty Seconds*. New York: Farrar, Straus & Giroux, 1980.

BLOOM, P. N., *Advertising Competition and Public Policy: A Simulation Study*. Cambridge, Mass.: Ballinger, 1976.

BURKE, J. D., *Advertising in the Marketplace*, 2nd ed. New York: Gregg Div., McGraw-Hill, 1980.

BURTON, P. W., AND W. RYAN, *Advertising Fundamentals*, 3rd ed. Columbus, Ohio: Grid, 1980.

BUSCH, H. T., AND T. LANDECK, *The Making of a Television Commercial*. New York: Macmillan, 1980.

CHASE, C., AND K. L. BARASCH, *Marketing Problem Solver*. Radnor, Pa.: Chilton, 1977.

DAVIS, M., *The Effective Use of Advertising Media*. London: Business Books, 1981.

DeLOZIER, M. W., *The Marketing Communications Process*. New York: McGraw-Hill, 1976.

DUNN, S. W., AND A. M. BARDAN, *Advertising: Its Role in Modern Marketing.* Hinsdale, Ill.: The Dryden Press, 1978.

Evaluating Advertising: A Bibliography of the Communication Process. New York: Advertising Research Foundation, 1978.

EWEN, S., *Captains of Consciousness: Advertising and the Social Roots of the Consumer Culture.* New York: McGraw-Hill, 1976.

FARBEY, D., *The Business of Advertising.* London: Associated Business Press, 1979.

FOWLES, J. *Mass Advertising as Social Forecast: A Method for Future Research.* Westport, Conn.: Greenwood Press, 1976.

GARBETT, T. F., *Corporate Advertising: The What, the Why, and the How.* New York: McGraw-Hill, 1981.

GILSON, C. C., AND H. W. BERKMAN, *Advertising Concepts and Strategies.* New York: Random House, 1980.

JEWLER, A. J., *Creative Strategy in Advertising.* Belmont, Calif.: Wadsworth, 1981.

JUGENHEIMER, D. W., AND P. B. TURK, *Advertising Media.* Columbus, Ohio: Grid, 1979.

JUGENHEIMER, D. W., AND G. E. WHITE, *Basic Advertising.* Columbus, Ohio: Grid, 1980.

KLEPPNER, O., *Advertising Procedure*, 7th ed. Englewood Cliffs, N.J.: Prentice-Hall, 1979.

LEIGH, J. H., AND C. R. MARTIN, JR., *Current Issues & Research in Advertising.* Ann Arbor: University of Michigan, 1980.

LEYMORE, V. L., *Hidden Myth: Structure and Symbolism in Advertising.* New York: Basic Books, 1975.

LITTLEFIELD, J. E., ed., *Readings in Advertising: Current Viewpoints on Selected Topics.* St. Paul: West Publishing Co., 1975.

MILLER, E. G., *The Art of Advertising.* New York: St. Martin's Press, 1980.

PARKER, R. B., *Mature Advertising: A Handbook of Effectiveness in Print.* Reading, Mass.: Addison-Wesley, 1980.

PERCY, L., AND J. R. ROSSITER, *Advertising Strategy: A Communication Theory Approach.* New York: Praeger, 1980.

PRESTON, I. L., *The Great American Blow-Up: Puffery in Advertising and Selling.* Madison: University of Wisconsin Press, 1975.

QUERA, L., *Advertising Campaigns: Formulation and Tactics.* Columbus, Ohio: Grid, 1977.

RUNYON, K. E., *Advertising and the Practice of Marketing.* Columbus, Ohio: Chas. E. Merrill, 1979.

SANDAGE, C. H., V. FRYBURGER, AND K. ROTZOLL, *Advertising Theory and Practice*, 10th ed. Homewood, Ill.: Richard D. Irwin, 1979.

SCHULTZ, D. E., AND D. G. MARTIN, *Strategic Advertising Campaigns.* Chicago: Crain, 1979.

WADEMAN, V., *Money-Making Advertising: A Guide to Advertising That Sells.* New York: John Wiley, 1981.

WRIGHT, J. S., D. S. WARNER, W. L. WINTER, JR., AND S. K. ZEIGLER, *Advertising*, 4th ed. McGraw-Hill, 1977.

CHAPTER

11

PUBLIC RELATIONS

PREVIEW

After completing this chapter, we should be able to:

Relate the philosophy and scope of public relations.
Define public relations.
Describe the profession of public relations.
Discuss the publicity function.
Understand the process of dealing with the working press.
Apply public relations practices.
Explain eight steps used to plan and develop a public relations campaign.
Discuss the economics of public relations.
Speculate on future issues facing public relations.

Public relations is directly related to advertising. In fact, sometimes there is a very fine line separating the two. Whereas advertising is concerned with selling a product or service, public relations is concerned with creating a favorable image (Figure 11–1) for the company or organization that produces the product or service. As responsible consumers of mass communication, we need to be aware that many of the messages we receive through the mass media are concerned with public relations. Just how

Figure 11-1 Public relations campaigns are designed to create a favorable image for the company and its products or services. (The Equitable Life Assurance Society of the United States)

thin that line is that separates public relations from advertising is evident when a fast-food chain sponsors a bike-a-thon for a national charity. In the charity ads, the food company's name and trademark are used in the same way they are used to sell sandwiches, yet the message solicits participation in the bike-a-thon. What the company is trying to do is create a favorable impression for itself as well as interest in its products.

PHILOSOPHY AND SCOPE

Why bother with public relations? Why not just concentrate on selling sandwiches? That may be satisfactory if the company's only goal is to sell sandwiches at their current locations. But what if the chain wants to expand? Perhaps the next community in which it plans to build a restaurant has had bad experiences with a similar food chain. As the request for the company's restaurant comes before the zoning board, there is much negative reaction to the application. However, the company officials remind the board and the concerned citizens about their involvement in local charities through their national bike-a-thon. This public relations event may be just what is needed to garner approval for the building application.

A major criticism of public relations is that too often it is similar to shutting the barn door after the horse has escaped. Effective public relations programs should help prevent problems in image and public opinion before they occur, not afterwards.

LINKING INSTITUTIONS AND THE PUBLIC

Many public relations firms work closely with professional organizations that act as a national voice for certain industries. For example, the American Gas Association helps to identify critical issues concerning the gas industry and to gain public support for the industry through national campaigns. The Mortgage Bankers Association represents much of the banking industry and presents journalism awards for stories related to banking. The contest, along with publicizing the banking industry to the news media, also promotes special features, articles, and documentaries carrying the message of the financial world to the public.

Professional organizations on the state level also carry on public relations campaigns and media awards programs. For example, a state health association conducts an annual awards contest to recognize media organizations for excellence in three categories: best in-depth factual presentation of a health matter, best promotional activity on a health matter, and best support given to public health programs on a continuing basis.

DEFINING PUBLIC RELATIONS

The definition of public relations is somewhat nebulous since it involves so many varied functions, depending upon the particular public relations campaign or institution involved. In 1948 Denny Griswold, editor of *PR News*, defined it by saying:

> Public relations is the management function which evaluates public attitudes, identifies the policies and procedures of an individual or organization with the public interest, and plans and executes a program of action to earn public understanding and acceptance.

Today that definition encompasses a diversity of job titles, such as "public relations manager," "director of public information," "public affairs officer," and "coordinator of university relations."

THE PROFESSION OF PUBLIC RELATIONS

The professional opportunities associated with these titles are many. For instance, public information officers operate in virtually every branch and at all levels of government. Virtually every educational institution and every major corporation employs people in similar functions. Many corporations consider public relations important enough that they create a separate division under the direction of a vice-president. Charitable and religious organizations must also involve themselves in public relations, as must hospitals. In some cases these organizations have complete media divisions which are responsible for producing syndicated radio and television programs, producing documentaries, and even publishing books.

Public relations involves many different functions. An awareness of the interrelationship between two of these functions—publicity and press relations—is important to an understanding of how public relations operates.

THE PUBLICITY FUNCTION

Publicity deals directly with the *gatekeepers* who control the flow of news. The forces directed toward such gatekeepers can be tremendous. These people are usually bombarded with telephone calls from press agents, piles of press releases on everything from new products to politicians, tickets to free dinners at which a politician is appearing or a company is delivering its latest annual report (Figure 11–2), and countless other tactics from people and organizations all trying to receive free media exposure. If they successfully receive this free exposure, it is often more valuable than media exposure obtained through advertising campaigns. For example, if a politician makes a favorable impression on the evening news, the publicity can be more credible than if he or she appears in a paid political advertisement.

Figure 11-2 Annual Reports are "corporate images" which not only provide a public relations function but also "sell" the company.

Those whose job it is to obtain free publicity work very hard at it, sometimes with limited results. Many newsroom personnel are so accustomed to press releases that they often do not bother to open mail from certain organizations. In many cases the press releases are tossed away because the person trying to obtain free publicity has done one of two things.

First, they have inundated the media with almost daily press releases. Rarely does a single subject or person warrant that much publicity. After all, if you were a regular reader of a newspaper and saw that every issue has a story about a local politician, you would begin to grow suspicious of the paper's credibility.

Second, many press releases try to masquerade as news. The press release begins with a lead sentence that might be used to introduce a major international event; the second paragraph reveals, however, that the politician is simply speaking at a fund raiser. The gatekeeper thus loses trust in the source of the press release and tends to shy away from using future releases.

APPLIED PUBLIC RELATIONS

How do public relations professionals avoid these pitfalls and create a strong working relationship with the press?

Researching
Outlets

Become aware of your local media. Read, not skim, the stories in the local newspaper and concentrate on the content of local broadcast news. Observe what these media carry as news and ask yourself *why* these stories appear. What is it about a particular story that attracted their attention? You'll find the stories usually contain news of interest to local readers, listeners, or viewers, something that affects their lives.

Keeping
Contact

Begin to develop an extensive mailing list of all newspapers, radio, and television stations in your area, as well as wire services, regional magazines, even corporate and institutional publications. Update the mailing list every three or six months, verifying the name and title of every broadcast news director and every newspaper and publication editor. Store the list in a memory typewriter or word processor to allow those addresses to be individually but electronically typed directly on an envelope. A release is less apt to be thrown out when it is packaged in an "individually typed" envelope rather than encased with an impersonal mailing label.

If you cannot do the job for whatever reason, assign a media contact person, responsible for maintaining congenial relationships with the press. If, as in the case of small firms, no one has time to assume an additional task, hire a part-time consultant. With one person responsible for press liaisons, your organization can maintain consistent, concentrated local press relations.

Being Effective	If you are designated to be in charge of press relations, there are a number of ways to increase your effectiveness. First, introduce yourself to the media in your region. As with any other business, you must know your "territory" and your "clients"—the editors of area newspapers and news directors of local radio and television stations.

Don't forget the wire services. These gatekeepers control the news pipeline to print and broadcast subscribers throughout the state and have access to the regional and national wires. Their job is to deliver news of interest to their readers, listeners, and viewers, but they cannot be everywhere at once. Remember, you are an additional "reporter." If you're able to tell them that story accurately and fairly, they'll come to depend upon you as a news source.

Check back with these press contacts. When a reporter wins an award, write or call your congratulations. Similarly when a reporter writes or broadcasts a particularly good story or editorial, write or call your appreciation. Occasionally, if not offending other members of the press, schedule exclusive interviews. "Exclusives" are bread and butter for the press.

Using Press Releases	The cardinal rule for developing an effective press release is to make certain the subject of your release is actually "news." If you gain a reputation for sending out "fluff," the end result will be an ineffective public relations program. Remember, one of the best compliments the press can bestow upon those in public relations is that of a trusted news source.

Write your release so that it can be used easily. First and foremost, be brief. Radio journalists have approximately 30 to 60 seconds to devote to an individual story. Television journalists have about two minutes. Newspaper space is also limited by the amount of advertising in the issue. Include your name and phone number on your release for reporters wishing more information. Type your message double-spaced with wide margins so that is is easy for reporters and their editors to read as well as to rewrite or change to suit their editorial needs.

Include in your one-page story the following: Who, What, When, Where, Why, and How. Your story should answer the questions, "What happened?" "Who did it happen to?" "When did it happen?" "Where did it happen?" "Why did it happen?" "How did it happen?"

Use "inverted pyramid style" of writing. Include the most important facts at the top of your story, saving the background information for later paragraphs. Time and space limitations may require an editor to omit part of your story, usually the last part but at least your most important information will be saved because it is in the first paragraph.

Write the press release in the present or even the future tense, if possible. The past tense infers that the news is old, and the chances are less that the release will be used. Misspelling a name, using an incorrect address, or giving a wrong date will cost you your credibility.

A press release sent to newspapers and stations across a broad region will be more effective if it has a local angle. It may necessitate writing more than one version of the release. Most reporters are extremely busy. Some cannot take time to "localize" a story.

Follow up on your press release with a phone call to key media people. Make certain they received the release. Ask if they have any questions. This "extra mile" can make the difference in press coverage.

Meeting Deadlines

Pay attention to deadlines for area media. Make certain your press release arrives in time. There is nothing more aggravating to public relations people and reporters than to receive a newsworthy press release too late to print or air it. If you are running out of time and must choose between media, consider hand-delivering the release to the wire services. If they use your release, it will be electronically transmitted to most media in the state within minutes. Find out if some of the major media outlets have an electronic data transmission system, whereby documents can be electronically transferred. If they do, your company may want to buy such a system.

Visualizing a Television Message

When you're writing a press release for television, ask yourself if your release would be more effective with an illustration. Ask yourself, could the story be enhanced with a slide, film clip, or videotape. Some stations, for example, prefer to make their own slides. Remember, quality control is especially important for television.

Handling Press Conferences

Suppose your company has something newsworthy enough that it wants to call a press conference. How do you plan for a press conference? Again, make certain that what your company wants to publicize warrants a press conference. Reporters are busy people and resent spending valuable time at a trumped-up event. If you have been carefully nuturing your credibility, reporters will attend.

Have a press kit prepared beforehand with press releases, background information, and copies of any charts or graphs that might help explain your story.

Dealing with Bad News

An accident hits your company. A corporate official is arrested. Suddenly you have reporters everywhere. What do you do? You do not hide your head in the sand and hope they will go away. What you do is to prepare for the eventuality long before it happens. As we said earlier, effective public relations should be able to close the barn before the horse escapes, not after.

Appointing a corporate spokesperson is a must. It may be someone the press can talk to until someone in authority can be reached. Inform other personnel who the spokesperson is and that any official statement should come from that individual. The intent of this request is not to restrain people from making comments, but rather to present an official and knowledgeable voice, sometimes assuring that only one story is released and that stories that are related contain verified facts.

The person selected as a spokesperson should be able to handle questions from the press as openly and as honestly as possible. "No comment" sometimes conjures up the image of a cover-up. If you won't tell your story, the press will simply get the story elsewhere, and it may not be what you wanted said. A war of words, however, is inadvisable. Remaining professional and above it all is essential, especially when a reporter has an axe to grind. Try to avoid awkward situations before they start by developing and keeping good media liaison. Finally when you don't know the answers, say so.

THE PUBLIC RELATIONS CAMPAIGN

In our previous example you were an in-house public relations professional working for a corporation. Now imagine you are a public relations consultant hired to coordinate and develop a public relations campaign. In this case your client is a regional government agency which has received funding to promote carpooling. Carpooling is especially important to the government agency since it serves an area bordered by three fairly large cities that surround a mammoth industrial park. The roads leading into the park are simply not sufficient to carry the traffic caused by the area's rapid industrial expansion. Yet development in the park was designed to blend in with and protect the natural terrain. Highway and parking lot expansion are therefore unacceptable. Your job is to develop a coordinated public relations campaign which will encourage the employees of companies in the park to carpool or vanpool. The planning and execution of the campaign centers around an eight-step procedure.

Analyzing the Need

First, analyze the need. In the carpooling example you know a problem exists—the limited highways to transport workers to the industrial park and the desire to keep natural terrain and avoid constructing additional parking lots.

From a public relations perspective you need to do three things: (1) convince the companies located in the park of the importance of carpooling, (2) gain their participation in publicizing the program to their employees, (3) persuade the employees to carpool. You should make a basic research survey to determine basic *demographic* characteristics of the area and the awareness workers already have of available carpooling.

Establishing Objectives

Next, establish your goals. They must be realistically obtainable yet challenging. You need to know what your goals are to provide a firm foundation and direction for your campaign.

What goals do you establish, and how can you tell if the program is successful? In the example, the results of your needs analysis research will help answer those questions. In other public relations campaigns the goals may be less exact, less easily measured. Your research reveals that a 20 percent participation rate will offset any traffic congestion predicted over the next ten-year period. Therefore you need to enlist 20 percent of the employees in the industrial park who are commuting to work to join the carpooling program. You also want to convince 50 percent of the companies in the park to participate in the carpooling program and to help publicize the program to their employees. If you reach those goals, then the ridesharing program will be a success.

Now that you understand the need and your goals, begin to develop the actual campaign. Arrange a news conference to announce the program to the press. At the news conference you will want to have an official of the government agency, representatives of local business, and a representative from the U.S. Department of Transportation which has provided the grant to publicize the program.

Besides launching the program at a news conference, you can get additional publicity by buying ads in newspapers (Figure 11–3) and on radio, making posters and brochures available for area businesses, creating local radio public service announcements, sending out press releases, and tying in television public service messages produced by the U.S. Department of Transportation (Figure 11–4).

Since you want to reach drivers, radio is an important advertising medium, so plan to buy "drive time," that time when people are commuting to and from work. You might hire a free-lancer who is skilled at developing

TRI-A-RIDE
to work.

It's Free.
TRI-A-RIDE will match you, free-of-charge, with other commuters in the Triangle Area who travel your route to work. You can join them to share the ride, share the gas, and save some money. We'd like to help you get started.

Call 549-9999.

Triangle Area Ridesharing is a carpool matching system sponsored by the Triangle J Council of Governments.

Figure 11-3 Effective campaigns can involve cross publicity with different media, such as this newspaper ad and the television public service announcement illustrated in Figure 11-4.

sign up for ridesharing

Public Service Announcement available in 30 second length on video tape.

U.S. Department of Transportation

Listen to me, I'm going to tell you how you can

save energy, fight inflation, clean up the air, and reduce our dependence on foreign oil.

Just like that... and you can save money too.

Hundreds of dollars a year. How? Don't drive alone.

Share the ride to work in a carpool, vanpool. Use public transportation. Sign up for ridesharing, sign up for independence.

 ENERGY EFFICIENCY

A Public Service of the United States Department of Transportation Washington, D.C. 20590

Carpool-Vanpool, Lorne Green: 30 sec. January

Figure 11-4 A television public service announcement to which an ending can be added which will "localize" the announcement for a specific community.

voice characters and sound effects to develop a "Professor Carpool" character to call attention to the carpooling program. Advertising can be used to support and reinforce your public relations efforts.

*Pretesting
the Plan*

When you write a term paper, you know the final draft will be better if you or someone else spends time editing it. The same preparation strategy holds true for both advertising and public relations. Once messages are disseminated through the mass media, there is no way to call them back. You could send additional messages to correct mistakes, but it would be costly and might not be effective. You could lose an account, ruin your reputation with a client, and be out of business.

To increase their effectiveness, pretest your ideas before implementing them. Pretesting can range from simply showing a copy of a press release to someone else in the office to actually testing the entire campaign in a real-life setting. The former is vital as a very minimal check on accuracy. The misspelling of names on a press release can creep in unnoticed until it's published in the newspaper. Sometimes the color and wording of a brochure may mean one thing to one person and something entirely different to someone else. Finding this out before the brochures are printed can save thousands of dollars, not to mention misunderstandings.

*Revising
the Plan*

Taking into consideration all of the information gleaned through pretesting, you now might want to make revision in your plan. In the case of your carpooling program, you discovered in pretesting that each business was unique and communicated with its employees in different ways. Whereas one business was satisfied to place the posters on conspicuous bulletin boards, other companies wanted to send a flyer to each employee in their pay envelope. Another wanted to run advertisements in the newspaper along with the corporate *logo*. Still another wanted to run the ads in the company newsletter along with special feature stories in the company magazine. Based on these initial contacts, you might revise your original strategy of sending posters and literature to each company and instead hand-deliver the materials. This would permit you to discuss the plan with corporate public relations representatives and tailor the plan to each company's need.

*Implementing
the Plan*

Once all of the pretesting and revision has taken place, you are ready to fully implement the plan. You develop a coordinated advertising plan using the same visual theme in all print advertising and billboards. It also employs the same color combination and a visual logo of a wooded area on all the literature publicizing the program. You purchase "drive-time" radio time to air your commercials when prospective carpoolers would be driving to and from work. You then meet with representatives of each company in the industrial park to explain the support already available through the placement of billboards, newspaper, radio, and television advertising.

Evaluating Effectiveness

Since you have already established criteria for determining a successful program, your job of evaluating effectiveness will be relatively easy. You can determine from polling the various corporate participants if 20 percent of their employees began taking part in the carpooling program. You can easily check to see if you achieved your goal of 50 percent participation by the companies operating in the industrial park.

In the example, percentages make it easy to determine if you reached your goal. However, keep in mind that evaluating the effectiveness of other types of campaigns is more difficult. Say, for example, that a company wants to improve its "corporate image." Measuring corporate image is sometimes difficult and requires attitude or "image" surveys, which are more complex than simply reading percentages. First, good surveys which get at the heart of the issues are expensive. Some companies do not want to commit the funds necessary to achieve a good base from which to build an effective public relations campaign and then measure its effectiveness. Second, unless the surveys are designed and administered by people skilled in research methodology, they can miss measuring the very issues the company wants to examine. For example, asking people how they feel about the "industrial plant's impact on the community" may garner opinions on everything from pay scales to pollution. Third, some companies try to link public relations effectiveness to increased sales, blaming it for losses when the overall marketing plan may actually be at fault.

Reviewing Procedures

The minute a campaign is completed is the perfect time to sit down and say, "If I did it again, what would I do differently?" Review the answers to those questions now while the decisions and actions are still fresh in your mind so that the next time a similar campaign occurs, you will have learned from your efforts.

Although "reviewing procedures" is listed as the last step in your campaign, keep in mind that the process of reviewing procedures is important at every stage of a campaign. Change is inevitable, and everyone involved in the campaign should keep an open mind to suggestions while keeping prepared for the unexpected.

THE ECONOMICS OF PUBLIC RELATIONS

Much of the income ad agencies receive comes from media commissions. Other fees for talent, printing, and graphic design can be charged to clients and credited to the agency's account. While there are similarities between the way an ad agency receives income and the way public relations firms are paid, there are distinctions between the two.

The Fixed-Fee Agreement

The *fixed-fee agreement* is an agreement between the public relations firm and a client to perform services for a prearranged fee. The client allocates a budget for public relations services, and it is up to the firm to stay within that budget. For example, assume a company wants to participate in a fund-raising drive for handicapped children. The company determines it can spend a certain amount of money on the project. It then contracts for a fixed fee with a local public relations firm for the firm to handle its participation in the charity. In another case a company may be opening a new plant and will contract with a local public relations firm to work with the corporate in-house public relations director and coordinate efforts at the plant opening. The local public relations firm's participation is important since it will be much more sensitive to the "personalities" and needs of the local media than will the corporate public relations people who may be located hundreds of miles away.

If printing and media buys are necessary, these are figured into the fixed fee before it is quoted and agreed to by the client and firm. Important to the fixed-fee agreement is an accurate estimate of expenses by the public relations firm. Cost overruns will usually be met with opposition, and if the firm wants to keep the account, and in some cases its reputation, it must absorb any losses incurred by underestimating the cost of its services.

Fixed-Fees with Billing Agreements

Along with the standard fixed-fee arrangement we just discussed, a public relations firm may also bill the client for such additional services as advertisements placed with media, graphics design, talent, and printing expenses. Depending on the agreement with the client, the billing arrangement may involve the firm tacking on a 15 percent commission to the cost for these services. In other words, if a graphics designer charges the public relations firm $100, the firm charges the client an additional 15 percent or $115, and the firm keeps the $15 as income. In this instance, the firm operates much like an advertising agency.

For the client the fixed-fee with billing arrangement creates a somewhat open-ended economic relationship, but for the firm, it is an economic lifesaver since it eliminates the risk of underestimating.

Consultants

In addition to fully staffed public relations firms, individual public relations consultants are also in the field working with companies. Many times these specialists work on a single campaign or in a trouble-shooting capacity to determine how to solve a particular public relations problem. A consultant usually works on a flat-fee basis charged to the client.

FUTURE ISSUES IN PUBLIC RELATIONS

Public relations is not new, but it is becoming increasingly important in a society where the lines of communication between our institutions and the public are not always open. Moreover, with new technology developing constantly, there are new ways to communicate and new ways to change public opinion. One hundred years ago the local newspaper was the only medium of distribution short of posters to communicate mass messages. Today we have access to everything from direct-mail flyers to press releases which arrive in our living room via a home computer with direct access to news bureaus, commodity futures, and the latest stock market quotations.

We can only guess about how people will be using these new technologies to make decisions. The news stories which once draped the inside pages of a newspaper may be hidden behind the circuits of a central computer and appear only as single index line on a video display terminal. What new skills will be needed to convince the consumer to "call up" the story which will communicate the message the public relations person has been hired to disseminate? How will these new electronic opinions be formed?

What we may see as we become increasingly individualized in our use of the mass media is a general emotional distance occurring between the public and our institutions. In the past the opinions we held of a local business may have resulted from the interpersonal communication we had with the owner of that business. Tomorrow our opinions may be determined by how well its products are displayed on the screen of the cable television shoppers' guide.

SUMMARY

Effective public relations prevents problems before they start. In general terms, public relations has two interrelated functions: generating publicity and press relations.

People working in public relations are found in all levels of government, business, the military, law enforcement, and education, among other fields. The activities of such individuals range anywhere from writing press releases to producing documentaries and publishing books.

We discussed examples of applied public relations, using corporate examples. A corporate public relations person working in a small business finds much of the work involves good relations with local media. In addition, keeping contact lists, being able to prepare press releases for print and broadcast media, the ability to coordinate successful press conferences, and being able to deal with good as well as bad news are important qualifications.

The public relations consultant works in a somewhat broader perspective and is many times responsible for coordinating or planning complete public relations campaigns. A step-by-step process toward effective campaigns includes analyzing the need, establishing objectives, developing a plan, pretesting the plan, revising the plan, implementing the plan, evaluating effectiveness, and reviewing procedures.

The fixed-fee agreement, the fixed-fee with billing, and consultation are three economic relationships a public relations firm can establish with its clients.

The future of public relations will include expanded responsibilities for those who work to bridge the gap and keep communication channels open between institutions and the public. Working with and understanding the role of new media technologies will be equally important to the future of public relations.

CUTLIP, S. M. AND A. H. CENTER, *Effective Public Relations,* 5th ed. Englewood Cliffs, N.J.: Prentice-Hall, Inc., 1982.

GUBERMAN, R., *Handbook of Retail Promotion Ideas.* Reading, Mass.: Addison-Wesley, 1981.

HARRIS, M., AND P. KARP, *How to Make News and Influence People,* Blue Ridge Summit, Pa.: TAB Books, 1976.

NEWSOM, D., AND A. SCOTT. *This is PR: The Realities of Public Relations*, 2nd ed. Belmont, Calif.: Wadsworth, 1981.

PEAKE, J., *Public Relations in Business.* San Francisco: Harper & Row, Pub., 1980.

REILLY, R. T., *Public Relations in Action.* Englewood Cliffs, N.J.: Prentice-Hall, 1981.

ROSS, R. D., *The Management of Public Relations: Analysis and Planning External Relations.* New York: John Wiley, 1977.

STRANG, R. A., *The Promotional Planning Process.* New York: Praeger, 1980.

WEINER, R., *Profession's Guide to Publicity.* New York: Richard Weiner, Inc., 1976.

CHAPTER

MASS MEDIA NEWS

PREVIEW

After completing this chapter, we should be able to:

Distinguish between the gatekeeper chain and gatekeeper group.
Describe news diffusion and the effect of high intensity and low intensity news.
Define source credibility and media credibility.
Explain how economics affect the gatekeeper.
Understand that legal restrictions are imposed on the working press.
State how deadlines can affect the flow and content of news.
Describe the role that personal and professional ethics play in the gatekeeper's performance.
Realize how competition can affect a gatekeeper.
Distinguish between news value and the news hole.
Discuss attention factors in media messages.
Talk about the influence of peer group pressure and feedback upon gatekeepers.
Explain the problems involved in processing news under crisis conditions.

Of all the messages processed through mass communication, news is certainly one of the most important. But the news we read in the evening newspaper or watch on television does not reach us through a set of formulas. Many forces are at work in this process, including human forces which are subject to mistakes, misjudgments, misunderstandings, and biases.

In this chapter we shall study the qualities of news, what affects its dissemination, and those forces that affect the gatekeepers who process it. We shall begin by examining the difference between gatekeeper chains and gatekeeper groups.

THE GATEKEEPER CHAIN

There is a *gatekeeper chain* when more than one *gatekeeper* processes the same news story with a *limited amount of feedback* from other gatekeepers in the chain. To understand the concept, imagine that you are a newspaper reporter assigned to the scene of a flood (Figure 12–1). You interview people, survey the damage, and write up the report. You (G_1) then call your story back to the city desk reporter (G_2) who takes down all the information and rewrites your story to read:

> The Clearwater River overflowed its banks today near the downtown section of Pineville. First reports are that two persons sustained minor injuries and three homes were destroyed.

The city editor (G_3) then reads the story and changes it to:

> Flash flooding hit Pineville today as the Clearwater River overflowed its banks, destroying homes and injuring residents in the area.

Now the story goes to a major wire service bureau in the state. The bureau receives a continual inflow of information for all over the region and uses this information to prepare a report for its subscribers. At the wire service a reporter (G_4) works to collate all the information about flood damage. Reports are coming in from all over the state, telling of property damage and numerous injuries. Compiling all of this information, the wire service story is sent to subscribers and reads:

> Flash floods swept over the state today doing millions of dollars in damages and injuring more than 100 persons. Pineville and other cities were hit by the sudden storms.

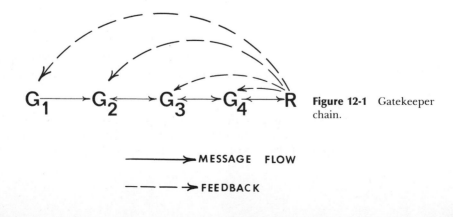

Figure 12-1 Gatekeeper chain.

Obviously the story that reaches the wire service subscribers is entirely different from the one you originally reported from the scene at Pineville. Nevertheless, word for word, there have been millions of dollars in damages, more than 100 persons have been injured, and Pineville is one of the communities which has been hit. On the other hand, a person who read the wire service description and had relatives in Pineville could easily have been left with the impression that the town had been swept off the map. Rearrangement of the factual material, minor changes made in the story by various gatekeepers, and the merging facts at the wire service all led to a variation in the story.

News distortion in a gatekeeper chain can be frequent, especially when a central clearinghouse for information, such as a wire service or other news bureau, has conflicting information from which to compile a report. Crowd estimates can be particularly difficult. Different news organizations covering the same story can report significant variations in the estimates of a crowd. A political rally, protest, convention, or other news event may look either like a small gathering of a few friends or a large assembly, depending on who is looking. When these variations are transmitted back to the wire service, there is bound to be distortion.

In some cases, chains of gatekeepers, working without checking and rechecking information, can produce embarrassing consequences. An example was the reported shooting of a Washington, D.C. Mayor, Marion Barry:

> . . . WRC, the NBC owned-and-operated television station in Washington, D.C., . . . at 9:46 P.M. on June 29 broke the story that Mayor Marion Barry had been shot and critically wounded and was being rushed by helicopter to Andrews Air Force Base Hospital. The bulletin was based on a tip from a caller identifying himself as mayoral assistant James Taylor; it had been confirmed by a WRC producer who, ignoring the number for the mayor's command center on file in the newsroom, had phoned the contact number that the caller had supplied.
>
> . . . WDVM-TV, the CBS affiliate in Washington, D.C., . . . at 9:56 P.M. reported that Barry had been shot and that his condition was "listed as critical" by "officials" at the hospital. Alerted to the story when its news people heard on the station's two-way radio scanners that WRC was organizing a crew to go to Andrews, WDVM . . . confirmed the story for itself with a call not to the hospital, but to base headquarters. As luck would have it, a spokesman at the command post did indeed know about the shooting—having just heard the bulletin on WRC.
>
> . . . CBS radio and NBC radio, on the strength of the WDVM announcement, aired reports of the shooting on their 10 P.M. newscasts.
>
> . . . UPI . . . at 10:06 P.M. ran an "urgent" on the shooting, fudging the absence of its own confirmation by attributing the story to WDVM.
>
> . . . WJLA-TV, the ABC affiliate, and WTTG-TV, a Metromedia station, both prompted by the UPI "urgent," aired reports of the shooting without troubling to confirm it.
>
> . . . ABC's west coast edition of World News Tonight, after learning from its Washington bureau that all three major local television stations had reported the shooting of Mayor Barry, went on the air with the story at 7:11 P.M. Pacific time. (The network did not bother to give viewers an update, since, according to producer Steve Skinner, the news went to "only eleven or twelve states.")

... The Associated Press at 10:34 P.M.—after more than thirty minutes of hanging tough and explaining to clamoring clients that it had not put the story on the wire because it was unable to confirm it ... sent out the first accurate account of the evening: the shooting of Mayor Barry was, in fact, a hoax.[1]

THE GATEKEEPER GROUP

Now we shall examine a *gatekeeper group* (Figure 12–2). Gatekeeper groups can operate at any point within a gatekeeper chain. The advantage that such groups have is that they permit interaction among gatekeepers. Interpersonal communication among members of the group results in greater accuracy, simply because the information can be discussed and checked before it is disseminated to the public. The message is clarified, changed, rewritten, and evaluated by each member of the group.

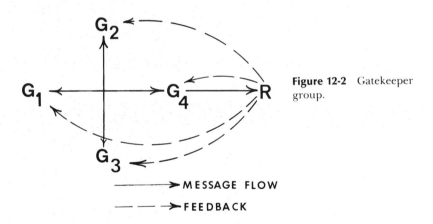

Figure 12-2 Gatekeeper group.

Consider what might have happened to *the flood story* at any point in the gatekeeper chain if there had been a gatekeeper group. The conversation among the group might have sounded like this:

OK, what have you been able to pick up?
Well, it wasn't too bad at Pineville, just some homes lost.
I checked with the sheriff, and he said the two injuries were to children.
Were they hurt very badly?
No, but the family dog drowned and a ten-year-old girl almost drowned trying to save it.
That might be good to note. Stories like this can become too impersonal.
Good idea. I wouldn't have thought of that.
I'll write up a draft, and then you can check it over.
OK. I'll see if there's an update.
The interaction permitted a check and a recheck of the story's content.

Gatekeeper chains and gatekeeper groups have many different combinations. The presence or absence of either does not mean news distortion *will* occur. It simply means it *can* occur, and as consumers or practicing professionals of mass communication, we should be aware of this potential.

New developments in electronic journalism have eliminated certain uses of the gatekeeper group without necessarily producing distortion. For instance, a television news correspondent in a foreign country may send a report by satellite to a news bureau in New York. From there the report may be retransmitted to subscribing stations. The report remains relatively unchanged from the time it was originally prepared. The only real distortion might be technical *"noise,"* such as visual or audio interference.

Although the gatekeeper chain and gatekeeper group are in a sense a "road map" of the flow of news, other factors are pertinent to *how news is diffused* into society and *how we react* to it.

NEWS DIFFUSION

News diffusion is defined as *the process by which news is disseminated to the receiving public.* To understand news diffusion, let's see what happens when the story about the flood reaches the public. An executive of a fertilizer company buys a copy of the paper at the newsstand, reads the story about the flood, and is alarmed at the reported damage to farms owned by a number of his customers in the heart of the flood region. He goes back to the office and immediately tells his colleagues about the flooding. They in turn tell other colleagues, and within a ten-minute period, almost the entire office is clustered around the radio to hear news updates on the flooding.

The experience of the fertilizer company executive illustrates what happens when news of high value reaches the public. In this case the news was disseminated through interpersonal communication. Then, those who heard about the event through interpersonal communication turned to the mass media for additional information. Within a relatively short time it had reached many other people who were also affected by the event. To recapitulate, when news of high value enters a social system, (1) it diffuses very rapidly; (2) much of the diffusion process is through interpersonal communication; (3) there is a tendency to search out mass media to learn more about the event; and (4) there is a desire to tell other people about the event.

Now let's consider what might occur when the news is of low value. Let's assume the executive purchased the newspaper, but that this edition contained a story about an economic upturn in agricultural industries. When he returns to the office, the sales manager walks in, and the executive tells her about the economic forecast he has just read. She replies with a quick "that sounds good" and continues with her work. About half an hour later another colleague goes out for a coffee break, returns with the same edition of the newspaper, and reads about the predicted economic upturn. He mentions it to the executive who says he already has seen the item. About this time some members of the sales force stop by the office to ask about new accounts. The sales force leaves, and there is no mention of the item in the newspaper. Meanwhile the radio plays softly in a corner of the office. Now ask yourself, what is different about the diffusion of news in this case?

First, we can see that although the economic forecast affected the employees of the fertilizer company, it was not of immediate concern to them as was the news of the flooding. Second, the diffusion process occurred less through interpersonal communication and more through individual purchases of the evening newspaper. Third, no one hurried to gather round the radio to hear the latest updates. As the radio continued to play background music, many people in the office remained unaware of the news. Comparing the diffusion patterns of the two events, we see that both interpersonal and mass communication participated in the diffusion process, but that these varied depending on the value of the event.

Many other factors will affect news diffusion: the time of day an event occurs; when an item is released by the media; to what audience and through what medium it is first released; and the education, age, sex, and other demographic characteristics of the audience, to mention a few.

SOURCE AND MEDIA CREDIBILITY

Ever since the ancient Greeks noted that a message delivered by one spokesperson had more impact than the same message delivered by a different spokesperson, the concept of *ethos* or credibility has been accorded much attention. Research into interpersonal communication has investigated how the source of a message can affect its reception, a concept called *source credibility*. We know, for instance, that the leader of a nation will have more credibility when talking about foreign policy than the factory worker expounding on his preferences to a hometown audience. The factory worker, on the other hand, may have more credibility than the national leader when the subject is factory production. Besides the effects of message and source on the ultimate reception of a message, we must also reckon with the role of different media. Their contribution to a story's believability is called *media credibility*.

Research has suggested some general trends about media credibility, trends that *do not* necessarily remain constant but do reflect the public's perception of the news media. For example, in the 1930s when radio first appeared as a medium, it quickly jumped ahead of newspapers as the most credible news source. Whether it was really more credible or contained fewer inaccuracies than newspapers is debatable. Yet the public clearly preferred hearing the news over the radio, and there were several reasons for this. First, the medium was new. Second, the dimension of sound added a realism to mass communication that was even reflected in Franklin D. Roosevelt's increased political stature. His "fireside chats" were not only novel but also instrumental in cementing a closer bond between the people and the president of the United States.

On Halloween night in 1938, radio's credibility as a mass medium was vividly demonstrated when actor Orson Welles broadcast his famous radio drama, *The War of the Worlds*. Its theme was a takeover of the East Coast of the United States by spaceships from another planet. Despite repeated announcements that the play was merely a radio drama, Welles succeeded in producing mass panic among thousands of listeners, who actually waited in fear for the Martians to swallow their community. Even today's highly refined television techniques cannot command this same blind belief.

Since the 1930s, research has examined the public's changing perceptions of media credibility. We know, for example, that newspapers have regained much of the overall credibility that they lost to radio in the thirties and early forties. We have also seen television surge ahead as today's most credible medium. *However, we should be cautious in assuming that messages received via other types of mass communication are therefore less credible.* Television's enormous credibility is attributable not only to the tremendous impact it has on our lives but also to its two dimensions of sight and sound. People also spend more time with television than with any other medium.

It is also important to consider each message and source separately in judging media credibility. For example, few members of the financial community would contest the fact that the *Wall Street Journal* covers economic news more credibly than any television station does. However, if you were to ask a rodeo rider which medium he considered more credible for rodeo news, *Rodeo Sports News* or his favorite television station, *Rodeo Sports News* would undoubtedly be the winner.

Certain characteristics inherent in different media lend themselves to different types of messages. The ability of television to capture the motion and color of major sporting events is unequaled by any other medium. A detailed contour map necessary to understand a complex story on the environment can, on the other hand, hardly be reproduced on a television screen.

FORCES AFFECTING NEWS SELECTION

Although we may feel that after reading a newspaper and a news magazine, listening to various radio newscasts throughout the day, and watching a local and national television news program, we have been exposed to all the news that could possibly happen in one day, such is not the case. Reporters are constantly faced with a multitude of stories from which to choose, scores of events to report, and a myriad of decisions to make about what should appear in print or on the air. Why are some stories chosen and others are not? Why do some stories carry pictures and others do not? Why are some stories on the front page or lead a broadcast while others are either buried or do not ever appear? All of these questions are summarized by one: What forces affect gatekeeper decisions?

Economics   With the exception of noncommercial media, such as campus radio stations or some campus newspapers, most media are commercial, profit-making businesses. Our context is the free world countries where the majority of media operate as free enterprises. And an economic fact of life is that these media must make a profit or go out of business.

For example, the ability of a newspaper to afford to send investigative reporters to cover a story will have a direct bearing on the type and amount of information the public receives. Labor costs and newsprint costs also affect the operation of a newspaper. Perhaps economic considerations might force a newspaper to reduce the number of pages. Even if it does cut back, however, the number of advertising pages, the newspaper's bread and butter, will probably not be affected. News will be what suffers.

Economics can affect messages on other media. Television stations can be very expensive to operate. Purchasing and maintaining electronic equipment as well as trained personnel can be costly. Like newspapers, television has certain basic operating costs. Engineers, directors, and producers all draw on the station's payroll. The evening anchorperson is not trained to repair a $100,000 color camera. In television, when personnel cuts take place, the news department may be the first to go.

Radio is no different. In some cases economics can play havoc with this medium. At many radio stations one or two persons staff the entire news department. Eliminating one position may reduce the department's ability to cover news by fifty percent. Economic considerations such as permission to make long-distance telephone calls and freedom from other on-air duties at the station all can affect how well a news team can gather and disseminate news to the public.

Legal Restrictions

The media most affected by legal restrictions are radio and television. One example of these legal shackles is the Fairness Doctrine, which requires radio and television stations to present all sides of a controversial issue. Although this may seem like common sense, it can place a station in a position of "bookkeeper," such as when a group of California stations found themselves faced with actually measuring the time given certain issues and then providing an equal amount of time for the opposing side. Moreover, the issues must be balanced over all types of programming, not merely advertising or editorials. News programming is included under this umbrella, as is entertainment programming. We shall learn more about these legal restrictions in other chapters.

Nor are newspapers immune from regulations. A reporter can be called to testify in a criminal case and be requested to reveal the sources of confidential information. Although the reporter can refuse the request and will usually win a contempt of court action brought against him or her because of this refusal, the threat of subpoenas may be enough to discourage the practice of using "unnamed" sources. It may also discourage these sources from openly revealing information to a reporter.

Deadlines

Every reporter lives with deadlines. The ever-present deadline can make the difference between gaining an exclusive story or being "scooped" by a competitor, between being able to report all the facts or just some of them, between being able to use a story or being forced to hold it for lack of information. For news reporters, deadlines mean working under extreme pressure on a daily basis, pressure that forces them to spew forth their ideas, thoughts, and words at an often unsettling pace.

In the broadcast media the pressure of deadlines is even more acute. Because radio and television can air news almost as it happens, deadlines literally come every minute. Of course, problems with accuracy arise when stories are broadcast too soon after a news event occurs. It takes time to gather news and prepare a story. Even when a story is reported live, there are many background details that cannot be reported without time and effort.

Deadlines and news reporting are always companions. To be a responsible consumer of news you need to know how they work together. When we read or hear news, we assume accuracy. We must, however, be alert to certain cues which may help us gauge the degree of this accuracy. Such phrases as *"at press time"* and *"at least one source"* alert us to missing gaps in a story or missing links in a chain of information.

Personal and Professional Ethics

Assume you have just written a story for your newspaper about a local resident arrested on a charge of drunken driving. As you are preparing to send the story to your editor, the owner of the paper walks in and kills your story because that particular resident had spent $50,000 in advertising last year. What would you do? Many reporters would quit immediately in disgust. Although economic concerns are undeniably important, the professional journalist cannot condone the suppression of newsworthy information, and his or her function is finding and publishing the truth. For the owner to have suggested compromising the newspaper's integrity for the sake of advertising would not only be considered poor journalism but also prostitution of the press and a request to participate deliberately in a breach of ethics. Or what would you do if you opened your mail and found two free tickets to cover a local political rally? Marked "complimentary," the tickets are what journalists call *freebies.* Would accepting the tickets prejudice your coverage of the rally? Even it if would not, should you still accept them? What if buying the tickets was simply too expensive, and you had the choice of either accepting the tickets as freebies or not covering the rally? What if the competition accepted the tickets and covered the rally, gaining considerable reader or viewer interest in the report? Answers to these questions are not easy.

Freebies can range from tickets to a church supper to excursions to a foreign country, which also are called *junkets.* Some newspapers have a policy against accepting freebies. If the function is important and requires paid admission, then the newspaper will purchase admission passes. The policy against freebies tries to prevent any opportunity, regardless of how small, for biased reporting. The paper wants its readership to receive objective news coverage and does not want freebies to endanger that objectivity.

The author's own experiences in covering stories have often involved personal ethics. On one occasion two fugitives from a mental institution stole a car and headed for the state line. After their capture there was an opportunity to take pictures of them as they emerged from the squad car in police custody. However, the following day, when it came time to use the story, a superior made the decision not to use the names of the two fugitives or their pictures. The case fell into the realm of crimes committed by suicidal and mentally ill persons. The story that reached the public mentioned only that a stolen car had been recovered and that two escapees from the state correctional institution had been taken into custody.

About two months later a similar incident forced another judgment of personal and professional ethics. On an early Sunday morning the static on the police monitor was broken by a report of a sniper in a ravine shooting at police cars with a high-powered rifle. One officer whose car had been hit was keeping the man "pinned down" until assistance arrived. As the morning progressed, a number of other law enforcement officers arrived at the scene. It was determined that the sniper, who had escaped from the same state correctional hospital, had a high-powered rifle with a telescopic sight and ample ammunition. Unsuccessful attempts by law enforcement officials to entice the man to surrender prompted a decision that a group of officers, armed with rifles, form a human line and walk side by side toward the ravine, all the time requesting the man to surrender. Nightfall was rapidly approaching, and many felt that in darkness it would be easy for the man to escape and threaten the lives of area residents. As the police line moved to a ridge above the ravine, the fugitive shot one of the officers in the stomach. Immediately the line opened fire. The fugitive's body, riddled with holes, was a somewhat gruesome sight. Nevertheless, the same superior who had determined not to use the pictures or names of the fugitives who had stolen the car, made the decision to use pictures of the dead sniper as well as his name and all the details surrounding the event. Why that decision?

A number of personal and professional reasons were behind that decision. For one, the police officer died. In addition, this reporter's superior had been employed by a federal law enforcement agency before becoming a journalist. Moreover, the police officer had been a high-ranking official in one of the communities served by the news medium. The incident, unlike that of the stolen car, had occurred in broad daylight, and the standoff with police officers had lasted for almost eight hours. The activity also took place on the only main highway connecting two major communities. All traffic for an eight-hour period was either stopped or detoured. In short, it was an incident of which the public became very much aware, especially in an area in which events of this magnitude were not that common. Thus, the story captured more attention than it might have, had the event occurred in a high crime area.

Similar personal and professional decisions are made every day by gatekeepers responsible for reporting news to the public. Ask yourself what decisions you might have made had you been the news executive. Would you have used the story with the pictures? Would you have used film of the event if it had been available?

Competition

Concern over the possibility of another medium nabbing a scoop story (Figure 12–3) is typical of competition among the news media. This competition is inherent in a free press and usually fosters the reporting of more than one opinion or approach to a story. Competition can also nurture the growth of true investigative journalism. Media in competition will sometimes take the extra initiative to explore an issue in depth rather than be satisfied with superficial information.

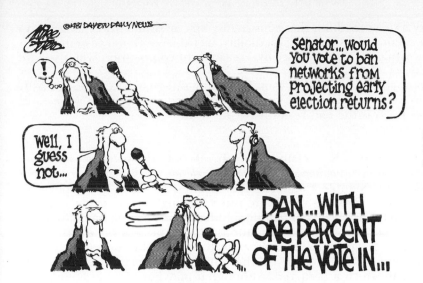

Plain economics encourages competition in many areas. Larger markets, for instance, have the financial base to support more than one news medium; large metropolitan areas can support even more than one newspaper. Some smaller communities, however, face information control by a single news medium that may be biased on certain issues. In such cases competition would have a positive effect on freeing the flow of information to the public.

Negative aspects of media competition surface particularly in the electronic media, in which the ability to air news almost simultaneously as it occurs breeds frenzied competition. The result can be news distortion. For example, put yourself in the seat of a radio news cruiser that has just received a call to cover a labor dispute at a major industrial plant. Also enroute to the event is another news cruiser from a competing station. Both cruisers are equipped for live, on-the-scene broadcasts. Both of you, sensing the other's presence, begin live reports. You describe a group of men fighting and report that it is the result of another flareup at the picket line. After the broadcast you get out of the news cruiser to learn some details. You discover the fight you were reporting was actually a rough-and-tumble football game. You are shocked. Had you not been quite as concerned about the competitive edge, you would have taken the time to investigate all the details. Your actions were inexcusable, to say nothing of being unprofessional and irresponsible. You may also have opened yourself and your station to a libel suit. Except under extreme crisis conditions, such as a natural disaster, the impression that listeners spend their time switching back and forth from one station to another just to see who airs the news first is a fallacy.

One of the nation's leading broadcast news consultants reacts negatively to the common practice among broadcast journalists of listening to the competition's newscasts. Such a practice, he contends, is a waste of time and effort since the listeners or viewers who are tuned to your station will not know what the competition is scooping you on in the first place.

Certainly a news medium that consistently airs or prints information days after an event occurs will lose credibility. Yet the continual dissemination of misinformation due to hasty overreaction to competition will also lose credibility.

Competition in itself is beneficial and safeguards a free press. It must, however, be taken in its proper perspective so that both a free and *responsible* press is the end result.

News Value

The term *news value* is a relative term. It refers to the *value or importance of an event or the potential impact of an event in relation to other events or potential news stories.* For example, the news value of the story about the sniper who shot the police officer was very high. But it was high *in comparison* to other events that may have been happening simultaneously or that had happened on previous occasions in the community. Note the words "in the community." The geographical sphere of influence of the message also will affect its value. Again, the story of the sniper had its highest value on the community in which it occurred. Although it may have had enough value to be selected as news by a gatekeeper in a neighboring community, its relative value there might have been less.

Another factor influencing news value is the number of people affected by an event. For example, the sniper's actions caused many hundreds of people to be stopped or detoured from their normal route of travel. The fact that a high-ranking police officer was shot affected everyone in the community in which he worked. All the people affected by an event contribute indirectly to the news value of the story.

The News Hole

The *news hole* is directly related to news value. To understand this concept, imagine a large auditorium full of students, each of whom wants to spend the day on a bused field trip. But only one bus load can go. When the instructor looks over the auditorium, everyone in the room tries to gain attention. Some shout. Others wave their hands and hold up signs. Still others become the object of attention by sheer accident, such as having a sign fall on their heads. Still, only a small percentage will be able to make the trip since space is limited. Now compare the students to all the events in society competing for the attention of the gatekeepers in the media. Some events may be deliberate attempts to gain attention, such as issuing a press release. Other events attract attention by accident, such as the sniper shooting. Certainly many of the events to which a gatekeeper is exposed can become news stories, but the news hole is only so big. There are only so many pages to a newspaper and so much time allotted to an evening television newscast.

The size of the news hole is also determined by the number and news value of events that attract the gatekeeper's attention. A busy news day may fill the news hole to capacity, leaving little room for press releases. We, the public, are exposed to only a fraction of the information that *could* be reported to us. What we do receive is determined by the *size* of the news hole in relation to the number and value of the messages that vie for attention in the limited space or time at the gatekeeper's disposal.

Attention Factors

Many things besides news value draw our attention to messages in the media. Although certain stories in themselves often command our attention, others may need help in the form of visual or aural stimuli. A story about a robbery, for example, might make the front page because an accompanying picture attracts attention to it. Audio actualities on radio and film or videotape on television all can attract attention to the newscast.

Although both the print and broadcast press have been accused of sensationalism, the use of pictures, newsfilm, and audio actualities do make a difference in which stories are reported as well as their location in the news hole. Certainly we should not assume that members of the press choose news only because of these added factors. If something important happens to a community, it will make news regardless of the visual or aural stimuli it contains. However, these factors *do make a difference* for stories with minimal or average news value. For example, if an editor has two stories about a beauty pageant and can only use one story, the one with the accompanying photograph of the queen may have an advantage.

Research suggests that more information communicated in the audio portion of a television newscast will be remembered by viewers when that audio is accompanied by interesting video. A study conducted at the University of Florida at Gainesville reported:

> Increased information gain from the interesting video occurred because the pictures aroused the subjects' curiosity and interest; thus viewers paid more attention and used the audio to explain the absorbing pictures. When the interesting video ended and the newscaster's head reappeared, the (viewers) may have found less to arouse their interest; thus the less interesting talking head may have caused less attention, and subjects may have listened less intently.[2]

As consumers of mass communication, we need constantly to keep in mind that these attention factors can make a difference. Ask yourself the next time you read a story on the front page of a newspaper or see the lead story on the evening newscast: Is it there because of its news value or because it had a picture, newsfilm, or audio actuality to accompany it?

Peer Group Pressure

One effective means of peer group pressure is the increasing number of local newspaper columnists who keep an eye on the broadcast press through regular columns about radio and television. Items that have appeared in newspaper columns include analyses of internal hiring practices and broadcast employee qualifications. Some broadcasting stations have also aired programs critical of the work of newspaper journalists. Such peer group pressure among media personnel can make gatekeepers look seriously at their work and the implications it has for the public.

Numerous *journalism reviews* keep a watchful eye on members of the press. The nationally famous *Columbia Journalism Review* is one example, and there are other journalism reviews in large cities which treat the activities of the press in their own locale.

Lack of peer group pressure can have just the opposite effect. This condition, which exists especially in small communities, is reflected in an almost narrow-minded reporting of the issues. Consider the life of a newspaper reporter in a small town that has no local radio or television station. Also imagine that the reporter has no one else on the staff to assist with newsgathering and reporting. What happens? Stated succinctly, the reporter can get into a rut, and the public suffers. Day in and day out the reporter sees the same people and reports the same news, but at no time is his or her work scrutinized. The basic facts can be correct, but the stories reflect a narrow line of thought that pervades the limited number of news sources. Isolation and lack of peer group pressure thus have resulted in a daily diet of limited reporting.

Perhaps the reporter develops what is commonly called a "police complex," in which the only real news the community receives comes from the police blotter and the traffic fatality list. Meanwhile, the other issues affecting the community go unnoticed and unchecked. This kind of reporting could permit a slow takeover by a corrupt government, it might even seem, with the tacit approval of the press.

Reacting to Feedback

Perhaps the most common form of feedback to the press is the letter to the editor. Although not necessarily representative of the general public, letters to the editor have been a traditional part of journalism since a free press began to flourish.

Some newspapers may even employ an *ombudsman* whose sole responsibility is to review feedback from the readership. Reaction to this feedback may prompt moderate changes such as a new emphasis on the coverage of a particular series of events. On the other hand, it may influence editorial comment or even necessitate special feature articles.

You should never discount the impact of reader or viewer feedback. Your own letter to the editor or the head of a major broadcasting complex can be a key indicator to personnel on what the public is thinking and why. One letter indicates to management that there are many other people who undoubtedly feel the same way but just did not take the time to write. One letter may be all it takes to prompt a reporter to question a news source, check an additional source, or conduct an in-depth interview that reveals a serious problem affecting the community.

PROCESSING NEWS UNDER CRISIS CONDITIONS

In recent years increased attention is being given by both news organizations and the public to mass media news disseminated under crisis conditions. Such acts as terrorist campaigns, frequent world conflicts, and inevitable natural disasters all create abnormal conditions within the media. The work load becomes tremendous, and schedules are carried out under great tension. The media become a clearinghouse for information, both incoming and outgoing. There is also far more information processing than under noncrisis conditions. A radio station, for example, may typically schedule a newscast once every hour. During a crisis, however, the same radio station may switch its format to continuous all-news programming in order to serve its stricken community. The station's staff may also change roles in a crisis. The program and music directors may completely disregard their regular duties to aid the news staff. In addition, the news director will usually assume charge of all on-air programming.

The reality of crisis reporting impacted the Pacific Northwest when Mount St. Helens erupted into an active volcano. Coverage of the exploding mountain, injury and death, and blankets of ash covering thousands of square miles became the lead story on front pages around the world. But reporting the crisis was not easy. Professor Ron Lovell of Oregon State University examined some of the problems in reporting the eruption and talked to reporters about their experiences.[3] He found reporters faced a major problem getting news out of the area because of the military. Used to a chain-of-command approach, the National Guard sent information first to central command posts and then back to the scene before reporters could gain access to the facts they needed for stories.

Limited information was also a problem. One reporter commented, "We started off dealing with the county sheriff which was OK. Then one day the army moved in. They believed it was war. We were not told anything but bits and pieces."[4] The military information breakdown caused some reporters to go to great lengths to obtain information. One reporter stated, "We started doing things we were not proud of, like sneaking around and dressing someone in a uniform to get into the medical morgue tent. This would not have happened if the military had not been in charge."[5]

News media also faced the difficulty of filing stories for two different audiences, national and local. One wire service editor pointed out, "When you have something like this happen, you have a main story written for national consumption—the flood, the devastation, the body count, the atmospheric effects."[6] Yet at the same time, local items demand attention. "What about Yakima and Spokane? What's happening to agriculture and the water supply?" Relatives wanted information about missing kin. Where had the bodies been taken? This was the local news slant.

Problems arising from these abnormal conditions vary. Two university professors, Galen Rarick and James Harless, investigated what happens to local radio stations and their personnel during a natural disaster. Under a grant from the National Association of Broadcasters, they investigated the operations of stations when faced with one of three different types of disasters—flood, blizzard, or tornado. They found a major problem for station personnel during a disaster was transportation. They found that four-wheel drive vehicles were almost indispensable. Without four-wheel drive, tire chains had to be used for many hours at a time, causing tires to "overheat and pop," leaving personnel stranded and unable to provide needed information to their community. Rarick and Harless also found that if reporters had two-way radios installed in their vehicles, they would not have to waste time searching for a telephone to relay their reports. Station personnel also felt that walkie-talkies would be beneficial and, for stations that could afford it, auxiliary power and transmitting equipment. Management agreed that "if you are off-the-air, you are nothing."

Rarich and Harless also found that news personnel had to be careful of whom they used as news sources. One reporter found the public to be no more than 80 percent accurate in reporting details of a snowstorm. In the case of tornados, people were so "frightened and shocked" after it hit that they could not remember what happened. Government agencies may be reliable sources for accurate information, but their helpfulness varies town to town. A classic case cites a local official who could not even find the key to the courthouse!

SUMMARY

This chapter dealt with mass media news. Two forces that have a significant effect on news processing are the gatekeeper group and the gatekeeper chain. The gatekeeper chain allows for little interpersonal communication between gatekeepers and consequently fosters a greater opportunity for distortion. The gatekeeper group, on the other hand, permits gatekeepers to check and recheck each other's decisions and therefore reduces the opportunity for distortion.

Closely related to the gatekeeper's responsibility is the process of news diffusion. News of high value will be diffused faster than news of little value. As in processing, rapid diffusion will increase the possibilities for distortion. In high intensity situations we are more apt to communicate and to receive important news by word of mouth than from mass media.

The medium that disseminates the news can also affect how we perceive it. Because society is so attuned to television, it is generally accorded more credibility than other mass media in the face of conflicting news reports. Media credibility is, however, not an absolute, but a relative term. Each medium has its own forte, lending its superior credibility for a particular message and source.

Many factors work together to influence the selection and treatment of mass media news. These include (1) economics, which refers to the profit-loss structure of media operating as part of a free enterprise system; (2) regulations legislated by local, state, and federal governments to control the operations of the media and to ensure freedom of the press; (3) deadlines, which limit the time in which a gatekeeper can collect news before it is necessary to disseminate it; (4) personal and professional ethics, those forces on which gatekeepers often base decisions in selecting information to become news; (5) competition, the safeguard of a free press in a democracy; (6) news value, which signifies the importance of one event in relation to other events; (7) the news hole, which refers to the total amount of available space or time in which to present messages in order of decreasing value; (8) attention factors, visual or aural stimuli that enhance a story; (9) peer group pressure, those decisions that are influenced by colleagues; and (10) reaction to feedback, the communication received from the audience.

Under crisis conditions different forces act upon the media and alter this news selection and dissemination process. Increased dissemination of news, demands on the media to provide information, and difficulty in gathering information are just some of the problems that can occur.

Almost Midnight: Reforming the Late-Night News. Beverly Hills, Calif.: Sage Publications, Inc., 1980.

BABB, L. L., ed., *Of the Press, by the Press, for the Press and Others Too. . . .* New York: Houghton Mifflin, 1976.

BAKER, B., *Newsthinking: The Secret of Great Newswriting.* Cincinnati: Writer's Digest Books, 1981.

BEHRENS, J. C., *The Typewriter Guerrillas: Closeups of 20 Top Investigative Reporters.* Chicago: Nelson/Hall, 1977.

CANTRIL, A. H., ed., *Polling On the Issues: Twenty-One Perspectives on the Role of Opinion Polls in the Making of Public Policy.* Cabin John, Md.: Sven Locks Press, 1980.

COLLINS, J. E., *She Was There: Stories of Pioneering Women Journalists.* New York: Julian Messner, 1980.

CROZIER, E., *American Reporters on the Western Front, 1914–1918.* Westport, Conn.: Greenwood Press, 1980.

DOWNIE, L., *The New Muckrakers.* New York: Mentor Books, 1978.

DYGERT, J. H., *The Investigative Journalist: Folk Heroes of a New Era.* Englewood Cliffs, N.J.: Prentice-Hall, 1976.

EDGAR, P., ed., *The News in Focus: The Journalism of Exception.* South Melbourne: Macmillan of Australia, 1980.

ENGLISH, E., AND C. HACH, *Scholastic Journalism.* Ames: Iowa State University Press, 1978.

FISHMAN, M., *Manufacturing the News.* Austin: University of Texas Press, 1980.

GANS, H. J., *Deciding What's News: A Study of CBS Evening News, NBC Nightly News, Newsweek, and Time.* New York: Pantheon, 1979.

GIBSON, M. L., *Editing in the Electronic Era.* Ames: Iowa State University Press, 1979.

HAGE, G., AND OTHERS, *New Strategies for Public Affairs Reporting: Investigation, Interpretation, and Research.* Englewood Cliffs, N.J.: Prentice-Hall, 1976.

HALBERSTAM, D., *The Powers That Be.* New York: Knopf, 1979.

HILDERBRAND, R. C., *Powers and the People: Executive Management of Public Opinion in Foreign Affairs, 1897–1921.* Chapel Hill: University of North Carolina Press, 1981.

HOHENBERG, J., ed., *The Pulitzer Prize Story II, 1959–1980.* New York: Columbia University Press, 1980.

HOUGH, G. A., 3rd, *News Writing,* 2nd ed. Boston: Houghton Mifflin, 1980.

HULTENG, J., *The News Media: What Makes Them Tick?* Englewood Cliffs, N.J.: Prentice-Hall, 1979.

JOHNSTONE, J.W.C., E. J. SLAWSKI, AND W. W. BOWMAN, *The News People: A Sociological Portrait of American Journalists and Their Work.* Urbana: University of Illinois Press, 1976.

KIRSCH, D., *Finance and Economic Journalism: Analysis, Interpretation and Reporting.* New York: New York University Press, 1979.

MALONEY, M., AND P. M. RUBENSTEIN, *Writing for the Media.* Englewood Cliffs, N.J.: Prentice-Hall, 1980.

McCOMBS, M., D. L. SHAW, AND D. GREY, eds., *Handbook of Reporting Methods.* Boston: Houghton Mifflin, 1976.

MERRILL, J. C., *Existential Journalism.* New York: Hastings House, 1977.

METZLER, K., *Newsgathering.* Englewood Cliffs, N.J.: Prentice-Hall, 1979.

MEYER, P., *Precision Journalism: A Reporter's Introduction to Social Science Methods*, 2nd ed. Bloomington: Indiana University Press, 1979.

MITFORD, J., *Poisoning Penmanship: The Gentle Art of Muckraking*. New York: Knopf, 1979.

MOLLENHOFF, C. R., *Investigative Reporting*. New York: Macmillan, 1981.

NORDENSTRENG, K., AND H. I. SCHILLER, eds., *National Sovereignty and International Communication*. Norwood, N.J.: Ablex, 1979.

PICKETT, C. M., ed., *Voices of the Past: Key Documents in the History of American Journalism*. Columbus, Ohio: Grid, 1977.

POWERS, R., *The Newscasters*. New York: St. Martin's Press, 1978.

RICHSTAD, J., AND M. McMILLAN, eds., *Mass Communication and the Press in the Pacific Islands: A Bibliography*. Honolulu: East-West Center, University Press of Hawaii, 1978.

RUBIN, B., *Media Politics & Democracy*. New York: Oxford University Press, 1977.

RUBIN, B., *How Others Report Us: American in the Foreign Press*. Beverly Hills, Calif.: Sage Publications, Inc., 1979.

SCHWOEBEL, J., *Newsroom Democracy: The Case for Independence of the Press*. Iowa City: School of Journalism, University of Iowa, 1977.

SPRAGENS, W. C., *From Spokesman to Press Secretary: White House Media Operations*. Washington, D.C.: University Press of America, 1980.

TICHENOR, P. J., G. A. DONOHUE, AND C. N. OLIEN, *Community Conflict and the Press*. Beverly Hills, Calif.: Sage Publications, Inc., 1980.

WENDLAND, M. F., *The Arizona Project*. Mission, Kans.: Sheed Andrews & McMeel, Inc., 1977.

WICKER, T., *On Press*. New York: Viking, 1978.

WILDE, G., AND M. ACKERSVILLER, *Accident Reporting in the Canadian Daily Press*. Kingston, Ont.: Department of Psychology, Queen's University, 1977–1979.

WILLIAMS, P. N., *Investigative Reporting and Editing*. Englewood Cliffs, N.J.: Prentice-Hall, 1978.

CHAPTER

MASS COMMUNICATION AND NEW TECHNOLOGIES

PREVIEW

After completing this chapter, we should be able to:

Describe the concept of cable television.
Identify the components of a cable system.
Be aware of the communication possibilities of two-way cable.
Explain pay cable.
Explain cable radio.
Explain the applications of fiber optics.
Explain the applications of microwave technology.
Understand multipoint distribution systems.
Trace the development of satellites from Sputnik through the present.
Explain COMSAT and INTELSAT.
Recognize the operation of domestic, educational, and direct broadcast satellites.
Analyze the political concerns over satellite communication.
Describe subscription-pay TV.
Compare and contrast teletext with videotex.
Be aware of the experiments in electronic newspapers and magazines.
Talk about newspapers and cable origination.

Trace the development of home video recorders and videodiscs.

Discuss the changes in television receiver design.

Explain low-power TV.

Detail the development and media applications of computer technology.

Explain the lure of a home computer and video games.

Describe teleconferencing and cellular radio systems.

Speculate upon the impact of new technologies on mass communication.

New technology is rapidly changing the way we receive and consume mass media. The actual definition of mass communication is changing to encompass more specialized media. Where once the printed press meant mostly newspapers, books, and magazines, today we can tune in electronic editions of the *Wall Street Journal* and *Better Homes and Gardens.*

Cable television which once meant a few more television channels today means a two-way communication system in many cities where services such as banking, shopping, security, and even medical monitoring are possible. The decision in 1982 to permit A.T.&T. to enter into home information systems and other new technologies may mean that those same services will soon be available on a widespread basis via telephone lines.

This chapter will examine these new technologies which are part of the communication and information revolution. We will also place them in a historical perspective while investigating their implications for our society.

CABLE TELEVISION: THE BASIC CONCEPT

The only communities capable of financially supporting several television stations are large population centers. The residents of these large cities have thus long enjoyed good reception of all the major network programs as well as those produced by independent stations. During television's early years, however, people living far away from these centers had no recourse but to sit in front of their sets, watching distant signals blurred by interference. People began investing in every type of complex antenna system imaginable, and a maze of television antennas covered rooftops everywhere.

In the late 1940s there was a breakthrough in the previously futile efforts to receive clear, interference-free television signals from distant stations. A large antenna was placed on a hilltop high above the average terrain, from which the distant signals would be carried by shielded wires, called *cables*, directly into home television receivers. Thus began the development of *cable television,* also called *community antenna television* (Figure 13–1) or *CATV.* Residents whose televisions were connected to a community antenna paid a monthly rental fee for the service. Others could, of course, still use their rooftop antenna but usually sacrificed good

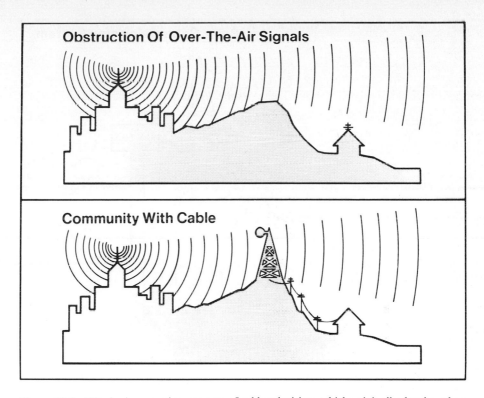

Figure 13-1 The basic operating concept of cable television, which originally developed as a means of receiving distant television signals. The concept has now been expanded to include significantly increased channel capacity and two-way capabilities. (NCTA)

reception. It soon became evident, especially in outlying areas, that the way to receive quality television signals and have a wide selection of channels was to link onto the local cable system. With the development of color TV sets, which accentuate poor reception, cable television became even more helpful.

CATV refined its system even further, including the application of sophisticated transistorized electronic equipment and improvements in the construction of the cable. Both developments made it feasible to send many more channels via cable without having to eliminate intermediate channels because of interference. Instead of receiving about half a dozen programs on the VHF spectrum, a cable subscriber could receive all 12 channels if the cable system carried all 12. Still other developments in cable expanded this 12 channel capacity to carry as many as 40 or 50 separate channels, and fiber optics can handle as many as 1000 channels.

COMPONENTS OF A CABLE SYSTEM

To understand how a cable system operates (Figure 13–2), let's examine its parts.

Basic Cable Television System

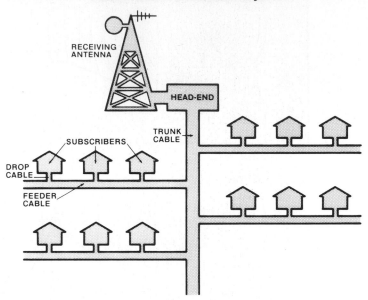

Figure 13-2 A basic cable television system is divided into three major components: the "head end" which includes the receiving antenna and a combination of human and hardware technology, the "distribution system" carrying the signals along different routes and includes trunks and feeder cables, and "home connections" which include the drop cable that connects to the home terminal. (See also Figure 13-4.) (NCTA)

Figure 13-3 Although glass fibers (Figure 13-7) are being employed in some areas, cable systems primarily use coaxial cable, which includes an inner metal conductor, a plastic foam cover, a metal outer conductor, and a plastic sheathing cover over that. (NCTA)

Coaxial Cable

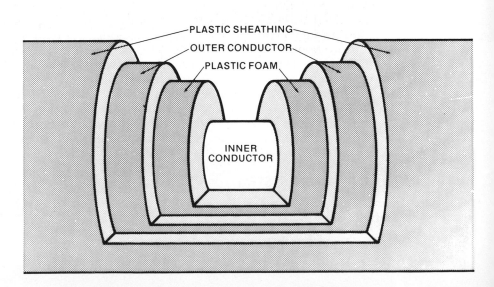

Head End   The center of any cable system is the *head end*. The head end is a combination of human beings and technology. The human side includes the personnel who actually operate the cable system. The head end's technical components include the *receiving antenna* system which receives the signals from a distant television station. The receiving antenna system usually is a tall tower on which are attached a number of smaller antennas specially positioned for receiving the distant signals. The tower can be located anywhere from a hillside outside of town to the top of a mountain far from a residential area. Installing the tower and antennas entails major construction, using everything from lumber cutting crews to giant helicopters.

The head end may also be television production facilities such as cameras, lights, and other studio hardware, depending on the size of the cable system and how much locally originated programming there is in the studio. The facilities can range from a small, black and white camera to full-scale color production equipment. With all of this in mind, we will define the head end as *the human and hardware combination responsible for originating, controlling, and processing signals over the cable system.*

Distribution System   Another important cable system component is the *distribution system*, which disperses the programming. The main part of the distribution system is the cable itself. A *coaxial cable* (Figure 13–3), which is used in most cable systems, consists of an inner metal conductor shielded by plastic foam. The foam is then covered with another metal conductor, and that in turn is covered by plastic sheathing. This protected cable may either be strung on utility poles or buried underground. The primary cable, or main transmission line, is called the *trunk cable*. It usually follows the main traffic arteries of a city, branching off into a series of smaller *feeder cables*, also called *subtrunks*. The feeder cables usually travel into side streets or into apartment complexes.

Home Connection   The actual connection to the home is made with a *drop cable*. This coaxial cable goes directly into the house where it connects with a *home terminal*. The home terminal, in turn, connects directly to the back of the television set. In most cable systems the home terminal is simply a splicing connector that adapts the drop cable to a two-wire connector which fits onto the two screws on the back of every television set. In two-way cable the home terminal is more complex and may even include a small keyboard. Some cable systems install these more sophisticated home terminals even though two-way cable may not be operative yet on the system. When it does become operative, the system and the subscriber will be ready.

TWO-WAY CABLE

Two-way cable systems, sometimes called two-way interactive television, permit the subscriber to feed back information to the head end. They are able to bring a wide variety of services, such as shopping, banking, and education into the home.

Figure 13-4 Two-way cable systems provide more than mere television programming. These systems include a home terminal that allows the customer to receive such services as electronic mail, bank-at-home, and home medical monitoring. (Warner Communications, Inc.)

Figure 13-5 Security systems are one service some predict will be a major function of cable systems. (Reprinted from the Sept. 15, 1980 issue of *TVC* magazine)

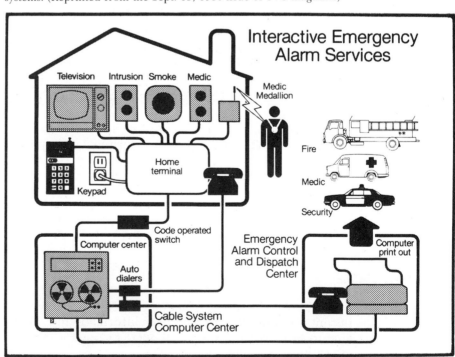

Uses of Two-Way Cable

In education, for example, special questions appear on the screen at regular intervals in the program. Students answer the questions on a home terminal (Figure 13–4), which can be as complex as a typewriter keyboard or as simple as a touch-tone telephone. The home terminal is hooked into a central computer, which aids the instructional process in two ways. First, it notifies the student if he or she has selected the right answer. Second, it tells the instructor how many students have selected the right answer. If the proportion of correct answers is low, the instructor can repeat the lesson.

Banking services permit the home subscriber to deposit and transfer funds. Shopper services permit the subscriber to electronically purchase goods through the home terminal and then receive the goods via direct delivery, as with groceries, or through the mail. Security (Figure 13–5), and medical monitoring are other applications.

Feedback Loops

Subscribers communicate with the system's central computer through *feedback* loops.

Two-Way Cable Transmission Techniques

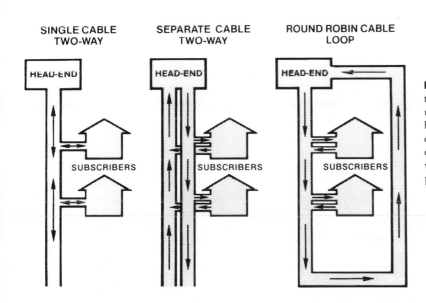

SINGLE CABLE TWO-WAY

SEPARATE CABLE TWO-WAY

ROUND ROBIN CABLE LOOP

Figure 13-6 Two-way cable transmission systems open up new services for subscribers. Different systems are cable of different functions, depending upon the type of wired transmission employed. (NCTA)

Feedback loops (Figure 13–6) are generally of three types. One is a single cable used for both transmitting to and receiving from the subscriber. Another uses two separate cables. Incoming signals reach the subscriber through one cable, and outgoing signals return from the subscriber to the head end using the second cable. A third, called a *round robin cable loop*, is an adaption of single cable but with separate drop cables.

PAY CABLE

Pay cable is defined as *the delivery of information and/or services to cable subscribers by assessing fees beyond the regular rental fee.* Pay cable should not be confused with *subscription TV* or *pay TV*, terms defining a special over-the-air TV distribution system where the signal is "scrambled" as it leaves the transmitter and is descrambled using a special device on the home receiving set. The advantage of pay cable is the opportunity to see first-run movies, exclusive viewings of major sports events, and other special entertainment programs.

Subscribing

People can subscribe to pay cable in a number of ways. The simplest is to pay a monthly fee to the cable company in order to receive a special channel of exclusive programming. The subscriber pays this set fee regardless of how much he or she views the pay cable channel. Or the subscriber can pay on a per-program basis. In this system, two-way capability is necessary so that the subscriber can signal the cable company to send the desired program into his or her home.

Economics and Competition

One of the main arguments in favor of pay cable is its ability to broadcast to small, select audiences, something over-the-air broadcast stations cannot do. The problem is economic. To obtain profitable advertising revenue, over-the-air station programming must attract audiences in the millions, especially network programming. Programs which cannot achieve this type of saturation are many times kept off the air. Fine arts programming, educational programs, and similar fare are on what the pay-cable components base their appeals. By charging for programs, the need for advertising revenue on pay cable is eliminated, or at least substantially reduced.

Arguments also exist against pay cable. Commercial broadcasters claim that pay cable destroys the free system of broadcasting upon which the nation's broadcast communication systems were built. Other groups claim that pay cable discriminates against the poor who cannot afford the additional rates. The opposing arguments intensify with suggestions that pay cable could make exclusive contracts with program producers, placing programs on pay cable which would normally have attracted an audience large enough to warrant airing them on over-the-air broadcast stations. That suggestion makes commerical broadcasters bristle.

Theater owners showing first-run movies have still another argument against pay cable. They contend that when first-run movies are made available through pay cable, people will stay at home and watch them instead of going to the neighborhood movie theater. Examples supporting and denying these contentions are used by both proponents and opponents of pay cable.

CABLE RADIO

Television is not the only medium channeled by cable systems. This wired concept also applies to radio. The principle for cable radio is the same as it is for television. Distant station programming is cabled into a local community. As expected, commercial radio broadcasters vehemently oppose cable radio. Radio is a very local medium. When a small community's cable system imports one or more stations from outside the local market, the radio broadcaster feels the economic pinch. The importation usually translates into a reduced audience and, consequently, reduced advertising dollars. The problem is not as serious for television since many communities do not have local television, but few do not have local radio stations.

FIBER OPTICS

Fiber optics (Figure 13–7) are thin strands of glass fiber through which light passes. This light, which travels at a very high frequency, carries the broadcast signals. The use of fiber optics dramatically increases the amount of information that can be carried on any single cable system.

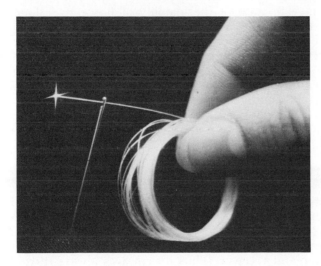

Figure 13-7 Fiber optic cable, tiny glass fibers through which light waves pass, dramatically increases the channel capacity of a cable system. These cables are also finding widespread use in telephone systems. (Western Electric)

Controlling the Fiber Optic Marketplace

Control of something usually gives power to the controller. It is no different with fiber optics. This time, the telephone companies could be in the driver's seat. Before development of fiber optics, only the cable companies had a channel capacity large enough to transmit and receive computer data directly into the home. The telephone company's home hookups were just not satisfactory for transferring those large amounts of information. Fiber optics has changed all of that. Telephone companies already have an established system of installation much larger than that of the entire cable industry. Their personnel, equipment, and even utility poles are ready now to install fiber optics in any home, anywhere.

Application of Fiber Optics

A future scenario even envisions telephone companies with their own television stations and networks feeding a "wired nation." The social implications of such a phenomenon are far-reaching. How would the computer of the future adapt to such a system? Behavioral scientists are currently studying how children are affected by constant association with television from birth. What will be the future of fiber optics and its ability to adapt in-the-home computer technology to television? Children may grow up not only watching television but also "communicating" with a central computer which continually processes and adapts to his or her programming likes and dislikes. It is all possible with the increased channel capacity that fiber optics offers. A future educational program may project a math instructor to a national viewing audience with individual computer terminals, enabling viewers to work the problems at home. At the same time the math instructor could look at the computerized results on his or her computer terminal and determine thousands of miles away how well the lesson is being understood.

The Future Transition

The future transition of fiber optics is not clear. It definitely has renewed interest in CATV, especially by the telephone companies which were at a disadvantage because of the inability of home telephone wires to carry multiple television channels. Both the cable industry and the telephone companies are interested in the transmission of data communications, such as connecting two distant computers, to which fiber optics will be essential.

Economics will partially dictate the future. Although telephone companies have fiber optics at their disposal, they have already invested billions of dollars in current hookup systems. Converting to the new fiber optics hardware, depreciating the billions of dollars, are serious economic questions which telephone companies will need to consider.

MICROWAVE TECHNOLOGY

Not all broadcast transmissions use standard AM, FM, and TV frequencies. At higher frequencies *microwave* transmission is used. *Microwaves are very short electromagnetic waves.* The higher the frequency, the farther the electromagnetic waves will travel in a direct line-of-sight path between transmitter and receiver. Thus microwaves always travel by line-of-sight transmission. The current state-of-the-art in microwave technology has barely scratched the potential of this multifaceted carrier of information.

Relaying Television Programming

A network television program may travel many thousands of miles before it reaches your local television station. The path it follows may very well use microwave relay systems. Microwave antennas (Figure 13–8) dot almost every landscape from the roofs of skyscrapers to the peaks of snowcapped mountains. Using high frequency line-of-sight transmission, these systems can carry crystal clear signals over long distances through a series of relay antennas which are approximately thirty miles apart. Their advantage is the lower cost and increased efficiency of transmission over traditional land-line systems.

Consider, for example, a television station in the rugged Colorado mountains which receives its network signal from Denver. To string a cable over the Rocky Mountains would be far too costly. Instead microwave towers on mountain tops all within sight of each other become the path over which the signal travels.

But mountain country is not the microwaves' only domain. Because flat areas are free from natural obstructions, microwave systems are scattered over the plains of the farm belt and the deserts of the Southwest for an efficient transmission system.

Keep in mind that the program you receive in your home does not arrive there directly by microwave. The local television station receives the signal via microwave, then retransmits it to your home receiver at a frequency regularly assigned to television transmission. You also should be aware that the television station probably does not own the microwave system, but rather rents its frequency, just as it would rent a line from the telephone company. Many private companies, including major telephone companies, own microwave systems. These systems currently comprise about 30,000 transmission miles in the United States alone.

Figure 13-8 Microwave transmission systems can be less expensive than cable and are especially necessary in rough terrain where the expense of laying cables is prohibitive. Pictured here is the Boulder Junction, Colorado radio relay tower in the foothills of the Rocky Mountains. (A.T.& T.)

Cable Relay and Interconnection

While the first cable systems erected high antennas and received signals direct from television stations, today a cable company can receive distant signals via microwave relay. The signals are relatively free from interference and, through the microwave relay network, can be received over much greater distances with clearer reception than taking the signals directly off the air from a distant television station (Figure 13–9).

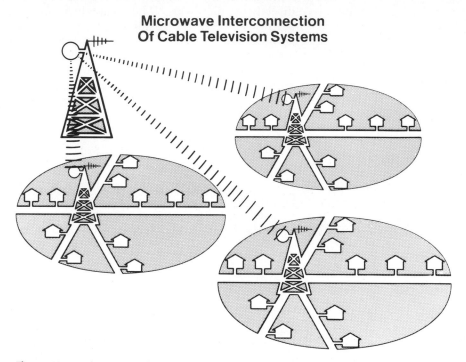

Microwave Interconnection Of Cable Television Systems

Figure 13-9 Microwave relay systems are also employed in cable systems, where a main antenna sends television signals via microwave to outlying antennas, which in trun are connected via cable to subscribers in local communities. (NCTA)

Satellite Relay Systems

Ground-based microwave systems are not the only route used to carry television programming. Widespread use of microwave satellite transmission is evident in any week's television fare. Because space is a vacuum, microwaves travel over long distances unimpeded by the earth's heavy atmosphere near ground level. This permits a transmitting station in London, for example, to transmit a television picture by microwave to a satellite thousands of miles in space, which relays it back to an earth-receiving station in the United States. Satellites are used to bring television signals to many outlying regions in which even microwave links would be too costly (Figure 13–10).

Electronic Newsgathering

The application of microwave to electronic newsgathering (ENG) has given television the flexibility that only radio once enjoyed. A mobile van and portable camera can provide live programming from a community arts fair or live aerial scenes (Figure 13–11) of a football stadium, and the unrehearsed moments of a newly elected politician's acceptance speech can give television news a dynamic dimension. New developments in microwave ENG systems now bounce the microwave beam off the side of a building to a relay antenna, permitting the eyes of a live television camera to peer into almost every nook and cranny of the largest metropolitan areas.

Figure 13-10 Ground-based portable microwave systems are used to receive and send signals via satellite. (Transportable Earth Stations, Inc.)

Figure 13-11 The Goodyear blimp "Mayflower" contains a microwave system which sends television signals via microwave to a ground antenna. The ground antenna then sends the signals to the television control console, which in turn sends them to network control centers and eventually to local stations or cable systems which then "redistribute" the signal, either over-the-air or via cable, to home viewers. (The Goodyear Tire and Rubber Company)

Although you may receive television programs through your local cable system, the original signal probably reached the local cable company through a microwave-signal relay link. A cable company often leases a microwave channel, receives the direct-broadcast signal from a television station, then retransmits it by microwave to a cable system in a community many hundreds of miles away from the original television station.

MULTIPOINT DISTRIBUTION SYSTEMS

Another use of microwave sends special programming to subscribers. For example, a signal is sent from a studio control center via microwave to a receiving dish antenna on top of a skyscraper or tower. From there it is retransmitted by microwave to other microwave-receiving antennas on top of high-rise apartment complexes and hotels. Hotel and apartment television sets are then connected by cable directly to the microwave-receiving antenna on top of the building. These *multipoint distribution* (Figure 13–12) systems can not only receive but also initiate live programming from a studio just as a local television station can. The studio programs are then sent over the system to subscribers.

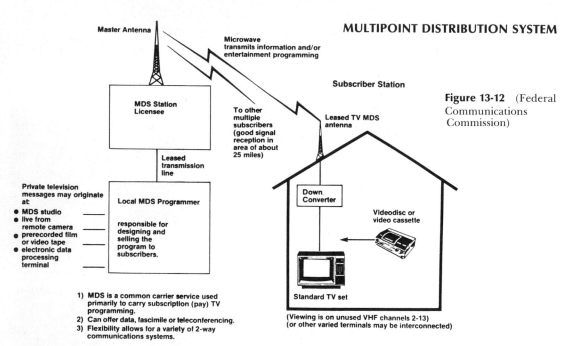

MULTIPOINT DISTRIBUTION SYSTEM

Master Antenna

Microwave transmits information and/or entertainment programming

Subscriber Station

Figure 13-12 (Federal Communications Commission)

MDS Station Licensee

To other multiple subscribers (good signal reception in area of about 25 miles)

Leased TV MDS antenna

Leased transmission line

Private television messages may originate at:
- MDS studio
- live from remote camera
- prerecorded film or video tape
- electronic data processing terminal

Local MDS Programmer

responsible for designing and selling the program to subscribers.

Down Converter

Videodisc or video cassette

Standard TV set

1) MDS is a common carrier service used primarily to carry subscription (pay) TV programming.
2) Can offer data, facsimile or teleconferencing.
3) Flexibility allows for a variety of 2-way communications systems.

(Viewing is on unused VHF channels 2-13) (or other varied terminals may be interconnected)

THE DEVELOPMENT OF SATELLITES

We have already learned in Chapter 2 about how satellite technology is applied to such things as facsimile transmission of newspaper pages. We will now learn how satellites operate.

Figure 13-13 Telstar, launched in 1962, ushered in the ear of live satellite-relayed television pictures.

Telstar   The modern era of communication satellites used in broadcasting began on the night of July 10, 1962. On that night political figures in England, America, and France waited as a NASA–A.T.&T.-launched payload named Telstar (Figure 13–13) roamed through outer space. Its antennas homed in on signals from North America, amplified them ten million times, and retransmitted them back to earth to receiving antennas in England and France. The telecast lasted less than an hour, not because the program ended, but because the satellite passed out of sight of the signals from earth. Telstar made international history during this marriage of satellite technology and broadcasting. In fact, 1960s television seized every opportunity to use this technology for its programming. The Ecumenical Conference in Rome was seen in Europe and the United States via satellite. European audiences watched the American reaction to the unveiling of the Mona Lisa at the National Gallery of Art. The Olympics in Japan traveled around the world via Telstar. A new era in international television had arrived.

Synchronous   The satellites in themselves, however, were not as important as their
Orbit   sophisticated control and guidance systems. Engineers at Hughes Aircraft
Satellites   Company tried their first launch of a *synchronous* orbit satellite in February, 1963. The synchronous orbit satellite, if successful, would reach a point

in space where it would rotate at a speed that would synchronize with the speed of the earth's rotation. The satellite would therefore appear stationary, even though traveling at several thousand miles per hour. This attempt, Syncom I, ended in failure, however.

Undaunted, Hughes engineers tried again with Syncom II in July of that same year. This time the launch was successful, and at 22,300 miles in space over the equator and the Atlantic Ocean, synchronous orbit was achieved. The U.S. Navy ship *Kingsport,* sailing off the coast of Nigeria, received the loud and clear message, "Kingsport, this is Lakehurst, New Jersey. How do you hear me?" The second era of satellite broadcasting had begun. No longer was it necessary to interrupt a political speech, concert, play, or correspondent's report simply because the satellite had left the range of the earth station's signals. Continuous live coverage could now take place, and hours of uninterrupted live programming became possible.

COMSAT
and
INTELSAT

By now the world was taking an active interest in satellite development. In the United States, Congress had created the quasi-governmental Communications Satellite Corporation (COMSAT) with passage of the Communications Satellite Act of 1962. COMSAT became the early planner of satellite systems on an international scale when it evolved as the manager of the International Satellite Consortium, a cooperative effort governing and developing world satellite systems. The consortium established itself under two international agreements originally signed by 14 countries and eventually ratified by 54. In 1974 it became the International Telecommunications Satellite Organization (INTELSAT) with a membership of more than 80 nations and presided over by a secretary general. Today it has approximately 100 members and is responsible for about 95 percent of the world's communiction traffic.

On April 6, 1965, Early Bird became the first INTELSAT satellite to be launched into orbit. It was followed by a long series of INTELSAT spacecraft which orbited the earth (Figure 13–14) and provided a worldwide system of communication, not only for broadcasting but also for computer data, telephone communication, two-way radio communication, weather monitoring, and other uses.

The satellites which led up to the current INTELSAT V system included the INTELSAT II series launched during 1967 and positioned over the Atlantic and Pacific Oceans. This series provided communication to two-thirds of the earth's surface. INTELSAT III satellites became operational between 1968 and 1970 and were positioned over the Atlantic and Indian Oceans. With global communication now possible, the next step was to improve and increase the capabilities of satellite communication.

Four improved INTELSAT IV satellites were launched between 1971 and 1973, followed by the launching of INTELSAT IV-A. The IV-A satellites, six in all, utilized improved technology called *beam separation.* Beam separation allowed the same frequency to be used for transmitting a signal both to and from the satellite, creating a more efficient use of the frequency. Moreover, improved antenna systems permitted a more highly directed "beam" (Figure 13–15) to an earth station, eliminating the power normally wasted by beaming signals over ocean areas, for example.

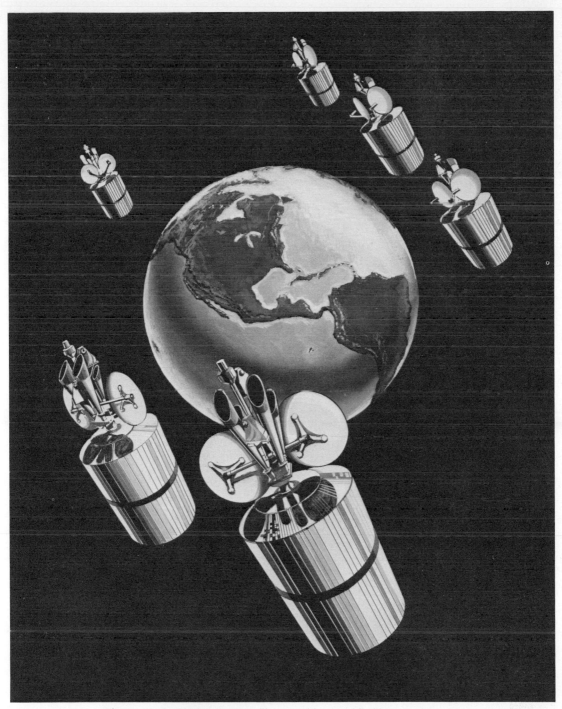

Figure 13-14 INTELSAT satellites provide a world-wide space network.
(Courtesy, Hughes Aircraft Company)

The INTELSAT V system (Figure 13–16) is the most sophisticated satellite communication program yet developed. It will meet the communication needs of much of the world during the 1980s. It consists of a seven-satellite system, with the contract for development awared to AeroNutronic Ford. With a 50-foot wing span when their solar panels are deployed, these satellites measure 22 feet in height. They consist of three primary modules: antenna, communications, and support subsystem. Since even at the high frequencies of GH2, or *gigahertz* (billions of cycles per second), overcrowding is beginning to occur, the INTELSAT V series will have alternate frequency capability with twice the capacity of the INTELSAT IV-A series.

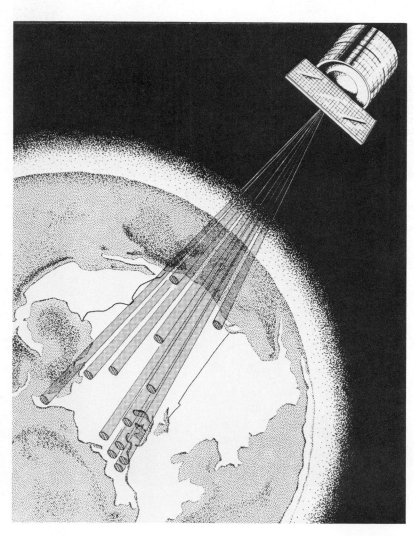

Figure 13-15 Improvements in satellite antenna systems facilitate "directed" beam transmission to satellite earth stations, improving the quality of signals and providing better use of available frequencies. (Bell Laboratories)

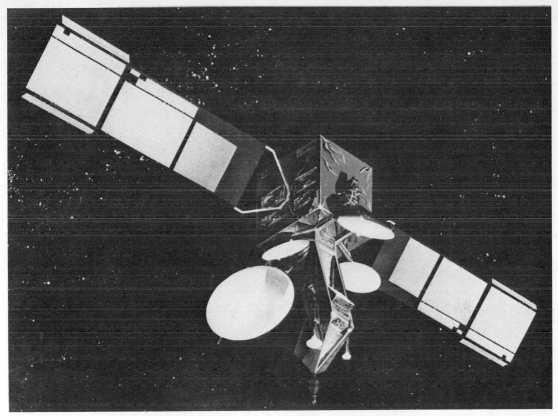

Figure 13-16 The INTELSAT V spacecraft measures approximately 50 feet from the tip of one solar panel "wing" to the other and has twice the capacity of previous INTELSAT spacecraft. (Aeronutronic Ford)

DOMESTIC SATELLITE SYSTEMS

Along with the global communication of the INTELSAT satellites, there are numerous domestic satellite systems.

RCA Satcoms One, begun in December, 1973, is operated by RCA. RCA formed a wholly owned subsidiary company to operate its domestic satellite system, RCA American Communications, Inc. (RCA Americom), which became part of the RCA Communications group. A network of earth stations complements the RCA system. The RCA Satcom satellites (Figure 13–17) permit their antennas to face the sun whenever it is in view, thus improving the power over previously launched satellites. When the sun is not in sight, the satellites are powered by nickel cadmium batteries. In addition to this antenna design, Satcom employs three advances in satellite technology: (1) a special high-capacity antenna that can carry up to 24 simultaneous color television channels; (2) the use of graphite fiber epoxy composition materials, insuring strength yet providing less weight in constructions; and (3) a special lightweight amplifier.

Figure 13-17 RCA's Satcom satellites, which are part of RCA's domestic satellite system, have 75 square feet of solar cells mounted on two panels that are continuously pointed at the sun. The cells produce 740 watts of power, sufficient to charge its batteries and drive the operating functions of the 1,000-pound spacecraft. (RCA)

Western Union also employs a domestic satellite system (Figure 13–18), called *Westar*. The system is capable of carrying a variety of information, including voice and video circuits. Along with mobile facilities (Figure 13–19), sending and receiving earth stations operate in New York, Atlanta, Chicago, Dallas, Los Angeles, San Francisco, and Washington. In cooperation with NASA, Western Union has also developed a tracking and data relay satellite (Figure 13–20).

Figure 13-18 Western Union's Westar satellite system includes three identical domestic communications satellites, which are used for the transmission of voice, data, video, and facsimile communication. Westar I and Westar II were launched in April and October, 1974 respectively, while Westar III was launched in August, 1979. (Western Union)

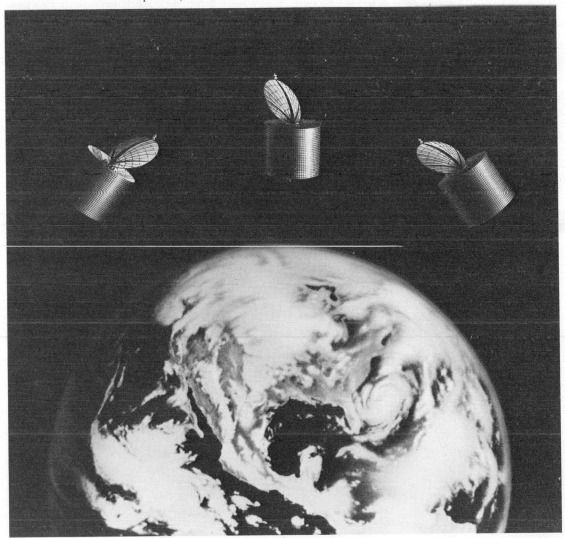

Figure 13-19   Western Union's Westar Mobile Earth Station provides portable ground connection to any of the Westar satellites. (Western Union)

Figure 13-20   The latest generation of the Western Union-NASA tracking and data relay satellites. (Western Union and TRW Defense and Space Systems Group)

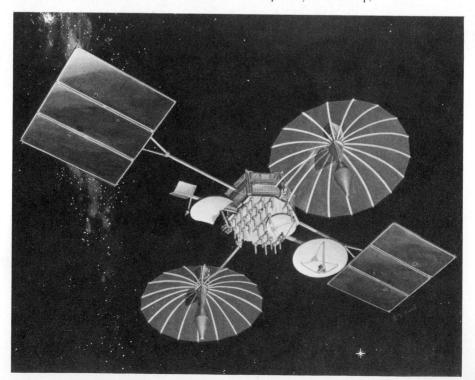

General Telephone & Electronics (GTE) announced the development of a domestic satellite system in 1981. Initially the system will consist of three satellites (Figure 13–21) and will provide communication for all 50 states. Each satellite will have a 16-channel capacity, with 1984 the first launch date.

Figure 13-21   One of three satellites which are part of the GTE Satellite system. Operational in 1984, the system covers much of North America and Hawaii. (GTE and RCA)

OSCAR: AMATEUR RADIO SATELLITE

While the major corporations and government consortiums receive most of the attention when we talk about satellite communication, a group of amateur radio operators, called "hams," are also experimenting with their own satellites as part of the Oscar series. Information gained from their experiments is being applied to improving satellite communication among broadcasters and other users.

Figure 13-22 The ATS-6 satellite launched a new series of educational television experiments by bringing direct, in-school programming to outlying areas. (NASA)

APPLICATION TECHNOLOGY SATELLITES

Commercial television is not the only benefactor of satellite systems. In the United States, NASA developed the Application Technology Satellite program (ATS) (Figure 13–22) for educational purposes. It launched six such satellites in all, with the sixth sending satellite signals to small earth stations. This was the key to important applications of satellite technology, from log cabin schools in the mountains of Idaho to mud huts across the world in India.

In the United States, such towns as Gila Bend, Three Forks, Battle Mountain, Wagon Mound, Sundance, and Arapahoe all participated in the ATS experiments. The local school yard had a new visitor in the form of a microwave dish and its strange antenna with corkscrew wires around a long metal tube. With the help of their visitor, students could sit in a classroom in West Yellowstone and talk via satellite to a classroom in Denver. Where no land-line or microwave system had been developed, the ATS-6 satellite would beam a signal simultaneously across half a continent.

The program generated a cooperative, although somewhat reluctant, effort between state governments. For example, issues affecting the local autonomy of schools usually formed a political thicket, but the Federation of Rocky Mountain States, composed of Arizona, Colorado, Idaho, Montana, New Mexico, Utah, and Wyoming, joined together to bring two-way educational television to the outlying communities in the eight-state region. In some areas the satellite-receiving systems were hooked directly into the local cable systems or microwave translator systems, permitting the signals to be received at home. The ATS project also provided similar educational television programming for the eastern United States, especially Appalachia.

After the American experiments, special earth-controlled rockets on the satellite shifted the ATS-6 from the Galápagos Islands to a new orbit over Kenya in Africa. From that position in 1976 it conducted educational television experiments in India where some of the population had never even seen television or motion pictures. Programs on modern agriculture, health, and family planning were part of the television fare. After the Indian experiments the satellite traveled back into the Western Hemisphere, stopping along the way for demonstrations sponsored by the United States Agency for International Development (USAID).

DIRECT BROADCAST SATELLITES

Considerable attention has been given to the development of high-powered satellite systems primarily designed to beam signals direct to small home antennas (Figure 13–23). Canada's CTS (Communications Technology Satellite) satellite became a prototype system in 1976. Japan and Germany followed. In the United States COMSAT, through its Satellite Television Corporation, and numerous other firms instituted plans to begin a direct broadcast satellite system in the mid-1980s.

Direct broadcast satellites could radically change the entire telecommunications industry, especially as it relates to the home consumer.

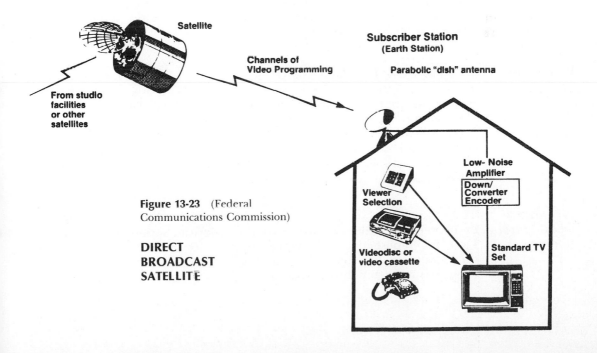

Figure 13-23   (Federal Communications Commission)

DIRECT BROADCAST SATELLITE

Satellites will be able to bring exceptionally clear pictures with 1000 + -line resolutions as opposed to the current United States 525-line resolution of standard broadcast. Households everywhere, regardless whether it was served by a cable system, could receive satellite signals with a rooftop dish antenna. Cable, in turn, might be used more as a two-way communication medium for interactive home computer networks, home security devices, and other formats far removed from traditional entertainment programming.

SATELLITE BUSINESS NETWORKS

The increased use of computers and the necessity to transmit data over long distances has seen satellite communication taking on greater significance in business and industry. One of the first satellite systems for data transmission developed in the 1980s and involved COMSAT General, IBM, and Aetna Life and Casualty. Another system (Figure 13–24), developed by Xerox Corporation, is proposing three main functions: *document distribution,* data transmission, and *teleconferencing.* With the document distribution function, a variety of sending and receiving terminals and work stations are linked together with the satellite being the coordinating relay device. With this linkage, advanced printing devices and mail distribution centers (bottom left of office portion in Figure 13–24) allow rapid delivery of documents. With data transmission, interactive terminals (lower center of office portion in Figure 13–24) can send and receive data with direct line quality. High-speed computer-to-computer applications (top center of office portion in Figure 13–24) allow individual computer processors and files to be located where they best support a customer's business. Teleconferencing applications permit a work conference atmosphere (far right of office portion in Figure 13–24) to include high-quality, still-frame video, hard copies on demand and voice capability. Data is routed through an equipment connection to a rooftop antenna, which sends and receives signals to the satellite.

POLITICAL ISSUES AND CONTROL OF SATELLITES

Americans are conditioned to the idea that the First Amendment to the Constitution is a universally held principle of law and morality—it is not. Its jurisdiction applies only within United States' boundaries. When other countries become involved, as they immediately do with direct broadcast satellite communication, new issues of international law and understanding arise.

Legalities and Cultural Integrity

These issues were summarized by Paul L. Laskin and Abram Chayes in an essay prepared under the auspices of the American Society of International Law and published by the Aspen Institute for Humanistic Studies.[1] In their summary they contended that there is no way to ensure that television programs sent from direct broadcast satellites would remain inside national

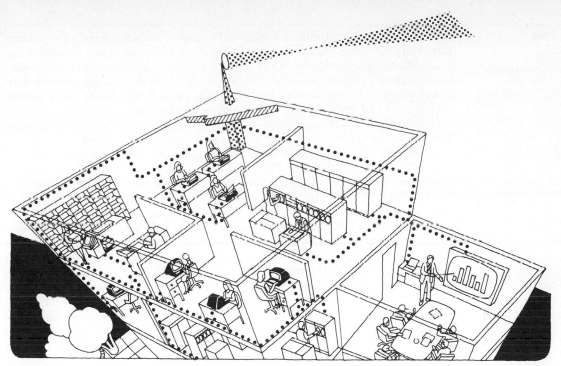

Figure 13-24 Xerox Corporation's Telecommunications Network (XTEN) has three main functions: document distribution, data transmission, and teleconferencing. (Xerox)

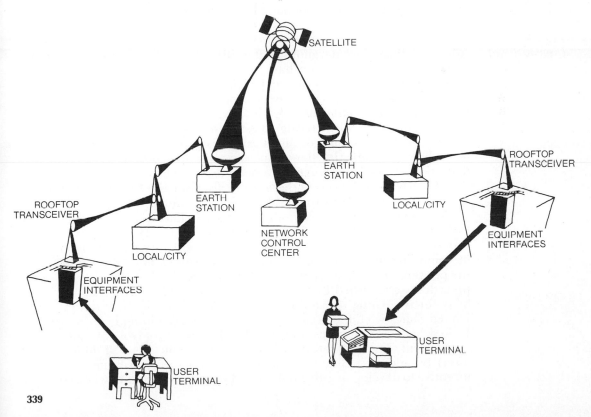

boundaries. For example, a nation surrounded by a ridge of high mountains may effectively keep within its boundaries television signals sent from a land-based transmitters. However, signals from satellites do not respect such natural terrain and can spill over into bordering nations. Even new developments in satellite technology that permit signals to be directed within areas of approximately 100 miles in diameter still cannot provide directional coverage to match the irregular political boundaries. Most satellite coverage areas must be circular. When spillover does occur, it can easily threaten a nation's culture, integrity, or even its security.

There is also the fear that the superpowers may be in a position to dominate world development of satellite communiction. Because the United States, for example, has the technology as well as the economic base to develop a worldwide system of satellite communication, other countries, especially the less developed ones, are resistant to American programming, especially programming from the major commercial networks. These nations also fear that bad American programs may drive out or keep out the good ones.[2]

Commercialism is another contested issue. Countries in which commercials are not a major part of the television fare are afraid that the influence of United States' programming will ignite a commercial bombardment. There is also the fear that commercials of one country would tend to create a desire for goods of that country and, as a result, provide unfair competition to local industries. In addition, certain societies are apprehensive that commercial programming will create a thirst for consumer goods and portray consumer-oriented societies too positively. Such examples may disrupt national plans for orderly social and economic development.

International Law

Added to these considerations is the difficulty of formulating any international law. Laskin and Chayes noted: "Where the Anglo-American countries, for example, proceed pragmatically, formulating the rules of legal behavior as they acquire experience, the civil law tradition tends to rely on the codification of rules in advance of action."[3] Such concepts become important when trying to establish systems in which agreements will *precede* the beginning of direct satellite communication into a country, or if the regulatory function is to begin *after* the broadcasts commence, determining when there may be a need to control them.

Clearly the solutions to these issues are not easy. In the United States the only two documents that really reflect any attempt to govern satellite communication are the Communications Satellite Act of 1962 and the Communications Act of 1934 as amended. The 1962 legislation was concerned mainly with setting up COMSAT, creating a common channel of communication and control with other nations and ultimately fixing the position of the United States with INTELSAT. The 1962 law followed precedents established by the 1934 legislation in that the FCC's responsibility for regulating television programming within the boundaries of the United States would logically carry over to programming beamed outside United States' boundaries. Beyond this, however, control is vague, if not nonexistent. This regulatory gap in American policy toward international direct broadcast satellite communication is not necessarily negative. The incentive to develop new technology and programs stagnates when constant rewriting of government regulations leaves companies uncertain of definitive guidelines. To prevent this from happening to satellite communication, many of the issues and incentives for developing an international system of direct broadcast satellites have purposely been kept in the discussion stage.

SUBSCRIPTION/PAY TV

Traditional over-the-air television transmission has allowed anyone who has a home receiver to receive the programming. Now, however, there is a growing interest in what is called *subscription TV* or *pay TV*, which means a new potential for the medium. With pay TV the signal is scrambled as it leaves the station transmitter and descrambled with a special attachment on the home receiving set. The individual pays a monthly fee for the descrambler attachment and can receive such special programming as first-run movies, sports, and other programs generally not available to nonsubscribers.

A number of cities are becoming competitive pay TV markets, with subscribers willing to pay fees substantially above the costs for standard cable services. Chicago, Los Angeles, and Detroit are three examples of pay TV markets, and fees can run approximately $25 per month, with an installation and deposit fee of $100. Major companies such as Time, Inc. see pay TV as having a substantial future and have made substantial investments in pay TV systems.

TELETEXT

Also gaining attention is the use of *teletext*, a system where a computer is connected with a television transmission system and can send data to home receivers equipped with a special decoder (Figure 13–25). The home

Example of Teletext

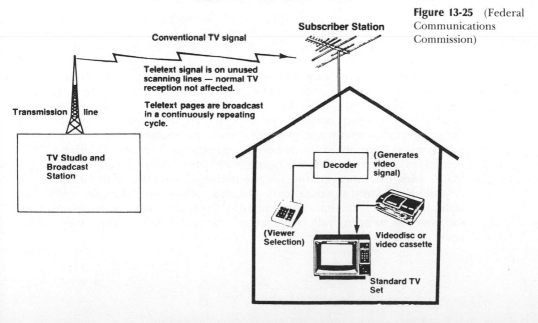

Conventional TV signal

Subscriber Station

Teletext signal is on unused scanning lines — normal TV reception not affected.

Teletext pages are broadcast in a continuously repeating cycle.

Transmission line

TV Studio and Broadcast Station

Decoder

(Generates video signal)

(Viewer Selection)

Videodisc or video cassette

Standard TV Set

Figure 13-25 (Federal Communications Commission)

viewer can select either standard television programming, the teletext signal, or both superimposed. Teletext can send electronic "pages" of information using scanned lines of the television picture not visible without an encoder. The system pioneered in Britain with the operation of IBA's ORACLE (Figure 13–26) and the BBC's CEEFAX operation. The system gained attention in the United States after experimental progress was made with a prototype unit installed at Bonneville International Corporation's KSL-TV in Salt Lake City.

The information potential for teletext is almost limitless. From grocery lists to newspaper pages, the system promises still new frontiers in communication as television becomes an even larger part of our information society.

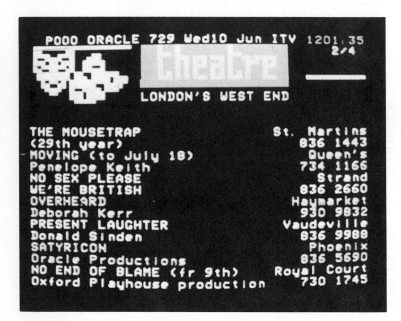

Figure 13-26 Teletext systems allow transmission of textual information. They pioneered in Britain with the Independent Broadcasting Authority's Oracle system. (Courtesy, Independent Broadcasting Authority)

VIDEOTEX

While teletext involves the over-the-air broadcast of information, *videotex* employs a wired connection between a central computer and a home receiver. The wired connection, via telephone or cable systems, permits a two-way relationship between the user and the transmission system. Both videotex and teletext are generic terms, meaning they refer to many different types of broadcast or wired connections. Videotex (Figure 13–27) resembles teletext in that the home user can select pages of information. With videotex, however, the user gets the information immediately as it is "called up" from the data bank whereas with teletext the user must wait, although usually less than a minute, until the transmission system completes its cycle of sending all other pages before sending the page which corresponds to the one requested.

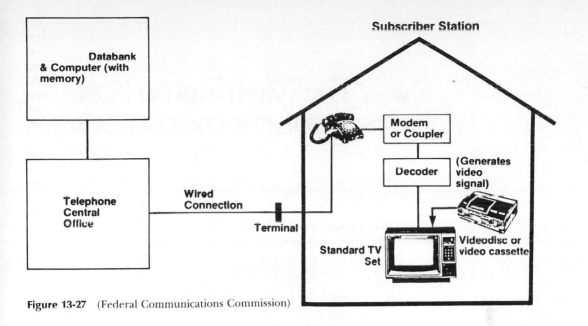

Figure 13-27 (Federal Communications Commission)

THE ELECTRONIC NEWSPAPER

While few are predicting that the newspaper of today will vanish, new technology is creating the potential for expanded distribution of newspapers. Publishers are watching closely the developments in new technology, such as the experimental distribution system, teletext and videotex, which we have already discussed.

The Columbus (Ohio) Dispatch and CompuServe

In 1979 a Columbus, Ohio computer software company named CompuServe introduced a videotex service which enabled anyone with a home computer and the proper equipment to connect via telephone with the CompuServe main computer. By calling a local number in most larger cities, the home computer enthusiast can link up with the central data base. Today that data base includes the electronic editions of major newspapers as well as other information services.

The first newspaper to use the CompuServe system was the *Columbus (Ohio) Dispatch*. Brought together with CompuServe by the Associated Press, the *Dispatch* offered its first electronic pages on July 1, 1980. A *Dispatch* executive reported the paper spent about $50,000 on the first six months of the experiment, compared to about $4 million a year just for the paper and ink used to print classified ads for the regular editions of the *Dispatch*. The program which tied the CompuServe computer to a computer at the *Dispatch* involved about 300 hours of programming time.

Other newspapers joined in the CompuServe system and were made available with the *Columbus Dispatch*. Such familiar names in American newspapering included the *Washington Post* (Figure 13–28), the *Los Angeles Times*, the *Atlanta Journal*, the *Atlanta Constitution*, the *San Francisco Chronicle*, and the *San Francisco Examiner*.

Figure 13-28 Electronic newspaper delivery is available to anyone with a computer and the ability to access, via telephone, the newspaper's data storage. (Courtesy, *The Washington Post*)

```
COMPUSERVE INFORMATION SERVICE

1 NEWSPAPERS
2 FINANCE
3 ENTERTAINMENT
4 COMMUNICATIONS
5 COMPUSERVE USER INFORMATION
6 SPECIAL SERVICES
7 HOME INFORMATION
8 EDUCATION
9 MICRONET PERSONAL COMPUTING
0 ELECTRONIC SHOP-AT-HOME
ENTER YOUR SELECTION NUMBER,
OR H FOR MORE INFORMATION.
```

```
1 THE COLUMBUS DISPATCH
2 THE NEW YORK TIMES
3 VIRGINIAN-PILOT & LEDGER-STAR
4 THE WASHINGTON POST
5 THE SAN FRANCISCO CHRONICLE
6 THE SAN FRANCISCO EXAMINER
7 THE LOS ANGELES TIMES
8 MINNEAPOLIS STAR AND TRIBUNE
9 ATLANTA JOURNAL CONSTITUTION
10 ST. LOUIS POST-DISPATCH
11 MIDDLESEX DAILY NEWS

LAST MENU PAGE. KEY DIGIT
OR M FOR PREVIOUS MENU.
```

```
       1 TALK TO US
       2 FRONT PAGE

3 OTHER NEWS      4 GOVT./POLIT.
5 SPORTS          6 BUSINESS
7 OPINION         8 LEISURE
9 ACCENT          10 NUTRITION
        11 WEATHER
        12 TERMINAL TREATS
        13 BROWSE

LAST MENU PAGE. KEY DIGIT
OR M FOR PREVIOUS MENU.
```

```
COLUMBUS DISPATCH     PAGE CDP-12

      THE COLUMBUS DISPATCH

1 BRIEFS          2 WORLD
3 U.S.            4 WASHINGTON
5 OHIO            6 LOCAL NEWS
7 AP WORLD        8 AP U.S.
9 AP WASHINGTON   10 AP REGIONAL


LAST MENU PAGE. KEY DIGIT
OR M FOR PREVIOUS MENU.
```

```
!6

COLUMBUS DISPATCH     PAGE CDP-26

5 CITY WON'T SHUT GATES ON ANGEL
6 "HE'S MY HERO," SAYS SISTER
7 UNITED WAY SHOCKS SUPPORTER
8 READING PROGRAM CONTINUES
9 INJURED MOTORIST DIES
0 BLOOD SUPPLY

LAST MENU PAGE. KEY DIGIT
OR M FOR PREVIOUS MENU.
```

```
!5

COLUMBUS DISPATCH  PAGE CDP-2901

 BY ALAN CROCKETT
 DISPATCH STAFF REPORTER
  CITY OFFICIALS AND SOME
COMMUNITY LEADERS ARE TAKING A
WAIT-AND-SEE ATTITUDE ABOUT THE
GUARDIAN ANGELS COMING TO WALK
THE STREETS OF COLUMBUS.
  ERIC BREWER, A SPOKESMAN FOR
THE CIVILIAN VOLUNTEER GROUP,
SAID TUESDAY A LOCAL CHAPTER
COULD BE STARTED BY MID-MARCH.
THE GUARDIAN ANGELS
```

Figure 13-29 The ComPuServe Information Service provides subscribers with access to a variety of information. The Columbus, Ohio *Dispatch*, for example, can be accessed by a sequence of commands on a home computer that is interfaced, via telephone, with a computer storing the *Dispatch*'s stories.

Using a home computer and a "*modem*" to couple the telephone to the computer and by dialing the access number, the subscriber is linked with the data base (Figure 13–29) which provides a "menu" of available information, which includes the list of electronic newspapers. After selecting the newspaper, the subscriber searches an index of categories such as front page, sports, weather, and leisure. From these categories the subscriber selects a given story from coded headlines, and the story then appears in textual form on the video display terminal or home television set. Since the system is two-way, the subscriber can "electronically write" letters to the editor.

Dow Jones Information Services

The resources of Dow Jones are also available, such as the *Wall Street Journal* and *Barron's Business and Financial Weekly*. Many of the stories are available on *Dow Jones News* within seconds after they are filed by the reporter.

Information is available on over 6000 companies. A subscriber can receive stock information, keyed by company code, on his or her home video display terminal by asking for headlines or stories of specific companies or industries. Subscribers can therefore receive financial information that previously was only accessible through newspapers, clipping files, archives, or directories.

Major stories are held for 90 days. A text search is available to locate stories older than 90 days. Using a key word search system, such as the name of a company or subject, a subscriber can get a complete chronological history of a company. The data base can be especially helpful for examining companies which are not on the stock exchange.

Edited versions of features from the *Wall Street Journal* are available each business day beginning at 7:00 A.M. Eastern Time. Among items available to subscribers are the front page, editorials, front page–section 2, market news, and back page.

Knight-Ridder's Viewdata Experiment

The newspapers involved in the CompuServe system and the Dow Jones Information Service we have just discussed are heavily editorial in nature. Another electronic newspaper experiment has incorporated substantial advertising into its delivery. Knight-Ridder, a company with over 30 newspaper properties in the United States, began delivering news and advertising copy in its Miami market in 1980.

Subscribers for the *viewdata* delivery system were selected by determining their needs for the services provided by the system. In a joint agreement with Southern Bell, the Knight-Ridder system offered two-way capacity using A.T.&T. equipment which had been designed in cooperation with Knight-Ridder engineering talent. Each member of a participating household was assigned a password which gave him or her access to the central computer through a home terminal. Knight-Ridder furnished all of the equipment necessary for the home subscriber, including a specially designed RCA television receiver permitting somewhat higher quality of graphics than many television sets offer.

Various firms provided information, advertising, and education. Editorial information was made available from the *Miami Herald*, American

Cancer Society, Associated Press, and the *Congressional Quarterly*, among others. Some of the firms providing advertising included Sears, J. C. Penney, Eastern Airlines, Shell Oil, B. Dalton, Southeast Banking Corporation, and Service Merchandise Corporation. Actual transactions could be made on the two-way system, such as buying groceries through the home terminal and having the store deliver the groceries to your home. Quizzes on boating and driver's education were included as part of the material on education.

The results of these various experiments in electronic newspapers will determine if the technology has outdistanced demand and whether we will soon be able to obtain a newspaper on a home visual display terminal.

NEWSPAPERS AND CABLE ORIGINATION

Although the electronic journalism we have just been talking about primarily involves distribution of pages of text, in some cities newspapers have made the complete transition to "broadcast" journalism. Today television stations compete for viewers with the "newspaper channel" on the local cable system. For example, in Des Moines, Iowa, the newsroom for the *Register* and *Tribune* sports a television studio from which an anchorperson broadcasts newsbreaks much like the newspaper's television counterparts. Other newspapers are operating similar cable news systems. It may only be a matter of time before the local newspaper finds itself playing the television ratings game.

ELECTRONIC MAGAZINES

Similar to the way newspapers are being electronically distributed, magazine publishers are experimenting with electronic editions. *Women's Day* (Figure 13–30), *Better Homes and Gardens,* and *Popular Science* are some of

Figure 13-30 Features from *Woman's Day* and the ability to purchase items advertised in the electronic pages of that magazine are part of an experimental CBS system. (CBS)

the forerunners in the field. Electronic distribution offers special advantages for magazine publishers, since magazines are expensive to produce and the audience is highly specialized. Yet one of a magazine's special appeals is its ability to produce high-quality illustrations, which as of now cannot be duplicated on a video screen.

Information is made available to the electronic magazine subscriber in much the same way that it is available to subscribers of electronic newspapers. Everything from recipes to feature articles can be stored and then indexed and called up on the home video screen. When distributed through two-way videotex systems, the subscriber can purchase goods and services from the magazine simply by pressing the correct key on the home computer keyboard and typing in an account number, such as VISA or Mastercard.

HOME VIDEO RECORDERS

When the CBS affiliates met in Chicago in 1956, Ampex unveiled what stockholders were told was a practical system for the recording and reproduction of TV pictures on magnetic tape. It brought wide acclaim and launched the era of videotape. In 1957 RCA introduced its version, which could reproduce images in color as well as black and white. Then in June, 1962, Machtronics introduced a portable videotape recorder, and many manufacturing companies, such as Sony, Memorex, Arvin Industries, and Panasonic, began manufacturing videotape components and systems.

The next revolution came with the introduction of the videocassette by Sony. Introduced in April 1969, the videocassette has entered every facet of television, from libraries and instructional resource centers to the newsroom. Home videocassette recorders are becoming more common despite court challenges on copyright issues contesting the legality of in-home recording.

VIDEODISCS

While cassette videotapes are making an impact, videodiscs are also changing the industry. The videodisc's potential lies with its capability to distribute television programming directly to homes, completely bypassing television stations. Pushed to its full potential, it means that videodiscs can be duplicated and shipped inexpensively anywhere in the world for playback on home players which operate much like a standard phonograph. Videodiscs are already being produced for distribution to the home market, and in the future you'll be able to pick up a catalogue and order your favorite television program much as you order your favorite album through a record club. Producers who are now involved in syndication to television stations may find themselves bypassing the stations and the networks to deal directly with the consumer.

These developments do not mean that television stations will start signing off the air, just as radio stations didn't succumb when 45 rpm and $33\frac{1}{3}$ rpm records came on the market. However, viewers will have more choices about what they watch and when. Your favorite magazine may one day be sent to you each month as a television documentary, and the book-of-the-month club selection may arrive in the form of a five-part television special, all via the mail. It may sound futuristic, but the technology to provide those services is already available and being used.

LOW-POWER TV (LPTV)

The FCC in 1980 initiated a procedure and issued a Notice of Proposed Rulemaking for the purpose of developing regulations and issuing licenses to a new class of television station providing low power broadcast service (LPTV) to areas which had previously been denied coverage or were under-served by existing stations. When the new service becomes operable, stations operating with low power (1000 watt UHF and 100 watt VHF) will be permitted to operate much like larger stations but with a limited coverage area (Figure 13–31).

Low-power television stations are much like the numerous *translator* stations around the United States that rebroadcast the signals of other stations. The difference between a translator and a low-power station is that the LPTV station can originate programming. The application procedure is less complex than for a full-service station—specifically, in the areas of proposed programming and community needs and ascertainment surveys, which are not required to the full extent that they are for a full-service station. At the same time, however, a full-service station is

Figure 13 31

ILLUSTRATIVE LOW POWER
TELEVISION STATION COVERAGE

VHF (Channels 2 - 13)

Transmitter Power Output	Transmitting Antenna Gain	Effective Radiated Power*	Transmitting Antenna Height**	Approx. Useful Coverage Distance***
1 watt	5	5	100'	3.5
1 watt	5	5	500'	8.0
1 watt	5	5	1000'	11.0
10 watts	5	50	100'	6.2
10 watts	5	50	500'	14.0
10 watts	5	50	1000'	19.5

UHF (Channels 14 - 83)

10 watts	10	100	100'	2.9 mi.
10 watts	10	100	500'	6.5 mi.
10 watts	10	100	1000'	9.0 mi.
100 watts	15	1500	100'	6.5 mi.
100 watts	15	1500	500'	12.5 mi.
100 watts	15	1500	1000'	18.0 mi.
1000 watts	15	15000	100'	10.0 mi.
1000 watts	15	15000	500'	21.0 mi.
1000 watts	15	15000	1000'	26.5 mi.

* Technically, the loss in the cable between the transmitter and the transmitting antenna should be taken into account in calculating the ERP. The reduction in ERP that would occur has been approximated by using a lower than normal antenna gain.

** The "height above average terrain" which will coincide with the height above ground level only for flat terrain. Variation in terrain will cause variation in coverage.

*** Distance is to the "Grade B Contour"—At the extremes of this coverage distance, outside antennas will generally be necessary for adequate reception.

protected from interference, and should a full-service station decide to apply for the frequency used by a low-power station, the full-service station will be given priority consideration even if the LPTV station is already licensed and operating.

An applicant wanting to own and operate a LPTV station should consult the FCC's latest rules at the time of making the application and should be prepared to demonstrate that the applicant is legally qualified, financially able, and has made the necessary technical arrangements and engineering surveys to go on the air.

CHANGES IN TELEVISION RECEPTION AND TRANSMISSION

We have ventured a long way from the television set of the 1930s which consisted of a large console cabinet and a small screen, sometimes reflected on a mirror-topped lid. Today the people who manufacture and sell television receivers are making changes which are designed to appeal to the consumer as well as to incorporate the latest technology into receiver design.

Stereo Television

The one advantage radio has had over television has been in the quality of its sound. Although the picture is there, the sound of an orchestra or a rock concert coming through a small single speaker on a television set leaves a lot to be desired in sound quality. Now companies are looking more seriously at improving television sound by manufacturing sets with stereo capabilities.

For television stations, however, broadcasting in stereo involves tremendous changes in transmitting equipment as well as increased costs. Stereo television, therefore, is limited primarily to videodiscs and some cable applications.

Cable-Ready Television

Presently a viewer who wants to subscribe a cable service offering pay TV or more than 13 channels must contract with the cable company for a home converter that increases the channel capacity of the set. Some television set manufacturers, sensing the increased demand for cable, are now marketing sets with built-in cable capacity, thus ostensibly eliminating the need for the separate converter. The success of the new sets will depend on the willingness of consumers to pay the additional price for cable capacity and of cable companies to permit their own converters to be substituted for built-in converters.

Component Television

With more sophisticated uses of television, such as interactive video and stereo, manufacturers are examining the appeal of component television. Component television already exists to some degree, since anyone who buys a home computer, videotape recorder, or videodisc system is buying another component for the television. Component television is designed to appeal to the person who is highly aware of sound and video technology and has probably purchased a stereo by buying components.

Large-screen *Television*	Ever since television was invented, people have been trying to increase the size of the screen while retaining a clear picture. Unfortunately many attempts have been less than successful since the intensity and brightness of the picture was lost on the large screen. Major improvements in the brightness and intensity of the picture are now making large-screen projection systems comparable to smaller screened sets.
High- *Definition* *Television*	At the same time the intensity of the large screen is improving, high-definition television is improving overall picture quality. In the United States, for example, a picture is typically scanned 525 times per second. With new high-definition systems the number of scans per second increases to over 1000. This permits large-screen projection without the graininess or the appearance of "lines" on the television picture.
Digital *Television*	Microprocessing has radically changed the entire world of electronics and telecommunications. Increasingly smaller components and computer circuitry are incorporated into new applications of technology, from microwave ovens to space shuttle controls. Television receiver design is also approaching the point where receivers will incorporate digital circuits, thus eliminating many of the interference patterns now seen on sets. Miniaturization will completely change the way a television signal is picked up and received. Such things as shadows, ghosts, and other distractions will disappear. The improved quality will also permit sharper pictures resulting in improved graphic displays from teletext and videotex systems.

COMPUTER TECHNOLOGY

When station KDKA broadcast the results of the Harding-Cox election returns in 1920, few people could have imagined that giant computers would someday predict with uncanny accuracy the outcome of national elections hours and sometimes days before all the votes were counted. The average citizen who sits in front of a television set and watches an election night broadcast is perhaps not aware of the full scope of the computer's power. The publisher whose newspaper must go to press a short time after the polls close, however, fully appreciates its predictive capacity when trying to avoid headline errors such as the famous boner made by the nation's major newspapers in predicting the outcome of the 1948 presidential election. Harry S. Truman went to bed listening to broadcast reports of his loss, only to awake the next morning as president-elect of the United States. The ability of the computer to analyze data from selected voting precincts, to use voting trends from previous years, to plot trends and probabilities, and to predict victories has given added credibility to all media.

Today's newspaper owes its greatly increased efficiency to computer technology (Figure 13–32). The ability of a major national newspaper to compose pages and advertisements, edit copy, set type, and effect regional distribution, all by computer, has become commonplace. Computers have also reduced errors in newspaper production. In the past, "scissors and

Figure 13-32 Computer technology has greatly increased the efficiency of the modern newspaper. Computer editing, for example, streamlines much of the work once done by mechanical typesetting machines. (MVP Editing System, Courtesy, Mergenthaler Linotype Company)

paste" manuscripts were marked with pencil and passed through many different copy desks. With computers the copy is now clean, and erasures and changes are edited electronically instead of manually. Type is set automatically through electrical impulse instead of by hand. Even the spacing of the lines and margins has been computerized.

In most applications to mass communication, the basic operation of a computer is information storage and retrieval. The three major components of the computer are *input, processing,* and *output.* Data, usually in the form of numbers, are entered into the computer by one or more mathematical operations. The answer is then typed on a teleprinter or displayed on a visual display terminal. In our example of election night news coverage, information about previous voting trends first is stored in the computer. This might include the similarity in voting of key precincts to the total overall vote of a given area; how this has affected previous elections; and the percentage of voters 18 to 24 years of age and how frequently they vote as their parents do. On election night when the votes are tabulated in the sample precincts, the information previously stored in the computer is combined with the new vote totals and then processed. The result is a prediction of voting results based on sample data collected in the current election as well as on information collected from previous elections.

The computer can also be used in broadcasting. For example, the chief engineer at a modern broadcasting complex can go directly to a visual display terminal (Figure 13–33) or can read computer printout data on the operation of the station's transmitter or automation system. In the past the same engineer would have to spend much time each day walking around with a clipboard taking meter readings required by the FCC. Now the computer receives data directly from the transmitter and translates this into a printout of the meter readings. The computer also stores these data for future reference. For example, by reviewing a list of the times the transmitter was off the air, the engineer can tell what the operating time of many key instruments is. She can then prepare for future equipment failures by replacing these instruments before they wear out.

New developments in computer technology have also been applied to radio and television production. A disc jockey can sit at the controls of a radio station and, with a keyboard and VDT nearby, automatically select the next song to be aired. A television program is recorded on magnetic videotape in much the same way that sound is recorded on magnetic audiotape. If a section of videotape needs to be edited, you find that portion of the tape and then electronically edit it. You may have two videotapes and want to blend video from both of them onto a third tape.

Figure 13-33 Computer logging systems are becoming standard features in broadcasting. (Harris Corp., Broadcast Products Division)

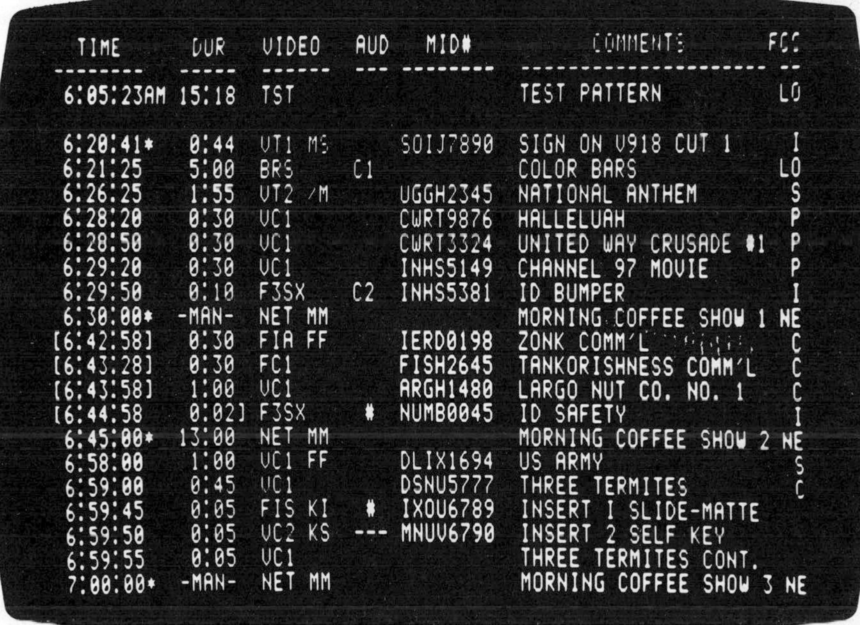

TIME	DUR	VIDEO	AUD	MID#	COMMENTS	FCC
6:05:23AM	15:18	TST			TEST PATTERN	LO
6:20:41*	0:44	VT1 MS		SOIJ7890	SIGN ON V918 CUT 1	I
6:21:25	5:00	BRS	C1		COLOR BARS	LO
6:26:25	1:55	VT2 /M		UGGH2345	NATIONAL ANTHEM	S
6:28:20	0:30	VC1		CWRT9876	HALLELUAH	P
6:28:50	0:30	VC1		CWRT3324	UNITED WAY CRUSADE #1	P
6:29:20	0:30	VC1		INHS5149	CHANNEL 97 MOVIE	P
6:29:50	0:10	F3SX	C2	INHS5381	ID BUMPER	I
6:30:00*	-MAN-	NET MM			MORNING COFFEE SHOW 1	NE
[6:42:58]	0:30	FIA FF		IERD0198	ZONK COMM'L	C
[6:43:28]	0:30	FC1		FISH2645	TANKORISHNESS COMM'L	C
[6:43:58]	1:00	VC1		ARGH1480	LARGO NUT CO. NO. 1	C
[6:44:58]	0:02	F3SX	#	NUMB0045	ID SAFETY	I
6:45:00*	13:00	NET MM			MORNING COFFEE SHOW 2	NE
6:58:00	1:00	VC1 FF		DLIX1694	US ARMY	S
6:59:00	0:45	VC1		DSNU5777	THREE TERMITES	C
6:59:45	0:05	FIS KI	#	IXOU6789	INSERT I SLIDE-MATTE	
6:59:50	0:05	VC2 KS	---	MNUV6790	INSERT 2 SELF KEY	
6:59:55	0:05	VC1			THREE TERMITES CONT.	
7:00:00*	-MAN-	NET MM			MORNING COFFEE SHOW 3	NE

You may want to dissolve or slowly change from one tape to another. Simply turn on the tape machines, and the computer will automatically edit, stop, and start the tapes exactly when you command it. Also, you might want to insert a sound effect at the moment a specific picture appears. By giving pre-edit commands to the computer, the exact picture and sound combination will occur automatically. The time segments on the computer are very detailed, down to tenths and even hundredths of a second. The ability to edit in such detailed segments permits almost error-free editing.

Computers in broadcast newsrooms can store stories and on command print a typed copy for the anchorperson with an additional copy for the teleprompter (Figure 13–34).

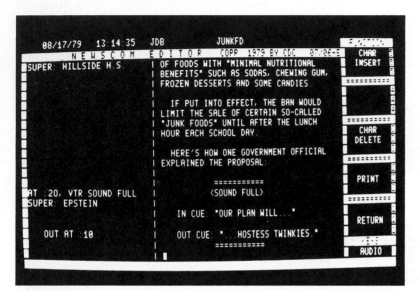

Figure 13-34 A hard copy television story from the NEWSCOM system. (Station Business Systems)

HOME COMPUTERS

In 1972 a toy called "Odyssey" tested the home video market waters. It made an economic splash, and never again would the television set be merely a passive home entertainment device. As consumers began to buy the "Odyssey" game, which cost under $100, other companies saw the growing market potential for home interactive games. By the 1980s numerous devices were being marketed to the consumer, all of which in some way involved a video screen. Some were games; others were sophisticated home computers that could perform functions ranging from storing mailing lists to performing complex mathematical analyses. The technology of microelectronics allowed the development of smaller and more compact computers (Figure 13–35).

Home computer manufacturers soon found that the consumer was ready to invest in this new technology, and this meant new revenue for a number of companies. Two of the early entrants into the field were Tandy,

Figure 13-35 With the aid of microelectronics, small personal computers are combining portability with larger storage capability. (TRS-80® Pocket Computer and Interface. Radio Shack No. 26-3505. Used with permission of Radio Shack and Tandy Corporation)

with its Radio Shack division, and Apple. IBM added its line as did companies which had predominantly been involved in video games, such as Atari and Mattel. Projections for the home computer market are positive. Market analysts predict a doubling of sales during the 1980s. Major companies such as Apple are expected to see continued growth, with other companies fighting hard for a share of Apple's market. However, Japanese firms are expected to enter this field and compete competitively for the consumer's dollar just as they have with other electronic devices.

With the increase in the number of companies entering the computer business it is not surprising that specialty computer stores are also growing. Much like the television and radio appliance stores of the 1950s, these new retail outlets permit the consumer to choose from a variety of brands and a variety of options.

Home computer networks are also developing, and access to such networks are as close as a telephone. The latest news from Associated Press, stock market quotations from Wall Street, and commodity markets from Chicago and Europe are just some of the information to which a home computer has access. Satellite data transmission adds even more flexibility to the system. A child growing up in a computer household may very well spend as much time in front of a home computer keyboard as the child of the 1970s spent watching television.

VIDEO GAMES

In 1972 a computer engineer designed a new game. It used electronics instead of the mechanical components of pinball. It employed a video screen with a set of hand controls, and it used computer technology in place of the random bounce of a metal ball bearing flinging off of pinball flippers. The game was named "Pong," and it wasn't long before the computer engineer had formed a company to which a much larger company took notice. When Warner Communications made the decisin to develop its Atari subsidiary and actively became involved in video games, it acquired "Pong." It was a wise choice. The operating revenues of Atari in 1980 were one-third of the total revenues of the large Warner Communications conglomerate. Few people could predict the growth of video games which as an industry is now larger than either the recording industry or the motion picture industry.

While "Pong" is considered the forerunner of video games, other companies and other countries in addition to the United States dot the history of video games. The Japanese, long important in electronics, entered the International market in 1978 when Taito marketed "Space Invaders." In Japan this new culture shock even affected the banks; the Bank of Japan tripled production of the 100-yen piece used to feed the thirsty "Space Invaders" machines. In the first year of production Taito placed 100,000 units in operation, and Japanese players spent the equivalent of $600 million playing "Space Invaders." In the United States a company named Bally, through its Midway division, began licensing "Space Invaders" in 1978, and in less than two years had placed 60,000 units in operation around the country.

With the popularity of the arcades, it wasn't long before Atari, which had already started with "Pong," obtained the rights to offer "Space Invaders" through home game devices that could hook up to a television set. The popularity of the arcade version propelled the home version into Atari's most successful video game.

"Space Invaders," "Galaxian," "Asteroids," "Missile Command," "Pac Man" and "Battlezone" remain some of the classics of video game technology. And when their popularity wanes, others replace them. Industry experts have determined the peak interest for a game ranges between six months and a year. The challenge for a company is to consistently be able to manufacture new games to replace the old ones.

From a strictly competitive standpoint video games cannot be ignored by other mass communication-related industries. They are gaining an increasingly larger share of the recreational "media" time available to young adults, mostly teenage males. Whenever an industry becomes larger than the recording or the motion picture industry, it must be taken seriously.

TELECONFERENCING

Increased energy costs reflected in increased transportation costs have made many companies consider different ways to bring business leaders together for corporate decision making. The telecommunications industry, realizing this need, is combining the telephone and television. The A.T.&T. system is labeled *Picturephone Meeting Service* and consists of full-color television facilities installed in meeting rooms in major cities. Using strategically placed cameras and monitors, executives in different parts of the country can carry on discussions in full view of one another.

Whether the system will receive widespread use will be determined by two things: (1) the cost of the system for smaller companies which may not be able to justify the expenditure of installing or leasing the meeting and production facilities, and (2) whether executives really find the system can replace the naturalness and effectiveness of good interpersonal communication in direct contact face-to-face situations.

CELLULAR RADIO TELEPHONE SYSTEMS

Mobile telephones have traditionally been the tool of rich and busy executives who can afford both the luxury of telephones in their cars or who demand the convenience of a mobile phone. One consistent problem with mobile telephone service has been that limited frequencies allow only about one dozen people to talk on mobile telephones in one geographical area at one time.

By approving a block of space on the electromagnetic spectrum for a new "cellular" mobile telephone service, the FCC may make mobile telephones more accessible. Cellular mobile telephone systems (Figure 13–36) operate by using a series of radio transmitters with limited coverage, as opposed to a single transmitter covering a wide area. A person making a telephone call from a mobile phone automatically connects with the closest transmitter that is connected to land lines. A computer switching system transfers calls automatically from one transmitter to another.

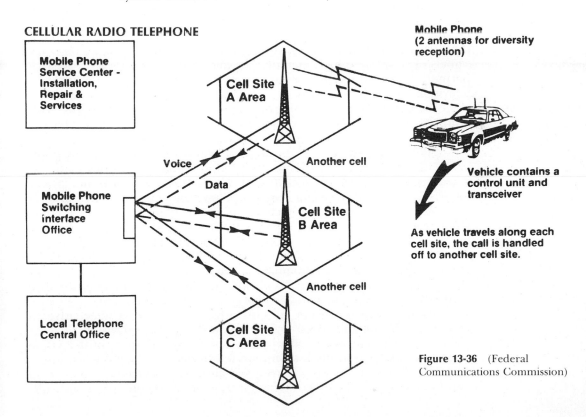

CELLULAR RADIO TELEPHONE

Mobile Phone Service Center - Installation, Repair & Services

Cell Site A Area

Voice

Another cell

Mobile Phone Switching interface Office

Data

Cell Site B Area

Another cell

Local Telephone Central Office

Cell Site C Area

Mobile Phone (2 antennas for diversity reception)

Vehicle contains a control unit and transceiver

As vehicle travels along each cell site, the call is handled off to another cell site.

Figure 13-36 (Federal Communications Commission)

Throughout our discussion of new technologies we can see that the future may judge the real difference in media to be the "content" rather than the "technology" of a particular medium. Moreover, our answer to the question of what mass communication is may change substantially when cable channels number in the hundreds and when interactive video and home computers become commonplace. While in times of world crises we may be tuned with millions of others to a single message on a single medium, other times may find us searching out the hundreds of specialized messages which fit our needs, correspond to our views, and serve our individualized purposes.

When newspapers begin broadcasting local news programs, when television stations begin distributing teletext newspapers, when *Better Homes and Gardens* arrives via cable or telephone, our life style and the way we consume media messages will change. As responsible consumers of mass communication, we can be alert to these changes by learning about and adapting to the ways new technologies will affect our society.

SUMMARY

This chapter has examined new technologies which are changing our society and the traditional ways we approach the study of mass communication. We began our discussion with cable television which started in the 1940s as a means of improving the reception of distant television signals. Today cable has expanded its role to include interactive systems permitting people in some areas of the country to enjoy a multitude of television channels and conduct such tasks as banking and shopping.

Pay cable offers such things as first-run movies and other programming features not generally available through standard cable or television programming. In some cities cable radio is also available.

Although *coaxial* cable is used in many cable systems, telephone companies are beginning to install fiber optic cable which consists of tiny strands of glass through which light waves travel. Fiber optics greatly increases channel capacity and opens the way for new interactive services.

Microwave and satellite technology are playing a part in everything from ground-based relays of television pictures to sending data transmission through space. Another means of distributing television programming is through subscription, or pay television in which the signal is scrambled at the transmitter and unscrambled at the home receiver.

Teletext is a one-way transmission system using television signals to send electronic pages of text. Videotex is a two-way interactive system.

Home video recorders and videodiscs are offering alternatives to other over-the-air and wired services. New designs in television receivers include stereo television, cable-ready television, component television, large-screen television, high-definition television, and digital television.

Home computers are offering still another dimension to mass communication. Merging two technologies, television and computers, are video games which are competing vigorously for the entertainment dollars once spent on motion pictures. Merging telephone and television are picture-phones which permit personal communication with the added dimension of video. Cellular radio is opening up the prospects for the more widespread use of mobile telephones.

OPPORTUNITIES FOR FURTHER LEARNING

ADLER, R., AND W. S. BAER, eds. *The Electronic Box Office Humanities and Arts on the Cable*. New York: Praeger, 1974.

BABE, R. F., *Cable Television and Telecommunications in Canada: An Economic Analysis*. East Lansing: Michigan State University Press, 1975.

CHU, G. D., AND B. CASSAN, eds., *Modern Communication Technology in a Changing Society: A Bibliography*. Honolulu: East-West Center, 1977.

Control of the Direct Broadcast Satellite: Values in Conflict. Palo Alto, Calif.: Aspen Institute Program on Communications and Society, 1974.

Direct Broadcast Satellite Communications: Proceedings of a Symposium. Washington, D.C.: National Academy of Sciences, 1980.

FEDIDA, S., AND R. MALIK, *Viewdata Revolution*. New York: Halstead Press, 1979.

GILLESPIE, G., *Public Access Cable Television in the United States and Canada*. New York: Praeger, 1975.

GRUNDFEST, J., AND S. N. BROTMAN, *Teletext and Viewdata: The Issues of Policy, Service, and Technology*. New York: Aspen Institute for Humanistic Studies, Program on Communications and Society, 1979.

HALLMARK, C. L., *Lasers: The Light Fantastic*. Blue Ridge Summit, Pa.: TAB Books, 1979.

HILLS, P., ed., *The Future of the Printed Word: The Impact of the Implications of the New Communications Technology*. Westport, Conn.: Greenwood Press, 1980.

KALBA BOWEN ASSOCIATES, *Direct Broadcast Satellites: Preliminary Assessment of Prospects and Policy Issues*. Washington, D.C.: National Association of Broadcasters, 1980.

LEDUC, D. R., *Cable Television and the FCC: A Crisis in Media Control*. Philadelphia: Temple University Press, 1973.

MEYER, J., ET AL., *The Economics of Competition in the Telecommunications Industry*. Cambridge, Mass.: Oelgeschlager, Gunn & Hain, 1980.

NATIONAL RESEARCH COUNCIL, *Telecommunications for Metropolitan Areas: Opportunities for the 1980's*. Washington, D.C.: National Research Council for the Department of Commerce, 1978.

PELTON, J. N., *Global Communications Satellite Policy*. Mt. Airy, Md.: Lomond Books, 1974.

PELTON, J. N., AND M. S. SNOW, eds., *Economic and Policy Problems in Satellite Communications*. New York: Praeger, 1977.

POLCYN, KENNETH A., *An Educator's Guide to Communication Satellite Technology*. Washington, D.C.: Academy for Educational Development, Inc., 1973.

QUEENEY, K. M., *Direct Broadcast Satellites and the United Nations*. The Netherlands: Sijthoff & Noordhoff, 1978.

RICE, D. M., "Direct Broadcast Satellites: Legal and Policy Options," In U.S. Federal Communications Commission, Network Inquiry Special Staff, *Preliminary Report on Prospects for Additional Networks*. Washington, D.C.: Federal Communications Commission, 1980.

RULE, J., D. McADAM, L. STEARNS, AND D. UGLOW, *The Politics of Privacy: Planning for Personal Data Systems as Powerful Technologies.* New York: Elsevier, 1980.

SIEGEL, E., ed., *Videotext: The Coming Revolution in Home/Office Information Retrieval.* White Plains, N.Y.: Knowledge Industry Publications, 1980.

SIRICO, L. J., JR., *How to Talk to the Telephone Company: Playing the Telephone Game to Win.* Washington, D.C.: Center for the Study of Responsive Law, 1979.

SMITH, D. D., *Communication Via Satellite: A Vision in Retrospect.* The Netherlands/ Boston: A. W. Sijthoff, 1976.

SNOW, M., *International Commercial Satellite Communications.* New York: Praeger, 1976.

TAYLOR, L., *Telecommunications Demand: A Survey and Critique.* Cambridge, Mass.: Ballinger, 1980.

Viewdata and Videotext, 1980–81: A Worldwide Report. Transcript of Viewdata '80. First World Conference of Viewdata, Videotex, and Teletext. White Plains, N.Y.: Knowledge Industry Publications, 1980.

CHAPTER

WIRE SERVICES, SYNDICATES, AND NETWORKS

PREVIEW

After completing this chapter, we should be able to:

Explain the wire service concept.
Trace the history of the three major wire services.
Understand the different ways in which individual media use a wire service.
Describe the bureau's role in gathering news.
Discuss the subscriber's role in gathering news.
Identify specialized wire services.
State how new technology is affecting wire service operations.
Explain the role of a feature syndicate.
Discuss the world of syndicated comics.
Trace the development of cartooning and syndicates.
Be aware of the broad scope of syndicates.
Talk about the process of merchandising comics.
Tell how networks operate.
Describe the network-affiliate relationship for both commercial and noncommercial networks and their affiliates.
Define regional, informal, and sales networks.

Although the media themselves are key links in bringing communication to a mass public, they are supported by many other media services. This chapter examines three such services that support both the print and broadcast media. First, few newspapers could successfully gather regional and national news without the help of wire services. Broadcasters would have similar difficulties. Second, neither the comics nor single panel cartoons, among other features, would appear in most newspapers or magazines without the help of syndicates. Many radio and television programs also reach the airwaves through this syndicated service. Third, both radio and television stations would have a difficult time filling their programming schedules without the services of some type of network. Let us begin by discussing wire services.

THE WIRE SERVICE CONCEPT

CBS news commentator Walter Cronkite once described working in a wire service as being in the "hot seat" of journalism. His analogy is not far from the truth. Sometimes called *press associations* or *news services*, wire services are essential information support systems for many mass media. Radio and television stations, newspapers, and specialized publications such as news magazines all use wire services as a source for their presentations. The most familiar wire services are the Associated Press (AP), United Press International (UPI), and Reuters. Stop and listen carefully to a television or radio news program. You will hear many reporters introduce the news program with a reference to the wire service. The reporter may say, "And now from the wires of United Press International," or "The Associated Press stated today. . . ." What follows is a story originally sent to subscribing media through a system of leased telephone lines and teletypes or teleprinters. Much of the national and international news offered by radio and television stations or newspapers comes from the wire services. Even networks rely heavily on wire services. It is obviously impossible for every radio and television station or newspaper to have correspondents throughout the world. The wire service is an important link in providing information to these media and consequently to the public.

*In the
Beginning:
AP and
Reuters*

Wire services in America date back to 1846. During that year eight newspapers in upstate New York—The *Syracuse Daily Star, Auburn Tocsin, Rochester Democrat, Buffalo Pilot, Auburn Advertiser, Buffalo Gazette, Rochester American, Syracuse Journal,* and *Utica Gazette*—formed a cooperative to exchange and disseminate news from the state capital in Albany. The cooperative used the services of William Lacy, an employee of the *Albany Daily Argus,* to compile and file dispatches from Albany. The group became known as the New York State Associated Press.[1]

In 1848 New York City newspaper publishers formed a newsgathering organization called the New York City Associated Press, later to evolve into today's Associated Press.

Such cooperatives became necessary as mass transportation systems not only increased the potential number of newspaper subscribers but also created a demand for news content beyond the provincial reporting that permeated local presses of the era. The system became more efficient with the development, in the same decade, of the telegraph as a major communication link. It provided instant news to places that just a few years earlier had waited for months to learn of events happening a mere hundred miles away.

**Reuter's
Pigeon
Service**

In 1851 Paul Julius Reuter began his first full year of operating a European carrier pigeon service relaying economic news to bankers between Aachen, in what is now West Germany, and Brussels, Belgium. The distance between the two points, 100 miles, was a large gap in the already developed telegraph network, and Reuter was able to bridge this gap. Soon Reuter hired help to run his own pigeon service and moved to London to try to develop a stronger base for his operation and also to have access to the coming Atlantic Cable. Although the London stockbrokers were eager for economic news, the London newspapers were not. It was not until 1858, after Reuter had provided a free trial service to the newspapers, that they entered into an agreement allowing them to receive general news from Europe.

**Dissension
in the AP
Ranks**

In the United States the AP was responsible for much of the news disseminated during the Civil War. The journalistic prowess and objective reporting of the AP even gave it exemption from censorship orders by the government. After the war ended, the AP struggled with some organizational problems. Specifically, the Western Associated Press complained that it was not receiving enough quality news from the New York headquarters bureau, which was controlled by New York interests. The Western Associated Press claimed that when the New York press learned of a big story, instead of turning it into the wire service for distribution, they would simply hold on to it. This practice, known as getting a "scoop," continues even today. Although the AP is legally entitled to all news gathered by its subscribers, there is no contractual agreement binding the subscriber to relay a major scoop immediately to the wire service.

The split between the two factions of AP temporarily healed, and the wire service expanded its operation with the development of its own leased lines for exclusive AP distribution. However, the split appeared again in 1891 when an investigative team of the western group went to New York and discovered that some of the key AP people had a secret news trade agreement with and were shareholders in a rival organization called United Press. This United Press was no relationship to the later service that eventually evolved into UPI. The outcome of the investigation was the formation of the Associated Press of Illinois, which was incorporated as a nonprofit organization and became the foundation for the modern AP. AP of Illinois also entered into agreements with foreign press associations, including Reuters, which increased its coverage of foreign news.

**John
Vandercook
and United
Press**

In 1897 the old United Press went out of business and left the new AP without any real competition. At about the same time a 25-year-old New York correspondent with the Scripps-McRae newspapers was beginning his career as a foreign correspondent and pursuing the opportunity to develop and enlarge the international wing of the Scripps-McRae Press Association. His name was John Vandercook. Seven years after his successful foreign assignment, he walked into his boss's office and asked E. W. Scripps for a promotion. He got it and began a 15-month position as editor of the *Cincinnati Post*. Not satisfied with being an editor, Vandercook again approached Scripps with an even weightier proposition. Since the end of the old United Press in 1897, the Scripps papers had not fared well. Their own Scripps-McRae Press Association was no match for AP, but membership in the rival wire service was not an attractive prospect. Vandercook proposed consolidating the Scripps-McRae Press Association with the East Coast Publishers Association and the Scripps News Association, which served the West Coast members of the Scripps chain. Scripps bought the idea, and the three merged into a new press association called United Press. United Press prospered even after Vandercook's death a year later in 1907. In 1958 it merged with the International News Service to form United Press International. During the years between its founding and the merger, it also became the first major supplier of news to broadcasting stations and gave the broadcast media equal status with newspapers in helping to determine wire service policies. It also launched UPI Audio to provide radio stations with audio actualities, correspondent reports, and regularly scheduled newscasts. AP began a similar audio service, AP Radio, in 1974.

Meanwhile, Reuters was developing its own sizable list of subscribers in the United States and especially in Europe. It continues to support many individual European bureaus that specialize in news services for specific countries. In 1967 it terminated agreements with AP and has since made great strides on its own, including the development of general and specialized services for the news media and such financial institutions as the Reuters Financial Report, Reuters Commodity Report, Reuters Money Report, and Reuters Metals Report.

USING A WIRE SERVICE

To understand how wire services function and how they are used by individual media, let's eavesdrop on a conversation at a local radio station. We are standing in the newsroom as the news director walks in. It is 6:00 A.M., and part of the news team is already sitting around having coffee. The "sitting around" will stop shortly; the coffee will remain a constant friend throughout the day.

News Director: What's it look like today, gang?

Reporter: We've had a big night. The jury on the Simpson case didn't get in until 1:30 this morning.

News Director: Did you get the story finished?

Reporter: I roughed out a draft and called it in to the wire service. They sent out a story on the morning split. They included some background information that we had overlooked. I had forgotten that Simpson had also been involved in that bank holdup five years ago.

News Director: Anything else breaking?

Reporter: Yea. Remember the hustler on the loan fraud case in Gaines-ville? Well, the wire says he tried it again last night and picked an undercover state trooper for his customer.

News Director: Call the state police headquarters and see if you can interview the trooper. We'll use it as an audio actuality.

Reporter: Already did that. Also there are some stories on the wire about the Boy Scout troop that uncovered the Indian ruins. It has some local interest for Scouts in this area. There is even a good kicker story on the wire which should make you think about stopping your smoking, boss.

News Director: What's that?

Reporter: Some guy was out riding with his girlfriend in his convertible last night. She was driving, and he was sitting in the passenger seat smoking a cigarette. The wind hit the cigarette ashes and burned a hole in his pants. He jumped up in the open convertible just as his girlfriend took a sharp S-curve. He fell out of the car and is in the hospital with a concussion.

From our conversation, let's examine the uses of a wire service. Keep in mind that a similar conversation could have taken place in a television station or a newspaper newsroom.

Backgrounding *Stories* From the wire the news team acquired additional information about local stories. Although the reporter had the information about the jury in the Simpson trial, the wire service filled in the details that gave greater depth to the story. The wire service also added another dimension to the station's news programming, an *audio actuality*, the recording of the "actual" sounds in the news. A portion of the station's interview with the state trooper will be used in the local newscast as an audio actuality. A television station or newspaper could accomplish the same thing with videotape. Our radio reporter also used the wire service as a source of new information—the story about the Boy Scout troop uncovering the Indian ruins. The wire even had a *kicker* story. This refers to the closing story of a newscast, which is in many cases a humorous anecdote, such as that about the fellow who fellow who fell out of his convertible.

We also heard some newsroom jargon during the conversation. For example, the word *split* was used to refer to a given news report sent over the wire. In wire service terminology, there are state splits, regional splits, morning splits, evening splits, and so forth. A split is simply a feature newscast on a particular region or a specialized interest, such as business, agriculture, weather, or sports.

Audio *Services* Along with the printed copy a wire service also offers *audio feeds* to subscribers. The audio feed is sent via telephone lines to local radio stations where it is either recorded or aired live. Audio feeds can be a single story or a complete newscast, such as UPI Audio or AP Radio provide. When your local radio station airs an interview with an interna-tional leader, the chances are that the interview was recorded first on location, then sent to the wire service headquarters by telephone where it was recorded and added to an "audio file" with other prerecorded stories. At a given time all of the prerecorded stories in the wire service's audio file are sent to all subscribing stations through leased telephone lines. If you were responsible for preparing a radio newscast, you would learn which prerecorded stories were available by checking the wire service audio *billboard* which periodically clears the teletype.

Picture Wires

Many of the pictures you see in the newspaper are also prepared by the wire services. Most newspapers subscribe to a *picture wire*. The next time you read the newspaper or look at a news magazine, examine the photographs. Probably under one of them will be the words *AP Wire Photo* or *UPI Wire Photo*. In each case the picture was transmitted through a special photo transmission system to the newspaper or magazine. New developments in wire photo transmission have made it possible to transmit photos of almost lifelike quality. Using a process similar to color television, color pictures can also be transmitted.

Video Feeds

Television stations can also benefit from wire service photographs. For example, video systems make it possible for television stations to receive daily video feeds of both still and motion pictures from the wire service. These are recorded on the station's videotape recorders and are later used in television newscasts.

Cable and Home Information Services

Wire services are actively involved in delivering news to cable systems. Condensed reports from the various wires are fed into a *character generator* for display on the home subscriber's television screen. Stories change slowly enough for easy comprehension. Computer storage of wire stories permits those with home computers and telephones to have direct access to wire service stories.

THE BUREAU'S ROLE IN GATHERING NEWS

The major wire services have bureaus throughout the world staffed with experienced reporters, photographers, and editors all responsible for gathering and disseminating news to subscribers (Fig. 14–1). In the United States, wire service bureaus are located in state capitals and metropolitan centers. Many of the major bureaus are responsible for disseminating world news that they receive from other wire service bureaus. In wire services, then, we have one of the most important *gatekeepers* of mass communication. In any given 24-hour period, wire service bureaus determine the news that billions of people will hear, see, and read.

Reporters, Photographers, and Technicians

When a major story breaks, a wire service bureau may dispatch a reporter, photographer, and technician to cover the event. In many cases one person performs all of these tasks. The nature of the wire service as news supplier to subscribers over a wide region requires that it carry the big stories and leave less important or local interest stories for individual broadcast

Figure 14-1 Modern wire service bureaus are a combination of people and electronic equipment. High-pressure news processing centers, these bureaus process millions of words of information daily, distributing it worldwide. (United Press International)

stations and newspapers to carry. When major news does break, wire service reporters are under considerable pressure to get as much accurate information over the wire as soon as possible. After all, a large group of professional journalists depend on these first-hand reports. Added to this is the pressure of competition among rival wire services.

Covering Major Events   An example of one enterprising wire service reporter in action is the account of the late UPI reporter John Gregory. Late one afternoon when Gregory was with UPI's Indianapolis Bureau, a passenger jet collided with a small plane above the Indianapolis airport; both planes crashed, killing all aboard. It was one of the country's largest air disasters. Gregory left the office and, in the process of driving to the scene of the event, pulled into a service station to ask directions. There he encountered a student on a school bus who had been an eyewitness to the event. Gregory directed the student to a telephone at the gas station, called UPI Audio headquarters in New York, and instructed the student to tell the wire service audio bureau about his eyewitness account of the crash. The New York bureau recorded the student's remarks. Continuing on his way to the scene, Gregory again stopped to ask for directions, this time at a nearby farmhouse. He was met at the door by a lady who had been picking vegetables outside when the crash occurred and had therefore been another eyewitness. In a few moments Gregory had placed another call to UPI Audio in New York, and the woman was giving her eyewitness account of the event. Subscribers to UPI Audio thus had access to eyewitness interviews ready for airing on their evening newscasts, something that most other stations could not match. Gregory followed up the story that night with data on casualties, flight plans of the aircraft, and background information on the personal lives of passengers who never reached their destination. It was an example of what working at a wire service and being on the "hot seat" is like.

THE SUBSCRIBERS' ROLE IN GATHERING NEWS

Not all the work in gathering news falls on the shoulders of the wire service. It would be simply impossible for a wire service bureau to cover every news item in its assigned area, so they count on their subscribers to tip them off to major stories and to provide in-depth coverage of others. It is this willingness on the part of subscribers to contribute news to the wire service that improves the quantity and quality of news sent to all subscribers and, consequently, to the public. For example, AP is organized as a news cooperative and is entitled to all of the news that its subscribers gather. UPI is not automatically entitled to news that subscribers gather but does not operate at a disadvantage to AP. Both arrangements work equally well. AP simply puts into contractual terms what UPI has in an unwritten agreement. In some instances subscribers are paid a nominal fee for their efforts. This token payment does not buy subscriber loyalty, however. The wire service's ability to provide a significant amount of important, accurate news on a regular basis is what keeps a subscriber renewing his or her contract.

Theoretically the more subscribers a wire service has, the more information can be fed to the wire service from local areas and thus distributed to all other subscribers. In some states the dominance of one wire service has created a lopsided situation, resulting in that wire service disseminating more stories of better quality.

SPECIALIZED WIRE SERVICES

Our discussion of wire services has centered on the major wire services of AP, UPI, and Reuters. There are also many specialized wire services serving specific news markets. We have already mentioned those furnished by Reuters. Another example is the Commodity News Service headquartered in Chicago and Kansas City. The Commodity News Service provides a series of specialized market analysis wire services of specific types of information. For example, it offers the Lumber Instant News (LIN), carrying such information to the lumber industry as daily cash prices of plywood, forest ranger reports, construction trends, and mortgage and financial information. This information is not only of interest to the mass media located in the heart of the lumber country but also provides an important service for the lumber industry, a subscriber to the LIN wire. Commodity News Service also offers the Farm Radio News (FRN) and Grain Information News (GIN), both offering crop reports, market quotations for the United States and Canada, and information on planting conditions. Also available are the Activity Commodity Trading News (ACT), Livestock Feed and Market News (LFM), and Poultry and Egg News (PEN).

The Public Relations Wire, another specialized wire service, is for the exclusive use of companies or other institutions and individuals who want to disseminate press releases through a wire service rather than through the mail. Sending a press release over a wire service provides an aura of importance and urgency that the mail cannot convey. The income for the wire comes from two sources—subscribers, such as newspapers, broadcasting stations, and networks, and companies which pay a fee to have their news releases distributed.

At first you might ask, "Why would any medium want to subscribe to a public relations wire?" The answer lies in its content and in the speed of distribution. Certainly much of the information received from such a source is biased in favor of the company or institution that distributes it. On the other hand, special feature information from a particular company or institution—discussing a major industrial development, executive transfers, or quarterly earnings—may be of interest to a specific public. Highly competitive media, such as the networks or media that carry a significant amount of financial news, find the wire informative and rely on it for information a day or two in advance of the mails—and therefore well ahead of the competing media.

WIRE SERVICES AND NEW TECHNOLOGY

New technology has greatly increased the efficiency of the wire service. For instance, it is now possible to transmit wire photos through the process of *electrostatic transmission.* Using specially prepared paper, this system processes pictures to subscribers as glossy prints on dry paper ready for printing. Before the electrostatic process, subscribers still had to develop wire photos for printing. The new system, pioneered by UPI, not only facilitates the work of the photo editor on a major newspaper but also makes it possible to use photos received only minutes before press time.

The computer has also been important to wire service operation and is now responsible for the storage and retrieval of most copy disseminated from wire service bureaus worldwide. No longer is the typewriter the standard piece of equipment in the wire service bureau. It has been replaced by the visual display terminal (VDT), a television screen with a keyboard on which are typed the stories to be sent to subscribers. The stories are then edited and stored in a computer until ready for transmission. At any point during the transmission process, an editor can call forth on the VDT a list of stories currently stored in the computer and then determine which stories are to be sent and in which order.

*Access
to Stories*

There are tremendous advantages to a computerized wire service system. Besides speed and efficiency, local news editors *access* to stories formerly available only to national wire service editors. An editor in Iowa, for example, might want a feature article on harvest conditions in other parts of the world. Previously the national wire service editor would control the dissemination of such features. Now the Iowa editor can scan the list of wire service stories on file in New York and call forth on his or her own

VDT a completed story about harvesting. If the Iowa editor likes the story, a command to the computer will order that complete story automatically typed on the local teletype, ready for printing.

Even the teletype is succumbing to new technology and is being replaced by the quiet, compact teleprinter. Used in many bureaus and newsrooms throughout the world, the teleprinter eliminates the familiar drumming sound of the teletypes associated with radio newscasts for decades. The small, boxlike machine sitting on a stylish base joins the silent VDTs in newsrooms where the only sounds are those of conversation, not of pounding typewriters and clicking teletypes.

Increased Channel Capacity

Channel capacity is another important consideration of wire services. By channel capacity we mean *the number of words a wire service can transmit during a given time period.* In effect, this determines the amount of information a subscriber can receive. In the past the channel capacity of standard teletype systems with information transmitted over telephone lines was limited to approximately 66 words per minute. However, new developments in technology, including high-speed teleprinters and cable systems, have the potential channel capacity of 70,000 words per second. Although the average newsroom will never receive that much news, developments such as these allow subscribers to receive an almost unlimited amount of news in any 24-hour period.

The future of wire services depends on their ability to remain free and independent suppliers of news. They are currently facing serious price squeezes. If they can survive this era financially intact, and there is every indication that they will, new technology such as satellite communication may aid in disseminating the news to their subscribers much more economically.

FEATURE SYNDICATES

The next time your read the comics or your favorite feature column in the newspaper, notice in the corner of one of the panels or columns the small print reference to the copyright of a *syndicate*. King Features Syndicate, United Features Syndicate, and National Newspaper Syndicate are some of the most important information systems for the newspaper and magazine industries. These publishers subscribe to syndicates in the same way they subscribe to wire services. In the past seventy years the role of the syndicates has steadily increased in size and importance. Moreover, newspapers long ago learned that the features they carry often determine the size and loyalty of their readers. Although people turn to the newspaper for news, they also depend on the newspaper for entertainment—entertainment that is just as important to the lifeblood of the newspaper as programming is to radio and television. It is mostly for this that the syndicates, sometimes called *feature* or *press syndicates*, operate.

Even books can become an important part of syndicate publication. Many times a syndicate will purchase the rights to a book and release it piecemeal before the complete publication is made available to the public. Along with providing good reading material for many magazines, the author and publisher also receive beneficial promotion. Records of special events are also syndicated. For example, many of the Apollo astronauts syndicated the stories of their adventures in space.

SYNDICATED COMICS

Of all the syndicated features, perhaps none reflects the concept more than the comics. Throughout this century comic strips (Figure 14–2) have reflected virtually every segment of life and have stereotyped such characters as the fighting soldier and the kid down the street. Every family with children can identify with such strips as *Dennis the Menace, Blondie,* and *Tiger.* The world of law enforcement has been accorded its share of attention through decades of *Dick Tracy.* We have watched this world-famous police officer tackle criminals with such crime fighting devices as two-way wrist radios and, later, two-way wrist television. The universal experience of romance has been captured in such popular strips as *Juliet Jones* and *Mary Worth.*

Figure 14-2 Comic strips, illustrated here in the "comic book" packaging technique used by some newspapers, are syndicated through major newspaper syndicates. (Courtesy, *The South Middlesex Daily News,* Framingham, Massachusetts)

Although not new, direct social commentary has become acceptable comic material and has gained popularity and loyalty among comic enthusiasts. One of the most successful is the strip *Doonesbury*, created by a 25-year-old Yale student named Garry Trudeau. The strip, an outgrowth of the turbulent late 1960s, first appeared in the *Yale Daily News* before being discovered and syndicated by Universal Press Syndicate. This comic has taken an almost no-holds-barred approach to current issues. In fact, some newspapers have refused to run certain episodes that pertain, by name, to some of the highest officials in government. Treatment of such issues as the energy crisis, protest marches, hippies, drugs, communal living, and life at the White House is common. Current estimates by Universal list the readership at 18 million.

Political cartoons have also made an important contribution to syndication. In fact, popular political cartoonists are valuable commodities for syndicates. *Doonesbury* is an example of a comic strip with political content; however, most of the more famous political cartoons are drawn in a single panel.

Figure 14-3 Syndicated cartoonist Paul Conrad of the *Los Angeles Times*. (Courtesy, *Los Angeles Times*)

Bill Mauldin's cartoons brought the trenches of World War II home to millions. One of his most famous appeared years later in 1963 when, after President John F. Kennedy was assassinated, Mauldin drew a caricature of the statue of Abraham Lincoln at the Lincoln Memorial holding his head in his hands and crying. Such political cartoonists as Jeff MacNelly, Jack Ohman, Don Wright, Paul Conrad (Figure 14–3), Mike Peters, Jules Feiffer, Tony Auth, Bob Gorrell, and Steve Benson have influenced and touched readers far beyond the circulation boundaries of their home newspapers.

The
Readership

The impact and readership of comic strips are astounding. Unofficial estimates for the comics alone range in the vicinity of 100 million readers per day. The comic strip characters have also traveled beyond the pages of newspapers to special radio and television programs. For example, Charles Schulz's Charlie Brown is not only a favorite among newspaper comic readers everywhere but has also starred in several prime-time television specials. In addition, his dog Snoopy adorns the dormitory rooms of countless students as a cuddly stuffed pillow dog, a perky poster, or in the form of countless other knickknacks.

Panel
Cartoons

Panel cartoons are also popular syndicate features. These are cartoons contained in a single frame instead of a series of frames. Popular single-frame cartoons include *Dennis the Menace, Marmaduke*, and *Grin and Bear It*. Editorial panel cartoons are syndicated in virtually every major newspaper in the free world.

As long as people continue to enjoy and identify with comic strip characters, syndicate publications will continue to thrive. With the ability to adapt to changing moods, issues, and experiences, the features of a syndicate can live almost indefinitely, appealing to generation after generation. Although the high cost of newsprint and other expenses associated with newspaper production have cut many pages from the print medium, the loyalty of readers to the comics and other features has been too steadfast for editors and publishers to gamble with removing some of the most popular characters of our daily lives.

CARTOONING AND SYNDICATE DEVELOPMENT

The roots of mass circulation cartoons date back to the early 1800s in Europe.

European
Roots of
Cartooning

In France the Paris newspaper *Charivari* used cartoons as early as 1838, and they became an established medium in French politics and society. The influence of *Charivari* soon spread to London, and in 1841 *Punch* was founded with a subtitle of the *London Charivari*. The cover drawing by Richard Doyle appeared on the publication from 1849 until 1956 when it was replaced by the policy of publishing a different cartoon each week in color. Still, Mr. Punch and his dog Toby were found inside

Figure 14-4 *Punch* was founded in 1841 with the subtitle, *London Charivari*. Mr. Punch and his dog, Toby, became standard features on the cover of the publication for over a century. (*Punch*, August 13, 1881. Source: *U&lc*)

the publication as a reminder of the heritage *Punch* (Figure 14–4) had acquired and its tradition in British journalism.

From both the success of *Punch* and *Charivari* came the publication of *Yellow Book* in London in 1894, and in Germany, the *Simplicissimus* appeared in 1896.

Cartooning in America

In the United States Benjamin Franklin added wit and wisdom to the *Pennsylvania Gazette* in 1754 with his broken snake (Figure 14–5) and the caption, "Join, or Die," which called for the colonies to unite against the British. In what could be compared to frontier comic books, frontiersman Davy Crockett published his cartoon-filled almanacs which appeared in the 1830s.

Figure 14-5 Early cartooning is evident in the "Join or Die" broken snake which appeared under the pen of Benjamin Franklin in 1754 issue of the *Pennsylvania Gazette*.

Harper's Weekly featured the cartoons of Thomas Nast during the 1860s. In a later series, Nast's scathing caricatures of New York's Tammany Ring and Boss Tweed contributed to their downfall. Tweed offered Nast a half-million dollars if he would leave New York to study art in Europe. But Nast stayed, and Tweed was run out of the country, only to be recognized in Europe by Spanish officials who had seen Nast's cartoons. When arrested and extradited, Tweed was said to have in his possession a complete set of the Nast caricatures.

During the late 1800s Frank Leslie's *Illustrated Newspaper* carried cartoons as did the *New York Daily Graphic*. In the 1870s and 1880s the *New York World* became famous for the work of cartoonist Walt McDougall, whose cartoon titled "The Royal Feast of Belshazzar," published during the 1884 presidential campaign, established the editorial cartoon as a regular feature in American nespapers. Other publications with an emphasis on graphic humor were *Puck* (Figure 14–6) introduced in 1877; *Judge* (Figure 14–7) introduced in 1881; and *Life*, introduced in 1883. *Life* should not be confused with the magazine *Life* which appeared in 1936.

Early Syndicate Development

By the late 1800s cartoons were so popular that they spawned the growth of feature syndicates by which more than one newspaper could share the work of the best cartoonist-illustrators. One of the best-known cartoons offered by a feature syndicate was the *Yellow Kid*.

Figure 14-6 *Puck*, an early magazine devoted to graphic humor, was introduced in 1877.

SEIZING THE DEMOCRATIC OPPORTUNITY.

The reduction of the McKinley tariff is the real issue in American politics.—*Democratic press.*

Figure 14-7 *Judge*, like *Puck*, also contained graphic humor and was introduced in 1881.

For all of its impact, the *Yellow Kid*, which we learned about in Chapter 2, had "accidental" beginnings. In 1893 Joseph Pulitzer bought a four-color press in order to print famous works of art in the Sunday supplements of the *New York World*. The idea didn't work. The Sunday editor argued that the new equipment should be tried on comic art. By this time Pulitzer had acquired the services of Richard F. Outcault, who created a cartoon which was set in the New York tenement district. One of the characters was a bald-headed boy in a nightshirt. One day in 1895 press foreman Charles Saalberg was experimenting with a new, quick-drying yellow ink and tried it out on the nightshirt of the bald-headed kid. The reaction of readers made the character an instant success, and the *Yellow Kid* was born.

Following the *Yellow Kid*, the *Katzenjammer Kids* were born, and they were joined in the early 1900s by such strips as *Mutt and Jeff* and in 1917 by *The Gumps*.

Figure 14-8 "Bringing Up Father" was developed by King Features Syndicate. The comic strip's popularity spilled over into a Broadway feature and sheet music.

Hearst and King Features	Hearst also guided the founding of King Features Syndicate which was responsible for producing comic strips and other features for the Hearst newspapers as well as for subscribers. *Happy Hooligan* and *Bringing up Father* (Figure 14–8) appeared along with book reviews, fashion features, and reproductions of art. M. Koenigsberg became the first president of King, and some of his early writers included George Bernard Shaw and William Jennings Bryan. Today King is responsible not only for its printed features but also for the production of radio features and cooperative ventures into motion pictures, such as the film *The Yellow Submarine*.
John Dille and Buck Rogers	Another syndicate pioneer, John Flint Dille, founded the National Newspaper Syndicate in 1916. Dille, who had an interest in science and the intellect, combined these qualities in 1929 to create the popular *Buck Rogers in the 25th Century*. The series was the forerunner of science fiction. One of the characters in the series, the famed Dr. Huer, differed from the usual athletic hero. He was an intellectual who was responsible for applying the discoveries of science to the imagination and creating mind-expanding adventures. He planted in many young readers of the era a hunger for scientific knowledge which undoubtedly influenced many of their professional careers. Along with becoming a successful and profitable entrepreneur, Dille wanted to give some social significance to his enterprise. So at a time when the word "psychology" still belonged to the realm of skepticism and suspicion, Dille launched the feature called *Let's Explore Your Mind*, written by Dr. Albert Edward Wiggam. Dille's son, Robert C. Dille, now heads National.

Many other feature syndicates developed concurrently. The principal wire services also entered the feature syndication field. Many major newspapers have syndicated their best writers and artists, including the *Washington Post, Chicago Tribune, New York Times, Los Angeles Times,* and *Denver Post.* Individual writers and artists have also independently syndicated their material for distribution.

SCOPE OF SYNDICATES: GOLF TO GALL BLADDERS

The scope of content found in contemporary syndicate features is as broad as the tastes of the readership they serve. For example, our preoccupation with the sport of golf has prompted the syndicated "golf tips" of such sports immortals as Arnold Palmer, Gary Player, Sam Snead, Cary Middlecoff, Jack Nicklaus, and many others. *Mark Trail's Outdoor Tips* and the Publisher Hall Syndicate's *Jimmy 'The Greek' Snyder*, plus many other sports cartoons, are further examples. Syndicated columnists themselves are popular with many readers. Jack Anderson has become a journalistic legend with his inside scoops on happenings in government. Other syndicated political columnists included on editorial pages include Rowland Evans, Robert Novak, and Carl Rowan. In some areas, regional columnists are also popular.

In addition, such specialized features as *Ann Landers* have gained tremendous loyalty among readers. Victor Riesel writes about the labor movement and has a wide following in areas in which a significant percentage of the readership are union members or come from union families. Hobbies have always been popular syndicated subjects, and many run on a seasonal basis, such as those dealing with gardening and landscaping. Medicine is also a popular feature, and the number of famous doctors writing syndicated columns has increased steadily. One of the most famous is Dr. Spock, the "baby doctor," whose column is found not only in newspapers but in magazines as well. Dr. Brady's health advice was syndicated by the National Newspaper Syndicate for over fifty years. National also syndicated the column by Dr. Lindsay Curtis entitled *For Women Only*, which deals exclusively with women's health problems.

HOW TELEVISION NETWORKS OPERATE

Most television stations operate on a profit. They derive their income from advertising, and their expenditures are primarily personnel salaries. But paying the number of people necessary to produce 18 hours of daily local programming would bankrupt the average television station. To produce a full day of local programming would require numerous sets, production crews, and theater and film crews, just to name a few. Because of the limited number of people a local station is capable of reaching, it cannot charge enough for advertising to offset the cost of all that production. Thus the network provides its *affiliate* stations with high-quality programming. Most stations need only to supplement this programming with two or three local shows per day, usually news programs. Since a network can charge more for advertising because of the large national audience it reaches, it can afford to provide programming with the talent capable of attracting and keeping sizable audiences.

Networks also act as a distribution system for commercials as well as for entertainment, news, and other types of programming. A national advertiser, usually through an advertising agency, can purchase advertising time on a network and reach millions of people without having to contract with each individual station. The three major commercial networks are all in competition for a share of the total national television viewing audience. The number of viewers a network is able to capture, measured in ratings, determines how much money it can charge for a segment of advertising. Certain special audience characteristics, such as the age and income of the audience, will also affect charges for network advertising. For example, a certain type of sports programming may appeal to a special type of audience, such as a predominantly male viewership with an average income of over $20,000 a year. Obviously this type of listener is much more capable of purchasing sponsors' products than is an audience of equal size but with little buying power, such as a group of preschoolers. Thus advertising on this type of programming will be more expensive.

The local television station is bound by an *affiliate contract* with the network but is not obligated to carry all of the available network programming. Naturally it is a rare occasion when a local affiliate will not carry network programming, although it does happen. The local station, not the network, is responsible to the FCC for meeting the needs of the station's local community. Thus when a local station feels that some type of programming may be objectionable to its audience, it may decide not to air the program or to shift it to another time period.

The networks must keep attuned to the needs and desires of their local affiliates. A network could not survive if its affiliates objected to its programming and refused to broadcast it, because sponsors could no longer be guaranteed a specific audience for commercials. Some advertisers might also object to sponsoring programs distasteful to the public. Therefore the networks must program shows that appeal to the great majority of the national audiences.

THE NETWORK-AFFILIATE RELATIONSHIP

A broadcast network is basically as strong as its affiliate stations. Remember that without the affiliates there would be no network. To understand the network-affiliate relationship, it first is necessary to understand the communication occurring between the two. The key element is *feedback*, feedback from the affiliate to the network management.

Commercial Networks

Affiliates make their opinions known to network management through a group of delegates, usually certain station managers of the network's affiliate stations. If local stations have complaints or opinions they wish expressed to the network, they tell their delegates, who in turn meet with the network's management. Although no network will act on isolated complaints, when affiliate feedback on an issue becomes substantial and is well represented geographically and demographically, then the networks will make efforts to remedy the situation.

Another method of feedback to commercial networks is provided through the *clearance ratio*. If a network plans to broadcast material of questionable taste, it will notify all the affiliates well in advance of the forthcoming program and then air it on closed circuit to all network stations for their perusal. If enough of the stations decide they do not want to air the program, the network will realize that it will suffer from the low ratings the program will undoubtedly receive. It is then up to the network to decide whether (1) to air the program at all; (2) to reschedule the program for another time period; (3) to permit local affiliates to videotape the program, then air it at a later hour; or (4) to cancel the program entirely.

How do the affiliates make their programming decisions? They do so by being responsive to the feedback they receive from their viewing audience. By carefully monitoring the *ratings*, broadcast management can determine what is suitable for local audience consumption. However, communicating their preferences to local broadcast management is the public's responsibility. Only when individuals take time to communicate their reactions to the local broadcaster can the local broadcaster, in turn, relay that feedback to the networks.

*Public
Broadcasting*   In the Public Broadcasting Service, feedback has a much different form from that originating from commercial affiliates. This feedback comes mainly from what is called the *Station Program Cooperative* (SPC). The SPC utilizes direct feedback in the form of financial commitment from affiliate stations to determine which *pilot* programs will make up over one-third of the programming distributed by PBS.

The SPC operates essentially in the following manner. As the person responsible for determining what program will be funded under the SPC system, you will first develop a set of national program needs using all of the feedback information mentioned before. Based on these needs you will solicit proposals from program producers. From this information you will then prepare a catalogue of the program proposals for use by the individual public broadcasting system's licensees in planning their next season's programming.

This selection process by the individual licensees initiates a direct feedback procedure that eventually determines which program will be funded and which program will be dropped from further consideration. The first step in this feedback process is a *bidding round* in which the licensees indicate their interest in specific programs. At this point there is no financial commitment by the licensee. From this information the SPC official then determines which programs are the top contenders for selection by affiliate stations. After a second bidding round, during which the stations begin to commit themselves financially, some programs are tentatively accepted, and others are dropped from the list. The final step, a *purchase round*, involves stations making final commitments and programs being selected.

REGIONAL, INFORMAL, AND SALES NETWORKS

Along with the major radio and television networks, other types of networks affect the flow of information to the public. These are the regional, informal, and sales networks.

Regional networks provide programming and information to specific geographic areas. They are incorporated into the regular programming of the station in much the same way as national network programming is. The regionals' supplemental programming, especially news, figures importantly in attracting local audiences. An audience in Maine, for instance, is more interested in news of Maine and new England than in new of Alabama. With the advent of *CATV*, regional networks have become increasingly important to individual stations. CATV takes the station's signal beyond its primary broadcast *contours* into many outlying communities. Since for most broadcasting stations the cost of sending reporters to cover all these surrounding areas is prohibitive, the regional network solves the problem.

Informal networks are news networks created by a professional group of radio or television news personnel. There is no contract or written document spelling out services or agreements. Such networks are in existence everywhere and are a big help to participating stations.

Let's assume that you are working as a radio reporter in a large city and want to carry news of three surrounding cites. To do so, you develop an association with news personnel at a station in each of three surrounding cities and call on them whenever you need information about a story in their community. The advantage of this informal network is that because the desired story is important local news, the originating station will probably cover it in depth and can provide additional background information that other networks, including a wire service, might not have. Usually called *co-ops*, these informal networks can consist of anywhere from 2 to 15 or more newspersons who exchange news on a fairly regular basis.

Sales networks are designed principally for advertising. Although participating stations may occasionally receive programming material, this is not the network's main purpose. A sales network is usually a group of stations linked together through some common bond to benefit all member stations financially. As with informal networks, this bond can be aided by a permanent communications system, such as teletypes or leased transmission lines. The networks are often formed by advertising agencies or broadcast station representatives.

For example, there might be one such network in an area noted for its vacation opportunities or tourist attractions. Let us assume that this area consists of three states and that you are responsible for buying advertising for a chain of restaurants in the three-state area. You decide to purchase commercials on different radio and television stations in the area and are looking for an inexpensive group rate. However, since the stations do not often voluntarily cooperate—mostly because they are competing businesses and are perhaps miles apart—an advertising agency in the area might contact the group of stations and ask if they would like to join together in a *tourist network*. The advertising agency or station representative would then sell commercials for all number stations, taking a commission from the total price of the commercials. All stations would benefit from the sale as would you, the advertiser, who would receive a group purchase discount. The difference between this type of network and the others is that dissemination of information is not the primary service provided by the network; its benefits come from group purchasing power.

SUMMARY

In this chapter we have studied wire services, syndicates, and networks. Wire services are responsible for supplying the bulk of news to the mass media, which in turn disseminate it to the public through broadcast and printed news reports. Specialized wire services carry news designed for specialized audiences such as the agricultural and business communities.

The concept of a wire service actually found its first application in the nineteenth century with carrier pigeon service between towns not connected by telegraph. The first modern wire service was Associated Press, which did not acquire its present form until a dispute between its western and eastern factions resulted in the formation of the Associated Press of Illinois. United Press International became the first supplier of news to broadcast stations. Reuters, AP, and UPI are the three major wire services.

Syndicates are another principal source of information for mass media, especially newspapers. The syndicate concept, which dates back to the end of the last century, has now been applied to everything from books to cartoons. Based on this same syndicate principle, many broadcasting stations are also using syndicated programming.

Broadcast networks, especially television networks, are responsible for providing much of the programming aired by affiliate stations.

In commercial broadcasting, networks are made aware of the concerns of their affiliates through affiliate representatives and organizations. In public broadcasting, affiliates directly participate in what becomes network programming through the station program cooperative.

Regional, informal, and sales networks are also sometimes formed by stations to accomplish a specific, common goal such as lower group rates for advertising.

OPPORTUNITIES FOR FURTHER LEARNING

BERGER, A., *The Comic-Stripped American*. Baltimore: Penguin, 1974.

CAMPBELL, R., *The Golden Years of Broadcasting: A Celebration of the First 50 years of Radio and TV on NBC*. New York: Simon & Schuster, 1976.

DREHER, C., *Sarnoff: An American Success*. New York: Quadrangle/*The N.Y. Times*, 1977.

ESTREN, J., *A History of Underground Comics*. New York: Quick Fox Inc., 1974.

FRIENDLY, F. W., *Due to Circumstances beyond Our Control . . .* New York: Random House, 1977.

HORN, M., ed., *The World Encyclopedia of Comics*. New York: Chelsea House, 1976.

HORN, M., ed., *The World Encyclopedia of Cartoons*. Detroit: Gale Research, 1980.

JOHNSON, J. J., *Latin America in Caricature*. Austin: University of Texas Press, 1980.

KOREN, E., *"Well, there's your problem": Cartoons by Edward Koren*. New York: Pantheon, 1980.

LEE, S., *Origins of Marvel Comics*. New York: Simon & Schuster, 1974.

MACY, J. W., *To Irrigate a Wasteland, the Struggle to Shape a Public Television System in the United States*. Berkeley: University of California Press, 1974.

NELSON, R. P., *Cartooning*. Chicago: Henry Regnery, 1975.

OLIPHANT, P., *Oliphant!* Kansas City: Andrews and McMeel, Inc., 1980.

PALEY, W. S., *As It Happened*. New York: Doubleday, 1979.

QUINLAN, S., *Inside ABC*. New York: Hastings House Publishers, 1979.

ROBINSON, J., *The Comics: An Illustrated History of Comic Strip Art*. New York: Putnam's, 1974.

WEINER, R., *Syndicated Columnists*. New York: Richard Weiner, Inc., 1976.

CHAPTER

REGULATORY CONTROL OF MASS COMMUNICATION

PREVIEW

After completing this chapter, we should be able to:

Describe the closed and open systems of communication.

Outline the provisions of the Wireless Ship Act of 1910, the Radio Act of 1912, the Radio Act of 1927, and the Communications Act of 1934.

Discuss the organization and effectiveness of the Federal Communications Commission (FCC).

Explain the provisions of Section 315.

Specify which programming is exempt under Section 315.

Describe the Fairness Doctrine and its 1974 and 1976 reports.

Tell how cable is regulated.

Discuss copyright laws.

Relate the history and activities of the National Telecommunications and Information Administration.

Explain the role that the Federal Trade Commission (FTC) plays in governing advertising messages.

Know how a complaint to the FTC is processed.

Discuss the functions of the International Telecommunication Union (ITU).

386

REGULATORY
CONTROL OF
MASS
COMMUNI-
CATION

Freedom from regulatory control of American mass media is guaranteed by the constitution. In other countries, legislation either guarantees the free flow of information via the media or establishes very strict controls over such messages. However, because space on the electromagnetic spectrum is limited, American electronic media operate *under* government control, originating from such agencies as the Federal Communications Commission on a national level or the International Telecommunication Union (ITU) on an international level. To understand control of mass communication, we shall begin by examining a theoretical model of control. Keep in mind as we examine the model of control that different media have different regulatory needs. Broadcasting, because it is a limited resource, has more regulations than magazines do, but although magazines are not regulated by a federal agency as such, they are affected by a complex array of postal regulations. In different countries the control of media varies, and the limitations on the print or broadcast media in one country can be entirely different in another.

A MODEL OF CONTROL

One way to view control of mass communication is through a model developed by Osmo Wiio, professor and director of the Helsinki Research Institute for Business Economics.[1] In Wiio's model, mass communication is viewed on a two-dimensional, open-closed continuum of the receiver system (the audience) and the message system (the media) as shown in Figure 15–1. The left vertical line of the model represents the audience,

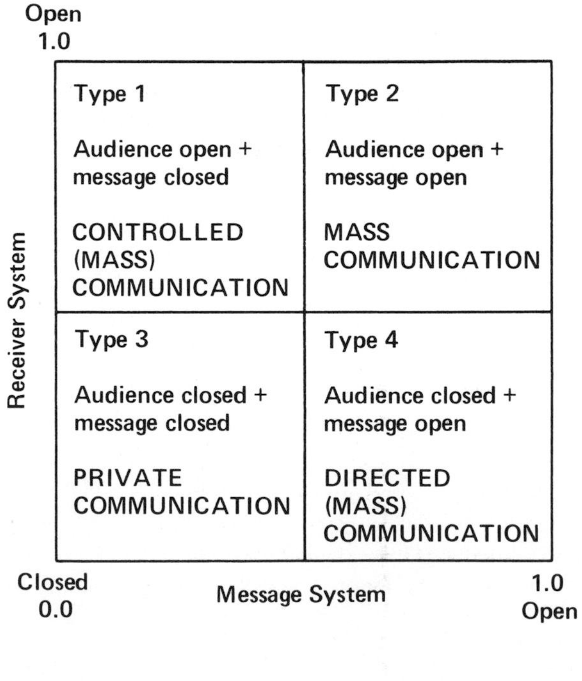

Open
1.0

Type 1 Audience open + message closed CONTROLLED (MASS) COMMUNICATION	Type 2 Audience open + message open MASS COMMUNICATION
Type 3 Audience closed + message closed PRIVATE COMMUNICATION	Type 4 Audience closed + message open DIRECTED (MASS) COMMUNICATION

Receiver System

Closed
0.0   Message System

1.0
Open

Figure 15-1 Osmo Wiio's model of communication. The most open system represented in the model appears as Type 2 (upper right). A closed system is represented by Type 3 (lower left).

387

REGULATORY
CONTROL OF
MASS
COMMUNI-
CATION

and the bottom horizontal line represents the message system. A numerical range of 0.0 to 1.0 is used to characterize the degree of control, with 1.0 representing the most open system, and 0.0 representing the most closed system. Thus the most *closed* system—for example, a Type 3 private telephone system—is actually private communication, not mass communication at all. Type 2, uncontrolled mass communication, which directs its mesages to anyone who can hear them, represents the other end of the spectrum, a completely *open* mass communication system.

Each medium operates under varying amounts of control and for an audience at some position on the open-closed continuum. For example, a company magazine is more closed both in terms of message and audience than is a major metropolitan newspaper. Certain messages within the same medium may also be more closed than others. Consider the local television cable system that provides a fairly wide range of programs for its viewers. Some channels, however, may be accessible only to those viewers who pay an additional fee to the cable system. In this case the system itself represents a more open position on the model, and given cable channel represents a more closed position. It is important to realize that the model is not meant to be a tidy classification of media. It is presented to help you conceptualize the various dimensions of control that affect mass communication. As you read about the specific agencies and regulations, consider how they would interrelate with the model we have just discussed. In addition, remember that many of these "controls" are not controls in the traditional sense but are actually safeguards to ensure our system's "openness."

EARLY BROADCAST LEGISLATION

The twentieth century had barely begun when it became clear that Marconi's invention was quickly getting out of hand. Interference, jamming, and crowded frequencies were just some of the conditions that caused the United States to bring radio under government control.

The Wireless Ship Act of 1910

The Wireless Ship Act of 1910 was the first piece of legislation to affect directly the new "wireless" communication that later became known as radio. Basically the law made it illegal for any "ocean-going steamer" (Figure 15–2) carrying more than fifty persons to leave a United States port for a trip of more than 200 miles without ship-to-ship and ship-to-shore communication equipment (Figure 15–3) operated by a trained technician. Enforcement of this regulation was the duty of the Secretary of Commerce and Labor, who had the authority to arrest the "master" of any ship violating the order. The courts were authorized to slap a maximum $5000 fine on the "master" for that violation. The act accomplished three things: (1) it provided an impetus for the beginnings of the radio industry; (2) it was evidence that Congress recognized the potential of the new medium; and (3) it sparked research and development of wireless communication for improving long-distance radio service.

Figure 15-2 Early wireless regulation primarily involved commerce matters related to ship-to-shore communication. Early ocean-going vessels required large antenna structures, since the shipboard wireless did not have the sophistication or power of modern radio communication systems. Today, a shipboard satellite antenna can transmit and receive data from anywhere in the world and automatically pilot the location of a vessel. The vessel shown here is passing under New York's Manhatten Bridge prior to World War I. (Naval History Photograph, U.S. Navy)

Figure 15-3 A vessel's wireless was a complex array of wires and equipment, as evidenced by this wireless room of the Lusitania. (Marconi Copyright, The Marconi Company Limited, Chelmsford, Essex)

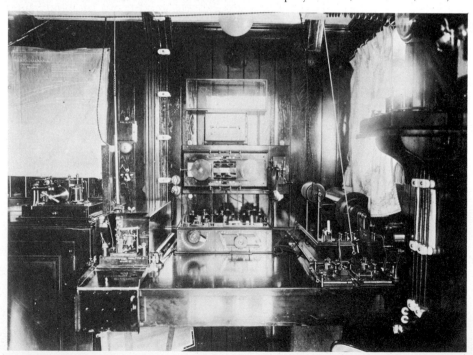

The Radio Act of 1912

Congress soon realized that it would be necessary to keep track of who owned and controlled the two-way communication equipment so the President of the United States could gain control of it during wartime, should that become necessary. Thus Congress passed a second piece of legislation, the Radio Act of 1912. This act decreed that anyone operating a radio transmitter first had to have a license; that the only people who could obtain a license were citizens of the United States and Puerto Rico or corporations chartered in either the United States or Puerto Rico; that the owners and location of the equipment be identified; and that there be some estimate of the distance over which the transmitter could send messages. The act also provided for separation between the frequencies of stations to eliminate interference, but it left these decisions more up to the owners of the transmitters than to the government.

Yet the 1912 act really had no practical way of controlling the development of commercial broadcasting for mass public consumption, for radio was far more than shipping and commerce. Experimental stations began testing the airwaves. The 1920s arrived with KDKA broadcasting the Harding-Cox election and WGN carrying Chicago Cubs and White Sox baseball, Big Ten football, and the Indy 500. Radio was suddenly everywhere. Broadcasters also realized that with an audience of this size they could charge for messages sent over the airwaves. Excitement and turmoil within the industry were mounting. To fight off competition, stations began to operate with more and more power.

By the 1920s the airwaves were in complete chaos, but the courts overruled the Department of Commerce and Labor's attempts at control.

Figure 15-4 Herbert Hoover, then Secretary of Commerce of Labor and later a U.S. President, called a series of National Radio Conferences during the 1920s to try and straighten out the conflicts arising from the inadequate laws governing radio. (A.T.& T.)

390

REGULATORY
CONTROL OF
MASS
COMMUNI-
CATION

Secretary of Commerce and Labor Herbert Hoover (Figure 15–4) then called a series of National Radio Conferences to propose legislative solutions to some of radio's crowding problems. The conferences brought together everyone from the military, to private owners of broadcasting stations, to amateur radio operators. Finally after a number of false starts with inadequate legislative proposals, Congress responded to the problem by passing the Radio Act of 1927.

The Radio Act of 1927

The Radio Act of 1927 recognized for the first time the need for broadcasting to be in "the public interest, convenience, and necessity," although in 1927 programming was not the issue it is today. Legislators also paid heed, both legal and political, to the fact that the airwaves, unlike the print media, were limited in their capacity to transmit messages at any one time. Only so much of the *electromagnetic spectrum* could be efficiently used for broadcasting; this scarce resource thus needed to be controlled.

The 1927 legislation also established the first governmental body to control broadcasting—the Federal Radio Commission—a five-member group appointed by the President. The Act of 1927 contained some significant legislation that still applies to broadcasting today. It established a system of call letters for radio stations, a systematic method of license renewal and equipment modification, and qualifications for station operators. It also gave government the power to revoke licenses, to provide for inspection of station apparatus, and to assign frequency and power limits to stations while retaining the regulatory provisions of the 1912 legislation on communication for ships at sea.

The Communications Act of 1934

The Radio Act of 1927 remained in force until 1934 when Congress, on the recommendation of President Franklin D. Roosevelt, passed the Communications Act of 1934. This act identified broadcasting as a separate entity apart from both the "utility" or "power" concept and apart from "transportation." The act replaced the Federal Radio Commission with the Federal Communications Commission and became the main piece of legislation, as later amended, under which the American system of broadcasting now operates.

THE FEDERAL COMMUNICATIONS COMMISSION

Of all governmental agencies the FCC (Figure 15–5) is second to none in its direct and profound effect on the lives of virtually everyone. The FCC is, whether directly or indirectly, the governmental body responsible for regulating relatively all of the messages millions of people see and hear every day through the broadcast media. Although the commission has no broad power to censor the content of broadcasting, it does have the power to ensure that those in broadcasting are responsible and consider the public "interest, convenience, and necessity." By one sweep of the regulatory hand or even by the suggestion of a major policy statement, it can affect the content of prime-time television, give networks second thoughts about children's television programming, give a politician equal air time,

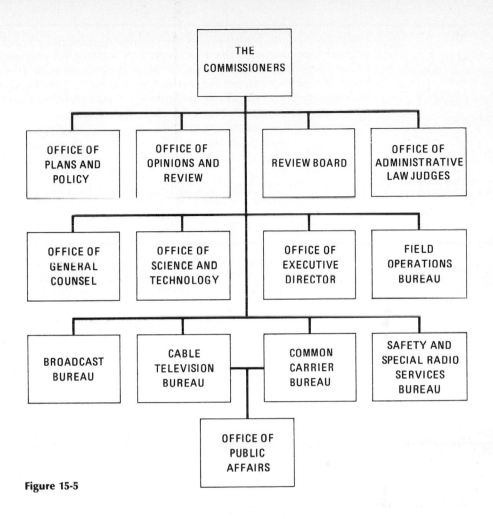

Figure 15-5

and affect the daily operation of every local broadcasting operation in the country, which in turn affects each citizen.

Organization   The commission consists of seven FCC commissioners appointed by the President with the advice and consent of the Senate. In recent years their appointment has come under close scrutiny in confirmation hearings, a sign of the importance of mass communication to our society in general and the control of that communication in particular. The Communications Act prohibits the commissioners from having any conflicting interests while serving on the commission. It also sets their terms for seven years and limits to four the members from any one political party.

Effectiveness   There are arguments on both sides of the fence as to how effective the FCC is. On the one hand, the commission has been criticized for being too lenient in broadcast programming regulation and allowing the networks,

392

REGULATORY
CONTROL OF
MASS
COMMUNI-
CATION

the broadcasting industry, and the politicians the upper hand. Others have argued that although the FCC is in fact a regulatory agency, it can very easily come into conflict with the First Amendment to the Constitution. Over the years the commission has increased in size to more than 2000 employees, a development indicative of the trend toward government bureaucracy. However, the FCC does patrol the operation of thousands of commercial broadcasting stations and many times that number of two-way radio stations operated by citizens, local governments, and municipalities. The surge of interest in citizens' band radio has also increased the commission's workload.

As with any governmental agency, many commission actions and decisions take their cue from developments within the industry. This is because in order to regulate an industry effectively and fairly, one first needs to know how that industry works. To obtain this feedback, the FCC initiates a system of "opinion filings" in which broadcasters file with the commission their opinions on pending rules and regulations. The FCC, in turn weighs these opinions, because significant industry opposition to a proposed regulation might result in more lawsuits than in compliance, once it is passed.

Many of the decisions the FCC makes are not popular with the industry, and many should not be. The commission is caught between regulating an industry that must operate in the public interest and being the instrument of a political process that is ultimately accountable to Congress. The commission can even face pressures from the industry directed at members of Congress. Comments from broadcasters are not ignored in Congress, and a high level of criticism against any governmental agency can cause everything from investigative inquiries to budget hassles. As new technology continues to affect our lives, and as Congress continues to define its regulation of electronic mass communication, the work of this regulatory body will become significantly more important.

SECTION 315

Of those sections found within the Communications Act of 1934, perhaps none has been more discussed than Section 315. It has had a profound effect on the operations of political broadcasting. Section 315 concerns the ability of political candidates to gain access to the airwaves during political campaigns. It states:

> If any licensee shall permit any person who is a legally qualified candidate for any public office to use a broadcasting station, he shall afford equal opportunity to all other such candidates for that office in the use of such broadcasting station: *Providing*, that such license shall have no power of censorship over the material broadcast under the provisions of this section.

Pros and Cons of Access

Section 315 has received serious criticism from candidates and broadcasters alike. To understand these feelings, imagine that you have just filed candidacy for your city council and plan to make arrangements to purchase advertising time on one of the radio stations in your community. You

393

REGULATORY
CONTROL OF
MASS
COMMUNI-
CATION

make an appointment with the sales manager to discuss the amount of money you have to spend and the type of political announcement you will make. You look at the station's rate card and discover that by purchasing 100 commercials, you will obtain a discount. You are not sure you can afford 100 commercials and are relieved to hear the sales manager say that you can purchase a lesser number of commercials and still receive the discount rate. He explains that under Section 315, you are entitled to the "lowest unit charge" and therefore will receive the station's "discount rate" for purchasing 100 commercials even though you will only purchase 50 commercials. The discount rate for 100 commercials is $5 per commercial. You can afford to purchase 50 commercials for a total of $250. You agree to the contract and then explain that you want to use the station's facilities to produce your commercials. The sales manager quotes you a per-hour rate for the use of the facilities. Returning the next day to produce your commercials, you tie up the facilities for about two hours. Finally with the help of the program director, you produce an acceptable commercial. After you leave, the sales manager goes in to talk with the general manager.

Sales Manager: Well, that job is finished. We tied up the main studio for two hours and all for $250 in advertising. I could have used the same time to produce a commercial for the hardware store worth $500 in advertising.

General Manager: Yes, I know. This Section 315 is getting to be a real headache. We haven't heard the end of it, either. You know that when the opponent hears that commercial, she'll be in here wanting to buy time, and we'll be faced with the same tied-up facilities and low sales that we were on this one. What do you think? Would it be a good idea simply to refuse to sell political advertising next year and instead offer free time to all the candidates?

Sales Manager: Do you have any idea how many people are running for city council? This place would be like a zoo. We would have every candidate in here who wanted to state a case. This way, the cost of purchasing commercials at least keeps the crowd down.

General Manager: Yes. It also keeps our profits down.

The conversation between the sales manager and the general manager illustrates just one of the issues surrounding Section 315—money. A station does not realize much profit from political commercials. In addition, because a station is required to permit all candidates for any one office to purchase time, every candidate is assured equal access and equal rates. Besides this, since a radio station is allowed to program only so many minutes per hour of commercials and since Section 315 says stations must grant candidates access to these minutes, many other advertisers who would pay more for commercials and who may be long-term, good customers may have to be pushed off the air to accommodate political advertisements. But remember the positive side of Section 315. Without it, candidates with smaller campaign budgets might not be able to use the broadcast media to bring their campaign to the public.

Exempting
News
Programming

One area that is exempt from the provisions of the law is news programming. Section 315 states that the equal time provisions do not apply to:

1. bona fide newscasts;
2. bona fide news interviews;
3. bona fide news documentaries (if the appearance of the candidate is incidental to the presentation of the subject or subjects covered by the news documentary); or
4. on-the-spot coverage of bona fide news events (including but not limited to political conventions and activities incidental thereto). [A 1975 ruling by the FCC added press conferences and political debates broadcast live in their entirety to this exemption.]

If you interviewed a candidate and aired his or her remarks in a newscast, you would have to decide whether to air the comments of the opposing candidate. Although you would want to exercise your responsibility to seek out both sides of an issue, the opponents could not demand equal time based on Section 315. An example of this exemption occurred with the *CBS Morning News*, which covered a story about an ex-convict running for sheriff in the state of Virginia. The story showed the candidate campaigning, interviewed him, and told of his background, which had included time served at a number of prisons for felony convictions. When the report was broadcast, there was even a campaign poster behind Hughes Rudd, the CBS news commentator, which said "vote for" and the name of the candidate. Although the man was an officially declared candidate, the news about his campaigning came under the exemption provisions of Section 315.

A station, of course, cannot completely refuse access to candidates and close itself off from its community. For instance, it cannot refuse free time and also refuse to sell political advertising. That would be denying "reasonable opportunity for the discussion of conflicting views on issues of public importance." The main purpose of Section 315 is to assure minority candidates and candidates with limited funds at least a minimal access to the broadcast media. Although there is continued criticism of the law, so far it is the best measure the FCC has to assure candidates an opportunity to be heard.

THE FAIRNESS DOCTRINE

The Fairness Doctrine goes beyond political broadcasting to the overall treatment of controversial issues. The issues are not limited to politics as codified in Section 315 but go beyond them to include other issues deemed important to the community served by the broadcasting station.

The Fairness
Doctrine
is Issued

In the spring of 1948 the FCC began a series of hearings on the subject of editorializing by the broadcast media.[2] Out of these hearings arose the Fairness Doctrine, which pertains to the responsibility of every broadcaster

395

REGULATORY
CONTROL OF
MASS
COMMUNI-
CATION

to provide station facilities for the expression of controversial issues and all sides of those issues.[3] In a statement on the matter, the commission noted on June 1, 1949, that editorializing was "consistent with the licensee's duty to operate in the public interest." The commission went on to emphasize the responsibility of the licensee to seek out opposing views on controversial issues, commonly referred to as the "seek out" rule. The 1949 report also charged the licensee with the responsibility to "play a conscious and positive role in bringing about a balanced presentation of opposing viewpoints."

Since 1949 the FCC has periodically issued a series of statements on the interpretations of the Fairness Doctrine. Among these is the "personal attack" rule requiring notification and offers of equal time to people verbally attacked on the air.

The 1974 Report

Reopened hearings on the doctrine in 1974 led to the issuing by the FCC of the "Fairness Doctrine Report: 1974." That report specifically exempted product advertisements from the doctrine's jurisdiction. The 1974 report also attempted to create an atmosphere of flexibility in interpreting the doctrine. The concern of the FCC, the broadcasters, and the public was that there were no guidelines for any of the groups to follow in defining such important concepts as "a controversial issue" or "reasonable opportunity for contrasting viewpoints." The commission summed up its feelings on these matters as follows:

> The Fairness Doctrine will not ensure perfect balance and debate, and each station is not required to provide an "equal" opportunity for opposing views. Furthermore, since the Fairness Doctrine does not require balance in individual programs or a series of programs, but only in a station's overall programming, there is no assurance that a listener who hears an initial presentation will also hear a rebuttal. However, if all stations presenting programming relating to a controversial issue of public importance make an effort to round out their coverage with contrasting viewpoints, these various points of view will receive a much wider public dissemination.

The 1974 report has not reduced the debate over the Fairness Doctrine. When cable television systems fully utilize their multichannel capacity and when citizen groups take advantage of their opportunities to help determine programming on these channels, the restricted broadcasting "spectrum" will expand as will its potential for disseminating information. Perhaps then both the implied and stated controls that comprise the Fairness Doctrine may be unnecessary.

Reconsidering the Fairness Doctrine

The commission decided to reconsider the Fairness Doctrine in 1976 after citizens' groups wanted more access to broadcasting. The FCC generally reaffirmed its decisions in the 1974 report. It felt that the doctrine should continue to be applied to advertisements that pertain to public issues, not to specific products. It agreed that broadcast editorials should come under the doctrine's aegis and reaffirmed the right of the broadcaster to decide how the doctrine should be applied on a local basis. In the case in which the FCC did have to intervene, it was felt that the probable action would be simply to require the station to provide time for opposing viewpoints.

REGULATING CABLE

The barrage of rules and regulations that has evolved since cable television became a major carrier of media content boggles the mind. Federal legislation is almost equal in amount to the combined regulations governing commercial radio and television broadcasting, and when we add to this the maze of local and state regulations, we may stand back in amazement. At least with standard broadcasting stations, the federal government has the responsibility for making and enforcing the laws. Such is not the case with cable. Regulations enacted by local municipalities abound, establishing standards for the local cable operator on everything from fees to program content. They have legislated to which poles cables can be attached, where they must be underground, why cable operators cannot work on actual television sets, and numerous other regulations. Officials at all levels of the regulatory ladder have discovered the potential of cable systems, and state and FCC lawmakers also want a voice in controlling them. There are no clearly defined rules or court precedents giving the FCC *exclusive* jurisdiction. Thus in many areas there are significant conflicts, if not confusion, over exactly who has jurisdiction over the case.

At the local level, control stems from municipalities' ownership of right of ways and from communities' realizations that the system has much more potential than merely bringing distant entertainment radio and television to the community. It can reach local school children with information about their schools. It can broadcast meetings of the city council and bring the workings of municipal government into living rooms with a realism that the local newscast or newspaper would find hard to match. With so many channels available to community groups, almost anyone can gain access to a local cable channel and disseminate a message to area cable subscribers. Moreover, there is the problem of categorizing cable in relation to other media. Legal precedent has suggested that the printed press and broadcast press are equal under the First Amendment rights of free speech and free press. However, is cablecasting the same as broadcasting? What would happen, for instance, if a cable company's news programs became justifiably critical of the city council in a community in which the city council had control over the cable company's franchise? These and other questions have posed many regulatory quandaries. Simple answers are just not available.

When a municipality becomes involved in cablecasting, problems of jurisdiction among the three governmental levels are bound to occur. Whenever state and local laws conflict, the state law will almost always have the advantage in an appeal. Similarly, in a conflict between state and federal laws, the federal law will usually take precedent. Thus, to avoid problems with possible appeals, many states and localities have borrowed regulations that closely resemble federal legislation.

In 1976 a complete revision of United States copyright statutes took place, with most of the new statutes taking effect on January 1, 1978. The new law was much more extensive than the old 1909 legislation, now including photocopy technology, cable television, and other changes that had evolved in the sale and distribution of copyrighted material.

For example, libraries received some measure of protection in reproducing copyright works with their photocopy equipment, a practice common to every college and university. Although the new law did not absolve the person desiring to make the copy from penalties, it gave libraries some immunity if they posted a public notice next to the photocopy machines stating that the use of the machine to reproduce material may be governed by copyright law.

This new law also clearly spelled out the fair use of copyright material. In particular, material used by reporters, critics, scholars, or teachers for noncommercial purposes became somewhat exempt from copyright restrictions. The key test of copyright infringement was whether someone other than the copyright holder used the reproduced documents for *profitable gain* and whether such reproductions *reduced the demand* for the original copyrighted work. The new law also extended copyright protection for life plus 50 years for authors and 75 years for copyright holders.

Certain activities of the broadcasting industry also came under this new law. Users of instructional television programs gained more jurisdiction to use copyrighted material without clearance and payment of fees if the taping and showing of the program was directly related to the teaching function. Negotiations began immediately after the law was passed to establish the rates that public broadcasters would pay for the use of copyrighted musical works licensed under the performance rights societies, such as *ASCAP, BMI*, and SESAC. SESAC did not wait for the other two to arrive at rates and instead sent public broadcasters a licensing agreement that many signed and returned with the requested licensing fee. Other stations waited to see what ASCAP and BMI would do. Professional organizations even joined together to resist payment of the licensing fees. A copyright royalty tribunal was formed under the law with jurisdiction to establish terms of the royalty payments to performers and fees to broadcasters.

As for cable television systems, the copyright law permits them to obtain a compulsory license and pay a single fee for both the license and rebroadcasting signals not only from FCC-licensed stations but also from similarly licensed stations in Canada and Mexico. Cable systems can also carry other signals that FCC rules permit them to carry. Locally originated programming, however, is separate from the compulsory license, and carrying it subjects the cable system to certain copyright fees similar to those paid by commercial broadcasters for airing copyrighted works.

As with all new legislation, this copyright law will undergo numerous court tests to become defined precisely, but it is a welcome relief to all media and related industries to have updated guidelines to a very complicated issue.

In 1978 President Jimmy Carter signed an executive order creating the National Telecommunications and Information Administration (NTIA) in the U.S. Department of Commerce. The idea was not new. It evolved in 1970 when President Richard Nixon coordinated the advisory functions on telecommunication, including both domestic and international radio and television and other electronic communication services, under the Office of Telecommunications Policy (OTP) in the Office of the President. He concurrently created the Office of Telecommunications (OT) in the Department of Commerce. The OTP's purpose first was to advise the president. The OT's purpose was to *conduct research* in order to make intelligent recommendations for telecommunications policy.

Both the OT and OTP worked closely, in theory but not always in practice, with other agencies of government. For example, they consulted with the FCC about frequency assignments and policy affecting domestic broadcasting stations. They worked with the State Department on relations with other countries concerning such issues as satellite communication and mutually cooperative efforts to establish communication systems abroad. They also worked with the Office of Management and Budget to gain insights into and policy recommendations for the fiscal aspects of a national telecommunication policy. In addition, they worked with the Defense Department on the role of telecommunications in wartime and in peacetime defense policy.

Unfortunately both the OTP and the OT came in less than ideal political times. First, Vice President Spiro Agnew lashed out at the media in a speech made in Des Moines, Iowa, in 1969, criticizing the supposed concentrated power and news bias in the three commercial television networks. The speech received wide publicity and alerted the networks that the White House was jumping into the communications policy arena. Then the OTP's first director, Clay Whitehead, delivered a famous speech to a group of journalists in Indianapolis, implying that radio and television stations could improve their chances for a five-year license renewal if management took an active interest in how their news departments functioned. Implied pressure from the executive branch over the license renewals of Florida television stations combined with the criminal implications of the Watergate scandal sent the Nixon administration to a low ebb among much of the public and the media establishment. President Carter, realizing the political liability of having the OTP located in the Office of the President and sensing the need for better cooperation between the OTP and other agencies of government, instituted the executive order creating the the NTIA.

Specifically, the order initiated five actions:

1. Transferred all functions of the Office of Telecommunications Policy to the Department of Commerce.
2. Abolished the Office of Telecommunications Policy.
3. Abolished the Office of Telecommunications.

399

REGULATORY
CONTROL OF
MASS
COMMUNI-
CATION

4. Established an assistant secretary for communications and information in the Department of Commerce.

5. Formed the National Telecommunications and Information Administration with the assistant secretary for communications and information as the NTIA director.

Although the NTIA's charge is still one of advising the President and is still an executive branch agency, moving it out of the Office of the President has at least presented the appearance of detachment and has opened the potential for better cooperation with other agencies of government. How effective that cooperation will be remains to be seen.

Similar in many ways to the old Office of Telecommunications, the NTIA has four primary functions, or *program elements*, as NTIA calls them:

1. *Policy Analysis and Development*, which includes analyzing the issues surrounding common carrier industries such as telephone communication, options for deregulating cable and broadcasting, international telecommunications, and protection of privacy in data communications.

2. *Telecommunications Applications*, which includes such concerns as improving telecommunications in rural areas, stimulating minority ownership in broadcasting and cable TV stations, coordinating local and state telecommunications policy, and working on user-industry cooperation in developing satellite systems for public service activities.

3. *Federal Systems and Spectrum Management*, which includes assessing the federal use of the electromagnetic spectrum and evaluating the procurement plans of other federal agencies.

4. *Telecommunications Sciences*, the research arm of NTIA, which studies climatic effects on radio waves, studies various direct broadcast systems for public service use, and develops user-oriented standards for federal data communication systems.

The elements we have been discussing are just *some* of those perceived by NTIA at its inception. Only the future will determine what road the new agency will take, how much it will become involved in politics, and how effective it will be in formulating policy and dealing with federal agencies.

THE FEDERAL TRADE COMMISSION

We need only look at a collection of bygone advertisements to see why current advertising controls exist. A perusal of old medicine ads for example, would bring to view labels for everything from horse liniment to castor oil, all capable of curing everything that could possibly ail man, woman, or beast. Their claims to cure were outdone only by those to prevent, claims that, figuratively speaking, promised the fountain of youth overnight—or in three doses! When the medicine wagon rolled through the frontier West, there was not much concern over the outlandish claims that the barker made. However, when the twentieth century saw mass circulation magazines roll off the presses, when it heard radio commercials jingling their way across the countryside, and when television began to assure "miracle" results, advertising was due for some regulation.

History of the FTC

The Federal Trade Commission was formed in 1914 by enactment of the FTC Act. The act's purpose was succinctly stated in its phrase: "Unfair methods of competition in commerce are hereby declared unlawful." Closely related to the FTC Act was the Clayton Act, also passed in 1914, which guarded against corporate mergers that would lessen competition. Since that date the FTC Act has been amended many times. Some of the most familiar pieces of legislation emerging from the Commission are the 1966 Fair Packaging and Labeling Act and the 1969 Truth in Lending Act, which requires full disclosure of credit terms. The FTC has five commissioners who are appointed, as are those of the FCC, by the President with the advice and consent of the Senate for seven-year staggered terms. No more than three commissioners can be from the same political party, and the President designates one of those people as chairperson.

FTC Organization

The organization of the FTC revolves around its commissioners and various departments. The Office of Public Information acts as a liaison between the FTC and the public and is charged with three primary functions: (1) informing the public about the enforcement activities of the FTC; (2) keeping the commission advised on public information policy; and (3) coordinating the public information programs of the FTC regional offices.[4] Working under the direction of the FTC chairman, the executive director is the chief administrative officer of the FTC. The administrative law judges conduct trials in cases in which the FTC has issued a complaint. They serve as the initial fact-finders and have tenure much like federal judges. Advising the FTC in questions of law and policy is the general counsel who acts as the FTC's chief law officer. The general counsel represents the commission in federal courts. The secretary is responsible for keeping the minutes of FTC proceedings and also acts as the custodian of the FTC's records. The signature of the secretary appears on all FTC orders. This person also handles requests from the public for information via the Freedom of Information and Privacy Acts. Planning the activities of the FTC is the Office of Policy Planning and Evaluation. This office has three functions: (1) to evaluate the commission's programs every six months and suggest new ones for it to undertake; (2) to develop questions to elicit the information needed by the commission to assess where the public's interest lies in a given matter; and (3) to determine the effect of previous FTC decisions on the public.[5]

Three key bureaus handle most of the tasks that affect both consumers and practitioners of broadcast advertising. They are the Bureau of Competition, responsible for enforcing the antitrust laws; the Bureau of Economics, advising the commission on the economic impact of its decisions; and the Bureau of Consumer Protection, charged with investigating trade practices alleged to be unfair to consumers. The Bureau of Consumer Protection is one of the closest allies of the public, helping to guard it against deceptive advertising. Formed in 1971, the bureau brought together under one roof all of the various consumer-related activities that had been performed by the FTC.[6]

To better understand the FTC's enforcement process, (Figure 15–6), let's imagine that you have received a complaint from the FTC, alleging that you are airing false and deceptive commercials.[7] The first notice you would probably receive from the FTC would be a letter. You would then have the opportunity to reply to that letter and explain your position. The FTC at this point may decide that your arguments have merit and simply decide not to pursue. But if the FTC is not satisfied with your arguments, it may proceed to subpoena all pertinent records, such as the details of any product-testing you may have undertaken.

Examining the records takes us to Step 3 in the review process. If the records clearly show your claims not to be deceptive, the FTC may consider your case closed. If, on the other hand, it is not content with your test results and still feels the advertising to be deceptive, enter Step 4, the beginning of negotiation. Two developments will normally take place during this phase. First, you may offer a consent order, stating that you will agree to remedy the problem, perhaps by taking your commercials off the air. The FTC then has an opportunity either to accept or to reject your consent agreement. If the commission accepts your agreement, it will be placed on the public record for sixty days. During that time other parties can file pro or con comments on the agreement. If the evidence builds up against you, the FTC can actually withdraw from the consent agreement and begin formal proceedings.[8] Second, if the consent order is signed, that usually ends the matter at Step 5.

Let us assume that the evidence built up against you during the sixty-day period was substantial and that the FTC decides to proceed to Step 6 and issue a complaint. Moving to Step 7, an administrative law judge rules on that complaint. In Step 8 the law judge issues a decision, which is then reviewed by the FTC commissioners in Step 9. Once again, you have two options. In step 10 the FTC can decide either (1) to affirm or modify the decision of the law judge or (2) to dismiss the complaint. We'll assume that it was not your lucky day, and that the FTC decided to uphold the decision of the administrative law judge, which was to prohibit you from using the commercials in any future advertising. Once again, you have two choices awaiting you in Step 11. You can either accept the FTC decision and tell your ad agency to move on some new commercials, or you can tell your lawyers to appeal the FTC decision to the circuit court.

Regardless of which decision you make at Step 11, one thing is certain: the road to the court has been both long and rough. You undoubtedly spent large sums of money fighting the case through the commission, and you will now face additional expense in the appeals process. Keep in mind that although you may feel as though you have been overwhelmed by the power of a high federal agency, the FTC would contend that such safeguards are for the benefit of the public. For the commission, enforcement powers are a stern warning to advertisers to see that their advertising meets the standards of truth and accuracy.

*Celebrity
Endorsements*

The FTC has been especially careful in recent years to scrutinize the use of celebrities in advertising. For one, the FTC expects celebrities who use their name or picture with a product to use the product. Also, in some

THE FTC ADVERTISING REVIEW PROCESS

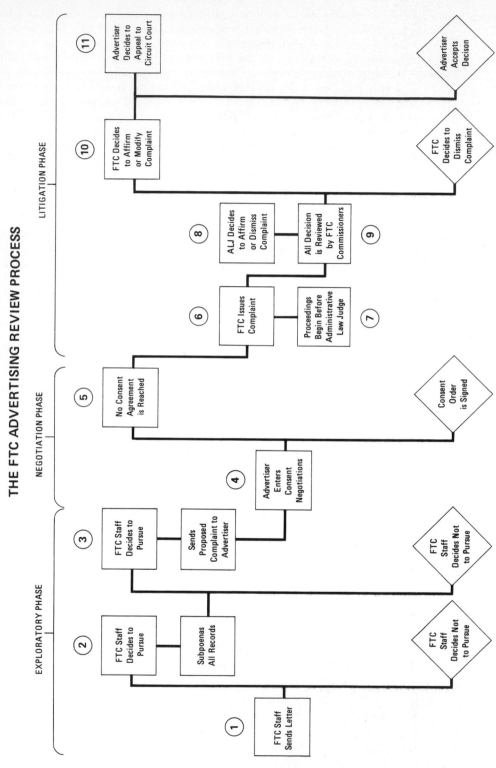

Figure 15-6 (Reprinted with permission from the July 11, 1977 issue of *Advertising Age*. Copyright 1977 by Crain Communications, Inc.)

403

REGULATORY
CONTROL OF
MASS
COMMUNI-
CATION

cases, the FTC has gone so far as to hold celebrities responsible for the quality of the products or services they advertise. Stringent controls such as these can make manufacturers, advertising agencies, and celebrities alike be careful of what products they represent and what they say about the products.

INTERNATIONAL TELECOMMUNICATION UNION

The International Telecommunication Union is a United Nations organization responsible for coordinating the use of telecommunication between nations. It does not have the enforcement powers of the Federal Communications Commission. Rather, it is a collective body of sovereign states and is only as strong as the willingness of the sovereign states to abide by its treaties. In other words, if a country violates an ITU agreement, no "field office" will revoke licenses or impose forfeitures. ITU's sovereign states view it not so much as an independent agency but as an arena in which to negotiate the uses of telecommunications.[9] And as that arena, it has been effective.

The principal functions of the ITU include:

1. Effective allocations of the radio frequency spectrum and registration of radio frequency assignments;
2. Coordinating efforts to eliminate harmful interference between radio stations of different countries and to improve the use made of the radio frequency spectrum;
3. Fostering collaboration with respect to the establishment of the lowest possible rates;
4. Fostering the creation, development, and improvement of telecommunication equipment and networks in new or developing countries by every means at its disposal, especially its participation in the appropriate programs of the United Nations;
5. Promoting the adoption of measures for ensuring the safety of life through the cooperation to telecommunication services;
6. Undertaking studies, making regulations, adopting resolutions, formulating recommendations and opinions, and collecting and publishing information concerning telecommunications matters benefiting all Members and Associate Members.[10]

SUMMARY

Our chapter began with a discussion of different theories of control over mass communication, pointing out that controls differ among print and broadcast media, and among countries. The electronic media that have evolved in the course of the twentieth century are a far cry from the colonial presses that the founding fathers had in mind when they wrote the Constitution. In the public interest, therefore, Congress sought more definitive controls to regulate the new media and accordingly formulated such legislation as the Wireless Ship Act of 1910, the Radio Act of 1912,

404

REGULATORY
CONTROL OF
MASS
COMMUNI-
CATION

the Radio Act of 1927, and the Communications Act of 1934. From this legislation the 1934 law created the Federal Communications Commission, the governmental body responsible for the control of electronic communication. The commission is under the direction of seven FCC commissioners, each serving a seven-year term.

Two of the most familiar regulations of standard radio and television programming are Section 315 of the Communications Act of 1934 and the Fairness Doctrine, a special 1949 ruling of the FCC. Section 315 covers political broadcasting, and the Fairness Doctrine sets up guidelines for unbiased treatment of controversial issues.

Cable is primarily regulated by local governments. Some states control cable but still relinquish much of the authority to local governments. The 1976 Copyright Act included provisions for cable television and the payment of copyright fees through a Copyright Tribunal.

The newest regulatory agency of government is the National Telecommunications and Information Administration. Formed under an executive reorganization order in March, 1978, this agency of the executive branch combines the duties of the former Office of Telecommunication Policy in the Office of the President with the former Office of Telecommunications in the Department of Commerce. The four program elements or functions of the NTIA are policy analysis and development, telecommunications applications, federal systems and spectrum management, and telecommunications sciences.

The Federal Trade Commission continues to police advertising. Its powers range from requesting information to major cease-and-desist orders which it may institute after an advertising review process takes place.

The International Telecommunication Union operates on the international level. Formed in 1865 to control telegraph communication, it has evolved to its current status as part of the United Nations. The ITU's areas of concern range from international spectrum allocations, to satellite development, to broadcasting in developing nations.

OPPORTUNITIES FOR FURTHER LEARNING

Applicability of the Fairness Doctrine in the Handling of Controversial Issues of Public Importance. Washington, D.C.: Federal Communications Commission, 1964 (FCC 64–611).

BITTNER, J. R., *Broadcast Law and Regulation.* Englewood Cliffs, N.J.: Prentice-Hall, 1982.

BOSMAJIAN, H. A., *Obscenity and Freedom of Expression.* New York: Burt Franklin & Co., 1976.

BOTEIN, M., *Legal Restrictions on Ownership of the Mass Media.* New York: Seminars, Inc., 1977.

COMPAINE, B. M., ed., *Who Owns the Media? Concentration of Ownership in the Mass Communications Industry.* White Plains, N.Y.: Knowledge Industry Publications, 1979.

GINSBURG, D. H., *Regulation of Broadcasting: Law and Policy Towards Radio, Television and Cable Communications.* St. Paul, Minn.: West Publishing Co., 1979.

405

REGULATORY
CONTROL OF
MASS
COMMUNI-
CATION

Gordon, G. N., *Erotic Communications: Studies in Sex, Sin, and Censorship*. New York: Hastings House, 1980.

Hyman, A., and M. B. Johnson, eds., *Advertising and Free Speech*. Lexington, Mass.: Lexington Books/D. C. Heath, 1977.

John and Mary Markle Foundation and the Twentieth Century Fund, eds., *Global Communications in the Space Age: Toward a New ITU*. New York: Markle Foundation and Twentieth Century Fund, 1972.

Kahn, F. J., ed., *Documents of American Broadcasting*, 3rd ed. Englewood Cliffs, N.J., Prentice-Hall, 1978.

Krasnow E. G., and L. D. Longley, *The Politics of Broadcast Regulation*. New York: St. Martin's Press, 1978.

LeDuc, D. R., *Cable Television and the FCC*. Philadelphia: Temple University Press, 1973.

Levin, H. J., *Fact and Fancy in Television Regulation: An Economic Study of Policy Alternatives*. New York: Russell Sage Foundation, 1980.

Mosco, V., *The Regulation of Broadcasting in the United States: A Comparative Analysis*. Cambridge, Mass.: Harvard University Program on Information Technologies, 1975.

Noll, R. G., M. J. Peck, and J. J. McGowan, *Economic Aspects of Television Regulation*. Washington D.C.: The Brookings Institution, 1973.

Paletz, D. L., R. E. Pearson, and D. L. Willis, *Politics in Public Service Advertising on Television*. New York: Praeger, 1977.

Rivers, W. L., and M. J. Nyhan, eds., *Aspen Notebook on Government and the Media*. New York: Praeger, 1975.

Signitzer, B., *Regulation of Direct Broadcasting from Satellites: The UN Involvement*. New York: Praeger, 1976.

Simon, J. F., *Independent Journey: The Life of William O. Douglas*. New York: Harper & Row, Pub. 1980.

Wallestein, G. D., *International Telecommunication Agreements*. Dobbs Ferry, N.Y.: Oceana Publications, 1977.

Will, T. E., *Telecommunication Structure and Management in the Executive Branch of Government: 1900–1970*. Dedham, Mass.: Horizon House and Thomas E. Will, 1978.

CHAPTER

LEGAL ISSUES AND THE WORKING PRESS

PREVIEW

After completing this chapter, we should be able to:

List and discuss the four theories of the press.
Discuss the application of the Constitution to freedom of the press.
Explain the concept of reporters' shield laws.
Describe the major thrusts of freedom of information laws.
Trace the history of cameras in the courtroom from the Lindbergh trial to today.
Identify the use of television in legislative proceedings.
Explain gag rules from both the judicial and journalism points of view.
Understand rights of the student press.
Understand rights of the basic concepts of libel law.
State the four areas in which invasion of privacy can occur.
Describe the implications of search and seizure for the press.
Discuss the functions of the National News Council.

As we learned in Chapter 1, mass communication does not occur in a vacuum. Many different controls affect the final message the public receives—government regulations, codes of ethics, and court orders, among others. This chapter examines some of the controls that both safeguard and in some ways hamper the working press.

First, however, we shall attempt to place these various controls in a broader perspective by studying four theories of how the press functions in society.

THEORIES OF THE PRESS

In their classic book, *Four Theories of the Press*, Fred S. Siebert, Theodore Peterson, and Wilbur Schramm outline four theories which have characterized the operation of the press in society. The oldest of these is the *authoritarian* theory.

Authoritarian Theory

The authoritarian theory evolved in the sixteenth and seventeenth centuries, spreading throughout Europe with the invention of the printing press. It was associated with such reigning families as the Tudors in England, the Bourbons in France, and the Hapsburgs in Spain. In modern society it has at various times found its way into the governments of Japan, Imperial Russia, Germany, and Spain, as well as some Asian and South American countries.

The authoritarian theory views humans as subservient to the state and as instruments of the state's natural, if not divine, right to maintain order and further the state's existence. The press in such a society is viewed as an instrument for disseminating the state's position to the populace, informing the populace what is right and wrong based on the state's interpretations of issues, and providing official policy statements of the ruling elite. The state, after determining its objectives, uses the press as a means of obtaining those objectives. The press becomes a means to an end rather than an instrument of criticism of either means or ends. In writing about the authoritarian theory, Siebert points out that in its early stages, the state used the press negatively by making sure that the press did not interfere with the attainment of national ends. Later the press, and for that matter the mass media in general, was used positively as an instrument for helping the state achieve its ends.

Under the authoritarian theory who owned the press was of equal importance as how the press was used. In early England the private sector was permitted to own the press, but that sector contained only wealthy friends of the Crown who did not abuse their ownership privilege by criticizing it. Later, government use of the media spawned various official journals that echoed the government line. Eventually these government media were joined by other private media. Herein was the difficulty of the authoritarian theory—how to control the private press.

The control took various forms. We already discussed the permits to publish that were granted by the government to the privileged few. This "patent" system existed for about 200 years in England. Then in the seventeenth century, the system began to collapse because of the success of the competing private press. The government next decided to limit the number of journeymen trained as apprentices for the monopolists, but this method soon disintegrated. Because ownership of the press was

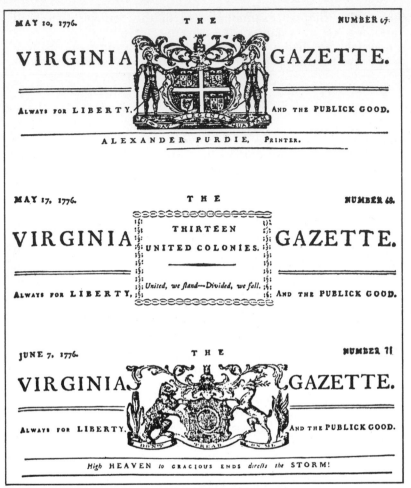

Figure 16-1 Three different mastheads of the *Virginia Gazette*, showing the growing spirit of independence and the change from the authoritarian to the libertarian press. (*The Printer in 18th-Century Williamsburg.* Williamsburg, Va: Colonial Williamsburg, 1955)

limited, the apprentices found that they could not get jobs when they reached the journeyman stage and instead began to operate their own presses illegally. A third method of control was outright censorship, requiring state approval of the content of selected works. Yet censoring proved so unpopular that it also did not succeed. A fourth method, again rather unsuccessful, was trying a person under the laws of treason or sedition for printing material unfavorable to the state.

In the United States the transition from authoritarian to *libertarian* press occurred more abruptly than in some other countries. The signing of the Declaration of Independence set forth new principles for freedom of expression. Indicative of this transition was the change in the *Virginia Gazette* published in Williamsburg, Virginia, in 1776 (Figure 16–1). The masthead of May 10, 1776, reflects British dominance with its coat of arms. A week later the masthead took on the revolutionary spirit, replacing the coat of arms with the words "Thirteen United Colonies" and the slogan, "United, we stand—divided, we fall," By June 7, 1776, independence was declared with a new coat of arms and the slogan "Don't Tread on Me."

Today the authoritarian system of the press is still in operation in many parts of the world. In Communist countries, in nations under dictatorial control, and in some third-world countries, a free press is little more than a theory without practice.

Libertarian Theory

The libertarian theory developed slowly in the sixteenth century, being refined in the eighteenth century as libertarian principles found their way into nations' constitutional framework. In theory a libertarian press is the exact opposite of an authoritarian press. Libertarianism places the individual above the state, not below it, and humans are viewed as rational beings who, although imperfect as individuals, will collectively arrive at the best decision for the general welfare of society.

Fred Siebert, in discussing the development of libertarianism, credits its transition from authoritarianism to the efforts of four men: John Milton (Figure 16–2) in the seventeenth century, John Erskine and Thomas Jefferson (Figure 16–3) in the eighteenth century, and John Stuart Mill

MILTON.

Figure 16-2 John Milton, one of the men upon whose philosophy the libertarian press was based.

Figure 16-3 Thomas Jefferson was one of the leading supporters of a libertarian press in Colonial America.

in the nineteenth century. Milton argued that people had the capacity to distinguish between right and wrong and good and bad. As a result, to make decisions, people should have "unlimited access to the ideas and thoughts of other men." Erskine argued that people seeking to enlighten others, and not intending to mislead, should be able to address the universal reason of a whole nation on what is believed to be true. John Stuart Mill felt that people had the right to think and act as they pleased if they did not infringe on the rights of others. Jefferson, borrowing from Milton's ideas, felt that the collective aggregate of a people, if intelligent and informed, could arrive at sound decisions. The press was the instrument to inform the people and therefore had to be free of control. In 1774 when Jefferson published his *Summary View of the Rights of British America* (Figure 16–4), it set the stage for the libertarian press.

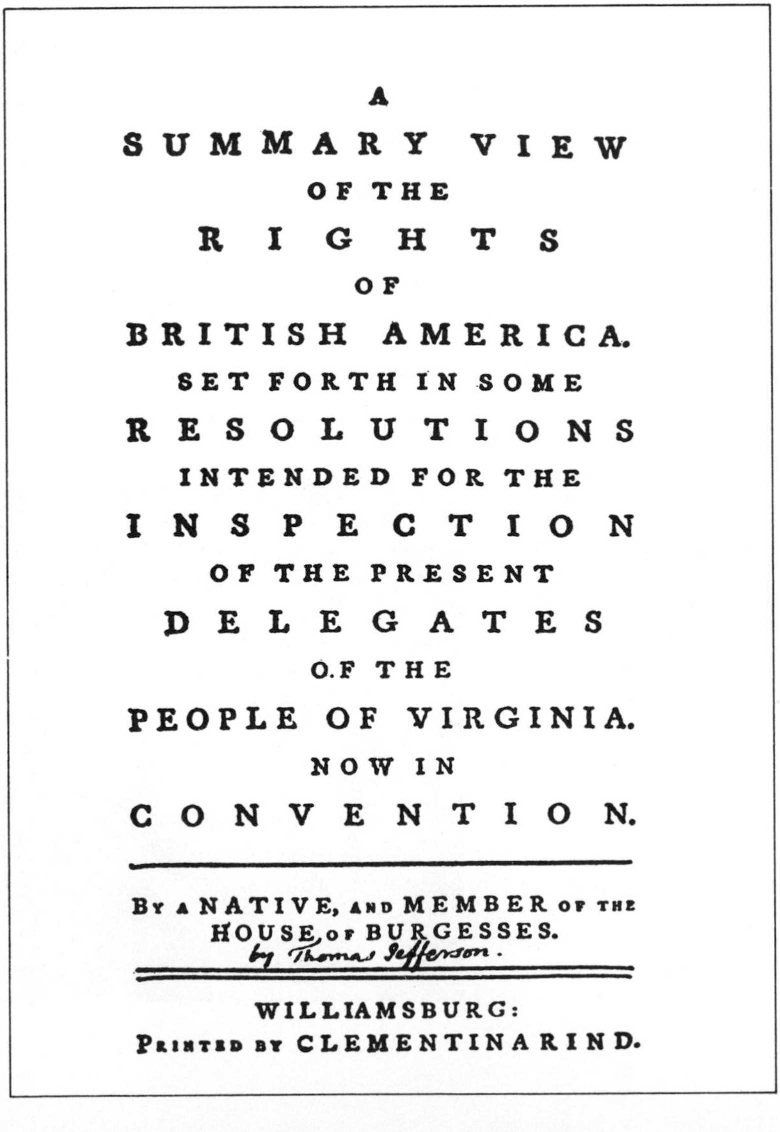

A

SUMMARY VIEW

OF THE

RIGHTS

OF

BRITISH AMERICA.

SET FORTH IN SOME

RESOLUTIONS

INTENDED FOR THE

INSPECTION

OF THE PRESENT

DELEGATES

O.F THE

PEOPLE OF VIRGINIA.

NOW IN

CONVENTION.

By a NATIVE, AND MEMBER OF THE HOUSE OF BURGESSES.
by Thomas Jefferson.

WILLIAMSBURG:
PRINTED BY CLEMENTINA RIND.

Figure 16-4 Published by Thomas Jefferson as a pamphlet in 1774, this piece gave Jefferson the stature to be selected to write the Declaration of Independence. The pamphlet is a classic example of the beginnings of the libertarian press in America. (*The Printer in 18th-Century Williamsburg*. Williamsburg, Va: Colonial Williamsburg, 1955)

Gradually the rights of the press and libertarianism began to gain ground. The road started in the courts where charges of *seditious libel*, or publishing language that incites rebellion against the state, were continually overthrown, since the jury had the right to determine if a person was guilty of printing the allegedly libelous piece. Since the jury was interested more in independence from the Crown than in supporting the decisions of Crown-appointed judges, even when a judge ruled material libelous, more often than not the jury simply claimed that the accused did not print the piece and therefore was not responsible for its dissemination. Eventually libertarianism, with its freedom of the press, became part of the constitutional doctrine both in the United States and later in England.

Social Responsibility Theory

By the twentieth century the printed press had been through the era of yellow journalism and was beginning to see the first glimpses of radio and motion pictures. Political ideas could persuade from such platforms as the airwaves and the giant screen.

In this atmosphere of the industrial revolution and a multimedia society developed a theory of a *free but responsible* press. It held that a press has the right to criticize government and institutions but also has certain basic responsibilities to maintain the stability of society. Nurturing this theory is the rise of professional associations associated with journalism such as the American Society of Newspaper Editors and the Society of Professional Journalists, Sigma Delta Chi. Both started near the turn of the twentieth century, and both have codes of ethics encouraging responsible actions by their members. Furthermore, the Communications Act of 1934, by which broadcasting is governed, is built upon the phrase "in the public interest, convenience, and necessity."

We see open criticism of the press in many journalism reviews and books. Theodore Peterson, writing about the *social responsibility* theory, points out that this criticism has its roots in Will Irwin's series on the press which appeared in *Colliers* magazine as early as 1911; in Upton Sinclair's *The Brass Check*, appearing in 1919; and in George Seldes' *Freedom of the Press*, written in 1935. All based their criticisms on dangers inherent in the increased reliance on advertising by the press. Even though the press is expected to be commercially independent of government control, profits achieved at the expense of public service are taboo. This concept permeates everything from the monopolistic practices blamed on the film industry in the 1930s to the cross-ownership controversy of newspaper and broadcasting properties in the 1970s. Within the framework of open and free press criticism, codes of ethics or government regulation, and guidelines for responsible action by members of the press lies the social responsibility theory.

Soviet-Communist Theory

In *Four Theories of the Press*, Wilbur Schramm writes about the *Soviet-Communist theory* of the press, aptly beginning his discussion by noting that when a reporter from the United States and one from the Soviet Union get together, "The talk is apt to be both amusing and frustrating. . . ." Their different frames of reference are simply incompatible. The American loathes the Soviet reporter's life with a government-controlled press.

Figure 16-5 Inside PRAVDA. (Courtesy, MTV Finland, from the documentary on PRAVDA)

The Soviet reporter loathes the American's association with a "corrupt," "venal," "irresponsible" press "controlled by special interests."

To understand the Soviet-Communist theory of the press, one must examine not only the basic Soviet political implications as derived from Marxist doctrine but also the Soviet interpretation of the word "freedom." You may be surprised to learn that the Soviet Constitution guarantees both free speech and a free press. In addition, the principal tenet of Soviet political life is one of unity. The rise of the working class, the revolution, was a movement of unity within Soviet society. This joining together of the people into a classless society has become the philosophy of the Soviet state. Thus freedom from the Soviet point of view is freedom from the oppression of a class—upper, middle, lower—society.

Schramm explains that mass communication in the Soviet-Communist theory is an instrument of the state. The two large Soviet newspapers, *Pravda* (Figure 16–5) and *Izvestiya*, are the best examples. International propaganda publications such as *Soviet Life* magazine reflect the Soviet-Communist theory. In *Four Theories of the Press*, Schramm writes, "The point is, that Soviet mass communication do not have integrity of their own. Their integrity, such as it is, is that of the state. They are 'kept' instruments, and they follow humbly and nimbly the gyrations of the Party line and the state directives." Mass communication is integrated with other instruments of the state, such as schools, the police, and even assemblies as instruments protecting the Communist philosophy. Yet while the press is considered an instrument of unity, it is also considered an instrument of revelation to provide enlightenment and to prepare the masses for unity and eventually revolution. The press is an "agitator, propagandist, and organizer."

Broadcasting (Figure 16–6) under the Soviet-Communist theory likewise is designed not so much to serve the public but to inform it. Programming is again the instrument of the state, and the medium is important to it because of the large numbers of people that broadcasting can reach.

Figure 16-6 Inside Soviet television. (Radio Moscow)

Our discussion of the four theories of the press should be viewed not so much as categories in which various mass media can be placed but rather as different variations of media systems. These systems can apply to different media across different countries or even different media within one country. They represent the roots of not only the press in society but of mass communication in general. Keep this in mind as we now turn our attention to more specific legal issues and to the working press.

FREEDOM OF THE PRESS: THE CONSTITUTION

The association of the working press with the Constitution is closest to the First Amendment: "Congress shall make no law abridging the freedom of speech, or of the press." To give some assurance that a state could not completely negate the U.S. Constitution, the Fourteenth Amendment was passed, stating, "No State shall make or enforce any law which shall abridge the privileges or immunities of citizens of the United States nor shall any state deprive any person of life, liberty, or property, without due process of law." The Fourteenth Amendment was not affirmed by the courts until 1925, in the case of *Gitlow* v. *New York*. Gitlow was the business manager of a newspaper that had published a "Manifesto" supporting Communist revolution in the United States. In this case the Supreme Court declared, "For present purposes we may and do assume that freedom of speech and of the press—which are protected by the First Amendment from abridgement by Congress—are among the fundamental personal rights and liberties protected by the due process clause of the Fourteenth Amendment from impairment by the states."[1]

Yet the Constitution has not stopped the states from passing countless laws affecting the confidentiality of sources for both print and broadcast journalists, from passing laws affecting the right of access to public meetings or cameras in the courtroom, nor from passing laws governing cable television. Continually in broadcasting, the twentieth-century concept of the electromagnetic spectrum as a limited resource has been used as a basis for more legislation and interpretation, although not without criticism. Former CBS commentator Eric Sevareid, addressing a meeting of the National Association of Broadcasters, remarked, "I could never understand why so basic a right as the First Amendment could be diluted or abridged simply because of technological change in the dissemination and reception of information and ideas."[2]

The broadcast press has had to fight continually for its rights as an equal partner with the print media under the First Amendment. This fight has entailed visible lobbying efforts by the National Association of Broadcasters (NAB). Spokespersons for the broadcasting industry have been equally vocal. CBS's William S. Paley remarked that the First Amendment freedom "presupposes, in us as broadcasters, a greater sense of responsibility. If we fail to see the dimensions of that responsibility and to measure up to them, we are in for constant threats of restrictions and policing."[3]

With the rhetoric has come some judicial support for the First Amendment's application to broadcasting. In the case of *CBS* v. *the Democratic National Committee*, Justice William O. Douglas wrote:

> My conclusion is that the TV and radio stand in the same protected position under the First Amendment as do newspapers and magazines. The philosophy of the First Amendment requires that result, for the fear that Madison and Jefferson had of government intrusion is perhaps even more relevant to TV and radio than it is to newspapers and other like publications.[4]

A panel of five justices of the New York Supreme Court affirmed the right of WABC-TV to show a documentary about conditions in a children's home.[5] Presiding Justic Harold A. Stevens wrote:

> While the protection of freedom of the press is not absolute, the burden of demonstrating a condition which warrants a prior restraint is indeed a heavy one. Television broadcasting falls under the umbrella of protection afforded the press, for it too, in matters such as the subject under review, is engaged in the dissemination of information of public concern.[6]

Ironically, while affirming the right to show the documentary, the court stopped the broadcast for five days to give the children's home time to appeal.

The spirit of the First Amendment is inherent in other laws, one example being the Communications Act of 1934 and its amendments. Section 326 of the Communications Act of 1934 states, "Nothing in this Act shall be understood or construed to give the Commission the power of censorship over the radio communications . . . shall interfere with the right of free speech by means of radio communication."

Although the U.S. Constitution remains the umbrella document under which legal theory functions in America, it is only a small part of the total regulatory scheme affecting the working press.

REPORTERS' SHIELD LAWS

Reporters' shield laws are designed to protect the anonymity of a reporter's sources of information. The laws received great attention in the early 1970s when the courts with interesting frequency began jailing journalists for not divulging their sources of information. One of the most publicized cases involved *Los Angeles Times* reporter William Farr, who refused to divulge the source of information he had received from an attorney during a murder trial. Farr served some time in jail. As a result of several other similar cases, a number of states began realizing that the Constitution did not give journalists sufficient protection and that there was a real need either to legislate new reporters' shield laws or to strengthen old ones. By 1980 more than twenty states had shield laws. Two states whose legislatures instituted typical changes were Indiana and Oregon. Indiana had had a shield law on the books since 1941, but it had become outdated. This, accompanied by the preceding reasons, prompted the legislature to change the law in 1971 and 1973. Following is the new law. The portion crossed out belongs to the 1941 law.

Section 1. IC 1971, 34-3-5-1 is amended to read as follows: Sec. 1. Any person connected with, or any person who has been so connected with or employed by, a weekly, semiweekly, triweekly, or daily newspaper that conforms to postal regulations, which shall have been published for five (5) consecutive years in the same city or town and which has a paid circulation of two per cent (2%) of the population of the county in which it is published, newspaper or other periodical issued at regular intervals and having a general circulation or a recognized press association; a wire service as a bona fide owner, editorial or reportorial employee, who receives or has received his or her principal income from legitimate gathering, writing, editing and interpretation of news, and any person connected with a commercially licensed radio or television station as owner, official, or as an editorial or reportorial employee who received or has received his or her principal income from legitimate gathering, writing, editing, interpreting, announcing or broadcasting of news, shall not be compelled to disclose in any legal proceedings or elsewhere the source of any information procured or obtained in the course of his employment or representation of such newspaper, periodical, press association, radio station, or television station, or wire service, whether published or not published in the newspaper or periodical, or by the press association or wire service or broadcast or not broadcast by the radio station or television station by which he is employed.

Although Indiana's 1941 shield law may seem rather shortsighted by today's standards, it was felt conclusive enough for that era. Today, however, there are many other considerations. Technology and judicial precedent have created a need for more inclusive shield laws.

An example of this inclusiveness is the Oregon shield law. In the Oregon law the scope of the media covered under the statute is much broader than in the Indiana law. Although a court might interpret the Indiana law as being just as broad, the Oregon law specifically states, "Medium of communication has its ordinary meaning and includes, but is not limited to, any newspaper, magazine or other periodical, book, pamphlet, news service, wire service, news or feature syndicate, broadcast station or network, or cable television system. . . ."

Laws as encompassing as Oregon's are rare. Not all states are explicit in their definition of media, and reporters working for magazines or writing books are not always protected as fully as newspaper journalists are. Although judicial precedent has firmly established radio and television as being "press" in the traditional sense, there still are many legal frontiers to be conquered before shield laws can be said to have universal application.

Reporters are also faced with the fact that orderly judicial procedures must be followed when a court order demands that a reporter reveal confidential sources of information. Courts have also ruled that reporters are not exempt from appearing and testifying before grand juries. Even the strongest shield laws may not prevent a judge from issuing a contempt order, and although a reporter may win a case on appeal, he or she may in the meantime spend considerable time in jail and be faced with huge legal fees.

FREEDOM OF INFORMATION LAWS

Closely related to reporters' shield laws are *freedom of information laws*. Both are designed to help guarantee the ability of the news media to disseminate truthful, accurate, and complete information. Freedom of information laws attempt to assure the press access to (1) meetings of governmental bodies and (2) documents that are classified or are part of public officials' files and reflect possible corrupt activities in government. These laws exist not only on a national level, as was so vividly brought to the public's attention during the Vietnam War and the Watergate era, but also on the state level.

For the news media the most common contact with freedom of information laws is in the area of open meetings. Investigative journalism is, of course, concerned with open records legislation, but the average reporter preparing information for daily public consumption is also concerned with whether he or she will be admitted to the local meeting of the city council or whether the executive meeting of the zoning board is going to shut the door to the news media. A report written by Professor John Adams of the University of North Carolina at Chapel Hill and funded by the American Newspaper Publishers Association listed eleven different classifications of open meetings laws.[7]

1. Include a statement of public policy in support of openness,
2. Provide for an open legislature,
3. Provide for open legislative committees,
4. Provide for open meetings of state agencies or bodies,
5. Provide for open meetings of agencies and bodies of the political subdivisions of the state,
6. Provide for open County Boards,
7. Provide for open City Councils (or their equivalent),
8. Forbid closed executive sessions,
9. Provide legal recourse to halt secrecy,
10. Declare actions taken in meetings which violate the law to be null and void,
11. Provide for penalties for those who violate the law.

Of all the classifications, the four most common types of open meetings legislation currently in operation include open state agencies, open county-local agencies, open county boards, and open city councils. For the average reporter these are the most common types of governmental bodies to which he or she would need access.

Two other key areas in which the press would like to see open information laws enforced are executive sessions and actions taken in meetings that violate the law. When important decisions must be made before they can be voted on in public, many governmental bodies may call executive sessions. The problem with these closed sessions is that they can easily become a habit. When such issues as budgets, firing employees, planning raises, and similar items arise, public reaction and concern can be significant. Voting and deciding behind closed doors and then merely "rubber stamping" the decisions at the public meetings of these agencies deprives the public of the information they need as constituents of elected officials.

The real teeth in open meetings laws are found in Points 10 and 11. Any law is only as good as its ability to be enforced. Laws are strong when they void any action taken in closed session and even stronger when they provide penalties for those who violate the law. When the news media have this type of legislation protecting their ability to report, the free flow of information to the public is much more open.

CAMERAS IN THE COURTROOM

In 1935 when Bruno Richard Hauptmann was tried for the kidnapping of the son of famed aviator Charles Lindbergh, the courtroom resembled a county fair more than a judicial proceeding. Reporters were falling over reporters, vendors were selling souvenirs, and when the judge barred cameras from the courtroom, one reporter still managed to sneak a camera into court and snap a picture (Figure 16-7) that bannered in papers across the country.

The American Bar Association approved its famous Canon 35 two years after the Lindberg trial. Amended in 1963 to include television, Canon 35 which later became Canon 3A(7), forbade either taking photographs of or broadcasting court proceedings. Individual states were quick to affirm Canon 35's principles and to place it in statutes affecting court proceedings. The Federal Rules of Criminal Procedures, specifically Rule 53, carries the prohibition of cameras to federal courts. A special committee of the Judicial Conference of the United States reaffirmed Canon 35 in 1968, calling for prohibition of "radio or television broadcasting from the courtroom or its environs, during the progress of or connection with judicial proceedings. . . ." Clearly from the standpoint of the courts and many lawyers, there is popular support for the Sixth Amendment's position guaranteeing a fair trial.

Figure 16-7 Richard "Dick" Sarno's photo of the sentencing of Bruno Hauptman in the Lindberg kidnapping trial. (*The New York Sun*)

Such claims for constitutional priority are not founded in merely supposition or conjecture. The annals of case law are filled with overturned verdicts, appeals, and charges of biased juries, because the news media have been less than restrained in their coverage. Cases that stand out include *Rideau* v. *Louisiana*.[8] In this case the suspect was interviewed by a country sheriff, and the interview was filmed and played on local television. The suspect's confessions made during the interview and the subsequent televising of those confessions prompted the defense attorney to request a change of venue. A denial and subsequent guilty verdict were all that was needed for the United States Supreme Court to reverse the conviction and state that the jury should have been drawn from a community whose residents had not seen the televised interview.

The case of Texas businessman Billie Sol Estes added fuel to this constitutional fire. Estes was tried and convicted of swindling. An appeals court affirmed the conviction, but when the case reached the United States Supreme Court in 1965 in *Estes* v. *State of Texas*, the conviction was reversed.[9] Massive national publicity surrounded the trial, and when it first went to court, the trial judge permitted television coverage of portions of the trial. In fact, the initial hearings were carried live. The scene was described by Justice Clark, who delivered the opinion in the case:

> Indeed, at least 12 cameramen were engaged in the courtroom throughout the hearing taking motion and still pictures and televising the proceedings. Cables and wires were snaked across the courtroom floor, three microphones were on the judge's bench, and others were beamed at the jury box and the counsel table. It is conceded that the activities of the television crews and news photographers led to considerable disruption of the hearings.

Justice Clark summarized four areas in which television could potentially interfere with a trial: (1) Television can have an impact on the jury. The mere announcement of a televised trial can alert the community to "all the morbid details surrounding" the trial. "Every juror carries with him into the jury box those solemn facts and thus increases the chance of prejudice that is present in every criminal case." (2) Television can impair the quality of testimony. "The impact upon a witness of the knowledge that he is being viewed by a vast audience is simply incalculable. Some may be demoralized and frightened, some cocky and given to overstatement; memories may falter. . . ." (3) Television places additional responsibilities on the trial judge. Along with other supervisory duties, the judge must also supervise television. The job of the judge "is to make certain that the accused receives a fair trial. This most difficult task requires his undivided attention." (4) On the defendant, television "is a form of mental if not physical harassment, resembling a police line-up or the third degree. The inevitable close ups of his gestures and expressions during the ordeal of his trial might well transgress his personal sensibilities, his dignity, and his ability to concentrate. . . ."

The Supreme Court's decision, however, did not stop the courtroom access of omnipresent television cameras. Breakthroughs did occur in 1972 when the American Bar Association's House of Delegates approved a Code of Professional Responsibility, permitting the use of television in the courtroom for such activities as prerecording testimony and playing

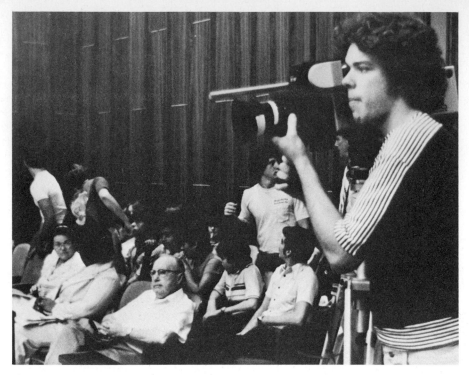

Figure 16-8 A televised trial under experimental guidelines in the state of Florida. States have been given the option to set their own guidelines for televised trials. (George Chase and WPBT-TV)

Figure 16-9 The work of the courtroom artist still remains a paramount part of television journalism. This scene is the work of Walt Stewart of KRON-TV in San Francisco. (Courtesy, Walt Stewart)

back the videotape to present evidence. Another breakthrough came in 1974 when the Washington State Supreme Court instructed a county superior to select a trial and to experiment, for "educational" purposes, with televising it. The experiment was generally successful.[10] In Las Vegas, Nevada, the fall of 1976 saw KLAS-TV televise in color a criminal court trial. Sixty hours of courtroom activity, including interviews with the defendant, jury, and attorneys, were videotaped and edited for a three-part, prime-time special. And one of the most publicized trials took place in Florida in 1977 when a teenager was accused of murder. The trial was televised (Figure 16–8), and segments appeared regularly on network television, calling national attention to the camera-courtroom issue. A few weeks later, when the verdict was read in an Indiana kidnapping case, cameras were again present, and the courtroom once again made national television.

In 1981 the Supreme Court ruled in the case of *Chandler v. Florida* that the Florida guidelines were not unconstitutional. It paved the way for states to develop their own guidelines and controls over cameras in court without being overly concerned about those controls being ruled unconstitutional.

The future of camera coverage of court proceedings will depend on the willingness of the courts to recognize the public's right of access to trials, their permission in court for the apparatus necessary to capture the actual sounds and sights of the court in session, and the willingness of the press to use restraint and the highest professional attitude and activity while covering a trial. Certainly not all of the courts across the country are going to open their doors to cameras overnight. The process will be slow and gradual, and many trials will remain closed at the request of the parties involved. Meanwhile, the familiar and talented courtroom artists will continue their craft of capturing on sketch pad (Figure 16–9) the activity barred from the eyes of the news cameras.

TELEVISION AND LEGISLATIVE PROCEEDINGS

While many broadcasters have been fighting to gain access to the courtrooms, others have been lobbying for access into legislative chambers, especially on the state level. One reason for this effort is to offset the lopsided coverage that the executive branch of government always receives. Another reason is the public's right to know. Critics argue that the legislature is where the real coverage should take place, since this is where an informed public needs to exert its opinions through its elected representatives. Although the U.S. House of Representatives voted in 1977 to permit television cameras in its chambers for certain proceedings, many state bodies have lagged behind.

Two factors have continually snarled the full-scale coverage: (1) the necessity to garner enough votes to pass a full-coverage measure and (2) the inability to muster a plan for the coverage. Sticky points include whether cameras should show all of the chamber. Can the gallery be seen? Do the cameras need to be in fixed positions? Who will determine what will and will not be televised? Will the charismatic representatives steal the show from their less "polished" counterparts? Will politicans play to the cameras instead of doing their job?

Nevertheless, the broadcast press is making progress. After court pressure was brought by a Chicago station, the Illinois Commerce Commission opened up its sessions to television coverage in 1977. Temporary guidelines were issued pending the adoption of permanent ones. Those guidelines restricted cameras and recording equipment to a designated area in the back of the hearing room. Television lights could not be set up outside the designated area; camera persons could have access to other areas of the room before the conference was called to order; and microphones could not be placed on the staff tables at the front of the room nor on the commissioner's bench. Photo journalists had similar restrictions placed upon them and were prohibited from using flash bulbs during the conference.

Such specially called conferences are just a brick on the road to unrestricted coverage of the day-to-day business of the legislative process. But again, as with the courts, as television cameras become smaller and less conspicious, and as broadcast journalists act more responsibly, there are bound to be greater opportunities for legislative coverage.

GAG RULES

In their attempts to assure a fair trial and to secure the "dignity" of the court, some judges have placed restraints on the press by keeping them from reporting those aspects of the trial that the judges feel might interfere with the judicial process. Such actions are commonly called "gag rules" and create a direct conflict between the news media and the judiciary in the issue of free press versus fair trial. Gag rules have ranged from attempts to keep all news media from reporting any and all aspects of a trial, to orders stifling just one particular reporter. In many cases reporters have been held in contempt of court for publishing or broadcasting information the judge has deemed unacceptable for public consumption via the news media.

Scope of Gag Rules

In recent years gag rules have become increasingly common. Although there seems to be little constitutional foundation to such rules and they are almost always voided when appealed, this has not hampered their frequent issuance. For instance, in California, Superior Court Judge J. A. Leetham barred journalists from reporting the identity of witnesses in a murder case. The same gags were placed on defendants, documents, and exhibits. The gag rule was eventually struck down by an appeals court.[11] An Ontario, California judge issued a gag rule against publication of the names of certain witnesses, also in a murder trial. A well-publicized gag rule resulted when a Baton Rouge, Louisiana judge, Gordon E. West, prohibited reporting news of a pretrial hearing involving a civil rights worker. Two reporters, Gibbs Adams of the *Morning Advocate* and Larry Dickinson of the *State Times*, defied the gag rule and were consequently fined and held in contempt of court. The rule was overturned by an appeals court, but the contempt citation was upheld, leaving the clear directive that, although a gag order may later be struck down in an appeal, it should be obeyed until that appeal has been completed.[12] In Texarkana, Arkansas, an editor was found in contempt of court for reporting the verdict in a rape case. That decision was also overturned by a higher court.[13]

*The Judicial
Dilemma*

Although these judicial decisions may seem arbitrary to you, place yourself behind the bench for a few moments and consider what might go through your own mind. You are considering a controversial murder case which has received considerable publicity. You, as a judge, have the responsibility to guide the attorneys in the search for truth. It is your responsibility to secure the defendant a fair trial and to see that everyone is equally represented in the case. You know from previous decisions that if you do not adhere to the rules of the court, the final decision in the case will be appealed, and your own actions will be held accountable in the appeal. If there is considerable pretrial publicity and an appeals court rules that the defendant is entitled to a new trial, then this reflects on the operation of your own courtroom, especially if during the trial the defendant's attorney requested a change of venue for the trial based on that very pretrial publicity. Perhaps you are an elected judge and are caught between giving the press complete freedom to do and say what they please and thus risk the dignity of your court, or attempt to gag them and thus incur their ire which could have an effect on your chances in the next election. Even if the press is responsible in your community, you may still wrestle with the question of what should be done and how it will affect your political career. On the other hand, you may be asking yourself, "If I issue a gag rule and in my opinion protect the dignity of the court, then when the gag rule is subsequently struck down, what does that action create?" In trying to protect the dignity of the court and the due process of law under one constitutional amendment, you successfully nullify the effect of another one. Thus, from behind the bench, it is a real dilemma, one which is not easily solved.

Now place yourself in the shoes of the reporter assigned to cover the case. From the morning that the case first appeared on the police log, you have worked to provide complete and impartial information about it. You have based your activities not only on the fact that you have a job to do but also that the public has a right to know. As a journalist, you have the responsibility to report the activities of the government and the courts and to point out any deficiencies which might exist. Now comes the day of the trial. The judge issues you an order to not publish any information about the case. You are faced with some rather unpleasant alternatives. You can defy the judge and publish the story. You can also land in jail and be fined in the process. On the other hand, you can abide by the judge's ruling and tell your peers back at the office why you sold out. Suppose you decide at least to take the issue to a higher court to try and have the gag rule reversed. Chances are you will be successful, but in the meantime, you will have missed the story. At the very least, you will have spent valuable time and money and may face the situation again when the judge decides to issue another gag rule. There is no easy solution to your dilemma any more than there is an easy solution to the judge's dilemma.

Occasionally the press has agreed to voluntary silence arrangements with the judge. For example, in Cartersville, Georgia, Judge Jefferson L. Davis simply calls a conference with the reporters whenever he wants information withheld from publication. He explains why, and the arrangement seems to work.[14] Yet Cartersville is not Los Angeles or New York, and what may work in a small Georgia community may not prove feasible in a major city. Moreover, many journalists would claim it should not work. That is not the job of a journalist.

In an article in *Time* magazine, the following incident was reported. When two persons accused of murder were brought to trial in Pennsylvania, the judge informed the press that the cases for the two defendants had been separated, and each was to receive a separate trial. The press agreed to withhold reporting the first trial so as not to prejudice the second trial. The news media, including radio and television stations as well as newspapers, went along with the judge and not only failed to cover the proceedings but omitted any public mention of the trial. When it was over, the press was divided on whether they had made the right decision.[15]

The problem of ensuring a free press but at the same time according a defendant a fair trial is a dilemma far from nearing a solution. Gag rules will probably continue to be issued, and journalists will probably continue to defy them, as will judges persist in citing members of the news media for contempt. This is one of those gray areas in regulatory posture that places law, journalism, and the Constitution right in the middle.

RIGHTS OF THE STUDENT PRESS

The courts' continued support of First Amendment principles as they apply to the student press depends on the responsible actions of student reporters. Although the legal issues are complex, generally the college press is afforded somewhat more freedom than the high school press. One reason for this greater freedom is because college students are usually of legal adult age, over 18 in most states, and can therefore assume some of the responsibility for their actions that the school district must assume for high school journalists.

Any school system typically finds itself in the awkward position of being an instrument of the state, supported by taxpayers' dollars. As a result, schools can exercise control over the student press when the content of the press directly and specifically affects the maintenance of the school system. In other words, calls for revolution in a school newspaper, especially in a high school newspaper, can be a sticky legal issue. For example, in one case the Supreme Court ruled, "The First Amendment can be abridged by state officials if their protection of legitimate state interests necessitates an invasion of free speech."[16] This does not, however, sanction blanket authority to censor anything disagreeable to a school administration. Specific actions affecting the control of a student press must be based on evidence. Moreover, money, once appropriated, cannot be withdrawn or threatened to be withdrawn as a means of controlling press content. Firing a student editor can be just as touchy, especially if it is done under the guise of an infraction of school rules.

As a result of the obscure legal issues, many student newspapers have tried to become independent of their parent institution. Yet how independent a student newspaper is from the school usually does not matter until the paper becomes involved in a libel suit. Attorneys can in "independent" status and can be quick to name regardless of how independent the paper claims purporting to show this association can center on spaper being widely publicized in school literature, ures to school catalogues; articles written in jour- aculty direction finding their way into print, the handling some of the newspaper bookkeeping; or university being used to house the newspaper; inistered through the school directly benefiting the

arnalists have the opportunity in a high school or experience both responsible reporting and the Taking advantage of both opportunities can be a und for a professional career or for better under- evaluation of the press. Most of the student publi- faculty advisors. Students who fail to take advantage who look upon them as potential censors instead of ned about a responsible press are failing to tap a ich can pay off in later years.

LIBEL AND SLANDER

Amendment gives reporters the ability to pursue truth, , and generally take a no-holds-barred attitude toward the exercise of a free press, there are certain legal safeguards against irresponsible journalism that may libel a person, institution, business, or other identifiable entity.

Definition

Libel is defined as *the publication of material that identifies and defames a person, resulting in that person's exposure to hatred, contempt, ridicule, and causes him or her to be shunned or avoided.* Closely related to libel is *slander,* which can apply to broadcasting, and is the *voicing of defamatory statements about someone to another person.* Libel and slander are in some ways interchangeable. For example, someone who is libeled on a radio newscast may also be slandered, inasmuch as the actual "publishing" of the news story was in the form of an oral presentation. A test to determine whether something is libelous has three parts: publication, defamation, and identification. If a person is written about in a newspaper or mentioned during a broadcast and that mention defames the person, then publication, defamation, and identification have occurred and the person may have been libeled.

Avoiding Libel

It is as important to understand libel as it is to avoid it. Most reporters have some knowledge of mass communication law, and although every case is different and every jury and judge can make a different interpretation of that law, there are guidelines for staying out of libel court. Of these, nothing is more important than to *avoid mediocre reporting practices*. Journalism is extremely serious business. A name misspelled, a false association with the scene of a crime, or an implied immoral act may wind up as a lawsuit in the millions of dollars. There is no substitute for accuracy, regardless of how big the story or how tight the deadline. Second, truth, although a defense against libel, may not hold up in court unless the *truth can be proved*. Simply saying that something is fact, yet not being able to prove it in court may not be enough. A reporter cannot *assume* something is true simply because someone says it is. Regardless of how close to the truth a source may seem to be, documents may be necessary to defend a libel suit. A third way to avoid libel is to *make sure the story is objective*. Words can often bring on a libel suit. If a reporter writes that someone is a swindler, that reporter had better be sure the person has been tried in court and convicted of swindling before using the noun in print. Even then it is safer to say that the person was "found guilty" in a court of law rather than using the word "swindler." Quotations can be particularly difficult. A reporter may accurately report a quotation. However, if the quotation is an untrue statement, regardless of how accurately it is reported, the reporter and his or her respective medium are open to charges of libel. Finally, if an error is made and a libelous statement is reported, a *full and complete retraction* should be made. Although only a few states make it a complete defense against libel, a retraction can nevertheless reduce the damages.

Libel Per Quod, Libel Per Se

Courts can award two types of damages in libel cases. One type results from what is termed libel *per quod* and the other from libel *per se*. Libel per quod refers to libel from association. For example, a newspaper gossip column reports that two public school teachers, Mr. Smith and Miss Jones, are going to make it legal and get married next week. The comment merely refers to their upcoming wedding but could infer that they have been living together, which a conservative school board might not consider the best publicity for their teachers. Smith and Jones might decide to sue for libel. If they did, it would be considered libel per quod. On the other hand, if the paper reported the Mr. Smith, who happens to be happily married, is getting a divorce to marry Miss Jones, when in fact it is not the case, Smith might decide to sue on grounds of libel per se, that the words themselves are libelous.

Defense Against Libel

When the press does find itself in libel court, it has three primary defenses. The first is *truth*. In some states, truth is an absolute defense against libel. In other words, regardless of how defamatory a statement or story is, if it can be proved true, then the plaintiff has little recourse but to live with the consequences without receiving any damages. The second defense is *reporters' privilege*. For example, comments made by politicians in a governmental forum, such as a legislature, are primarily immune from libel actions. Statements made by witnesses, judges, and lawyers in open court are also poor arguments in a libel case. In addition, comments made by heads of governmental agencies in the official discharge of their duties can also be freely reported on as long as the reporter does not show malice in reporting them.

A third defense is *fair comment*—comment about books, artistic works, and performers and others in the public light. However, recent Supreme Court decisions have greatly narrowed this privilege by narrowing the definition of a public figure. Simply putting someone in the news does not make him or her a public figure. When fair comment is employed, malice cannot be the motive, and the statements must be opinions, not statements about what the reporter believes to be *fact*. Other defenses also exist beyond the three primary ones stated. For example, having permission to report something can be a defense. It must be proved, however. Consent in writing is much better than someone's verbal consent. Permitting the person to reply is another defense, and if the statute of limitations has expired, the person libeled has little recourse.

In recent years, libel suits have increased in frequency, and the press is not always held in high esteem among juries. So despite a defense of free press, truth, a retraction, or reporters' privilege, the reporter and the medium can find themselves paying significant damages. In fact, the problem is becoming so serious that some insurance companies are considering discontinuing libel insurance. Those companies that still have the insurance have raised their premiums so high that they are almost prohibitive for many small newspapers and broadcast stations. Yet the risk of libel judgments running into the millions of dollars can lead only to bankruptcy. The result is the need, more than ever, for responsible journalists.

INVASION OF PRIVACY

In its search for truth, the press deals daily with the issue of invasion of privacy. How far can the press go to gather information without infringing on the rights of others, specifically the right of privacy? Both statutes and judicial precedent have established parameters within which reporters must work to gain information. Going outside these parameters can result in actions against the press for invasion of privacy and, depending on what is reported, libel or slander.

Generally, four areas must be avoided to avoid an invasion of privacy action:[17]

1. *Physical intrusion*—breaking into someone's office or home is clearly off limits, although if the police raid the office or home and you accompany them, you would at least be on safer grounds. Good taste still can be considered. If the police arrest the occupant and drag him nude into the street and you film that and show him nude on the evening news, you may find yourself in court for invasion of privacy. Similarly, bugging a telephone or using a telephoto lens can get a reporter into the same kind of trouble, especially if a private citizen is involved and no crime has been committed. Even if a crime has been committed, publishing the picture or the results of the wiretap can be extremely serious and good cause for legal action.

2. *Appropriation*—showing a person's picture or using a person's name for

commercial purpose without his or her permission can also be costly. Although this type of privacy invasion mostly concerns the advertising department of a newspaper or broadcasting station, the reporter taking the photograph or providing it to the commercial department for use can be named a defendant.

3 .*Public disclosure*—exposing private, embarrassing facts about an individual can provoke legal action against the reporter. A patient hospitalized for obesity would have a case if a reporter took a picture of the individual in the hospital and published the photo without the person's permission.

4. *Placing a person in false light*—file photos can be particularly troublesome in this area. Publishing a picture of a policeman in conjunction with a story about a police corruption probe when the policeman in the photo is in no way connected with the probe would definitely be cause for legal action.

Much like libel, responsible reporting is the best insurance against an invasion of privacy suit.

SEARCH AND SEIZURE

In 1978 the Supreme Court ruled that police could search for criminal evidence believed in possession of a third party. The decision arose from a case concerning the *Stanford Daily* at Stanford University. The ruling had frightening implications for a free press. At the extreme, it means that a corrupt government can use police action to secure documents from reporters who may be trying to expose that corruption. At the very least, it threatens every reporter who has ever worked on a story that may have criminal implications. If all police forces were without the taint of corruption and every officer of the law carried the banner of a free press, perhaps the ruling would not be as serious. But they are not. It was not surprising that the press was concerned about the ruling, and trade publications were quick to point out its dangers. *Broadcasting* magazine, in an editorial, noted, "It will be a public-spirited cop indeed who chances upon evidence of a journalistic investigation of the local police and keeps it secret."

Some protection against search and seizure occurred with the passage of the Privacy Protection Act in 1981. The law made it "unlawful for a government officer or employee investigating or prosecuting a criminal offense to search for a work product possessed by someone reasonably believed to have a purpose to disseminate information to the public."

While the law provides some protection, it does not stop a zealous prosecutor from seeking the search warrant and worrying about appealing its validity later. Distinctions in the law also exist between "work product" and "documentary materials." Also the law provides little protection if the prosecutor can argue that the material would be destroyed if a subpoena were issued.

The threat of a search warrant rests in the fact that it is a surprise document thrust in the front door and not subject to challenge. Instead of issuing a subpoena and having it challenged in court, a police officer can show up at the front door of a newspaper and, as one executive commented, "break the door down." Moreover, when the warrant is requested from the judge, no one from the press will be there to argue against its issuance. Although the Supreme Court suggested that judges be careful of protecting First Amendment concerns when issuing warrants, the press found little solace in this, pointing out that local officials on the magistrate level will likely be less than cognizant of First Amendment principles, especially when police officers and prosecutors are standing in front of them demanding a search warrant in the name of law and order.

ALTERNATIVE CONTROLS: THE NATIONAL NEWS COUNCIL

When news reporters were being jailed over shield-law issues and the administration of President Richard Nixon was protesting the press coverage it was receiving, the National News Council became a reality. Supported by a grant from the nonprofit Twentieth Century Fund, the council was charged with the responsibility of considering the accuracy and fairness of news disseminated by national newsgathering organizations. Anyone can bring a complaint before the council as long as he or she waives filed legal proceedings against the newsgathering agency in regard to the complaint.

After some well-publicized criticism, the council finally became a reality in early 1973 and in July of that year formally announced its 15 members, representing people from a wide range of backgrounds. William B. Arthur, a former editor of *Look*, was named executive director. Roger J. Traynor, a former chief justice of the California Supreme Court, became chairman, and the former city editor of WCBS-TV, Ned Schnurman, was named associate director. Three years later the council increased its size to 18 members, permitting two additional representatives from the media and one from the general public.

Ironically Richard Nixon's criticism of the press coverage of his administration was not handled by the news council, mostly because it could not gain the cooperation of the Nixon administration officials to substantiate the charges.

Other cases have come before the council. A CBS television documentary about the life of President Franklin Delano Roosevelt was criticized for misleading the viewers into assuming that troops had killed marchers during a Washington, D.C., protest in 1932. The council said the complaint brought against CBS was warranted. The *Washington Post* also received council scrutiny when the *Post* edited a UPI story and thus, the council claimed, changed the reported thrust of a speech by a woman's rights advocate.

The scope of the council has expanded beyond the national press to include press that may not be national in initial circulation but that deals with issues of a national concern or concern for journalists. Certainly the future of such a body depend on the ability of the council to obtain three things—money, public support, and media support. Without any one of these, it cannot succeed. The thought by some that the council might turn into a type of hatchet body was not justified. While criticizing some media, it found that other complaints were not warranted. Currently the council operates much like a watchdog without teeth. It can investigate and comment, but it cannot take action against the media, short of attempting to publicize its findings.

SUMMARY

Our discussion of legal issues and the working press began by examining four theories of the press as discussed by Siebert, Peterson, and Schramm. Of these theories, the authoritarian theory is the oldest and is based on the assumption that the individual is subordinate to the state. The press functions as an instrument of the state under this theory, with limited private control of the press for selected individuals who will publish the state's position on issues affecting society. As the authoritarian theory began to deteriorate, it was gradually replaced by the libertarian theory, which espouses a free press. Libertarianism envisions a society in which the individual is the concern of society, and society's goal is the achievement of the greatest happiness possible for the largest number of people. In the twentieth century, partly based on criticism of the role of advertising in the press, the social responsibility theory of the press arose. This theory suggests that while a free press exists, it must operate within certain safeguards to ensure that it will be both a free and a responsible press. The Soviet-Communist theory is an example of a press that is not only an instrument of the state but one that is integrated with other instruments to maintain the theory of unity in Soviet society.

The basic legal document affecting the press in America is the First Amendment of the U.S. Constitution. Even when the federal government becomes directly involved in regulating mass media, the free press–free speech concept applies. Indicative of this is the Communications Act of 1934, which prohibits direct censorship of the media by government.

Our chapter also discussed reporters' shield laws, those laws protecting the confidentiality of reporters' news sources. Because of the lack of specificity of the Constitution with regard to safeguarding the confidentiality of news sources, individual states have enacted shield laws to strengthen their own commitment to freedom of the press. Closely related to shield laws are freedom of information laws which guard against the secrecy of governmental record keeping and meetings. Measures that control the press in the coverage of judicial poceedings include Canon 3A(7) of the American Bar Association and gag rules. Canon 3A(7) was designed to prevent cameras in the courtroom but is slowly being revoked by both courts and forward-thinking judges. Gag rules are issued by judges to thwart journalists from reporting news of court proceedings.

The student press enjoys many of the same rights as other media. There are, however, some restrictions placed on high school newspapers, and the student press that receives funds from a tax-supported college or university retains the somewhat precarious position of being an extension of the state. Whatever the relationship to the funding source, a student press provides an opportunity for students to learn from responsible advisors and to gain experience in reporting practices which can be beneficial in later professional careers.

Libel laws are among those safeguards that ensure a responsible press. Publication, identification, and defamation are three facts that can spell libel and a court suit for reporters. Similarly, invading someone else's privacy can also cause legal difficulties. Recent Supreme Court rulings have lifted the press's immunity from police search and seizure tactics. Placed in the same category as other businesses, the press is concerned about the possible abuse of this search and seizure privilege and the use of warrants to silence any record of possible criminal activity.

Alternatives to legal controls on the working press can be found in the activities of the National News Council. Operable in 1973, the council operates mainly as a watchdog.

OPPORTUNITIES FOR FURTHER LEARNING

American Newspaper Publishers Association, *ANPA: To Advance the Cause of a Free Press, 1978–79*. Reston, Va.: ANPA, 1978.

ANDERSON, D. A., A *"Washington Merry-Go Round" of Libel Actions*. Chicago: Nelson-Hall, 1980.

BARTLETT, J., ed., *The First Amendment in a Free Society*. New York: H. W. Wilson, 1979.

BERN, W., *The First Amendment and the Future of American Democracy*. New York: Basic Books, 1976.

Current Developments in Copyright Law, 1980. New York: Practicing Law Institute, 1980.

DENNISTON, L. W., *The Reporter and the Law: Techniques of Covering the Courts*. New York: Hastings House, 1980.

DEVOL, K. S., *Mass Media and the Supreme Court: The Legacy of the Warren Years*. New York: Hastings House, 1976.

FRANKLIN, M. A., *Cases and Materials on Mass Media Law*. Mineola, N.Y.: Foundation Press, 1977.

Freedom vs. Control: The United States and World News Flow. Grand Forks, N.D.: ICD Publications, International Communication Division, Association for Education in Journalism, 1979.

GILLMOR, D. M., AND J. A. BARRON, *Mass Communication Law*, 3rd ed., St. Paul: West Publishing Co., 1979.

HEMMER, J. J. JR., *Communication under Law, Vol. 2: Journalistic Freedom*. Metuchen, N.J.: Scarecrow, 1980.

JEHLE, F. F., *Libel: An ABP Practical Guide*. New York: American Business Press, 1981.

JOHNSTON, D. F., *Copyright Handbook*. New York: R. R. Bowker, 1978.

LOFTON, J., *The Press as Guardian of the First Amendment*. Columbia: University of South Carolina Press, 1980.

PATTON, W. L., *An Author's Guide to the Copyright Law*. Lexington, Mass.: Lexington Books/D. C. Heath, 1980.

PEMBER, D., *Mass Media Law*. Dubuque, Iowa: Wm. C. Brown, 1977.

POWERS, R., *The Newscasters*. New York: St. Martin's Press, 1977.

REDDICK, D., *The Mass Media and the School Newspaper*. Belmont, Calif.: Wadsworth, 1976.

RUCKELSHAUS, W., AND E. ABEL, eds., *Freedom of the Press*. Washington, D.C.: American Enterprise Institute for Public Policy Research, 1976.

SANFORD, B. W., *Synopsis of the Law of Libel and the Right of Privacy*. Cleveland: Baker Hostetler & Patterson, 1977.

SIEBERT, F. S., T. PETERSON, AND W. SCHRAMM, *Four Theories of the Press*. Urbana: University of Illinois Press, 1956.

SIMONS, H., AND J. A. CALIFANO, Jr., eds., *The Media and the Law*. New York: Praeger Special Studies, 1976.

TRAGER, R., AND D. L. DICKERSON, *College Student Press Law*, 2nd ed. Athens, Ohio: National Council of College Publications Advisers. 1979.

ZUCKMAN, H. L., AND M. J. GAYNES, *Mass Communications Law in a Nutshell*. St. Paul: West Publishing Co., 1977.

CHAPTER

AUDIENCE
AND EFFECTS
OF MASS COMMUNICATION

PREVIEW

After completing this chapter, we should be able to:

Distinguish between audience demographics and audience psychographics.

Realize the pitfalls in researching an audience.

Describe the bullet theory.

Understand that subgroups have an effect on how we receive and react to mass communication.

Explain the concepts of two-step flow and opinion leaders.

Realize the interpersonal influence acting on mass communication.

Define the individual differences approach, categories approach, and social relationships approach of reacting to messages from the mass media.

Discuss selective exposure, selective perception, and selective retention.

Identify highbrow, middlebrow, lowbrow, and postbrow film audiences.

Describe Stephenson's play theory.

Explain the uses and gratifications approach to the consumption of media messages.

Define the agenda-setting function of media.

Outline the socialization process of media.

Be aware of the studies and inquiries into the effects of televised violence.

Understand the concept of diffusion of innovations.

Ever since the press began to exert an influence in society, people have been concerned about the effects of the press. Today that concern ranges far beyond the press. Scan the topics in an evening newspaper, listen to radio or television, or read a news magazine, and you will realize why there is concern about the effects of mass media on our lives. The impact of editorials on the election process, the influence of televised violence in contributing to or in alleviating real-life violence and teenage delinquency, and the effect of comic books—all of these have entered the discussions of legislators, parent-teacher associations, and academicians.

The purpose of this chapter is to examine the effects of mass communication on our lives. Before doing this, however, it is necessary also to understand the audience for mass communication. We shall learn how we view the audience in terms of its demographic and psychographic characteristics and then shall discuss some of the pitfalls in studying the audience and effects.

AUDIENCE DEMOGRAPHICS

With a mass audience, it is often difficult to find certain segments of the population to which specific mass media messages are to be directed. For example, a successful advertising campaign for a Rolls Royce must first select an audience whose income level is high enough to afford it. As a result, media buyers must rely on *demographics* to categorize the population. *Demographic characteristics are the basic statistical data on such things as age, sex, education level, income, and ethnic background.* They are used more often than any other method to pinpoint a certain mass audience and thus to determine such things as how much an advertiser will be charged for airing a commercial during a particular television program at a specified time.

Demographics can be applied to local media that serve a given geographic area as well as to national media. For instance, your local radio station reaches a specific portion of the total community listeners, which again can be identified as a group because of its demographic characteristics. If you were to walk into the manager's office at the local station and ask him what the characteristics of his station's audience are, he might reply, "We reach the upper-income, middle-aged male." Further investigation might reveal that his station programs a lot of play-by-play sports which attract this type of audience.

Similarly, if you were to walk into the office of a network executive and ask what type of audience her network prime-time programming reaches on Wednesday nights, she might say, "The middle-income individual whose median age is 34." In each case, both media executives identified their audience by demographic characteristics.

Now for comparison, let's examine what would happen if you walked into the office of a media manager who was responsible for publishing a magazine called *Skiers*. The publisher would certainly be able to tell you the demographic characteristics of her audience. However, this would not be the only important quality of the audience. Of equal importance would be their interest in skiing. They would be joined, not so much because of their demographic characteristics, but because they liked to ski. Advertisers, although wanting to know the average income of the audience, would be mainly interested in them because of this skiing interest. It would be an ideal place to advertise ski apparel, ski equipment, and ski resorts. On the other hand, if an advertiser wanted to reach an audience predominantly in their mid-twenties, all hobbies or other interests aside, he would want to find another mass medium that would accurately reflect this demographic feature. Perhaps network television or radio would be a better medium in this instance.

As a result of certain demographic characteristics, media specialists and researchers have become very proficient in determining media habits of the mass audience. Although new research techniques are being developed to supplement audience demographics, demographics still remain the foundation for categorizing the mass audience.

AUDIENCE PSYCHOGRAPHICS

One of the new research frontiers that scrutinizes the mass audience is called *psychographics*. Psychographics attempts to define and to distinguish the psychological characteristics of the mass audience. Examples are attitudes, opinions, values, or self-esteem.

Psychographics come into play when the traditional demographic characteristics are not sufficient to play a media buy or to explain our reaction to media messages. For instance, age and income may very well help to determine attitudes toward welfare payments. However, if these were the only characteristics you considered when planning a media persuasion campaign to revise the welfare system, you would have little success. Many other characteristics of the mass audience help determine attitudes toward welfare, and it is imperative for the media buyer to look directly at those attitudes, disregarding, for the moment, demographic characteristics.

After sampling audience attitudes, you may discover that unfavorable attitudes toward the current welfare system are held by middle-income people. Based on psychographic information about these individuals, you plan your media campaign to reach them. Had you assumed that the attitudes of all income groups were alike, your media campaign would have been needlessly expensive. Moreover, had you assumed that certain attitudes toward welfare followed directly from membership in specific age and income groups and had not investigated these attitudes, your media campaign would have failed miserably. Based on the information you have received, you may also discover that you will need to use different media to reach these middle-income individuals. Perhaps they watch more television than other income groups do, or read certain consumer magazines. Your media campaign will then have the greatest chance for success if advertisements are placed in these media.

RESEARCHING THE AUDIENCE AND EFFECTS: SOME PITFALLS

What we know about the characteristics of the mass audience and the effects that mass communication has on this audience is the result of about four decades of research, a short span of time when we consider how long, for example, the print media have been with us. There is still much to learn.

Methodology and Theory

For instance, in Chapter 1 we learned there were three basic types of communication—intrapersonal, interpersonal, and mass communication. Research in each of these three areas has proceeded from a different methodological base. In intrapersonal communication, highly controlled laboratory experiments have employed sensitive electronic measurements of such physiological processes as brain waves and galvanic skin response. Interpersonal communication research has been mostly under closely controlled laboratory conditions, frequently in the college classroom. In many cases this research has consisted of students receiving some type of message and then being tested for attitude change. Mass communication research, on the other hand, has consisted of mostly field or survey research, in which the sample population responds either to a questionnaire or to a home interview.

Experimental vs. Survey Methodologies

When people have tried to structure a theoretical base for all types of communication from these three very different types of data, results have been less than ideal. Psychologist Carl Hovland, in discussing the subject of attitude change, summarized the differences in results obtained through research using experimental and survey methodologies.[1] Among these differences were such things as the *length of the message* used to test attitude change, the *influence of experimenters*, the *difference in interpersonal reaction*, and the *elapsed time after exposure to the message*. These differences, among others, reflect some of the difficulties in researching the mass audience and studying the effects of mass communication.

Imagine that you are a researcher hired to test viewers' reactions to a new television commercial for a certain brand of soap. You arrange for a group of people not currently using that brand of soap to gather in a classroom, sit quietly, and watch the commercial. You then elicit their opinions about new soap. Their answers suggest they have changed their opinion about their current brand of soap and will try the new one. You are excited; your commercial works. But does it? You select a community in your area, purchase time on a local television station, and wait for sales to go up. But they do not. What happened?

To answer the question, review some of the carefully controlled conditions of your "laboratory." Recall first that your group watched the entire commercial from start to finish. But what happened outside the laboratory? Many people only saw part of the commercial. They may have headed for the refrigerator at the very instant the commercial appeared. This limited exposure naturally affected their reaction to the commercial. Second, when your group entered the classroom setting, they perceived your wishes and reacted accordingly. This influence was not present in the home environment. Third, you also asked your group to sit quietly. They were not permitted to talk to each other. Yet when viewers saw the commercial in their home environment, the situation was entirely different. They would interact freely, and their reactions may have been exactly opposite to those expressed in the classroom. Perhaps one member of the family told the rest that the brand of soap featured in the commercial was not any good, and the rest of the family believed her. When you showed the commercial in the classroom, you tested for attitude change immediately after the airing. But after waiting a few weeks to compile the results of your mass communication campaign, you discovered what you could not find out from the interpersonal, classroom setting—that after a few weeks, people's preferences for soap returned to what they had been before the commercial.

Of course, there are many other factors, all making the results of your research misleading. These four conditions are just some of the ones that make researching the mass audience a difficult process. Although you wanted to obtain as truthful and as valid results from your research as you could, moving research out of the laboratory made it possible for many unknown variables to interfere with the results.

In the following pages, keep in mind that the results of research can vary with different methodologies. Human communication is a very complex phenomenon. It is not easily defined, let alone completely understood.

EARLY APPROACHES TO UNDERSTANDING EFFECTS: THE BULLET THEORY

Early theories held that the mass audience was an unidentifiable group of people with separate life styles, who were individually affected by the various mass media with which they came in contact. Reaction to mass media was thus seen as an individual rather than a collective experience. This approval to understanding the effects of mass communication was termed the *hypodermic or bullet theory*. Two assumptions that can easily be drawn from such an approach are (1) people receive information directly from the mass media and not through an intermediary, and (2) that reaction is individual, not based on how other people might influence them.

REVISING THE BULLET THEORY

As psychologists and sociologists began to work with the bullet theory, it just did not seem to explain why people reacted the way they did to messages from the mass media. Gradually the idea of *subgroups* began to emerge.

Subgroups   This concept of a subgroup, a "mass within a mass," provided new insights into how we, as members of a mass audience, both receive information from the mass media and react to that information. For example, we can receive information directly by watching television, listening to the radio, reading a newspaper, leafing through a magazine, or some other form of direct contact with the media. On the other hand, some of our knowledge is derived from *other people* who have been exposed to the media and who have, in turn, relayed the message to us. In a sense, these people who relay the message to us play the role of *gatekeeper*. And, just as the gatekeeper working in the media both expands and restricts our informational environment, so the person delivering interpersonal communication may both expand and restrict our informational environment.

To understand this concept, let's imagine an executive of a large fertilizer company is sitting at lunch reading the financial page of the local newspaper. That afternoon he leaves the office and on the way out meets the office manager. They stop to chat for a moment, and in the course of their conversation, the executive suggests that the office manager consider purchasing agribusiness stocks as an excellent personal investment. The office manager mulls over the advice of the executive. She has heard about a number of the agribusiness stocks and feels that they might make a good investment. However, until now, she has never been influenced to the point of buying. Her conversation with the executive changed all that. She values his advice. He has made many successful investments in the stock market. She also knows that he reads a large number of financial magazines, the financial page of the local newspaper, and specialized economic publications that offer tips on potential investments. Based on the executive's advice she decides to purchase the agribusiness stocks.

Opinion Leaders and the Two-Step Flow

The above example illustrated two important concepts in understanding the mass audience—the *two-step flow* and *opinion leaders*. First, let us study the two-step flow. This theory was posited by three researchers, Paul Lazarsfeld, Bernard Berelson, and Hazel Gaudet, who studied the 1940 American presidential campaign.[2] In the process of interviewing people about the election, they found that much of the voters' information about the campaign came from other people. This concept has been expanded upon since that time, but the primary hypothesis remains essentially the same—that much of the information disseminated by mass media comes to the individual's attention secondhand from people who relay their interpretation of it. The case of the executive reading the financial news in the newspaper and then suggesting that the office manager buy stock was an example of the two-step flow.

In addition, the executive *influenced* the office manager's opinion of the stocks—he was an opinion leader. This concept, which also evolved from the research of Lazarsfeld, Berelson, and Gaudet,[3] hypothesizes that relayers of information from mass media can also influence the attitudes and decisions of the receivers.

Interpersonal Influence

We all are acquainted with someone we respect for his or her opinions on world affairs. This other person is usually very much attuned to the mass media and may read more than one newspaper per day, some news magazines, and also listen to a number of radio and television news presentations. We may thus tend to rely on this person's judgments of world affairs. Type of medium may also determine how and with what influence an opinion leader functions. For example, some opinion leaders are attuned to more specialized media which give them an authoritative stance on specific subjects. You, as students, are in class to learn about mass communication. You rely on your instructor to provide you with recent and authoritative information. Your instructor, because of his or her interest in mass communication, most likely reads scholarly journals on the subject, journalism reviews, radio-television columns in the local newspaper, and probably watches television programs on issues surrounding mass media in society. Because your instructor is so attuned to the mass media, especially when it concerns his or her area of expertise, you rely on this person as an opinion leader.

Now imagine for a moment that you cut class and miss a lecture in which the instructor relates new research findings that he or she read about in a scholarly journal. You know you probably will be penalized when it comes time for an examination, so you borrow another student's class notes. When you choose the student, you pick someone that you feel took good notes and could relay to you an accurate interpretation of the instructor's remarks. You were again seeking someone who, for you, would be an opinion leader. Notice that more than one person was involved in relaying information to you from the mass media—in this case, the scholarly journal. Both the instructor and your fellow student became opinion leaders. Thus, *although this process is still referred to as the two-step flow, it may involve more than just one relay person.*

In addition to the indirect communication we receive via the two-step flow, we may turn directly to the media either to receive more information, to reinforce an opinion presented to us by an opinion leader, or to form our own opinions. For instance, assume that the information about new research published in the scholarly journal seems strange to you. You feel that despite the authoritative posture of both your teacher and your friend, you just cannot accept it as valid. Instead you decide to refer to the journal and read the article yourself. In this case you use media as a *check* and *reinforcement* for the information that you received from the opinion leader. What actually occurred was an interrelationship between the media and the opinion leader, an interrelationship that ultimately determined how you were informed and influenced by media content.

UNDERSTANDING REACTION TO MEDIA MESSAGES

If we accept the idea that different individuals and groups affect how we react to messages from the mass media, we can begin to understand the different approaches to explaining these reactions. These approaches can be grouped into the individual differences, categories, and social relationships approaches.

Individual Differences Approach	The *individual differences* approach proposes that each of us has unique qualities that result in our *reacting differently* to media messages. Professors Melvin De Fleur and Sandra Ball-Rokeach in their book *Theories of Mass Communication* state:

> Individual differences perspective implies that media messages contain particular stimulus attributes that have differential interaction with personality characteristics of audience members. Since there are individual differences in personality characteristics among such members, it is natural to assume that there will be variations in effect which correspond to these individual differences.[4]

Variables in these differing effects are partially caused by the audience's *exposure, perception*, and *retention* of media content, which we shall discuss later in this chapter.

Although at first the individual differences approach may seem like the bullet theory, it is more complex and takes into consideration the differences among individuals in accounting for different reactions to the same message.

Categories Approach	Another approach to the mass audience and the effects of media content is the *category* approach.[5] Its origin stems from the needs of advertisers to reach more specialized audiences. Although the simplest way to group an audience into categories is by demographics—sex, age, income—researchers are looking more and more at the physiographic—values, beliefs, attitudes, life styles—components of the audience. Looking at the audience through categories can be much more complex than the old bullet theory. Notice we said, *can be*. For the ad buyer wanting to reach 18- to 21-year-old females, the application of the theory becomes mechanical. But for social scientists wanting to know how categories of people think and how they interact with other categories of people, the approach becomes much more involved. Moreover, if we want to use these interrelationships to understand how people react to mass communication, the process becomes even more sophisticated. Buying an ad to reach the homemaker is one thing; buying an ad to reach the homemaker who *interacts* with another homemaker viewing a competing commercial is something else.

Social Relationships Approach	Concentration on this interaction and the people taking part in it would describe the *social relationships* approach to studying the audience and media effects. The importance of interpersonal communication becomes evident in the social relationships approach, as does the realization that although the media can help disseminate the initial message, how it is retransmitted, discussed, and rediscussed among audience members will significantly determine the effect of the message.

After considering the different approaches to studying the audience and the effects of mass communication on an audience, we can readily see that not only do the three approaches overlap, but that in some ways, all come into play in the communicative process. It is much like viewing that process through different colored glasses. A psychologist concerned with an individual's behavior might feel more comfortable with an individual differences approach, although that same psychologist would be foolish to ignore the other approaches. Similarly, an advertiser wanting to reach a specific type of audience might be concerned with categories but cannot ignore the interrelationships among people that demand the attention of the social relationships approach.

SELECTIVE EXPOSURE, PERCEPTION, AND RETENTION

In discussing the individual differences approach, we talked about exposure, perception, and retention. Each influences our interaction with the media and how they affect us. For instance, research has taught us that we selectively expose ourselves to certain types of programming, the process being called *selective exposure*. If a politician is delivering a televised address, you might tune in the program because you agree or disagree with the politician. For either reason, you selectively exposed yourself to the program.

Second, the perceptions you hold prior to watching the televised address will also affect your reaction to it. If you are extremely loyal to the politician, you might agree with everything she says regardless of *what* she says, so much so that if her opponent said the same thing, you might completely disagree with him. You would be guilty of *selective perception*. It is not a serious crime, but one that can considerably distort how you react to messages.

Third, because of your selective perception, you may retain only those portions of the address with which you agree. If you perceive the entire address as favorable, you may remember all of it. If you perceive it as unfavorable, you may wipe it entirely from your mind. If parts of the address affect you positively, those may be the portions that you remember while forgetting the negative elements. Or the negative elements may be the very ones you remember. Either way, how you originally perceived the address determines what you retain, a process called *selective retention*.

Our focus on selective exposure, perception, and retention may take on new importance as media become more specialized. In the past with only a few major television networks from which to choose, the chances were still great we would be exposed to messages which might present opposing views to our own. Now that we can choose from a multitude of specialized media, the theory of selective exposure suggests we will select those which support our beliefs and which have programming and information appeaing to our own interests. Furthermore, the more we use those media, the more the people responsible for programming will send information which appeals to us. Will a medium's continual reinforcement of our beliefs and opinions and our continual reinforcement *by choice*—selective exposure—of programming which supports our interests may make us a society of psychological isolates with narrow and dogmatic views continually fed by programmers sending more and more specialized messages?

For the most part, our discussion has been in the context of how the media influence the audience or how the mass audience reacts to the media content. Our study has been primarily one-sided, and we have so far failed to consider the *interactive* qualities of our media-audience relationship. We have been asking the question, "What do the media do *to* people?" instead of "What do people do *with* media?" This same myopic approach was noted by well-known media researcher and scholar Elihu Katz, who stressed that much media research proceeded from a "bookkeeping" outlook indicative of the first question, rather than to a "functional" or "uses and gratification" approach, indicative of the second question.[6] Let's look at this "functional" concept in more detail so that we can become aware of how the mass audience interrelates with the mass media.

Film: Highbrow, Middlebrow, Lowbrow, Postbrow

One of the ways that we can study this concept is through film audiences. The motion picture has become an established medium of mass communication. Over the past sixty years it has touched on virtually every segment of society, has dealt with every subject, and has reached every audience. Yet for these audiences, it has had many different meanings and has performed many different functions.

Louis M. Savary and J. Paul Carrico, in writing about motion pictures and their audiences, divide the film audience into three distinct groups— *highbrows, middlebrows*, and *lowbrows*.[7] For each audience, film performs a different function and has a different meaning. For example, the highbrows look at the medium as an artistic expression and derive intellectual satisfaction from a well-executed film. They may attend a movie more than once, not necessarily because they like the plot or the actors, but because they want to study the work of a famous director or review the camera techniques. For the lowbrow audience the experience is entirely different; perhaps it is an excuse to get out or an escape from life's daily routine. Between these two groups are the middlebrows, somewhat knowledgeable in what a good motion picture consists of and able at least to differentiate between a really good and really bad film.

Savary and Carrico typify the current audience for films as belonging to none of the three types previously mentioned. Still predominantly in their late teen and young adult years, they are more sophisticated than past generations. Having taken courses in film, they have a much deeper understanding of the medium and its social implications. Savary and Carrico have labeled this knowledgeable generation the "postbrow" or "no-brow" audience.

Stephenson's Play Theory

Using a data-gathering procedure called *Q-sort*, William Stephenson did extensive research on how different types of audiences, expressed as typical individuals, feel about the media. From this research has evolved Stephenson's play theory, which suggests that we use the media as a means of escaping into a world of "play" not accessible at other times.[8] Those researchers familiar with Stephenson's data-gathering methods have given considerable support to Stephenson's theory as well as to his methodologies. Others have been severely critical, like Professor David Chaney who contends that "Stephenson . . . fails to move beyond an individualistic level of description. While the importance of audience commitment is understood, his concern with finding a methodological demonstration of his argument leads his audience to be conceived as only a conglomeration of individuals."[9]

Professor Deanna Campbell-Robinson of the University of Oregon provides a more generous view of Stephenson's methodologies. Conducting research on the uses of television and film by upper-middle-class professionals, she suggested that Stephenson's technique could be used for a direct examination of people's attitudes toward media and be able to demonstrate "(1) that within any single, demographically defined audience group, several attitude or 'taste' groups exist and (2) that similar taste groups exist within other cases."[10] Further support for Stephenson has been offered by Wilbur Schramm who generalized that Stephenson, with a style of writing like McLuhan's, could have been the guru of modern media.[11]

Uses and Gratifications

Moving from the specific to the general, Stephenson's play theory is part of a wider body of research and theory centering on what *uses* we make of media and what *gratifications* we gain from exposing ourselves to media. Research of these uses and gratifications has been conducted in populations ranging from farmers in less developed countries to American homemakers. The research has not escaped vigorous debate, however, not only on the different types of uses and gratifications but also on the very methodologies that attempt to identify them.

Part of the debate is a conflict between the individual differences approach and the social categories approach to the study of media effects. Consider a television program. We could argue that a soap opera provides certain role models for homemakers or college students. We could also contend that reaction to soap operas cannot be classified in demographic terms but, rather, in psychographic terms. Soap operas have certain *uses* for people possessing specific motivations or certain psychological characteristics. Or we could argue that even this approach is unsatisfactory since each individual is different, and many different individuals may have many different uses for the same soap opera. How we learn what uses these many different people or groups of people make of the media is still another dilemma. Do we individually test them in tightly controlled laboratory situations, psychologically wiring them up to get at the depths of their thought processes?

What has the research told us about uses and gratifications? Sampling a few of these studies, Professor Deanna Campbell-Robinson studied upper-middle-class professionals. She discovered the presence of "information absorbers," people who passively absorb information from television without actively interpreting it. Another group she labeled "analytical artists" who use television to increase their understanding of themselves, other people, and the world. Researcher Neil Weintraub suggested that radio gives teenagers awareness, makes their day pass more quickly, and also tells them what is happening.[12] Researcher Lawrence Wenner examined the elderly and found that one use of television among this group was companionship.[13]

One of the earliest studies on the uses of the media was conducted by Herta Herzog who examined the reasons that people listen to radio soap operas. Conducting in-depth interviews, Herzog found three reasons: compensation, wish fulfillment, and advice.[14]

Consider the area of *compensation through identification*. As members of society, we assume certain roles and must make decisions based on these roles. Naturally we seek to receive approval or recognition for what we do. *Direct approval* comes from someone telling us that we are doing the right thing. *Indirect approval* comes from our knowledge or assumption that others are doing the same things that we are. The soap opera thus provides a form of indirect approval. The person watching sees other people experiencing the same relationships, trials, and tribulations that he or she experiences. It may be meeting a new neighbor, having a love affair, splurging for a new coat, or whatever. The important thing is that there are, even though only portrayed on the television screen, people living similar lives and having experiences similar to our own.

The person who views soap operas as a means of *wish fulfillment* has a different functional relationship with the medium. This individual wishes that those things taking place on the screen were happening to her or him but is not actually experiencing them. In this situation the audience uses the program to fantasize about the lives of other people. Perhaps their environment is unpleasant, drab, or routine, and they have neither the ability nor the real desire to change their life style. Yet simply by exposing themselves to the soap opera, these viewers are given the opportunity to fantasize.

Anyone who has ever watched any soap opera will notice the development of a series of plots and subplots that represent human relations problems to be solved—an in-law spending too much time at her married child's home, a member of the family suffering from alcoholism, or a neighbor with marital problems. The viewer is faced with the question of how to deal with these situations. The soap opera provides the answers. This type of viewer is seeking *advice* on what he or she should do in his or her own life when faced with similar situations.

Researcher Ronald Compesi examined the gratifications identified by the viewers of the popular soap opera *All My Children*.[15] Using people in Eugene, Oregon, Compesi asked 221 viewers who volunteered for the study to respond to 52 statements designed to measure the gratification *All My Children* had for the viewers. After submitting the data to statistical analysis, the following statements, in rank order, described the gratifications viewers received from watching the program:

1. *Entertainment*. Viewers use the program as entertainment or fun.
2. *Habit*. Viewing the program was described as something to which the viewers looked forward. It was described as being part of the viewer's routine.
3. *Convenience*. The program is seen at a convenient time.
4. *Social Utility*. The program is used as a tool for social interaction with

others. People view the program with friends and enjoy talking about the program with friends.

5. *Relaxation or Escape from Problems.* Watching the program reduced tension in viewers.

6. *Escape from Boredom.* Viewers watch the program when they are bored and have nothing else to do or because there is nothing else worth watching on television.

7. *Reality Exploration or Advice.* The program is used to help solve problems in the viewer's own life. *All My Children* provides advice and is a personal reference point to help the viewer understand his or her own life as well as others' and to provide an accurate reflection of reality.

The statements are indications of the gratifications people *may* receive from watching the program, not necessarily *do* receive. For example, Compesi noted that the "reality exploration or advice" statements had "a strong reality orientation that is disagreed with by the fans in this study."

Television news has also been found to have uses and gratifications for viewers. Researcher Mark R. Levy categorized five different areas of uses and gratifications based on statements by viewers of television news.[16] One category defined by Levy is *surveillance-reassurance*. The surveillance-reassurance category is exemplified by such viewer statements as "TV news makes me realize that my life is not so bad after all," "I watch TV news so I won't be surprised by higher prices," and "TV news helps me keep track of what is happening to people like myself." Another category is *cognitive orientation*. In this category Levy grouped viewer statements such as "I like to compare my ideas to what the commentators say" and "Watching TV news keeps me in touch with the world." Levy's third category is *dissatisfactions*. Statements in this category include "The TV news programs try to make things seem more dramatic than they really are" and "By the time I see the TV news at night, I've already read or heard about most of the headline items." The fourth category Levy labels *affective orientation*, characterized by such statements as "After a hard day, watching the TV news helps me relax," "I feel sorry for the newscasters when they make mistakes" and "Television news is sometimes very exciting." Levy's fifth category of uses and gratifications is *diversion*, characterized by such viewer statements as "When the newscasters joke around with each other, it makes the news easier to take," "TV news satisfies my sense of curiosity," and "I enjoy hearing funny, different, or strange things on the news."

Researcher Eileen Lehnert examined the uses 18- to 34-year-olds have for newspapers.[17] Using in-depth Q-sort techniques to examine the opinions of 71 Michigan State University students, Lehnert identified four "types" of readers:

1. *Information Stalker.* "Information stalkers are almost obsessed with the quest for information. They want a newspaper to cover a wide range of topics, and they're so intent on this that they're willing to forego comics and features for articles of a more serious nature."[18]

2. *Consumer Advocates.* "Useful information is of paramount importance to Consumer Advocates. They are interested in getting the most for their

money, and they expect their newspapers to help them secure that end."[19]

3. *Fascinated Feature Reader.* "The Fascinated Feature Readers desire entertainment from a newspaper. They want well-written bright stories about famous and interesting people's lifestyles."[20]

4. *Opinion Seekers.* The Opinion Seeker is totally enamored with the search for opinions on a wide range of topics. The editorial page is a continual source of delight."[21]

An interesting comparison to Lehnert's study can be found in research completed by Judee Burgoon and Michael Burgoon.[22] Examining five different markets—Niagara Falls, New York; Binghamton, New York; Rockford, Illinois; Salinas, California; Stockton, California—they examined the functions people have for the daily newspapers. Although varying from city to city, four functions stood out:

1. *Immediacy and Thoroughness.* The newspaper is important for obtaining "immediate knowledge of big news events, getting full details of those events and getting the day's headlines."[23]

2. *Local Awareness and Utility.* The readers want to keep "informed on local happenings and explaining how important events and issues relate to the local community."[24]

3. *Redundancy and Entertainment.* The newspaper provides additional information on things experienced personally, supports and repeats other information sources. It serves to entertain and provide "unusual stories for conversational fodder."[25]

4. *Social Extension.* Newspapers "serve as surrogates for other people or for social experiences, such as providing conversational tidbits, offering vicarious experiences and helping to shape opinions."[26]

Stop and consider your own uses and gratifications of the messages you receive from mass media. What do television soap operas mean to you? Why do you watch television news? What meanings do films have for you?

Agenda-Setting Function

With the advent of sophisticated means of measuring the relationship between mass media and media audiences has come the development of preliminary theoretical concepts, which state that media not only inform us but also influence us as to what is important to know.[27] In other words, the media create an *agenda* for our thoughts and influence us in what seems important. For example, if the media in a local community provide considerable coverage of a local bond issue, the residents of the community may very well perceive the bond issue as being of great importance to the community, even if it is not. The media coverage of issues in a political campaign may help us to perceive certain issues as being more important than others and consequently influence our decisions about candidates based on how they address themselves to those issues.

Major research on the agenda-setting function of the mass media is now being conducted at a number of universities. There are some problems associated with this research, however. One of the most troublesome is monitoring all media that affect an individual and then determining how they actually do affect the person. For instance, a major market may have upwards of fifty different media channels bombarding a population. Keeping track of all of these media messages is an awesome task. By first determining which media are important to certain population groups and then concentrating on these media, the control of intervening variables has permitted at least a preliminary theoretical base for the agenda-setting function.

The Broad
Context
of Functional
Use

The uses and gratification, or functional relationships, described here are only a few of the many ways a person attuned to the various mass media can interact with them. The importance of these functional relationships is in the context of the mass audience, and it is on this level that they will affect societal development. For instance, if you personally need a new dress and cannot find one you like in the store, you may order one from a catalogue. The catalogue, a medium directed to a specialized audience, has a very identifiable use—to order merchandise—and each individual purchaser's decision will affect only that person. On the other hand, the content of television and film affects millions. Yet we have seen that researching the mass audience is difficult. When we do understand more about our functional relationship to the mass media, we will undoubtedly have a far greater insight into how we use media, instead of how media use us.

    This emphasis on future research is important. Some of the criticism of media has been that media give us exactly what we want to consume, and as we consume, media managers and planners provide us with more of the same. If we are, in the broader sense of an entire society, interrelating with media in a functional sense, then we need to know more about this relationship. We need to know such things as how media affect our political system, how our attitudes and values are formed, and what effect media have on this formation. Answers to these questions will come from more than just a "bookkeeping" approach to mass media research. Perhaps as students of mass communication, you can help find these answers.

SOCIALIZATION

Closely related to how we use media is their effect on our social development in acquiring culture and social norms. Although a significant amount of research centers on media, especially broadcasting's effects on the socialization of children, we know that socialization continues throughout our lives. As with other approaches to studying effects, the content of messages can mean different things to different people. For example, the effect of a violent television program on a group of male adults can be in sharp contrast to the effect of that same program on a group of small children, whose world and ideas are just being formed and whose socialization process is much less developed than that of the adults. The adult might go to bed thinking how great John Wayne was as the hero. The child may have frightful nightmares about evil forces affecting his or her ability to survive in the world.

Here again, research has opened up a plethor of debate. And here again, different methodologies are used. As responsible consumers of mass communication, we should recognize these. Since socialization does not occur simply by being exposed to a single message, we must draw from a wide body of research across many disciplines to begin to theorize exactly how media affect our socialization process. Moreover, that data must be drawn over time. Few studies examine socialization over time. Most ask a given group of individuals what meaning mass media has for them and then group the results under the heading of socialization or uses and gratifications research. Although studying the research on these different audiences is valuable, studying the *same* individuals over a *longer* time period is much more desirable.

Stages in Studying Effects on Socialization

Socialization research has three stages. First, numerous studies have examined the "content" of media messages. Such elements as the image of women in advertisements, hero figures in movies, and acts of violence on television have told us much about what we see or hear. The second stage of this research tells us if people exposed to the message actually perceive or recognize it. Were the children who saw a given television program able to recognize examples of good behavior and prosocial messages? The third stage of investigation must determine what effect the messages have once they are received.

Studying the Results

From socialization research we have learned that children can identify certain prosocial content themes. For example, CBS has actively supported various research projects on this issue. Even though beneficial from a public relations standpoint, the research has been conducted under responsible scrutiny.[28] Examining the program *Fat Albert and the Cosby Kids*, research in three cities—Cleveland, Philadelphia, and Memphis—revealed that almost nine out of ten children who had seen an episode of *Fat Albert* received one or more messages of social value. Some of the prosocial messages reported being received included "Take care of younger children," "Father's job is important," "Support a friend in trouble," "Be honest," and "Be friendly; don't be rude, nasty, jealous, or mean."

Similar research by CBS showed that older children were more likely to receive more abstract messages than younger children were. For example, in studying the program *Shazam*, about a Superman figure, about half the 7- to 8-year-olds received the message "obey your parents," whereas about three-fourths of the 10- to 11-year-olds and the 13- to 14-year-olds received that message. Only 4 percent of the 7- to 8-year-olds received the message "be independent," whereas 11 percent of the 10- to 11-year-olds and 25 percent of the 13- to 14-year-olds received the message. Examining the program *Isis*, about a superhuman female figure, the research discovered that girls were more likely than boys to comment on Isis' concern for others and her beauty, while boys mentioned her superhuman qualities as often as did girls.

Analyzing the effects of broadcasting on socialization, we can conclude that parents can have responsibility in the relationship and should not permit television to become a surrogate parent.[29] Watching television with very young children, then discussing the results while referring to the prosocial lessons that may appear is one positive use of the medium. This same process was common in pretelevision times as parents read storybooks to children, then discussed the content of the books. Children apparently learn from television, and such broadcasting practices as stereotyping the roles of certain classes of people can therefore become a child's perception of reality.

The amount of television and when and how it becomes part of children's lives can also influence how they relate to their environment. Studying three towns in Australia that had three different availabilities of television, researchers found that the content viewed was directly related to the context in which it was viewed.[30] When television experience was restricted to mostly an informative-educational context, children perceived it to be far more than just entertainment. Whereas high levels of television viewing tended initially to decrease the involvement in such outside activities as sports, the involvement returned to normal levels after the novelty wore off.

There are also content and context variables in research on the political socialization of children. Political knowledge, news discussion, public affairs interest, and seeking information about news events were investigated by Professors Charles K. Atkin and Walter Gantz.[31] They found that the amount of news viewing to be associated mildly with children's political awareness, with the highest correlations being among older children. The amount of exposure to television news has some relationship to children's knowledge of politics, but more so among middle-class youngsters than among working-class youngsters. Many children in the research reported being stimulated to seek further information after watching television news, and to some degree this desire for more information increased with the amount of news exposure.

Advertising can also influence the socialization process. For example, one study showed children three different eyeglass advertisements with a woman giving a testimonial.[32] One advertisement showed the woman dressed as a court judge, another as a computer programmer, and the third as a television technician. The children who saw that woman in a particular role were more apt to choose that occupation as appropriate for women.

There is still a great deal to be learned about mass media's relationship to the socialization process. Because socialization among children centers on the broadcast media, broadcasting has been singled out as the basis for research. However, we need to understand the influences of other media in the socialization process. Even though children may not be able to read yet, what images are being formed and what behavior patterns are being developed by children leafing through a magazine and seeing the pictures? What indirect socialization may occur as parents discuss the content of media in the presence of children? How do newspapers affect the socialization process when children are exposed to special inserts designed for younger readers? What influence do comics have among children old enough to consume comics? These questions need to be investigated and answered before we can make intelligent conclusions about how the media affect our lives and the learning process.

The importance of understanding the role of media in socialization has resulted in efforts to develop ways in which children can be taught to be critical consumers of television and other media. Perhaps as these receivership skills become more a part of growing up, more positive socialization will take place.

VIOLENCE ON TELEVISION

Violence in media can be traced back to ancient pictographics which displayed such sacrificial acts as carving a heart out of a person's chest, ceremonial torture methods used to bestow adulthood on children reaching puberty, and other activities that by today's standards, if shown, would never make late-night television. Awareness of the effects of violent programming in general and on television in particular began in 1952 during television's formative years when Senator Estes Kefauver's subcommittee investigated juvenile delinquency. Testimony by authorities charged television with being responsible not only for showing violence but also for prompting juveniles to imitate it. The issue might have vanished from public attention except for that afternoon in 1963 when a sniper's bullets killed President John F. Kennedy. Ironically it was television that brought three days of national mourning into American living rooms in what was hailed as the medium's finest hours. That same medium would later be blamed by its critics for causing the warped minds that were responsible for similar events.

The Surgeon General's Report

The bloodshed was not over. Black leader Martin Luther King, Jr., was next to fall to an assassin's bullet. Then another assassin killed Senator Robert Kennedy as he was celebrating with hundreds of campaign workers his victory in the 1968 California presidential primary. The entire era had been spiced with dinnertime details of the Vietnam War, plus political protests at the 1968 Democratic presidential convention. What many saw as inevitable finally occurred as the American government examined the issue of violence on television and committed $1 million to a study, with additional funds for administrative and publishing costs. The project, titled "The Surgeon General's Study of Television and Social Behavior," involved leading social scientists and produced a multivolume work which, when completed, posed as many questions as it had answered. The summary report of the study stated:

> There is a convergence of the fairly substantial experimental evidence for short-run causation of aggression among some children by viewing violence on the screen and the much less certain evidence from field studies that extensive violence viewing precedes some long-run manifestations of aggressive behavior. This convergence of the two types of evidence constitutes some preliminary evidence of a causal relationship.

From this statement it is easy to see how the press and critics jumped on the report with varying interpretations. The reactions ran from the *New*

York Times's headline of "TV Violence Held Unharmful to Youth," to then FCC Commissioner Nicholas Johnson's comparing the network executives responsible for programming to child molesters.

Since the report was released and the public's attention was drawn to the issue, the press has been filled with reference to television's causal relationship to violent behavior. To examine what trends do exist in the research on this subject, we'll center our discussion on learning theory.

Effects of Televised Violence: The Role of Learning Theory

Four theories predominate in the violence-media relationship. The *catharsis theory* suggests that we build up frustrations in our daily lives which are released vicariously by watching violent behavior. This theory claims that there are actual benefits gained from televised violence. This theory is the least supported of the four, although the results of some studies have provided limited support for the idea.[33] The *aggressive cues theory* suggests that exposure to violence on television will raise the level of excitement in the viewer, forming a catalyst to trigger already learned behavior resulting in violent acts being repeated in a real-life setting.[34] Closely aligned to the aggressive cues theory is the *reinforcement theory*, suggesting that televised violence will reinforce behavior already existing in an individual.[35] Inherent in such a theory is the probability that the violent person, because of violent tendencies, perceives violent behavior as a real-life experience, whereas the nonviolent person may perceive the violent program as entertainment without becoming psychologically involved with the program. The *observational learning theory* suggests that we can *learn* violent behavior from watching violent programs.[36]

Clearly all of the theories have merit, and none should be discounted. Moreover, research is examining new variations of these four principal approaches. The observational learning theory, for example, could apply more strongly to very young children who are in their formative years of growth when their environment has a significant effect on what they learn. In essence, if television becomes a surrogate parent, it could certainly teach behavior. Later in the child's life, with the behavior well manifested, violence learned in the formative years could be reinforced. For a child who is hyperactive or easily excitable, the aggressive cues theory might be used to explain easily heightened emotions from exposure to televised violence. Even the catharsis theory could apply to the business executive who uses television to unwind and vicariously vent his or her frustrations through the actions of others.

We immediately begin to see all sides of the violence debate surfacing. Current research is concentrating primarily on children, partly because of funding for such research and partly because of a general feeling that children may very well be the most affected by television violence. In this arena the violence debate is becoming public with considerable pressure and visibility from citizens' groups.

Along with suggesting the causal relationship of televised violence to aggression, the widely quoted research of George Gerbner, Director of the Annenberg School of Communication at the University of Pennsylvania, is used to support the arguments. For more than a decade Gerbner and his associates have compared violence on television among the major networks, then plotted their data over time, providing a running record of the number of violent acts representative of each new television season. Two often-discussed measures are Gerbner's Violence Index, measuring the actual acts of violence, and the Risk Ratio, describing the risk of encountering violence. The index is used mainly to count violent acts on television; the ratio is a bit more complex. It measures the aggressors and the victims, dividing the larger into the smaller with the final figure preceded by a plus sign if aggressors exceed victims and a minus sign if victims exceed aggressors. CBS employs a different violence measuring device, prompting continuing debate over which measure is more accurate and representative of actual violence.[37]

Effects
of Portrayal
on
Aggressive
Behavior

The research on televised violence is now voluminous, with more studies on the way. What the research is telling us about the relationship between the portrayal of violence and aggressive behavior was summarized by Professor George Comstock in the *Journal of Communication*. He stated that the evidence suggests:

1. Cartoon as well as live portrayals of violence can lead to aggressive performance on the part of the viewer.
2. Repeated exposure to cartoon and live portrayals of violence does not eliminate the possibility that new exposure will increase the likelihood of aggressive performance.
3. Aggressive performance is not dependent on a typical frustration, although frustration facilitates aggressive performance.
4. Although the "effect" in some experiments may be aggressive but not antisocial play, implications in regard to the contribution of television violence to antisocial aggression remain.
5. In ordinary language, the factors in a portrayal which increase the likelihood of aggressive performance are the suggestion that aggression is justified, socially acceptable, motivated by malice, or pays off; a realistic depiction; highly exciting material. The presentation of conditions similar to those experienced by the young viewer, including a perpetrator similar to the viewer and circumstances like those of his environment, such as a target, implements, or gives other cues resembling those of the real-life milieu.
6. Although there is no evidence that prior repeated exposure to violent portrayals totally immunizes the young viewer against any influence on aggressive performance, exposure to television portrayals may desensitize young persons to responding to violence in their environment.[38]

In concluding our discussion of televised violence, we should remember that accompanying the issue are numerous policy decisions that can affect the future of television programming. If a causal link is established and if legislators feel that something should be done to curtail the violence, then major First Amendment issues of free speech will arise. Yet this curtailment may have legal precedent. A recent court decision giving the FCC the authority to control programming that airs when children may be present indicates a shift toward some type of control over entertainment programming, control that in the past had been limited to the vagueness of the Fairness Doctrine and indecent programming.

DIFFUSION OF INNOVATIONS

As consumers of mass communication, we are constantly exposed to material that both informs and persuades—information about new discoveries in technology, products designed to make our life easier, inventions, and other innovative procedures. The importance of mass communication in convincing us of the worthiness and benefits of various innovations has been under research and investigation for some time.[39] There are *no concise formulas* to express the importance of mass communication in convincing us to acquire these products, because each of us is unique, as is each product and each situation. But some general trends are discernible and can aid in our understanding of this process.

To understand the process, imagine that you are considering purchasing a new portable electric typewriter. Your old manual typewriter just does not work well anymore, and you *need* a new one. While reading a magazine, you happen to stumble across an ad for such a typewriter, and the ad catches your eye. The new electric portable has a cartridge ribbon system, which means you do not have to change ribbons, and also has a separate cartridge from which to make erasures. You glance at all the features the ad presents and then flip to another article in the magazine.

The next day you happen to be watching television, and a commercial appears that shows the typewriter you first became *aware* of while reading the magazine. Now you are really *interested*. There it is in living color with all of its new features. You then decide to discuss the machine with some of your friends who also have similar portable electric typewriters. While you are discussing it, you are constantly *evaluating* its features. Next, you make a trip to the office supply store and further investigate the typewriter. There you encounter the sales clerk who explains the features to you and asks you if you would like to borrow the typewriter on a *trial* basis until you make up your mind. You think that idea is great, bring the typewriter back to your room, and begin using it in your school work. Finally, after about two weeks of trying it out, you decide you like the typewriter and *acquire* it. Of course, you could have decided to reject the typewriter in favor of a different model.

The process that led up to your decision to buy the typewriter had several steps. First, you had a *need* to purchase the typewriter. Your old typewriter just was not satisfactory. Second, you became *aware* of the new typewriter. Your accidental encounter with it in the magazine alerted you to its many features. Your second exposure to the typewriter, this time on the television commercial, created an *interest* sufficient to discuss it with your fellow students. These discussions helped you *evaluate* the typewriter in comparison to your old one and others on the market. Then you made the decision to go one step farther. You made arrangements at the office supply store to take the typewriter on a *trial* basis. After the trial period, you then decided to *acquire* the typewriter.

SUMMARY

There are many variables in researching the audience and the effects of mass communication. As a result, it has become difficult to develop a theoretical base for studying them and to provide a link with research in intrapersonal and interpersonal communication.

Early explanations centered on the bullet theory that stated that people were individually affected by mass media. Gradually, though, we became aware that subgroups influenced how we consumed mass media. Research began to tell us that messages reached us not only from the media but also from other people. In fact, these other people could influence us even more than the media could. How we reacted to messages began to be explained in three different but interrelated theoretical frameworks: individual differences, categories, and social relationships. How we react to messages can also be explained by how we selectively expose ourselves to media as well as how we perceive and retain that to which we are exposed.

Although we need to know how we react to media, we also need to understand how we use media. Our discussion centered on such concepts as the lowbrow, middlebrow, and highbrow film audiences; Stephenson's play theory's uses and gratifications; and the agenda-setting function of media. How we learn and how our behaviors develop from media messages is called the socialization process. Although television and children are the major emphases of current media research, we also need to examine other media audiences and their effects. Violence on television is one of the most visible issues on the effects of mass communication. Current studies of learning theory have shown that there may be some trends that link aggressive behavior with viewing televised violence.

Mass communication is also important to the diffusion of innovations. From products found in commercial advertising to new innovations in developing countries, we are learning more about how the media influence our decisions to accept new products and services.

OPPORTUNITIES FOR FURTHER LEARNING

BAGGALEY, J., M. FERGUSON, AND P. BROOKS, *Psychology of the TV Image*. New York: Praeger, 1980.

BLUMLER, J. G., AND E. KATZ, eds., *The Uses of Mass Communications: Current Perspectives on Gratifications Research*. Beverly Hills, Calif.: Sage Publications, Inc., 1974.

CATER, D., AND S. STRICKLAND, *TV Violence and the Child*. New York: Russell Sage Foundation, 1975.

CBS Office of Social Research, *Communicating with Children through Television*. New York: CBS, 1977.

CHAFFEE, S. H., ed., *Political Communication: Issues and Strategies for Research*. Beverly Hills, Calif.: Sage Publications, Inc., 1975.

CHANEY, D., *Processes of Mass Communication*. London: The Macmillan Press Ltd., 1972.

COMSTOCK, G., S. CHAFFEE, N. KATZMAN, M. McCOMBS, AND D. ROBERTS, *Television and Human Behavior*. New York: Columbia University Press, 1979.

Davis, D. K., and S. J. Baran, *Mass Communication and Everyday Life: A Perspective on Theory and Effects*. Belmont, Calif.: Wadsworth, 1981.

Frank, R. E., and B. M. Greenberg, *The Public's Use of Television: Who Watches and Why*. Beverly Hills, Calif.: Sage Publications, Inc., 1980.

Gantz, W., *Uses and Gratifications Associated with Exposure to Public Television*. Washington, D.C.: Corporation for Public Broadcasting, Office of Communication Research, 1980.

Gordon, T. F., and M. E. Verna, *Mass Communication Effects and Processes: A Comprehensive Bibliography, 1950–1975*. Beverly Hills, Calif.: Sage Publications, Inc., 1978.

Katz, E., *Social Research on Broadcasting: Proposals for Further Development*. London: BBC, 1977.

Kraus, S., and D. Davis, *The Effects of Mass Communication on Political Behavior*. University Park: Pennsylvania State University Press, 1976.

Lemert, J. B., *Does Mass Communication Change Public Opinion After All?* Chicago: Nelson-Hall, 1981.

Lerner, D., and L. M. Nelson, eds., *Communication Research—A Half-Century Appraisal*. Honolulu: East-West Center, University Press of Hawaii, 1977.

Lesser, G. S., *Children and Television: Lessons from Sesame Street*. New York: Random House, 1974.

McAnany, E. G., J. Schnitman, and N. Janus, *Communication and Social Structure: Critical Studies in Mass Media Research*. New York: Praeger, 1981.

Milgram, S., and R. L. Shotland, *Television and Antisocial Behavior: Field Experiments*. New York: Academic Press, 1973.

Monge, P. R., and J. N. Cappella, eds., *Multivariate Techniques in Human Communication Research*. New York: Academic Press, 1980.

Moody, K., *Growing up on Television: The TV Effect: A Report to Parents*. New York: Times Books, 1980.

Pearce, W. B., and V. E. Cronen, *Communication, Action, and Meaning: The Creation of Social Realities*. New York: Praeger, 1980.

Piepe, A., M. Emerson, and J. Lannon, *Television and the Working Class*. Lexington, Mass.: Lexington Books/D.C. Heath, 1975.

Ries, A., and J. Trout, *Positioning: The Battle for Your Mind*. New York: McGraw-Hill, 1981.

Rogers, E. M., and F. F. Shoemaker, *Communication of Innovations: A Cross Cultural Approach*, 2nd ed. New York: Free Press, 1971.

Ross, R. S., and M. G. Ross, *Understanding Persuasion*. Englewood Cliffs, N.J.: Prentice-Hall, 1981.

Rubin, B., *Political Television*. Belmont, Calif.: Wadsworth, 1967.

Schramm, W., and D. F. Roberts, eds. *The Process and Effects of Mass Communication*, 2nd ed. Urbana: University of Illinois Press, 1971.

Shaw, D., and M. E. McCombs, eds. *The Emergence of American Political Issues*. St. Paul: West Publishing Co., 1977.

Sherif, C. W., M. Sherif, and R. E. Nebergall, *Attitude and Attitude Change: The Social Judgment–Involvement Approach*. Philadelphia: Saunders, 1965.

Sveriges Radio, *Uses and Gratifications Studies: Theory and Methods*. Stockholm: Sveriges Radio, 1974.

Winick, C., ed., *Deviance and Mass Media*. Beverly Hills, Calif.: Sage Publications, Inc., 1978.

Winick, M., P., and C. Winick, *The Television Experience: What Children See*. Beverly Hills, Calif.: Sage Publications, Inc., 1979.

CHAPTER

MEDIA ETHICS
AND
SOCIAL ISSUES

PREVIEW

After completing this chapter, we should be able to:

Discuss conflict of interest in the practice of journalism.

Describe some of the ethical issues which arise when journalists become "diplomats."

Define entrapment.

Be aware of the ethics involved in a reporting situation which may endanger someone's life.

State the ethical dilemmas surrounding the practice of reporters selling advertising time and space.

Identify the ethical decisions required when dealing with unnamed sources.

Talk about the practice of criticizing competitors.

Ponder the ethics of accepting free gifts.

Explain checkbook journalism.

Understand the ethics involved when cooperating with officials.

Describe some of the ethics surrounding the quest for awards.

Be aware of press codes.

Discuss censorship of the press from the time of the American Revolution to today.

Discuss the concept of media as "big brother."

Be aware of media's portrayal of women.

Be aware of media's portrayal of the elderly.

Professor Gideon Sjoberg, a sociologist at the University of Texas, suggests that "The major ethical orientation of most people in the modern world is that of system loyalty or system maintenance. Indeed, commitment to the nation-state has been the basic ethical orientation during the past century and a half of most politicians, citizens, and scholars. . . . In contradistinction to the system ethic, we need one that transcends any given social system." In this chapter we will examine a few instances in which a media professional's ethics may come face to face with this system ethic. Which ethic will blink first?

CONFLICT OF INTEREST

The term *conflict of interest* generally describes a situation in which a person becomes involved, knowing that he or she has divided loyalties. Certain politicians are often said to be guilty of this, but the same could be said of certain media professionals. The media professional who is less than careful can find a conflict of interest creeping into daily decision making which, if the issue is serious enough, can reflect on the credibility of his or her organization and even the industry. Let's discuss some conflicts of interest people in media might face. Although these examples deal primarily with journalists, they may apply with equal distinction to advertisers, public relations specialists, producers, creative personnel, management, and other people employed in mass media organizations.

Employment

Although some news directors may feel that reporters should never work for a news organization while holding another job, economic reality often forbids this ideal situation to exist. The ethical problem arises when the reporter is assigned to cover a newsworthy event at the organization which employs him or her.

Consider the reporter who has a part-time job with a local manufacturing plant. One day it is discovered that the head of the manufacturing plant has been diverting corporate funds for personal use. Since the reporter knows the inner workings of the company and has contact with many of the people who work there, the news director feels the reporter is the ideal choice to cover the story. Upon arrival at the plant, the reporter is met by some of the middle-management people who tell him if he covers the story, he doesn't need to bother reporting for work in the morning.

What decision does the reporter make? It might be his one chance for a major story. Perhaps he has been waiting to prove his ability to the editor or news director. If so, he could cover the story and take his chances on finding another job. But suppose he can't find another job. Should we then blame the editor or news director who never should have assigned the reporter to the story in the first place because of his obvious conflict of interest? Perhaps, but what if there was no one else who could have covered the story as responsibly?

Interns

Now let's consider another example, one which is repeated daily in newspapers, advertising agencies, broadcasting stations, and other media everywhere. Student interns have traditionally been an inexpensive form of help for media organizations. The internship gives the student an opportunity to gain valuable experience, and it gives the organization an opportunity to look for new talent before it commits a major investment in payroll. While working as an intern, especially as a reporter, it is not unusual for the college student to be dealing with issues affecting his or her school. In many cases the student may be the very person who has the most knowledge about the institution and the issues affecting it. But the question becomes, can the student be sufficiently removed from the issue, especially if it becomes controversial and involves highly polarized opinions, to cover it objectively?

Involvement With a News Source

Personal involvement with a news source can be another area for potential conflict of interest. This is especially true when reporters are consistently assigned to cover a certain assignment, or "beat," such as reporting the daily activities of a police department. Many reporters assigned to the police beat develop a close association with members in the police department. These contacts provide a rich resource for news stories. A police beat reporter becomes a friend, an associate, even a "pal" of a police officer. But what if the reporter's police officer friend is involved in a scandal? Can the reporter be far enough removed from the scandal story to objectively cover it? How would you react to such a story if you were a police beat reporter? How would you handle the story if your family and that of the police officer were close personal friends? What if you were in love with the police officer? Even if you did reach a point where you felt it was time to remove yourself from the story, what if you were working for a small radio station and you were the only news person employed by the station? Would you quit your job as opposed to covering the story? Would you give up your friendship or your love to cover the story? These are tough ethical questions, but ones that are easier to answer now than when you might be confronted with them in an actual situation.

Conflict With a Superior

A difficult ethical dilemma everyone may face, no matter what profession he or she may be working in, is a conflict of interest that may develop with a superior. While working as a radio news director, I was approached one morning by a supervisor who pointed out that an individual who had been arrested the night before for drunken driving was a very big advertiser on the station. With that statement, the hint had been made to "kill," or to not air the story, or at least to play it down. It was almost news time. To make matters even worse, the same individual, whose company carried his name, sponsored the newscast.

Having never been confronted with that type of situation before, I thought seriously about killing the story, at least for that single newscast, in order to have more time to think. I was still trying to decide when we came into the first commercial of the newscast, and I asked the program director for his opinion. He placed the decision back on my shoulders.

Although very concerned about the consequences, I aired the story as scheduled. Fortunately there were no consequences, and the incident was never mentioned again. Later, when I served in station management, my temptation to suggest to the news department that a story be covered one way or the other was tempered by my realization of the personal trauma that can result when faced with pressure from management.

Supporting the Status Quo

We began this chapter with a quotation by Professor Gideon Sjoberg of the University of Texas. Professor Sjoberg also warns that "large-scale bureaucracy seems to generate a secret side, and part of that secret tends to become a dark side where a great deal of manipulation takes place." He suggests that much of this manipulation is for the purpose of maintaining the bureaucracy, especially for those who hold the power. Many reporters operate within this secret domain. It is here that the big stories arise. Yet it is also here that problems can arise. While working in this secret domain and developing many of the close contacts with sources, many journalists can lose their ethical perspective. Professor Sjoberg suggests that journalists can find themselves so sucked into the system that they actually perpetuate what they are assigned to report.

Many reporters, especially new ones, are susceptible to the glamour of their profession. Some others should never be allowed near a reporting job. The daily hobnobbing with high political officials or celebrities and the immediate public acceptance by being associated with the "media" can be a heady experience. But herein lie the temptations that can subtly push even the best professionals away from personal ethics and toward the "system-specific ethic" that Professor Sjoberg warns us about.

Consider a small-town reporter. Each day the reporter talks to the same people, reports the same news, and as long as the basic facts are correct, the resulting story reflects a very narrow line of thought. Without realizing it, the reporter becomes little more than a propaganda instrument for a system which uses the press to give the public what the power brokers feel the public should hear.

JOURNALISTS AS DIPLOMATS

A graduate school history professor named Floyd Fithian, who later became a congressman, once asked me an examination question which went something like, "It's now the year 2000, and many of the great names in media have passed away only now to come before the court of St. Peter and be charged with going beyond their role as journalists to makers of history. The prosecutors in the case are President Richard Nixon, President Lyndon Johnson, President John Kennedy, and President Dwight Eisenhower. Name the people who are charged with these offenses and record the testimony of the court."

Throughout its history the press has inadvertently and perhaps sometimes intentionally become deeply involved in the course of events. The Mideast peace talks of the late 1970s and the Iranian hostage crisis of the early 1980s brought to national attention the role of journalists in international relations. In the Mideast peace talks former CBS news anchor Walter Cronkite, in a satellite interview with Egyptian President Anwar Sadat and another with Israeli Prime Minister Menachem Begin, discussed the possibility of a meeting between the two leaders. Cronkite's discussion has been construed as the diplomatic bridge which resulted in an invitation for Sadat to visit Israel.[1]

During the Iranian hostage crisis, when it was difficult for the State Department to open up communication with Iranian officials, a number of network television reporters managed to speak through interpreters to high-ranking members of the Iranian government, including the Ayatollah Khomeini. State Department officials were somewhat concerned over the role played by American journalists, and many felt Iranian demonstrations took place for the benefit of the cameras. Nevertheless, the interviews provided significant insight into the complex gaps in policies and ideologies that existed between Iran and the United States.

When we consider the traditional role of the press as that of scrutinizing government rather than playing a part in it, we begin to ask some major ethical questions. Is it inappropriate for journalists to become makers of history? Is it impossible for journalists to avoid becoming makers of history? Should the television networks be criticized for taking such an active role in diplomacy during the Mideast peace talks and the Iranian hostage crisis? Were the networks actually supporting United States' foreign policy and taking an active role in formulating that policy? If they were, should they have been?

ENTRAPMENT

What kind of ethical questions arise when entrapment becomes part of the methods used by an investigative journalist to get a story? Do truth and accuracy prevail when people are lured into unnatural choices which may result in conduct which could lead to stories of corruption, bribe taking, illicit sex, or a host of other headlines? Although media codes of ethics are quick to discourage acceptance of free tickets, free meals, or junkets, they are very shaky or nonexistent on the area of entrapment.

CBS news producer Barry Lando brought the subject to the attention of an Ohio journalism conference when he asked the question, "How many of you here tonight would like to be the subject of a hidden camera?"[2] Lando surmised that in the area of entrapment, the journalist must make his or her own internal decisions about ethics.

He cited examples of a CBS *60 Minutes* news crew committing crimes which could be classified as misdemeanors or felonies while going after a story. In one instance he pointed to the example of a reporter who obtained a checking account by using a false social security card as well as establishing credit under the name of a dead woman.[3] He cited another example of a *60 Minutes* crew purchasing pornographic film and then asked whether that would be considered entrapment. Although admitting a code of ethics would be difficult to draw up on the issue of entrapment, Lando did blame the confusion on the lack of responsible guidelines for the press. He said that reporters who are quick to attack the government for spying do not hesitate to use bugging, tapes, and spies to invade privacy for the "higher good" of being able to expose misconduct or illegal activity.[4]

Imagine that you are working for a television station and have the opportunity to report a major story about corruption. You feel the only way to obtain the story is to use hidden tapes or cameras and record the actual voices of the politicians involved in a pay-off. Would you resort to electronic bugging to get the story? Suppose there is no hint of corruption, but you decide to test the ethical standards of your local politicians anyway. You set up a fake influence-buying scheme and entice the politicians with large sums of money to participate. As a journalist, would your actions be ethical? Would you turn over to law enforcement officers the names of those politicians who succumbed to your temptations so that the evidence could be used to prosecute them?

ENDANGERING LIFE

What kind of ethical decisions become involved when the actual reporting process may endanger someone's life? Are there any general guidelines that *can* exist? Or can such problems be solved only on an individual and local basis, each situation different, each situation with new demands?

Kidnapping: Two Examples

While I was working as a radio news director, the station received a call one morning about a kidnapping. The police asked that we not release either the name of the victim or that a crime had even occurred. They felt that if the kidnapper knew the authorities and the press were involved, he or she might harm the victim. The radio stations all agreed to the request and aired nothing about the story. Later that afternoon the victim was released. The police again requested the story be held so that they might have complete freedom to apprehend the suspect. By late afternoon we were aware that the local afternoon newspaper and the local television station's 6:00 P.M. newscast would carry the details of the kidnapping regardless of any news embargo the radio stations had participated in during the day. We explained to police that we could appreciate their dilemma, but because the newspaper and the television stations were going to release the story, we would not be able to hold it past 5:00 P.M., the time of our major newscast of the day. By 6:00 P.M. the radio stations had carried the story, the evening newspaper was on the streets with all of the available details, and the television stations were airing the report. Later that evening the police apprehended the suspect in one of the local rooming houses.

The kidnapping posed a number of ethical situations, one of which was whether the media has the responsibility of withholding information if a human life is in danger. What would have happened if the kidnapper had decided to take other victims? By keeping the information secret, the public was unaware that a kidnapper was at large or even that a crime had been committed. And was the life of the victim actually in danger? Do police departments who make such requests and journalists who comply with them labor under the false assumption that a kidnapper will automatically harm a victim whenever publicity about the crime is released? Some argue that the publicity itself may be as rewarding as the ransom.

Consider another case, this one involving a New York television station which aired a report of the husband of a kidnapping victim following the instructions of the abductors. The station did withhold airing the film until after the safe release of the man's wife. But after the release, the station aired the film which showed the husband making a telephone call and later waiting for further instructions at a New Jersey fast food restaurant.[5] The station came under severe criticism for having filmed the conversation in the first place. Some of the criticism came from the FCC, which decided to look into the possibility that Section 605 of the Communications Act had been violated by the station's possible unauthorized interception of the FBI's nonbroadcast frequency. The FBI, itself, was critical, saying that when someone's life was in danger, it was not a time to "sneak around and try and get a scoop."[6] Another New York City news director suggested that the story would have been reported eventually, and therefore the scoop was unnecessary, especially since it was not a case of a "life or death need to know."[7]

Reporters as Intermediaries

There are numerous examples of reporters arriving at a scene, picking up a telephone, and actually calling someone committing a crime while the crime is in progress. More than one reporter has spoken to a fugitive while the police stand by attempting to save hostages or make a capture. Often when a police officer speaks with a criminal, he or she is trained in negotiation techniques and tactics. Few reporters have received such training. Are the questions of an untrained reporter justified when those questions could endanger lives? Daily decisions and tough decisions must be made when reporting the story may interfere with law enforcement or place the lives of individuals in danger.

SELLING TIME AND SPACE

When the owner of a Minneapolis radio station found that the station was losing money, he instructed the news department to start selling commercials. His action gained considerable publicity in the trade press, especially when it was learned that the news department was practically the entire station, since the station operated with an all-news format. When questioned about a possible conflict of interest, the owner indicated the practice was common in small markets, and that he was simply applying it to a larger market.

In the glamour of the media, we sometimes forget that, especially in small markets, reporters sometimes must double as sales personnel. An owner of a small weekly newspaper may be forced, from an economic standpoint, to act as both journalist and account executive. If the owner is fortunate enough to be able to hire a reporter, that reporter may not be able to make enough money without supplementing his or her income with commissions from advertising sales. Nevertheless, the practice is generally looked down upon by many journalists, albeit ones in major markets who have never had to face the economic reality of making a living while remaining a part of the profession.

What about the ever-present conflict that can exist when a reporter is asked to be part of the sales department? A past president of the Radio/Television News Directors Association said that the Minneapolis situation represented an "impossible conflict of interest that will destroy the credibility of radio and television news. . . . The entire credibility of the journalist depends upon the public knowledge that he is independent of all other considerations than serving the public by presenting factual information, fairly and accurately. . . . We sympathize with the economic problems of radio and television owners, but we submit that the record of radio and television stations across the country in presenting . . . accurate and impartial news while . . . maintaining economic viability is substantial."[8] Other people may be less critical. One radio station manager was quoted as saying, "If I were in this situation and had the problems, I'd say, 'Look, everybody has to get out and push, and put the station over. If anybody here thinks they are too damn important to push the station, don't let the door hit your back.'"[9]

Certainly when the economic situation permits it, keeping news department as far away from selling advertising as possible is in the best interests of everyone. If a reporter is receiving a commission from a local department store's advertising, he or she might be unable to turn down the opportunity to cover a store's grand opening, even when it might not be considered ligitimate news. Similarly if a store employee runs afoul of the law, that same reporter may find it difficult to give the story fair and equitable treatment. As long as the mass communication industry is primarily in the business of making a profit, these situations will arise.

UNNAMED SOURCES

In the early 1970s a series of disclosures about undercover political shenanigans leading to the break-in of the Democratic party headquarters in Washington, D.C., eventually brought about the resignation of President

Figure 18-1 While some campus newspapers are responsible forums of journalism, others can become the political tools of faculty, administrators, or zealous students. (Copyright, 1980, G. B. Trudeau. Reprinted with permission of Universal Press Syndicate. All rights reserved)

DOONESBURY   **by Garry Trudeau**

Richard Nixon. Watergate, as it became known, created a new wave of investigative journalism, spurred in part by the hero label tagged on the two *Washington Post* reporters who uncovered the story, and reinforced by the movie *All The President's Men*, starring Robert Redford and Dustin Hoffman. In its wake Watergate also generated a wave of irresponsible reporting in which many immature, unqualified journalists attempted to imitate those reporting techniques (Figure 18–1).

Abusing the Privilege

With the Watergate era came the frequent use of the "unnamed source" in news reports. It was almost as if some media preferred to use that term in order to leave the impression that they had a secret investigative reporting team at work, rather than mention the person responsible for providing the information. Some reporters even began to use unnamed sources as a lazy way to get information, avoiding the necessity to check documents and facts to make sure a story was accurate and probable. The result of this abuse was some sloppy investigative reporting and the publication and broadcast of untrue information.

Reconsidering the Practice

Today in retrospect, the use of the unnamed source has taken on a questionable value as the press has begun to realize the unnamed source can leave an image of questionable reporting tactics. Any journalist faced with using the unnamed source should ask some hard questions about the information he or she is receiving.

1. Is the information provided by the unnamed source critical to the story or could it be eliminated without sacrificing content or credibility?
2. Does the unnamed source have something to gain by the publication or broadcast of the story?
3. Will you be able to tell the public precisely why the individual does not want his or her name revealed? If you can't, determine whether you should be skeptical of the information.
4. Has the individual ever been used as an unnamed source before, and were the quotations correct?
5. Is the unnamed source giving you information that he or she has obtained from another party? If so, you are talking to the wrong individual.
6. What will the public think about the use of an unnamed source? Will that use detract from the story's or the news department's credibility?

Unnamed, Reliable, and Confidential Source

In addition, it is important to distinguish among an unnamed source, a reliable source, and a confidential source. A *reliable source* is always an unnamed source, but the opposite is not necessarily true. Before you use the word "reliable" in place of "unnamed," be sure the individual is actually credible. A *confidential source*, on the other hand, is usually one who is not quoted, but rather serves as a source of background information for the story.

CRITICIZING COMPETITORS

During a series of civil protests in a midwestern community, a local reporter had become so involved with the issues that he began to lose the ability to report objectively about what was taking place. He even began fabricating reports that were favorable to his cause. Other members of the press were aware of his actions but did not take issue with them publicly until the reporter was arrested one night for taking part in one of the protests. That action pushed him over the line, and the pent-up frustrations other reporters had of his unprofessional antics touched off open criticism. Two weeks later he was relieved of his responsibilities and left the community. What still to this day remains unanswered is why no member of the press had spoken out against the individual before he was arrested, even when members knew he was being dishonest. Had the press been scrutinizing similar misconduct by politicians or even doctors or lawyers, such actions could have made news.

The same ethical question is faced by other media professionals. The ad agency that criticizes another ad agency for the seemingly unethical manner of landing an account may be correct but may appear as being a poor loser. How far will you go to report other members of your profession who display obvious unethical conduct? What forces do you expect to act upon you which may affect whether you publicize such conduct?

ACCEPTING FREE GIFTS

Freebies are everywhere. Some of them can creep in almost unnoticed. To thwart their possible influence, some media organizations place a monetary limit on accepting free gifts. To others, this practice may seem hypocritical. There are those who feel that any gift, regardless of how small, should not be accepted. On the other hand, nothing more than mere politeness may be involved. While working as a journalist, I frequently interviewed a senator during small personal breakfast chats. Nothing more than coffee was ever consumed, but I can remember his legislative aide picking up the tab on occasion. At the time I never thought much about it, but in view of some recent concern over accepting freebies, there are those who would say that personal ethics should prevent even this amount of gratuity. Others would argue that the individual should determine whether he or she can remain objective after accepting a gift, be it complimentary dinner tickets or international travel.

Even campus media are not immune. I have watched students who champion the antifreebie policy and the Code of Ethics of the Society of Professional Journalists, Sigma Delta Chi and yet accept every invitation by the university president's office to have lunch with every V.I.P. brought to campus. Somehow it has not occurred to some of them that the story about the V.I.P. on campus is just as important to the university as good publicity is for a politician or a local manufacturer who wants to display a new product.

There seem to be few qualms about accepting press credentials to legitimate news events, especially among sports reporters. One sports writer commented, "I can't report the game if I'm standing outside, and there is little doubt that seats on the basketball floor within five feet of the coaches' bench would cost a premium that some organizations simply would not pay."

That comment brings up the other side to the freebie issue. All of the ethics in the world will have little effect if management refuses to support an antifreebie policy. And few managers, especially in small operations, are going to purchase the high-priced tickets that some charity or political fund-raising functions demand. Even though the event may be the biggest news item of the week in some small communities, profit-and-loss-oriented managers would tell reporters to find the first door if they demanded that the station pick up the tab for dinner tickets.

Freebies have been around as long as business has—and will continue to be. In the end, the ethics of freebies reduces to the ethics of the individual.

CHECKBOOK JOURNALISM

Checkbook journalism is commonly defined as the payment of money to a newsmaker for the privilege of quoting that newsmaker. Opinions are mixed on the ethical considerations involved with such an act. Some who have paid the price have reaped major career benefits. One of the more famous cases of checkbook journalism occurred when David Frost, a British television personality, captured a major international scoop by conducting a series of paid interviews with former President Richard Nixon. Nixon, who had not granted interviews since his resignation from office, reportedly received $1 million for the series of interviews, which lasted 28¾ hours. In an appearance at the Washington Press Club after the broadcast, Frost defended the checkbook journalism issue by noting that payment for a televised interview compensated the interviewee for the loss of editorial control he or she would have if the interview were to appear in print.

CBS may have thought deeply about the checkbook issue when it coughed up a reported $10,000 to an informant who claimed he could locate the missing body of Jimmy Hoffa, the former president of the International Brotherhood of Teamsters who disappeared mysteriously in the mid-1970s. Then CBS News President Richard Salant was quick to point out that the payment "was a standard procedure payment to a free-lance journalist, consultant, or informant for services rendered, and thus was in no way to be confused with 'checkbook journalism' or paying for hard news."[10] Salant was also interviewed on the *CBS Evening News* by one of his own correspondents and asked if he thought the payment had been a mistake or reason to review CBS's news policy after the network apparently had to forfeit the money. Salant replied, "No, I don't think it raises a question of policy. It may have been a mistake in the sense that so far it's gone off on a tangent, and the body hasn't appeared yet. It won't be a mistake if they find the body."[11] They didn't.

COOPERATING WITH OFFICIALS

Almost ten years ago the Society of Professional Journalists, Sigma Delta Chi passed a resolution which condemned the use of press cards or other credentials by any person for any purpose other than gathering information for broadcast or publication. It highlighted the delicate relationship that exists between reporters and government agencies, both of which at times may find it advantageous to cooperate with each other for mutual gain. Most journalists consider cooperating with a government, even a police department, a breach of ethics and the opposite of what a free press is designed to do—report on government, not be a part of it. Nevertheless, history is filled with cases of news media–government agency cooperation which have caused journalists and professional associations alike to condemn such activity. Such cooperation has ranged from exchanging press credentials to helping the Central Intelligence Agency.

For example, a Salt Lake City police department employee was asked to leave a news conference when he showed up under the guise of being a staff member of a fictitious "Channel 6" news organization in Utah. The imposter was discovered when he appeared at a press conference called by Iranian students at the University of Utah.[12] In another Utah incident three policemen were reported to have posed as reporters for the *Los Angeles Times*, during which time they attempted to arrest a suspect for refusing to send his children to public school.[13]

In Welch, West Virginia, an editor and publisher of a daily newspaper staunchly defended his decision to permit a state police trooper to use his paper as a cover while investigating drug traffic.[14] And in Fort Lauderdale, a Florida police officer was issued false United Press International (UPI) press credentials. UPI protested, and the police department's public information unit apologized to the wire service.[15]

The above incidents faced a barrage of criticism from various media circles. In the case of the Utah Channel 6 incident, the Radio/Television News Directors Association (RTNDA) issued a statement saying, "We believe such action seriously damaged the credibility and independence of the news media, and seriously hampered the free flow of information."[16] In the West Virginia incident one newspaper editorialized, "The prostitution of the Welch newspaper is deplorable. It is a glaring example of the newspaper that has failed itself, failed its profession and failed its readers. . . . Anytime a newspaper lets itself be used by government, it becomes an extension of that government and loses its right to report and protest abuses. . . ."[17] The executive secretary of the West Virginia Press Association questioned the practice of police posing as reporters "because of the problems legitimate reporters will face in the future in trying to gather news or maintain confidential sources of information."[18] The West Virginia University chapter of the Society of Professional Journalists, Sigma Delta Chi passed a resolution claiming the "action would make it difficult for newspersons subpoenaed before courts and grand juries to argue they should not be viewed as the right arm of law enforcement agencies."[19] Another resolution passed by the Ohio Valley–Kanawha chapter stated, "We especially deplore any active collaboration in such subterfuge by members of our own organization. . . ."[20]

Journalism offers numerous awards for which reporters, editors, and media compete to reaffirm their ability to practice their craft. On the prestigious side are the Pulitzer Prizes for print journalism and the Peabody Awards for broadcasting. Somewhere down the prestigious scale are certificates given out for almost anyone who enters a particular competition to local and regional awards where a diligent effort is made by judges to recognize and reflect quality reporting.

Awards serve various functions, depending upon the people and organizations involved. Some, which recognize achievement in a particular field of journalism such as health, business, and the law, are designed to capture publicity for that field. For reporters, awards are a recognition of achievement which can serve to boost self-confidence, impress peers and bosses, and advance a professional career. For the media, awards can impress and attract advertisers who keep the publication or station afloat.

Ethical questions arise when the pressure to win awards dictates the content of stories. Should a newspaper or station cover a story with the expressed intent of winning an award? Let's assume you work for a newspaper in a market where another newspaper competes aggressively for awards. Each year the competition publicizes its awards and sends a brochure with its accomplishments to each advertiser. Given this atmosphere, is your newspaper justified in assigning reporters to cover stories on the sole basis that the stories can be entered in the awards competition?

Such pressure for recognition even permeates the most prestigious awards. A Washington, D.C. reporter was awarded a Pulitzer Prize for her story about an eight-year-old heroin addict, but just after the award was announced, it was determined that the story had been fabricated. The reporter was subsequently stripped of the award. Although the reporter primarily shouldered the brunt of the resulting bad publicity, her superiors had to share the blame because they had permitted the story to develop without sufficiently questioning its content. Laced with unattributed statements, the story still managed to move through the Pulitzer selection process and receive the award.

The Pulitzer Prize incident raises a series of questions, not all of which neatly fit into the ethical questions surrounding awards competitions. How much responsibility can be placed upon a reporter if an atmosphere exists at a newspaper or a station which permits a fabricated story to evolve? Are the editors and the reporter's superiors equally at fault? Is there something wrong with a selection process that allows a fabricated story to receive an award? Is the pressure for awards, success, and recognition in some journalism arenas so great that it interferes with the job of being a responsible professional? If the answer to that question is "yes," should media that want to be truly ethical simply stop competing for awards?

Before leaving our discussion of some of the media's ethical dilemmas, we need to realize that even though we may never actually work in the media and face these tough decisions, such decisions affect the content of what we read and hear. The next time you hear or read an award-winning story, reflect upon the process behind it.

PRESS CODES

The press, because of its foundation in the First Amendment, has been the least controlled of any American institution of mass communication. Although certain regulations have been placed on broadcast journalism through the Communications Act of 1934, the news media have generally operated with only conscience as a guide. Unfortunately some journalists are less scrupulous than others, and in many cases this laissez-faire atmosphere has resulted in journalism of less than good taste. Yet there is an attempt by some professional organizations to encourage responsible journalism practices, more through social and professional sanctions than through concerted attempts at enforcement. Three codes among many that reflect these thoughts are the Code of Ethics of the Society of Professional Journalists, Sigma Delta Chi; the Code of Broadcast News Ethics of the Radio/Television News Directors Association (RTNDA); and the Code of Ethics of the American Society of Newspaper Editors.

The Society of Professional Journalists, Sigma Delta Chi (SPJ, SDX)

The Society's code charges journalists to exercise boldness in reporting the news but cautions them to do so responsibly. This particular code was cited frequently during the Nixon era when journalists were facing jail sentences for refusing to divulge their sources of information. The code is divided into six areas: (1) responsibility, (2) freedom of the press, (3) ethics, (4) accuracy and objectivity, (5) fair play, and (6) pledge.

Under *responsibility*, the code reminds the journalist of two forces. These are in the "mission of the mass media," which is based on the public's right to know, and the great trust that the public places in the news media. *Freedom of the press* is expressed as the "right of people in a free society." The code endorses journalists' "responsibility to discuss, question, and challenge actions and utterances" of government and institutions, both public and private. The *ethics* section is concerned with such things as journalists' refusing freebies, moonlighting, and personal life styles that might reflect negatively on the profession. News judgment, overcoming obstacles in gathering news, and protecting the confidentiality of sources are also covered. The *accuracy and objectivity* section stresses "truth" as the ultimate goal and charges journalists to distinguish between news and opinions, to recognize editorializing, to keep informed, and to label clearly their "own conclusions and interpretations." *Fair play* treats the right to reply, invasion of privacy, handling details of vice and crime, correcting errors, and accountability to the public. Compliance with the code is entirely voluntary, being signified by a *pledge* charging journalists to "censure and prevent violations of these standards."

Radio/ Television News Directors Association (RTNDA)

The *RTNDA* is composed mainly of those responsible for directing the news operation of a broadcasting station. Membership dues are based on the size of the station's news staff, and associate memberships are available to educators and other practicing broadcast news professionals. The Code of Broadcast News Ethics of RTNDA has ten articles, within which are found the major issues affecting most working broadcast journalists. Many

469

of these articles parallel those of the *SPJ, SDX*. For instance, there are similarities in the areas of rights of privacy, overcoming obstacles, keeping informed, confidentiality of sources, and censuring other professionals who violate the code. The RTNDA's unique qualities surface in such areas as broadcasting court proceedings. This section calls for journalists to "conduct themselves with dignity" when covering such proceedings, as do the NAB's Standards for Broadcasting Public Proceedings. Other articles within the RTNDA Code cover the individual's right to a fair trial, the use and abuse of news *bulletins*, and guarding against sensationalism.

American Society of Newspaper Editors

Similar to both the codes of Sigma Delta Chi and RTNDA is the Code of Ethics of the American Society of Newspaper Editors. It stresses, "A journalist who uses his power for any selfish or otherwise unworthy purpose is faithless to a high trust." Two other sections pertain to freedom of the press and the independence of the press. The latter states, "Promotion of any private interest contrary to the general welfare, for whatever reason, is not compatible with honest journalism." Editorialism is also discussed when the code warns that "editorial comment which knowingly departs from the truth does violence to the best spirit of American journalism; in the news columns it is subversive of a fundamental principle of the profession." Other concepts include the use of headlines and fair play—the opportunity for the accused to be heard.

Code Enforcement

The Achilles' heel of every journalism code is, of course, the actual ability to enforce sanctions on violaters. With protection of the press well established in law, there are few ways to force reporters to make public the "secrets," "confidential sources," and other "protected" information that may be necessary to investigate some aspect of a journalist's ethical conduct. The journalism profession is full of stories, some rumor and unfortunately some fact, of serious breaches of professional ethics despite the professional organizations' noble guidelines. Fear of retaliation, lack of concern, and desire to avoid publicity for the competition, combine to make attack or censure by one medium on another a rare occurrence.

CENSORSHIP

The issue of censorship will always be in the forefront of any discussion of mass media. The forces that act toward greater control of media content and those that act against it are present in all societies. We tend to think of censorship as something negative, but we have yet to define this phenomenon that spans all media and all types of media content.

Earlier in this text we learned how Colonial governments virtually controlled the fledgling publishing industry in early America. Today we would have little difficulty in defining such control as a form of censorship. If an eighteenth-century newspaper wanted to publish articles critical of the government, the owner would usually find himself out of work; his government subsidy would be cut off, his presses might be confiscated, and he might even be deported to England. In retrospect we can see that it took the American Revolution to free the press from its shackles. Yet if there had been no government control over the press during its formative years, would the republic have survived and prospered as much as it did? Did our republic need a period of time simply to gain a foundation and population, even if it was the recipient of a daily diet of censored news? If the American Revolution had occurred earlier, would the country have had the solidarity to conquer suppression? These rhetorical questions could be debated for hours. Yet when India's Prime Minister Indira Gandhi censored the press during nationwide upheavals in 1975, many gasped in amazement at how such a dictatorial attitude could be displayed. An ambassador to India appearing on a television news program was not nearly as taken back by the action, commenting that in the early stages of a democracy when certain political forces could actually harm it, censorship was necessary.

During the War Between the States, we again saw the press shackled, this time by generals who were unhappy with the newspaper coverage they were receiving. In other wars in which Americans took part, notably World War II, the press voluntarily complied with government orders to withhold news from the public. In such cases are the members of the press guilty of censorship just as much or more than the officials who order the news embargo? Are such embargoes ever justified? Would you comply with such an embargo if you were a reporter covering the battlefront?

We have already learned about shield laws that protect the confidentiality of news sources and freedom of information laws that guarantee the press and public access to public records. What about laws against censorship? What about the reporter who is subpoenaed before a grand jury to identify his or her source of information for a story? Can a zealous prosecutor use this same threat of subpoena to wrest this information from a reporter before the journalist is even called before the grand jury? Having been through this experience, will the reporter tend in the future to avoid the hassle represented by such a threat by shunning controversial stories? Is the prosecutor then, with this threat of subpoena, guilty of news censorship? Is the judge who issues a gag order preventing or trying to prevent pretrial publicity guilty of censorship?

The molders of our Constitution could not have foreseen the advent of electronic media. When these media did make their impact felt, government found itself as an umpire in assigning portions of the electromagnetic spectrum to specific radio and television stations. The FCC and its regulatory actions came about by necessity. When sex-talk shows scintillated the airwaves, the FCC let explicit on-air discussion of sexual activities go only so far. It then decreed that continuing such programming could provoke action against the licensee.

In 1978 the Supreme Court upheld the FCC's decision to take action against a New York radio station that broadcast comedian George Carlin's album about seven words you cannot say on television. Court cases and rulings such as the Fairness Doctrine have now established a legal precedent for determining the content of broadcast programming, yet there has been little solid legal ground on which to justify similar controls in the print media. Consider the broadcast manager who operates a station in a large city where there are ample opportunities for the public to obtain diversified programming. The FCC can admonish the manager that he or she has certain programming guidelines to follow. But, wait a moment—is this government control any different from the control placed on the pre-Revolutionary press? Are the actions of the FCC a form of censorship?

What about the small newspaper that receives a sizable share of its advertising from a large business in the community? Can the threat of withdrawing that advertising make an editor think twice about giving the big business unfavorable publicity? Is this form of economic censorship any different from what the early Colonial printer faced when he printed news unfavorable to the politicians subsidizing his enterprise?

What about the student press? At many colleges and universities the campus newspaper as well as the campus radio and television station receive subsidies from the parent institution. What happens when these media grow critical of the college or university administration? The loss of such subsidies, especially when the broadcast media are noncommercial and prohibited by law from selling commercials to raise money, can become instantly crippling.

Other censorship issues focus on the internal operations of mass media. Take a labor dispute, for example. Perhaps the labor union strikes after newspaper management refuses to consider a union-proposed wage package. As negotiations progress, it is clear that nonunion labor will be called in to run the presses. On the day before the strike the presses are "accidentally" damaged beyond immediate repair and cannot operate. Is this action a form of censorship? Is it a means of stopping the free flow of information to the public? Does censorship exist when the purpose of an action is not directly to inhibit the free flow of information but to protect workers' rights?

None of these answers is easy. Remember, censorship can be obvious. It can be the court order that keeps a newspaper story from being published. It can be the network executive's decision to scrap an evening television show that the executive views as too sexually explicit for a home viewing audience. Yet even these rather obvious forms of censorship can be seen as decisions in the public interest, actions that protect other constitutionally guaranteed freedoms. In this "in-between" area lie many of the cases involving censorship. Continued discussion of individual situations as well as a reasonable definition of the issues are necessary to make sure that decision makers do not stray too far in either restricting our freedoms or ruining our social order.

MEDIA AS "BIG BROTHER"

Sitting in your room, you reach over to switch the channel on the television set from the instructional television program you have been watching as a class assignment. You feel that you know the material being shown in the program and are ready to be tested on it in class. As you turn the dial to another channel, a warning light flashes on a master control console in the basement of a building at the other end of the campus. There, a lab assistant quickly traces the source of the alarm light to your room and, in a special notebook, records a check next to your name. It is not the first time you have changed channels in the middle of a televised course assignment. At the end of the semester you receive a lower grade than the one you expected. In a consultation with the instructor, you are told you did not watch the assigned programs and made fun of the course to friends who would stop by your room. That is why your grade was lowered. You discover that a two-way interactive cable system was hooked to your television set which made it possible for the master control to monitor what channels you watched and also to listen in to conversations in your room. You are shocked and file a lawsuit claiming that your privacy has been invaded.

Our example brings to light some of the concerns that recent technological capabilities have placed in the minds of the public. Many people feel we are no longer "secure" in our homes as guaranteed by the Fourth Amendment to the Constitution. We have become the watched instead of the watchers, the invaded instead of the invaders. The thought of an unseen, unknown, ever-present "big brother" looms over us as we become pawns to a technological society. Although the example in the preceding paragraph was fictitious, it is well within the confines of technology at this very moment. We are increasingly faced with policy decisions that affect our rights to privacy and our ability to maintain confidential such items as our medical records, financial statements, and educational transcripts.

Among the media under fire in this issue, cable television perhaps more than any other has captured the limelight, mostly because of its two-way operability. The hardware already exists to monitor when television sets are on or off and to what channel a set is tuned. Hooked to central computers these systems can be used for opinion polling and similar data-gathering exercises. Obviously one of the first concerns of the public is how to control such a system. The federal government, the logical governing body, has in recent years discredited itself with news of snooping into citizens' private affairs and violating the same safeguards that it has been charged with protecting. Reports from Washington reveal that the CIA, in the name of national security, has actively participated in opening mail—approximately a quarter-million letters—and the National Security Agency (NSA) has even monitored messages sent via overseas telephone and cable in attempts to find people suspected of being involved in political dissent. Computers at NSA were programmed to activate on such key words as "assassination" and to identify the sender and receiver of such messages. Certain communication companies have been charged with routinely turning some messages sent through company facilities over to government officials. Such massive surveillance measures create a gloomy picture for those who feel that technology has already invaded our privacy and shows no signs of retreating.

MEDIA'S PORTRAYAL OF WOMEN

The women's rights movement has been responsible for much more than merely identifying women as a target audience. It has produced a groundswell of attention on how the media portray women. Public interest groups have been particularly vocal, and sometimes very effective in getting the attention of media decision makers.

The major attention over the portrayal of women in mass media has tended to concentrate on television, most obviously because of the dominance of the medium but also because other media, such as specialty magazines, do treat women as competent professionals, since this is the target audience the magazine reaches.

Women in Television

Although any study can be criticized on methodological grounds, research has shown some definite trends in television's projection of women. Professors Alice E. Courtney and Thomas W. Whipple of York University in Toronto, Canada, summarized four research projects investigating the image of women in television commercials.[21] One of the four studies was done in Canada, the others in the United States. Results were fairly consistent. The first of these applied to the *appearance* of males and females in television commercials. Results showed that "men were overwhelmingly present as voice-overs, the announcing or authority figures employed . . ." in television commercials. A positive point was found in the proportion of males and females as product representatives in television commercials; three studies investigated this concept and found a fairly equal balance between males and females. Three research studies investigated occupational data. Courtney and Whipple's survey showed that females were "over-represented in family/home occupations while males dominate the media/celebrity and business/sales/management occupations. Furthermore, women are still seen in a more limited variety of occupational roles than they actually perform." Courtney and Whipple did state, though, that this imbalance seems to be changing. Researchers William J. O'Donnell and Karen J. O'Donnell examined the roles of men and women in prime-time television commercials.[22] Their research concluded that an equal number of men and women appeared as visible product representatives, but women were more likely to represent domestic products. Men were more likely to represent nondomestic products and women were three times as likely as men to appear as product representatives in a home setting. Men were almost three times as likely to appear in settings outside the home. They concluded, "The picture presented by television commercials is unchanged—the home is the woman's domain."

Researchers George Gerbner, Larry Gross, Nancy Signorielli, and Michael Morgan examined the images of prime-time television characters and found that "women actually outnumber men among characters in their early twenties (Figure 18–2), when their function as romantic partners is supposed to peak, but then their numbers fall to 4 or 5 times below the number of men as their usefullness in the world of television declines."[23] Their research also showed that "the age distribution of females, compared to that of males, favors young girls and women under 35. Men are mostly concentrated, with almost a third of their total numbers, in the 35 to 44-age bracket. The character population is structured to provide a relative abundance of younger women for older men, but no such abundance of younger men for older women."[24]

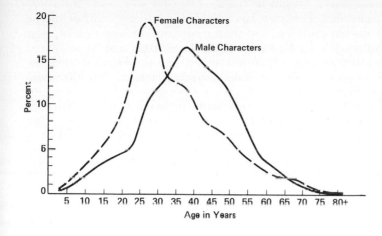

Figure 18-2 Percentages of all prime-time TV characters by chronological age and gender. (Source for Figures 18-2 through 18-6: G. Gerbner, L. Gross, N. Signorelli, and M. Morgan, "Aging with Television: Images on Television Drama and Conceptions of Social Reality," *Journal of Communication* (Winter, 1980, p. 40)

Further analysis showed that "women on television 'age' faster than men. As women age, they are cast for roles (Figure 18–3) that decrease their romantic possibilities. . . ."[25] When social age (young adult, settled adult, and older person) are compared with chronological age, the study showed that "as early as the teen years, the percentage of female major characters (38 percent) assigned to the older social and dramatic category of young adults is greater than the percentage of males of the same age (30 percent) assigned to such roles. In their twenties, only 26 percent of the men but 33 percent of the women are cast as settled adults (the rest, of course, young adults). Among characters from 55 to 64, only 22 percent of the men but 33 percent of the women are cast as old characters. Among characters 65 and over, 28 percent of the men still play settled adult roles and 72 percent are cast as old, but 90 percent of women of the same chronological age are cast as old."[26]

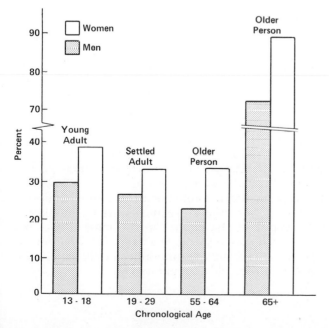

Figure 18-3 Percentages of major prime-time TV characters cast in social age categories by their chronological age and gender.

**Women
in the Print
Media**

Despite the publicity that television has received in this area, other media have also come under criticism for their portrayal of females. At the University of Illinois, Cheris Kramer directed research that investigated the stereotypes of women's speech found in cartoons published in the *New Yorker, Playboy, Cosmopolitan*, and the *Ladies' Home Journal*.[27] Students who analyzed the speech of women in the cartoon captions found it to be "ineffective and restricted." It could not "deal forthrightly with a number of topics, such as finance and politics. . . ." Kramer went on to report that students "in writing about how they determined the sex of the speaker of the captions characterized the stereotyped women's speech as being stupid, naive, gossipy, emotional, passive, confused, concerned, wordy, and insipid."

**Ms., Miss,
or Mrs.**

Even journalism has had many problems in accurately reflecting the new title of "Ms." when covering a story. One editor of a major paper summed up the use of Ms. by saying that it was mostly common sense. If you were aware that a person did not like the title Ms., then you did not use it. If the person was a senior citizen, then usually the term Miss or Mrs. was more appropriate. Many women in the news found themselves referred to by their last names on second reference just as their male counterparts were. A resolution passed by the 7000-member Women in Communication called on the wire services to "eliminate the use of courtesy or social titles for newsmakers who happen to be female or extend such usage to newsmakers who happen to be male, and . . . to adopt the practice of identifying all newsmakers by gender and marital status directly and only when pertinent to the story. . . ."

How media will portray women in the future will be determined by how many changes media planners make on their own, how much pressure is placed on them by women and men, and what economic indicators suggest about the profit or loss of changing portrayals. Although economic indicators may seem like a poor excuse for discouraging changes, it is indeed a powerful motivation and one to be reckoned with, especially when dealing with media decision makers.

MEDIA AND THE ELDERLY

Only in recent years has there been a serious and detailed study of the relationship of the elderly to mass media. The fruits of those labors, both in scholarly circles and within media organizations, have finally recognized the traditional stereotype of the elderly as just that. As a group, the elderly are not necessarily a depressed, socially isolated burden of society. The media, however, have not paid serious attention to this group of people; one reason being simply that they did not represent the affluent middle-aged consumers of society and were therefore neglected by media for economic reasons. The portrayal of the elderly in the mass media has been characterized by either such spoofs as the *Over The Hill Gang* on the late-night television movie or public service announcements asking for "young" volunteers to work with the "old" people in society.

The research by Gerbner and his colleagues just cited also examined the images of the elderly. They found that "as males age, proportionately more are portrayed as 'bad' (Figure 18–4). For females, proportionately more girls are portrayed as 'bad' than are young or middle-aged women. More older women, though, are portrayed as 'bad.' The most obvious and important difference is that proportionately fewer older characters are 'good,' while the proportion of 'bad' older characters (especially men) is greater than in the younger age groups."[28]

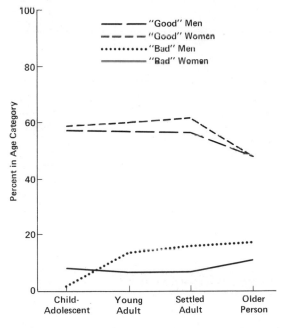

Figure 18-4 Percentages of "good" and "bad" major prime-time TV characters in social age categories by gender.

Their research went on to point out, "The percent of successful men increases with age, but as women age, the percent who are successful see-saws and then drops to 16 percent (Figure 18–5). In fact, more older women are unsuccessful than are successful."[29]

In addition, their research showed that "the elderly, especially older men, are less likely to portray serious roles (Figure 18–6) than are characters of younger age, and older men are much more likely than younger men to be cast in a comic role."[30]

There has also been an effort to call attention to the plight and "portrayed plight" of the elderly, especially in radio and television fare. One organization that actively supports fair treatment of the elderly in media is the Gray Panthers. They appeared before the Television Code Review Board of the National Association of Broadcasters to lobby for a change in the NAB Television Code that would alert broadcasters to be sensitive to portrayal of the aged. Whereas the code had previously alerted the broadcasters to material dealing with sex, race, creed, religion, or ethnic background, the word *age* has now been added. The board itself said the inclusion was directed not only toward the elderly but to all ages.

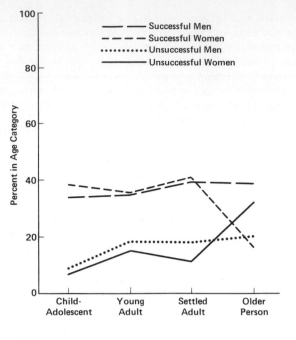

Figure 18-5 Percentages of successful and unsuccessful major prime-time TV characters in social age categories by gender.

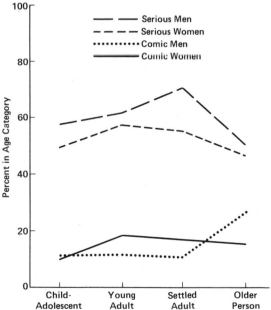

Figure 18-6 Percentages of comic and serious prime-time TV characters in social age categories by gender.

Special Features and Functional Uses

Scholarly research has made a systematic investigation of the ways in which the elderly use media. Many newspapers are now beginning to carry special syndicated features as well as local news and special sections devoted to the elderly. The content of these publications varies greatly, but most have common themes of activities for the elderly and programs

478

in which the elderly are participating. There also are special consumer tips for the elderly, such as advice on money management and nutrition as well as medical information. More publications are now directed exclusively toward the elderly, such as the magazine *Retirement Living*. Many are official journals of organizations whose membership mainly consists of the elderly. Such publications also provide an avenue for advertisers to reach this target audience at what is usually a more efficient cost per thousand than through other media.

There are also many functional uses of media for the elderly. For instance, soap operas permit the elderly to identify with characters with whom, because of their own life style, they have little real contact. Such identity can help reduce the feeling of isolation that often occurs when one lives alone.

The real groundwork for a beneficial relationship between the elderly and the media will be laid when media content reflects the true characteristics of this audience and portrays them realistically rather than stereotypically. Untapped frontiers are available for cable television to "involve" the elderly with media. Such factors as a special broadcast seminar permitting two-way interaction among shut-ins can help alleviate the loneliness that some elderly persons face and can actually stimulate a "neighborly" environment for them, thus creating new and vital interpersonal relationships.

SUMMARY

Chapter 18 looked at the ethics and social issues confronting mass media. On the subject of media ethics we saw how questionable actions occurred within both the print and broadcast media. We also saw that within any single medium lies the potential for responsible professional and ethical practices or a blatant violation of those principles. Discussed were a number of ethical problems faced by working media professionals. Among them are conflict of interest, journalists as diplomats, entrapment, endangering life, selling time, unnamed sources, criticizing competitors, accepting free gifts, checkbook journalism, cooperating with officials, and the quest for awards.

Censorship of the media is an age-old philosophical issue. Procensorship arguments champion the need to protect social order, whereas anticensorship arguments argue the necessity for the free flow of information in a democracy. Media as big brother is another issue constantly facing us. Although this fear has been particularly applicable to two-way television, other types of technology, such as computers, are also a perceived threat to many people. Policy making on such issues often comes to a stalemate when the need for government control is pitted against the necessity to prevent abuse of that control.

Content of the media has also become an important social issue. For example, women and the elderly are two groups that have been portrayed as possessing negative qualities which are not accurate or reflective of women or the elderly in society. Although these images are changing, there needs to be considerable improvement.

BABB, L. L., ed., *Of the Press, by the Press, for the Press, and Others Too. . . .* New York: Houghton Mifflin Company, 1976.

BARBER, J. D., *The Pulse of Politics: Electing Presidents in the Media Age.* New York: W. W. Norton & Co., Inc., 1980.

BROWN, L., *The Reluctant Reformation.* New York: D. McKay, 1974.

FRIEDMAN, L. J., *Sex Role Stereotyping in the Mass Media: An Annotated Bibliography.* New York: Garland Publishing, 1977.

GALNOOR, I., ed., *Government Secrecy in Democracies.* New York: Harper & Row, Pub., 1977.

GRABER, D. A., *Mass Media and American Politics.* Washington, D.C.: Congressional Quarterly Press, 1980.

GREWE-PARTSCH, M., AND G. J. ROBINSON, eds., *Women, Communication, and Careers.* New York: K. G. Saur, 1980.

HERZ, M. F., assisted by L. RIDER, *The Prestige Press and the Christmas Bombing, 1972: Images and Reality in Vietnam.* Washington, D.C.: Ethics and Public Policy Center, 1980.

HOCKMAN, S., AND S. WONG, *Satellite Spies: The Frightening Impact of a New Technology.* Indianapolis: Bobbs-Merrill, 1976.

HULTENG, J. L., *The Messenger's Motives: Ethical Problems of the News Media.* Englewood Cliffs, N.J.: Prentice-Hall, 1976.

JOAN, P., AND A. CHESMAN, *Guide to Women's Publishing.* Paradise, Calif.: Dustbooks, 1978.

LAUDON, K. C., *Communication Technology and Democratic Participation.* New York: Praeger Special Studies, 1977.

LEE, C. C., *Media Imperialism Reconsidered.* Beverly Hills, Calif.: Sage Publications, Inc., 1980.

MERRILL, J. C., AND R. D. BARNEY, eds. *Ethics and The Press.* New York: Hastings House, 1975.

MILLER, C., AND K. SWIFT, *The Handbook of Nonsexist Writing for Writers, Editors, and Speakers.* New York: Lippincott & Crowell, 1980.

PATTERSON, T. E., *The Mass Media Election: How Americans Choose Their President.* New York: Praeger, 1980.

PHELAN, J. M., *Disenchantment: Meaning and Morality in the Media.* New York: Hastings House, 1980.

ROSHCO, B., *Newsmaking.* Chicago: University of Chicago Press, 1975.

RUBIN, B., ed., *Small Voices and Great Trumpets: Minorities and the Media.* New York: Praeger, 1980.

THAYER, L., ed., *Ethics, Morality and the Media: Reflections on American Culture.* New York: Hastings House, 1980.

WILLIAMS, F.R.L., AND F. FROST, *Children, Television, and Sex-Role Stereotyping.* New York: Praeger, 1981.

GLOSSARY
OF
MEDIA TERMS

A   **AAAA**   American Association of Advertising Agencies.
Advocacy advertising   advertising championing preventive action against conditions affecting the public welfare.
AEJ   Association for Education in Journalism.
Affiliate   station that airs network programming is said to be an "affiliate" of that network.
AM   amplitude modulation.
Annual billings   money billed advertisers for commercials carried in a medium over a one-year period.
ANPA   American Newspaper Publishers Association.
ASCAP   American Society of Composers, Authors, and Publishers.
Audio actuality   the recording of the "actual sounds" in the news for incorporation into radio newscasts.
Audio feeds   stories, live or recorded, distributed by wire services to subscribers.
Authoritarian   characterized by media that are either "private or public" and "are chiefly instruments for effecting government policy, though not necessarily government owned."
AWRT   American Women in Radio and Television.

B   **BEA**   Broadcast Education Association.
Beam Separation   separates the transmission impulses of a satellite increasing its information capacity.
Billboard   (1) a wire service feed listing all the prerecorded stories in the wire service's current audio file; (2) a major publication of the recording industry; (3) a slang term for outdoor advertising bulletin.

BMI Broadcast Music Incorporated.

Bulletin (1) important news usually disseminated as an interruption in normal broadcast programming; (2) wire service (audio or video) feed to subscribers.

Bullet theory theory that suggests the mass audience is an unidentifiable group of people affected by messages received from the mass media and independent of an interpersonal influence. For the most part, replaced by the two-step flow theory, taking into consideration the role of interpersonal communication in the dissemination and influence of media messages.

Business magazine category of magazines targeted to readers in business and industry. Subcategories include such areas as professional and trade magazines.

C

CATV community antenna television, or cable TV.

Channel capacity amount of information that a channel of communication can hold. The number of words a wire service can transmit during a given time period.

Character generator computer-based storage of letters and numbers which can be typed electronically onto a television screen to provide textual information.

Charts another term for record charts where songs are listed in order of popularity.

Clearance ratio the proportion of affiliate stations that clear a network for airing.

Coaxial cable heavy cable consisting of an inner wire core surrounded by a layer of plastic, metal-webbed insulation, and a third layer of plastic.

Consumer magazines category of magazines reaching a more general mass audience and not specifically targeted to one of the other magazine subcategories such as business, farm, and religious magazines.

Contour the geographic area covered by a broadcast station's signal.

Co-ops also called *informal networks*, (1) broadcast news networks created by a group of radio or TV news personnel; (2) trade-out advertising agreements between advertisers and the individual advertising outlet.

Corrective advertising advertising that attempts to correct previous false or misleading advertising.

Counter advertising advertising directed against a product or service.

CPB Corporation for Public Broadcasting.

D

Demographics data on such things as age, sex, education level, income, and ethnic background.

Demo session a preliminary recording session.

Diary method of broadcast rating measurement in which viewers or listeners keep a record of the programs and stations they tune in at periodic intervals.

Directional stations radio stations, primarily in the AM band, that utilize directional antennas to keep their signals from interfering with those of other stations.

Direct-wave propagation radio wave pattern in which signals travel through direct line-of-sight transmission.

Distribution system term used to describe the system of cables that distributes programming to subscribers.

Document distribution sending documents via data transmission.

Drop that section of a cable that brings the signal from the trunk or subtrunk directly into a subscriber's home receiver.

E

Electromagnetic spectrum an atmospheric yardstick used to measure varying levels of electromagnetic energy, called frequency.

Electromagnetic waves electrical impulses traveling through space at the speed of light. Used to transmit radio and television signals.

Electrostatic transmission   a system used to transmit wire service pictures. Subscribers receive glossy prints on dry paper ready for printing, thereby eliminating the need for the subscriber to develop the photo himself or herself.

ETV   television programming designed for educational purposes.

F

Farm magazine   category of magazines targeted to readers interested in farming. Subcategories include state and vocational magazines.

Feedback   reactions of a receiver to a message from a sender.

Fiber optics   glass fibers which transmit information via light waves.

FM   frequency modulation.

Freebies   ranging from excursions to foreign countries to tickets to a church supper, these complimentary offerings are designed to entice journalists to cover a story.

Freedom of information law   Law permitting access to government documents and meetings by the press and the public.

Frequency   (1) broadcast rating term to indicate how often a viewer has tuned to a given station (2) position on the electromagnetic spectrum.

G

Gatekeeper   any individual directly involved in the relay or transfer of information from one individual to another through the use of a mass medium.

Gatekeeper chain   chain of gatekeepers where little interaction can take place and ample opportunities for distortion exist.

Gatekeeper group   a group of gatekeepers among whom there is the opportunity for interaction to take place.

Gazetta   the Italian coin used as an admission price to hear a reader announce the day's news events.

Geostationary   or *synchronous*, an orbiting satellite that travels at the same speed in proportion to the earth's rotation and thus appears to remain stationary over one point of the earth.

GH2   Gigahertz. One billion hertz or one billion cycles per second.

H

Head end   the human and hardware combination responsible for originating, controlling, and processing signals over the cable system.

Hertz   last name of Heinrich Rudolph Hertz commonly used as abbreviation for "cycles per second" in referring to electromagnetic waves.

Home terminal   receiving set for cable TV transmissions that can be either one-way or two-way.

Horizontal publication   publication directed at a certain managerial level but cutting across several different industries.

Households using television (HUT)   a term used in broadcast ratings to describe every household using television.

House organ   a direct-mail piece in the form of a newsletter or company magazine that is sent to all members of a certain organization.

Hypodermic theory   See "bullet theory."

I

ICA   International Communication Association.

Image advertising   advertising dealing with issues confronting a particular company or industry. Usually designed to place the sponsor in a favorable light.

Impressions   the number of times a person is reached by an advertisement.

Industrial magazines   subcategory of business magazines. See "business magazines."

Informal networks   broadcast news networks created by a professional group of radio or TV news personnel. These networks are also called co-ops.

In-house agencies   advertising agencies operating within a company solely to promote its products.

Institutional magazines a type of business publication directed toward a specific institution.

In-the-can films movies that have already been seen in movie theaters but whose income is assured through re-releases and release to television.

ITV instructional television, programming specifically designed for direct or supplemental teaching.

J

Junkets excursions for journalists, compliments of someone seeking news coverage of an event.

K

KHz Kilohertz. 1000 hertz or 1000 cycles per second.

Kicker Closing story of a newscast, often a humorous anecdote.

Kinetoscope forerunner of the motion picture developed by Thomas Edison, it was a crude device with a peephole through which a viewer could see pictures move.

L

Libertarian describes a press privately owned and providing a check on government in addition to meeting other needs of society.

Logo a symbol, usually simple in design, which becomes the visual identity of a company or product.

M

Market research research, usually conducted by advertising agencies, into the potential market for products.

Mass communication process by which messages are communicated by a mass medium to a large number of people.

Master control console heart of a television control room operation through which both the audio and video images are fed, joined together, and improved, perhaps through special effects for the "on-air" image.

Master record the master session is recorded on this record, from which additional records are pressed.

Master session the final recording session in which a song is put onto tape. Costing many thousands of dollars, this uses full orchestration, a major control console, and a recording engineer.

Media credibility the believability of a medium in which a message appears. For example, one particular newspaper might be considered more believable than another newspaper.

Meter method a broadcast ratings measurement in which a monitoring device installed on TV sets is connected to a central computer, which then records channel selection at different times of the day.

MHz Megahertz. One million hertz or one million cycles per second.

Microwave a very short wave frequency located above the area on the electro-magnetic spectrum where standard broadcast transmission takes place.

Modem electronic coupler connecting a computer and telephone permitting access to other computers and data bases.

MPA Magazine Publishers' Association.

MPAA Motion Picture Association of America.

Municipal advertising advertising which stresses the favorable attributes of a municipality. Used many times to try and attract business to an area.

N

News diffusion the process by which news is diffused to the receiving public.

News hole available space or time for a news story to appear or be aired based on the news value of competing stories and the space or time taken up by competing stories.

News value the value or importance of an event or the potential impact of an event in relation to other events or potential news stories.

Noise something that interferes with the communication process.

Ombudsman personnel who accept feedback from readers on any issue, from suggestions to complaints.

Opinion leaders people who influence thinking on a particular subject(s) because their opinions are respected.

Pay cable a system in which cable subscribers pay an additional amount beyond the standard monthly rental fee in order to receive special programming.

PBS Public Broadcasting Service.

Personalized book a "gift" book where the actual name of the person receiving the book is interwoven into the story through quick printing by computer. Personalized books are frequently directed toward children.

Picture wire wire services through which photo transmission takes place.

Pilots sample broadcasting programs produced either by networks or production companies for possible programming adoption.

Pirated records and tapes illegally recorded music sold in violation of copyright and contractual agreements with artists.

Playlists form of feedback for the recording industry in which individual radio stations list the songs popular in their listening area for a given time period.

Production companies commonly called production houses, these businesses produce broadcasting programs for adoption either by networks or by individual stations via syndication.

Product research research, usually instigated by advertising agencies, into a company and its product.

Professional magazines a type of business publication directed at readers in a specific profession, such as law.

Projection an estimate of the characteristics of a total universe based on a sample of that universe.

Psychographics study of the psychological characteristics of the mass audience.

Public broadcasting the operation of the various noncommercial radio and television stations in the United States.

Public service advertising advertising supporting non-profit causes and organizations and provided free as a service to the public by the print or broadcast media where the ads appear.

Random sample a selection in which every item in a universe has an equal chance of being chosen.

Rating a percentage of the total number of households or persons tuned to a station or program during a certain time period.

Reader profiles research surveys designed to ascertain both the demographic and the psychographic characteristics of specialized audiences.

Reader service card a device that gives magazine readers an opportunity to request additional literature and information about an advertiser's products by circling a corresponding number on a reply card.

Readership survey detailed analysis of a newspaper's audience.

Regional networks a system that provides broadcast programming and information to specific geographic regions of the country.

Relay satellite Echo I became the first artificial device capable of bouncing messages back to earth.

Religious category of magazines targeted to readers with an interest in religion. Denominational magazines fall into this category.

Repeater satellite the United States' Courier 1-B became the first of a series of satellites that could both receive and retransmit signals back to earth.

Research service businesses that specialize in providing research on current topics for subscribers, primarily newspapers and broadcast executives.

RTNDA Radio Television News Directors Association.

Sales networks a group of broadcasting stations linked together by a financial agreement to benefit all member stations by offering advertisers a joint rate.

Sampling the process of examining a small portion of something to estimate what the larger portion is like.

Saturation the percentage of the total number of households that subscribe to a given medium.

SCA Speech Communication Association.

Seditious libel criminal libel against the government.

Semantic noise interference with the communication process because of a misunderstanding caused by a cliché or slang.

Share a percentage of households *using* television or people *listening* to radio who are tuned to a *particular* station or program during a certain time period. A station's "share" is its percentage of households using television or people listening to radio. Not to be confused with "rating."

Shield Law law protecting the confidentiality of reporter's sources.

SNAP Society of National Association Publications.

Social responsibility theory espousing privately owned media "unless the government has to take over to ensure public service."

Social Responsibility Advertising ads sponsored by organizations or companies admonishing us to act responsibly when consuming products or participating in activities. Responsibility in drinking, safe driving, and similar ads fall under this type of advertising.

Source credibility the believability of a sender of communication.

Soviet-Communist theory system of state-owned media functioning as a propaganda instrument of the government.

SPJ, SDX Society of Professional Journalists, Sigma Delta Chi.

Split a given news report compiled by a wire service.

Standard advertising ads paid for by the company or organization that has products to sell or services to render.

Station program cooperative (SPC) concept in public broadcasting that utilizes direct feedback in the form of financial commitment from affiliate stations to determine which programs will compose about one-third of the programming distributed by PBS.

Station representative person or firm representing a number of different radio and television stations and selling time on those stations to advertisers. See also, "time broker."

Subgroups the "mass within a mass" on which the concept of the mass audience is based.

Subtrunk secondary cables branching out from the main trunk in a cable TV system to carry the signal to outlying areas.

Synchronous or *geostationary*, a satellite that travels at the same speed in proportion to the earth's rotation and thus appears to remain stationary over one point of the earth.

Syndicated programming programming distributed directly to stations instead of through network distribution channels. The group of stations airing the programs sometimes are collectively called a "network."

Syndicates companies whose business it is to promote and sell comics, columns, and other special features to newspapers.

T

Target audience any group of persons who have a common bond, such as shared demographic and/or psychographic characteristics.

Teleconferencing communication between individuals or groups using two-way video and audio systems.

Teletext One-way over-the-air transmission system using the vertical blanking interval of television to send textual information.

Television household a broadcast rating term used to describe any home with a television set, as distinguished from a household using television.

Tie-ins term used to describe a marketing strategy, frequently used in book publishing, where different advertising media "tie in" or "tie together" a common message about a product. An example would be television commercials, floor displays, and billboards promoting a book.

Time broker person or company that sells large blocks of time to advertisers. See also, "station representative."

Trade magazines subcategory of business magazines. See "business magazines."

Trade-out an exchange of merchandise for a service; for example, in advertising, a merchant will trade the use of a product for an equivalent amount of advertising in print or broadcast media.

Translators television transmitting antennas, usually located on high natural terrain.

Trunk main line of a cable system

Two-step flow process by which information disseminated by mass media is (1) received by a direct audience and then (2) relayed to other persons second-hand.

U

Universe the whole from which a sample is chosen; in broadcast ratings, this can be the sample area, metro area, or rating area.

V

Value structures a normative, conceptual standard of the desirable that predispositionally influences individuals in choosing among personally perceived alternatives of behavior.

VDT visual display terminals. Data from electronic keyboards and computers appear on a device similar to a television screen.

Vertical advertising publication reaching different levels of a specific business or profession.

Vertical publications a category of business publications designed to reach people at all levels within a given profession.

Videotape tape through which visual images are "magnetically" recorded.

Videotex Generic term for two-way transmission systems, primarily of graphic and textual information. The system's two way capacity permits the consumer to perform such tasks as shopping and banking using the system.

Viewdata A type of videotex system.

NOTES

CHAPTER 1

[1] Richard Maisel, "The Decline of Mass Media," *Public Opinion Quarterly*, 37 (Summer 1973), 159–70.

CHAPTER 2

[1] Eric W. Allen, "International Origins of the Newspaper: The Establishment of Periodicity in Print," *Journalism Quarterly*, 7 (December 1930), 309–19.

[2] See: Jon G. Udell, *Economic Trends in the Daily Newspaper Business, 1946 to 1970*. (Madison, Wisconsin: Bureau of Business Research and Service, 1970), p. 9. See also: *Facts about Newspapers 1978*, American Newspaper Publishers Association; Jon G. Udell, *Future Newsprint Demand 1970–1980* (Madison, Wisconsin: Bureau of Business Research and Service, 1971).

[3] Jon G. Udell, *The U.S. Economy and Newspaper Growth: 1963–1973 and the Future Outlook*, ANPA Newsprint and Traffic Bulletin, no. 31, October 24, 1974.

[4] Gerald L. Grotta, "Prosperous Newspaper Industry May be Heading for Decline," *Journalism Quarterly*, 51 (Autumn 1974) 498–502.

CHAPTER 3

[1] Frank Luther Mott, *A History of American Magazines 1965–1885*, vol. 3 (Cambridge, Mass.: Harvard University Press, 1938), p. 5.

[2] Theodore Peterson, *Magazines in the Twentieth Century* (Urbana: University of Illinois Press, 1964), p. 23.

[3] Ibid., p. 23.

CHAPTER 4

[1] Two publications contributed significantly to the discussion of book publishing in colonial America: *The Printer in Eighteenth Century Williamsburg* (Williamsburg, Va.: Colonial Williamsburg, 1974); and *The Bookbinder in Colonial Williamsburg* (Williamsburg, Va.: Colonial Williamsburg, 1973). For the reader with the opportunity to visit Williamsburg, the authentic recreation based on sound historical documentation of early printing and bookbinding processes is part of Colonial Williamsburg.

[2] See F. L. Shick, *The Paper Bound Book in America* (New York: R. R. Bowker Company, 1958).

CHAPTER 5

[1] *Columbine*, 2 (April/May, 1974).

[2] Ibid.

[3] John Fink, *WGN: A Pictorial History* (Chicago: WGN, Inc., 1961), p. 11.

[4] Wilbur Schramm, "Reading and Listening Patterns of American University Students," *Journalism Quarterly*, 22 (March 1945), 23–33.

[5] *Welcome South Brother* (Atlanta: WSB Radio, 1974), p. 17.

[6] "Annual Report of Research in Progress," Institute for Communication Research, Stanford University, 1972–73.

CHAPTER 6

[1] Excerpt from "Preface," p. vii, in *Public Television: A Program for Action, The Report and Recommendations of the Carnegie Commission on Educational Television* (New York: Harper & Row, Pub., 1967).

[2] Ibid.

CHAPTER 7

[1] Edwin Emery and Michael Emery, *The Press and America*, 4th ed. (Englewood Cliffs, N.J.: Prentice-Hall, 1978), p. 365–66.

[2] The author gratefully acknowledges the help of the following source in preparing this section of the chapter on "landmarks,": John Faber, *Great News Photos and the Stories Behind Them*, 2nd ed. (New York: Dover Publications, Inc., 1978).

[3] Alfred Eisenstaedt, *Studio Photography*, (February 1979), p. 27.

CHAPTER 9

[1] The author is indebted to the Recording Industry Association of America for furnishing significant information used in this chapter. Other sources that proved particularly useful included: Harry Dichter and Elliott Shapiro, *Handbook of Early American Sheet Music 1768–1889* (New York: Dover, 1977). Material for the section on the prerecording era is found in this source. Also especially useful in preparing this chapter were: Oliver Read and Walter L. Welch, *From Tin Foil to Stereo* (Indianapolis: Howard W. Sams and Co., Inc.; Bobbs-Merrill, 1976); Ronald Gelatt, *The Fabulous Phonograph* (Philadelphia: Lippincott, 1955).

CHAPTER 10

[1] Andrew Kershaw, "The Next Ordeal or the Biggest Problem of the Next Ten Years," Speech delivered to the annual meeting of the Association of National Advertisers, Hot Springs, Virginia, October 1974.

[2] James T. Lull, "Counter Advertising: Persuasability of the Anti-Bayer TV Spot," *Journal of Broadcasting*, 18 (Summer 1974), 353–60.

[3] Walter L. Thomas, *A Manual for the Differential-Value Profile* (Ann Arbor, Mich., Educational Service Company, 1966). p. 6.

CHAPTER 12

[1] The account of the story is from *Columbia Journalism Review*, September/October, 1981.
[2] M. Edwardson, D. Grooms, and S. Proudlove, "Television News Information Gain from Interesting Video vs. Talking Heads," *Journal of Broadcasting* 25 (Winter 1981), 23.
[3] R. Lovell, "Mount St. Helens: Reporting a Disaster," *The Quill* 68 (December 1980), 12–16.
[4] *Ibid.*
[5] *Ibid.*
[6] *Ibid.*

CHAPTER 13

[1] Paul L. Laskin and Abram Chayes, "A Brief History of the Issues," *Control of the Direct Broadcast Satellite: Values in Conflict* (Palo Alto, Calif.: Aspen Institute Program on Communications and Society, 1974), pp. 3–14.
[2] Ibid.
[3] Ibid.

CHAPTER 14

[1] R. A. Schwarzlose, "The Nation's First Wire Service: Evidence Supporting a Footnote," *Journalism Quarterly* 57 (Winter, 1980), 555–62.

CHAPTER 15

[1] Osmo A. Wiio, "System Models of Information, Communication and Mass Communication: Reevaluation of Some Basic Concepts of Communication," Paper presented at the annual meeting of the International Communication Association, Montreal, 1973. See also Osmo A. Wiio and Leif Aberg, "Open and Closed Mass Media Systems," Paper presented at the annual meeting of the International Communication Association, Chicago, 1975; and Osmo A. Wiio, *Systems of Information, Communication, and Organization* (Helsinki, Finland: Helsinki Research Institute for Business Economics, 1975)
[2] *In the Matter of the Mayflower Broadcasting Corporation and the Yankee Network, Inc.* (WAAB), 8 FCC 33, 338, January 16, 1941.
[3] *In the Matter of Editorializing by Broadcast Licensees*, 13 FCC 1246, June 1, 1949.
[4] *Your F.T.C.: What It Is and What It Does* (Washington, D.C.: Federal Trade Commission, 1977).
[5] *Ibid.*
[6] *Ibid.*
[7] *Ibid.*
[8] *Ibid.*
[9] Harold K. Jacobson, "The International Telecommunication Union: ITU's Structures and Functions," in *Global Communications in the Space Age: Toward a New ITU*, ed. John and Mary R. Markle Foundation and the Twentieth Century Fund, 1972, p. 40.
[10] *Ibid.*

CHAPTER 16

[1] *Gitlow v. New York* 268 U.S. 652, 666 (1925). The reference was a "casual statement not necessary to the decision." See: Donald M. Gillmor and Jerome A. Barron, *Mass Communication Law* (St. Paul: West Publishing Co., 1974.) p. 1.
[2] Eric Sevareid. Speech delivered at the "First Amendment Confrontation" during the fifty-fifth annual convention of the National Association of Broadcasters, March 28, 1977.
[3] Paley's remark was quoted by Archibald Cox, Carl Miloeb University Professor at Harvard University, during a speech by Cox to the Anti-Defamation League of B'nai B'rith on the occasion of Paley's receiving the First Amendment Freedoms Award, December 7, 1976, in New York City.
[4] *CBS v. Democratic National Committee*, 412 U.S. 94 (1973), William Small, "The First Amendment/Radio and Television: Treated Like Distant Cousins," *The Quill*, 64 (September 1976), 32.

[5] "State Court Holds Free-Press Rights Are Applicable to Broadcasting," *Broadcasting*, 45 (April 12, 1976), 59.

[6] Ibid.

[7] John B. Adams, *State Open Meeting Laws: An Overview* (Columbia, Mo.: Freedom of Information Foundation, 1974).

[8] *Rideau v. Louisiana*, 373 U.S. 723, 10 L. Ed. 2d 663, 83 S. Ct. 1417 (1963).

[9] *Estes v. State of Texas*, 381 U.S. 532, 85 S. Ct. 1628, 14 L. Ed. 2d 543 (1965).

[10] "Cameras in the Courtroom," *The Quill*, 63 (April 1975), 25.

[11] Roger M. Grace, "The Courts v. the News Media: Is the Conflict Necessary?" *Case and Comment*, 79 (March/April 1974), 3–10.

[12] Stan Crock, "A Flurry of Gag Rules," *The Quill*, 62 (March 1974), 21. *United States v. Dickinson*, 465 F. 2d 496 (5th Cir. 1972).

[13] Grace, "The Courts v. the News Media."

[14] Ibid.

[15] "York's Strange Silence," *Time*, November 18, 1974, pp. 88–89.

[16] *Dennis v. United States*, 341 U.S. 494, 510 (1951).

[17] See: *NAB Highlights* October 31, 1977, p. 3; Donald M. Gillmor and Jerome A. Barron, *Mass Communication Law* (St. Paul: West Publishing Company, 1974), 287–88.

CHAPTER 17

[1] Carl I. Hovland, "Reconciling Conflicting Results Derived from Experimental and Survey Studies of Attitude Change," in *The Process and Effects of Mass Communication*, ed. Wilbur Schramm and Donald F. Roberts (Urbana: University of Illinois Press, 1971), pp. 493–515.

[2] Paul Lazarsfeld, Bernard Berelson, and Hazel Gaudet, *The People's Choice* (New York: Columbia University Press, 1948).

[3] Ibid.

[4] Melvin DeFleur and Sandra Ball-Rokeach, *Theories of Mass Communication* (New York: David McKay Co., Inc., 1975), p. 205.

[5] A discussion of how the categories approach evolved from the bullet theory and how it fits into current communication theory is found in Wilbur Schramm and Donald Roberts, *The Process and Effects of Mass Communication* (Urbana: University of Illinois Press, 1971), pp. 4–53.

[6] Elihu Katz, "Mass Communications Research and the Study of Popular Culture," *Studies in Public Communication*, vol. 2 (1959), as discussed in David Chaney, *Process of Mass Communication* (London: The Macmillan Press, Ltd., 1972), pp. 11–36.

[7] Louis M. Savary and J. Paul Carrico, eds., *Contemporary Film and the New Generation* (New York: Association Press, 1971), pp. 15–19.

[8] William Stephenson, *The Play Theory of Mass Communication* (Chicago: University of Chicago Press, 1967).

[9] Chaney, pp. 20–21.

[10] Deanna Campbell Robinson, "Television/Film Attitudes of Upper-Middle Class Professionals," *Journal of Broadcasting*, 19 (Spring 1975), 196. Also discussed under the text subheading "Uses and Gratifications."

[11] Wilbur Schramm, *Men, Messages, and Media: A Look at Human Communication* (New York: Harper & Row, Publishers, Inc., 1973).

[12] Neil Weintraub, "Some Meanings Radio Has for Teenagers," *Journal of Broadcasting*, 2 (Spring 1971), 147–52.

[13] Lawrence Wenner, "Functional Analyses of TV Viewing for Older Adults," *Journal of Broadcasting*, 20 (Winter 1976), 77–88.

[14] Herta Herzog, "What Do We Really Know about Daytime Serial Listeners," in *Radio Research, 1942–1943*, ed. Paul F. Lazarsfeld and Frank Stanton (New York: Duell, Sloan and Pearce, 1944).

[15] R. J. Compesi, "Gratifications of Daytime TV Serial Viewers," *Journalism Quarterly*, 57 (Spring 1980), 155–158.

[16] M. R. Levy, "The Audience Experience with Television News," *Journalism Monographs*, 55 (April 1978).

[17] E. Lehnert, "The Youth Market's Ideal Newspaper," *Newspaper Research Journal* 2 (Spring, 1981), 3–15.

[18] *Ibid.*, 6.

[19] *Ibid.*

[20] *Ibid.*, 9.

[21] *Ibid.*, 11.

[22] J. K. Burgoon and M. Burgoon, "The Functions of the Daily Newspaper," *Newspaper Research Journal*, 2 (Spring 1981), 29–39.

[23] *Ibid.*, 32.

[24] *Ibid.*

[25] *Ibid.*

[26] *Ibid.*

[27] Bernard C. Cohen, *The Press and Foreign Policy* (Princeton, N.J.: Princeton University Press, 1963). See also: Maxwell McCombs and Donald Shaw, "The Agenda-Setting Function of Mass Media," *Public Opinion Quarterly*, 36 (1972), 176–87.

[28] CBS Office of Social Research, *Communicating with Children through Television* (New York: CBS, 1977).

[29] For example: Charles R. Corder-Bolz, "Television Content and Children's Social Attitudes," *Progress Report to the Office of Child Development* (Washington, D.C.: Department of Health, Education, and Welfare, 1976).

[30] John P. Murray and Susan Kippax, "Children's Social Behavior in Three Towns with Differing Television Experience," *Journal of Communication*, 28 (Winter 1978), 19–29.

[31] Charles K. Atkin and Walter Gantz, "The Role of Television News in the Political Socialization of Children." Paper presented at the meeting of the International Communication Association, Chicago, April 1975.

[32] Charles Atkin and Mark Miller, "The Effects of Television Advertising on Children: Experimental Evidence." Paper presented at the 1975 meeting of the International Communication Association. A review of recent research on television and advertising can be found in the *Journal of Communication*, 27 (Winter 1977).

[33] Seymour Feshbach, "The Stimulating vs. Cathartic Effects of a Vicarious Aggressive Experience." *Journal of Abnormal and Social Psychology* 63 (1961), 381–85.

[34] Leonard Berkowitz, *Aggression: A Social Psychological Analysis* (New York: McGraw-Hill Book Company, 1962).

[35] Joseph Klapper, *The Effects of Mass Communication* (New York: The Free Press, 1960).

[36] Albert Bandura and Richard Walters, *Social Learning and Personality Development* (New York: Holt, Rinehart & Winston, 1963).

[37] *The Journal of Broadcasting*, 21 (Summer 1977) features a discussion of Gerbner's methodology, CBS' criticism, and Gerbner's response.

[38] George Comstock, "Types of Portrayal and Aggressive Behavior," *Journal of Communication*, 27 (Summer 1977), 189–98.

[39] Everett M. Rogers and F. Floyd Shoemaker, *Communication of Innovations: A Cross Cultural Approach*, 2nd ed. (New York: The Free Press, 1971).

CHAPTER 18

[1] "Journalists as Diplomats," *Broadcasting*, (November 21, 1977), 38–39.

[2] *The Quill*, (June, 1978), 20.

[3] *Ibid.*

[4] *Ibid.*

[5] "Scoop Backfires," *Broadcasting*, (August 13, 1979), 46.

[6] *Ibid.*

[7] *Ibid.*

[8] "Short's News Team Doubles in Sales," *Broadcasting*, (June 19, 1978), 56.

[9] *Ibid.*

[10] "CBS Gets Stung for $10,000 Hoping to Find Hoffa's Body," *Broadcasting*, (December 15, 1975), 51.

[11] *Ibid.*

[12] "Utah Cops, Disguised as Mild-Mannered Reporters," *Broadcasting*, (February 5, 1979), 76.

[13] *Ibid.*

[14] "Policemen Who Pose as Reporters," *The Quill*, (April, 1977), 10.

[15] *Ibid.*

[16] "Utah Cops," 76.

[17] "Policemen Who Pose as Reporters," 10.

[18] *Ibid.*

[19] *Ibid.*

[20] *Ibid.*

[21] Alice E. Courtney and Thomas W. Whipple, "Women in TV Commercials," *Journal of Communication*, 24 (Spring 1974), 110–18.

[22] William J. O'Donnell, "Update: Sex-Role Messages in TV Commercials," *Journal of Communication*, 28 (Winter 1978), 156–58.

[23] G. Gerbner, L. Gross, N. Signorelli, and M. Morgan, "Aging with Television: Images on Television Drama and Conceptions of Social Reality," *Journal of Communication* (Winter 1980), p. 40.

[24] *Ibid.*

[25] *Ibid.*, 42.

[26] *Ibid.*, 42–43.

[27] Cheris Kramer, "Stereotypes of Women's Speech: The Word from Cartoons." Paper presented at the annual meeting of the Speech Communication Association, Chicago, Illinois, December 1974.

[28] Gerbner et al., 43.

[29] *Ibid.*

[30] *Ibid.*, 45.

INDEX